# California Judges Benchbook

# SEARCH AND SEIZURE

Second Edition

Honorable George Brunn, Retired

CJER

CALIFORNIA CENTER FOR JUDICIAL EDUCATION AND RESEARCH
San Francisco, California

CEB

CONTINUING EDUCATION OF THE BAR ▪ CALIFORNIA
Oakland, California

Library of Congress Catalog Card No. 01–135596

Printed in the United States of America
ISBN 0-7626-0637-1

CR-33590

# ABOUT CJER

The California Center for Judicial Education and Research (CJER), as the Education Division of the Administrative Office of the Courts (AOC), is responsible for developing and maintaining a comprehensive and quality educational program for the California judicial branch. Formed in 1973 as a joint enterprise of the Judicial Council and the California Judges Association, CJER supports the Chief Justice, the Judicial Council, and the courts by providing an extensive statewide educational program for judicial officers and court staff at both the trial and appellate levels. It includes orientation programs for new judicial officers, court clerks, and administrative officers; continuing education programs for judicial officers, court administrators, and managers; an annual statewide conference for judicial officers and court administrators; video and audiotapes; and judicial benchbooks, benchguides, and practice aids.

# Consultants for Search and Seizure Benchbook

Hon. Jerome T. Benson
Superior Court of California,
County of San Francisco

Hon. Gregory M. Caskey
Superior Court of California,
County of Shasta

Hon. Larry P. Fidler
Superior Court of California,
County of Los Angeles

Mark Hutchins, Esq.
District Attorney
County of Alameda

Hon. William A. McKinstry
Superior Court of California,
County of Alameda

Hon. William R. Pounders
Superior Court of California,
County of Los Angeles

Scott Spear, Esq.
Public Defender
County of Alameda

# Foreword

This book is the first of a series of volumes that will replace the criminal law benchbooks published in 1991. The two other benchbooks in this series will be Felony Sentencing and Domestic Violence Cases in Criminal Courts, which was first published in 1996.

We are pleased that the California Continuing Education of the Bar is making these benchbooks available to attorneys pursuant to its special responsibility as the educational arm of the State Bar.

These benchbooks will give judges a practical working tool to conduct criminal proceedings fairly, correctly, and efficiently. They are written from the judge's point of view, giving the judge concrete advice on what to look for and how to respond. These benchbooks will also give attorneys an illuminating and indispensable insight into the judges' policies and practices in criminal proceedings.

We sincerely thank the author of this benchbook, retired Judge George Brunn, and the judges who served as consultants and whose names appear in the preface for their dedication and hard work in preparing this benchbook.

The text covers case law through the 2000–2001 term of the U.S. Supreme Court, and through volumes 26 C4th 589, and 88 CA4th, and statutes and rules effective as of July 1, 2001.

We recognize that the area of law that this work covers is a dynamic one, and we welcome comments, criticisms, and suggestions for its improvement. We hope that each person using this benchbook will become a contributor, editor, and critic as this work is updated and expanded through future supplements. Please address all correspondence regarding the contents of the benchbook to:

CJER Publications Department *or* cjerpubs@jud.ca.gov
455 Golden Gate Ave., 6th Floor
San Francisco, CA 94102–3660

In this way, each reader can help CJER to serve the working needs of California's judges.

Karen M. Thorson
CJER Director

# Preface and Acknowledgments

Search and seizure law employs balancing tests. This book, too, strives to strike a balance. It is not an "everything you have always wanted to know" treatise; Professor Wayne R. LaFave has written an excellent one in five volumes. I highly recommend it to everyone who works extensively in this field. The present work is designed as a working tool for California judges. If you feel it contains more than anyone needs to know about the subject, I will not quarrel with you. I use as my excuse the nature of the field, including California's special contribution—procedures that almost rival the substantive law in complexity.

Fourth Amendment law and procedure has continued to receive the active attention of the courts and the state legislature in the 12 years since I wrote the first edition. Paradoxically, as the exclusionary rule has shrunk, the law has become more complicated. I have extensively reworked the book to discuss new developments and to make it more useful. Some topics, such as e–mail search warrant applications, are covered here for the first time. Discussion of other subjects, such as good faith, have been reorganized and expanded.

In addition to introducing the text, a preface is intended to fulfill two functions. The first is to permit easy identification of the guilty party. The shortcomings, whether of omission or commission, are mine. I hope that you will make the next edition a better one by your suggestions.

The second function is the pleasant one of gratefully acknowledging the many individuals who provided invaluable assistance in preparing this book. I would like to thank the following judges who served as consultants for the book and who commented on the manuscript and made many helpful suggestions: Hon. Jerome T. Benson, San Francisco Superior Court; Hon. Gregory M. Caskey, Shasta Superior Court; Hon. Larry P. Fidler, Los Angeles Superior Court; Hon. William A. McKinstry, Alameda Superior Court; and Hon. William R. Pounders, Los Angeles Superior Court. Also sharing their expertise were Mark Hutchins, Esq., of the Alameda County District Attorney's Office, and Scott Spear, Esq., of the Alameda County Public Defender's Office. I am also thankful to CJER staff attorneys Barry Harding and Robert Schindewolf for their careful and thoughtful editing, to Dennis Matsura and Christine Acker for coordinating the production of the book, to Debra Landis for providing legal research assistance, to Iris Okura for copyediting, to Jenny A. Jones for preparing the index, and lastly, but by no means least, to Mary McCormick for efficiently and capably inputting the manuscript onto the computer. They deserve the credit for whatever merits the book may have.

January 2002 Hon. George Brunn (Ret.)

# Contents

# 1

# The Fourth Amendment and the Exclusionary Rule

## I. [§1.1] SCOPE OF CHAPTER

The chapter begins with brief overviews of the development of the exclusionary rule (§§1.2–1.8) and its nature and functions (§§1.9–1.14). The chapter next discusses the application of the exclusionary rule to various proceedings (§§1.15–1.24), the extent to which the rule and the Fourth Amendment afford protection against searches and seizures by private citizens (§§1.25–1.27), and the good-faith exception to the exclusionary rule (§§1.28–1.42). After a brief discussion of the effect of bad faith on the part of the officer conducting the search (§1.43), the chapter concludes with an analysis of "fruit of the poisonous tree" issues (§§1.44–1.62).

There are many exclusionary rules, such as the hearsay rule and rules blocking admission of coerced confessions. In this book, "exclusionary rule" refers to the set of rules that determine under what circumstances evidence obtained in violation of the Fourth Amendment is inadmissible.

## II. DEVELOPMENT OF THE EXCLUSIONARY RULE

### A. [§1.2] Constitutional Provisions

The Fourth Amendment to the U.S. Constitution states:

> The right of the people to be secure in their persons, houses, papers, and effects, against unreasonable searches and seizures, shall not be violated, and no Warrants shall issue, but upon probable cause, supported by Oath or affirmation, and particularly describing the place to be searched, and the persons or things to be seized.

The amendment is part of the Bill of Rights and reflects a long struggle on both sides of the Atlantic against governmental assertion of nearly unlimited powers to search and seize. 1 LaFave, Search and Seizure, pp 3–5 (3d ed 1996), hereafter cited as LaFave.

The California Constitution contains a nearly identical provision (Cal Const art I, §13), but it no longer has a role in how California courts shape and apply the exclusionary rule. See §1.7.

### B. [§1.3] Origin of Exclusionary Rule

The U.S. Supreme Court first excluded evidence obtained by an illegal search in *Weeks v U.S.* (1914) 232 US 383, 34 S Ct 341, 58 L Ed 652 (evidence taken by U.S. marshal in warrantless search of defendant's home inadmissible in federal prosecution for unlawful use of mails). The court said that attempts to obtain convictions "by means of unlawful seizures . . . should find no sanction in the judgments of the courts, which are charged at all times with the support of the Constitution . . ." 232 US at 392. Otherwise, the Fourth Amendment would be "of no value, and . . . might as well be stricken from the Constitution." 232 US at 393.

### C. The Exclusionary Rule in California

#### 1. [§1.4] Pre-*Cahan*

California's treatment of evidence obtained in violation of the Fourth Amendment or its state counterpart has gone through four major phases.

Until 1955, California had no exclusionary rule relating to the products of unreasonable searches and seizures, with an exception noted below. *Weeks v U.S.* (1914) 232 US 383, 34 S Ct 341, 58 L Ed 652, discussed in §1.3, did not apply to state court prosecutions. *Wolf v Colorado* (1949) 338 US 25, 33, 69 S Ct 1359, 93 L Ed 1782 (exclusionary rule may be effective in deterring unreasonable searches, but is not an essential ingredient of the privacy rights guaranteed by the Fourth Amendment as made applicable to the states by the 14th Amendment). The *Wolf* court noted that 30 states had rejected *Weeks.* 338 US at 38.

The only exception was that state courts had to suppress evidence that was obtained by means that shock the conscience. *Rochin v California* (1952) 342 US 165, 209–210, 72 S Ct 205, 96 L Ed 183. However, this principle, which continues to be in effect, rests not on the Fourth Amendment but on due process grounds.

#### 2. [§1.5] *Cahan* to *Mapp*

Beginning with *People v Cahan* (1955) 44 C2d 434, 282 P2d 905, California courts fashioned their own exclusionary rule. *Cahan* said this was the only practical way to enforce the guaranties in the state and federal constitutions against unreasonable searches and seizures; when courts admit illegally obtained evidence, they are in the morally incongruous position of flouting constitutional rights while insisting that its citizens obey the law. 44 C2d at 446–447.

In this era, California courts were not bound by the federal exclusionary rule. 44 C2d at 450–451 (federal decisions that overly restrict right to conduct reasonable searches can be rejected).

#### 3. [§1.6] *Mapp* to Proposition 8

By 1960, the majority of states had joined California in excluding illegally obtained evidence. See *Elkins v U.S.* (1960) 364 US 206, 224–225, 80 S Ct 1437, 4 L Ed 2d 1669. This was one factor that led the U.S. Supreme Court to decide in *Mapp v Ohio* (1961) 367 US 643, 81 S Ct 1684, 6 L Ed 2d 1081, that all evidence obtained by searches and seizures in violation of the U.S. Constitution is inadmissible in state courts. 367 US at 651, 655.

After *Mapp,* the minimum scope of the exclusionary rule in the state and federal courts was the same; in addition, states continued to be free under their own constitutions to exclude evidence that would be admitted in a federal prosecution. For example, California courts but not federal courts gave a defendant standing to invoke the rule even when a search violated another person's Fourth Amendment rights rather than those of the defendant. *People v Martin* (1955) 45 C2d 755, 759–761, 290 P2d 855; *Rakas v Illinois* (1978) 439 US 128, 140, 99 S Ct 421, 58 L Ed 2d 387.

*Mapp* treated the exclusionary rule as an essential part of the Fourth and 14th Amendments. Later cases, although not overruling *Mapp,* make it clear that the rule is a judicially created remedy rather than a personal constitutional right. See, *e.g., U.S. v Calandra* (1974) 414 US 338, 348, 94 S Ct 613, 38 L Ed 2d 561.

### 4. [§1.7] From Proposition 8 to the Present

In 1982, California voters approved Proposition 8, which added §28(d) to article I of the state constitution. That section specified that relevant evidence in a criminal trial shall not be excluded, except under a statute enacted by two-thirds of the legislature.

Article I, §28(d), federalized California's search and seizure law. It barred suppression of evidence seized in violation of California law but not in violation of the Fourth Amendment. *California v Greenwood* (1988) 486 US 35, 38, 108 S Ct 1625, 100 L Ed 2d 30; *In re Lance W.* (1985) 37 C3d 873, 879–880, 210 CR 671. For example:

- The standing requirements developed by the U.S. Supreme Court apply in California courts. *In re Lance W., supra.*

- The California rule that warrantless searches of garbage left outside for collection is illegal was superseded by the contrary decision in *California v Greenwood, supra.*

*Greenwood* upheld Proposition 8 against the contention that it violated due process.

*Status of lower federal court decisions.* In determining federal law, lower federal court decisions are not controlling but are "persuasive and entitled to great weight," especially when numerous and consistent. *Etcheverry v Tri-Ag Serv., Inc.* (2000) 22 C4th 316, 320–321, 93 CR2d 36.

*Status of pre-Proposition 8 decisions.* Pre-Proposition 8 California cases that rest on the Fourth Amendment remain binding on trial courts in the absence of a U.S. Supreme Court or California decision to the contrary. *Auto Equity Sales, Inc. v Superior Court* (1962) 57 C2d 450, 455, 20 CR 321; *People v Neer* (1986) 177 CA3d 991, 1000, 223 CR 555. Pre-Proposition 8 decisions should not be devalued "in favor of the views of lower federal courts from around the country merely because" they were decided before the effective date of Proposition 8. *People v Camacho* (2000) 23 C4th 824, 830 n1, 98 CR2d 232.

### 5. [§1.8] Chart: The Exclusionary Rule in California Courts

| | |
|---|---|
| Before *Cahan* (1955) | No exclusionary rule. |
| *Cahan* (1955) to *Mapp* (1961) | State-fashioned rule; federal rule not controlling. |
| *Mapp* (1961) to Prop 8 (1982) | Federal rule plus exclusion based on independent state grounds. |
| After Prop 8 (1982) | Federal rule as applied by U.S. Supreme Court; for status of pre-Proposition 8 California decisions, see §1.7. |

## III. RELATION OF FOURTH AMENDMENT TO EXCLUSIONARY RULE

### A. [§1.9] Underlying Issues When Fourth Amendment and Exclusionary Rule Invoked

A suppression motion may raise one or more of the following issues:

- Was there a search or a seizure within the meaning of the Fourth Amendment? The everyday meaning of "search" and the Fourth Amendment meaning differ. See §1.10.
- If so, was the search or seizure unlawful? This question is the topic of chaps 2–5.
- If so, does the exclusionary rule apply? The Fourth Amendment and the exclusionary rule are not congruent; evidence that is the product of an illegal search or seizure is not always excluded. See §§1.15–1.24, 1.28–1.62.

### B. [§1.10] Meaning of "Search" and "Seizure"

In the context of the Fourth Amendment, "search" and "seizure" have specialized meanings.

*Search.* Generally, a "search" is a governmental intrusion upon, or invasion of, a citizen's personal security in an area in which he or she has "a reasonable expectation of privacy." *People v Mayberry* (1982) 31 C3d 335, 341, 182 CR 17. In accord is *U.S. v Jacobsen* (1984) 466 US 109, 113, 104 S Ct 1652, 80 L Ed 2d 85 (search occurs when expectation of privacy that society considers reasonable is infringed); *Conservatorship of Susan T.* (1994) 8 C4th 1005, 1014, 36 CR2d 40.

For example, a police officer who trespasses on open fields does not violate reasonable privacy expectations; the officer's observations, therefore, do not amount to a search, even if the property is posted with "No Trespassing" signs and the officer climbed over fences. *U.S. v Dunn* (1987) 480 US 294, 304, 107 S Ct 1134, 94 L Ed 2d 326. On the other hand, a police entry into the garage of a single-family dwelling violates reasonable privacy expectations and therefore the lawfulness of the entry becomes the key issue. *People v Baker* (1986) 187 CA3d 562, 567, 231 CR 877 (entry without warrant, consent, or exigent circumstances unlawful).

The limitation of the Fourth Amendment to *governmental* intrusions is discussed in §§1.25–1.27. For a detailed discussion of reasonable privacy expectations, see §§5.2–5.8.

*Seizure.* A seizure of property is any "meaningful interference with an individual's possessory interest in that property." *U.S. v Jacobsen, supra.* The Fourth Amendment protects property as well as privacy. *Soldal v Cook County* (1992) 506 US 56, 62, 113 S Ct 538, 121 L Ed 2d 450. A seizure of a person occurs when a reasonable person would believe that he or she is not free to leave. *U.S. v Mendenhall* (1980) 446 US 544, 554, 100 S Ct 1870, 64 L Ed 2d 497; for discussion, see §§3.6–3.9.

## C. Nature and Function of Exclusionary Rule

### 1. [§1.11] Evidentiary Nature of Rule

The exclusionary rule is an evidentiary rule and functions by making certain evidence obtained in violation of the Fourth Amendment inadmissible. The rule also generally prohibits testimony about an illegally obtained object. See §1.54.

For discussion of a Fourth Amendment requirement that is not primarily evidentiary, see §1.16 (right to early determination of lawfulness of arrest). For the effect of an illegal search or seizure on jurisdiction, see §1.12.

### 2. [§1.12] Effect of Violation on Jurisdiction

A Fourth Amendment violation does not affect a court's jurisdiction to try the defendant. The prosecution may and often does go to trial on the parts of the evidence that were not suppressed. Also, the illegality of a defendant's arrest—even kidnapping by law enforcement agents—blocks only the use of any evidence derived from that illegality. *U.S. v Alvarez-Machain* (1992) 504 US 655, 661, 112 S Ct 2188, 119 L Ed 2d 441; *Ker v Illinois* (1886) 119 US 436, 444, 7 S Ct 225, 30 L Ed 421; see also §§1.44–1.62.

### 3. [§1.13] Purposes of Exclusionary Rule

The main purpose of the exclusionary rule is deterring unreasonable searches and seizures. See, *e.g., Pennsylvania Bd. of Probation & Parole v Scott* (1998) 524 US 357, 363, 118 S Ct 2014, 141 L Ed 2d 344; *Terry v Ohio* (1968) 392 US 1, 12, 88 S Ct 1868, 20 L Ed 2d 889; *Elkins v U.S.* (1960) 364 US 206, 217, 80 S Ct 1437, 4 L Ed 2d 1669.

Second, the rule keeps courts from participating in and, in effect, condoning unlawful invasions of constitutional rights. *Terry v Ohio, supra*; *People v Cahan* (1955) 44 C2d 434, 445, 282 P2d 905.

Moreover, courts have said that failure to require government to obey the law breeds contempt for the law; government, like citizens, may not use unlawful means to achieve laudable ends. 44 C2d at 446. Otherwise the system of constitutional restraints on which our liberties rest would be endangered. *Mapp v Ohio* (1961) 367 US 643, 660, 81 S Ct 1684, 6 L Ed 2d 1081.

### 4. [§1.14] Exceptions to Exclusionary Rule

Courts have come to stress the deterrence function of the rule almost exclusively. This has given rise to a growing number of exceptions to the exclusionary rule in situations in which courts believe that the costs of applying it outweigh the benefits of deterrence or that such benefits are negligible under the particular circumstances.

For example:

- *In U.S. v Leon* (1984) 468 US 897, 916, 104 S Ct 3405, 82 L Ed 2d 677, the court justified the "good faith" exception by saying that excluding evidence seized under an invalid search warrant that the officer reasonably and in good faith believed to be valid would have no significant deterrent effect. For discussion of the good-faith exception, see §§1.28–1.42.

- More recently, in *Pennsylvania Bd. of Probation & Parole v Scott* (1998) 524 US 357, 363, 118 S Ct 2014, 141 L Ed 2d 344, the court used a cost-benefits approach to conclude that illegally obtained evidence can be introduced in parole revocation hearings. California had anticipated this analysis and conclusion. *In re Martinez* (1970) 1 C3d 641, 648, 83 CR 382. For further discussion, see §1.21.

- In *U.S. v Calandra* (1974) 414 US 338, 349, 94 S Ct 613, 38 L Ed 2d 561, the court used the same rationale to hold that a witness could not refuse to answer questions before a grand jury on the ground that they were based on illegally obtained evidence. See also §1.15.

- In *People v Beuer* (2000) 77 CA4th 1433, 1439, 92 CR2d 572, the court held that illegally obtained evidence was admissible in an unrelated criminal trial. The evidence in question had not resulted in charges against the defendant but was used in an unconnected subsequent drug prosecution to show knowledge and intent. The court said that application of the exclusionary rule would not serve any deterrent function under these circumstances.

## IV. APPLICATION OF EXCLUSIONARY RULE TO VARIOUS PROCEEDINGS

### A. Application to Stages of a Criminal Case

#### 1. Pretrial Phases

##### a. [§1.15] Grand Jury Testimony and Indictment

A grand jury witness may not invoke the exclusionary rule to refuse to answer questions based on illegally obtained evidence. *U.S. v Calandra* (1974) 414 US 338, 349, 94 S Ct 613, 38 L Ed 2d 561 (deterrent benefits outweighed by harm to grand jury functions).

Two questions remain:

(1) What is the effect of the provision of Pen C §939.6 that the grand jury shall only receive evidence that would be admissible at trial over objection? In light of Proposition 8 (see §1.7), Pen C §939.6 is probably superseded by *Calandra* and does not help a witness before a grand jury. See 4 Witkin & Epstein, California Criminal Law, *Illegally Obtained Evidence* §18 (3d ed 2000).

(2) May a defendant challenge a grand jury indictment on the ground that it rests on illegally obtained evidence? Neither *Calandra* nor any other U.S. Supreme Court decision answers this question. Lower federal courts usually answer it in the negative. See 1 LaFave, p 164. However, California has long treated challenges to indictments like those to informations. See *People v Sherwin* (2000) 82 CA4th 1404, 1410, 98 CR2d 888; *Cummiskey v Superior Court* (1992) 3 C4th 1018, 1027, 13 CR2d 551; *Smith v Superior Court* (1978) 76 CA3d 731, 733, 143 CR 109 (defendant who wants to avoid use of illegally obtained evidence "may move to set aside an indictment or information"); Pen C §995.

☛ **Judicial Tip**: Trial courts should continue to permit Fourth Amendment challenges to indictments under Pen C §995. The test is whether there is sufficient lawful evidence to establish probable cause of defendant's guilt. *Cummiskey v Superior Court, supra.*

##### b. [§1.16] Bail and Probable Cause Hearing

When the defendant is in custody pursuant to a warrantless arrest, the

Fourth Amendment requires a relatively quick determination of probable cause; defendant must be released absent a warrant or probable cause to arrest. *Gerstein v Pugh* (1975) 420 US 103, 116–119, 95 S Ct 854, 43 L Ed 2d 54; *In re Walters* (1975) 15 C3d 738, 742–743, 126 CR 239. In misdemeanor cases, this is done under a Pen C §991 motion; for discussion of procedure, see §§4.95–4.102 (procedure is nonadverserial; determination made by review of documents). In felony cases, the preliminary hearing serves this function.

In light of the right to an early probable cause determination, search issues are almost never raised in bail hearings, and there is no controlling decision as to whether such issues may properly be raised at that stage.

#### c. [§1.17] Preliminary Hearing

A defendant is entitled to assert the exclusionary rule at the preliminary hearing. Pen C §1538.5(f); for discussion of procedure, see §§6.54–6.59. Use of suppression motions at this stage declined after Pen C §1538.5 was amended to eliminate the right to a de novo suppression hearing following the filing of the information.

#### d. [§1.18] Diversion/Deferred Entry of Judgment

Evidence suppressed on Fourth Amendment grounds cannot serve as the basis for a prosecutorial determination of ineligibility for diversion or deferred entry of judgment. *People v Dyas* (1979) 100 CA3d 464, 467–468, 161 CR 39; Pen C §1538.5(d) (suppressed evidence inadmissible in trial or other hearing); see *People v Brackett* (1994) 25 CA4th 488, 498, 30 CR2d 557. But see *People v Flores* (1987) 196 CA3d 475, 486, 241 CR 835 (dictum questioning validity of *Dyas* after passage of Proposition 8).

### 2. [§1.19] Trial: Impeachment of Defendant

California follows the federal rule permitting the use of previously suppressed evidence for impeachment purposes. *People v Moore* (1988) 201 CA3d 877, 885, 247 CR 353; *U.S. v Havens* (1980) 446 US 620, 627–628, 100 S Ct 1912, 64 L Ed 2d 559.

The permitted use extends only to the impeachment of the defendant, not of defense witnesses. *James v Illinois* (1990) 493 US 307, 313, 110 S Ct 648, 107 L Ed 2d 676. *James* supersedes *People v Johnson* (1989) 211 CA3d 392, 395–396, 259 CR 388, which has allowed impeachment of defense witnesses by evidence obtained in violation of the Fourth Amendment.

### 3. Posttrial Phases

#### a. [§1.20] Sentencing

Before Proposition 8, evidence suppressed on Fourth Amendment grounds could not be considered in imposing sentence. *People v Belleci* (1979) 24 C3d 879, 888, 157 CR 503; Pen C §1538.5(d) (suppressed evidence inadmissible in trial or other hearing). The U.S. Supreme Court has not ruled on this issue. Some lower federal courts permit such consideration absent a showing that the police obtained the evidence to enhance the sentence. 1 LaFave, p 174. *Belleci* rests on Pen C §1538.5(d) rather than on the scope of the exclusionary rule. See *In re Michael V.* (1986) 178 CA3d 159, 168, 223 CR 503. Some courts have held that Pen C §1538.5(d) no longer controls in view of Proposition 8. *People v Moore* (1988) 201 CA3d 877, 885, 247 CR 353; *People v Brewster* (1986) 184 CA3d 921, 926–927, 229 CR 352. But the California Supreme Court has applied Pen C §1538.5(d) to a post-Proposition 8 case, using it to hold previously suppressed evidence inadmissible when the prosecution refiles charges. *Schlick v Superior Court* (1992) 4 C4th 310, 314–316, 14 CR2d 406. Such a result is not compelled by the Fourth Amendment. Accordingly, some judges believe that *Belleci* still controls.

*Belleci* does not apply to juvenile delinquency disposition hearings. *In re Michael V., supra*; for discussion, see §1.22.

Defendant cannot raise a suppression issue for the first time at the sentencing hearing. Pen C §1538.5(m); *People v Parrott* (1986) 179 CA3d 1119, 1124, 225 CR 293.

#### b. [§1.21] Parole and Probation Revocation Hearing

The exclusionary rule generally does not apply to revocation hearings. *Pennsylvania Bd. of Probation & Parole v Scott* (1998) 524 US 357, 363–364, 118 S Ct 2014, 141 L Ed 2d 344; *In re Martinez* (1970) 1 C3d 641, 648–650, 83 CR 382.

Previously suppressed evidence, however, may not be used in such a hearing. *People v Zimmerman* (1979) 100 CA3d 673, 675, 161 CR 188. *Zimmerman* antedates Proposition 8 and rests on a reading of Pen C §1538.5(d) (suppressed evidence inadmissible at trial or other hearing), rather than on an application of the exclusionary rule. To date, *Zimmerman* and Pen C §1538.5(d) seem to have survived Proposition 8. See *Schlick v Superior Court* (1992) 4 C4th 310, 314, 14 CR2d 406. For discussion of searches of parolees and probationers, see §§5.141–5.156.

## B. Application to Other Proceedings

### 1. [§1.22] Juvenile Court

The exclusionary rule applies to juvenile court proceedings filed under Welf & I C §602, *i.e.,* delinquency proceedings. See *In re Tyrell J.* (1994) 8 C4th 68, 75–76, 32 CR2d 33; *In re Michael V.* (1986) 178 CA3d 159, 169, 223 CR 503; Welf & I C §700.1. It does not apply, however, to disposition hearings, the equivalent of adult sentencing hearings. 178 CA3d at 170; see *In re Shannon B.* (1994) 22 CA4th 1235, 1247, 27 CR2d 800. Thus, a court may consider previously suppressed evidence at the disposition hearing.

The procedure for invoking the exclusionary rule in juvenile court is governed by Welf & I C §700.1 and Cal Rules of Ct 1419. Pen C §1538.5 does not apply to juvenile court proceedings. *In re David G.* (1979) 93 CA3d 247, 252, 155 CR 500.

Dependency hearings are not subject to the exclusionary rule. *In re Robert P.* (1976) 61 CA3d 310, 320–321, 132 CR 5.

☛ **Judicial Tip**: Questions about the applicability of the exclusionary rule should not be confused with issues concerning the Fourth Amendment rights of minors in relation to school authorities. For discussion, see §§5.157–5.160.

### 2. [§1.23] Civil and Quasi-Criminal Proceedings

The exclusionary rule is inapplicable to actions that are purely civil. *U.S. v Janis* (1976) 428 US 433, 454, 96 S Ct 3021, 49 L Ed 2d 1046 (tax refund suit); *I.N.S. v Lopez-Mendoza* (1984) 468 US 1032, 1042, 104 S Ct 3479, 82 L Ed 2d 778 (deportation proceeding); *Conservatorship of Susan T.* (1994) 8 C4th 1005, 1017–1020, 36 CR2d 40 (conservatorship proceeding).

The exclusionary rule, however, does apply in quasi-criminal proceedings such as

- *Civil narcotics commitment proceedings* (Welf & I C §§3100–3200 applicable to persons not convicted of a crime). *People v Moore* (1968) 69 C2d 674, 682, 72 CR 800 (proceedings involve loss of liberty and have same objectives as criminal law enforcement).

- *Forfeiture proceedings. One 1958 Plymouth Sedan v Pennsylvania* (1965) 380 US 693, 700, 85 S Ct 1246, 14 L Ed 2d 170 (object of proceeding is to penalize for commission of offense). However, items such as narcotics whose contraband nature is clear or can be shown without resort to illegally obtained evidence may be forfeited even if they were seized by unlawful means. 380 US at 699.

### 3. [§1.24] Administrative Proceedings

The exclusionary rule has limited application to administrative proceedings. It is generally not applied when doing so would have little or no deterrent effect. See, *e.g., Emslie v State Bar* (1974) 11 C3d 210, 229, 113 CR 175 (evidence illegally seized by police may be used in state bar disciplinary proceeding); *Finkelstein v State Personnel Bd.* (1990) 218 CA3d 264, 271, 267 CR 133 (evidence from search in connection with office move may be considered in disciplinary hearing); see also cases collected in *Conservatorship of Susan T.* (1994) 8 C4th 1005, 1017 n9, 36 CR2d 40.

A different result follows when an agency conducts an illegal search for evidence of an employee's crime and then tries to use that evidence in disciplinary proceedings against the employee. *Dyson v State Personnel Bd.* (1989) 213 CA3d 711, 722, 262 CR 112 (exclusionary rule deters such conduct as much as it deters unlawful police searches).

The exclusionary rule also applies to administrative proceedings that depend on a judicial probable cause determination. *Goldin v P.U.C.* (1979) 23 C3d 638, 668, 153 CR 802 (discontinuance of telephone service; agency need only consider facial validity of search warrant affidavits).

An agency is not bound by a determination in a criminal case that a search was illegal. *Gikas v Zolin* (1993) 6 C4th 841, 857, 25 CR2d 500 (Pen C §1538.5(d) inapplicable to administrative proceedings). Pen C §1538.5 does not apply to such proceedings. *Goldin v P.U.C., supra.*

## V. SEARCHES AND SEIZURES BY PRIVATE CITIZENS

### A. [§1.25] General Rule

The Fourth Amendment and its exclusionary rule generally apply only to searches and seizures by the government or its agents, not to the actions of private individuals. *U.S. v Jacobsen* (1984) 466 US 109, 113, 104 S Ct 1652, 80 L Ed 2d 85; *Burdeau v McDowell* (1921) 256 US 465, 475, 41 S Ct 574, 65 L Ed 1048; *People v De Juan* (1985) 171 CA3d 1110, 1120, 217 CR 642.

This principle simplifies suppression issues with respect to the validity of an arrest and the lawfulness of a search or seizure:

- Whether a citizen's arrest was valid is immaterial because invalidity is not a ground for suppression. *People v Cheatham* (1968) 263 CA2d 458, 461, 69 CR 679.

- Whether a purely private search or seizure of an object was lawful is immaterial because the unlawfulness of a private search or seizure is not a ground for suppression. *People v De Juan, supra*. For further discussion, see §§4.107–4.111.

But searches by local, state, and federal government employees come within the Fourth Amendment regardless of whether they are conducted by civil or criminal authorities and whether they seek evidence of a crime. *New Jersey v T.L.O.* (1985) 469 US 325, 335, 105 S Ct 733, 83 L Ed 2d 720 (school officials); see *Michigan v Tyler* (1978) 436 US 499, 506, 98 S Ct 1942, 56 L Ed 2d 486 (firefighters entering private premises to fight fire); *Camara v Municipal Court* (1967) 387 US 523, 528, 87 S Ct 1727, 18 L Ed 2d 930 (housing inspectors).

*New Jersey v T.L.O., supra,* supersedes California decisions such as *In re Guillermo M.* (1982) 130 CA3d 642, 645, 181 CR 856, and *People v Scott* (1974) 43 CA3d 723, 726, 117 CR 925, that took a narrower view of which searches by government employees are subject to Fourth Amendment protection.

☛ **Judicial Tip**: The *applicability* of the Fourth Amendment is a very different question from the *scope* of constitutional protection, which courts give to particular types of searches. For example, school officials may search students on less than probable cause. *New Jersey v T.L.O., supra*; see §5.157.

### B. [§1.26] Police Participation or Instigation

Insulation from the exclusionary rule disappears when private individuals act jointly with the police (*Stapleton v Superior Court* (1968) 70 C2d 97, 101–102, 73 CR 575), at the direction or request of the authorities (*People v Fierro* (1965) 236 CA2d 344, 347, 46 CR 132), or as agents of the police (*People v Tarantino* (1955) 45 C2d 590, 595, 290 P2d 505). Suppression will also be ordered when police officers sit idly by and do nothing when they have knowledge that a private citizen is violating or is about to violate the privacy rights of another; but mere consultation between a private citizen and police does not create a joint operation. *People v North* (1981) 29 C3d 509, 513–516, 174 CR 511. Similarly, a police officer who tells a citizen, "If you happen to run across a hammer or anything, let me know," is not requesting a search; the citizen's search remains purely private. *People v Wharton* (1991) 53 C3d 522, 579, 280 CR 631.

*Private search followed by police search.* When a citizen turns over a package or other materials to the authorities, the latter may conduct a warrantless search provided it does not exceed the scope of the private search. *U.S. v Jacobsen* (1984) 466 US 109, 115, 104 S Ct 1652, 80 L Ed 2d 85; *Walter v U.S.* (1980) 447 US 649, 656, 100 S Ct 2395, 65 L Ed 2d 410.

### C. [§1.27] Acts of Security Guards

*People v Zelinski* (1979) 24 C3d 357, 366, 155 CR 575, applied the exclusionary rule to searches of shoplift suspects by store security personnel on the ground that such action was not purely private; in the court's view, the security employees were fulfilling a public function in bringing violators of the law to justice.

The decision rested on the California Constitution rather than on the Fourth Amendment. In the aftermath of Proposition 8, courts of appeal have held that the exclusionary rule no longer applies to searches by private security guards. *In re Christopher H.* (1991) 227 CA3d 1567, 1576, 278 CR 577; *People v Taylor* (1990) 222 CA3d 612, 619, 271 CR 785; *People v Brouillette* (1989) 210 CA3d 842, 846, 258 CR 635. The U.S. Supreme Court has not ruled on the underlying issue. The California Supreme Court has not expressly overruled *Zelinski,* but has held in a different context that the conduct of store employees in arresting customers does not implicate the Fourth Amendment. *Jones v Kmart Corp.* (1998) 17 C4th 329, 334, 70 CR2d 844 (plaintiffs cannot maintain civil action predicated on violation of Fourth Amendment rights by store employees because employees' conduct is not state action).

## VI. GOOD FAITH AND BAD FAITH

### A. *Leon* and Its Extensions

#### 1. The *Leon* Good-faith Exception

##### a. [§1.28] Basic Principle

*Leon* and its progeny create exceptions to the Fourth Amendment exclusionary rule. *U.S. v Leon* (1984) 468 US 897, 104 S Ct 3405, 82 L Ed 2d 677. The *Leon* good-faith exception allows the introduction of evidence obtained under a defective warrant issued by a neutral and detached magistrate if the officers who executed the warrant acted in the reasonable good-faith belief that the warrant was valid. *U.S. v Leon, supra* (search warrant lacked probable cause); *Massachusetts v Sheppard* (1984) 468 US 981, 988, 104 S Ct 3424, 82 L Ed 2d 737 (error in search warrant regarding items to be seized); see also summary of *Leon* in *Arizona v Evans* (1995) 514 US 1, 11, 115 S Ct 1185, 131 L Ed 2d 34. For discussion of the meaning of good faith, see §1.29; for illustrative applications, see §§1.30–1.32.

*Leon* reflects the court's view that applying the exclusionary rule under such circumstances would not significantly deter violations of the Fourth Amendment. 468 US at 920.

*Arrest warrants. Leon* applies to arrest warrants, as well as to search warrants. *Arizona v Evans, supra*; *People v Palmer* (1989) 207 CA3d 663, 666, 255 CR 55.

*Warrantless searches and seizures.* For the extension of the good-faith concept to warrantless searches and seizures under limited circumstances, see §§1.33–1.36.

#### b. [§1.29] Meaning of Good Faith

Good faith is defined as "objectively reasonable reliance" on a warrant. *U.S. v Leon* (1984) 468 US 897, 920, 104 S Ct 3405, 82 L Ed 2d 677. In determining whether reliance on a warrant was reasonable, the inquiry is whether a well-trained police officer should reasonably have known that the warrant was invalid. *People v Camarella* (1991) 54 C3d 592, 596, 286 CR 780; *Bay v Superior Court* (1992) 7 CA4th 1022, 1031, 9 CR2d 339.

*Reasonable reliance.* When the defect consists of insufficient facts to establish probable cause, the issue is whether the warrant is so lacking in the indicia of probable cause that it would be unreasonable for a well-trained officer to believe that sufficient cause existed. *U.S. v Leon, supra*, 468 US at 923; *People v Camarella, supra.* Similarly, when a search warrant is overbroad, the test is whether a well-trained officer should have recognized that the description was so general that the warrant could not reasonably be regarded as valid. This would be the case, for example, if an officer executing the warrant "could only speculate whether an item of property was among the items to be seized." *Bay v Superior Court, supra.*

Objective reasonableness is determined without considering the fact that a magistrate accepted the affidavit, because every invalid warrant was issued by a magistrate, but not every invalid warrant is saved by *Leon. People v Camarella, supra*; but see *People v Bell* (1996) 45 CA4th 1030, 1056, 53 CR2d 156.

The prosecutor has the burden of establishing objectively reasonable reliance. *U.S. v Leon, supra*, 468 US at 924; *People v Camarella, supra.*

#### c. Illustrative Applications

#### (1) [§1.30] Warrant Lacks Probable Cause

Reliance was found *reasonable* in the following cases:

- Although the information was stale and uncorroborated, the affidavit was more than "bare bones" and the police investigation had been extensive. *U.S. v Leon* (1984) 468 US 897, 904, 104 S Ct 3405, 82 L Ed 2d 677.

- The combination of an anonymous tip and corroboration by state information made it a close question whether the affidavit established probable cause. *People v Camarella* (1991) 54 C3d 592, 606, 286 CR 780.
- The affidavit failed to link the residence to be searched to the suspect or his activities, but the officers knew defendant lived at the residence and could easily have cured the defect. *People v Bell* (1996) 45 CA4th 1030, 1055, 53 CR2d 156.

Reliance was found *unreasonable* in the following cases:

- The affidavit stated that a known drug dealer parked behind the residence to be searched. However, the affidavit contained no information, and the officers had none, that the dealer lived in the residence or used it. *People v Hernandez* (1994) 30 CA4th 919, 924–925, 35 CR2d 916.
- The affidavit recited two informants' reports of heavy foot traffic but did not corroborate any suspicious activity. *Bailey v Superior Court* (1992) 11 CA4th 1107, 1114, 15 CR2d 17 (court noted that officers could readily have conducted surveillance and that to uphold such a warrant "would leave an important part of law enforcement to well-intentioned tyros or those with the least competence").
- The affidavit was based on an anonymous uncorroborated tip concerning the identity of a bank robber. *People v Johnson* (1990) 220 CA3d 742, 750, 270 CR 70.
- The affidavit stated that drug addicts are prone to steal things to support their habits. *Doe v Broderick* (4th Cir 2000) 225 F3d 440, 452.

### (2) [§1.31] Defective or Overbroad Descriptions

Reliance was found *reasonable* in the following cases:

- The search warrant in a homicide investigation mistakenly authorized a search for controlled substances, rather than for the items listed in the supporting affidavit. The actual search was limited to the latter objects. *Massachusetts v Sheppard* (1984) 468 US 981, 986–988, 104 S Ct 3424, 82 L Ed 2d 737.
- The search warrant listed several categories of items; one was overly

broad. *People v Bradford* (1997) 15 C4th 1229, 1293, 65 CR2d 143 (homicide).

- The district attorney's office accidentally omitted the description of the items to be seized in the affidavit and the search warrant, but the search did not exceed the scope of what the warrant would have authorized. *People v Rodrigues-Fernandez* (1991) 235 CA3d 543, 552–553, 286 CR 700; see also *People v Alvarez* (1989) 209 CA3d 660, 665, 257 CR 445.

- The search warrant purported to authorize the search of a fraternity house, but the affidavit only established grounds to search defendant's room. The officers limited their search to that room. *People v MacAvoy* (1984) 162 CA3d 746, 760–763, 209 CR 34.

Reliance was found *unreasonable* in the following cases:

- The search warrant described the business premises by a mailbox number; the premises that were searched were several miles from the mailbox. *U.S. v Williamson* (10th Cir 1993) 1 F3d 1134, 1136 (no reasonable officer could believe that a warrant so lacking in meaningful description was valid).

- The warrant authorized seizure of property and records that were evidence of violation of specified federal statutes. *U.S. v Spilotro* (9th Cir 1986) 800 F2d 959, 964. In accord is *U.S. v Leary* (10th Cir 1988) 846 F2d 592, 606–610.

#### (3) [§1.32] Unsworn Statement

The good-faith exception applies to a search warrant based on an unsworn "Statement of Probable Cause" and on a sworn affidavit that contains no facts. *People v Leonard* (1996) 50 CA4th 878, 884, 57 CR2d 845. Courts are generally forgiving toward formal defects.

### d. [§1.33] Neutrality of Magistrate

The good-faith exception does not apply when "the issuing magistrate wholly abandoned his judicial role in the manner condemned in *Lo-Ji Sales, Inc. v New York* . . .; in such circumstances, no reasonably well-trained officer should rely on the warrant." *U.S. v Leon* (1984) 468 US 897, 923, 104 S Ct 3405, 82 L Ed 2d 677. In *Lo-Ji Sales, Inc. v New York* (1979) 442 US 319, 326–328, 99 S Ct 2319, 60 L Ed 2d 920, the magistrate who issued a search warrant for obscene material participated in the search. For further discussion of the need for a neutral and detached magistrate, see §§2.53–2.54.

#### e. [§1.34] Search Warrant Based on Illegally Obtained Evidence

The good-faith exception does not apply to a search warrant based on illegally obtained evidence, such as evidence from a prior unlawful entry. *People v Machupa* (1994) 7 C4th 614, 629–631, 29 CR2d 775; *People v Ingham* (1992) 5 CA4th 326, 333, 6 CR2d 756. Here the Fourth Amendment violation originates with the police, not with the magistrate.

#### f. [§1.35] Affidavit Containing False Statements or Omissions

The good-faith exception does not apply when the search warrant affidavit includes material false statements that the affiant made recklessly or knowingly. *U.S. v Leon* (1984) 468 US 897, 923, 104 S Ct 3405, 82 L Ed 2d 677. Here the exclusionary rule deters efforts to mislead the magistrate. Even if the magistrate is not misled, misstatements and omissions have a bearing on whether an officer reasonably believed in the existence of probable cause. *People v Maestas* (1988) 204 CA3d 1208, 1216, 252 CR 739.

Omission of evidence favorable to a finding of probable cause does not render *Leon* inapplicable. *People v Lim* (2000) 85 CA4th 1289, 1297–1298, 102 CR2d 604.

#### g. [§1.36] Sealed Affidavit

The good-faith exception does not apply to a search pursuant to a telephonic search warrant when the entire transcribed oral statement is sealed and kept from the defendant. *Swanson v Superior Court* (1989) 211 CA3d 332, 339–340, 259 CR 260 (*Leon* does not excuse due process violation). The due process problems with sealed affidavits may be reduced by following the in camera review procedure developed by *People v Hobbs* (1994) 7 C4th 948, 972–975, 30 CR2d 651. For further discussion, see §2.51.

### 2. The *Krull* Extension of *Leon*

#### a. [§1.37] Unconstitutional Statutes

Probable cause to arrest a person for violating a particular statute or ordinance is not affected by the subsequent invalidation of the statute or ordinance. The arrest under the invalidated statute or ordinance remains lawful; so does an otherwise valid search incident to such an arrest. *Michigan v DeFillippo* (1979) 443 US 31, 37, 99 S Ct 2627, 61 L Ed 2d

343; see *In re Hector R.* (1984) 152 CA3d 1146, 1152, 200 CR 110. The exclusionary rule, however, long applied to searches under statutes that were invalidated because they authorized unreasonable searches. See, *e.g., Ybarra v Illinois* (1979) 444 US 85, 96 n11, 100 S Ct 338, 62 L Ed 2d 238 (statute authorized search and detention of person on premises being searched pursuant to warrant); *Torres v Puerto Rico* (1979) 442 US 465, 471, 99 S Ct 2425, 61 L Ed 2d 1 (statute permitted search of luggage of persons entering Puerto Rico); *Almeida-Sanchez v U.S.* (1973) 413 US 266, 272–274, 93 S Ct 2535, 37 L Ed 2d 596 (statute authorized vehicle search without probable cause within border areas).

In *Illinois v Krull* (1987) 480 US 340, 349–350, 107 S Ct 1160, 94 L Ed 2d 364 (search of auto junkyard under state inspection statute invalidated by state court because it gave officers unbridled discretion), the court created a good-faith exception to the exclusionary rule for police who reasonably rely on the search authorization of a statute that is subsequently declared unconstitutional. The court treated the case as analogous to *Leon* and concluded that the exclusionary rule would not be a deterrent under the circumstances; the court equated the situation of *DeFillippo* from the perspective of deterrence.

*Krull* recognizes exceptions to its rule parallel to those in *Leon*: statutes that result from a complete abandonment by the legislature of its responsibility to enact constitutional laws and statutes whose "provisions are such that a reasonable officer should have known that the statute was unconstitutional." 480 US at 355.

Invalid legislation should not be confused with misinterpretation of a statute by the police. Such errors are generally not condoned; to rule otherwise would encourage ignorance and misinterpretation. For further discussion, see §1.42.

### b. [§1.38] Reliance on Invalid Search Condition

Search conditions may pose at least two types of good-faith problems: the court may find the particular condition invalid, or the officer's information that the defendant is subject to a search condition may be erroneous. The former situation is discussed below, the latter in §1.40.

A search under a condition later found invalid is analogous to a search under a statute that is subsequently found unconstitutional. Accordingly, the good-faith exception applies. *People v Fleming* (1994) 22 CA4th 1566, 1573, 28 CR2d 78 (search condition improperly imposed as part of diversion grant; court relied on *Leon* rather than *Krull*; court rejected argument that reliance unreasonable in light of established law that diversion grants may not include search condition).

### 3. The *Evans* Extension of *Leon*

#### a. [§1.39] Erroneous Warrant Information

Much more common than the *Krull* problem is a detention or arrest based on erroneous information received through official channels. For example, the police computer or information network shows an outstanding warrant for the defendant, although the warrant has in fact been recalled. This is the situation addressed by *Arizona v Evans* (1995) 514 US 1, 115 S Ct 1185, 131 L Ed 2d 34.

In *Evans,* the court clerk had failed to notify the sheriff's department that the court had recalled the warrant. *Evans* used *Leon* principles to hold that under the circumstances, the arresting officer could reasonably rely on the police computer system that showed the existence of the warrant. Thus, evidence obtained as a result of the detention or arrest was not excluded. 514 US at 14–16.

The court differentiated between mistakes of law enforcement organizations and those of other agencies. In the latter case, the exclusionary rule is unlikely to have a significant deterrent effect, according to *Evans*.

Reliance on erroneous information when the error originates outside law enforcement is not automatically reasonable. 514 US at 17 (dissenting opinion); *In re Arron C.* (1997) 59 CA4th 1365, 1369, 69 CR2d 852 (law enforcement officials are collectively responsible for keeping official channels free of outdated, incomplete, and inaccurate information; test is not merely good faith of individual officer in field, but good faith of agency of which officer is a part). Thus, cases that involve faulty warrant information may present two distinct issues:

(1) Who made the initial mistake?

(2) Did the arresting agency take reasonable steps to keep its information system current to make reliance on it reasonable?

Responsibility is not always easy to determine. For example, in *U.S. v Santa* (2d Cir 1999) 180 F3d 20, 25–30, the court that had issued the warrant had in fact notified a law enforcement agency of the recall, but that agency had no responsibility for the information system used by the arresting agency. *Santa* upheld the arrest under *Evans*.

#### b. [§1.40] Erroneous Information Regarding Search Condition

The good-faith exception also applies to reliance on erroneous information that an individual is subject to a search condition. *People v Downing* (1995) 33 CA4th 1641, 1650–1653, 40 CR2d 176 (computer error by court clerk showed defendant on probation subject to search condition). As with erroneous warrant information, reliance is unreasonable when the error originates with the police. *Miranda v Superior Court* (1993) 13 CA4th 1628, 1636, 16 CR2d 858.

Errors by a probation or parole officer are treated like those of court personnel. *In re Arron C.* (1997) 59 CA4th 1365, 1370–1372, 69 CR2d 852 (probation officer); *People v Tellez* (1982) 128 CA3d 876, 880, 180 CR 579 (parole officer). But see *People v Howard* (1984) 162 CA3d 8, 20–21, 208 CR 353 (criticized in *In re Arron C., supra*, 59 CA4th at 1372).

Probation and parole officers possess some of the powers of law enforcement, but for the purposes of good-faith exception they are not regarded as adjuncts of law enforcement. 59 CA4th at 1371. *Arron C.* involved a juvenile offender; the dissent noted that juvenile probation officers have a dual role as peace officers and as aides to the juvenile court.

### B. Good-Faith Mistakes

#### 1. [§1.41] Mistakes of Fact

A good-faith mistake of fact, *i.e.*, an objectively reasonable one, will generally not invalidate a search or seizure. *Illinois v Rodriguez* (1990) 497 US 177, 185–186, 110 S Ct 2793, 111 L Ed 2d 148. This includes reasonable mistakes concerning

- The identity of the person arrested or detained. *Hill v California* (1971) 401 US 797, 802–804, 91 S Ct 1106, 28 L Ed 2d 484; *People v Saucedo* (1995) 33 CA4th 1230, 1239, 40 CR2d 153; *People v Superior Court* (McBride) (1981) 122 CA3d 156, 162, 175 CR 723.

- The place to be searched under a search warrant. *Maryland v Garrison* (1987) 480 US 79, 84–86, 107 S Ct 1013, 94 L Ed 2d 72; for further discussion, see §§2.66–2.68.

- The authority of a person to consent to an entry or search. *Illinois v Rodriguez, supra*; *People v Jacobs* (1987) 43 C3d 472, 481, 233 CR 323; for further discussion, see §§5.128, 5.130.

These decisions rest on a fundamentally different ground than *Leon*, even though they also speak of objective reasonableness or good faith (for good faith, see, *e.g.*, *Hill v California, supra*, 401 US at 803; *People v Jacobs, supra*, 43 C3d at 481). In *Leon* and its progeny, the police had violated the Fourth Amendment and the court carved out exceptions to the exclusionary rule. In the mistake-of-fact cases, the courts hold that a search and seizure under a reasonable mistake of fact is not a violation of the Fourth Amendment because it satisfies the reasonableness requirements of the Amendment. Thus, to satisfy the "reasonableness" requirement of the Fourth Amendment, the appellate courts generally demand not that the many factual determinations regularly made by agents of the government always be correct, but that they always be reasonable. *Illinois v Rodriguez, supra*, 497 US at 185.

### 2. [§1.42] Mistakes of Law

An officer's erroneous interpretation of California law or of a local ordinance is generally unreasonable. *People v Lopez* (1987) 197 CA3d 93, 101, 242 CR 668 (good faith does not excuse erroneous belief that statute prohibiting possession of open container of alcohol in vehicle on highway applies to a vehicle in a parking lot); *In re Arthur J.* (1987) 193 CA3d 781, 785–788, 238 CR 523 (good faith does not excuse mistake regarding hours covered by local curfew ordinance). Dictum in *People v Souza* (1993) 15 CA4th 1646, 1653, 19 CR2d 731, suggests that good faith can excuse a possible misinterpretation of the Vehicle Code's open container provisions.

Courts usually view mistakes of law as unreasonable because when the wording of a statute or ordinance is reasonably clear, a contrary ruling would provide an incentive to remain ignorant of the law. *People v Teresinski* (1982) 30 C3d 822, 832, 180 CR 617. When the law of another state is involved, these considerations are weaker; a misinterpretation of foreign law may be reasonable under some circumstances. *People v Glick* (1988) 203 CA3d 796, 802, 250 CR 315.

The result is different when the officer is mistaken about *what* offense defendant committed as long as the officer knew facts that constituted grounds to detain or arrest the defendant. See, *e.g., People v Smith* (1984) 151 CA3d 89, 98–99, 198 CR 623 (mistake as to Vehicle Code section violated). Such errors generally do not violate the Fourth Amendment, because the reasonableness of the officer's actions is determined objectively and does not depend on the officer's subjective beliefs. See §3.50.

## C. [§1.43] Bad Faith: Pretext Stops and Searches

Just as claims of good faith are determined objectively, so are claims that the police acted in bad faith. An officer's bad faith does not invalidate an otherwise lawful search or seizure based on probable cause to believe a violation of the law has occurred. *Whren v U. S.* (1996) 517 US 806, 810–813, 116 S Ct 1769, 135 L Ed 2d 89.

*Whren* upheld a traffic stop made after the officer had seen the driver commit a minor traffic offense, even though the "real" reason for the stop was the officer's hope of finding drugs. The court said that using the traffic violation as a pretext to stop the vehicle was immaterial as long as a legal basis for the stop existed. In accord is *People v Miranda* (1993) 17 CA4th 917, 922–926, 21 CR2d 785.

*Whren* differentiated searches whose validity does not depend on probable cause, for instance, inventory searches and administrative inspections. Such searches may not be used as a pretext to look for contraband or evidence of criminal violations. *Florida v Wells* (1990) 495 US 1, 4, 110 S Ct 1632, 109 L Ed 2d 1; *People v Williams* (1999) 20 C4th 119,125–127, 83 CR2d 275; *People v Valenzuela* (1999) 74 CA4th 1202, 1207–1209, 88 CR2d 707.

Probation searches differ from inventory and administrative searches, at least when the circumstances show a possible probation violation. *People v Woods* (1999) 21 C4th 668, 678–679, 88 CR2d 88 (upholding search of probationer's residence under search clause although purpose of search was to look for incriminating evidence against another resident).

For discussion of using a search warrant as a pretext for an exploratory search, see §2.114.

## VII. FRUIT OF THE POISONOUS TREE

### A. [§1.44] What Is Excludable?

The exclusionary rule is applied most commonly to evidence that stems directly from a Fourth Amendment violation, such as things found after an illegal detention or arrest ("primary evidence"). It also applies, to a degree, to secondary or derivative evidence "that is the product of the primary evidence, or that is otherwise acquired as an indirect result of" the Fourth Amendment violation. *Murray v U.S.* (1988) 487 US 533, 536–537, 108 S Ct 2529, 101 L Ed 2d 472; *People v Williams* (1988) 45 C3d 1268, 1299, 248 CR 834. In short, the exclusionary rule bars use of "the fruit of the poisonous tree," a phrase that the U.S. Supreme Court first used in *Nardone v U.S.* (1939) 308 US 338, 341, 60 S Ct 266, 84 L Ed 307.

The major issue in fruit of the poisonous tree cases is the extent to which derivative evidence is excluded. The underlying consideration is that the evidence in question may be so far removed from the initial illegality "that the deterrent effect of the exclusionary rule no longer justifies its cost." *U.S. v Leon* (1984) 468 US 897, 911, 104 S Ct 3405, 82 L Ed 2d 677; *U.S. v Ceccolini* (1978) 435 US 268, 278–280, 98 S Ct 1054, 55 L Ed 2d 268.

Evidence is not fruit of the poisonous tree "simply because it would not have come to light but for the illegal actions of the police. Rather, the more apt question in such a case is whether, granting establishment of the primary illegality, the evidence to which instant objection is made has been come at by exploitation of that illegality or instead by means sufficiently distinguishable to be purged of the primary taint." *Wong Sun v U.S.* (1963) 371 US 471, 488, 83 S Ct 407, 9 L Ed 2d 441 (interior quotation marks omitted). For example, a defendant's statements made shortly after he was arrested without a warrant or probable cause are inadmissible, as are narcotics found as a result of the statement. However, a statement made several days after an illegal arrest and after defendant was released on his own recognizance and returned voluntarily to the police station has "become so attenuated as to dissipate the taint." 371 US at 491. For a discussion of attenuation, see §1.45. In addition to attenuation, evidence may also be free of taint if it rests on an "independent source" or would have been inevitably discovered. For discussion, see §§1.58–1.62.

## B. Attenuation

### 1. [§1.45] Basic Principles

Attenuation is a doctrine under which derivative evidence that would otherwise be excludable as fruit of the poisonous tree may nevertheless be admitted under the theory that a variety of factors contribute to remove the taint from the unlawful conduct and the evidence. There is no bright line that determines attenuation. The three key factors are, in order of increasing importance:

(1) The time lapse between the unlawful police conduct and the obtaining of the evidence sought to be suppressed—the shorter the time, the less likely is attenuation of the illegality;

(2) The presence of intervening circumstances; and

(3) "[P]articularly, the purpose and flagrancy of the official misconduct." *Brown v Illinois* (1975) 422 US 590, 604, 95 S Ct 2254, 45 L Ed 2d 416.

Usually no single fact is dispositive. *Brown v Illinois, supra.* Courts often give less weight to the time factor than to the others. See *Lozoya v Superior Court* (1987) 189 CA3d 1332, 1341, 235 CR 77. The *Brown* analysis applies to all types of evidence with the possible exception of courtroom identification testimony. See §1.53. The material that follows discusses attenuation in the context of different kinds of evidence.

☛ **Judicial Tip**: It is important to avoid a mechanical application of factors. The central inquiry is whether the police exploited their unlawful conduct or whether the evidence is an incidental by-product of it.

## 2. Applications

### a. Confessions Following Illegal Arrest, Detention, or Search

#### (1) [§1.46] Voluntariness and *Miranda* Warnings

When a defendant confesses or makes admissions after an illegal detention, arrest, or search, a *Miranda* admonition does not, in itself, make defendant's statements admissible. *Miranda* compliance is a factor to be considered, but is not a sufficient intervening act. *Miranda* bears on voluntariness; involuntary statements are inadmissible under the Fifth Amendment. For Fourth Amendment purposes, a confession that follows unlawful police conduct must not only be voluntary but also "sufficiently an act of free will to purge the primary taint." *Brown v Illinois* (1975) 422 US 590, 602, 95 S Ct 2254, 45 L Ed 2d 416, quoting *Wong Sun v U.S.* (1963) 371 US 471, 486, 83 S Ct 407, 9 L Ed 2d 441. Even a spontaneous outburst during an illegal detention may be subject to suppression. *People v Boyer* (1989) 48 C3d 247, 269, 256 CR 96; *In re Peter G.* (1980) 110 CA3d 576, 585, 168 CR 3; see §1.47.

The reason that *Miranda* warnings alone are not adequate attenuation is that a contrary rule would encourage unlawful arrests for the purpose of questioning. *Brown v Illinois, supra.*

#### (2) [§1.47] Chart: Attenuation as to Confessions After Unlawful Arrest or Detention

| *Name of Case* | *Time Lapse* | *Intervening Factors* | *Misconduct* |
|---|---|---|---|
| (1) *Attenuated* | | | |
| *Wong Sun v U.S.* (1963) 371 US 471, 491, 83 S Ct 407, 9 L Ed 2d 441 (confession of Wong Sun) | Several days | Arraignment, O.R., voluntary return to give statement | Arrest without probable cause |
| *Rawlings v Kentucky* (1980) 448 US 98, 107, 100 S Ct 2556, 65 L Ed 2d 633 | 45 minutes | *Miranda* admonition; spontaneous reaction to discovery of drugs in another's purse | Detention while search warrant sought |

| *Name of Case* | *Time Lapse* | *Intervening Factors* | *Misconduct* |
|---|---|---|---|
| *People v Beardslee* (1991) 53 C3d 68, 109, 279 CR 276 | 11 years | *Miranda* admonition; police illegality occurred in another state; exemplary conduct by local police to whom defendant gave statement | Police perjury |
| *People v Gonzalez* (1998) 64 CA4th 432, 447, 75 CR2d 272 (Paul's Kitchen confession) | 1 day | *Miranda*; questioning by officers from wholly unrelated agency | Lack of probable cause, but arresting officers knew nothing about crime involved in confession |
| *People v De Juan* (1985) 171 CA3d 1110, 1123–1124, 217 CR 642 | Probably an hour or less | *Miranda* admonition; defendant told he was not under arrest; defendant said he wanted to clear matter up | Police allowed private investigators to unlawfully arrest and transport defendant; threats by investigators |
| (2) *Not attenuated* | | | |
| *Wong Sun v U.S., supra*, 371 US at 486 (confession of Toy) | Minutes | None | Arrest without probable cause |

| *Name of Case* | *Time Lapse* | *Intervening Factors* | *Misconduct* |
|---|---|---|---|
| *Brown v Illinois* (1975) 422 US 590, 604–605, 95 S Ct 2254, 45 L Ed 2d 416. In accord: *Dunaway v New York* (1979) 442 US 200, 218–219, 99 S Ct 2248, 60 L Ed 2d 824 | Approx. 2 hours | *Miranda* | Arrest without probable cause and for purpose of questioning |
| *Taylor v Alabama* (1982) 457 US 687, 690–691, 102 S Ct 2664, 73 L Ed 2d 314 | 6 hours | 3 *Miranda* warnings; confession followed conversation with friends; arrest warrant filed before confession | Same |
| *People v Boyer* (1989) 48 C3d 247, 269, 256 CR 96 | Less than 4 hours | *Miranda* admonition; "consent" to accompany officers; defendant volunteered "I can't live with it" | Same; consent not free; statement after defendant told repeatedly he could not live with his guilt |
| *People v Gonzalez* (1998) 64 CA4th 432, 446–447, 75 CR2d 272 (Mac's Liquor confession) | 3 1/2–5 1/2 hours | *Miranda* admonition | Lack of probable cause; defendant arrested to see what might turn up |
| *Lozoya v Superior Court* (1987) 189 CA3d 1332, 1341–1346, 235 CR 77 | 4 days | Prior unattenuated admissions; possibly, confrontation with codefendant's statement | Same; egregious questioning |

☛ **Judicial Tips**:

- The judge should initially focus on the purpose of the unlawful arrest or detention. When circumstances indicate that a major purpose was to interrogate defendant, claimed intervening factors are less persuasive.
- The defendant might make several statements. The fact that some may be unattenuated does not automatically prevent attenuation of later ones (see *People v De Juan, supra*), but a second confession is presumed to have followed from the compulsion of the first (*People v DeVaughn* (1977) 18 C3d 889, 899, 135 CR 786).
- The defendant's voluntary return to the police station after being released is a compelling attenuating factor. Prolonged, aggressive questioning works against attenuation.
- The effect of a spontaneous statement depends on its relation to the preceding interrogation, if any. See *Rawlings v Kentucky, supra*; *People v Boyer, supra*.

### (3) [§1.48] Confession After Confrontation With Product of Illegal Search

A defendant might be lawfully arrested and then confess after being shown or told about evidence that the police found during an unlawful search. Assuming standing, such a confession is inadmissible; it flows from an exploitation of the illegality. *People v Stoner* (1967) 65 C2d 595, 599–600, 55 CR 897; *People v Johnson* (1969) 70 C2d 541, 546–549, 75 CR 401. Some judges believe that attenuation is possible when, for example, the unlawful search was conducted in an unrelated matter. See also *Rawlings v Kentucky* (1980) 448 US 98, 108, 100 S Ct 2556, 65 L Ed 2d 633 (spontaneous statement after incidental exposure to evidence admissible).

Confrontation with an unlawfully obtained confession has the same effect as confrontation with physical evidence that resulted from an illegal search. *People v DeVaughn* (1977) 18 C3d 889, 899, 135 CR 786.

### (4) [§1.49] Fruits of Unlawful Confession

The fruits of an unlawful confession are also inadmissible. Thus, in *Harrison v U.S.* (1968) 392 US 219, 88 S Ct 2008, 20 L Ed 2d 1047, defendant's first conviction for felony murder was reversed because the trial court had admitted his unlawfully obtained confessions. Defendant had testified at the first trial, admitting presence at the scene of the crime but denying its commission. In the second trial, the prosecutor read this testimony to the jury. Defendant was again convicted. The U.S. Supreme Court reversed, holding that the testimony could not be used unless the prosecution proved that defendant's decision to testify had not been compelled by the introduction of the illegally secured confessions. 392 US at 224–226. In accord is *People v Spencer* (1967) 66 C2d 158, 163–167, 57 CR 163.

In contrast, an accomplice's unlawfully obtained confession does not block his testimony against the defendant when he has previously been advised on the record by his attorney that his confession may well be inadmissible and that without it there will be no case against him, and when, after such advice, he has made an arm's length plea bargain. *People v Johnson* (1989) 47 C3d 1194, 1226, 255 CR 569 (these attenuating factors established that decision to testify was an exercise of accomplice's free will and not a consequence of any further exploitation of the confession).

In *People v Vasila* (1995) 38 CA4th 865, 873–874, 45 CR2d 355, a coerced confession led to the recovery of weapons and to further incriminating statements the next day. The court suppressed the weapons and the additional statements as fruits of the unlawful interrogation. In contrast, evidence seized as a result of a noncoercive *Miranda* violation is admissible. *People v Whitfield* (1996) 46 CA4th 947, 955, 54 CR2d 370 (court held earlier decisions to the contrary no longer control). The U.S. Supreme Court has not decided this issue; the Ninth Circuit has the same view as *Whitfield*. See, *e.g., U.S. v Henley* (9th Cir 1993) 984 F2d 1040, 1044.

A "public safety" exception makes firearms found as a result of questioning that did not comply with *Miranda* admissible under certain circumstances. *New York v Quarles* (1984) 467 US 649, 655–656, 104 S Ct 2626, 81 L Ed 2d 550; *People v Sims* (1993) 5 C4th 405, 450, 20 CR2d 537. However, this rule is an exception to *Miranda* and not to the principle that bars the fruits of unlawful confessions. See *New York v Quarles, supra*; *People v Sims, supra*.

### b. Identification Evidence

#### (1) [§1.50] Fingerprints and Other Physical Evidence of Identity

The poisonous tree doctrine applies to fingerprints. Prints taken after an arrest without probable cause are inadmissible, especially when the arrest was for the purpose of obtaining them. *Davis v Mississippi* (1969) 394 US 721, 727, 89 S Ct 1394, 22 L Ed 2d 676; *Hayes v Florida* (1985) 470 US 811, 813, 105 S Ct 1643, 84 L Ed 2d 705 (same result when police persuaded defendant to come to police station for printing by threatening to arrest him if he did not). The same holds true of other forms of identification evidence such as palmprints (*People v Rosales* (1984) 153 CA3d 353, 364, 200 CR 310) and handwriting exemplars (*People v Sesslin* (1968) 68 C2d 418, 428, 67 CR 409).

Attenuation principles also apply. Prints routinely taken after an unlawful arrest in another unrelated case may usually be used to identify a defendant lawfully arrested on the new charges. See *People v McInnis* (1972) 6 C3d 821, 825–826, 100 CR 618 (discussed in §1.52); *People v Reserva* (1969) 2 CA3d 151, 156, 82 CR 333. Prints taken after an arrest on probable cause but in violation of *Payton v New York* (1980) 445 US 573, 576, 100 S Ct 1371, 63 L Ed 2d 639, are in all likelihood admissible on the basis of *New York v Harris* (1990) 495 US 14, 16, 110 S Ct 1640, 109 L Ed 2d 13 (confession admissible under these circumstances).

A valid holding order is a sufficient intervening act; prints taken thereafter are admissible. *People v Solomon* (1969) 1 CA3d 907, 910, 82 CR 215. Advising defendant that he does not have to provide a handwriting exemplar is not an adequate intervening event. *People v Sesslin, supra.* For attenuation purposes, such advice is analogous to *Miranda* admonitions. See §1.46.

For a discussion of the application of inevitable discovery to fingerprints, see §1.61.

### (2) [§1.51] Showups and Lineups

Evidence that a victim or witness identified defendant at a showup or lineup held after an illegal arrest is usually inadmissible as a clear exploitation of the illegality. See, *e.g., U.S. v Crews* (1980) 445 US 463, 472, 100 S Ct 1244, 63 L Ed 2d 537. However, attenuation is possible. For instance, in *Johnson v Louisiana* (1972) 406 US 356, 365, 92 S Ct 1620, 32 L Ed 2d 152, before the lineup defendant had been brought before a magistrate who set bail and advised him of his rights. The court viewed this as a sufficient intervening factor. The result might be different if the arrest were made for the purpose of having a witness identify the defendant.

A consent to be in a lineup after an arrest for such a flagrantly improper purpose is invalid. *In re Dung T.* (1984) 160 CA3d 697, 716–717, 206 CR 772. In contrast, a consent to accompany the officers to the police station in order to be photographed is valid if it is not a submission to an assertion of authority. *People v Farley* (1979) 90 CA3d 851, 863, 153 CR 695.

### (3) [§1.52] Photo Lineups

When evidence concerning identification from photographs is in issue, it is important to differentiate between two situations. In one, defendant's picture was taken after an unlawful arrest in the matter before the court and a witness identified this photograph from a group of mugshots. Testimony that such an identification was made is inadmissible as fruit of the illegality, at least when the arrest lacked probable cause or was made for the purpose of photographing defendant, and there were no significant intervening circumstances. *U.S. v Crews* (1980) 445 US 463, 472, 100 S Ct 1244, 63 L Ed 2d 537 (pretext arrest so that suspect could be photographed).

In the second situation, a witness viewed a photo lineup that included a mugshot of the defendant taken after an unlawful arrest in an unrelated case. Here courts are likely to find attenuation and admit evidence of the photo lineup and of in-court identification without inquiring whether the latter is independent of the former. *People v McInnis* (1972) 6 C3d 821, 825–826, 100 CR 618. See also *Lockridge v Superior Court* (1970) 3 C3d 166, 170, 89 CR 731; *People v Thierry* (1998) 64 CA4th 176, 182, 75 CR2d 141.

In *People v McInnis, supra,* the court said that a contrary ruling would give defendant a crime insurance policy in perpetuity by providing him with "immunity because another constable in another jurisdiction in another case" blundered. 6 C3d at 826. However, there is no attenuation when the police photographed defendant during an illegal detention in order to use the photo in future criminal investigations. *People v Rodriguez* (1993) 21 CA4th 232, 240, 26 CR2d 660; see *People v Thierry, supra,* 64 CA4th at 183.

### (4) [§1.53] In-Court Identification

The exclusion of pretrial identification evidence does not dictate the same result for courtroom identification of the defendant. A victim or witness may make an in-court identification when it rests on an independent recollection of the encounter with the defendant and was not biased by unlawful pretrial identification procedures. *U.S. v Crews* (1980) 445 US 463, 472, 100 S Ct 1244, 63 L Ed 2d 537; *People v Teresinski* (1982) 30 C3d 822, 827, 180 CR 617; *People v Thierry* (1998) 64 CA4th 176, 184, 75 CR2d 141; *People v Rodriguez* (1993) 21 CA4th 232, 241, 26 CR2d 660.

It is not sufficient for the witness to testify that the identification is based on the original encounter. Testimony regarding specific observations must show that the in-court identification is not affected by the illegal prior identification. *U.S. v Crews, supra*; *People v Nation* (1980) 26 C3d 169, 181, 161 CR 299; *People v Martin* (1970) 2 C3d 822, 831, 87

CR 709. For factors to be considered, see *U.S. v Wade* (1967) 388 US 218, 241, 87 S Ct 1926, 18 L Ed 2d 1149. It is undecided whether the court also needs to apply the *Brown* factors discussed in §1.45. *U.S. v Crews, supra.*

☛ **Judicial Tip**: Many judges believe explicit findings are especially useful in these situations. For example, when the court denies a suppression motion, the record may be unclear in the absence of findings whether in-court identification testimony is allowed because (1) the underlying arrest was lawful as were the pretrial identification procedures; (2) the arrest was not lawful, but attenuation makes the pretrial identification and, hence, the courtroom identification admissible (*i.e.*, the *McInnis* situation discussed in §1.52); or (3) the pretrial identification was not attenuated, but the courtroom identification is independent (the *Crews* situation). Findings can also demonstrate that the court gave careful attention to the relevant factors. Some judges make alternative findings whenever possible.

### c. [§1.54] Testimony of Witness

When the authorities find a witness as a result of a Fourth Amendment violation, courts are considerably more likely to permit the witness to testify than to admit other products of the illegality. *U.S. v Ceccolini* (1978) 435 US 268, 279, 98 S Ct 1054, 55 L Ed 2d 268. The poisonous fruit doctrine applies to testimony, but *Ceccolini* holds that the illegality is more readily attenuated than in the case of physical evidence because the cost of excluding live witness testimony is often greater. 435 US at 280.

In *Ceccolini,* an officer on break visited a friend who worked in a flower shop. He went behind a counter, saw an envelope with money sticking out, picked it up, looked inside, and observed betting slips. He did not mention this to his friend, but reported it to his superiors who in turn passed the information on to the FBI. The FBI had been investigating gambling in the town; it had surveilled the flower shop, owned by defendant, a year earlier. Four months after the police officer's observations, an FBI agent interviewed the shop employee, and she agreed to testify. The court held that she could do so, noting the following factors (435 US at 275):

- The witness was not a putative defendant. This is an important factor (see *People v Superior Court* (Sosa) (1982) 31 C3d 883, 894, 185 CR 113), but not critical (*People v Johnson* (1989) 47 C3d 1194, 1226, 255 CR 569 (testimony by accomplice)).

- The testimony was voluntary and not induced by the authorities. A witness's earlier involuntary statements are significant (*People v Superior Court* (Sosa), *supra*), but do not necessarily make the testimony involuntary. *People v Johnson, supra* (intervening plea bargain and full on-the-record advice by witness's counsel). See also *People v Douglas* (1990) 50 C3d 468, 500, 268 CR 126.

- Substantial time lapsed between the illegal search and contact with the witness.

- The relation between the witness and the defendant was known before the search.

- The illegally obtained evidence was not used in questioning the witness.

- The officer did not make the search with the intent of finding a witness. The egregiousness of police conduct is an important factor (*People v Superior Court* (Sosa), *supra*), but courts have found attenuation despite highly flagrant illegalities if they were committed by other police agencies or in unrelated matters (*People v Douglas, supra*; *People v Superior Court* (Sosa) (1983) 145 CA3d 581, 588, 194 CR 525 (different case from one with same name referred to above)), and intervening circumstances ensure that the testimony is truly voluntary (*People v Johnson, supra*; *People v Superior Court* (Sosa), *supra*, 145 CA3d at 589).

The two major considerations are "the degree of free will exercised by the witness" and the closeness "of the connection between the illegal police conduct and the testimony sought to be suppressed." *People v Ford* (1984) 150 CA3d 687, 703, 198 CR 80. See *People v Superior Court* (Sosa), *supra*, 31 C3d at 893; *People v Cella* (1983) 139 CA3d 391, 403, 188 CR 675. Even wholly voluntary testimony is not permitted when it is tied closely to the illegality. Thus, when police unlawfully seize property they suspect to be stolen, its owner cannot testify that he identified it at the police station. *People v Dowdy* (1975) 50 CA3d 180, 187, 123 CR 155.

The result in *Dowdy* is also an application of the principle that when the exclusionary rule prohibits introduction of an object into evidence, the rule also prohibits testimony about that object (see *Murray v U.S.* (1988) 487 US 533, 536, 108 S Ct 2529, 101 L Ed 2d 472) or other efforts to bring it before the court (*Silverthorne Lumber Co. v U.S.* (1920) 251 US 385, 391, 40 S Ct 182, 64 L Ed 319 (prosecution cannot subpoena records that had been illegally seized and returned to defendant under court order)).

### d. [§1.55] Consent

Consent to search that is the product of unlawful police conduct is invalid absent a showing of attenuation. *Wong Sun v U.S.* (1963) 371 US 471, 486, 83 S Ct 407, 9 L Ed 2d 441; *People v Henderson* (1990) 220 CA3d 1632, 1651, 270 CR 248. Such a showing "requires at least an intervening independent act by the defendant or a third party which breaks the causal chain linking the illegality and evidence in such a way that the evidence is not in fact obtained by exploitation of that illegality." *People v Superior Court* (Keithley) (1975) 13 C3d 406, 410, 118 CR 617 (interior quotation marks omitted); see *Wong Sun v U.S., supra.*

An illustration of an independent act is *People v Boyer* (1989) 48 C3d 247, 276, 256 CR 96. There defendant's consent was arguably invalid. Defendant's cotenant also gave consent, although only after she learned that defendant, who was in custody, had assented. The court held that the cotenant's consent was not tainted by any improper police conduct toward defendant because the particular circumstances showed that the cotenant made an independent decision. Those circumstances included her conversation with defendant, without any suggestion that his consent was coerced, and her consultation with her counsel.

Factors that bear on attenuation include the proximity of the consent to the officers' illegal conduct (the closer, the more tainted), whether the illegality led to observation of the item for which they obtained consent, whether the unlawful conduct was flagrant, whether defendant was advised that he could refuse consent, whether the consent was volunteered rather than requested, and whether the police purpose underlying the illegality was to obtain consent. *People v Henderson, supra,* 220 CA3d at 1651.

For discussion of consent to be in a lineup, see §1.51.

### e. [§1.56] Search Warrants

Generally, a search warrant that depends on information acquired by an illegal search is invalid. *People v Chapman* (1984) 36 C3d 98, 113, 201 CR 628; see *People v Machupa* (1994) 7 C4th 614, 623, 29 CR2d 775 (search warrant based on prior warrantless unlawful entry not saved by good-faith exception). However, attenuation principles may allow the admission of evidence seized under such a warrant. For example, in *People v Coe* (1991) 228 CA3d 526, 531, 279 CR 362, police had seized tools from the defendant under a search warrant that was quashed. The police marked and photographed them before returning them to the defendant.

Two years later, the police found the tools at the scene of a burglary, traced them to the defendant by the markings, and on that basis obtained a search warrant. The court held that the evidence found under the second warrant was admissible, even though there would have been no probable cause for it without the markings and photographs of the tools. The time lapse was substantial; there were intervening circumstances—defendant committed a new crime and abandoned the tools when he fled the scene of the burglary; and the police illegality was not flagrant and had occurred in an unrelated matter. Thus, all three *Brown* factors pointed to attenuation.

Abandonment is an attenuating circumstance when, as in *People v Coe, supra*, it is not brought about by police illegality; however, it is not an attenuating circumstance when it occurs during an illegal detention. *People v Verin* (1990) 220 CA3d 551, 555, 269 CR 573.

For application of the independent source doctrine to search warrants, see §§1.58–1.59.

#### f. [§1.57] Subsequent Investigation

Unlawfully obtained evidence can properly be used to continue or reopen an investigation of defendant. See *U.S. v Ceccolini* (1978) 435 US 268, 279, 98 S Ct 1054, 55 L Ed 2d 268. For example, when police officers find drugs during an illegal search of defendant's car, they may decide to set up an undercover buy. Depending on the flagrancy of the initial illegality, defendant's voluntary decision to sell may be a sufficient intervening factor. *People v Caratti* (1980) 103 CA3d 847, 850, 163 CR 265; see *People v Eastmon* (1976) 61 CA3d 646, 653, 132 CR 510.

While an illegal search does not immunize a suspect against subsequent surveillance or investigation, the police cannot turn ambiguous conduct observed during the investigation into probable cause for arrest by factoring in unlawfully obtained information. *Lozoya v Superior Court* (1987) 189 CA3d 1332, 1340, 235 CR 77; *People v Maxwell* (1978) 78 CA3d 124, 131, 144 CR 95. But see criticism of *Maxwell* in *People v Coe* (1991) 228 CA3d 526, 533, 279 CR 362.

### C. Independent Source

#### 1. [§1.58] Basic Principles

The "independent source" doctrine is a doctrine under which evidence obtained in violation of the Fourth Amendment may nevertheless be admitted if the evidence is also discovered by a source independent of the violation. The underlying policy is that the police should not be put in a worse position than they would have been absent any error or violation. *Nix v Williams* (1984) 467 US 431, 443, 104 S Ct 2501, 81 L Ed 2d 377.

Thus, subject to an important condition discussed below, an illegal entry does not taint a search pursuant to a warrant based on information known to the police before the entry. *Murray v U.S.* (1988) 487 US 533, 542, 108 S Ct 2529, 101 L Ed 2d 472; *Segura v U.S.* (1984) 468 US 796, 814, 104 S Ct 3380, 82 L Ed 2d 599. Such a warrant rests on a source that is independent of the Fourth Amendment violation. *Segura* supersedes *People v Shuey* (1975) 13 C3d 835, 850, 120 CR 83 (when defendant would not consent to search, police detained him for three hours while obtaining search warrant; evidence obtained during execution of warrant suppressed). *People v Bennett* (1998) 17 C4th 373, 389 n5, 70 CR2d 850.

This principle applies to unlawful entries for the purpose of securing the premises (*Segura v U.S., supra*; *People v Lamas* (1991) 229 CA3d 560, 282 CR 296; *People v Angulo* (1988) 199 CA3d 370, 375, 244 CR 819), to illegal entries to confirm officers' suspicions that the premises contain contraband (*Murray v U.S., supra*; *People v Freeman* (1990) 219 CA3d 894, 904, 268 CR 603), and to blocking persons from entering premises while officer obtains a search warrant. *People v Bennett, supra* (alternate holding).

The evidence in dispute will be admissible regardless of whether it was discovered for the first time during the execution of the warrant as in *Segura* or observed during the unlawful entry as in *Murray, Freeman,* and *Angulo.*

The search, however, rests on a "genuinely independent source" only if "no information gained from the illegal entry affected either the law enforcement officers' decision to seek a warrant or the magistrate's decision to grant it." *Murray v U.S., supra,* 487 US at 540, 542. In short, "what counts is whether the actual illegal search had any effect in producing the warrant." 487 US at 542 n3.

### 2. [§1.59] Practical Problems

The easy case is one in which (1) the officers started to prepare the search warrant application before the time of the illegal entry (or other evidence shows that the decision to seek a warrant was made before the entry), and (2) observations during the entry were not part of the search warrant application or otherwise conveyed to the issuing magistrate. These circumstances clearly satisfy the requirements of *Murray v U.S.* (1988) 487 US 533, 540, 108 S Ct 2529, 101 L Ed 2d 472.

When the affidavit includes observations made during the illegal entry, the illegally obtained information is excised, and if the remaining information supplies probable cause, the warrant is valid. *People v Weiss* (1999)

20 C4th 1073, 1074–1075, 86 CR2d 337, disapproving *People v Koch* (1989) 209 CA3d 770, 787–788, 257 CR 483, which also required that the decision to issue the warrant was not influenced by the illegally obtained information.

However, a magistrate's decision to issue a warrant based on an affidavit that includes tainted information is not entitled to the considerable deference reviewing courts normally give a warrant. *People v Weiss, supra,* 20 C4th at 1082–1083.

## D. Inevitable Discovery

### 1. [§1.60] Basic Principles

Inevitable discovery is a principle under which derivative evidence may be admitted if it would have been discovered regardless of the underlying illegality. The term "inevitable discovery" is a misnomer, however; "[t]he test is not one of certainty, but rather of a reasonably strong probability." *People v Superior Court* (Tunch) (1978) 80 CA3d 665, 681, 145 CR 795. See *People v Boyer* (1989) 48 C3d 247, 278, 256 CR 96.

The U.S. Supreme Court accepted inevitable discovery in *Nix v Williams* (1984) 467 US 431, 104 S Ct 2501, 81 L Ed 2d 377. In that case, defendant's incriminating statements, unlawfully obtained, had led the police to thc victim's body. The court held that evidence concerning the body was "admissible because a search had been under way which would have discovered the body, had it not been called off because of the discovery produced by the unlawfully obtained statements." See *Murray v U.S.* (1988) 487 US 533, 539, 108 S Ct 2529, 101 L Ed 2d 472. The rationale for the inevitable discovery exception is the same as for the independent source rule: Without it the government would be in a worse position than if the illegality had never occurred. *Nix v Williams, supra,* 467 US at 444; see §1.58.

Significant factors in applying the inevitable discovery exception are pursuit by the police of a broad-based investigation at the time of the illegality (see *Nix v Williams, supra*; *People v Boyer, supra*) and the likelihood that "usual and commonplace police investigative procedures" would have led to the evidence irrespective of the Fourth Amendment violation (*People v Boyer, supra*; *People v Superior Court* (Tunch), *supra*).

Care is needed "to prevent application of the inevitable discovery exception from subverting the safeguards of the exclusionary rule. . . . There is much danger that a mechanical application of the doctrine will encourage unconstitutional shortcuts." *People v Superior Court* (Tunch), *supra* (interior quotation marks omitted). *Tunch* suggested that one limitation on inevitable discovery, as in the case of attenuation, is the purpose and flagrancy of the official misconduct. 80 CA3d at 682. However, *Nix v Williams, supra*, and California decisions subsequent to *Tunch* do not appear to give weight to this factor. In other words, courts do not subject application of the inevitable discovery and independent source exceptions to the kind of analysis they use to decide attenuation. Nevertheless, many judges believe that *Tunch*'s cautionary statements are sound and that the prosecution bears a "heavy burden" (*People v Superior Court* (Tunch), *supra*, 80 CA3d at 682) in seeking to establish the admissibility of evidence under the inevitable discovery exception.

### 2. [§1.61] Applications

Inevitable discovery applies to many types of evidence, among them:

- *Fingerprints.* Prints taken following defendant's arrest are admissible, even if the arrest is unlawful, when the police have latents as well as defendant's prints from a prior arrest. "It is inconceivable that a match-up would not have been made." *People v Rosales* (1987) 192 CA3d 759, 769, 237 CR 558.

- *Physical evidence. Nix v Williams* (1984) 467 US 431, 443, 104 S Ct 2501, 81 L Ed 2d 377; *Green v Superior Court* (1985) 40 C3d 126, 136, 219 CR 186; *People v Huston* (1989) 210 CA3d 192, 221–222, 258 CR 393; *People v Jaquez* (1985) 163 CA3d 918, 930–931, 209 CR 852; *People v Superior Court* (Tunch) (1978) 80 CA3d 665, 682–683, 145 CR 795.

- *Testimony of witness. People v Boyer* (1989) 48 C3d 247, 277, 256 CR 96.

- *Blood sample. People v Clark* (1993) 5 C4th 950, 992, 22 CR2d 689 (inevitable because 30 minutes after blood drawn, defendant admitted ingesting drugs).

### 3. [§1.62] Limitation: Argument That Search Warrant Inevitably Would Have Been Obtained

An unlawful warrantless search cannot be justified on the ground that a search warrant would inevitably have been obtained; this "would constitute a practical repeal of the Fourth Amendment." *People v Ruggles* (1981) 125 CA3d 473, 488, 178 CR 231, vacated on other grounds in *California v Ruggles* (1982) 459 US 809, 103 S Ct 34, 74 L Ed 2d 47. The court issued a new opinion in *People v Ruggles* (1985) 39 C3d 1, 216 CR 88. See *People v Robles* (2000) 23 C4th 789, 800–801, 97 CR2d 914. But see *People v Russell* (1987) 195 CA3d 186, 190, 240 CR 456.

2

# Search Warrants

## I. [§2.1] SCOPE OF CHAPTER

This chapter discusses the requirements for issuing and executing search warrants, including those transmitted by telephone, fax, or e-mail.

Sections 2.2–2.14 outline the constitutional and statutory framework of search warrant law, including grounds for issuing a search warrant, the special master procedure and a checklist for using it (§§2.5–2.7), other special limitations, and the geographic jurisdiction of the issuing magistrate.

The requirements for affidavits are the topic of §§2.15–2.51. The heart of the affidavit, its statement of probable cause, is examined in detail (§§2.22–2.43). The warrant itself is the focus of §§2.52–2.77, with special attention to the need for adequate description of persons and places to be searched and of the property to be seized (§§2.64–2.77).

Sections 2.78–2.129 cover the execution of search warrants, including questions related to promptness of execution, night service, the detention of persons during the execution, the seizure of items not covered by the search warrant, the presence of third parties, videotaping of the search, the use of dogs, unduly prolonged or intense searches, the receipt, return and inventory, searches conducted by special masters, and securing the premises pending issuance of a warrant.

The chapter concludes with procedural guides to telephonic, fax and e-mail warrants (§§2.130–2.131), and with a form of an affidavit to be executed by special masters (§2.132).

This chapter is limited to warrants issued under the Penal Code. For administrative inspection warrants, see CCP §§1822.50–1822.60 (inspections relating to buildings, fires, safety, health, labor, or zoning); Health & S C §§41510 (air pollution), 43012 (vehicle pollution); Fish & G C §15501 (aquaculture).

## II. CONSTITUTIONAL AND STATUTORY FRAMEWORK

### A. [§2.2] Constitutional Provisions

The Fourth Amendment specifies that warrants be issued "upon probable cause, supported by oath or affirmation, and particularly describing the place to be searched, and the persons or things to be seized." See §1.2. Virtually identical language in the California Constitution does not serve as an independent basis for excluding illegally obtained evidence. See §1.7.

### B. [§2.3] Statutory Definition of Search Warrant

Penal Code §1523 long defined a search warrant as an order in writing, signed by a magistrate, commanding a peace officer to search for personal property and bring it before a magistrate.

Presently, the section also includes an order to search for "a person or persons, a thing or things." The reference to persons was added to provide a mechanism for compliance with *Steagald v U.S.* (1981) 451 US 204, 101 S Ct 1642, 68 L Ed 2d 38, which held that search of a person's home, under an arrest warrant for another individual, violates the Fourth Amendment in the absence of a search warrant. Stats 1996, ch 1078, §8(a). It is not clear why "thing or things" was added to the statute, except possibly to make the section consistent with Pen C §1524(a), which speaks of "property or things" in delineating the grounds for issuance of a search warrant. For discussion of Pen C §1524, see §2.4.

### C. [§2.4] Statutory Grounds for Issuance

Penal Code §1524(a) authorizes search warrants for property that

(1) "was stolen or embezzled" (Pen C §1524(a)(1));

(2) was "used as the means of committing a felony" (Pen C §1524(a)(2));

(3) is "in the possession of any person with the intent to use it as a means of committing a public offense, or in the possession of another to whom he or she may have delivered it for the purpose of concealing it or preventing its being discovered" (Pen C §1524(a)(3));

(4) consists of any item or constitutes any evidence "that tends to show a felony has been committed, or . . . that a particular person has committed a felony" (Pen C §1524(a)(4)); or

(5) is evidence of the sexual exploitation of a child in violation of Pen C §311.3 or of the possession of matter showing sexual conduct of a person under the age of 18 in violation of Pen C §311.11 (Pen C §1524(a)(5)).

The first and third grounds apply both to felonies and misdemeanors; the second and fourth only to felonies. The last ground refers to particular misdemeanors. See Chrystie & Schirn, Search Warrants, p I-2 (10th ed California District Attorneys Association 2000), hereafter cited as

Chrystie & Schirn. Note that the statute does not authorize search warrants for property used to commit a misdemeanor or that is evidence of a misdemeanor, unless the property comes within subsections (a)(1), (3), or (5).

The statute also permits a search warrant "(w)hen there is a warrant to arrest a person." Pen C §1524(a)(6).

*Penal Code §1524 and the Fourth Amendment.* At one point the Fourth Amendment was construed to prohibit a search for or seizure of "mere evidence" of a crime. *Gouled v U.S.* (1921) 255 US 298, 304–306, 41 S Ct 261, 65 L Ed 2d 647. Penal Code §1524(a)(4) opted for a broader view, permitting a search for evidence tending to show commission of a felony. *People v Thayer* (1965) 63 C2d 635, 642, 47 CR 780, upheld the constitutionality of Pen C §1524(a)(4).

Subsequently, the U.S. Supreme Court rejected the "mere evidence" rule. *Warden v Hayden* (1967) 387 US 294, 87 S Ct 1642, 1647–1652, 18 L Ed 2d 782. Today a search warrant may be issued for "contraband or evidence of a crime." *See Illinois v Gates* (1983) 462 US 213, 238, 103 S Ct 2317, 76 L Ed 2d 527. The crime may be one committed in another state. *People v Kraft* (2000) 23 C4th 978, 1051, 99 CR2d 1.

## D. Limitations in Particular Situations

### 1. Papers of Lawyers, Doctors, Psychotherapists, and Members of Clergy

#### a. [§2.5] No Suspicion of Person Whose Place Is To Be Searched: Special Master Procedure

When the authorities seek a search warrant for the place of a lawyer, doctor, psychotherapist, or member of the clergy, the affidavit must so state. Pen C §1525. Warrants for documentary evidence in the possession of such professionals who are not suspected of criminal activity are subject to special requirements set out in Pen C §1524(a)–(f). These requirements are sometimes called the special master procedure. See, *e.g.,* Pen C §1543(a).

The court appoints a special master, selected from a State Bar list. Pen C §1524(a), (d); for a checklist for issuing warrants for documents of lawyers, doctors, psychotherapists, or clergymen, see §2.7. The court may dispense with the appointment if it determines after a reasonable effort to find a special master that none is available within a reasonable time. Pen C §1524(d). The special master accompanies the person serving the warrant and performs specified duties. The party served is entitled to a postsearch hearing to raise Fourth Amendment and privilege issues. Pen C §1524(c)(2); for discussion, see §§6.144–6.147.

The special master procedure applies to typical situations such as searches of a doctor's or lawyer's office for evidence of criminal activity by a patient or client or by another physician or attorney. When a proposed search extends to client files, "special care must be taken to avoid unnecessary intrusion on attorney-client communications." *Fenwick & West v Superior Court* (1996) 43 CA4th 1272, 1279, 51 CR2d 294.

### b. [§2.6] Suspicion of Criminal Activity by Person Whose Place Is To Be Searched

A person suspected of criminal activity related to the documents being sought is not entitled to the special master procedure. *People ex rel Lockyer v Superior Court* (2000) 83 CA4th 387, 404, 99 CR2d 646, disapproved on other grounds in 25 C4th 703, 718 n5; *McKirdy v Superior Court* (1982) 138 CA3d 12, 18–20, 188 CR 143. However, the magistrate in deciding whether to issue a warrant should consider the privacy rights of clients and patients, determining whether they are outweighed by a "predominant state need and sufficiently circumscribed means." *People v Hepner* (1994) 21 CA4th 761, 784, 26 CR2d 417; *McKirdy v Superior Court, supra.* A strong showing of suspected criminal fraud on the part of the doctor whose files were searched sufficed in *Hepner* and *McKirdy.*

The search warrant need not be limited to files that are known to contain evidence of fraud as long as the affidavit shows a fair probability that other files contain evidence of criminal intent or that the known cases are representative of more pervasive violations. *Andresen v Maryland* (1976) 427 US 463, 483, 96 S Ct 2737, 49 L Ed 2d 627; *People v Hepner, supra*, 21 CA4th at 780.

A lawyer whose files were seized is entitled to an in camera hearing on a motion objecting to disclosure of the documents on the ground that they are privileged. *People v Superior Court* (Laff) (2001) 25 C4th 703, 712–720, 107 CR2d 323; *People v Superior Court* (Bauman & Rose) (1995) 37 CA4th 1757, 1767, 44 CR2d 734; *PSC Geothermal Servs. Co. v Superior Court* (1994) 25 CA4th 1697, 1712, 31 CR2d 213. At the hearing the court determines whether the crime/fraud exception applies to the claimed privileges. The prosecutor must establish a prima facie case of fraud and a reasonable relation between the fraud and the attorney-client communication. *Bauman & Rose, supra*, 37 CA4th at 1769. The probable cause showing to obtain a search warrant may not satisfy the showing required to establish the crime/fraud exception. *Bauman & Rose, supra*. The fact that the attorney is a subject of suspicion does not obviate the privilege. *Bauman & Rose, supra*.

Proposition 8 does not eliminate the need to rule on disclosure of documents that are subject to the attorney-client or work product privilege because the proposition expressly exempts existing statutory rules of evidence relating to privilege. *Bauman & Rose, supra*, 37 CA4th at 1771.

A physician suspected of criminal activity does not have an equivalent right to assert the doctor-patient privilege. *Brillantes v Superior Court* (1996) 51 CA4th 323, 329, 58 CR2d 770 (differentiating doctor-patient and attorney-client privileges).

### c. [§2.7] Checklist: Issuance of Search Warrants for Papers of Lawyers, Doctors, Psychotherapists, or Clergymen

(1) *Determine whether the warrant seeks documents in the possession or under the control of a member of the special group.* This will usually be apparent from the affidavit. See Pen C §1525 (affidavit must so specify when applicable).

(2) *Determine whether there is probable cause to issue the warrant.* If yes, proceed to (3); if no, deny the application.

☛ **Judicial Tip**: This is done as with any warrant application, but often takes considerable time because of extensive attachments to the affidavit. The magistrate should not be rushed, especially in view of the added balancing the magistrate may have to undertake (see (3), below) and to reduce the risk of confusing quantity with quality.

(3) *Determine whether the person on whom the warrant will be served is suspected of criminal activity related to the papers being sought.* Pen C §1524(a). If yes, proceed to (a); if no, proceed to (4).

(a) Balance the state's needs for the documents and the breadth of the proposed search against the interests of clients or patients in the privacy of their records. See §2.5. Determine whether it is desirable and practical to narrow the scope of the warrant and/or whether the privacy concerns are sufficiently strong that the special master procedure should be utilized.

(b) If you determine to appoint a special master, proceed to (4); otherwise, issue the warrant as in other cases.

☛ **Judicial Tip**: In issuing search warrants for documents, it is especially important to impose meaningful restrictions on what may be seized. For a discussion, see §§2.69–2.72.

(4) *Select a prospective special master from the State Bar list and contact him or her by telephone.* Proceed to (5). If attorney cannot be reached, select another.

☛ **Judicial Tip**: The court should have a current list prepared by the State Bar of lawyers qualified to serve as special masters under Pen C §1524(a). If no list is available, the magistrate should contact the State Bar for names. Appointment of attorneys not on the list may undermine the search.

(5) *Advise the selected person of the matter and inquire whether he or she has any relationship with any of the parties involved.* See Pen C §1524(d). If there is a relation or if the person cannot serve for other reasons, repeat (4) and (5); otherwise, proceed to (6).

☛ **Judicial Tips**: (1) Some courts ask the special master to execute an affidavit that he or she has no conflicts of interest. For a form, see §2.132. (2) When reasonable efforts to find a special master prove unavailing, the magistrate may authorize the party seeking the warrant to conduct the search without one in the manner prescribed by Pen C §1524. Pen C §1524(d). Most judges consider it advisable to make a statement on the record reflecting such a determination and to note it on the warrant. It is even more important that the warrant clearly state the prescriptions applicable to special master searches because the person who will serve the warrant in lieu of a special master may not be fully familiar with them.

(6) *Appoint the special master.*
(a) Inform the master and the applicant of the appointment.
(b) Note the appointment on the warrant.

(7) *Review the scope of the warrant for possible overbreadth.* See §§2.69–2.72. Narrow the scope if necessary.

(8) *Issue the warrant.*

### 2. News Media

#### a. [§2.8] Penal Code §1524(g)

Penal Code §1524(g) prohibits issuance of a search warrant for items described in Evid C §1070, *i.e.,* sources of information and unpublished information provided to news media. The legislature enacted Pen C §1524(g) in response to *Zurcher v Stanford Daily* (1978) 436 US 547, 98 S Ct 1970, 56 L Ed 2d 525. *Zurcher* denied First and Fourth Amendment challenges to a warrant for the search of the *Stanford Daily* premises. The college newspaper was not suspected of a crime; the police were looking for photos to identify demonstrators who had attacked officers. 436 US at 559–562. *Zurcher* also said that state legislatures could enact statutory protections against search warrant abuses. 436 US at 567. For a discussion of *Zurcher* and its relation to Pen C §1524(g), see *PSC Geothermal Servs. Co. v Superior Court* (1994) 25 CA4th 1697, 1705, 31 CR2d 213.

The protected news media include newspapers, magazines, other periodicals, press associations, wire services, and radio and TV stations. Evid C §1070(a)–(b). For the definition of "unpublished information," see Evid C §1070(c).

For discussion of media presence during a search of other premises, see §2.117.

#### b. [§2.9] Federal Statute

The Privacy Protection Act (42 USC §2000aa) "generally prohibits government officials from searching for and seizing documentary materials possessed by a person in connection with a purpose to disseminate information to the public." *Citicasters v McCaskill* (8th Cir 1996) 89 F3d 1350, 1353. Exceptions include the following situations:

- There is probable cause to believe that the person who has the documents has committed certain crimes to which they relate;
- Immediate seizure is necessary to prevent death or serious injury; or
- Giving notice pursuant to a subpoena duces tecum is likely to result in the destruction, concealment, or alteration of the materials. 42 USC §2000aa(b).

The federal statute applies to acts of local officials, but a violation does not result in suppression of evidence. 89 F3d at 1355 (dictum that private cause of action is exclusive remedy).

☛ **Judicial Tip**: The nonexcludability of evidence obtained in violation of the federal statute or of Pen C §1524(g) does not lessen the importance of screening search warrant applications in this area carefully. If anything, such care is even more important, in the view of many judges. Substantial concerns are involved; violations may well lead to costly litigation.

### 3. [§2.10] Obscenity

The First Amendment makes a search warrant a prerequisite to the seizure of obscene material. *Flack v Municipal Court* (1967) 66 C2d

981, 983, 59 CR 872; *Walter v U.S.* (1980) 447 US 649, 654, 100 S Ct 2395, 65 L Ed 2d 410. In the absence of a search warrant, officers cannot seize such material even incident to a lawful arrest. *Roaden v Kentucky* (1973) 413 US 496, 502, 93 S Ct 2796, 37 L Ed 2d 757. Circumstances that present the officers with a "now or never" situation constitute an exception. *Roaden v Kentucky, supra*; *People v Superior Court* (Freeman) (1975) 14 C3d 82, 89, 120 CR 697. See also *Maryland v Macon* (1985) 472 US 463, 468, 105 S Ct 2778, 86 L Ed 2d 370 (purchase by an officer of materials in an adult bookstore is not a seizure). The First Amendment requires no greater showing of probable cause than for search warrants for other objects. *New York v P.J. Video, Inc.* (1986) 475 US 868, 875, 106 S Ct 1610, 89 L Ed 2d 871. It does, however, necessitate great particularity. For discussion, see §2.69.

An adversary hearing is not required before the issuance of a search warrant for films or books (*Heller v New York* (1973) 413 US 483, 488, 93 S Ct 2789, 37 L Ed 2d 745) except for large-scale seizures amounting to a substantial restraint. *Quantity of Books v Kansas* (1964) 378 US 205, 210, 84 S Ct 1723, 12 L Ed 2d 809; *Marcus v Search Warrants* (1961) 367 US 717, 731, 81 S Ct 1708, 6 L Ed 2d 1127. For a summary of these principles, see *New York v P.J. Video, Inc., supra*, 475 US at 873. However, there must be an opportunity for a prompt postseizure pretrial judicial determination of obscenity. *Heller v New York, supra*; *Suki, Inc. v Superior Court* (1976) 60 CA3d 616, 625, 131 CR 615; *People v Superior Court* (Loar) (1972) 28 CA3d 600, 616, 104 CR 876.

A search warrant for obscene films cannot validly authorize seizure of projectors. Such a seizure "prevents the lawful use of the projectors, as a means of expression protected by the First Amendment. . . ." *Porno, Inc. v Municipal Court* (1973) 33 CA3d 122, 126, 108 CR 797.

## 4. Bodily Intrusions

### a. [§2.11] In General

Applications for search warrants or similar orders authorizing bodily intrusions do not need to meet a standard greater than probable cause for minor intrusions such as taking blood for testing, but the more intense, undignified, or risky the proposed bodily invasion, "the greater must be the showing for the procedure's necessity." *People v Scott* (1978) 21 C3d 284, 293, 145 CR 876. See *Winston v Lee* (1985) 470 US 753, 761, 105 S Ct 1611, 84 L Ed 2d 662 (showing was inadequate to permit removal of bullet from suspect's chest because procedure would require general anesthesia, involve some medical risks, and prosecution had other adequate evidence); *People v Earp* (1999) 20 C4th 826, 882–883, 85 CR2d 857.

To determine whether the requisite "strong showing of need" (*People v Scott, supra*) has been made, privacy interests are balanced against societal interests. *Winston v Lee, supra*; *People v Scott, supra.* "Factors which must be considered include the reliability of the method to be employed, the seriousness of the underlying criminal offense . . ., the strength of law enforcement suspicions that evidence of crime will be revealed, the importance of the evidence sought, and the possibility that evidence may be recovered by alternative means less violative of Fourth Amendment freedoms." *People v Scott, supra.*

Procedures that endanger life or health may be impermissible regardless of probable cause. *Winston v Lee, supra.*

The police must seek and obtain authorization for the *specific* procedure; a warrant for the search of the person is insufficient. *Jauregui v Superior Court* (1986) 179 CA3d 1160, 1167, 225 CR 308 (administration of emetic). Warrantless bodily invasions are allowed only under a "limited range of exigent circumstances," such as "the need to prevent loss or destruction of evidence, or the existence of a medical emergency" *People v Scott, supra,* 21 C3d at 292; *People v Siripongs* (1988) 45 C3d 548, 568, 247 CR 729 (testing murder suspect's blood for drugs or alcohol in case he made statements is inadequate justification but harmless error because in the particular case a properly justified sample would inevitably have been drawn).

*Winston* expressly left open the question of whether an adversary hearing is required before authorization of a procedure such as surgery. *Winston v Lee, supra,* 470 US at 763 n6.

The Fourth Amendment, including the requirements of *Scott* and *Winston*, protects witnesses as well as defendants. *People v Earp, supra* (blood test); *People v Melton* (1988) 44 C3d 713, 738, 244 CR 867 (trial court properly denied defense requests for blood test of witness on stand in absence of probable cause to believe that he was testifying under influence of drugs); *People v Nokes* (1986) 183 CA3d 468, 476, 228 CR 119 (request for physical examination of child witness in connection with his sodomy testimony properly denied under the particular circumstances).

### b. [§2.12] HIV Blood Testing

The issuance of a search warrant for the purpose of HIV blood testing is stringently circumscribed, and the results may not be used in a criminal trial as evidence of guilt or innocence. Pen C §1524.1. Key requirements include:

- The person to be tested has been charged with a crime.
- The search warrant is requested by a victim of the crime or, under limited circumstances, of an uncharged sex crime.
- After the preliminary hearing and before sentencing, the court conducts an adversary hearing at which only affidavits, counteraffidavits, and medical reports are admissible.
- At the conclusion of the hearing, the court finds
- Probable cause to believe the defendant committed the offense; and
- Probable cause to believe that blood, semen, or other bodily fluids capable of transmitting the HIV virus has been transferred from the accused to the victim.

The local health officer makes provision for administering HIV tests and discloses the results only to the victim and the defendant, and only after the results have been confirmed by a confirmatory test.

See also Pen C §1202.1 (postconviction order to submit to AIDS testing); Health & S C §§121055, 121060 (orders for AIDS testing).

### 5. [§2.13] Motorized Battering Rams

The magistrate must employ a balancing test similar to the one required by *People v Scott* (1978) 21 C3d 284, 293, 145 CR 876 (for discussion of *Scott,* see §2.11) before authorizing use of a motorized battering ram that smashes through walls. *Langford v Superior Court* (1987) 43 C3d 21, 31, 233 CR 387. Such authorization is a precondition to the use of the device. 43 C3d at 30.

Police officers may use the authorization only if they determine at the scene that evidence is in the process of being destroyed or that resistance to the search poses a serious danger of injury to the officers, justifying deployment of the battering ram. 43 C3d at 31.

## E. [§2.14] Territorial Jurisdiction

The magistrate's jurisdiction to issue search warrants is not limited to his or her judicial district. A magistrate can properly issue a warrant for any location in the county in which the magistrate's court is located. *People v Smead* (1985) 175 CA3d 1101, 1103, 223 CR 303.

A magistrate has "jurisdiction to issue an out-of-county warrant if the magistrate finds that the search relates to a crime committed in the magistrate's county, and thus pertains to a present or future prosecution in that county." *People v Fleming* (1981) 29 C3d 698, 701, 175 CR 604.

A warrant for an out-of-county search unrelated to a crime in the issuing magistrate's county is invalid, but courts have upheld the search by applying the good-faith exception of *Leon* (*U.S. v Leon* (1984) 468 US 897, 104 S Ct 3405, 82 L Ed 2d 677). *People v Ruiz* (1990) 217 CA3d 574, 578–579, 265 CR 886; *People v Dantzler* (1988) 206 CA3d 289, 292, 263 CR 526.

A magistrate lacks jurisdiction to issue a search warrant to a peace officer of another county for a search in the magistrate's county. *People v Galvan* (1992) 5 CA4th 866, 870, 7 CR2d 195 (evidence admissible under *Leon* good-faith exception); Pen C §1528(a) (magistrate to issue search warrant "to a peace officer in his or her county").

## III. AFFIDAVIT REQUIREMENTS

### A. Written Affidavits

#### 1. [§2.15] General Rule

Generally the affidavit must be in writing and subscribed by the affiant. Pen C §1526(a); *Charney v Superior Court* (1972) 27 CA3d 888, 891, 104 CR 213. In *Charney*, the magistrate wrote an addendum to the affidavit after interviewing the affiant. The affiant did not subscribe the addendum; instead, the magistrate wrote, "Affiant has sworn to truth of above" and signed the addendum. The appellate court held the addendum invalid. Since the affidavit lacked probable cause, the court suppressed the evidence. The result might be different under the *Leon* good-faith exception discussed in §§1.28–1.40. See *People v Leonard* (1996) 50 CA4th 878, 885–886, 57 CR2d 845 (search warrant based on unsworn statement of probable cause and on affidavit lacking facts invalid, but evidence admissible under good-faith exception).

☛ **Judicial Tip**: The judge should not hesitate to discuss the affidavit with the affiant when it is presented to make sure that it satisfies all requirements. Handwritten changes and additions can be made, preferably in the affiant's handwriting. Each correction and other change should be initialed both by the magistrate and the affiant. Some judges recommend that the date also be written next to the initials. Any addenda should be properly subscribed to avoid *Charney* problems.

For discussion of telephonic search warrant, see §§2.19–2.20; of search warrants issued by fax or e-mail, see §2.21.

#### 2. [§2.16] Attachments and Papers in Addition to Affidavit

The affiant often attaches investigation reports, sometimes extensive ones, to the affidavit. See, *e.g., Kaylor v Superior Court* (1980) 108 CA3d 451, 453, 166 CR 598 (155 pages of police report). Occasionally an affiant presents documents separate from the affidavit. See, *e.g., People v Egan* (1983) 141 CA3d 798, 803, 190 CR 546 (separate request for night service). Attachments and separate papers become part of the affidavit only if they are incorporated by reference.

☛ **Judicial Tip**: The magistrate should initial each attached page of the affidavit after reading it and make sure that it

- States that the affiant read the attachments.
- Incorporates them by appropriate reference. The following is typical language:

On _____, 20____, your affiant received and read an official L.A.P.D. Crime Report No. ____, consisting of _____pages, which is attached hereto as Exhibit 1 and incorporated as if fully set forth herein.

- Indicates what, if anything, the affiant or other officers did as a result of the attached reports.
- Explains any omissions or errors in an exhibit. See Chrystie & Schirn, p IV-27. The magistrate may want to inquire whether there are any such omissions or errors and have the affiant add the response to the affidavit.

### 3. [§2.17] Subscription

Penal Code §1526(a) states that the magistrate must take the affidavit and cause the affidavit to be subscribed by the party. However, it is not fatal if the court clerk takes the affidavit instead. In *People v Chavez* (1972) 27 CA3d 883, 104 CR 247, the clerk had the affiant swear that the contents were true and had the affiant sign the affidavit. The clerk then took it to the magistrate while the affiant waited in an outer room. The magistrate read and approved the affidavit and issued a search warrant.

The court upheld the warrant, saying that Pen C §1526(a) should not be read literally and that there is no constitutional requirement that the magistrate personally take the affidavit. The court said that "the essence of the statute is not to require a face to face confrontation between the magistrate and the affiant, but that the magistrate shall have an opportunity to examine the affiant should any questions arise in his mind. . . ." 27 CA3d at 886.

☛ **Judicial Tip**: Most judges consider it poor practice to have the affidavit subscribed outside the magistrate's presence.

A different subscription problem arose in *People v Egan* (1983) 141 CA3d 798, 190 CR 546. The affiant presented the request for night service, including the facts justifying it, on a paper separate from the affidavit. The affiant signed the separate sheet, but it lacked a jurat (the "sworn to and subscribed before me" clause). The affidavit itself had a jurat that the magistrate signed after swearing the affiant and asking him whether the information was true.

The court held that the night service authorization was valid. Although it was not incorporated into the affidavit by reference, the magistrate considered it at the same time as the affidavit, regarded the documents to be one affidavit, and swore the affiant to the truth of all the facts. The prosecution had the right to establish that the showing for night service was made under oath. 141 CA3d at 803, 805.

In the simpler case, in which the affiant orally swears that his statements are true but the magistrate fails to sign the jurat of the affidavit, the result is unclear. The converse happened in *Clifton v Superior Court* (1970) 7 CA3d 245, 86 CR 612. The magistrate signed the jurat, but had forgotten to swear the affiant. However, the magistrate had asked him whether the statements were true and he had replied that they were. The court upheld the warrant, saying that the affiant's oral declaration before the magistrate would constitute an oath if the affiant were charged with perjury, even though he was not formally sworn. 7 CA3d at 254. See also *People v Superior Court* (Robinson) (1977) 75 CA3d 76, 78, 141 CR 917 (warrant upheld although magistrate forgot to sign it), *and Charney v Superior Court* (1972) 27 CA3d 888, 891, 104 CR 213, discussed in §2.15.

#### 4. [§2.18] Partial Loss of Affidavit

In *People v Curry* (1985) 165 CA3d 349, 211 CR 590, the last page of the affidavit was missing when the case came to hearing and no copy could be found. The magistrate vividly remembered the affidavit, including the fact that the last page only expressed the affiant's opinion that narcotics would be found on the premises. The portions of the affidavit before the court adequately covered probable cause. The court upheld the search warrant, emphasizing that it was doing so on the particular facts. A different result follows when the loss prevents adequate judicial review. 165 CA3d at 353, and cases cited.

### B. Sworn Oral Statement, Including Statement for Telephonic Search Warrant

#### 1. [§2.19] Statutory Basis and Use

As an alternative to written affidavits, Pen C §1526(b)(1) permits sworn oral statements that are subsequently transcribed. Affiants use them in two situations:

(1) An affiant appears before the magistrate and makes a probable cause statement verbally. See, *e.g., People v Goldberg* (1984) 161 CA3d 170, 180, 207 CR 431.

(2) The affiant phones the magistrate, states probable cause, and obtains the magistrate's verbal authorization to sign the latter's name to the warrant under Pen C §1528(b) ("the magistrate may orally authorize a peace officer to sign the magistrate's name on a duplicate original warrant"). The resulting warrant is the so-called telephonic (or, more accurately, telephonically authorized) search warrant.

The expression "telephonic search warrant" can give rise to the erroneous impression that the warrant itself is oral. All search warrants must be in writing. Pen C §§1523, 1528. The only thing different about a telephonic warrant is that the affiant signs the magistrate's name to a duplicate original search warrant.

The statutes do not mention statements by the affiant over the telephone, but have been interpreted to permit them. *People v Aguirre* (1972) 26 CA3d Supp 7, 10, 103 CR 153; *People v Peck* (1974) 38 CA3d 993, 999–1000, 113 CR 806. The procedure is constitutional. *People v Peck, supra.* No special circumstances need be shown for issuing a telephonic warrant. 38 CA3d at 1000.

The procedural requirements relating to sworn oral statements are discussed in §2.20. The telephonic search warrant itself, as distinguished from the affidavit, is discussed further in §2.59. For a step-by-step guide to issuing telephonic search warrants, see §2.130. For a discussion of transmission of affidavits by e-mail or fax, see §2.21.

### 2. [§2.20] Procedural Requirements for Sworn Oral Statement (Pen C §1526(b)(1))

(a) *Oath.* The affiant's oral statement must be under oath. If the magistrate does not administer the oath until the affiant has made the statement, the error is not prejudicial. *People v Aguirre* (1972) 26 CA3d Supp 7, 11, 103 CR 153.

(b) *Recording.* The statement must be recorded. This is usually done by tape recorder or other recording equipment. Counties vary in their practices as to location of this equipment. Some hook up a tape recorder to the telephone in a duty judge's home. (As to designation of a duty judge, see Pen C §810.) In other counties, police departments or the district attorney's office maintain recording equipment.

An inaudible recording is not fatal as long as the affiant can reconstruct the affidavit in a form that gives defendant an opportunity to controvert it. *People v Fortune* (1988) 197 CA3d 941, 951–953, 243 CR 189.

Penal Code §1526(b)(1) also permits recording by a certified court reporter. This alternative is useful when taking an oral statement in the courthouse.

(c) *Transcription.* The affiant's sworn oral statement must be transcribed. The transcribed statement constitutes the affidavit. The magistrate issues the warrant even though the affiant's statement has not yet been transcribed. *People v Peck* (1974) 38 CA3d 993, 998, 113 CR 806.

(d) *Certification.* The magistrate must certify the transcribed statement. If a court reporter has recorded affiant's statement, the reporter must also certify the transcript.

(e) *Filing.* The transcribed statement "shall be filed with the clerk of the court." Pen C §1526(b)(1).

(f) *Sealing.* The transcribed statement cannot be sealed or otherwise concealed from the defendant except "that portion which necessarily would reveal the identity of a confidential informant." *Swanson v Superior Court* (1989) 211 CA3d 332, 339, 259 CR 260. Concealment is a denial of due process; therefore, the officer's good faith in executing the warrant is immaterial. *Swanson v Superior Court, supra.* The proper procedure is for the court to give defense counsel an edited statement, deleting portions that would identify the informant. *People v Greenstreet* (1990) 218 CA3d 1516, 1519, 267 CR 377. A permissible alternative to an edited statement is a written affidavit prepared by the prosecutor for the defendant on order of the court. See *People v Hobbs* (1994) 7 C4th 948, 963, 30 CR2d 651. See §2.52.

The transcription, certification, and filing must be done "promptly." *People v Peck, supra,* 38 CA3d at 999. *People v Meza* (1984) 162 CA3d 25, 32, 208 CR 576, condoned a four-month delay in certification. *Meza* inquired whether the delay violated the defendant's due process rights and concluded it did not. The tape and transcribed statement were available to the defendant several months before the suppression hearing, and the certification was on file before the conclusion of the hearing.

☛ **Judicial Tips**: (1) Since there is a time gap between the oral statement and the certification of the transcription, some judges write down the essence of the oral statement very soon after it is made. (2) Suppression hearings often occur more quickly than in *Meza*. Transcription, certification, and filing should be completed well before the preliminary hearing so that the defendant can exercise his or her statutory right to make a Pen C §1538.5 motion at the hearing without having to waive time. See Pen C §859b (continuance of preliminary hearing).

### C. [§2.21] Transmission of Affidavit by Fax or E-Mail

In addition to telephonic transmission of affidavits, Pen C §1526(b)(2) permits transmission by fax or e-mail. Unlike so-called telephonic search warrants, a written affidavit is necessary from the outset of the §1526(b)(2) procedure. The required steps pertaining to the affidavit are (Pen C §1526(b)(2)(A) and (B)):

(1) The applicant phones the magistrate who administers the oath to the applicant during the conversation.

(2) The affiant signs the affidavit; a digital signature is required for e-mail transmission.

(3) The applicant transmits the affidavit, attachments, and proposed search warrant to the magistrate by fax or e-mail.

(4) The magistrate confirms receipt.

(5) The magistrate verifies that all pages have been received and are legible, and that the affiant's signature or digital signature is acknowledged as genuine.

For further discussion of issuing search warrants by fax or e-mail, see §2.60; for a procedural guide, see §2.131.

### D. Probable Cause

#### 1. [§2.22] Basic Standard

The basic standard for probable cause to issue a search warrant is "whether, given all the circumstances set forth in the affidavit . . . , there *is a fair probability that contraband or evidence of a crime will be found in a particular place.*" *Illinois v Gates* (1983) 462 US 213, 238, 103 S Ct 2317, 76 L Ed 2d 527 (emphasis added); *People v Bennett* (1998) 17 C4th 373, 391, 70 CR2d 850; *People v Hernandez* (1994) 30 CA4th 919, 923, 35 CR2d 916. For discussion of the good-faith exception to affidavits that do not meet this standard, see §§1.28–1.31.

#### 2. [§2.23] Contrast to Probable Cause for Arrest Warrant

The essential inquiry for probable cause to issue a *search* warrant differs from that for an *arrest* warrant. The latter is concerned with a suspect's probable guilt; the former with the existence and location of seizable property. *People v Cook* (1978) 22 C3d 67, 84 n6, 148 CR 605 (superseded on other points by Proposition 8 and *Franks v Delaware* (1978) 438 US 154, 98 S Ct 2674, 57 L Ed 2d 667); *People v Fernandez* (1989)

212 CA3d 984, 989, 261 CR 29 (extent of defendant's personal involvement not an issue in determining probable cause to search his apartment, as long as there is a factual basis for believing it might contain evidence of illegal activity); *People v Watson* (1979) 89 CA3d 376, 385, 152 CR 471 ("It is irrelevant that the affidavit did not directly implicate appellant in the sale of heroin. It is enough that it showed probable cause to believe that heroin would be found in the apartment."). A search warrant may issue for a place whose occupants are not suspected of any crime. See, *e.g., Zurcher v Stanford Daily* (1978) 436 US 547, 554, 563, 98 S Ct 1970, 56 L Ed 2d 525 (search of newspaper premises for photographic evidence of assaults by demonstrators).

Another important difference flows from the distinctive nature of search and arrest warrants. Probable cause to arrest requires a linkage between a suspect and a crime. Probable cause to search requires a double linkage, *i.e.*, one that links the items to be seized to an offense and another that connects them to the place to be searched. *People v Barnum* (1980) 113 CA3d 340, 346, 169 CR 840.

### 3. [§2.24] General Principles for Applying Standard

Affidavits are often written in haste by nonlawyers. In interpreting affidavits, both the magistrate's and the reviewing court's emphasis should be on practicality and common sense; hypertechnical constructions should be avoided. *Illinois v Gates* (1983) 462 US 213, 236, 103 S Ct 2317, 76 L Ed 2d 527; *U.S. v Ventresca* (1965) 380 US 102, 109, 85 S Ct 741, 13 L Ed 2d 684; *People v Mesa* (1975) 14 C3d 466, 469, 121 CR 473; *People v Superior Court* (Johnson) (1972) 6 C3d 704, 711, 100 CR 319.

Probable cause is not measurable by formulas; rather, its existence depends on the totality of circumstances. *Illinois v Gates, supra.* See also §2.33 (abolition of "two-prong test"). The affidavit carries with it a presumption of validity. *Franks v Delaware* (1978) 438 US 154, 171, 98 S Ct 2674, 57 L Ed 2d 667. A search warrant can rest on less persuasive evidence than a warrantless search. *Jones v U.S.* (1960) 362 US 257, 270, 80 S Ct 725, 4 L Ed 2d 697, overruled on other grounds (1980) 448 US 83, 85; *Skelton v Superior Court* (1969) 1 C3d 144, 150, 81 CR 613. Courts resolve doubtful or marginal cases in favor of the warrant (*U.S. v Ventresca, supra*; *People v Superior Court* (Corona) (1981) 30 C3d 193, 207, 178 CR 334), but must review the sufficiency of affidavits conscientiously to ensure that the magistrate had sufficient information and did not merely ratify the bare conclusions of others. *Illinois v Gates, supra*, 462 US at 239.

For application of guidelines, see, *e.g., People v Glenos* (1992) 7 CA4th

1201, 1206, 10 CR2d 363; *People v Meyer* (1986) 183 CA3d 1150, 1159, 228 CR 635; *People v Wilson* (1986) 182 CA3d 742, 747, 227 CR 528.

### 4. [§2.25] Key Determinations of Probable Cause

Judges find that determining probable cause is not always simple. "[T]he magistrate is required to make in effect two determinations: first he must satisfy himself that the facts are as the applicant states them to be, then he must consider whether these facts constitute probable cause for issuance of the warrant." *People v Cook* (1978) 22 C3d 67, 84 n6, 148 CR 605 (superseded on other points by Proposition 8 and *Franks v Delaware* (1978) 438 US 154, 98 S Ct 2674, 57 L Ed 2d 667, but approved on this point by *People v Frank* (1985) 38 C3d 711, 727, 214 CR 801); see Chrystie & Schirn, p IV-2.

In essence, probable cause requires (1) facts (§§2.26–2.35) (2) making it fairly probable (§2.36) (3) that "contraband or evidence of a crime" (§2.37) (4) "will be found in a particular place" (§§2.38–2.43). *Illinois v Gates* (1983) 462 US 213, 238, 103 S Ct 2317, 76 L Ed 2d 527.

### 5. [§2.26] Facts, Opinions, Expertise, Informants

Penal Code §1527 states that "[t]he affidavit or affidavits must set forth *the facts* tending to establish the grounds of the application, or probable cause for believing that they exist." (Emphasis added.) The requirement that probable cause rest on facts is a precondition of all the other requirements. *People v Frank* (1985) 38 C3d 711, 727, 214 CR 801 (search warrant for, among other things, defendant's personal diary; affidavit stated no facts permitting an inference that defendant had such a diary or kept it in the place to be searched; warrant held invalid as to that item).

Two major problems in this area concern the effect of opinions and conclusions in an affidavit and the credibility or reliability of the affiant's information, especially when it comes from unidentified informants.

#### a. [§2.27] Opinions and Conclusions

An affidavit that recites only opinions or conclusions is insufficient. *Illinois v Gates* (1983) 462 US 213, 239, 103 S Ct 2317, 76 L Ed 2d 527; *People v Smith* (1986) 180 CA3d 72, 86, 225 CR 348. "The magistrate must be presented facts and not conclusory statements if he is to perform his detached function and not become a rubber stamp for the police." *People v Pellegrin* (1977) 78 CA3d 913, 916, 144 CR 421. The affidavit should leave any significant inference-drawing to the magistrate. *People v Smith, supra,* 180 CA3d at 87. See also *Illinois v Gates, supra,* 462

US at 240 (key protection of requirement that warrants be based on probable cause is that magistrate rather than police officer draw inferences from the evidence).

Examples of impermissible conclusory statements are "Bert Jones is a heroin dealer" and "Jeff Smith has heroin at 12018 Tiara Street, North Hollywood." See Chrystie & Schirn, p IV-3. Others include affiant "has cause to suspect and does believe that" liquor illegally brought into the country is located on certain premises (*Nathanson v U.S.* (1933) 290 US 41, 44, 54 S Ct 11, 78 L Ed 159) and "affiants have received reliable information from a credible person and do believe" that heroin is stored in a home (*Aguilar v Texas* (1964) 378 US 108, 109, 84 S Ct 1509, 12 L Ed 2d 723). *Gates* approved these holdings, saying that "a mere conclusory statement . . . gives the magistrate virtually no basis at all for making a judgment regarding probable cause . . . [H]is action cannot be a mere ratification of the bare conclusions of others. In order to ensure that such an abdication of the magistrate's duty does not occur, courts must continue to conscientiously review the sufficiency of affidavits on which warrants are issued." *Illinois v Gates, supra,* 462 US at 239. See also *Rodriguez v Superior Court* (1988) 199 CA3d 1453, 1464, 245 CR 617 (statement that informant was at defendant's residence when heroin was sold is conclusory; *Rodriguez* is discussed further in §2.30); *Lee Art Theatre, Inv. v Virginia* (1968) 392 US 636, 637, 88 S Ct 2103, 20 L Ed 2d 1313 (affidavit for seizure of allegedly obscene materials cannot rest entirely on officer's conclusions that they are obscene). But see *New York v P.J. Video, Inc.* (1986) 475 US 868, 877, 106 S Ct 1610, 89 L Ed 2d 871 (affidavit that accurately describes the numerous acts of sexual intercourse in each film is sufficient).

The emphasis on nontechnical interpretation of affidavits sometimes leads courts to view what look like opinions or conclusions as factual statements. See, *e.g., People v Superior Court* (Brown) (1975) 49 CA3d 160, 166, 122 CR 459, upholding an affidavit framed entirely in terms of what affiant believed.

Conclusions and opinions are permissible, however, under two circumstances: the affiant's experience or expertise, or opinions based on logic or common sense. See §§2.28 and 2.29.

### (1) [§2.28] Affiant's Experience or Expertise

In determining probable cause, the magistrate may properly consider an affiant's opinion based on his or her training, experience, or expertise. See, *e.g., Johnson v U.S.* (1948) 333 US 10, 13, 68 S Ct 367, 92 L Ed 2d 436; *People v Mayoff* (1986) 42 C3d 1302, 1319, 233 CR 2.

It is not necessary that the affiant qualify as an expert witness in order to be able to form a reasonable opinion. *Wimberly v Superior Court* (1976) 16 C3d 557, 565, 128 CR 641.

Typical cases include:

- Opinions as to the nature of an observed item. *Johnson v U.S., supra* (opium odor); *Wimberly v Superior Court, supra* (marijuana); *People v Mayoff, supra* (marijuana).
- Opinion that contraband observed in location A will probably also be in location B. *People v Mayoff, supra* (paths from marijuana field to structures permitted experienced officer to conclude that structures were probably being used to cure, store, and hide marijuana); *People v Cleland* (1990) 225 CA3d 388, 392, 275 CR 126 (experienced officer may reasonably conclude that defendant, arrested on street with 12 baggies of marijuana and $451 was probably a dealer who had more marijuana at home); *People v Aho* (1985) 166 CA3d 984, 989, 212 CR 686 (training and experience to permit officer to conclude that defendant, factually linked to trading drugs for stolen property, probably kept controlled substances or stolen goods in his car or home). See also §2.39.
- Opinion concerning the significance of particular actions or words. *People v Andrino* (1989) 210 CA3d 1395, 1401, 259 CR 17 (upholding search warrant based on results of telephone pen register and trap, together with experienced officer's opinion that pattern of calls from known bookie to defendant indicated that the calls were made to make lay-off bets); *People v Veasey* (1979) 98 CA3d 779, 784, 159 CR 755 (expertise plus corroborating facts permits opinion that "a small thing of boy" refers to a $25 or $50 quantity of heroin).

The question for magistrates and reviewing courts is whether the combination of facts and the nature of the affiant's training and experience make the affiant's opinion a reasonable one under the particular circumstances. This is not always the case. For example, in *People v Pellegrin* (1977) 78 CA3d 913, 917, 144 CR 421, an officer experienced and trained in identifying marijuana saw a single marijuana plant growing in defendant's backyard. In his affidavit the officer said that the plant did not appear to be growing wild and that he knew cultivators who raised marijuana in their residences. The court held that there was no probable cause for the search of the residence. The officer's opinion that marijuana growers often keep the product in their homes is relevant only if there is evidence of marijuana cultivation. But the affiant's statement that the one plant he saw did not appear to be growing wild is purely conclusory because the affiant's expertise goes only to identifying marijuana. Hence there is no basis for inferring that marijuana was being cultivated.

#### (2) [§2.29] Logic or Common Sense

The magistrate may also consider the affiant's opinions when they follow logically from factual recitals in the affidavit or are based on common sense. For example:

- The affidavit in *People v Frank* (1985) 38 C3d 711, 214 CR 801, set out in great detail the facts of the crime (kidnap murder of young child) and many circumstances linking it to the defendant. The affidavit stated that defendant may have taken "the items which he used to perform these acts on [the victim] with him and, perhaps, also her clothes in his vehicle to his home." 38 C3d at 728. The court held that this was a reasonable and permissible inference from the detailed factual averments.
- The affidavit in *People v Meyer* (1986) 183 CA3d 1150, 228 CR 635, a welfare fraud case, set out detailed facts that defendant was operating a business while receiving welfare. The affidavit also stated that defendant kept business records at his home and sought authorization to search for them. The court upheld the search warrant and said that the statement referring to the business records was "a logical, common-sense assumption" and that personal knowledge was not a prerequisite for making it. 183 CA3d at 1162.
- The affidavit in *People v O'Leary* (1977) 70 CA3d 323, 138 CR 667, recited in detail that defendant was the consignee of two sizable marijuana shipments at two different addresses. "The affiant police officer, an eight-year veteran of the county sheriff's office, assigned to the narcotics investigation detail for the past four years, expressed the belief" in the affidavit that defendant "is trafficking in narcotics" and was using the two addresses as "'Stash pads' and places to sell narcotics." The court upheld the affidavit's conclusions as those of an experienced officer and "as compelled by the affidavit's evidentiary showing." 70 CA3d at 329.

#### (3) [§2.30] Opinions of Persons Other Than Affiant

The principles discussed in §§2.27–2.29 also apply to the opinions and conclusions of persons who provide information to the affiant. For example, in *Bailey v Superior Court* (1992) 11 CA4th 1107, 15 CR2d 17, two citizens told affiant about a lot of foot traffic to a certain apartment involving persons who stayed two or three minutes; the citizens suspected narcotics were being sold in the apartment, and prostitution conducted there. The court held that the observations were too limited to justify the conclusion. 11 CA4th at 1112–1113.

Similarly, an affidavit stating that an informant was present when heroin was being sold is impermissibly conclusory in the absence of facts to establish the informant's knowledge. *Rodriguez v Superior Court* (1988) 199 CA3d 1453, 1464, 245 CR 617.

### b. Reliability or Credibility of Information

#### (1) [§2.31] Police Officers' Personal Observations

Determining the reliability of information is straightforward when the affidavit consists largely or entirely of observations made personally by the affiant officer. Police officers are presumed to be reliable. *People v Hill* (1974) 12 C3d 731, 761, 117 CR 393, overruled on other grounds in 18 C3d 889, 896 n5. Affidavits based on the observations of officers are particularly trustworthy; such information need not be corroborated. *Skelton v Superior Court* (1969) 1 C3d 144, 154, 81 CR 613.

#### (2) [§2.32] Hearsay

Affidavits can and often do recite considerable hearsay and even double hearsay (see, *e.g., People v Love* (1985) 168 CA3d 104, 108, 214 CR 483); hearsay is inevitable whenever the affiant received information from others, whether they are police officers, citizen informants, or police informants (*People v Superior Court* (Bingham) (1979) 91 CA3d 463, 472, 154 CR 157). Hearsay can establish probable cause as long as the totality of circumstances indicates its overall reliability. *Illinois v Gates* (1983) 462 US 213, 241–242, 103 S Ct 2317, 76 L Ed 2d 527 (upholding search warrant based on corroborated tip of anonymous informant).

#### (3) [§2.33] Police Informants

Under the *Gates* test, "an informant's 'veracity,' 'reliability' and 'basis of knowledge' are all highly relevant . . .," but they are not "entirely separate and independent requirements to be rigidly exacted in every case"; "a deficiency in one may be compensated for . . . by a strong showing as to the other, or by some other indicia of reliability." *Illinois v Gates* (1983) 462 US 213, 230, 233, 103 S Ct 2317, 76 L Ed 2d 527. Before *Gates*, information from police informers or anonymous informants was subject to a two-prong test. The affidavit had to show (1) that the informant's statement is factual and based on personal knowledge, and (2) that the informant is credible or the information is reliable. *Aguilar v Texas* (1964) 378 US 108, 112–114, 84 S Ct 1509, 12 L Ed 2d 723; *Spinelli v U.S.* (1969) 393 US 410, 412–416, 89 S Ct 584, 21 L Ed 2d 637; *People v Superior Court* (Johnson) (1972) 6 C3d 704, 711, 100 CR 319.

Under current law, a magistrate needs to ask (1) whether the police informant's statement is factual rather than conclusory (see §2.30); (2) whether it rests on personal knowledge (such knowledge may be inferred from detailed factual allegations (*Alexander v Superior Court* (1973) 9 C3d 387, 391–392, 107 CR 483; *People v Murphy* (1974) 42 CA3d 81, 87, 116 CR 889)); (3) whether the police informant is credible (*e.g.,* a showing in the affidavit that he has supplied accurate information in the past); or (4) whether the information is reliable (*i.e.,* corroborated). *Gates* did not change the pertinence of these considerations; rather, it stressed that probable cause is to be determined in a common sense, practical fashion and not by formulas. Corroboration of information from anonymous or untested informants, other than citizen informants, remains essential, however. See, *e.g., People v Johnson* (1990) 220 CA3d 742, 749, 270 CR 70; for further discussion, see §2.35.

### (4) [§2.34] Citizen Informants

Information from a citizen-informant who is a victim of or witness to a crime is presumptively reliable (*People v Hill* (1974) 12 C3d 731, 757, 117 CR 393, overruled on other grounds in 18 C3d 889, 896 n5), once his or her status is inferable from the circumstances shown by the affidavit (*People v Smith* (1976) 17 C3d 845, 851, 132 CR 397 (affidavit failed to establish that informant, a parolee who spent 12 hours in an apartment where he observed marijuana packaging, was a citizen-informant)). Of course, reliability alone is not enough; the information must also constitute probable cause. See *e.g., Bailey v Superior Court* (1992) 11 CA4th 1107, 1112, 15 CR2d 17 (report of foot traffic to residence does not support conclusion of probable criminal activity; see §2.30).

For illustrations of sufficient and barely sufficient affidavits concerning citizen informants, see *People v Lombera* (1989) 210 CA3d 29, 32, 257 CR 222, and *People v Terrones* (1989) 212 CA3d 139, 145–149, 260 CR 355. The informant in *Lombera* reported seeing cocaine at a residence. The informant, while not identified in the affidavit, was interviewed in person by the affiant. The interview established the informant's ability to identify cocaine. His police record was checked; he had none. The court upheld the warrant.

In *Lombera,* the court stressed that the police should know the identity of the alleged citizen informant; such knowledge avoids the situation "in which an anonymous tipster, unknown to law enforcement, assumes the mantle of a citizen informant." 210 CA3d at 32.

In *Terrones*, another residential drug search case, the information came from two unnamed citizens and two other confidential informants. The affidavit said nothing about whether the police knew the identity or reliability of the citizen informants. The court had considerable difficulty upholding the warrant; it did so by concluding that the particular observations were consistent with those of concerned neighbors rather than participants in crime and that the details the citizens gave compensated for the lack of facts concerning their reliability, particularly because their observations were corroborated by the other two informants. 212 CA3d at 148–149.

☛ **Judicial Tip**: The issuing magistrate can often greatly reduce the risk of challenge to the sufficiency of an affidavit by having the affiant amend it to amplify sketchy references to informants.

After an affidavit is challenged, the affiant cannot amplify it by testimony at the suppression hearing. *People v Terrones, supra,* 212 CA3d at 145 n2 (affiant testified he had met the citizen informants and knew their names and addresses; court held such testimony cannot supply probable cause).

### (5) [§2.35] Illustrative Decisions Dealing With Informants

The following situations illustrate how courts have dealt with informants:

(a) *Uncontrolled buy.* In the familiar controlled buy situation, an officer accompanies a confidential reliable informant to a place near the location where the informant is to buy drugs or narcotics; the informant goes inside, returns with the drugs, gives them to the officer, and describes what took place. The informant is often strip-searched before the buy and sometimes wired as added measures of reliability.

In *People v Love* (1985) 168 CA3d 104, 214 CR 483 (2:1 decision), the buy was not made by informant X. Instead X went to a particular house with an unidentified Y, about whose background the affidavit said nothing. X waited outside while Y made the buy and showed his purchase to X. X told all this to the affiant-officer, including a description of what Y had produced. The officer had not supervised the buy or seen the purchased drugs, but stated that he concluded from X's description that they were methamphetamines. The court upheld the finding of probable cause. "[T]he affidavit hangs together and supports the common sense determination made by the magistrate." 168 CA3d at 111.

(b) *Anonymous tip followed by controlled buy.* In *People v Berkoff* (1985) 174 CA3d 305, 219 CR 878, the affiant-officer received an anonymous tip from a citizen about an unusual amount of pedestrian traffic at a specified apartment. The officer used a confidential, reliable informant to make a controlled buy from an occupant of the apartment. The court held an affidavit spelling out these facts to be valid ("the facts set forth in the affidavit provided the issuing judge with a substantial basis for concluding there was a fair probability that contraband would be found in defendant's apartment"). 174 CA3d at 311.

(c) *Anonymous tip followed by corroboration of noncriminal activity.* In *People v Rooney* (1985) 175 CA3d 634, 221 CR 49, an anonymous informant told the affiant-officer that defendant was accepting bets on professional football games at a specified phone number. The informant did not provide an address; the officer obtained it from the telephone company. The officer found that defendant had a prior arrest for bookmaking at the same address and observed defendant entering the apartment. The officer also called the number supplied by the informant and overheard a conversation between the informant and an unknown male about point spreads for professional football games. The affidavit recited these facts. The court held that the affidavit adequately corroborated the tip; "corroboration of an anonymous informant's tip does not require a showing of criminal activity" because "seemingly innocent activity became suspicious in light of the initial tip." 175 CA3d at 648–649.

In the absence of corroboration raising some suspicion, however, even several anonymous tips do not add up to probable cause. *Higgason v Superior Court* (1985) 170 CA3d 929, 216 CR 817 (anonymous telephone tips of drug sales not adequately corroborated by verification of alleged seller's physical description, residence, and vehicles). Further, anonymous tips, "without more, cannot serve to corroborate each other." 170 CA3d at 938.

*People v Johnson* (1990) 220 CA3d 742, 749, 270 CR 70, summarizes principles applicable to unverified information from anonymous or untested informants:

- Such information is unreliable unless corroborated.
- Adequate corroboration "must pertain to the alleged criminal activity; accuracy of information regarding the suspect generally is insufficient."
- "Courts take a dim view of the significance of 'pedestrian facts' such as a suspect's physical description, his residence and his vehicles."

- Corroboration is adequate if the police uncover "indications of criminal activity along the lines suggested by the informant."
- "Even observations of seemingly innocent activity provide sufficient corroboration if the anonymous tip casts the activity in a suspicious light." See, *e.g., People v Rooney, supra.*

(d) *Informant's observation of sale, but no showing of knowledge.* In *Rodriguez v Superior Court* (1988) 199 CA3d 1453, 1464, 245 CR 617, the affidavit stated that within two days prior to its preparation, a confidential reliable informant was at defendant's residence when heroin was sold from the residence. The court held that the affidavit was impermissibly conclusory because it contained no facts to establish the informant's knowledge. "No substance was observed or smelled, no bindle or other forms of packaging were noted, no exchange of drugs for money was observed." However, the court upheld the search under the *Leon* good faith doctrine.

(e) *Officer-affiant bases statement that informant is reliable on information from other officers.* In *People v Lopez* (1986) 181 CA3d 842, 844, 226 CR 714, the affidavit relied on information supplied by a confidential informant. Officers of other agencies supplied the affiant officer with all the facts regarding the informant's reliability; the affidavit contained no first-hand data concerning reliability. The court held that the affidavit met the *Gates'* totality-of-circumstances test.

### 6. [§2.36] Fair Probability

Once the affidavit sets out believable facts, the next inquiry is whether they establish a "fair probability" that items properly subject to seizure will be found in a particular place. *Illinois v Gates* (1983) 462 US 213, 238, 103 S Ct 2317, 76 L Ed 2d 527.

"Fair probability" means "that the facts available to the officer would warrant a man of reasonable caution in the belief that certain items may be contraband or stolen property or useful as evidence of a crime." *Texas v Brown* (1983) 460 US 730, 742, 103 S Ct 1535, 75 L Ed 2d 502 (interior quotation marks and citation omitted; warrantless search). California cases speak of "facts . . . such as would lead a person of ordinary caution or prudence to believe and conscientiously entertain a strong suspicion . . ." See, *e.g., People v Barnum* (1980) 113 CA3d 340, 345, 169 CR 840; *People v O'Leary* (1977) 70 CA3d 323, 327, 138 CR 667; *Skelton v Superior Court* (1969) 1 C3d 144, 150, 81 CR 613.

The belief need not be correct or more likely true than false. *Texas v Brown, supra* (plurality opinion). It is not measured by a preponderance of the evidence or other formulas. *Illinois v Gates, supra.* Observations need not point unequivocally toward a crime; observation of innocent behavior can corroborate other information. *Illinois v Gates, supra*; *People v Glenos* (1992) 7 CA4th 1201, 1207, 10 CR2d 363 (purchase of large quantity of freon and driving it to remote area in foothills support suspicion that evidence of methamphetamine manufacturing will be found); *People v Costello* (1988) 204 CA3d 431, 446, 251 CR 325. But see *People v Earp* (1999) 20 C4th 826, 882–883, 85 CR2d 857 (no probable cause for blood test that would only establish whether blood type is consistent with that of half of general population). Corroboration of pedestrian facts is often of little significance. See, *e.g., Higgason v Superior Court* (1985) 170 CA3d 929, 940, 216 CR 817, discussed in §2.35.

### 7. [§2.37] "Contraband or Evidence of a Crime"

While *Illinois v Gates* (1983) 462 US 213, 238, 103 S Ct 2317, 76 L Ed 2d 527, talks simply of "contraband or evidence of a crime," the kinds of property for which search warrants can be issued in California are defined and limited in Pen C §1524(a). See §2.4.

☛ **Judicial Tip**: Warrant forms often include boxes that indicate the applicable subdivision of Pen C §1524(a); the applicant for the warrant marks the appropriate box. The issuing magistrate should make sure that the facts set out in the affidavit match the box that was checked.

For requirements that search warrants (and hence affidavits supporting them) particularly describe the items to be seized and restrict them to those that have a direct connection to the crime under investigation, see §§2.69–2.72.

### 8. [§2.38] "Will Be Found in a Particular Place"

The inquiry into the likelihood that seizable property "will be found in a particular place" (*Illinois v Gates* (1983) 462 US 213, 238, 103 S Ct 2317, 76 L Ed 2d 527) involves three questions: Does the property *exist*? Is it in the *place* or places the police want to search? Is it there *now*? *People v Frank* (1985) 38 C3d 711, 727, 214 CR 801.

Affidavits for search warrants often recite criminal activity at length but are short on information that helps answer these questions. Officers frequently know many details of a crime but have scant concrete information about the present location of its fruits or of other physical evidence related to the offense.

To deal with these realities, courts draw practical inferences from the known facts. See §§2.39–2.40.

☛ **Judicial Tip**: Magistrates often find it helpful to recall that probable cause to search requires a double linkage: the items to be seized must be linked to an offense and they must also be linked to the place to be searched. See §2.23.

### a. Inferences From Known Facts

#### (1) [§2.39] Permissible Inferences

An affidavit often links a named suspect to a crime such as burglary. The affidavit describes the items taken, provides information as to the suspect's current residence, and requests a warrant to search the residence for the stolen property. Although neither the affiant nor the magistrate knows whether the items are at that location, their probable presence can be inferred from the known facts. *People v Superior Court* (Brown) (1975) 49 CA3d 160, 167, 122 CR 459; *People v Schoennauer* (1980) 103 CA3d 398, 410, 163 CR 161. This was stated more formally in *U.S. v Lucarz* (9th Cir 1970) 430 F2d 1051, 1055:

> The situation here does not differ markedly from other cases wherein this court and others, albeit usually without discussion, have upheld searches although the nexus between the items to be seized and the place to be searched rested not on direct observation, as in the normal search-and-seizure case, but on the type of crime, the nature of the missing items, the extent of the suspect's opportunity for concealment, and normal inferences as to where a criminal would be likely to hide stolen property.

*Drug Dealers*. In the case of drug dealers, evidence is likely to be found where the dealers live. *U.S. v Gil* (9th Cir 1995) 58 F3d 1414, 1419. For example, a controlled buy of heroin in the backyard of a residence permits a logical inference that narcotics were probably on the premises. *People v Gonzalez* (1990) 51 C3d 1179, 1206, 275 CR 729. See also *People v Tuadles* (1992) 7 CA4th 1777, 1785, 9 CR2d 780 (grounds to suspect defendant A imported marijuana provide probable cause to search his residence and also that of defendant B, whose telephone number defendant had used; court stressed affiant's expert opinion that large scale drug traffickers often use more than one location to serve different functions; affidavit contained no other information about B).

☛ **Judicial Tip**: Judges should review an affidavit carefully to ensure that it includes facts identifying the residence of the suspected dealer. For an illustration of insufficient facts, see §2.40.

*Other illustrations of permissible inferences*:

- A person who runs a business while collecting welfare checks might keep business records at home. *People v Meyer* (1986) 183 CA3d 1150, 1162, 228 CR 635.

- A child murderer might keep murder weapons at home. *People v Frank* (1985) 38 C3d 711, 728, 214 CR 801 (but not a permissible inference that a diary would be found in his residence in the absence of any factual basis for believing he kept a diary).

- Paths leading from marijuana patches to structures and affiant's opinion, based on experience, that cultivators often keep marijuana in nearby structures might indicate that marijuana is kept in the structures. *People v Mayoff* (1986) 42 C3d 1302, 1320, 233 CR 2; *Hart v Superior Court* (1971) 21 CA3d 496, 499, 98 CR 565 (observation of 30 marijuana plants in backyard provides probable cause to search residence). For limitations of inferences from growing marijuana, see §2.40.

#### (2) [§2.40] Impermissible Inferences

Illustrations of impermissible inferences include:

- The fact that a narcotics dealer parks a car behind a residence does not support an inference that the residence contained narcotics when the affidavit contained no information that the dealer lived there, used the residence, was seen carrying packages to and from it, or was even seen entering it. *People v Hernandez* (1994) 30 CA4th 919, 924, 35 CR2d 916.

- Probable cause that a resident has committed a crime at a particular location does not support an inference that evidence will be found there. *U.S. v Gil* (9th Cir 1995) 58 F3d 1414, 1418.

- Observation of a single marijuana plant growing in a backyard does not support an inference of cultivation. *People v Pellegrin* (1977) 78 CA3d 913, 917, 144 CR 421. Observing a small marijuana patch on a large ranch does not give rise to a reasonable inference that marijuana was growing elsewhere on the property or would be found in every residence on the ranch. *People v Joubert* (1983) 140 CA3d 946, 952, 190 CR 23. See §2.39.

### b. Current and Stale Information

#### (1) [§2.41] Basic Principles

A search pursuant to a search warrant is valid only if probable cause existed when the magistrate issued the warrant (for an exception, see

§2.43) *and* when it was executed. *Sgro v U.S.* (1932) 287 US 206, 210, 53 S Ct 138, 77 L Ed 260; *People v Cleland* (1990) 225 CA3d 388, 393, 275 CR 126. For discussion of the existence of probable cause when a warrant is executed, see §§2.78–2.82.

The element of time is crucial to the concept of probable cause. *People v McDaniels* (1994) 21 CA4th 1560, 1564, 27 CR2d 245. The freshness of the information is one of the factors that determine whether there is probable cause to believe that the articles covered by the warrant will be found at the place that is to be searched. *People v Hernandez* (1974) 43 CA3d 581, 586, 118 CR 53. "No clear cut rule, of course, tells us when the time span must be deemed too attenuated." *Alexander v Superior Court* (1973) 9 C3d 387, 393, 107 CR 483. An often-cited summary of the guiding principles comes from *Andresen v State* (1975) 24 MdApp 128, 172, 331 A2d 78, aff'd sub nom *Andresen v Maryland* (1976) 427 US 463, 96 S Ct 2737, 49 L Ed 2d 627:

> The likelihood that the evidence sought is still in place is a function not simply of watch and calendar but of variables that do not punch a clock: the character of the crime (chance encounter in the night or regenerating conspiracy?), of the criminal (nomadic or entrenched?), of the thing to be seized (perishable and easily transferable or of enduring utility to its holder?), of the place to be searched (mere criminal forum of convenience or secure operational base?), etc. The observation of a half-smoked marijuana cigarette in an ashtray at a cocktail party may well be stale the day after the cleaning lady has been in; the observation of the burial of a corpse in a cellar may well not be stale three decades later. The hare and the tortoise do not disappear at the same rate of speed.

### (2) [§2.42] Character of Criminal Activity

The character of the criminal activity is the factor to which appellate courts pay the most attention in determining whether evidence was sufficiently fresh for purposes of probable cause. *People v Wilson* (1986) 182 CA3d 742, 755, 227 CR 528. For example, courts treat sales of contraband differently from manufacture, cultivation, and possession of illegal substances. Probable cause evaporates more quickly in the former situation:

*Sales*. In *People v Greenwood* (1986) 182 CA3d 729, 733, 227 CR 539, rev'd on other grounds (1988) 486 US 35, 108 S Ct 1625, 100 L Ed 2d 30, foot traffic gave rise to a suspicion of drug selling in mid-February; the warrant was obtained in early April. The court held that the information was stale. Similarly, a lapse of 34 days between a controlled buy and obtaining a search warrant is too large in the absence of information that the activity is continuing. *Hemler v Superior Court* (1975) 44 CA3d 430, 433–434, 118 CR 564. Twenty days between sale and issuance is probably also too long. 44 CA3d at 434.

Twelve days from a controlled buy to issuance of the warrant is "on the fringe of unreasonableness," but was upheld in *People v Hernandez* (1974) 43 CA3d 581, 586, 118 CR 53.

*Manufacture, cultivation, possession.* In *People v Wilson, supra,* the last suspicious observation relating to methamphetamine manufacturing was made on February 1; the affidavit included information that manufacturing had been going on at the particular location for six months prior to February 1. The warrant was issued on March 12. The court held that the information was not stale.

Similarly, a lapse of six weeks from observation of marijuana cultivation to issuance of the warrant does not vitiate probable cause. *People v Brown* (1985) 166 CA3d 1166, 212 CR 907 (observer also noted that plants were immature and that an irrigation system was present). *Brown* said (166 CA3d at 1169):

> Rather than dealing with the often highly transitory activity of the sale of a substance such as cocaine or heroin [citation], we are presented with the cultivation of marijuana . . . The activity is continuing, rather than a one-time or irregular occurrence.

A gap of more than one year between the observation of possession and the issuance of the warrant makes the information stale. *Alexander v Superior Court* (1973) 9 C3d 387, 393, 107 CR 483.

Very limited corroboration of old information may suffice. In *People v Mikesell* (1996) 46 CA4th 1711, 1717–1718, 54 CR2d 708, the search warrant was based on suspicion that defendant was selling drugs from his home. The bulk of the information was one to four years old, but on the day before the warrant was issued, an officer observed many cars pulling into the suspect's driveway and leaving after the drivers knocked on the door without receiving an answer. Some of the cars returned later that evening when the suspect was home; all but one of the visitors stayed only a few minutes. The court said that the information as a whole painted an adequate picture of continuing drug sales.

#### c. [§2.43] Anticipatory Warrants

An anticipatory or contingent search warrant rests on a showing that probable cause will arise at a definite future time or upon occurrence of a specified event such as a controlled delivery. *People v Sousa* (1993) 18 CA4th 549, 557, 22 CR2d 264 (warrant based on planned reverse sting involving sale of marijuana to suspect). Such a warrant is valid at least as long as the anticipated event is not the sole component of probable cause. *People v Sousa, supra*. This is an exception to the principle that probable cause must exist when the magistrate issues the warrant.

☛ **Judicial Tip**: An anticipatory search warrant should clearly specify what events must occur before the warrant can be executed. This reduces the risk of premature execution. *People v Sousa, supra*, 18 CA4th at 561 n8 ("definitely the preferred practice"). However, failure to do so is not fatal if the contingency in fact occurred before the officers executed the warrant. *People v Sousa, supra* (application of good faith rule). But see *U.S. v Hotal* (9th Cir 1998) 143 F3d 1223, 1227 (face of warrant or affidavit must clearly, expressly, and narrowly specify triggering event).

The manner in which the contingency happens may destroy probable cause. For example, the warrant anticipates a controlled delivery of a package containing marijuana; the police leave the package at the door of an apartment; a brief time later and before anyone inside picks it up, they enter the apartment and search it. These circumstances do not provide probable cause. *U.S. v Vigneau* (1st Cir 1999) 187 F3d 70, 80.

When the warrant application rests on the expected delivery of contraband, it must include facts establishing probable cause to believe the contraband will be at the place to be searched when the warrant is executed. *U.S. v Loy* (3d Cir 1999) 191 F3d 360, 365. For example, delivery of child pornography to a post office box is not, without more, probable cause to believe that it will be taken to the residence to be searched. *U.S. v Loy, supra* (affiant's experience that collectors of child pornography usually keep it at home can supply probable cause, but not when defendant had told affiant that he keeps it in a storage facility; court applied good-faith exception).

## E. Misstatements and Omissions

### 1. [§2.44] Basic Principles

The basic principles governing alleged misstatements or omissions in affidavits are set forth in *Franks v Delaware* (1978) 438 US 154, 155–156, 171, 98 S Ct 2674, 57 L Ed 2d 667:

- In challenging the accuracy of an affidavit in support of a search warrant, the defendant is entitled to an evidentiary hearing only if

- The defendant makes a specific, factual offer of proof that the misstatements or omissions were deliberate or reckless on the affiant's part, *and*

- The defendant shows that the misstatement or omission is necessary to the finding of probable cause.
- Upon proof that a statement in the affidavit is a deliberate misstatement or was made in reckless disregard of the truth, the court disregards the statement and determines whether the remainder of the affidavit establishes probable cause. A materially false statement does not automatically invalidate the warrant.
- The defendant cannot challenge negligent misstatements or innocent mistakes.
- Omissions are treated analogously to misstatements: The court retests the affidavit for probable cause by adding to it any intentionally or recklessly omitted information that is material. *People v Meyer* (1986) 183 CA3d 1150, 1161, 228 CR 635. An omission is intentional if it is made with intent to deceive the magistrate; it is material if it makes the affidavit substantially misleading. *People v Kurland* (1980) 28 C3d 376, 384–385, 168 CR 667 (superseded as to consequences of omissions by Proposition 8 and *Franks v Delaware, supra*).

For further discussion, see §§2.45–2.48; for procedural matters, including discovery of whether misstatements or omissions occurred, see §§6.113–6.116.

A challenge under *Franks* can be made not only to the affiant's statements but to those of other officers and government agents on which the affidavit relies. *Hart v O'Brien* (5th Cir 1997) 127 F3d 424, 448; *U.S. v Wapnick* (2nd Cir 1995) 60 F3d 948, 956; see 2 LaFave, Search and Seizure, p 492 (3d ed 1996), hereafter cited as LaFave. The police cannot "insulate one officer's deliberate misstatement merely by relaying it through an officer-affiant personally ignorant of its falsity." *Franks v Delaware, supra*, 438 US at 164 n6.

### 2. [§2.45] Omissions Relating to Police Informants

Defendants often challenge affidavits that do not reveal everything the affiant knows about a confidential informant who supplied the affiant with information. Typically the challenged affidavit omits the informant's criminal background or fails to state promises the police made to the informant. Attacks along this line, like other attacks for alleged misstatements or omissions, rarely succeed. The omitted information is usually viewed as immaterial or regarded as not intentional or reckless, or the affidavit passes the add-and-retest procedure.

Courts consider the criminal history of police informers to be immaterial because "information provided by customary police sources is inherently suspect" and "[t]he details of their criminal pasts are not necessary to place the magistrate on notice of their potential unreliability." *People v Kurland* (1980) 28 C3d 376, 392–393, 168 CR 667; *People v Goldberg* (1984) 161 CA3d 170, 186–187, 207 CR 431 (fact that informant had been jailed many times and was on probation at the time not material because his criminality was apparent from other facts in the affidavit; omission of informant's alleged blackmailing of defendant material, but not shown to be reckless or intentional).

Deals between the informant and the authorities, indeed any circumstances of police pressure on informants, or indications that an informer "is seeking to avoid or mitigate personal difficulties with the authorities," *are* material. *People v Kurland, supra*, 28 C3d 376 at 395; *People v Cobb* (1983) 146 CA3d 290, 294, 194 CR 96. Omission of such information is occasionally intentional. *People v Cobb, supra* (DA policy not to put such information into warrants). Courts have repeatedly held, however, that such omissions are not fatal under the add-and-retest approach to the problem discussed in §2.44. See, *e.g., People v Lopez* (1985) 173 CA3d 125, 134, 218 CR 799 (police detective told informant that charges against him might be dismissed); *In re Larry C.* (1982) 134 CA3d 62, 68, 184 CR 505 (plea bargain); *People v Flores* (1982) 128 CA3d 512, 519, 180 CR 368 (police promises to help informant resolve pending charges; police payments and promises of payment). But see *People v Cobb, supra* (pre-Proposition 8 case, hence add-and-retest procedure not used for intentional omission).

Affidavits that state an informant has proved reliable in the past must also disclose any instances of unreliability. *People v Kurland, supra*, 28 C3d at 395. The effect of such an omission has not been determined and will probably depend largely on the particular facts.

☛ **Judicial Tip**: Magistrates can reduce the risk of a successful challenge to an affidavit by asking the affiant a few questions when the affidavit is presented and by having the affiant add the answers to the affidavit. For example: Is the informant currently in custody? Are charges pending against him or her? Have any promises or semi-promises or threats been made? Did the police give the informant financial assistance? A few questions asked early can prevent later legal tangles.

### 3. [§2.46] Multiple Omissions

Challenges to affidavits commonly include claims of multiple omissions. *People v Berkoff* (1985) 174 CA3d 305, 219 CR 878, illustrates how courts analyze such contentions. The affidavit recited receipt of an anonymous tip from a citizen-informant of unusual traffic at a specified apartment by visitors who stayed only a few minutes. The affidavit then described in detail a controlled buy of cocaine at the apartment made by a confidential, reliable informant. Defendant contended that the affidavit should have mentioned (1) the tip was several weeks old and therefore stale; (2) initial police surveillance of defendant's apartment following the tip indicated no unusual activities; (3) the police did not actually see the informant enter defendant's apartment; (4) cocaine arrests of persons other than defendant had occurred in the apartment building in October, the month of defendant's arrest; (5) the informant used PCP; (6) the informant had a criminal record, had criminal matters pending against her, and was a paid police informant. 174 CA3d at 309.

The court said that the first two omissions were immaterial in light of the controlled buy. The third was not an omission because the affidavit stated that the informant was in the affiant's sight at all times except when she entered the apartment. The fourth, cocaine arrests of other persons, was irrelevant because the confidential informant identified the particular person who sold her cocaine. As to omissions relating to the drug habits and background of the informant, the record showed that the affiant had no knowledge of these matters. 174 CA3d at 309–311.

### 4. [§2.47] Search Warrants Based on Prior Search

In *People v Ratliff* (1986) 41 C3d 675, 224 CR 705, the search warrant application rested in part on a prior consent search of the defendant's car. The defendant contended that the affidavit omitted a threat by the officers to "bust open" the trunk of the car unless the defendant consented. The court held that the trial court could reasonably conclude that no such threat was made "or that it merely consisted of a correct statement of the officers' legal remedies if consent were refused. Failure to disclose such immaterial matters to the magistrate would not taint issuance of the warrant." 41 C3d at 688.

Sometimes the affidavit omits the fact of a prior search altogether. Thus, in *People v Cook* (1978) 22 C3d 67, 93, 148 CR 605 (superseded on other points by Proposition 8 and *Franks v Delaware* (1978) 438 US 154, 98 S Ct 2674, 57 L Ed 2d 667), the affidavit failed to mention an earlier, warrantless search of defendant's house. The court held that the defendant was entitled to litigate the legality of the earlier search but could not challenge its omission from the affidavit. The omission was irrelevant because, when issuing a search warrant, "it is not the magistrate's function also to determine whether the facts alleged in the affidavit were lawfully obtained."

In other words, an earlier and allegedly illegal search raises a fruit of the poisonous tree problem but not an omission problem. A search warrant obtained on information acquired by an illegal search is itself illegal. *People v Chapman* (1984) 36 C3d 98, 113, 201 CR 628, disapproved on other grounds in 24 C4th 856, 867; *Raymond v Superior Court* (1971) 19 CA3d 321, 326, 96 CR 678. The prosecution has the burden of showing either

(1) That the prior warrantless search was lawful. *People v Duncan* (1986) 42 C3d 91, 97, 227 CR 654 (officer's earlier presence on premises due to exigent circumstances); *People v Cook, supra* (prior entry to confirm information illegal; classic unlawful confirmatory search); *People v Baker* (1986) 187 CA3d 562, 567–571, 231 CR 877 (legality of earlier consent search); or

(2) That the police obtained the information in the search warrant independently of any prior illegality. *Segura v U.S.* (1984) 468 US 796, 798, 104 S Ct 3380, 82 L Ed 2d 599 (illegal entry to secure premises while police obtain search warrant does not invalidate a search warrant that rests on information entirely unrelated to the illegal entry); *People v Gesner* (1988) 202 CA3d 581, 588, 248 CR 324; *People v Angulo* (1988) 199 CA3d 370, 374, 244 CR 819. The independent source doctrine also applies to evidence initially discovered during an illegal search and later obtained independently through activities untainted by the initial illegality. *Murray v U.S.* (1988) 487 US 533, 108 S Ct 2529, 101 L Ed 2d 472. For further discussion, see §§1.58–1.59.

Evidence obtained pursuant to a search warrant based on an earlier illegal search is not admissible under the good-faith exception of *Leon*, even when the affidavit discloses the prior search. *People v Machupa* (1994) 7 C4th 614, 630, 29 CR2d 775; *People v Murtha* (1993) 14 CA4th 1112, 1123, 18 CR2d 324.

### 5. [§2.48] Sting Operations

In *People v Truer* (1985) 168 CA3d 437, 441–444, 214 CR 869, the DEA ran a storefront operation selling chemicals to suspected drug makers. The affidavit stated that the defendant had ordered specified chemicals for illicit drug manufacture from a chemical supply company. The court held that failure to disclose the true nature of the supply company was material, but that adding this information to the affidavit would not diminish probable cause.

## F. Other Matters Outside Affidavit

### 1. [§2.49] Extrinsic Evidence To Clarify Ambiguities

In *People v Smith* (1980) 108 CA3d 843, 848, 166 CR 778, the affidavit stated, "Within the past seventy-two hours . . . X [a confidential reliable informant] advised me that X had been to a residence of a subject known to X as Gary Smith. . . ." It is not clear whether X had been there within 72 hours or that he was there at some unspecified earlier time and only told the affiant about it in the last 72 hours. The currency or staleness of X's information bore on the issue of probable cause. *Smith* held that "the prosecution had the right to produce evidence of the intended meaning of the language in the affidavit." 108 CA3d at 850–851. *People v Christian* (1972) 27 CA3d 554, 560, 103 CR 740, is in accord. See also 4 Witkin & Epstein, California Criminal Law, *Illegally Obtained Evidence* §95 (3d ed 2000).

Some judges note that both *Smith* and *Christian* were alternate holdings and suggest that they be used with caution. Claimed ambiguities should be resolved whenever possible within the four corners of the affidavit. See, *e.g., People v McDaniels* (1994) 21 CA4th 1560, 1564, 27 CR2d 245; *People v Smith, supra* (affidavit as a whole more important to interpretation than apparent grammatical meaning). The general rule is that probable cause is to be determined from the face of the affidavit. See, *e.g., People v Smith* (1976) 17 C3d 845, 852 n3, 132 CR 397 (only facts included in the affidavit can be considered for probable cause); *People v Schmidt* (1978) 83 CA3d 968, 975, 148 CR 426 (subsequent disproof of a fact does not invalidate warrant; issue is reasonable belief of affiant at time of application).

☛ **Judicial Tip**: It is often possible to eliminate ambiguities before signing the search warrant. A fine line often separates an effort to clarify an ambiguity in an affidavit from an attempt to add to the affidavit. "An otherwise insufficient affidavit cannot be rehabilitated by evidence concerning information possessed by the affiant when he sought the warrant but not disclosed to the issuing magistrate." *People v Superior Court* (Corona) (1981) 30 C3d 193, 204, 178 CR 334. Most judges are very reluctant ever to go outside the four corners of the affidavit.

### 2. [§2.50] Examination of Informant by Magistrate

In *Theodor v Superior Court* (1972) 8 C3d 77, 104 CR 226 (superseded as to consequences of misstatements by Proposition 8 and *Franks v Delaware* (1978) 438 US 154, 98 S Ct 2674, 57 L Ed 2d 667), the magistrate had written affidavits from an officer and from an undisclosed informer. The magistrate examined the latter under oath; the magistrate took notes but did not have the examination recorded and transcribed.

The court held that the magistrate had discretion under Pen C §1526 to so examine the informant-affiant. *Theodor v Superior Court, supra,* 8 C3d at 87. In a footnote the court also said, "[W]e find that, especially in view of the magistrate's extensive examination of the informant, the affidavits are sufficient. . . ." 8 C3d at 86 n4. The court spoke with approval of the magistrate's "thoroughness" in "taking additional measures to ensure that probable cause exists even when an affidavit on its face supports the issuance of a warrant." 8 C3d at 87.

Presumably such oral questioning enhances the magistrate's determination of credibility. Whether the magistrate can use this procedure in the more common situation of an informant who is not an affiant, *i.e.,* when the sole affiant is a police officer, is unknown. Many judges doubt that such a procedure would be proper unless the magistrate conducts the examination under oath and has it reported, transcribed, and certified so that it constitutes an oral affidavit under Pen C §1526(b). See §§2.19–2.20. The magistrate followed the latter course in *People v Goldberg* (1984) 161 CA3d 170, 207 CR 431. *Goldberg* held that the officer's affidavit by itself was insufficient but that the examination of the informer established his credibility and was therefore adequate probable cause. 161 CA3d at 183.

Some judges believe that questioning the informant risks compromising the magistrate's neutrality. They suggest that if the affiant is unable to establish credibility in the affidavit, it is preferable simply not to issue the warrant.

## G. [§2.51] Sealing of Affidavit; Hearing

The issuing magistrate may seal those portions of the affidavit that tend to reveal a confidential informant's identity. *People v Hobbs* (1994) 7 C4th 948, 963, 30 CR2d 651; *People v Seibel* (1990) 219 CA3d 1279, 1299–1300, 269 CR 313.

When a magistrate seals all or a major portion of the affidavit, the defendant is effectively blocked from showing misrepresentations or the materiality of the informant as a witness or, indeed, from litigating whether the affidavit provides sufficient probable cause for the search. See *People v Hobbs, supra,* 7 C4th at 972. To avoid a denial of due process, the reviewing court must conduct a particularly careful and thorough in camera hearing at which the court determines whether:

(1) The extent of sealing is necessary to avoid revealing the informant's identity; and

(2) There is a *reasonable* probability that the affidavit contains materially false statements or insufficient probable cause, depending on whether the motion before the court is to traverse or to quash the search warrant. *People v Hobbs, supra*; *PSC Geothermal Servs. Co. v Superior Court* (1994) 25 CA4th 1697, 1713, 31 CR2d 213 (standards for trial court review of sealing order).

When a court finds such a reasonable probability, the prosecutor has the choice of consenting to the disclosure of the sealed portions of the affidavit or losing the motion. *People v Hobbs, supra*, 7 C4th at 975.

At the in camera hearing, the prosecutor, but not the defendant or defense counsel, can be present. Defense counsel can submit written questions. The court can require the prosecutor to produce "materials or witnesses it requires. The materials will invariably include such items as relevant police reports and other information regarding the informant and the informant's reliability. Furthermore, because the defendant's access to the essence of the affidavit is curtailed or possibly eliminated, the lower court may, in its discretion, find it necessary and appropriate to call and question the affiant, the informant, or any other witness whose testimony it deems necessary to rule upon the issues." 7 C4th at 973. The hearing should be reported and may be videotaped. *People v Hobbs, supra.*

☛ **Judicial Tip**: Magistrates should approach requests for sealing all or major portions of a search warrant affidavit with particular caution. Much of the time the confidentiality of an informant can be adequately protected without taking such a drastic step, thereby avoiding substantial subsequent difficulties.

## IV. WARRANT REQUIREMENTS

### A. [§2.52] Summary of Requirements

A search warrant must meet the following statutory and constitutional requirements:

(1) *Affidavit.* It must rest on one or more sufficient affidavits. Pen C §§1526, 1527. See §§2.15–2.51.

(2) *Neutral magistrate.* It must be issued by a neutral magistrate. See §§2.53–2.54. In California, state Supreme Court and court of appeal justices are magistrates, as are superior court judges. Pen C §808.

(3) *Writing; form.* It must be in writing and substantially in the form prescribed by statute. Pen C §§1523, 1529. See §§2.55–2.56.

(4) *Signature.* It must be signed by a magistrate. Pen C §§1523, 1528(a), 1529. See §§2.57–2.58.

(5) *Peace officer.* It must be directed to a peace officer. Pen C §§1523, 1528(a). Certain persons other than peace officers may serve search warrants. See §2.61.

(6) *Affiant.* It must name the affiant. Pen C §1529; see §2.62.

(7) *Grounds.* It must specify the statutory ground(s) on which it is based. Pen C §1529; see §2.63. The permitted grounds are set out in Pen C §§1524(a) and 1524.1; see §2.4.

(8) *Particularity.* It must describe the person and place to be searched and the property to be seized with "reasonable particularity." Pen C §1529; US Const amend IV. See §§2.64–2.77. The same particularity requirement applies to affidavits. Pen C §1525.

☛ **Judicial Tips**: Particularity is the major requirement after probable cause and merits especially careful attention by issuing magistrates. It is good practice to double-check that the descriptions in the affidavit(s) match the ones in the warrant.

(9) *Night service.* When an affidavit requests night service, the magistrate must determine whether there is good cause for it and, if so, must expressly authorize it in the warrant. Pen C §1533. See §§2.84–2.88.

## B. Neutral Magistrate

### 1. [§2.53] Basic Principles

Lack of neutrality and detachment on the part of the person who issues the warrant violates the Fourth and Fourteenth Amendments and renders a warrant invalid. *Lo-Ji Sales, Inc. v New York* (1979) 442 US 319, 326, 99 S Ct 2319, 60 L Ed 2d 920; *Coolidge v New Hampshire* (1971) 403 US 443, 450, 91 S Ct 2022, 29 L Ed 2d 564. The test is an objective one, not how detached the magistrate feels. *Lo-Ji Sales, Inc. v New York, supra*, 442 US at 326–327; *Grimes v Superior Court* (1981) 120 CA3d 582, 586, 174 CR 623. The magistrate's conduct after issuing the warrant may erode neutrality. *Lo-Ji Sales, Inc. v New York, supra,* 442 US at 327; see §2.54.

*Good faith.* The good-faith exception is inapplicable when the magistrate actively participates in the search as in *Lo-Ji Sales. U.S. v Leon* (1984) 468 US 897, 923, 104 S Ct 3405, 82 L Ed 2d 677 (such complete abandonment of judicial role makes officer's reliance on warrant unreasonable). The result may be otherwise when the lack of neutrality is not reasonably apparent to the officer (see 2 LaFave, p 439), but there are no controlling decisions.

### 2. [§2.54] Illustrative Situations

*Prior contact with defendant*; *relation to victim.* Neutrality is not compromised by the fact that the magistrate previously heard cases involving the defendant, but it may be by the magistrate's relation to the victim or to the person seeking the warrant (*e.g.,* when the victim is the judge's clerk or when the affiant and the magistrate date). 2 LaFave, p 444.

*Assistance in affidavit preparation.* A magistrate does not jeopardize neutrality by helping the affiant add truthful and accurate information to an affidavit to make it sufficient. 2 LaFave, p 451.

*Magistrate as investigator.* In *Coolidge v New Hampshire* (1971) 403 US 443, 450, 91 S Ct 2022, 29 L Ed 2d 564, the court invalidated the warrant because it had been issued by the state Attorney General acting as a justice of the peace; the Attorney General was also in charge of the investigation relating to the warrant. While the particular events of *Coolidge* probably could not happen in California because only judges of California courts are magistrates (Pen C §808), an analogous situation has occurred. In *Grimes v Superior Court* (1981) 120 CA3d 582, 174 CR 623, a magistrate investigated a citizen's compliant about marijuana cultivation, turned the information over to the police, and then issued a search warrant for the property in question. The court invalidated the warrant: "In issuing the warrant Judge . . . ruled upon his own credibility." 120 CA3d at 586.

*Observation of search*; *participation.* Observation of the search by the issuing magistrate without participation in it does not reflect on the neutrality of the magistrate. *People v McCarter* (1981) 117 CA3d 894, 905, 173 CR 188. However, participation does. *Lo-Ji Sales, Inc. v New York* (1979) 442 US 319, 326, 99 S Ct 2319, 60 L Ed 2d 920 (magistrate took active role in search for obscene materials).

☛ **Judicial Tip**: Most judges consider being present at the execution of a search warrant a practice to be avoided. Being present may later put the judge in the difficult position of attempting to disregard information gained outside the record when making decisions pertaining to the search. Also, it may create an appearance of impropriety, and such appearances should be avoided whenever possible. See, *e.g., Grimes v Superior Court, supra*, 120 CA3d at 587. Neutrality aside, a judge's presence at the search may turn the judge into a witness who is subject to being questioned.

### C. [§2.55] In Writing

A search warrant must be in writing. Pen C §1523. The writing must exist *before* the search; a search cannot be validated retroactively by a search warrant obtained later. *Fixler v Superior Court* (1974) 38 CA3d 475, 480–481, 113 CR 285; *Bowyer v Superior Court* (1974) 37 CA3d 151, 161, 111 CR 628.

There is *no* exception to the writing requirement for telephonic search warrants. Despite their misleading name, a written warrant is essential and it must exist at the time of the telephone conversation between the magistrate and the affiant. *Bowyer v Superior Court, supra*; see Pen C §1528(b); *People v Morrongiello* (1983) 145 CA3d 1, 9, 193 CR 105. For discussion of affidavits for telephonic search warrants, see §§2.19–2.20. For discussion of affidavits transmitted by fax or e-mail, see §2.21. For telephonic search warrants generally, see discussion in §2.59.

### D. [§2.56] Form of Search Warrant; Questions for Issuing Magistrates

Penal Code §1529 prescribes the form of a search warrant. The statutory requirements are set out verbatim below, together with questions on the margins that the issuing magistrate may use as a checklist.

| | | |
|---|---|---|
| | County of ____________________ | |
| 1. County filled in? | The people of the State of California to any sheriff, marshal, or police officer in the County of ____________________. | 2. Addressed to a peace officer? |
| 3. All affiants named? | Proof, by affidavit, having been this day made before me by (naming every person whose affidavit has been taken), that (stating the grounds of the application), according to Section 1524, or, if the affidavit be not positive, that there is probable cause for believing that ____________________________ | 4. Statutory ground(s) stated? |

| | | |
|---|---|---|
| 5. Night service? | (stating the ground of the application in the same manner), you are therefore commanded, in the daytime (or any time of the day or night, as the case may be, according to Section 1533), to make search on the person of C.D. (or in the house situated ___________, describing it, or any other place to be searched, with reasonable particularity, as the case may be) for the following property, thing, things, or person: (describing the property, thing, things, or person with reasonable particularity); and, in case of a thing or | 6. Location adequately described? |
| 7. Property or person adequately described? | things or personal property, if you find the same or any part thereof, to bring the thing or things or personal property forthwith before me (or this court) at (stating the place). | 8. Place of return stated? |
| 9. Dated? | Given under my hand, and dated this ____ day of ______, A.D. (year). | |
| | E.F., Judge of the (applicable) Court | 10. Signed with name of office? |

☛ **Judicial Tip**: Noncompliance with formal requirements may not always invalidate the warrant, but it adds to litigation and does not favorably impress courts that subsequently deal with the warrant.

## E. [§2.57] Signature

A search warrant must be signed by the magistrate "with his or her name of office." Pen C §§1528(a), 1523. For the definition of a magistrate, see §2.52.

Two major questions arise concerning the signature requirement:

(1) What consequences flow from an omission of the signature? See §2.58.

(2) How is the signature requirement met when the search warrant is authorized via telephone, fax, or e-mail? See §§2.59–2.60.

### 1. [§2.58] Effect of Omitting Signature

Forgetting to sign the warrant is not fatal as long as the record is clear that the magistrate intended to sign it. *People v Superior Court* (Robinson) (1977) 75 CA3d 76, 78–80, 141 CR 917 (magistrate signed only jurat of affidavit; she testified that she intended to sign the warrant and failed to do so through inadvertence); *Sternberg v Superior Court* (1974) 41 CA3d 281, 291, 115 CR 893 (officer discovered omission of signature shortly after executing the warrant and had it brought back to the magistrate who then signed it).

*Robinson* illustrates how courts upheld defective warrants before the good-faith exception of *Leon* (75 CA3d at 80):

> The [fourth] amendment, of course, does not include an express requirement that the magistrate's signature be affixed to the warrant. The primary purpose of the amendment, as has been noted many times, is to require that decisions about the sufficiency and the reliability of evidence used to justify a search be made by a neutral and detached magistrate, rather than by an "officer engaged in the often competitive enterprise of ferreting out crime." (*Johnson v United States*, 333 US 10, 14 [92 L Ed 436, 440, 68 S Ct 367].) That is precisely what happened in the present case.

### 2. [§2.59] Telephonic Search Warrants

Penal Code §1528(b) sets out the procedure for issuing a so-called telephonic search warrant. The officer-affiant prepares an original and a duplicate original warrant. After taking the affiant's sworn oral statement over the phone (see §§2.19–2.20), the magistrate authorizes the affiant to sign the magistrate's name on the duplicate original, which is then served and returned. The officer brings the magistrate the original search warrant, often at the time of return of service. The magistrate then enters "the exact time of the issuance" on the original warrant, signs it, and files the original and duplicate original warrants with the court clerk. For a step-by-step guide, see §2.130.

The magistrate need not sign the original search warrant before the search. *People v Ramos* (1982) 30 C3d 553, 574, 180 CR 266, rev'd on other grounds (1983) 463 US 992, 103 S Ct 3446, 77 L Ed 2d 1171. Misplacement or loss of the unsigned original is not fatal. *People v Sanchez* (1982) 131 CA3d 323, 330, 182 CR 430 (original could not be found; duplicate original was "later signed by the Judge in the manner he would have done on the original").

Upon an appropriate second sworn oral statement, the magistrate can telephonically authorize an amendment to the search warrant. *People v*

*Morrongiello* (1983) 145 CA3d 1, 10, 193 CR 105 (amendment added authorization to search a duffel bag). The officer should make the change on the duplicate original before serving the warrant. Dictum in *Morrongiello* suggests that the search may be upheld even if the officer adds the amendment after executing the warrant. 145 CA3d at 12.

### 3. [§2.60] Issuance of Search Warrants by Fax or E-mail

Penal Code §1526(b) provides an alternative to telephonic search warrants. After taking affiant's oath over the phone, the affiant signs the affidavit and transmits it by fax or e-mail to the magistrate, together with all attachments and the proposed search warrant. A digital signature is used when the transmission is via e-mail. The magistrate confirms receipt and legibility of the papers with the affiant and verifies that affiant acknowledges his or her signature to be genuine. See §2.19.

If the magistrate decides to issue the warrant, he or she

(a) Causes papers received by e-mail to be printed;

(b) Signs the warrant that was transmitted;

(c) Notes on it the exact date and time of issuance;

(d) Notes on it that affiant's oath was administered orally over the phone;

(e) Transmits the signed search warrant via fax or e-mail to the affiant, who acknowledges receipt telephonically; and

(f) On acknowledgment of receipt, authorizes affiant to write "duplicate original" on the completed search warrant transmittal to the affiant. For a step-by-step guide, see §2.131.

This document then becomes a duplicate original and is ultimately returned together with the original search warrant.

## F. [§2.61] Direction to Peace Officer

By statutory definition a search warrant is an order "directed to a peace officer." Pen C §§1523, 1528(a). The term "peace officer" is defined expansively in Pen C §830 and following sections. However, the statutory search warrant form prescribed by Pen C §1529 is not addressed to any peace officer but to a "sheriff, marshal, or police officer." It is unclear whether the wording of Pen C §1529 is intended as a limitation. In the view of most judges it is not.

Persons other than peace officers may *apply* for a warrant, as distinguished from *serving* it. *People v Bell* (1996) 45 CA4th 1030, 1054–1055, 53 CR2d 156.

Without amending Pen C §1523, §1528, or §1529, the legislature has authorized specified public employees who are not peace officers but have had peace officer training to serve search warrants within the scope of their employment. See Pen C §§830.9 (animal control officers), 830.11 (designated employees of Departments of Financial Institutions, Real Estate and Insurance, and of Public Utilities Commission), 830.13 (investigators of county auditor-controller or director of finance), 831.5 (custodial officers of certain counties). As to federal employees and tribal law enforcement officers, see Pen C §830.6.

☛ **Judicial Tip**: When an authorized person who is not a peace officer will serve the warrant:

- The affidavit should so state and provide facts showing that person's statutory qualification; and
- The warrant should name that person and his or her title.

### G. [§2.62] Naming the Affiant

The statutory search warrant form mandates "naming every person whose affidavit has been taken." Pen C §1529. Affidavits by confidential informants constitute a judicially created exception in order to preserve the nondisclosure privilege of Evid C §1041. *People v Sanchez* (1972) 24 CA3d 664, 677, 101 CR 193, disapproved on other grounds in 9 C3d 687, 695 n8. For discussion of the sealing of affidavits, see §2.51.

### H. [§2.63] Specification of Grounds

Penal Code §1529 requires that the warrant state the ground or grounds "of the application." Penal Code §1524(a) lists the grounds for issuing a search warrant. See §2.4.

Search warrant forms usually include a preprinted statement of possible grounds; the officer who prepares the warrant indicates which ground applies.

☛ **Judicial Tip**: In examining the specification of grounds, it is helpful to make three inquiries: (1) Are the grounds indicated in the warrant? (2) Does the specification of grounds in the warrant match the specification in the affidavit? (3) Most important, does the affidavit adequately support the specification?

### I. [§2.64] Description of Persons and Places To Be Searched and Property To Be Seized

Many of the requirements discussed so far are formal. The need for particularity of description is central. It stems from the Fourth Amendment ("particularly describing the place to be searched, and the persons or things to be seized") as well as from the Penal Code. Pen C §§1528(a), 1529. Penal Code §1529 repeatedly speaks of description with "reasonable particularity." Particularity of description is necessary in the affidavit as well as in the warrant. Pen C §1525.

### 1. [§2.65] Description of Person To Be Searched

The person to be searched must be described with reasonable particularity. *Lohman v Superior Court* (1977) 69 CA3d 894, 900, 138 CR 403. The person can be identified by a name others use in referring to him or her, even if it is not his or her real name. See *People v McLean* (1961) 56 C2d 660, 663, 16 CR 347 (arrest warrant). However, a warrant for the search of two named "and other unidentified persons" is too broad because it "would allow an unlimited search of persons." *People v Tenney* (1972) 25 CA3d 16, 23, 101 CR 419, disapproved on other grounds in 16 C3d 869, 875.

In many cases the police do not have a full name or complete description. "A bare minimum description should include sex, race, approximate age, and probable location." See Chrystie & Schirn, p II-5.

Stating the likely location of the subject adds particularity (see Chrystie & Schirn, p II-1) and is important for another reason. In *Lohman v Superior Court, supra*, the search warrant directed the search of a particular ranch and two named individuals. One of the two was the defendant. However, the defendant was not searched at the ranch but at his brother's house nearby. The court held that "a search warrant authorizing a search of a person does not permit a search for that person at a residence not described in the warrant, even where officers have a reasonable basis to believe the person to be searched is present." 69 CA3d at 905.

☛ **Judicial Tip**: In reading a search warrant for a person, it is sometimes helpful to ask whether an officer with no knowledge of the case would be able to identify the person from the description without difficulty and whether the warrant would tell the officer where to find the person. See Chrystie & Schirn, p II-1.

For special requirements when the search of a person involves bodily intrusions, see §§2.11–2.12.

### 2. Description of Place To Be Searched

#### a. [§2.66] Key Issues

Place descriptions in search warrants can give rise to two distinct issues:

(1) Does the warrant permit searches of locations for which probable cause has not been shown?

(2) Does the warrant make it reasonably clear what place is to be searched?

The first issue is illustrated by *People v MacAvoy* (1984) 162 CA3d 746, 753–754, 209 CR 34. The affidavit established probable cause to believe that contraband would be found in one particular room of a fraternity house. The warrant authorized search of the entire house and was held too broad (see, however, §§1.28–1.31 regarding application of the good-faith rule). As to apartment houses, "the particular 'place' to be described means a single living unit, that is to say the residence of one person or family, and a warrant describing an entire building issued on probable cause to search only one apartment therein is void." *People v Govea* (1965) 235 CA2d 285, 300, 45 CR 253; *People v Estrada* (1965) 234 CA2d 136, 146, 44 CR 165.

As to the second inquiry, the governing principle is that the warrant "must sufficiently describe the premises to be searched so that the officer executing the warrant may, with reasonable effort, ascertain and identify the place intended." *People v Peck* (1974) 38 CA3d 993, 1000, 113 CR 806; *People v Dumas* (1973) 9 C3d 871, 880, 109 CR 304; *People v MacAvoy, supra*, 162 CA3d at 754.

Courts construe place description expansively. A warrant for the search of "the Minder residence, and the premises therein" permits search of a safe found one or two feet outside the house. *People v Minder* (1996) 46 CA4th 1784, 1787–1788, 54 CR2d 555. A warrant for the "premises located at 2128 W 242nd Street, . . . further described as a single family residence . . . there is a detached garage located to the rear (south) of the residence" authorizes search of the garage when the affidavit establishes probable cause for doing so. *People v McNabb* (1991) 228 CA3d 462, 467, 279 CR 11. See also *People v Weagley* (1990) 218 CA3d 569, 572, 267 CR 85 (warrant for apartment permits search of outside mailbox reasonably identifiable as corresponding to apartment).

Similarly, a warrant to search defendant's house and "appurtenant buildings" covers the garage and automobiles parked in it, provided, of course, that the affidavit shows probable cause to search the cars. *People v Elliott* (1978) 77 CA3d 673, 688, 144 CR 137. See also *People v Fitzwater* (1968) 260 CA2d 478, 486, 67 CR 190. But such a warrant does not permit search of a vehicle that is neither mentioned in the warrant nor parked in the building's garage. *People v Dumas, supra.*

A warrant that only gives a business's mailbox number is a totally inadequate description for a search of the business' premises. *U.S. v Williamson* (10th Cir 1993) 1 F3d 1134, 1136.

### b. [§2.67] Buildings With Multiple Occupants; Search of Wrong Apartment

The two issues discussed in §2.66 may overlap, especially when the warrant describes multi-occupancy structures. Thus, in *People v Estrada* (1965) 234 CA2d 136, 144, 44 CR 165, an often-cited case, the warrant referred to "the apartment house occupied by Manuel Estrada at 18 S. 19th Street, San Jose, the second story of a white house. . . ." The building had four apartments, two on the second floor, one of which was occupied by Estrada. Only his apartment was searched. The court held that by referring to Estrada the warrant enabled the officers to identify the particular apartment without difficulty; interpreted in this manner, the warrant was neither overly broad nor uncertain. With respect to the latter, the court said (234 CA2d at 148):

> If the description in the warrant limits the search to a particular part of the premises either by a designation of the area or other physical characteristics of such part or by a designation of its occupants, the business conducted there, or otherwise so that the officer executing the warrant can with reasonable effort identify the place to be searched, the warrant will meet Fourth Amendment requirements in respect to the description of the place to be searched.

*Estrada* might lead one to believe that a different result would follow if the officers entered and searched the wrong apartment, as in *Maryland v Garrison* (1987) 480 US 79, 80, 107 S Ct 1013, 94 L Ed 2d 72. The search warrant was for the person of Lawrence McWebb and "the premises known as 2036 Park Avenue third floor apartment." When the officers obtained the warrant they believed that there was only one apartment on the third floor. When they executed the warrant, they discovered that there were two and picked Garrison's (the defendant) instead of McWebb's. The court held (480 US at 85–88):

- The validity of the description must be determined by the information available to the officers at the time they obtained the warrant; subsequent events are immaterial.
- Under the particular circumstances, the police investigation preceding the issuance of the warrant caused the officers reasonably to believe that McWebb was the only tenant on the third floor.
- The search of Garrison's apartment was valid because the officers' mistake was objectively reasonable. The court found the case analogous to *Hill v California* (1971) 401 US 797, 803–804, 91 S Ct 1106, 28 L Ed 2d 484, in which the police arrested the defendant

in the mistaken but reasonable belief that he was another man, and the court upheld the validity of the arrest.

#### c. [§2.68] Erroneous Address

Courts sustain search warrants containing erroneous addresses as long as the warrant makes it clear that it authorizes the search of the premises of a particular, named person. *People v Superior Court* (Fish) (1980) 101 CA3d 218, 224–225, 161 CR 547 (search warrant gave wrong lot number, but referred to the house in question as occupied by Robert Fish; warrant gave physical description of Fish and house); *People v Lovett* (1978) 82 CA3d 527, 531, 147 CR 136 (warrant authorized search of 1227 1/2 West Washington instead of 1227; warrant also authorized search of defendant; court said magistrate obviously intended to authorize search of the premises occupied by defendant).

An erroneous address is also not fatal when the house to be searched is described accurately in other respects and there is no reasonable probability that the wrong house would be searched. *People v Amador* (2000) 24 C4th 387, 393, 100 CR2d 617.

These cases tend to stress the fact that the officers in fact searched the right house or apartment. See, *e.g.,* 24 C4th at 393; *People v Lovett, supra,* 82 CA3d at 532 ("Far more serious problems would have arisen had the police attempted to search the premises at 1227 1/2 about which nothing whatever had been said in the affidavit . . .").

A variation on the theme of mistaken address arises when the address given by the victim for the premises involved and the address in the search warrant do not match. This happened in *People v Duncan* (1981) 115 CA3d 418, 424–425, 171 CR 406. The affidavit included abundant facts showing that the address stated in the warrant was the right one. The court upheld the warrant against a contention that the differences in address negated probable cause.

### 3. Description of Property To Be Seized

#### a. [§2.69] Purpose and Definition of Particularity Requirements: "Meaningful Restriction" Test

Property descriptions in search warrants are often challenged on claims of overbreadth. Descriptions that are excessively broad or vague violate the particularity requirements. *People v Frank* (1985) 38 C3d 711, 722, 214 CR 801; *Burrows v Superior Court* (1974) 13 C3d 238, 250, 118 CR 166 ("It is axiomatic that a warrant may not authorize a search broader than the facts supporting its issuance"); *People v Holmsen* (1985) 173 CA3d 1045, 1048, 219 CR 598 ("papers showing or tending to show the trafficking of cocaine" may be too broad, but in any event is invalid because affidavit failed to show that such papers are likely to exist).

Courts often reiterate the following principles for determining whether a description of things to be seized is reasonably particular:

(1) "The requirement of particularity is designed to prevent general exploratory searches which unreasonably interfere with a person's right to privacy." *Burrows v Superior Court, supra*, 13 C3d at 249. See, *e.g., People v Frank, supra*, 38 C3d at 724; *People v Schilling* (1987) 188 CA3d 1021, 1030, 233 CR 744. The major danger is from warrants that allow "a general, exploratory rummaging in a person's belongings." *Coolidge v New Hampshire* (1971) 403 US 443, 467, 91 S Ct 2022, 29 L Ed 2d 564.

(2) The principle most often cited states that the requirement of reasonable particularity is "satisfied if the warrant imposes a *meaningful restriction* upon the objects to be seized." *Burrows v Superior Court, supra.* (Emphasis added.) See, *e.g., People v Schilling, supra*; *People v Tockgo* (1983) 145 CA3d 635, 645, 193 CR 503; *People v Barnum* (1980) 113 CA3d 340, 347, 169 CR 840.

(3) A "meaningful restriction" is one that leaves nothing to the discretion of the officer who conducts the search. *Marron v U.S.* (1927) 275 US 192, 196, 48 S Ct 74, 72 L Ed 231; *People v Frank, supra*; *People v Dumas* (1973) 9 C3d 871, 880, 109 CR 304. The warrant should set out "objective standards by which executing officers can differentiate items subject to seizure from those which are not." *Bay v Superior Court* (1992) 7 CA4th 1022, 1026, 9 CR2d 339; *U.S. v Spilotro* (9th Cir 1986) 800 F2d 959, 963.

(4) The particularity requirement "is to be accorded the most scrupulous exactitude when the 'things' are books, and the basis for their seizure is the ideas which they contain." *Stanford v Texas* (1965) 379 US 476, 485, 85 S Ct 506, 13 L Ed 2d 431.

As might be expected from principles framed so broadly, the meaningful restriction test is far easier to state than to apply. Sections 2.70–2.72 discuss illustrative applications.

☛ **Judicial Tip**: Descriptions of property, like place descriptions, often give rise to two distinct issues that merit separate treatment. First, does the affidavit provide probable cause to seize the particular property that the officers took? Secondly, does the warrant leave anything to the discretion of the officers conducting the search? In other words, does the warrant enable a reasonable officer to differentiate seizable items from others?

### b. "Meaningful Restriction" Test in Action

#### (1) [§2.70] Generic Descriptions

Descriptions of a generic nature such as "stolen property" fail to impose a meaningful restriction on the officer conducting the search and are invalid. *Thompson v Superior Court* (1977) 70 CA3d 101, 108, 138 CR 603 ("stolen property"); *People v Tockgo* (1983) 145 CA3d 635, 642, 193 CR 503 ("cigarettes . . . and any and all goods owned by" named victim).

The breadth of generality that is allowed depends to some degree on the ability of the investigating agency to identify the items in question more particularly. *People v Tockgo, supra*; *People v Lowery* (1983) 145 CA3d 902, 907, 194 CR 815; *People v Superior Court* (Williams) (1978) 77 CA3d 69, 78, 143 CR 382, disapproved on other grounds in 25 C3d 67, 76 n9. Thus, in *Tockgo*, the officers had information about unique markings of stolen cigarettes; the description should have included the markings to permit differentiation from other cigarettes that were not stolen property. Similarly, when the police know at the time they apply for the warrant that stolen drill bits have altered or defaced serial numbers, a description of "drill bits in sizes from 4" to 18" . . . having some defaced and altered serial numbers" is too broad. *People v Superior Court* (Williams), *supra.*

By contrast, *People v Lowery, supra*, rejected a contention that a description of computer chips was inadequate to permit the police to distinguish legitimate from stolen chips. The court said that there was no evidence that the police had information to make such a differentiation possible. The court applied the same principle in *Dunn v Municipal Court* (1963) 220 CA2d 858, 868, 34 CR 251. The warrant described the property as "deer or elk meat illegally possessed." In upholding the warrant, the court noted that a more particular description was not possible; meat does not have serial numbers or brand names.

The opportunity to collect information for a detailed description may be curtailed by emergency conditions. *People v Remiro* (1979) 89 CA3d 809, 831, 153 CR 89. Relatively broad descriptions are also more likely to be proper "in a complex case resting on the piecing together of many bits of evidence . . . than in a simpler investigation. . . ." *People v Kraft* (2000) 23 C4th 978, 1041, 99 CR2d 1 (interior quotation marks omitted).

Qualifying language often serves to narrow and save an otherwise overly broad description. See, *e.g., People v Schilling* (1987) 188 CA3d 1021, 1031, 233 CR 744 ("scientific evidence, including but not limited to fingerprints, powder burns, blood . . ."; the court said that under the particular circumstances, the officer could not detail in advance all the scientific evidence); *People v Barnum* (1980) 113 CA3d 340, 347, 169 CR 840 ("typewriter(s), tools, wires, . . . *which are the instrumentalities and evidence of crimes against the United States to wit: Title 18, United States Code, Sections 876 and 1716*" imposes a meaningful restriction "and left nothing to the discretion of the searching officers"; emphasis in original); *Nunes v Superior Court* (1980) 100 CA3d 915, 933, 161 CR 351 ("stolen property as indicated in the affidavit and attached police report" is sufficient as long as the affidavit contains adequate description). See §2.75 for further discussion of reference to affidavits to save descriptions in the warrant.

### (2) [§2.71] Papers and Other Documentary Evidence

All-encompassing clauses authorizing seizure of papers are often successfully challenged. By way of illustration, the following descriptions have been invalidated as overbroad:

- Checks, sales records, customers' correspondence and "[a]ny and all other records and paraphernalia connected with" the defendant's business. *Aday v Superior Court* (1961) 55 C2d 789, 793, 13 CR 415 (search of business suspected of publishing and distributing obscene materials).
- "[A]ll books, records, accounts and bank statements and cancelled checks of the receipt and disbursement of money and any file or documents" referring to four named persons. *Burrows v Superior Court* (1974) 13 C3d 238, 241, 118 CR 166 (search of office of lawyer suspected of misappropriating the funds of one client).
- "[B]ills and receipts for the purchase and repairs of metal numbering stamping equipment." *People v Superior Court* (Williams) (1978) 77 CA3d 69, 76, 143 CR 382, disapproved on other grounds in 25 C3d 67, 76 n9 (search of residence and mini-storage unit for stolen oil well drilling equipment). The court analyzed this clause of the warrant as if it only described "bills and receipts." 25 C3d at 78.
- "Documentary evidence tending to show the whereabouts of Theodore Frank during March 14 and 15, 1978, including, but not limited to credit card receipts, receipts from businesses, records of telephone toll calls made during that period of time; canceled checks made out or cashed on those dates, ledgers or personal diary notations which would indicate the whereabouts of Theodore Frank on those dates; . . . scrapbooks, newspaper clippings, photographs (developed or undeveloped), tape recordings or writings which could relate to the death of Amy [S.] and would indicate either participation and/or

an interest in that death by Theodore Frank. . . ." *People v Frank* (1985) 38 C3d 711, 723, 214 CR 801 (search of kidnap-murder suspect's apartment).

- "Evidence of indebtedness by [defendant] . . . , including but not limited to such items as bills, contracts, checkstubs, checks, bank-books, . . ." *Griffin v Superior Court* (1972) 26 CA3d 672, 692, 103 CR 379 (murder investigation).
- "Any papers showing names and addresses of associates of" defendant. 26 CA3d at 693.

A warrant authorizing seizure of virtually every document and computer file at a business cannot simply list categories of records without limitations or suggestions of how they relate to a specific criminal activity. *U.S. v Kow* (9th Cir 1995) 58 F3d 423, 427–428 (court also held *Leon* good-faith exception inapplicable).

One factor that courts sometimes consider is how broadly the searching officers interpret their authority. The seizure of large quantities of innocuous material tends to demonstrate the unlawful generality of the warrant. See, *e.g., People v Frank, supra*, 38 C3d at 727; *Burrows v Superior Court, supra*.

*Broad language with qualifying clause.* Broad language has been upheld if it is modified by a qualifying clause. For instance:

- "[A]ny papers or writings, records that evidence dealings in controlled substances including, but not limited to address books, ledgers, lists, notebooks, etc." *Toubus v Superior Court* (1981) 114 CA3d 378, 381, 170 CR 697. The court said that defendant's challenge to the warrant "ignores the qualifying clause . . . ; each record, book, etc. seized must evidence dealings in controlled substances. As so limited, the authorization is not 'overly broad.' " 114 CA3d at 386.
- "[C]orrespondence, address books, . . . directories and other documents which are the instrumentalities and evidence of" specified offenses relating to explosives. *People v Barnum* (1980) 113 CA3d 340, 347, 169 CR 840. Some statutes, however, cover a broad range of activity; a warrant's reference to them without other limiting features is not a sufficient restriction. *U.S. v Leary* (10th Cir 1988) 846 F2d 592, 601 (Arms Export Control Act) and cases there discussed.
- "[P]apers, books, records . . . and all other bookmaking property and paraphernalia, used or capable of being used for the purpose of recording or registering bets upon horse races. . . ." *People v*

*Barthel* (1965) 231 CA2d 827, 832, 42 CR 290 ("The warrant here fairly restricts, and the objects actually seized were the instrumentalities used in the commission of the crimes"). Here the officers' interpretation of the warrant to conduct a limited seizure worked in favor of validity.

- "[B]ooks, records, documents, papers, memoranda and correspondence, showing or tending to show a fraudulent intent, and/or knowledge as elements of the crime of false pretenses . . . together with other fruits, instrumentalities and evidence of crime at this [time] unknown." *Andresen v Maryland* (1976) 427 US 463, 480 n10, 96 S Ct 2737, 49 L Ed 2d 627. The court held that the latter, broad language did not permit a search for and seizure of any evidence of any crime but was limited by the qualifying clause to evidence relevant to the crime of false pretenses.
- Material "depicting minors (that is, persons under the age of 16) engaged in sexually explicit conduct." *U.S. v Hurt* (9th Cir 1986) 795 F2d 765, 772.

*Time Period.* As to the effect of a warrant's failure to limit the time period for which records can be seized, contrast *People v Lowery* (1983) 145 CA3d 902, 907, 194 CR 815 (warrant valid despite lack of time restriction because suspected illegal activity not limited to specific time period), and *Burrows v Superior Court, supra,* 13 C3d at 249 (offense under investigation occurred over a six-month period; court regarded the warrant's failure to restrict the record search to the relevant period as a factor in finding it overbroad).

### (3) [§2.72] Indicia-of-Occupancy Clauses

Search warrants for residences routinely include indicia-of-occupancy clauses such as "papers to show control of the residence, including rent receipts and utility bills" (*People v Holmsen* (1985) 173 CA3d 1045, 1048, 219 CR 598), or "[e]vidence tending to establish the identities of the occupants, users or owners of the residence, including, but not limited to . . ." (*People v Frank* (1985) 38 C3d 711, 722, 214 CR 801).

Such clauses are valid. *People v Nicolaus* (1991) 54 C3d 551, 574–575, 286 CR 628 (also held that searching officer who finds folder of papers may briefly examine them and seize them if they are incriminating); *People v Rogers* (1986) 187 CA3d 1001, 1009, 232 CR 294.

☛ **Judicial Tip**: An indicia-of-occupancy clause should include limiting examples when possible.

### 4. [§2.73] Special Requirement for Search of Premises of Certain Professionals

Penal Code §1525 mandates that the affidavit "specify when applicable, that the place to be searched is in the possession or under the control of an attorney, physician, psychotherapist or clergyman."

☛ **Judicial Tip**: Information that the premises are those of a specified professional should trigger a check by the magistrate as to the applicability of the special master provision of Pen C §1524(c). See §§2.5–2.7. Some judges suggest that the papers to be seized should be described with greater particularity than usual because patient and client privileges and privacy concerns will be implicated.

### 5. Judicial Techniques for Upholding Searches Based on Deficient Descriptions

#### a. [§2.74] In General

Courts have developed several approaches to validate, in whole or in part, warrants whose descriptions are facially inadequate or searches based on them. The *Leon* good-faith exception is the most widely used technique. See §§1.28–1.40. Others include:

- Referring to the affidavit to limit the description. See §2.75.
- On-scene identification by civilians of the particular place to be searched. See §2.76.
- Severance of invalid portions of the warrant. See §2.77.

#### b. [§2.75] Reference to Affidavit

Occasionally courts refer to the affidavit in order to narrow and validate an overly broad description. Thus, in *People v Peck* (1974) 38 CA3d 993, 1000, 113 CR 806, the warrant authorized search of an entire duplex; the affidavit concerned only the half occupied by the defendant and only that half was searched. The court upheld the warrant. In accord are *Nunes v Superior Court* (1980) 100 CA3d 915, 933, 161 CR 351; *People v Moore* (1973) 31 CA3d 919, 925, 107 CR 590; *People v Grossman* (1971) 19 CA3d 8, 12, 96 CR 437.

This approach is available only when the affidavit accompanies the warrant at the time it is served or the person executing the warrant has read the affidavit. *Bay v Superior Court* (1992) 7 CA4th 1022, 1027, 9 CR2d 339. See also *People v MacAvoy* (1984) 162 CA3d 746, 755,

209 CR 34 (affidavit must accompany warrant and be incorporated by reference).

### c. [§2.76] On-Scene Identification by Civilians

An on-scene identification by a civilian may supplement the particularity of a search warrant. In *People v Green* (1981) 117 CA3d 199, 207, 172 CR 582, the warrant authorized search of apartment No. 9 and "all storage areas designated for Unit #9." The storage rooms were unmarked, but an uninvolved tenant pointed out to the officers the storage room used by the occupant of apartment No. 9. The officers also had a key for the particular storage room. The court relied on these events to hold that the description was sufficiently particular and "vitiated any reasonable possibility that any other tenant's rights of privacy would be abrogated. . . ."

An overbroad description of things to be seized, however, cannot be saved by having the victim identify the items involved at the scene of the search. *People v Tockgo* (1983) 145 CA3d 635, 644, 193 CR 503 (warrant referred to property "determined by Certified Grocers to be stolen"; victim's security guard pointed out stolen items to the searching officers). "[T]he terms of the warrant, not the observations of a victim accompanying its execution, must provide the particularity required by the Constitution in order to render the warrant and the search valid." 145 CA3d at 646. But if the description is proper, the victim can assist the officers in the identification process, including pointing out items subject to seizure under the "plain sight" rule. *People v Superior Court* (Meyers) (1979) 25 C3d 67, 72–73, 157 CR 716; see *People v Superior Court* (Moore) (1980) 104 CA3d 1001, 163 CR 906; Pen C §1530 (search warrant to be served only by officers mentioned in its directions, "except in aid of the officer on his requiring it, he being present and acting in its execution"). For discussion of the application of the plain sight rule to the service of search warrants, see §§2.113–2.115.

### d. [§2.77] Severance of Invalid Portions of Search Warrant

Adequate descriptions in a search warrant may be severed from defective ones. The leading case permitting severance is *Aday v Superior Court* (1961) 55 C2d 789, 797, 13 CR 415. The description of things to be seized was overbroad except for two named books. The court held the warrant invalid only as to the portions that suffered from overbreadth. In *Aday*, the court said (55 C2d at 797):

> Although the warrant was defective in the respects noted, it does not follow that it was invalid as a whole. Such a conclusion would

> mean that the seizure of certain articles, even though proper if viewed separately, must be condemned merely because the warrant was defective with respect to other articles. The invalid portions of the warrant are severable from the authorization relating to the named books, which formed the principal basis of the charge of obscenity. The search for and seizure of these books, if otherwise valid, were not rendered illegal by the defects concerning other articles.

The severance principle has seen limited use, primarily in cases of overbroad descriptions of items to be seized. See *People v Smith* (1986) 180 CA3d 72, 89, 225 CR 348 (alternative holding); *People v Holmsen* (1985) 173 CA3d 1045, 1048, 219 CR 598; *People v McCarter* (1981) 117 CA3d 894, 901 n2, 173 CR 188; *People v Howard* (1976) 55 CA3d 373, 379, 127 CR 557 (alternative holding). One decision applied *Aday* to a description of location. *People v Joubert* (1983) 140 CA3d 946, 952, 190 CR 23 (warrant allowed search of large parcel for growing marijuana; court found probable cause to search only one particular area and severed the search of that area).

In *Aday,* the court said that severance will not always be allowed (55 C2d at 797):

> [W]e do not mean to suggest that invalid portions of a warrant will be treated as severable under all circumstances. We recognize the danger that warrants might be obtained which are essentially general in character but as to minor items meet the requirement of particularity, and that wholesale seizures might be made under them, in the expectation that the seizure would in any event be upheld as to the property specified. Such an abuse of the warrant procedure, of course, could not be tolerated.

In accord with the quoted statement, severance is not available when the valid portion of the warrant is a relatively minor part of it. *U.S. v Kow* (9th Cir 1995) 58 F3d 423, 428.

## V. EXECUTION OF WARRANTS

### A. Time of Execution

#### 1. 10-Day Requirement

##### a. [§2.78] General Rule

Penal Code §1528(a) provides that the warrant command the officer "forthwith to search." However, in this instance "forthwith" does not mean immediately. Penal Code §1534(a) specifies that a "search warrant shall be executed and returned within 10 days after date of issuance. A warrant executed within the 10-day period shall be deemed to have been timely executed and no further showing of timeliness need be made."

Section 1534(a) does not automatically validate all searches made within 10 days. The defendant can litigate the issue whether probable cause disappeared between the time of issuance and execution, but the effect of the statute is to place the burden of proof on the defendant. *People v Hernandez* (1974) 43 CA3d 581, 590, 118 CR 53; *People v McCarthy* (1978) 79 CA3d 547, 552, 144 CR 822. See also *People v Seibel* (1990) 219 CA3d 1279, 1299, 269 CR 313.

### b. [§2.79] Computation of Period

The 10-day period is "computed by excluding the day on which the search warrant is issued and by including the day on which" it is executed. *People v Clayton* (1993) 18 CA4th 440, 445, 22 CR2d 371.

*Last day on weekend.* When the 10th day falls on a weekend or holiday, a *return* on the next business day is proper (*People v Stevenson* (1976) 62 CA3d 915, 918, 133 CR 406), but a *search* may not be. See *People v Clayton, supra,* 18 CA4th at 446, cautioning "law enforcement against relying on the related general statutes authorizing extensions to the next business day when the last day for executing a search warrant falls upon a holiday." The court said that returning a search warrant is a ministerial act to which such statutes apply, but executing one is not.

*Service on day of issuance.* Excluding the first day in computing the 10-day period does *not* preclude law enforcement from executing the warrant on the day it is issued. *People v Clayton, supra.*

### c. [§2.80] Timely Service Followed by Delays

In *People v Kibblewhite* (1986) 178 CA3d 783, 785–786, 224 CR 48, the officers who served the warrant removed a safe to the police station and opened it four days later, still within the 10 days. The court held that they had complied with Pen C §1534.

In *People v Schroeder* (1979) 96 CA3d 730, 158 CR 220, timely service was made on banks and a timely partial return filed. The warrant sought voluminous documents and it took the banks several days after the 10-day period had lapsed. The court found no violation of Pen C §1534(a). The court stressed that the purpose of the 10-day requirement is to ensure that probable cause still exists when the warrant is served. 96 CA3d at 733.

The court reached the same conclusion in *People v Bowen* (1982) 137 CA3d 1020, 1034, 187 CR 614, when the police seized a car for laboratory examination and kept it for over five months. The seizure and return occurred within 10 days after issuance of the search warrant; the court regarded this as compliance with the statute even though the laboratory examination took much longer.

### d. [§2.81] Effects of Noncompliance

Penal Code §1534(a) states that after 10 days "the warrant, unless executed, is void." "Void" means that a search beyond the 10-day period is invalid (see *Sgro v U.S.* (1932) 287 US 206, 210–211, 53 S Ct 138, 77 L Ed 260), unless the search would be lawful without a warrant (*People v Larkin* (1987) 194 CA3d 650, 656, 239 CR 760).

A late return, as distinguished from a late search, results in suppression only if the defendant was prejudiced by the delay. *People v Head* (1994) 30 CA4th 954, 960, 36 CR2d 1 (loss of witness not sufficient); *People v Kirk* (1979) 99 CA3d 89, 92, 160 CR 184; *People v Couch* (1979) 97 CA3d 377, 381, 158 CR 647. In the view of most judges, prejudice warranting suppression is virtually impossible to show. For discussion of returns, see §2.126.

### e. [§2.82] Reissuance of Search Warrant

Officers who are unable to serve a search warrant within the required time sometimes ask a magistrate to reissue it. Such a procedure is permissible, even if it occurs after the 10-day period has expired. *People v Brocard* (1985) 170 CA3d 239, 241, 216 CR 231 (magistrate wrote at bottom of warrant: "Warrant reissued w/addendum to affidavit 7–12–83" and signed his name; affiant submitted sworn addendum to affidavit, but was not resworn as to original affidavit; procedure held valid).

☛ **Judicial Tip**: Requests for reissuance need scrutiny by the magistrate to determine whether probable cause still exists. Many judges and police departments prefer preparation of a new affidavit and warrant.

### f. [§2.83] Public Access to Records During 10-Day Period

Penal Code §1534(a) provides that "documents and records of the court relating to the warrant need not be open to the public until the execution and return of the warrant or the expiration of the 10-day period after issuance. Thereafter, if the warrant has been executed, the documents and records shall be open to the public. . . ." There is no exception for a search that furthers an ongoing investigation. *PSC Geothermal Servs. Co. v Superior Court* (1994) 25 CA4th 1697, 1714, 31 CR2d 213.

Public access to "documents and records" means the affidavit(s), return of the warrant, and other documents relating to the warrant, but probably not the property that was seized. *Oziel v Superior Court* (1990) 223 CA3d 1284, 1295, 273 CR 196 (court also held videotape of search not available to public).

For discussion of sealed affidavits, see §2.51.

### 2. Night Service

#### a. [§2.84] Statutory Provisions

Penal Code §1533 states:

> Upon a showing of good cause, the magistrate may, in his or her discretion, insert a direction in a search warrant that it may be served at any time of the day or night. In the absence of such a direction, the warrant shall be served only between the hours of 7 a.m. and 10 p.m.
>
> When establishing "good cause" under this section, the magistrate shall consider the safety of the peace officers serving the warrant and the safety of the public as a valid basis for nighttime endorsements.

The purpose of the second paragraph, added in 1986, is unclear. Courts have long considered officer and public safety as relevant factors. See, *e.g., Tuttle v Superior Court* (1981) 120 CA3d 320, 329, 174 CR 576 ("Safety of police officers is of extreme importance and is a factor which may be considered in determining cause for night service"; however, facts must be stated from which the magistrate can infer that nighttime service would lessen the possibility of a violent confrontation); *People v McCarter* (1981) 117 CA3d 894, 907, 173 CR 188 (officers had just received information "that one or more racially motivated, senseless murders had occurred the previous night and that another was contemplated"; public safety interest in averting more killings justified night service).

The fundamental purpose of Pen C §1533 is to guard privacy interests against "the peculiar abrasiveness of official intrusions" at night. *People v Maita* (1984) 157 CA3d 309, 322, 203 CR 685. More specifically, "the legislative purpose behind section 1533 is two-fold: (1) to require the magistrate to consider and determine whether he should exercise a discretion which authorizes a search peculiarly intrusive on the householder and especially dangerous to the officers; and (2) to enable the householder to know, from the face of the papers served on him, that the intrusion had, in fact, been authorized by a magistrate and that it was not the result of a mere whim or zealousness of the police." *Rogers v Superior*

*Court* (1973) 35 CA3d 716, 720, 111 CR 9; *Nunes v Superior Court* (1980) 100 CA3d 915, 923, 161 CR 351.

#### b. [§2.85] The 10 p.m. Deadline

In *People v Zepeda* (1980) 102 CA3d 1, 162 CR 143, the search warrant covered two residences. The officers completed the first search before 10 p.m., and started the search of defendant's residence after 10 p.m. The court upheld the latter search on the ground that the warrant was executed in "a single continuous transaction" that started before the deadline. In addition, the defendant was personally served with the warrant before 10 p.m. 102 CA3d at 7 (alternative holding).

In *People v Maita* (1984) 157 CA3d 309, 203 CR 685, the officers arrived at the location of the search before 10 p.m. The evidence was in dispute whether they entered before the deadline. The court said that even if they did not, the record was clear that the occupant knew "of the officers' presence and their intention to gain entry to the house well before 10 p.m." and that, therefore, Pen C §1533 was not violated. 157 CA3d at 322.

#### c. Good Cause

##### (1) [§2.86] Determined From Affidavit as Whole

Good cause for night service must appear from the affidavit; unsworn statements to the magistrate do not suffice. *People v Watson* (1977) 75 CA3d 592, 599, 142 CR 245. A statement of good cause can be on a separate sheet of paper submitted concurrently with the affidavit, as long as the magistrate regards it as part of the affidavit. *People v Egan* (1983) 141 CA3d 798, 803, 190 CR 546.

In deciding whether the affidavit shows good cause, the magistrate is not limited to facts, if any, that the affiant articulates as justifying night service; the magistrate considers the entire affidavit. *People v Lopez* (1985) 173 CA3d 125, 138, 218 CR 799 (good cause statement inadequate, but affidavit as a whole sufficient). The relevant inquiry is whether the "affidavit, read in a common sense manner and as a whole, reasonably supports the inference that the interests of justice are best served by the authorization of nighttime service. . . ." *People v McCarter* (1981) 117 CA3d 894, 906, 173 CR 188; *People v Cletcher* (1982) 132 CA3d 878, 882, 183 CR 480.

##### (2) [§2.87] Sufficiency of Showing

Good cause, like probable cause, does not lend itself to formulas. Courts have been liberal in upholding the magistrate's determination. An implied "finding of good cause . . . will not be disturbed on appeal absent an abuse of discretion." *People v Lopez* (1985) 173 CA3d 125, 138, 218 CR 799; see *People v Cletcher* (1982) 132 CA3d 878, 882, 183 CR 480.

Good cause "requires only some factual basis for a prudent conclusion that the greater intrusiveness of a nighttime search is justified by the exigencies of the situation." *People v Kimble* (1988) 44 C3d 480, 494, 244 CR 148, adopting the wording of *U.S. v Searp* (6th Cir 1978) 586 F2d 1117, 1121. The most frequently approved factor is the existence of facts from which the magistrate can infer that the objects of the search will disappear if the search is delayed. For example:

- Information that defendant is planning to leave the following morning. *People v Morrongiello* (1983) 145 CA3d 1, 13, 193 CR 105; *People v Mardian* (1975) 47 CA3d 16, 35, 121 CR 269, disapproved on other grounds in 43 C3d 1104, 1123.

- An inference from the affidavit that the suspect surmises or will soon know that he is under suspicion. *People v Egan* (1983) 141 CA3d 798, 806, 190 CR 546 (aerial surveillance and recent searches of neighboring marijuana patches by officers using marked police cars); *People v Cletcher, supra* (defendant may have seen informant observing stolen art piece in defendant's apartment); *People v Zepeda* (1980) 102 CA3d 1, 6, 162 CR 143 (informant married to suspect). See also *People v Siripongs* (1988) 45 C3d 548, 569, 247 CR 729 (homicide defendant's call from jail, speaking in Thai, gives rise to reasonable inference that he is giving instructions to dispose of evidence).

- Facts showing that particular stolen items are small and hence easily transferred, such as a camera and other small objects (*People v Siripongs, supra*), jewelry and coins (*People v Lopez, supra*) or money (*People v Zepeda, supra*), or that they are likely to be consumed (*In re Donald R.* (1978) 85 CA3d 23, 26, 149 CR 152, which involved stolen food, liquor, and cigarettes; informant had attended a party where some of the stolen items were in fact consumed).

In addition to the risk of disappearance, courts have given weight to factors such as the following:

- Facts indicating that night service would enhance public or officer safety. See §2.84. Other things being equal, the safety of the officer may be a consideration adverse to night service because execution of a warrant at night is "especially dangerous to the officers." *Rogers v Superior Court* (1973) 35 CA3d 716, 720, 111 CR 9.

- The fact that the location of the search needs to be kept under surveillance pending service of the warrant. This is not a decisive consideration and is given more weight if the location is not a residence. *People v Lowery* (1983) 145 CA3d 902, 909, 194 CR 815; *People v Flores* (1979) 100 CA3d 221, 234, 160 CR 839.
- The desirability of conducting the least intrusive search under the circumstances. *People v Morrongiello, supra* (search of duffel bag for cocaine after other searches were unsuccessful; defendant in custody; night search might facilitate release of defendant).
- Facts linking a search for recently stolen equipment to a recent homicide. *People v Kimble, supra.*

By way of contrast, the following statements, standing alone, are insufficient to justify night service. They share a common flaw in that they do not give rise to a reasonable inference that one of the factors discussed above is likely to exist.

- Investigation: marijuana cultivation. Statement: Drug distributors often utilize the cover of darkness to conceal their transportation and handling of contraband. Insufficient because growing marijuana usually does not disappear overnight. *Tuttle v Superior Court* (1981) 120 CA3d 320, 327–328, 174 CR 576.
- Investigation: possession of marijuana for sale. Statement: Facts indicating trafficking. Insufficient in the absence of facts showing that the activity occurred at night or that night service would enhance officer or public safety. *Rodriguez v Superior Court* (1988) 199 CA3d 1453, 1468, 245 CR 617; *People v Flores, supra*; *People v Watson* (1977) 75 CA3d 592, 596, 142 CR 245.
- Investigation: residential burglary-robbery. Statement: Affiant fears that the property sought will be disposed of. By itself this statement is not sufficiently specific. *People v Lopez* (1985) 173 CA3d 125, 138, 218 CR 799 (but court found sufficient specificity in other parts of affidavit; the stolen items were described and many "were small and readily concealed or transferred").
- Investigation: possession for sale. Statement: Defendant works and will not get home before 6 p.m. Insufficient because it does not show need for service after 10 p.m. *People v Watson, supra,* 75 CA3d at 598.
- Investigation: cultivation. Statement: Instances of violence are becoming more common in serving search warrants in remote cultivation

sites. Insufficient because no indication that night service would lessen risk. *Tuttle v Superior Court* (1981) 120 CA3d 320, 329, 174 CR 576.

☛ **Judicial Tips**: Routine requests for night service should be viewed skeptically. Residential searches in the middle of the night are especially intrusive (see §2.84). Night service should generally *not* be authorized when the court appoints a special master. See Pen C §1524.

#### d. [§2.88] Insertion of Direction for Night Service in Warrant

A magistrate who authorizes night service should "insert a direction in the search warrant that it may be served at any time of the day or night." Pen C §1533. Many current warrant forms contain a special night service authorization which the magistrate initials. See, *e.g., Nunes v Superior Court* (1980) 100 CA3d 915, 921, 161 CR 351. On other forms the magistrate puts an "X" in a box to indicate approval. See Chrystie & Schirn, p V-8.

☛ **Judicial Tip**: Particular care is needed when the police use the statutory form: "you are therefore commanded, in the daytime (or at any time of the day or night, as the case may be). . . ." Pen C §1529; see §2.56. This form sets out alternatives. Only daytime service is permitted unless the magistrate affirmatively and unmistakably approves the day or night alternative. See, *e.g., People v Mills* (1967) 251 CA2d 420, 422, 59 CR 589 (the court stressed that "[t]he householder is entitled to the assurance that the magistrate has considered and decided whether the facts justify a night search"). Underlining the words on the form that are in parentheses and initialing on the adjacent margin suffices. *People v Young* (1970) 12 CA3d 878, 881, 90 CR 924. When no householders are present at the time of the search, failure to affirmatively approve night service has been held not to be fatal because the reason for the rule has disappeared. *Tidwell v Superior Court* (1971) 17 CA3d 780, 786, 95 CR 213.

In *Nunes v Superior Court, supra*, the magistrate intended to initial the night service authorization but forgot to do so. The court upheld the search, noting that the defendant "was read the warrant (which contained the nighttime direction) and did not object to its service" and the officer did not realize that the magistrate had made a mistake. 100 CA3d at 926.

#### e. [§2.89] Effect of Violation of Pen C §1533

*Rodriguez v Superior Court* (1988) 199 CA3d 1453, 1467–1470, 245 CR 617, held that the Fourth Amendment does not mandate exclusion of evidence obtained in a nighttime search without good cause under Pen C §1533. See also *People v Swan* (1986) 187 CA3d 1010, 1017, 232 CR 288. Before Proposition 8, a search in violation of Pen C §1533 was invalid. See, *e.g., People v Cook* (1978) 22 C3d 67, 98, 148 CR 605, and cases there cited; *Tuttle v Superior Court* (1981) 120 CA3d 320, 174 CR 576.

Other courts apply the good-faith exception to save the search. *People v Swan, supra*; see *People v Lopez* (1985) 173 CA3d 125, 138, 218 CR 799. But see *Rodriguez v Superior Court, supra*, 199 CA3d at 1467 (reliance on nighttime endorsement unreasonable when affidavit includes no facts to show need for it).

The California Supreme Court has not ruled on either of these approaches, nor has the U.S. Supreme Court decided what limitations, if any, the Fourth Amendment imposes on nighttime searches. See 2 LaFave, pp 590–592.

## B. Knock-Notice

### 1. [§2.90] Statutory and Constitutional Bases

*Statutes.* The term "knock-notice" refers to the requirements of Pen C §1531 and its federal counterpart (18 USC §3109) that before entering a house to serve a search warrant, police officers give notice of their authority and purpose and be refused admission. *People v Mays* (1998) 67 CA4th 969, 971, 79 CR2d 519. Penal Code §1531 states:

> The officer may break open any outer or inner door or window of a house, or any part of a house, or anything therein, to execute the warrant, if, after notice of his authority and purpose, he is refused admittance.

The knock-notice rules of Pen C §844 (*arrest* warrants) are "substantially identical." *People v Gastelo* (1967) 67 C2d 586, 587, 63 CR 10. Decisions that interpret Pen C §1531 often cite cases arising under §844. See, *e.g.*, *People v Bencomo* (1985) 171 CA3d 1005, 1016, 217 CR 826; *Jeter v Superior Court* (1983) 138 CA3d 934, 938, 188 CR 351; *People v Gastelo, supra.* For many purposes, decisions applying the two sections "may be interchangeably cited." *People v Peterson* (1973) 9 C3d 717, 722 n7, 108 CR 835. But there are differences between the two sections; see §§4.80–4.81.

The statutes are codifications of common law. *People v Miller* (1999) 69 CA4th 190, 200, 81 CR2d 410.

*Fourth Amendment.* The common law principle that police officers should announce their presence and authority before entering a dwelling is also a requirement under the Fourth Amendment. *Wilson v Arkansas* (1995) 514 US 927, 934, 115 S Ct 1914, 131 L Ed 2d 976; *People v Mays, supra*. The U.S. Supreme Court has not yet developed an extensive body of case law in this area. See *Wilson v Arkansas, supra*, 514 US at 934–936 (dicta that pre-entry announcement not always necessary; Court leaves it to lower courts to develop exceptions); *U.S. v Ramirez* (1998) 523 US 65, 69, 118 S Ct 992, 140 L Ed 2d 191 (entry involving damage to property does not require higher standard of exigency); *Richards v Wisconsin* (1997) 520 US 385, 388, 117 S Ct 1416, 137 L Ed 2d 615 (exigent circumstances exception).

California courts treat unexcused violations of Pen C §844 or §1531 as Fourth Amendment violations. See §2.109.

### 2. [§2.91] Requirements Not Limited to Searches and Arrests

Penal Code §§844 and 1531 apply to entries for purposes other than serving search and arrest warrants. For example, knock-notice rules apply to entries for investigative purposes (*People v Miller* (1999) 69 CA4th 190, 200, 81 CR2d 410), to the securing of premises pending the issuance of a search warrant (*Machado v Superior Court* (1975) 45 CA3d 316, 320, 119 CR 344), and to warrantless searches conducted pursuant to parole and probation conditions (*People v Mays* (1998) 67 CA4th 969, 973, 79 CR2d 519; *People v Montenegro* (1985) 173 CA3d 983, 989, 219 CR 331).

### 3. [§2.92] Purposes of Knock-Notice

The basic purposes of knock-notice are the following:

(1) Protecting occupants and officers from violence;

(2) Protecting the privacy of occupants; and

(3) Avoiding needless destruction of property. *People v Hoag* (2000) 83 CA4th 1198, 1203, 100 CR2d 556; *People v MacAvoy* (1984) 162 CA3d 746, 768, 209 CR 34. See also *People v Gallo* (1981) 127 CA3d 828, 838, 179 CR 662 ("the statutory purpose is not that the officer must obtain a consensual entrance, but rather that the police not act so precipitously that the entrance violates privacy, endangers innocent persons who may be present . . . or . . . the police who may be injured by a frightened householder").

In interpreting Pen C §§844 and 1531, courts often refer to these purposes. See, *e.g., People v Hoag, supra*; *People v Miller* (1999) 69 CA4th 190, 200, 81 CR2d 410; *People v Howard* (1993) 18 CA4th 1544, 1551, 23 CR2d 212; see also §2.108.

## 4. "Breaking" and Consent

### a. [§2.93] Meaning of "Break" in Pen C §§844 and 1531

The word "break" used in Pen C §§844 and 1531 is a term of art that includes more than the physical breaking of a door or window. *People v Jacobs* (1987) 43 C3d 472, 480, 233 CR 323. Courts differentiate between outer and inner doors.

*Outer doors.* An entrance effected by opening a closed door is a "breaking." *People v Peterson* (1973) 9 C3d 717, 723, 108 CR 835 (unlatched screen door); *People v Castaneda* (1976) 58 CA3d 165, 170, 129 CR 755. Generally, a nonconsensual entry through an open door is also a breaking. *People v Bradley* (1969) 1 C3d 80, 87–88, 81 CR 457; *People v Miller* (1999) 69 CA4th 190, 201, 81 CR2d 410; *People v Zabelle* (1996) 50 CA4th 1282, 1286, 58 CR2d 105.

*Inner doors.* Entry through an open inner door is not a breaking. *People v Castaneda, supra*; *People v Livermore* (1973) 30 CA3d 1073, 1077, 106 CR 822. The more recent decisions reach the same conclusion about entry through a closed inner door. *People v Mays* (1998) 67 CA4th 969, 974, 79 CR2d 519; *People v Aguilar* (1996) 48 CA4th 632, 637–638, 55 CR2d 716; *People v Howard* (1993) 18 CA4th 1544, 1546, 23 CR2d 212. Earlier decisions were divided. See cases discussed in *People v Howard, supra.*

Repeated knock-notice may be required when the residence is unusually large, when the outer door does not provide access to the place to be searched, or when the warrant extends only to a single room. 18 CA4th at 1555.

Entrance into the room of a hotel guest is a breaking; a hotel room is considered a dwelling for purposes of the Fourth Amendment. *People v Zabelle, supra.*

### b. Consent

#### (1) [§2.94] Effect of Consent; Test

A consensual entry "is not considered a 'breaking.' " *People v Jacobs* (1987) 43 C3d 472, 480, 233 CR 323. However, the police can rely on consent only if the person granting it "had the authority to permit the entry or the police reasonably and in good faith believed she had such authority." 43 C3d at 481 and cases cited.

In *Jacobs,* the court held that the 11-year-old daughter of the occupants lacked authority to consent and that the officers could not reasonably believe that she had authority. Reliance on the consent of an occupant's daughter who appeared to be between 14 and 16, and who was in fact 16, is reasonable. *People v Hoxter* (1999) 75 CA4th 406, 413–414, 89

CR2d 259. In the leading case of *Duke v Superior Court* (1969) 1 C3d 314, 321, 82 CR 348, the court held that a cotenant who is outside the premises at the time cannot validly consent to police entry, and the officers cannot rely on such permission. The court emphasized that a contrary rule would frustrate the purposes of the statute. *People v De La Plane* (1979) 88 CA3d 223, 234, 151 CR 843, is in accord.

As to consent by a joint occupant given *inside* the premises, compare *People v Gomez* (1976) 63 CA3d 328, 334, 133 CR 731 (consent valid when defendant was sleeping in open bedroom), with *Young v Superior Court* (1976) 57 CA3d 883, 887, 129 CR 422 (joint occupant cannot validly consent to entry of closed bathrooms because occupants of closed bedrooms and bathrooms have high expectation of privacy).

Consent negates breaking; hence, officers making a consensual entry do not need to comply with Pen C §1531. When they do comply, however, and are refused admittance (or when compliance is excused), they have the right to "break" into the house; their right to enter does not depend on the occupants' permission. *People v Valdivia* (1980) 114 CA3d 24, 28, 170 CR 431.

Consent within the context of Pen C §1531 should not be confused with problems related to consent searches. See §§5.102–5.140. See also *People v Baker* (1986) 187 CA3d 562, 565, 231 CR 877 (officers obtained consent to search by stating they had a search warrant; court held consent is valid only if the warrant is valid).

#### (2) [§2.95] Nonverbal Consent

Consent may be nonverbal. "[A]ctions which clearly and unequivocally indicate" that "entry is invited" suffice. *People v Gomez* (1976) 63 CA3d 328, 334, 133 CR 731; *People v Harrington* (1970) 2 C3d 991, 995, 88 CR 161 (inviting gesture sufficient).

#### (3) [§2.96] Consent Obtained by Ruse

Since police with a valid search warrant have "the right to enter and search without permission it becomes immaterial that permission was obtained by a ruse." *People v Ramirez* (1970) 4 CA3d 154, 157, 84 CR 104 (officer in civilian clothes invited into residence after claiming he was looking for fictitious person).

Other examples:

- Invitation to enter after officers falsely told resident that "Pete" said they could pick something up at the house. *People v Evans* (1980) 108 CA3d 193, 195–196, 166 CR 315.

- Officer disguised as mail carrier with special delivery letter. *People v Rudin* (1978) 77 CA3d 139, 143, 143 CR 360.

- False name used to gain entry. *People v Kasinger* (1976) 57 CA3d 975, 978, 129 CR 483.

- Invitation to enter extended to narcotics agents who pretended to be cocaine buyers. *Toubus v Superior Court* (1981) 114 CA3d 378, 383, 170 CR 697.

Ruses to gain entry under Pen C §§1531 and 844 should not be confused with the use of similar ruses to effect an arrest in violation of the requirements of *People v Ramey* (1976) 16 C3d 263, 275–276, 127 CR 629. As to the latter, see, *e.g., In re Danny E.* (1981) 121 CA3d 44, 51, 174 CR 123, and cases cited. For discussion of *Ramey,* see §§4.61–4.79.

### 5. [§2.97] Meaning of "House" in Pen C §1531

Not every structure is a "house" within the meaning of Pen C §1531. The section does not apply to theaters and stores open to the public; such application would not accomplish the purposes of the statute. *People v Maita* (1984) 157 CA3d 309, 323, 203 CR 685 (theater); *People v Lovett* (1978) 82 CA3d 527, 532, 147 CR 136 (store).

On the other hand, garages, whether attached (*People v Gallo* (1981) 127 CA3d 828, 839, 179 CR 662) or detached (*People v Bruce* (1975) 49 CA3d 580, 587, 122 CR 648), are given the same protection as residences, unless they have "no private character" and are not "used for the comfort and convenience of those of the household." *People v Franco* (1986) 183 CA3d 1089, 1093, 228 CR 527; see *People v Murray* (1969) 270 CA2d 201, 203, 75 CR 625.

*People v Franco, supra,* treated a small inhabited hut on residential property as a house, noting that the test is the exhibition of a reasonable expectation of privacy.

*People v Bencomo* (1985) 171 CA3d 1005, 1015, 217 CR 826, dealt with a related problem. A five-foot concrete wall with a gate surrounded the residence to be searched. The gate was 20 or 30 feet from the front door and had no buzzer or bell. The court held that under the circumstances, Pen C §1531 did not apply to the gate in the wall. *Bencomo* stressed the particular facts; a different result may be in order if a gate includes a communication device or is located closer to the house. See also *People v Mayer* (1987) 188 CA3d 1101, 1109, 233 CR 832 (Pen C §1531 does not apply to fences).

### 6. Compliance With Pen C §1531

#### a. [§2.98] Summary of Requirements

Full compliance with Pen C §1531 requires officers to do the following before "breaking" into a house:

- Give notice of their presence to the occupants. See §2.99.
- Give notice of their authority. See §2.100.
- Give notice of their purpose. See §2.101. These announcements need not be made by uniformed officers. See *People v Schad* (1971) 21 CA3d 201, 206, 98 CR 439; *People v Negrete* (1978) 82 CA3d 328, 337–339, 147 CR 101.
- Give the occupants an opportunity to surrender the premises voluntarily. See §2.102.

For discussion of circumstances excusing compliance in whole or in part, see §§2.103–2.108. For discussion of consequences of an unexcused failure to comply, see §2.109.

#### b. [§2.99] Notice of Presence

Under Pen C §1531, officers must "knock or utilize other means reasonably calculated to give adequate notice of their presence to the occupants." *People v Ramsey* (1988) 203 CA3d 671, 680, 250 CR 309, quoting *Duke v Superior Court* (1969) 1 C3d 314, 319, 82 CR 348. Officers often knock, but this is not essential as long as their announcement is heard or likely to be heard by the persons in the house. See *People v Franco* (1986) 183 CA3d 1089, 1094, 228 CR 527; *People v Maita* (1984) 157 CA3d 309, 321, 203 CR 685.

As a practical matter, this requirement is not distinct from the announcement of authority. What matters is that the latter is loud enough so that it will probably be heard.

#### c. [§2.100] Announcement of Authority

Penal Code §1531 requires the officers executing the warrant to identify themselves as police officers. *Duke v Superior Court* (1969) 1 C3d 314, 319, 82 CR 348; *People v Ramsey* (1988) 203 CA3d 671, 680, 250 CR 309. Terse announcements are common: "Sheriff's Department" (*People v Alaniz* (1986) 182 CA3d 903, 906, 227 CR 575; "Police" (*Jeter v Superior Court* (1983) 138 CA3d 934, 936, 188 CR 351). For discussion on knocking, see §2.99.

### d. [§2.101] Announcement of Purpose

The officer must give "notice of his . . . purpose." Pen C §1531; *People v Alaniz* (1986) 182 CA3d 903, 906, 227 CR 575; *People v Neer* (1986) 177 CA3d 991, 994, 223 CR 555 ("we have a search warrant"). Knocking and waiting, without announcing presence and purpose, are not enough. *People v Pipitone* (1984) 152 CA3d 1112, 1119, 201 CR 18.

The announcement needs only to be made before the officer enters, not before the door is opened by an occupant. *People v Mays* (1998) 67 CA4th 969, 973, 79 CR2d 519. An announcement made during instead of before entry is not enough. *People v Keogh* (1975) 46 CA3d 919, 927, 120 CR 817 ("acceptance of such conduct would vitiate the underlying policy of the entry statutes"). But see §§2.103–2.104. A violation of Pen C §1531 is not cured by making the announcement after entry. *People v Franco* (1986) 183 CA3d 1089, 1094, 228 CR 527.

Unlike Pen C §844, Pen C §1531 does not require a demand for admittance. *People v Gallo* (1981) 127 CA3d 828, 838, 179 CR 662. In search warrant situations officers often do not make such a demand. See, *e.g., People v Alaniz, supra*; *People v Neer, supra*; *Jeter v Superior Court* (1983) 138 CA3d 934, 936, 188 CR 351. Occasionally a court states the Pen C §1531 requirements by quoting from a case that arose under §844. See, *e.g., People v Bencomo* (1985) 171 CA3d 1005, 1016, 217 CR 826 (officers to state "the purpose of their demand for admittance," quoting *Duke v Superior Court* (1969) 1 C3d 314, 319, 82 CR 348).

### e. [§2.102] Opportunity To Surrender Premises

Penal Code §1531 provides that officers may enter the premises if they are "refused admittance" after making the requisite announcements. This means the police must give the occupants "an opportunity to surrender the premises voluntarily." *Jeter v Superior Court* (1983) 138 CA3d 934, 936, 188 CR 351; *People v Neer* (1986) 177 CA3d 991, 996, 223 CR 555; *People v Montenegro* (1985) 173 CA3d 983, 989, 219 CR 331. An announcement followed by an immediate or nearly simultaneous entry does not comply with Pen C §1531. *People v Neer, supra*; see *U.S. v Moore* (10th Cir 1996) 91 F3d 96, 98.

☛ **Judicial Tip**: When dealing with this aspect of Pen C §1531, judges should differentiate cases decided under Pen C §844, which does not include a refusal-of-admittance requirement. See *People v Neer, supra*, 177 CA3d at 996 n3; *People v Schmel* (1975) 54 CA3d 46, 50, 126 CR 317.

*Reasonable opportunity.* Penal Code §1531 requires only that the occupants be afforded a reasonable opportunity to admit the officers; the statute does not require the occupants' permission or consent to the entry of the police. *People v Valdivia* (1980) 114 CA3d 24, 28, 170 CR 431; *People v Gallo* (1981) 127 CA3d 828, 838, 179 CR 662.

*Length of wait.* How long the officers must wait after making their announcement of authority and purpose before they can conclude that they have been refused admittance largely depends on the particular circumstances. Twenty to thirty seconds suffice when the officers see people just on the other side of the door. *People v Gallo, supra* (30 seconds); *People v McCarter* (1981) 117 CA3d 894, 906, 173 CR 188 (30 seconds); *People v Elder* (1976) 63 CA3d 731, 739, 134 CR 212 (about 20 seconds). See also *People v Nealy* (1991) 228 CA3d 447, 450, 279 CR 36 (20–30 seconds sufficient when officer sees car named in search warrant in front of building).

An occupant who verbally acknowledges the officer's presence is entitled to even less time. *People v Hobbs* (1987) 192 CA3d 959, 964, 237 CR 742 (five seconds); *People v Montenegro* (1985) 173 CA3d 983, 989, 219 CR 331. But see *People v Gonzalez* (1989) 211 CA3d 1043, 1051, 259 CR 846 (sole woman occupant's five-second hesitation natural under the particular circumstances).

On the other hand, a wait approximately as long as in *Elder* or *Gallo* is inadequate when the officers do not know whether someone is in the house. Under these circumstances the officers lack information to conclude that they are being denied entry. *Jeter v Superior Court* (1983) 138 CA3d 934, 937, 188 CR 351. An 18-second delay is probably insufficient to allow occupants of an average-sized apartment to answer a knock. *People v Trujillo* (1990) 217 CA3d 1219, 1226, 266 CR 473 (but entry upheld on theory of compliance with objective of statute). A 10-second wait rarely gives occupants time to reach the door before the officers break it open. See *U.S. v Jenkins* (10th Cir 1999) 175 F3d 1208, 1214–1215. The amount of time officers need to wait before entering is generally reduced during midday. *U. S. v Jenkins, supra* (upholding delay of 14–20 seconds).

Police department policies that purport to fix the length of the officers' wait are probably invalid. See *U.S. v Jenkins, supra*; *U.S. v Ward* (4th Cir 1999) 171 F3d 188, 193–194. Particular circumstances may nevertheless make the officers' conduct proper. *U. S. v Jenkins, supra.*

*Conduct showing refusal to admit.* Refusal to admit can be shown by the resident's conduct as well as by inaction, such as struggling with the officer (*People v Bencomo* (1985) 171 CA3d 1005, 1018, 217 CR

826), closing the door (*People v Thompson* (1979) 89 CA3d 425, 432, 152 CR 495), and noises such as shouting or running that "support an objectively reasonable belief the occupants had refused entry" (see *People v Neer* (1986) 177 CA3d 991, 996, 223 CR 555). Hearing movement inside an apartment is not, without more, a manifestation of a refusal of entry. *People v Trujillo, supra*, 217 CA3d at 1226.

### 7. Substantial Compliance

#### a. [§2.103] Meanings of "Substantial Compliance"

Substantial compliance with Pen C §§844 and 1531 is sufficient to satisfy the statutory mandates. See, *e.g., People v Peterson* (1973) 9 C3d 717, 724, 108 CR 835; *Duke v Superior Court* (1969) 1 C3d 314, 320, 82 CR 348; *People v Miller* (1999) 69 CA4th 190, 201, 81 CR2d 410. Courts use the term "substantial compliance" in at least three senses:

(1) They occasionally use it to lend meaning to an officer's announcement. *People v Miller, supra* (asking if anyone was home sufficient statement of purpose when officer was looking for resident whose small child was wandering on street).

(2) A specific substantial compliance doctrine affects solely the announcement-of-purpose requirement. For discussion, see §2.104.

(3) Some courts use the term to refer to a broader exception discussed in §2.105 for conduct that complies with the objectives of the statutes.

#### b. [§2.104] Announcement of Purpose

Compliance with the announcement-of-purpose requirement is excused when circumstances make the officer's purpose clear to the occupants or further announcement would be futile. *People v Rosales* (1968) 68 C2d 299, 302, 66 CR 1; *Duke v Superior Court* (1969) 1 C3d 314, 320, 82 CR 348; *People v Keogh* (1975) 46 CA3d 919, 927, 120 CR 817.

For example, *People v Hall* (1971) 3 C3d 992, 998, 92 CR 304, held that the announcement "police officers," followed by immediate screaming, makes further efforts futile. In *People v Cockrell* (1965) 63 C2d 659, 666, 47 CR 788, the officers knew that a marijuana sale had been made on the premises only minutes before they requested admittance. The court said that the purpose of the officers "was reasonably apparent." In *People v Sotelo* (1971) 18 CA3d 9, 18, 95 CR 486, the circumstances showed that a man "had just made a purchase of heroin and had a 'fix' on the premises"; the court concluded "it was highly improbable that the occupant did not understand the purpose for which the police sought to enter." *Sotelo* and *Cockrell* arose under Pen C §844; it is not clear whether it would be apparent to the occupants that the officers were serving a search warrant.

In *People v Montenegro* (1985) 173 CA3d 983, 986–989, 219 CR 331 (parole search), the parole agent knocked on the defendant's door and the defendant answered, "Okay, okay." A police officer then shouted, "Police, open the door," and the defendant did not respond. The court held that this showed that "defendant was aware of their presence and purpose" and that, therefore, "substantial compliance existed here."

The substantial compliance exception that excuses the announcement of purpose developed largely in the context of Pen C §844. Under appropriate circumstances, however, it also applies to Pen C §1531. *People v Montenegro, supra*; see *People v Webb* (1973) 36 CA3d 460, 465, 111 CR 524.

### c. [§2.105] Compliance With Objectives of Statute: The *Peterson* Principle

In addition to the narrow substantial compliance exception discussed in §2.104, courts have fashioned a broader one for conduct that falls short of the statutory requirements but does not violate the purpose of knock-notice requirements. Some decisions also refer to such conduct as substantial compliance. See, *e.g., People v Peterson* (1973) 9 C3d 717, 724, 108 CR 835; *People v La Jocies* (1981) 119 CA3d 947, 953, 174 CR 100. See also *People v Jacobs* (1987) 43 C3d 472, 485, 233 CR 323 (dissenting opinion).

Thus, in *People v Peterson, supra*, the officer knocked several times and saw through a closed screen door that two people were seated in the living area. After a minute "he opened the screen door, stood at the threshold, identified himself and, after stating he had a warrant for a search of the premises, entered." 9 C3d at 721. The court upheld the search on the following grounds:

- "No right of privacy was infringed" because the interior was visible to any member of the public and because the officers "did not physically intrude into the home until after the announcement." 9 C3d at 723.
- The procedure did not increase the risk of violence: The officers could clearly observe the occupants and, conversely, "the officers were immediately visible and announced their purpose to the occupants who were thus made aware of the situation and its demands." 9 C3d at 724.

Factually similar to *Peterson* and reaching the same result is *People v Uhler* (1989) 208 CA3d 766, 769, 256 CR 336.

Other examples:

- In *People v La Jocies* (1981) 119 CA3d 947, 953, 174 CR 100, the officers made a proper announcement; a woman answered the door; and the officers asked her to put the dogs in the backyard, opened the screen door, and entered. The court noted that "[t]he record does not reflect that the officers were either refused admittance or allowed [the occupant] a reasonable time in which to admit them." The court nevertheless upheld the search, saying that "[h]ere, neither appellant's privacy nor a violent confrontation was threatened by the officers' failure to delay their entry into the residence." For a similar case, see *People v Maita* (1984) 157 CA3d 309, 321, 203 CR 685 (officer made announcement to occupant in yard and entered house while occupant put dogs into garage). See also *People v Tacy* (1987) 195 CA3d 1402, 1421, 241 CR 400 (open door; closed screen door; eye contact with occupant prior to announcement; court held that entry immediately after announcement was in compliance with "[t]he spirit of Penal Code section 1531 . . .").

- In *People v Thompson* (1979) 89 CA3d 425, 152 CR 495, the uniformed officers who had a search warrant "were confronted with the problem of access to a veritable 'fortress.' " 89 CA3d at 432. They persuaded the defendant to open his locked iron front gate by staging a mock chase in front of his house and asking him to look at his parked car for possible damage. Only then did the officers announce their real purpose. The court upheld the search, concluding that the ruse "successfully avoided the various consequences that [the knock-notice] rule is designed to prevent." *In re William C.* (1977) 70 CA3d 570, 580, 138 CR 843, held that a "formal recitation of his [the officer's] identity" is unnecessary when the officer is in uniform and the occupant could see him clearly immediately after the knock. Such visibility, however, does not excuse the announcement of purpose. *People v Hayko* (1970) 7 CA3d 604, 608, 86 CR 726. See also *Greven v Superior Court* (1969) 71 C2d 287, 292, 78 CR 504, in which "the Supreme Court . . . made it clear that 'substantial compliance' cannot be achieved 'in the absence of an announcement by the officers identifying themselves as such.' " *People v Negrete* (1978) 82 CA3d 328, 339 n7, 147 CR 101.

- In *People v Constancio* (1974) 42 CA3d 533, 116 CR 910 (search pursuant to probation condition), the officers were apparently in civilian clothes. 42 CA3d at 537 n1. One officer knocked on the door and said he wanted to talk to Gail. The occupant opened the front door, leaving the screen door closed, and the officer said "It's Jim, and I want to talk to Gail." Then the officer opened the screen door and "standing on the threshold without entering," announced his identity and purpose. "The officers then entered." 42 CA3d at 537. The court upheld the search, saying that the case was identical to *People v Peterson, supra.* 42 CA3d at 546.

- In *People v Cohen* (1976) 59 CA3d 241, 246, 130 CR 656, the police went to the door of an apartment with the manager, who knocked, identified herself, and opened the door. The police officers then made the required announcement before entering. The court said the purpose of the statute had been "fully satisfied." 59 CA3d at 247 n4. *Cohen* distinguished *People v Keogh* (1975) 46 CA3d 919, 120 CR 817, on the basis that in *Cohen* "the officer asked the manager not to open the door." 59 CA3d at 246. The court did not explain how this difference bears on whether the procedure frustrates the purposes of the statute.

- In *People v Trujillo* (1990) 217 CA3d 1219, 1225, 266 CR 473, the officers knocked, properly announced themselves and their purpose, and waited 18 seconds before kicking in the door. The court held that under the circumstances, an 18-second delay probably did not constitute a refusal of admittance but that the case was close and the entry valid because of compliance with the purposes of the statute. In accord is *People v Hoag* (2000) 83 CA4th 1198, 1211, 100 CR2d 556 (15 seconds insufficient but under circumstances served policies underlying knock-notice).

### 8. Excused Noncompliance: Unoccupied Premises and Exigent Circumstances

#### a. [§2.106] Basic Principles

The "excused noncompliance" exception (the phrase is from *People v Webb* (1973) 36 CA3d 460, 465, 111 CR 524) delineates the conditions under which officers may make unannounced entries. They may do so under two very different sets of circumstances. The first is simple: Officers need not make the announcement of identity and purpose to enter unoccupied premises. *Hart v Superior Court* (1971) 21 CA3d 496, 499, 98 CR 565; *People v Ford* (1975) 54 CA3d 149, 154, 126 CR 396. An announcement would not serve any useful purpose. *Hart v Superior Court, supra.* The exception is more limited for entries under Pen C §844, requiring clear evidence of abandonment. *People v Bruce* (1975) 49 CA3d 580, 587, 122 CR 648. For a discussion of the differences between Pen C §§844 and 1531 in this respect, see *Hart v Superior Court, supra.*

The second situation of excused noncompliance is considerably more important as well as more complex. It gave rise to its own good faith rule long before the broader good-faith exception of *Leon.* As stated in *People v Dumas* (1973) 9 C3d 871, 877, 109 CR 304:

> strict compliance with . . . notice requirement may be excused "if the specific facts known to the officer before his entry are sufficient to support his good faith belief that compliance will increase his peril, frustrate the arrest, or permit destruction of evidence." [Citations.]

This exception, often called the exigent circumstances or emergency exception, was adopted by the U.S. Supreme Court in *Richards v Wisconsin* (1997) 520 US 385, 394, 117 S Ct 1416, 137 L Ed 2d 615 (police must have reasonable suspicion that knocking and announcing presence, under the particular circumstances, would be dangerous or futile or would inhibit effective investigation by, for example, allowing destruction of evidence).

#### b. [§2.107] Insufficient Exigent Circumstances; "No-Knock" Warrants

The crucial aspect of the exigent circumstances exception is the specificity of the facts known to the officers. Propensities, generalized beliefs, and even information that the occupant possesses firearms are not enough. *Richards v Wisconsin* (1997) 520 US 385, 394, 117 S Ct 1416, 137 L Ed 2d 615 (rule that exigent circumstances are always present in felony drug cases contravenes Fourth Amendment); *People v Gastelo* (1967) 67 C2d 586, 588, 63 CR 10 (propensity of narcotics violators to destroy the easily disposable evidence not sufficient); *People v Neer* (1986) 177 CA3d 991, 995, 223 CR 555 (officer's fear, not based on specific facts, that subjects of narcotics search warrant "would flee, destroy evidence or arm themselves" is generalized belief and not "objectively reasonable"); *People v Dumas* (1973) 9 C3d 871, 878, 109 CR 304 (information that defendant had rifle insufficient).

The absence of noise or other signs of activity, after a woman occupant had inquired who was there, is not an exigent circumstance when only five seconds elapsed since the officer's announcement. *People v Gonzalez* (1989) 211 CA3d 1043, 1050, 259 CR 846.

The facts giving rise to the emergency must exist "*at the time of entry*"; hence a magistrate cannot excuse compliance with Pen C §1531 in advance. *Parsley v Superior Court* (1973) 9 C3d 934, 939, 109 CR 563 (emphasis in original). *Parsley* rests on the construction of California's knock-notice statutes. The Fourth Amendment probably permits magistrates to issue so-called "no-knock" warrants when sufficient cause to do so is demonstrated beforehand. See *U.S. v Ramirez* (1998) 523 US 65, 68, 118 S Ct 992, 140 L Ed 2d 191; *Richards v Wisconsin, supra,* 520 US at 396 n7.

The requirement that the exigency exist at the time of entry does not mean that the officers must receive their first inkling of the emergency only shortly before entering; they can rely on advance information when it is reasonable to do so. *People v Dumas, supra*; see §2.108.

An exigency that permits a warrantless entry does not necessarily excuse knock-notice. In *People v Miller* (1999) 69 CA4th 190, 199, 81 CR2d 410, an officer entered a residence to look for the mother of a small child who had been wandering on the street. The court held that under these circumstances the entry was proper, but compliance with knock-notice was not excused.

### c. [§2.108] Illustrations of Sufficient Exigent Circumstances

In *U.S. v Ramirez* (1998) 523 US 65, 70–72, 118 S Ct 992, 140 L Ed 2d 191, the officers were looking for a prison escapee with a violent past, who had vowed that he would not do time and reportedly had access to a large supply of weapons. The court held that knocking and announcing was excused because the police had a reasonable suspicion that doing so might be dangerous to themselves or others. The court also held that it made no difference that the escapee was not found in the place the police entered and that an entry involving destruction of property does not require a higher standard of exigency.

In *Richards v Wisconsin* (1997) 520 US 385, 395–396, 117 S Ct 1416, 137 L Ed 2d 615, officers had a warrant to search defendant's hotel room for drugs. They knocked, defendant cracked the door open, saw the officers in uniform and quickly slammed the door shut. The court held that defendant's apparent recognition of the officers, combined with the easily disposable nature of the drugs, justified the officers' decision to enter without first announcing their presence and authority.

In *People v Dumas* (1973) 9 C3d 871, 877, 109 CR 304, the officers had information that the defendant possessed firearms and habitually answered the door with one. The court held that while the first fact alone was insufficient (see §2.107), the two pieces of information together justified an unannounced entry.

In *People v Zabelle* (1996) 50 CA4th 1282, 1286–1287, 58 CR2d 105, officers saw a man apparently asleep near heroin, but could not see his hands nor whether he might have anything in them. The court held compliance with knock-notice would have increased the potential for violence and was therefore excused.

In *People v Alaniz* (1986) 182 CA3d 903, 227 CR 575, the defendant had attempted to destroy evidence on three prior occasions when he was served with search warrants for narcotics. The court held that this, combined with the officer's knowledge that the defendant possessed an automatic pistol, justified forced entry immediately after the announcement. The court said: "A man's home may be his castle, but it is not a sanctuary for the destruction of evidence." 182 CA3d at 907.

In *People v De La Plane* (1979) 88 CA3d 223, 235, 151 CR 843, the court held sufficient the reasonable suspicion that defendant had recently committed an armed robbery. In *People v Henderson* (1976) 58 CA3d 349, 355, 129 CR 844, the court found exigent circumstances from the defendant's record of arrests for assaultive behavior and from his carrying a firearm during a recent altercation with a police officer.

A knock or announcement followed by immediate running by the occupant in a narcotics case has also been held to warrant immediate entry. *People v Mayer* (1987) 188 CA3d 1101, 1112, 233 CR 832; *People v Pipitone* (1984) 152 CA3d 1112, 1118, 201 CR 18; *People v Negrete* (1978) 82 CA3d 328, 336, 147 CR 101. In *Negrete,* the observations were detailed. The officer saw the defendant cut heroin and knocked; the defendant ran toward him in apparent recognition and then ran "back toward the easily flushable heroin." In *Pipitone,* which relied on *Negrete,* the officer "heard someone running, and . . . heard something—falling or rattling and saw a male through the doorway of the kitchen moving quickly." *People v Pipitone, supra,* 152 CA3d at 1116.

### 9. [§2.109] Effect of Unexcused Knock-Notice Violations

"An entry effected in violation of the knock-notice requirements of sections 844 and 1531 renders any subsequent search and seizure unreasonable within the meaning of the Fourth Amendment and thus requires exclusion of the evidence. . . ." *People v Franco* (1986) 183 CA3d 1089, 1095, 228 CR 527. See *People v Jacobs* (1987) 43 C3d 472, 484, 233 CR 323; *People v Neer* (1986) 177 CA3d 991, 997, 223 CR 555. For discussion of the Fourth Amendment basis of knock-notice rules, see §2.90. Whether Fourth Amendment and statutory requirements completely coincide awaits future decisions. Statutory and Fourth Amendment law probably differ with respect to "no-knock" warrants. See §2.107.

☛ **Judicial Tip**: Judges should continue to exclude evidence obtained after an unexcused entry in violation of Pen C §844 or §1531 until there is some final disposition with respect to the overlap of Fourth Amendment and statutory requirements. *Auto Equity Sales, Inc. v Superior Court* (1962) 57 C2d 450, 455, 20 CR 321; *People v Tacy* (1987) 195 CA3d 1402, 1413–1414, 241 CR 400.

## C. Conduct of Search

### 1. Detention and Search of Occupants During Execution of Warrant

#### a. [§2.110] Detention

The police have a limited right to detain persons on or near the premises being searched. The scope of the right depends on the nature of the premises and on the particular circumstances.

*Residential premises.* When the police search a residence, the right to detain is usually limited to occupants, as distinguished from visitors. *Michigan v Summers* (1981) 452 US 692, 703–705, 101 S Ct 2587, 69 L Ed 2d 340; see *People v Glaser* (1995) 11 C4th 354, 365–367, 370, 45 CR2d 425. For example, a person who knocked on the door of a residence being searched may not be detained merely because he or she did so; the fact that drugs had been sold from the place is not sufficient to justify detention. *People v Gallant* (1990) 225 CA3d 200, 207–210, 275 CR 50. In contrast, a person who enters without knocking acts like an occupant and may be detained. *People v Huerta* (1990) 218 CA3d 744, 749–750, 267 CR 243.

The limitation to occupants is relaxed when particular circumstances create a danger of harm to officers or to the person being detained. *People v Glaser, supra* (upholding brief detention of person who approaches residence in the dark by a backyard gate, is unresponsive to officers and cannot quickly be identified as nonresident); *People v Samples* (1996) 48 CA4th 1197, 1206, 56 CR2d 245 (upholding detention of driver of vehicle who parks near residence being searched; officers recognized passengers as persons for whom police also had search warrants and told all persons in car to exit it).

☛ **Judicial Tip**: Persons on premises may also be detained on reasonable suspicion of criminal activity. See *People v Glaser, supra,* 11 C4th at 370. The rule of *Michigan v Summers, supra,* merely provides a basis for detention in the absence of such suspicion.

*Business premises.* In a search of business premises open to the public, the right to detain hinges on whether "the circumstances create a reasonable suspicion of a relationship between the person and the place sufficient to connect the individual to the illegal activities giving rise to the warrant." *People v Ingram* (1993) 16 CA4th 1745, 1753, 21 CR2d 33 (wife's detention in driveway of husband's business proper during search of premises).

Detentions during the execution of an arrest warrant are governed by the same principles. *People v Hannah* (1996) 51 CA4th 1335, 1340–1347, 59 CR2d 806.

#### b. [§2.111] Search

*Pat search.* The right to pat search persons detained during the execution of a search warrant depends on whether there are reasons to believe they are armed and dangerous. See §§3.96–3.99. When a home is being searched for drugs, such danger exists, but the customers of a business being searched for narcotics may not be frisked without more. *Ybarra v Illinois* (1979) 444 US 85, 91–93, 100 S Ct 338, 62 L Ed 2d 238.

*Full search.* A search beyond a weapons pat-down of a person not named in the search warrant requires probable cause to believe that the person has evidence described in the warrant. *Ybarra v Illinois, supra*; *People v Reyes* (1990) 223 CA3d 1218, 1224, 273 CR 61. Residence in searched premises without more is not sufficient. *People v Reyes, supra.* These limitations on the search of persons present at the scene extend to the pants of a man lying within his reach as he steps out of the shower (*People v Reyes, supra*), but not to a resident's purse. *People v Berry* (1990) 224 CA3d 162, 167, 273 CR 509 (scope of warrant normally extends to personal effects likely to contain the contraband described in search warrant).

When occupants are arrested on probable cause developed during the course of the search, they may properly be searched. *Michigan v Summers* (1981) 452 US 692, 695, 101 S Ct 2587, 69 L Ed 2d 340.

### 2. Seizure of Property Not Described in Search Warrant

#### a. [§2.112] In General

Normally the police "may seize only the property described in the warrant." *People v Superior Court* (Meyers) (1979) 25 C3d 67, 72, 157 CR 716. Exceptions include:

- Property in plain view. See §§2.113–2.115.
- Property seized pursuant to a search conducted as incident to a valid arrest. *Skelton v Superior Court* (1969) 1 C3d 144, 155, 81 CR 613. See §§4.103–4.136.
- Property identified in the affidavit but inadvertently omitted from

the search warrant. *People v Russell* (1987) 195 CA3d 186, 188, 240 CR 456. For discussion of good faith, see §§1.28–1.40.

The related problem of police interception of telephone calls at the search scene is discussed in §2.116. The problem is related because such an interception is a seizure. *People v Drieslein* (1985) 170 CA3d 591, 600, 216 CR 244.

### b. The Plain-View Exception

#### (1) [§2.113] Basic Principles

In *Skelton v Superior Court* (1969) 1 C3d 144, 157, 81 CR 613 (leading case), the court formulated the "plain-view" or "plain-sight" exception as follows:

> When officers, in the course of a bona fide effort to execute a valid search warrant, discover articles which, although not included in the warrant, are reasonably identifiable as contraband, they may seize them whether they are initially in plain sight or come into plain sight subsequently, as a result of the officers' efforts.

In accord with *Skelton* is *People v Superior Court* (Meyers) (1979) 25 C3d 67, 73, 157 CR 716. See §2.114 for discussion of bona fide effort and §2.115 for discussion of reasonably identifiable contraband.

Note that under this formulation the plain-view exception extends to property that comes into view as the result of the officer's execution of the search warrant. For example, in *Meyers*, the officers properly looked through drawers and closet space in their search for specified stolen property (25 C3d at 71) and discovered additional stolen items. See also *People v Emanuel* (1978) 87 CA3d 205, 214, 151 CR 44 (in executing search warrant for narcotics, it is a "necessity" to search "every crevice of the house").

The discovery of the evidence need not be inadvertent as long as the scope of the search does not exceed that permitted by the terms of the warrant, and the incriminating character of the evidence is immediately apparent. *Horton v California* (1990) 496 US 128, 130, 136, 110 S Ct 2301, 110 L Ed 2d 112; *People v Kraft* (2000) 23 C4th 978, 1041, 99 CR2d 1.

#### (2) [§2.114] Good Faith ("Bona Fide Effort")

The officers who execute the search warrant must do so in good faith. They cannot use the search warrant as a pretext for conducting a general exploratory search; such a search renders the plain view exception inapplicable. *People v Albritton* (1982) 138 CA3d 79, 87, 187 CR 652; *People v McGraw* (1981) 119 CA3d 582, 600, 174 CR 711. Police conduct in flagrant disregard of the scope of the warrant may justify total suppression of the evidence seized. See *People v Kraft* (2000) 23 C4th 978, 1044, 99 CR2d 1; *People v Bradford* (1997) 15 C4th 1229, 1305–1307, 65 CR2d 145.

*Albritton* illustrates the use of a search warrant as a pretext. The warrant authorized a search for narcotics. An officer assigned to the auto theft division went along to assist in the execution of the warrant. He knew defendant's vehicle theft history, went into the garage to look for stolen vehicles, checked serial numbers, ran "want" checks, and seized the items that had positive want checks. The court noted that the officer's actions were totally unrelated to the search warrant and concluded that the officer used the warrant as a means to conduct his own investigation. The court held that he did not validly seize the stolen items. 138 CA3d at 88.

*Albritton* does *not* stand for a rule that officers serving a search warrant may never examine serial numbers. Subject to the good-faith limitation, they may do so. See §2.115.

In contrast to *Albritton, People v McGraw, supra*, found good faith under the following circumstances: The search warrant was for the proceeds of a burglary. The executing officers requested the presence of an officer from another city who was investigating other burglaries in which the defendant was a suspect; that officer helped identify property taken in those burglaries. The court said that he was present "not to explore but to match contraband to specific offenses." 119 CA3d at 603. *People v Williams* (1988) 198 CA3d 873, 885–887, 243 CR 914, and *People v Miller* (1987) 196 CA3d 846, 852, 242 CR 179, are in accord with *McGraw.*

### (3) [§2.115] Linkage Between the Property in Plain View and Criminal Behavior ("Reasonably Identifiable as Contraband")

Although *Skelton v Superior Court* (1969) 1 C3d 144, 157, 81 CR 613, speaks of "articles . . . reasonably identifiable as *contraband*" (emphasis added), the plain-view exception has a broader scope. It applies not merely to contraband such as stolen property but also to other evidence of crime. See, *e.g., People v Bradford* (1997) 15 C4th 1229, 1295, 65 CR2d 145 (objects that are evidence of crime, contraband, or otherwise subject to lawful seizure); *People v Miley* (1984) 158 CA3d 25, 35, 204 CR 347 (diagram); *People v Cooks* (1983) 141 CA3d 224, 297, 190 CR 211 (binder); *People v Guillebeau* (1980) 107 CA3d 531, 553, 166 CR 45 (shoes and newspaper).

The searching officers, however, cannot use the plain-view exception even in good faith to seize any articles of which they are suspicious. The officers must have information that links the articles to criminal behavior. This requirement, implicit in *Skelton's* comment about identifiability, was first stated in its present form in *People v Hill* (1974) 12 C3d 731, 763, 117 CR 393, overruled on other grounds in 18 C3d 889, 896 n5, but specifically approved on this point in *People v Superior Court* (Meyers) (1979) 25 C3d 67, 73, 157 CR 716: "The police officers who seize an article must be presently aware of some specific and articulable fact from which a rational link between the item seized and criminal behavior can be inferred. . . ." In short, the incriminating character of the object must be immediately apparent. *People v Bradford, supra.*

The linkage principle is often called the "nexus rule." *People v Superior Court* (Meyers), *supra*; *People v Miley, supra*; *Nunes v Superior Court* (1980) 100 CA3d 915, 928, 161 CR 351.

The nexus rule is most often invoked in stolen property cases. In *Nunes v Superior Court, supra,* the officers seized articles that they suspected would match the description of stolen items in police reports not in their possession. 100 CA3d at 932. The court held that such a "general suspicion" lacked the specificity required by the nexus rule.

Similarly, in *People v Murray* (1978) 77 CA3d 305, 311, 143 CR 502, the officers seized two television sets not described in the warrant. The court held the seizure improper under the plain-view doctrine because the sets "were not inherently identifiable as contraband nor were they identified at the scene as having obliterated serial numbers or other distinctive markings." Knowledge that the occupant of the premises was a fence and the discovery of 67 other TV sets, 20 of which had their serial numbers removed, did not supply a sufficient nexus because the officers could not tell whether or not the two sets in issue were stolen. 77 CA3d at 311.

The requisite linkage can be established in several ways. For example:

(a) By the officers' knowledge of the crime investigation giving rise to the warrant (*People v Lowery* (1983) 145 CA3d 902, 908, 194 CR 815; *Cooper v Superior Court* (1981) 118 CA3d 499, 511, 173 CR 520) or of other crimes (*People v McGraw* (1981) 119 CA3d 582, 599, 174 CR 711). For example, unlike *Nunes* and *Murray*, there is adequate linkage when an officer seized a TV set from defendant's residence knowing that (1) its size and brand matched those of a set taken in a particular burglary, (2) property taken in that burglary had been passed over a fence into defendant's backyard, and (3) the set had entered defendant's house at about the time of the burglary. *People v Rios* (1988) 205 CA3d 833, 840–841, 252 CR 653.

(b) By the identification of stolen articles made by other persons at the scene of the search. *People v Superior Court* (Meyers), *supra*, 25 C3d at 73–74 (identification by burglary victims); *People v McGraw, supra* (identification by police officer from another city).

(c) By the officers' discovery that serial numbers of items have been removed or matched the numbers on articles reported stolen. The officers can examine articles in plain view for serial numbers. *People v Schreier* (1984) 158 CA3d Supp 20, 205 CR 151 (officer had search warrant for cocaine, saw camera, ran serial number check over the telephone, learned camera was stolen, and seized it; seizure upheld under plain view doctrine); *People v Eitzen* (1974) 43 CA3d 253, 258 n3, 117 CR 772 (officers took serial numbers of several guns not described in warrant, checked numbers later and determined that the guns were stolen, and obtained a second search warrant to seize them; seizure held valid). See also *People v Murray, supra*, 77 CA3d at 310 (implicitly approves examining TV sets to determine if their serial numbers had been obliterated).

However, the right to examine serial numbers is limited. Moving items in plain view to look at the number is itself a search and is proper only when the officer has probable cause to believe they were stolen. *Arizona v Hicks* (1987) 480 US 321, 326, 107 S Ct 1149, 94 L Ed 2d 347. *Hicks* involved a lawful warrantless entry by police into an apartment, but the court's reasoning also applies to the discovery of items in plain view during the execution of a search warrant. *Horton v California* (1990) 496 US 128, 136–142, 110 S Ct 2301, 110 L Ed 2d 112; *People v Williams* (1988) 198 CA3d 873, 887–892, 243 CR 914 (court found probable cause).

### c. [§2.116] Police Interceptions of Telephone Calls at Scene of Search

In *People v Drieslein* (1985) 170 CA3d 591, 216 CR 244, while the officers were executing a narcotics search warrant at a house, the telephone rang. An officer picked up the phone and, pretending to be a drug buyer, talked to the defendant. The conversation led to an arrangement to purchase narcotics from the defendant and ultimately to his arrest. The court applied a nexus rule adapted from the plain view decisions, inquiring whether the officer could reasonably suspect that the call would be linked to criminal activity. 170 CA3d at 602. The court found an adequate nexus from the affidavit and the large amount of drugs and cash found in the premises. In addition to an objective linkage, the court required a subjective belief by the officer that the call was linked to criminal conduct and inferred such a belief from the fact that the officer gave the defendant a false name when he intercepted the call.

Other decisions do not use the word "nexus," but apply the same principle. *People v Vanvalkenburgh* (1983) 145 CA3d 163, 167, 193 CR 274 (discovery of a large amount of cocaine and cash "render incoming calls reasonably suspect"); *People v Sandoval* (1966) 65 C2d 303, 308, 54 CR 123 (information available to officers "rendered incoming telephone calls reasonably suspect"); *People v Harwood* (1977) 74 CA3d 460, 468, 141 CR 519 (officers had no reason to believe that defendant arrested a block from his house for selling cocaine "conducted his narcotics transactions after telephone calls to his residence").

### 3. [§2.117] Presence of Third Parties

The presence of media representatives at police invitation during the search of a private home violates the Fourth Amendment. *Wilson v Layne* (1999) 526 US 603, 611, 119 S Ct 1692, 143 L Ed 2d 818. The court based the decision on two reasons: high respect for the privacy of the home and the fact that the presence of reporters was not related to the objectives of the police activity. *Wilson v Layne* was a civil suit against the officers involved. It is undecided at the time this is being written whether such a violation would result in invocation of the exclusionary rule.

Third parties may, however, be present to assist the police in identifying property named in the warrant. See *Wilson v Layne, supra*. For further discussion, see §2.76.

### 4. [§2.118] Videotaping of Search

Videotaping by media violates the Fourth Amendment. See *Wilson v Layne* (1999) 526 US 603, 119 S Ct 1692, 143 L Ed 2d 818, discussed in §2.117. The legality of videotaping by police is undecided. Dictum in *Wilson v Layne* states that "it might be reasonable . . . as part of a 'quality control' effort to ensure that the rights of homeowners are being respected, or even to preserve evidence." 526 US at 613. Police videotaping of a scantily clad person on the premises is improper. See *U.S. v Stowe* (7th Cir 1996) 100 F3d 494, 500. So is release of a videotape to the media at least until the subject of the search has had an opportunity to litigate its validity. *Oziel v Superior Court* (1990) 223 CA3d 1284, 1292, 273 CR 196.

### 5. [§2.119] Use of Dogs

The police may use drug-sniffing dogs in executing a search warrant for heroin, cocaine, or marijuana. *People v Russell* (1987) 195 CA3d 186, 189, 240 CR 456. The warrant need not specifically authorize the use of such dogs. *People v Russell, supra*. The propriety of using a police dog for other purposes, such as security or to look for a person named in the warrant, is undecided. In the view of most judges, this would probably not result in an application of the exclusionary rule as long as the officers had an objectively reasonable basis for bringing the dog along.

### 6. [§2.120] Unduly Prolonged or Intense Search

A search "can become constitutionally infirm if unduly prolonged." *People v James* (1990) 219 CA3d 414, 420, 268 CR 105. The police may remain on the premises only as long as they reasonably need to carry out the search. 2 LaFave, p 673. No California court has invalidated a search pursuant to a search warrant on this ground.

A search may be as intense, in terms of what the officers may look into on the premises, as the nature of the objects to be seized makes reasonable. A search for documents or drugs can obviously cover many nooks and crannies that a search for stolen TV sets could not. See 2 LaFave, p 670.

☛ **Judicial Tip**: When a search is partly proper and partly excessive in terms of length or scope, the solution may be to admit the products of the former and exclude the results of the latter; in the event of flagrant misconduct, all the fruits of the search may need to be suppressed. 2 LaFave, p 680.

### 7. [§2.121] Multiple Searches

A search warrant authorizes only a single search of the subject premises. *People v James* (1990) 219 CA3d 414, 419, 268 CR 105. A search following an interruption or break is not necessarily an improper second search. In *James,* the court held that a meal break by the searching officers and the preparation of two inventories did not compel a conclusion that there were two searches.

### 8. [§2.122] Who May Execute

A search warrant may be served only by:

- Any of the officers mentioned in its directions,
- Persons aiding the officer at the officer's request and in his or her presence. Pen C §1530.

For discussion of searches by special masters, see §2.127.

### 9. Information to Householders

#### a. [§2.123] Copy of Warrants

The persons who execute the warrant need not read it to the householders or leave a copy with them. *Nunes v Superior Court* (1980) 100 CA3d 915, 935–937, 161 CR 351 (court notes that such a practice, while not mandatory, is desirable). The warrant need not even be present on the premises. *People v Rodrigues-Fernandez* (1991) 235 CA3d 543, 553, 286 CR 700 (defendant given copy later at police station). Special requirements apply to warrants that involve a special master. See §2.127.

Federal Rule of Criminal Procedure 41(d) requires federal agents to give a copy of the warrant to the householder. See *City of West Covina v Perkins* (1999) 525 US 234, 243, 119 S Ct 678, 142 L Ed 2d 636.

#### b. [§2.124] Receipt

Penal Code §1535 provides that when officers take property, they must give a detailed receipt to the person from whom it was taken or in whose possession it was found; in the absence of any person, the officers must leave the receipt in the place where they found the property. A receipt differs from an inventory; the latter is a sworn document. See §2.127. Courts occasionally confuse the two. See, *e.g., People v James* (1990) 219 CA3d 414, 420, 268 CR 105.

Failure to give a receipt does not invalidate the search. See *People v Phillips* (1958) 163 CA2d 541, 548, 329 P2d 621, disapproved on other grounds in 64 C2d 842, 844–845. *Phillips* rejected a contention that failure to take an inventory in defendant's presence and to give her a copy vitiated the warrant. The court treated the case as one under Pen C §1535. While the Fourth Amendment does not mandate a receipt, due process requires adequate notice that property was taken. See *City of West Covina v Perkins* (1999) 525 US 234, 240–241, 119 S Ct 678, 142 L Ed 2d 636.

#### c. [§2.125] Instructions on Reclaiming Property

The police need not give instructions or advice to owners who seek return of property no longer needed for investigation or prosecution. *City of West Covina v Perkins* (1999) 525 US 234, 240, 119 S Ct 678, 142 L Ed 2d 636 (California remedies for return are not so arcane as to necessitate instructions as long as law enforcement agents take reasonable steps to give notice that property was taken).

#### d. [§2.126] Return of Warrant and Inventory

Penal Code §1537 states:

> The officer must forthwith return the warrant to the magistrate, and deliver to him a written inventory of the property taken, made publicly or in the presence of the person from whose possession it was taken, and of the applicant for the warrant, if they are present, verified by the affidavit of the officer at the foot of the inventory, and taken before the magistrate at the time, to the following effect: "I. R. S., the officer by whom this warrant was executed, do swear that the above inventory contains a true and detailed account of all the property taken by me on the warrant.

The widely used phrase "return to the warrant" (see, *e.g., People v Guillebeau* (1980) 107 CA3d 531, 554, 166 CR 45) means "an inventory or list of all the property seized during service of the warrant." See Chrystie & Schirn, p X-18.

Penal Code §1534(a) requires the return of the search warrant "within 10 days after date of issuance." Penal Code §1538 provides that when the search warrant has been returned "[t]he magistrate must thereupon, if required, deliver a copy of the inventory to the person from whose possession the property was taken, and to the applicant for the warrant."

Statutory provisions concerning the return of search warrants have been held to be ministerial; violations do not cause exclusion of evidence unless the defendant shows prejudice. *People v Head* (1994) 30 CA4th 954, 960, 36 CR2d 1 (loss of potential trial witness as result of late return not sufficiently prejudicial; return more than a year after search); *People v Kirk* (1979) 99 CA3d 89, 95–96, 160 CR 184 (55-day delay in return; inventory made by criminalist); *People v Couch* (1979) 97 CA3d 377, 381, 158 CR 647 (untimely return); *People v Guillebeau* (1980) 107 CA3d 531, 554, 166 CR 45 (return omitted items taken pursuant to plain-view exception); *People v Phillips* (1958) 163 CA2d 541, 548, 329 P2d 621, disapproved on other grounds in 64 C2d 842, 844–845 (inventory not taken in occupant's presence; no copy given to her).

### 10. [§2.127] Execution of Search Under Special Master Procedure

When the court has appointed a special master, Pen C §1524 imposes special requirements for the execution of the warrant:

*Time of service.* The warrant shall be served during normal business hours whenever practicable. Pen C §1524(c)(3).

*Person served.* The warrant shall be served on the person who appears to have possession or control of the items sought. Pen C §1524(c)(3).

*Who executes warrant.* The person to whom the warrant is directed serves it, but the special master conducts the search if the person served fails to provide the items requested by the warrant. Pen C §1524(c)(1). The person who served the warrant may accompany the special master during the search, but may not participate in it or examine any of the items being searched. Pen C §1524(e).

*Duties of Special Master* (Pen C §1524(c), (d)):

- Accompanies person serving the warrant.
- Informs the party served of the items sought and that the party has the opportunity to provide them.
- Decides whether the party has provided the items.
- Conducts the search upon deciding that the party has failed to provide them.
- Seals any item that the party served states should not be disclosed or, in case no such party is found, any item that appears to the special master to be privileged.
- Takes sealed items to court for a hearing.
- Keeps all information confidential and divulges it only in direct response to inquiry by the court.

### 11. Securing Premises Pending Issuance of Warrant

#### a. [§2.128] Probable Cause Plus Exigency Rule

A nonconsensual entry to secure premises during the time the police obtain a search warrant or decide whether to seek one generally requires both of the following:

- Probable cause to search, and
- Exigent circumstances, usually an imminent danger that evidence will be destroyed. *People v Bennett* (1998) 17 C4th 373, 386, 70 CR2d 850; *People v Gentry* (1992) 7 CA4th 1255, 1265, 9 CR2d 742; *People v Camilleri* (1990) 220 CA3d 1199, 1206, 269 CR 862. For discussion of what constitutes a sufficient emergency, see §2.129.

This principle also applies to:

- The temporary detention of persons on the premises. *In re Elizabeth G.* (2001) 88 CA4th 496, 505, 105 CR2d 811 (occupants could move through house only with police accompaniment); *People v Gentry, supra.*
- The temporary prevention of persons from entering or reentering

the premises. *Illinois v McArthur* (2001) 531 US 326, 121 S Ct 946, 148 L Ed 2d 838, 847–848; *People v Bennett, supra.*

- The seizure of property on the premises pending issuance of the warrant. *People v Link* (1994) 26 CA4th 1272, 1277, 32 CR2d 149.

*Exceptions.* When there is no police entry, probable cause alone permits law enforcement to temporarily prevent others from entering the premises. *People v Bennett, supra*; but see *Illinois v McArthur, supra* (probable cause major factor supporting lawfulness of preventing resident's reentry without police accompaniment). Entry to secure unoccupied premises may also be lawful on the basis of probable cause without exigent circumstances. See *People v Gentry, supra*; *Segura v U.S.* (1984) 468 US 796, 798, 104 S Ct 3380, 82 L Ed 2d 599. An unlawful entry is not always fatal. See §§1.58–1.59 (warrant issued after improper entry valid if it rests on facts known to police before entry).

*Knock-notice.* An entry to secure premises is subject to knock-notice requirements. *Machado v Superior Court* (1975) 45 CA3d 316, 320, 119 CR 344. But those requirements are also subject to an exception for exigent circumstances. See §§2.106–2.108.

### b. [§2.129] Exigent Circumstances

Mere apprehension that evidence will be destroyed is insufficient. The officers must have "an objectively reasonable basis for believing there is someone inside the residence who has reason to destroy evidence"; the police need specific, articulable facts. *People v Gentry* (1992) 7 CA4th 1255, 1264, 9 CR2d 742; *People v Camilleri* (1990) 220 CA3d 1199, 1209, 269 CR 862; *People v Koch* (1989) 209 CA3d 770, 782, 257 CR 483, disapproved on other grounds in 20 C4th 1073, 1075.

Relevant circumstances include (*People v Bennett* (1998) 17 C4th 373, 385, 70 CR2d 850, quoting with approval *U.S. v Rubin* (3d Cir 1973) 474 F2d 262, 268–269):

- The degree of urgency involved and the time needed to get a search warrant.
- Reasonable belief that the contraband is about to be removed.
- Danger to officers guarding the site while the police seek a warrant.
- Information indicating that the persons who have the contraband are aware that the police are on their trail.
- The ready destructibility of drugs and the knowledge that drug traf-

fickers will make efforts to dispose of them rather than be caught with them.

Illustrations:

- Police accompany a wife at her request to a trailer in which she lives with her husband, so that she can remove her belongings. She tells one of the officers that her husband has drugs in the trailer under the couch. These are adequate exigent circumstances to prevent the husband's reentry into the trailer unless accompanied by an officer: there is good reason to fear that the husband suspected his upset wife of snitching and that he would destroy the drugs unless detained. *Illinois v McArthur* (2001) 531 US 326, 121 S Ct 946, 148 L Ed 2d 838, 848.

- Police arrest a gang member after a shooting and just after he dropped off a possible accomplice near the arrestee's residence. The police had not yet located the firearms. These circumstances permit the police to temporarily seize the residence and detain its occupants. *In re Elizabeth G.* (2001) 88 CA4th 496, 507, 105 CR2d 811.

- Police make a large cocaine buy, follow the seller to his source, and arrest him. The seller's supplier would expect prompt payment and would probably panic if left alone while police got a search warrant. These are adequate exigent circumstances to enter and secure the supplier's house. *People v Camilleri, supra.*

- A car passenger is properly arrested for possession of drugs found on his side of the vehicle. The officers lack exigent circumstances to enter his house while they seek a search warrant in the absence of information that anyone is there who is likely to become alarmed or that any other drug possessors are aware that the police are hot on their trail. *People v Koch, supra.*

- The police have information that a person is selling marijuana at a very fast rate from a car parked near his apartment. This is not an emergency that permits the police to enter the apartment. *People v Gentry, supra.*

*Burden of proof.* The prosecution has the burden of proving exigent circumstances, including a showing of insufficient time to obtain a warrant. *People v Camilleri, supra*, 220 CA3d at 1206; *People v Brown* (1989) 210 CA3d 849, 855, 260 CR 293.

*Police-created emergency.* The police may not create an emergency to justify an entry. *People v Shuey* (1975) 13 C3d 835, 849, 120 CR 83.

*Murder scene.* The scene of a murder is not an exception to the requirement of exigent circumstances. See *Flippo v West Virginia* (1999) 528 US 11, 14, 120 S Ct 7, 145 L Ed 2d 16; *Mincey v Arizona* (1978) 437 US 385, 395, 98 S Ct 2408, 57 L Ed 2d 290.

## VI. PROCEDURAL GUIDES TO TELEPHONIC, FAX, AND E-MAIL SEARCH WARRANTS

### A. [§2.130] Telephonic Search Warrants

**During the telephone conversation**

*(1) Record the conversation.* If the judge does the recording, he or she should check that the equipment is switched on and operating. If the recording is being done at the affiant's end, the judge should ask whether the recording equipment has been turned on.

*(2) Avoid unrecorded or unsworn statements.* Unrecorded or unsworn statements by the officer (or prosecutor, if one participates in the conversation) as to what the case is about should be discouraged. Such statements can create confusion in the officer's and judge's mind regarding what was said on the record for probable cause and what was not.

*(3) Identify all speakers.* All speakers should be asked to identify themselves; the judge should make sure that throughout the conversation, the identity of each speaker is clear.

*(4) Swear affiant.* The affiant should be sworn. Pen C §1526(b).

*(5) Take affiant's statement.* The affiant should make a statement of probable cause. The judge can ask questions. Pen C §1526(b).

☛ **Judicial Tip**: The judge should not hesitate to ask the affiant questions if any part of the oral statement is not clear. This is especially useful when the affiant speaks without having a written affidavit or outline.

*(6) Ask affiant to read search warrant.* The affiant should read the proposed search warrant. If changes are necessary, the affiant should make them identically both on the original search warrant and the duplicate original.

*(7) Include in judge's statement*:

- That probable cause exists to issue the search warrant, if the judge so finds.

- That the search warrant as read by the affiant shall issue.

- The date and time of issuance, which the judge will later have to enter on the original search warrant.
- That the affiant is authorized to sign the judge's name to the duplicate original search warrant. Pen C §1528(b).

*(8) Instruct officer-affiant*:

- The officer should bring the original and duplicate original search warrant to the judge. The officer often does this at the time he or she brings the return.
- Unless the judge is recording the conversation personally, the officer should be instructed to have the tape promptly transcribed and to deliver the tape and transcription.

**After the Telephone Conversation**

*(1) Once the search warrant is received, the judge should take the following steps* (Pen C §§1528(b), 1534(b)):

- Enter the exact time of *issuance* on the *original* search warrant.
- Check that the officer who served the warrant entered the exact time of *execution* on the *duplicate* original.
- Sign the original search warrant.
- Give both the original and the duplicate original search warrant to the clerk for filing.

*(2) To ensure proper transcription of the conversation, do the following* (Pen C §1526(b)):

- Check that the transcription and the tape are received promptly.
- Compare the transcription with the tape and make any needed corrections in the transcript.
- Certify the tape and transcription.
- Give the tape and transcription to the clerk for filing. These steps should be taken promptly. See §2.20.

### B. [§2.131] Warrants Transmitted by Fax or E-mail

**During the Telephone Conversation**

*(1) Identification of speakers.* The judge asks all speakers to identify themselves and makes sure that the identity of each speaker is clear throughout the conversation.

*(2) Initial applicant statement.* The applicant should state that an affida-

vit and search warrant are ready for immediate transmission by fax or e-mail.

*(3) Applicant data.* The judge obtains and makes a note of the applicant's telephone number and fax number or e-mail address.

*(4) Magistrate data.* The judge confirms that applicant has the magistrate's correct fax number, if different from the phone number, or e-mail address.

*(5) Oath.* The judge administers the oath to the applicant over the telephone.

*(6) Page information.* The judge inquires how many pages of affidavit, attachments, and warrant will be transmitted, unless this information was provided earlier in the conversation. It is important to make a note of the respective numbers of pages.

*(7) Signature.* The judge instructs the affiant to sign the affidavit and the affiant does so. If digital signature capabilities exist and e-mail transmission is planned, affiant provides a digital signature.

**After the Telephone Conversation**

*(1) Start equipment.* Judge and applicant turn on their fax machines or computers.

*(2) Document transmittal.* Applicant faxes or e-mails:

- The affidavit(s);
- All attachments to the affidavit(s);
- The search warrant.

*(3) Confirmation.* The magistrate confirms receipt and legibility of the correct number of pages of all documents.

*(4) Request for further transmission.* The magistrate requests

- Retransmission of any missing or illegible pages; and
- In case of e-mail, affiant's verification of the digital signature.

*(5) Decision whether to issue.* The magistrate reads the affidavit(s), attachments, and proposed search warrant and determines whether to issue the warrant.

*(6) Issuance of warrant.* A magistrate who has decided to issue the warrant should do the following:

- In case of e-mail transmission, make a hard copy of all papers;
- Sign the faxed or hard copy of the warrant;

- Note on the warrant the exact date and time at which it was issued; and
- Write "Original Warrant" on the signed warrant.

*(7) Warrant transmittal.* The judge transmits the signed warrant to the applicant via fax or e-mail and directs the applicant to *phone* the judge to acknowledge receipt.

*(8) Receipt acknowledgment.* Applicant telephones the magistrate and acknowledges receipt of the warrant. For an additional part of this telephone call, see (9) below.

*(9) Authorization for duplicate original.* In the same telephone conversation, the judge authorizes the applicant to write "duplicate original" on the copy of the warrant that the judge transmitted.

*(10) Filing.* The judge gives the "original warrant," affidavit, and attachments to the clerk for filing.

## VII. [§2.132] FORM: SPECIAL MASTER AFFIDAVIT

**I, ______________________________ declare that:**

**Name of special master**

**1. I am a member in good standing of the State Bar of California and designated by the State Bar as an attorney qualified to serve as a Special Master.**

**2. Pursuant to Penal Code §1524(d), I have no relationship with, or adverse interest to, as defined by the California Rules of Professional Conduct, any police or prosecutorial agency, or person or entity subject to search or involved in this pending matter.**

**I declare under penalty of perjury under the laws of the State of California that the foregoing is true and correct.**

**Dated: ______________________ ___________________________**

**Affiant**

# 3

# Temporary Detentions and Searches Incident to Temporary Detentions

## I. [§3.1] INTRODUCTION AND SCOPE OF CHAPTER

The term "temporary detention," as courts use it, covers restraints on a person's freedom more serious than in a casual police-citizen encounter, but not as serious as in an arrest. The most common temporary detentions are stopping motorists for traffic violations and so-called *Terry* or investigative stops on suspicion of criminal activity. Road blocks and border checks are other examples.

Fourth Amendment law governs temporary detentions, both as to what the police can do and the consequences of improper police actions. Sections 3.2–3.3 outline the Fourth Amendment issues. Next, sections 3.4–3.30 address the questions of what a temporary detention is and how it differs, on the one hand, from an arrest and, on the other, from less serious intrusions on liberty.

Sections 3.31–3.84 cover traffic stops and detentions based on suspicion that the detainee may be involved in criminal activity. This part of the chapter focuses on two major questions: What are the requirements for making a lawful stop? Under what circumstances does a temporary detention that was initially lawful become unlawful through undue prolongation or other police conduct?

Roadblocks and other detentions not based on individualized suspicion are the topic of §§3.85–3.94. Sections 3.95–3.107 discuss searches incident to a temporary detention.

## II. APPLICATION OF FOURTH AMENDMENT

### A. [§3.2] Stop and Frisk as Seizure and Search

The Fourth Amendment prohibits "unreasonable searches and seizures." A temporary detention of a person is a "seizure" within the meaning of the Fourth Amendment and a "frisk" is a search. *Terry v Ohio* (1968) 392 US 1, 16, 88 S Ct 1868, 20 L Ed 2d 889 (pedestrian stop); *Delaware v Prouse* (1979) 440 US 648, 653, 99 S Ct 1391, 59 L Ed 2d 660 (detention of vehicle and its occupants). The Fourth Amendment also requires that "no warrants shall issue, but upon probable cause. . . ." But *Terry* held that the legality of detentions should not be determined under the warrant clause of the Fourth Amendment but rather under the amendment's general proscription of unreasonable searches and seizures. California courts had earlier reached the same conclusion. See, *e.g., People v Mickelson* (1963) 59 C2d 448, 450, 30 CR 18. The circumstances short of probable cause that make temporary detentions and incidental searches reasonable seizures and searches are one of the main topics of this chapter.

Fourth Amendment considerations determine not only the conditions that make a temporary detention and an attendant search lawful, but also what constitutes such a detention. See §§3.4–3.30. A lawful stop does not necessarily permit a frisk or other search. See §§3.95–3.107.

### B. [§3.3] Effects of Unlawful Detention or Frisk

Evidence obtained as a result of an unlawful detention or of an unlawful frisk must generally be suppressed. See, *e.g., Delaware v Prouse* (1979) 440 US 648, 653–663, 99 S Ct 1391, 59 L Ed 2d 660; *Wilson v Superior Court* (1983) 34 C3d 777, 791, 195 CR 671; *People v Valenzuela* (1994) 28 CA4th 817, 830, 33 CR2d 802. For exceptions, see discussion of attenuation and inevitable discovery in §§1.45–1.62. The exclusionary rule extends to the following:

- Police observations during an illegal detention. *People v Spicer* (1984) 157 CA3d 213, 216–217, 203 CR 599 (officer saw gun in purse of vehicle passenger who was unlawfully detained).

- Evidence based on a consent search when the consent was given during an unlawful detention; such a consent is invalid. See *e.g., Florida v Royer* (1983) 460 US 491, 103 S Ct 1319, 75 L Ed 2d 229; *Wilson v Superior Court, supra*; *People v Valenzuela, supra.* An illegal detention *after* an otherwise proper consent generally does not invalidate the consent. *People v $48,715 United States Currency* (1997) 58 CA4th 1507, 1513, 68 CR2d 829. For discussion of consent to search that is requested after detention is no longer warranted, see §3.76.

- Lineup identification. *In re Dung T.* (1984) 160 CA3d 697, 712, 206 CR 772 (detained person improperly moved to police station for lineup; lineup identification inadmissible; in-court identification admissible only if independent of lineup).
- Fingerprints and footprints. *Hayes v Florida* (1985) 470 US 811, 814, 105 S Ct 1643, 84 L Ed 2d 705; *People v Harris* (1975) 15 C3d 384, 388–392, 124 CR 536.
- Statements by the defendant during an illegal detention. *Florida v Royer, supra.*

As to the effect of Proposition 8, Cal Const art I, §28(d), see §1.7.
The validity of a detention occasionally becomes an issue in contexts other than a suppression motion. See, *e.g., People v Smith* (1984) 151 CA3d 89, 98, 198 CR 623 (assault on a police officer; legality of detention determines whether officer was engaged in lawful performance of duties).

## III. WHAT CONSTITUTES A TEMPORARY DETENTION

### A. [§3.4] Temporary Detentions in the Spectrum of Police-Civilian Contacts

Fourth Amendment law recognizes that police-civilian contacts vary in their degree of intrusiveness from minimal to severe and that as the seriousness of the restraint of a person's liberty increases, so must the justification for it. See, *e.g., Florida v Royer* (1983) 460 US 491, 500, 103 S Ct 1319, 75 L Ed 2d 229; *In re James D.* (1987) 43 C3d 903, 911, 239 CR 663; *Wilson v Superior Court* (1983) 34 C3d 777, 784, 195 CR 671. These decisions recognize three levels of police-citizen interactions:

(1) *Consensual encounters.* The least intrusive contacts involve no restraint of liberty; courts do not regard them as seizures. *Florida v Royer, supra,* refers to such interactions as consensual encounters. The police may initiate them without any objective justification. *Wilson v Superior Court, supra.* See §3.5.

(2) *Temporary Detentions.* The second category of police-civilian contacts is the temporary detention. They generally require an objectively reasonable basis for suspecting the detainee of criminal activity and must be limited in duration, scope, and purpose. *In re James D., supra*; *Wilson v Superior Court, supra.*

(3) *Arrests.* Finally, "there are those seizures of an individual which ex-

ceed the permissible limits of a detention, seizures which include formal arrests and restraints on an individual's liberty which are comparable to an arrest, and which are constitutionally permissible only if the police have probable cause to arrest the individual for a crime." *Wilson v Superior Court, supra*; *People v Shields* (1988) 205 CA3d 1065, 1072, 252 CR 849.

A police-civilian contact is not limited to a fixed point on the spectrum. Casual encounters often become detentions. Detentions turn into arrests or into restraints tantamount to them.

## B. Differentiating Detentions From Less Intrusive Contacts

### 1. [§3.5] Contacts Not Amounting to Seizure ("Consensual Encounters")

> [L]aw enforcement officers do not violate the Fourth Amendment by merely approaching an individual on the street or in another public place, by asking him if he is willing to answer some questions, by putting questions to him if the person is willing to listen, or by offering in evidence in a criminal prosecution his voluntary answers to such questions. . . . Nor would the fact that the officer identifies himself as a police officer, without more, convert the encounter into a seizure requiring some level of objective justification. . . . The person approached, however, need not answer any question put to him; indeed, he may decline to listen to the questions at all and may go on his way. . . . He may not be detained even momentarily without reasonable, objective grounds for doing so; and his refusal to listen or answer does not, without more, furnish those grounds. . . . [Citations omitted.]

*Florida v Royer* (1983) 460 US 491, 497, 103 S Ct 1319, 75 L Ed 2d 229.

In short, consensual encounters are police-civilian interactions that "result in no restraint of an individual's liberty whatsoever—*i.e.,* no 'seizure.'" *Wilson v Superior Court* (1983) 34 C3d 777, 784, 195 CR 671. In accord is *In re James D.* (1987) 43 C3d 903, 911, 239 CR 663.

Although consensual contacts require no objective justification (see §3.4), initiating one solely on the basis of race may violate the 14th Amendment. See *Whren v U.S.* (1996) 517 US 806, 813, 116 S Ct 1769, 135 L Ed 2d 89; *U.S. v Travis* (6th Cir 1995) 62 F3d 170, 173 (court did not decide whether evidence resulting from such a violation would be suppressed).

### 2. Test To Determine Temporary Detention

#### a. [§3.6] *Mendenhall* Test

A temporary detention, unlike a consensual encounter, is a restraint of liberty: The person to whom the police is talking is no longer free to terminate the contact and walk away. Courts use an objective test to differentiate between the two types of contact. The *Mendenhall* test asks whether "in view of all the circumstances surrounding the incident, a reasonable person would have believed that he was not free to leave." *U.S. v Mendenhall* (1980) 446 US 544, 554, 100 S Ct 1870, 64 L Ed 2d 497; *Wilson v Superior Court* (1983) 43 C3d 777, 790, 195 CR 671. For discussion of objective nature of test, see §3.9.

The *Mendenhall* test, expressed in an opinion of only two justices, has been adopted by the U.S. Supreme Court. *California v Hodari D.* (1991) 499 US 621, 627, 111 S Ct 1547, 113 L Ed 2d 690; *Michigan v Chesternut* (1988) 486 US 567, 573, 108 S Ct 1975, 100 L Ed 2d 565 (crucial test is whether police conduct would have communicated to a reasonable person that he or she was not free to ignore the police presence); *Florida v Royer* (1983) 460 US 491, 497, 103 S Ct 1319, 75 L Ed 2d 229.

The test focuses on the particular show of police authority. *Florida v Royer, supra.* Blanket rules are disfavored. *Florida v Bostick* (1991) 501 US 429, 437, 111 S Ct 2382, 115 L Ed 2d 389 (disapproving state court rule that requesting bus passengers to consent to luggage search constitutes detention). For illustrative applications of the *Mendenhall* test, see §§3.10–3.28; for a summary of factors that courts consider, see §3.29.

An actual detention occurs only when a person submits to the police show of authority; a person who runs away is not detained while being chased. *California v Hodari D., supra.* The same principle applies to a car chase. See §§3.22, 3.24.

### b. [§3.7] Variants of *Mendenhall* Test

Under some circumstances the test is modified to ask whether a reasonable person would feel free to refuse an officer's request. For example, when officers ask bus passengers to agree to a luggage search, the issue is whether a reasonable person would believe under the particular circumstances that he or she could effectively decline to give permission. *Florida v Bostick* (1991) 501 US 429, 436, 111 S Ct 2382, 115 L Ed 2d 389; *U.S. v Washington* (11th Cir 1998) 151 F3d 1354, 1357 ("Absent some positive indication that they were free not to cooperate, it is doubtful a passenger would think he or she had the choice to ignore the police presence. Most citizens, we hope, believe that it is their duty to cooperate with the police"); *U.S. v Guapi* (11th Cir 1998) 144 F3d 1393, 1394.

An analogous inquiry needs to be made when dealing with a request to accompany an officer to the police station. *In re Gilbert R.* (1994) 25 CA4th 1121, 1125, 30 CR2d 676; see §3.23.

#### c. [§3.8] Who Is a Reasonable Person

The reasonable person test "presupposes an *innocent* person." *Florida v Bostick* (1991) 501 US 429, 438, 111 S Ct 2382, 115 L Ed 2d 389 (emphasis in original; court rejected argument that passenger carrying drugs in luggage would not consent to search).

The courts have not addressed the question of whether in the case of a minor, the standard is a reasonable minor or a reasonable adult. See, *e.g., California v Hodari D.* (1991) 499 US 621, 627, 111 S Ct 1547, 113 L Ed 2d 690; *In re James D.* (1987) 43 C3d 903, 913, 239 CR 663.

#### d. [§3.9] Objective Nature of Test

The *Mendenhall* test "is an objective one: not whether the citizen perceived that he was being ordered to restrict his movement, but whether the officer's words and actions would have conveyed that to a reasonable person." *California v Hodari D.* (1991) 499 US 621, 628, 111 S Ct 1547, 113 L Ed 2d 690.

The officer's subjective intention to detain is irrelevant except insofar as it is communicated to the defendant. *U.S. v Mendenhall* (1980) 446 US 544, 555, 100 S Ct 1870, 64 L Ed 2d 497. For example, in *In re Frank V.* (1991) 233 CA3d 1232, 1237, 285 CR 16, the officers intended to make a traffic stop, but the driver stopped before the officers signaled him to do so. The court held that no detention had taken place.

Before *Mendenhall* and Proposition 8, California courts had held that a detention occurs when an officer stops a person because of suspicion that he or she is involved in criminal activity. *People v Aldridge* (1984) 35 C3d 473, 477, 198 CR 538; *In re Tony C.* (1978) 21 C3d 888, 895, 148 CR 366. These cases no longer apply. *In re James D.* (1987) 43 C3d 903, 910, 239 CR 663.

### 3. Police-Pedestrian Contacts

#### a. In Airports

#### (1) [§3.10] In General

Cases that deal with questioning of persons in airports by drug enforcement agents are useful in showing the factors to which courts give particular attention. In these situations the agent's suspicions are aroused by observations that fall short of grounds for a detention, so that the validity of a subsequent search, often a consent search, depends on whether the initial contact was a detention or a consensual encounter.

### (2) [§3.11] Asking Person To Talk

No detention occurs if a police officer approaches a person in the airport and asks whether they might talk. *Florida v Rodriguez* (1984) 469 US 1, 5–6, 105 S Ct 308, 83 L Ed 2d 165 ("the initial contact between the officers and respondent, where they simply asked if he would step aside and talk with them, was clearly the sort of consensual encounter that implicates no Fourth Amendment interest"). Similarly, *Wilson v Superior Court* (1983) 34 C3d 777, 790, 195 CR 671, held that the officer did not detain the defendant "for federal constitutional purposes, merely by approaching him, identifying himself as a police officer, and asking if he might have a minute of his time." Asking for and examining a person's ticket is also permissible. *Florida v Royer* (1983) 460 US 491, 501, 103 S Ct 1319, 75 L Ed 2d 229; *U.S. v Mendenhall* (1980) 446 US 544, 555, 100 S Ct 1870, 64 L Ed 2d 497.

### (3) [§3.12] Advising Person of Freedom To Leave

The clearest case of consensual encounter is one in which the officer or drug enforcement agent explains to the civilian that he or she is free to leave. Thus, in *People v Profit* (1986) 183 CA3d 849, 878, 229 CR 148, the agent identified himself to the defendants, explained that he was conducting a narcotics investigation, and repeatedly advised them that if they did not want to talk to him, they were free to leave at any time. The court held that the contact was not a detention. The court stressed the explicit advice and also noted that there was not a threatening presence of several officers and that, while the agent looked at the airline tickets that defendants produced in response to a request for identification, the agent did not retain them. In accord is *People v Derello* (1989) 211 CA3d 414, 419, 259 CR 265.

Telling the persons contacted that they are free to leave is not mandatory (*U.S. v Mendenhall* (1980) 446 US 544, 558–559, 100 S Ct 1870, 64 L Ed 2d 497), although it "weighs heavily in favor of findings" that the contact was consensual (*People v Profit, supra,* 183 CA3d at 877). Courts sometimes note the absence of such advice as a factor in finding that the interaction was a detention. *Florida v Royer* (1983) 460 US 491, 503, 103 S Ct 1319, 75 L Ed 2d 229; *Wilson v Superior Court* (1983) 34 C3d 777, 791, 195 CR 671 (lack of such advice particularly significant once officer expresses suspicion); *U.S. v Guapi* (11th Cir 1998) 144 F3d 1393, 1395.

### (4) [§3.13] Transforming Encounter Into Detention

A consensual encounter often becomes a detention. In *Wilson,* the transformation occurred when the officer "advised Wilson that he was conducting a narcotics investigation and that he 'had received information that he [Wilson] would be arriving today from Florida carrying a *lot of drugs.*'" *Wilson v Superior Court* (1983) 34 C3d 777, 790, 195 CR 671 (emphasis in original). The court concluded that under those circumstances an ordinary citizen "would not feel at liberty simply to walk away from the officer." In *Florida v Royer* (1983) 460 US 491, 103 S Ct 1319, 75 L Ed 2d 229, the officers told Royer that he was suspected of transporting narcotics and asked him to accompany them to a room away from the public concourse, while retaining his ticket and driver's license. The court held that this was tantamount to an arrest and required probable cause. But see *People v Daugherty* (1996) 50 CA4th 275, 284–285, 57 CR2d 666 (officer's statement after initial contact that he interviews only narcotics suspects does not transform consensual encounter into detention).

#### (5) [§3.14] Other Circumstances

Reasonable persons might not feel free to leave even if not told that they are objects of suspicion. All circumstances of the encounter need to be considered. The greater the show of official authority, the more likely a person will feel that he or she cannot walk away. *U.S. v Mendenhall* (1980) 446 US 544, 100 S Ct 1870, 64 L Ed 2d 497, lists a number of significant factors that are important beyond the context of airport encounters. In *Mendenhall,* DEA agents approached the defendant in the airport's public concourse, identified themselves as federal agents, asked to see her identification and ticket, "and posed to her a few questions." The court said that "nothing in the record suggests that [she] had any objective reason to believe that she was not free to end the conversation . . . and proceed on her way." 446 US at 555.

*Mendenhall* stressed that the agents were not in uniform, did not display weapons, and did not summon the defendant but approached her and requested, rather than demanded, her identification and ticket. The court said "examples of circumstances" indicative of a detention "would be the threatening presence of several officers, the display of a weapon by an officer, some physical touching of the person of the citizen, or the use of language or tone of voice indicating that compliance with the officer's request might be compelled." 446 US at 554.

### b. [§3.15] On Streets

Cases involving police-civilian contacts on streets, in malls, and in parking lots often present difficult questions of whether the contact was a detention, whether it became a detention at some point and, if so, whether it was lawful.

The airport cases are helpful, particularly in articulating the factors to which they give weight. They are, however, not controlling because, "due in part to extensive antihijacking surveillance and equipment, reasonable privacy expectations are of significantly lesser magnitude" in airports than in other places. *Florida v Rodriguez* (1984) 469 US 1, 6, 105 S Ct 308, 83 L Ed 2d 165.

Sections 3.16–3.23 illustrate the approach of the courts.

#### (1) [§3.16] Casual Banter

In *People v Warren* (1984) 152 CA3d 991, 199 CR 864, an officer who was an avid fisherman and owned a fishing tackle store, saw the defendant walking down a seedy street at 10:50 p.m., clutching several fishing poles. The officer asked him, "How is fishing?" "Where do you fish?" "What kind of fish do you catch?" The court said that this was "typical banter between two anglers," and not a detention. The officer did not become suspicious until the defendant gave incredible answers that furnished grounds for detaining him. 152 CA3d at 996.

#### (2) [§3.17] Request for Identification and Explanation of Presence

Requesting civilians to provide identification or to explain their presence is not automatically a detention. *Brown v Texas* (1979) 443 US 47, 50, 99 S Ct 2637, 61 L Ed 2d 357. *U.S. v Mendenhall* (1980) 446 US 544, 556, 100 S Ct 1870, 64 L Ed 2d 497, summarizes *Brown*: "In that case, two police officers approached Brown in an alley, and asked him to identify himself and to explain his reason for being there. Brown refused. . . . *Up to this point there was no seizure.*" (Emphasis added.) The subsequent frisk and arrest of Brown, however, were illegal because his refusal did not create a valid basis for detaining or arresting him.

All circumstances surrounding the request need to be considered.

*No detention.* In the following situations, courts concluded that no detention occurred:

- A border patrol agent asked the defendant on a public street where he was born and whether he had any documents on him. The agent was part of a narcotics task force but questioned the defendant to determine his residence status. *People v Sanchez* (1987) 195 CA3d 42, 240 CR 413, held this to be a consensual encounter rather than a detention. "Not only was there nothing apparent in [the agent's] attitude or the nature of his inquiry to reflect compulsory compliance, but the incident occurred on a public street with no show of force or threats, express or implied." 195 CA3d at 47.

- An officer asked a person slumped over a park bench whether he was all right and to identify himself. *People v Clark* (1989) 212 CA3d 1233, 1237, 261 CR 181.
- An officer asked a man sitting on the hood of a car whether it was his car, why he was sitting there, and whether he had identification. *People v Lopez* (1989) 212 CA3d 289, 292, 260 CR 641.
- An officer asked a man sitting on a park bench whether he had identification, and the man handed him his driver's license. *People v Terrell* (1999) 69 CA4th 1246, 1254, 82 CR2d 231, held that the contact was a consensual encounter, stressing that the officer did not indicate, by words or conduct, that the defendant was not free to leave.
- An officer asked a woman who had been standing with others in front of an apartment complex to identify herself. She did and said she lived in one of the apartments. The officer then asked for confirming identification, requested that she walk toward him, which she did, talked to her for two or three minutes about posted "no trespassing" signs in the area, and asked her to take her hands out of her pockets. As she did so, she threw rock cocaine behind her. *People v Ross* (1990) 217 CA3d 879, 885, 265 CR 921, held that the entire encounter until the drug discarding was consensual, and was not at any time a detention.

☛ **Judicial Tip**: Some judges believe that in many circumstances a reasonable person would not feel free to walk away once an officer requests the opposite.

*Detention.* Courts found that a detention did take place in the following situations:

- Before asking pedestrians in a parking lot to identify themselves, an officer ordered them to put their packages on the ground and stand next to the police car. This exercise of authority is a clear restraint of freedom to walk away and hence makes the encounter a detention from the beginning. *People v Aldridge* (1984) 35 C3d 473, 477, 198 CR 538.
- Officers ordered youthful pedestrians to "stay there," patted them down, ordered them to sit on the curb, and photographed them. *People*

*v Rodriguez* (1993) 21 CA4th 232, 238, 26 CR2d 660. In accord is *People v Miles* (1987) 196 CA3d 612, 616, 242 CR 107 (detention occurred when officer told defendant to place his hands on his head and pat searched him).

- A person handed an identification card to the requesting officer. *People v Castaneda* (1995) 35 CA4th 1222, 1227, 42 CR2d 18, held that a person would not reasonably feel free to leave while the officer has the card and thus is detained rather than engaged in a consensual encounter.

#### (3) [§3.18] Request or Command

An important aspect of determining whether the police detained a civilian is whether they made a request or issued a command. The following are commands that make the contact a detention:

- "Hold it; police" or "Hold on; police." *People v Verin* (1990) 220 CA3d 551, 555, 269 CR 573.
- "Stop. Would you please stop," addressed to a pedestrian by an officer who drove his marked police car across traffic and stopped near the pedestrian. *People v Jones* (1991) 228 CA3d 519, 523, 279 CR 56.
- "Come down towards me. Step down off that landing." *People v Johnson* (1991) 231 CA3d 1, 10, 282 CR 114.
- "Come over here. I want to talk to you." *People v Roth* (1990) 219 CA3d 211, 213–215, 268 CR 66; see also §3.19.

In contrast, "Hey, can I talk to you?" is a request, not a command. *In re Manuel G.* (1997) 16 C4th 805, 811, 822, 66 CR2d 701 (court stressed that officer did not draw gun or stop minor from continuing what he was doing). So is "Hey, wait a minute, can we talk to you for a second?" *People v Garcia* (1981) 121 CA3d 239, 243, 246, 175 CR 296, disapproved on other grounds in 21 C4th 846, 866 n21.

The officer's tone of voice is often significant. See, *e.g., People v Bennett* (1998) 68 CA4th 396, 402, 80 CR2d 323 ("Can I talk to you for a moment?" in polite, conversational tone does not restrain pedestrian's liberty).

Not every order automatically transforms the contact into a detention. Telling a person to remove his hands from his pockets is not the same as a command to stay; both the nature and the manner of the order must be examined. *In re Frank V.* (1991) 233 CA3d 1232, 1239, 285 CR 16.

☛ **Judicial Tip**: In the view of some judges, the appropriate inquiry here is whether a person would reasonably feel free to disregard such an order, rather than whether he or she would feel free to depart. See *Florida v Bostick* (1991) 501 US 429, 436, 111 S Ct 2382, 115 L Ed 2d 389, discussed in §3.7.

#### (4) [§3.19] Officers in Patrol Vehicle

A pedestrian is not detained when officers in their vehicle merely follow him or her without attempting to talk to, stop, or block his or her course or activate a siren or flashing lights. Hence, items discarded by the pedestrian are not subject to exclusion as product of an unlawful detention. *Michigan v Chesternut* (1988) 486 US 567, 574, 108 S Ct 1975, 100 L Ed 2d 565.

More difficult circumstances were present in *People v Franklin* (1987) 192 CA3d 935, 939–940, 237 CR 840, a murder case. The officer pulled his patrol car directly behind a male pedestrian, shone his spotlight on him, radioed that he was making a pedestrian stop, and stopped his vehicle. The pedestrian approached the patrol car and repeatedly asked, "What's going on?" He appeared sweaty and jittery and the officer "asked" him to take his hands out of his pockets. The court held that this combination of circumstances was a consensual encounter. As to the effect of the officer's radio call, see also *In re Manuel G.* (1997) 16 C4th 805, 821–823, 66 CR2d 701; §3.9 (officer's subjective intent immaterial); as to telling persons to remove their hands from their pockets; see also §3.18.

Contrast *Franklin* with the following facts. Officers shine a spotlight on a male pedestrian, stop their patrol car, get out, and tell him that they want to talk to him. A person in this position would not feel free to walk away. *People v Roth* (1990) 219 CA3d 211, 213–215, 268 CR 66.

#### (5) [§3.20] Warrant Check

Running a warrant check on a pedestrian does not automatically convert a consensual encounter into a detention. *People v Bouser* (1994) 26 CA4th 1280, 1286–1287, 32 CR2d 163; see *People v Terrell* (1999) 69 CA4th 1246, 1251, 1254, 82 CR2d 231. The dissent in *Bouser* argued that few people would feel free to wander off before the warrant-checking process was completed. See *People v Bouser, supra,* 26 CA4th at 1289 (dissenting opinion).

#### (6) [§3.21] Observations During Officer's Approach

An officer may generally approach a person to talk to him or her without implicating the Fourth Amendment. See §3.5. Therefore, the officer's observations during the approach are lawful and may provide grounds for a detention or an arrest. For example, in *People v Rosales* (1989) 211 CA3d 325, 330, 259 CR 503, officers walked toward defendant to interview him. During their approach one of the officers identified himself, and defendant thrust his left hand into a pants pocket in which the officer had noticed a bulge. Walking toward defendant was not a detention. Therefore, the officers' observations of the defendant were lawful and gave the officers sufficient grounds to detain defendant.

Similarly, in *People v Divito* (1984) 152 CA3d 11, 14, 199 CR 278, as the officer walked toward the defendant, he noticed an odor of PCP emanating from the defendant's person. The officer stopped and searched the defendant and found PCP on him. The court held that the officer's initial approach was not a detention. Hence, the odor was lawfully smelled and provided a proper Fourth Amendment basis for detaining the defendant.

### (7) [§3.22] Foot Chase

A person who runs off at the approach of the police is not detained while being chased (*California v Hodari D.* (1991) 499 US 621, 625–626, 111 S Ct 1547, 113 L Ed 2d 690); a chase is not a seizure within the meaning of the Fourth Amendment (*County of Sacramento v Lewis* (1998) 523 US 833, 842–844, 118 S Ct 1708, 140 L Ed 2d 1043; *California v Hodari D., supra*).

In consequence, objects thrown or dropped by the defendant during the chase are admissible, regardless of whether the police had adequate grounds to detain him or her. *California v Hodari D., supra*; *People v Johnson* (1991) 231 CA3d 1, 11, 282 CR 114. In contrast, items discarded or thrown during an illegal detention are inadmissible. See, *e.g., U.S. v Davis* (10th Cir 1996) 94 F3d 1465, 1470.

For discussion of flight as a ground for detention, see §3.57.

### (8) [§3.23] Request To Accompany Officers to Police Station

Compliance with a request to accompany officers to the police station is a consensual encounter when a reasonable person in the particular circumstances would believe that he or she did not have to do so. *In re Gilbert R.* (1994) 25 CA4th 1121, 30 CR2d 676. Factors that affect the determination include whether the officers asked or ordered, and whether the request was accompanied by any threat, show of force, or physical restraint. 25 CA4th at 1125.

When a reasonable person would believe that he or she had to accompany the officers to the police station, the contact is an *arrest*, rather than a temporary detention. See §3.30.

### 4. Police Contacts With Persons in Vehicles

#### a. [§3.24] Drivers

When the police stop a car, a reasonable driver, almost by definition, would not feel free to leave until the officers had finished their business, nor would the driver be free to do so. Vehicle stops are, therefore, detentions of the driver. *Whren v U.S.* (1996) 517 US 806, 809–810, 116 S Ct 1769, 135 L Ed 2d 89; *Delaware v Prouse* (1979) 440 US 648, 653, 99 S Ct 1391, 59 L Ed 2d 660. Similarly, a bicyclist told to dismount is detained upon compliance (*People v Foranyic* (1998) 64 CA4th 186, 188, 74 CR2d 804), as is a driver at an inspection station who is ordered to pull over and park (*People v Valenzuela* (1994) 28 CA4th 817, 824, 33 CR2d 802).

A driver who pulls over voluntarily before the officer displays a gesture of authority, such as overhead lights or a siren, has not been detained. *In re Frank V.* (1991) 233 CA3d 1232, 1237–1238, 285 CR 16. Merely following a vehicle is not a detention. *People v Turner* (1994) 8 C4th 137, 180–181, 32 CR2d 762; *People v Rico* (1979) 97 CA3d 124, 130, 158 CR 573. Nor is a car chase; objects discarded during such a chase are deemed abandoned and admissible. *People v Green* (1994) 25 CA4th 1107, 1110, 30 CR2d 812; see §3.22.

#### b. Passengers

##### (1) [§3.25] Automatic Detention

In *Maryland v Wilson* (1997) 519 US 408, 117 S Ct 882, 137 L Ed 2d 41, the U.S. Supreme Court held that officers who make a traffic stop have the right to order passengers out of the vehicle, but did not decide whether the passengers had been detained. But the court said: "There is probable cause to believe that the driver has committed a minor vehicular offense, but there is no such reason to stop or detain the passenger." 519 US at 413. The court in *People v Cartwright* (1999) 72 CA4th 1362, 1369, 85 CR2d 788, viewed this as meaning that there is no automatic detention of the passenger. 72 CA4th at 1367. See also *People v Fisher* (1995) 38 CA4th 338, 344, 45 CR2d 57 (passenger not detained until asked to step out of car). But other courts have held that a traffic stop automatically constitutes a detention of passengers and that the lawfulness of the detention hinges initially on the lawfulness of the stop. See *People v Bell* (1996) 43 CA4th 754, 765, 51 CR2d 115 (passenger may therefore challenge legality of driver's detention); *People v Grant* (1990) 217 CA3d 1451, 1460, 266 CR 587.

### (2) [§3.26] Unlawful Detention

Often the issue before the court is not whether the passenger was automatically detained, but whether the conduct of the officer created an unlawful detention. For instance, asking a passenger for her license almost immediately after a DUI stop, without any prefatory remarks, is "pregnant with coercion"; a reasonable person would not feel free to refuse. *People v Spicer* (1984) 157 CA3d 213, 220, 203 CR 599. On the other hand, a request for identification that does not impart "any compulsion to comply" is not a detention. *People v Cartwright* (1999) 72 CA4th 1362, 1370, 85 CR2d 788; *People v Grant* (1990) 217 CA3d 1451, 1461, 266 CR 587. But once a person has handed identification papers to the officer, he or she would no longer reasonably feel free to leave. *People v Castaneda* (1995) 35 CA4th 1222, 1227, 42 CR2d 18.

The following acts also create a detention that requires justification:

- Ordering a passenger to remain in the car or to get back into it. *People v Castellon* (1999) 76 CA4th 1369, 1374, 91 CR2d 204; *People v Gonzalez* (1992) 7 CA4th 381, 383–384, 8 CR2d 640.

- Attempting to shine a flashlight into a passenger's eyes. *People v Lionberger* (1986) 185 CA3d Supp 1, 3–6, 230 CR 358.

- Directing a passenger to sit on the curb. *People v Cartwright, supra,* 72 CA4th at 1371.

Asking a passenger whether there is anything illegal in the vehicle or for consent to search is not ipso facto a detention; whether it is depends on whether the circumstances, particularly the officer's words and manner, indicate that compliance is required. *People v Cartwright, supra*; *People v Galindo* (1991) 229 CA3d 1529, 1535, 281 CR 155. Similarly, telling passengers to take their hands out of their pockets does not automatically create a detention or make a detention unlawful in the absence of justification. *In re Frank V.* (1991) 233 CA3d 1232, 1238, 285 CR 16; see §3.18.

### c. [§3.27] Parked Vehicles

Contacts with persons in parked vehicles, like police encounters with pedestrians, are not automatically detentions. The *Mendenhall* test applies: Would a reasonable person feel free to leave or refuse to respond? For instance, in *People v Harris* (1986) 184 CA3d 1319, 1321, 229 CR 400, the officer saw the defendant asleep or unconscious in a parked car. The officer woke him with difficulty and asked him to step out of the car to check on his well-being. He was unable to stand. The officer asked him whether he was on drugs. The defendant's affirmative answer led to his arrest and conviction of being under the influence of PCP.

The court said that asking the defendant to get out of the car was not a detention. "The only thing stopping appellant from leaving was his level of intoxication." 184 CA3d at 1322. The question to the defendant did not violate *Miranda* because he was not in custody.

Blocking a parked vehicle with a police car is a detention. *People v Wilkins* (1986) 186 CA3d 804, 809, 231 CR 1. So is aiming a squad car's emergency lights at a parked vehicle. *People v Bailey* (1985) 176 CA3d 402, 405, 222 CR 235. But see *People v Perez* (1989) 211 CA3d 1492, 1495–1496, 260 CR 172 (shining spotlight and high beam at parked vehicle without blocking it is not a detention). Once officers start writing a parking ticket, "*no one would have tried to walk away.*" *People v Castaneda* (1995) 35 CA4th 1222, 1227, 42 CR2d 18 (emphasis in original).

The officer's intention is irrelevant unless it is communicated to the defendant. See §3.6. Thus, in *People v Banks* (1990) 217 CA3d 1358, 1362, 266 CR 574, an officer received a radio transmission to stop defendant's car for a narcotics investigation. Defendant parked in the driveway of a motel; the officer stopped his unmarked car behind defendant; defendant got out of his car, saw the officer, and reentered the car. The officer ran toward defendant's car and saw him hand suspected contraband to a passenger. The court held no detention had occurred and that therefore, the officer's observations were lawful.

### 5. [§3.28] Factory Surveys

In *I.N.S. v Delgado* (1984) 466 US 210, 218, 104 S Ct 1758, 80 L Ed 2d 247, the court applied the *Mendenhall* test to the questioning of factory employees by immigration agents. Agents stationed themselves at exits, while others went through the workplace, asking employees about their citizenship and requesting aliens to produce identification documents. The court held that the employees had not been detained within the meaning of the Fourth Amendment. The court said that when people are at work, their freedom to move about is already restricted by their job obligations and that the questioning under the circumstances did not interfere with that limited freedom. The surveys were conducted pursuant to warrants or the employer's consent.

*Delgado* should be contrasted with *People v Shields* (1988) 205 CA3d 1065, 1072, 252 CR 849, in which the employer invited police to search common areas for drugs and to check whether any employee was under the influence of a drug. The court held that individual employees could not be detained and questioned without a particularized suspicion related to the specific employees. Information that some employees were suspected of being under the influence does not give rise to a right to detain every employee for investigation.

*Shields* distinguished *Delgado* on the grounds that (1) immigration agents have statutory authority to check for proper identification, and (2) federal cases have interpreted *Delgado* as permitting detentions of particular workers only on the basis of individualized suspicion. 205 CA3d at 1073.

☛ **Judicial Tip**: The initial inquiry in cases involving questioning of employees by the authorities should probably be whether a reasonable person would feel free to decline to answer. See §3.7.

### 6. [§3.29] Chart: Factors in Determining Whether Contact Was Consensual or a Detention

The following chart summarizes some of the factors courts regard as significant in characterizing the police-civilian encounter. The list is not exhaustive. It underscores the importance of considering all the circumstances of the police conduct.

| ***Indicative of Consensual Encounter*** | ***Indicative of Detention*** |
|---|---|
| Officer uses conversational tone of voice | Authoritative tone |
| Officer requests (but some "requests" are equivalent to demands) | Officer orders or demands |
| Absence of threats or drawn weapons | Use of threats or drawn weapons |
| Lack of physical restraints | Physical restraints are compelling indications of a detention or an arrest |
| Few officers | Many officers |
| Path not blocked | Path blocked |
| Officer promptly returns papers to the civilian | Officer holds papers |

| *Indicative of Consensual Encounter* | *Indicative of Detention* |
|---|---|
| Officer makes no accusations | Officers tells person he is suspected of a crime (accusations convert consensual encounter into detention) |
| Officer advises civilian that he need not talk with him (advice is not mandatory) | Absence of such advice |
| Officer explains reasons for encounter (explanation is not mandatory) | Lack of explanation |

### C. [§3.30] Temporary Detention Distinguished From More Serious Contacts

Three important consequences follow when a police-citizen encounter is or becomes more than a temporary detention (*Berkemer v McCarty* (1984) 468 US 420, 434–441, 104 S Ct 3138, 82 L Ed 2d 317; *People v Taylor* (1986) 178 CA3d 217, 226–230, 223 CR 638):

(1) The greater restraint of liberty is valid only if the police have probable cause to arrest.

(2) The existence of probable cause carries with it a broader right to search than the presence of facts that permit only a detention.

(3) *Miranda* requirements come into operation.

The line is crossed not only when the police formally arrest a person but also when the officers use "means that approach the conditions of arrest" (*Florida v Royer* (1983) 460 US 491, 499, 103 S Ct 1319, 75 L Ed 2d 229) or that are "comparable to an arrest" (*Wilson v Superior Court* (1983) 34 C3d 777, 784, 195 CR 671). See also *Hayes v Florida* (1985) 470 US 811, 815, 105 S Ct 1643, 84 L Ed 2d 705 (in the absence of probable cause to arrest, police cannot take suspect to police station for fingerprinting; court suggests that brief detention in the field for fingerprinting may be permissible); *Dunaway v New York* (1979) 442 US 200, 212, 99 S Ct 2248, 60 L Ed 2d 824 (police took suspect from home to police station and, without formally arresting him, questioned him for an hour; court held this was not a temporary detention); *Lozoya v Superior Court* (1987) 189 CA3d 1332, 1339, 235 CR 77. In *Dunaway* the court did not accept the officer's characterization of the encounter as a temporary detention. That principle also cuts another way, namely, when probable cause to arrest is in fact present, the search will be tested as one incident to an arrest, even if the officer believes he is only making a frisk pursuant to a *Terry* stop. *Peters v New York* (1968) 392 US 40, 68, 88 S Ct 1889, 20 L Ed 2d 917 (companion case to *Terry*); *People v Fay* (1986) 184 CA3d 882, 893, 229 CR 291; *People v Adams* (1985) 175 CA3d 855, 863–864, 221 CR 298. The converse is probably also true. When the police arrest a person without probable cause but with grounds to detain, the fruits of the search are admissible as long as the search or pat-down was one that was permissible in the case of a temporary detention. See *People v York* (1980) 108 CA3d 779, 785–786, 166 CR 717; *People v Baker* (1970) 12 CA3d 826, 841, 96 CR 760.

The officer's subjective, uncommunicated intent to arrest the defendant does not turn a valid temporary detention into an arrest. *U.S. v Hensley* (1985) 469 US 221, 228, 105 S Ct 675, 83 L Ed 2d 604. This rule parallels the principle that a consensual encounter is not transmuted into a detention by the officer's intent to detain the defendant. See §3.9. The underlying principle is that "[w]hether a Fourth Amendment violation has occurred 'turns on an objective assessment of the officer's actions . . .' and not on the officer's actual state of mind at the time the challenged action was taken." *Maryland v Macon* (1985) 472 US 463, 470–471, 105 S Ct 2778, 86 L Ed 2d 370; *Scott v U.S.* (1978) 436 US 128, 136, 98 S Ct 1717, 56 L Ed 2d 168; See *Whren v U.S.* (1996) 517 US 806, 813, 116 S Ct 1769, 135 L Ed 2d 89.

The question of when a temporary detention becomes an arrest or a situation tantamount to one is best discussed further in the context of the conditions for a valid detention. These conditions include, in addition to adequate grounds for the stop, the requirement that it be "limited in scope and duration." *Florida v Royer, supra,* 460 US at 500. The permissible scope and duration are related to the purpose of the stop. See, *e.g., Florida v Royer, supra* ("detention must be temporary and last no longer than necessary to effectuate the purpose of the stop"). The following sections discuss the proper grounds for detaining a person and the appropriate "scope and duration" of a temporary detention.

## IV. REQUIREMENTS FOR TEMPORARY DETENTIONS RELATED TO CRIME INVESTIGATIONS AND TRAFFIC VIOLATIONS

### A. Standard

#### 1. [§3.31] Objective Basis

To justify a temporary detention related to crime, "the detaining officers must have a particularized and objective basis for suspecting the particular person stopped of criminal activity." *U.S. v Cortez* (1981) 449 US 411, 417–418, 101 S Ct 690, 66 L Ed 2d 621. Applying *Cortez,* the court in *People v Souza* (1994) 9 C4th 224, 231, 36 CR2d 569, said:

> A detention is reasonable under the Fourth Amendment when the detaining officer can point to specific articulable facts that, considered in the light of the totality of the circumstances, provide some objective manifestation that the person detained may be involved in criminal activity.

In accord are *People v Avalos* (1996) 47 CA4th 1569, 1576, 55 CR2d 450 and *People v Fisher* (1995) 38 CA4th 338, 344, 45 CR2d 57. For a fuller statement, see *People v Conway* (1994) 25 CA4th 385, 388, 30 CR2d 533 ("the circumstances known or apparent to the officer must include specific and articulable facts which, viewed objectively, would cause a reasonable officer to suspect that (1) some activity relating to crime has taken place or is occurring or is about to occur, and (2) the person the officer intends to stop or detain is involved in that activity").

Such temporary detentions are sometimes called investigative or "*Terry* stops," after *Terry v Ohio* (1968) 392 US 1, 22, 88 S Ct 1868, 20 L Ed 2d 889, which upheld the detention of persons suspected of planning a robbery. See, *e.g.*, *Berkemer v McCarty* (1984) 468 US 420, 439, 104 S Ct 3138, 82 L Ed 2d 317. *Terry* created a limited exception to the general rule that all seizures of the person must be justified by probable cause to arrest for a crime. *Florida v Royer* (1983) 460 US 491, 498, 103 S Ct 1319, 75 L Ed 2d 229. Detentions other than *Terry* and traffic stops are discussed in §§3.85–3.94.

### 2. [§3.32] Totality of Circumstances

In assessing the reasonableness of a detention, "the totality of the circumstances—the whole picture—must be taken into account," including observations, information from police reports, "and consideration of the modes or patterns of operation of certain kinds of lawbreakers." *U.S. v Cortez* (1981) 449 US 411, 417–418, 101 S Ct 690, 66 L Ed 2d 621; *U.S. v Sokolow* (1989) 490 US 1, 8, 109 S Ct 1581, 104 L Ed 2d 1. The evidence must be viewed "as understood by those versed in the field of law enforcement." *U.S. v Cortez, supra,* 449 US at 418.

### 3. [§3.33] Level of Suspicion

The standard for a *Terry* stop has been called "reasonable suspicion" to contrast it with probable cause. *Alabama v White* (1990) 496 US 325,

330, 110 S Ct 2412, 110 L Ed 2d 301; *U.S. v Sokolow* (1989) 490 US 1, 7, 109 S Ct 1581, 104 L Ed 2d 1. Reasonable suspicion can be established with less information and less reliable information than that required to show probable cause. *Alabama v White, supra*; *People v Souza* (1994) 9 C4th 224, 230, 36 CR2d 569; *People v Johnson* (1991) 231 CA3d 1, 11, 282 CR 114. For further discussion, see §3.38. Detentions within the home require reasonable suspicion plus exigent circumstances. See §§3.40–3.41.

### 4. [§3.34] Objective Nature of Standard

The test for the propriety of a temporary detention is objective; it does not matter whether the police actually suspected the defendant of criminal activity as long as they had reasonable grounds for such a suspicion. *People v Lloyd* (1992) 4 CA4th 724, 733, 6 CR2d 105 (officer detained defendant as possible witness; detention upheld because of objective factual basis for suspecting defendant of burglary); *People v Uribe* (1993) 12 CA4th 1432, 1438, 16 CR2d 127; see *Whren v U.S.* (1996) 517 US 806, 811–813, 116 S Ct 1769, 135 L Ed 2d 89 (traffic stop as pretext for drug investigation lawful when officer observed traffic violation; for discussion, see §1.43); *Scott v U.S.* (1978) 436 US 128, 138, 98 S Ct 1717, 56 L Ed 2d 168 (claimed Fourth Amendment violations are tested by objective evaluation of police actions). But see *In re James D.* (1987) 43 C3d 903, 914, 239 CR 663.

Before Proposition 8, the officer had to subjectively entertain the suspicion in addition to its objective reasonableness. *In re Tony C.* (1978) 21 C3d 888, 893, 148 CR 366. While dictum in *In re James D., supra,* follows this aspect of *Tony C.*, later decisions recognize that the subjective element is inconsistent with U.S. Supreme Court decisions. *People v Lloyd, supra*; *People v Uribe, supra.* The objective test decisions in all likelihood supersede earlier decisions that an officer's inadequate statement of reasons for the detention invalidate it, despite facts known to the officer showing a sound basis for the stop. See *People v Bower* (1979) 24 C3d 638, 647, 156 CR 856; *People v Ferguson* (1981) 126 CA3d Supp 22, 26–31, 179 CR 437. *People v Lloyd, supra,* exemplifies the present state of the law on this point.

### 5. [§3.35] Availability of Less Intrusive Means

The ability of the police to verify or dispel their suspicion by means less intrusive than a temporary detention is not germane. *U.S. v Sokolow* (1989) 490 US 1, 11, 109 S Ct 1581, 104 L Ed 2d 1 (reasonableness of decision to stop suspect does not turn on availability of less intrusive investigatory techniques). That availability is, however, often important in determining whether a detention lasted too long. See *U.S. v Sokolow, supra*; for further discussion, see §3.71.

## B. Issues Concerning Application of Standard

### 1. [§3.36] Conduct Equally Consistent With Innocent Activity

Circumstances consistent with lawful activity do not render a detention invalid, when the circumstances, in their totality, also raise a reasonable suspicion of criminal activity. *U.S. v Sokolow* (1989) 490 US 1, 9–10, 109 S Ct 1581, 104 L Ed 2d 1; *People v Conway* (1994) 25 CA4th 385, 390, 30 CR2d 533; *People v Dolliver* (1986) 181 CA3d 49, 56, 225 CR 920. Earlier dictum to the contrary in *Irwin v Superior Court* (1969) 1 C3d 423, 427, 82 CR 484, was disapproved in *In re Tony C.* (1978) 21 C3d 888, 894, 148 CR 366.

### 2. [§3.37] Training and Experience of Officer

Officers necessarily base their judgments and decisions on their experience and skills. The training, experience, and expertise of the officer making the stop are appropriate factors in evaluating the grounds for a detention. *U.S. v Cortez* (1981) 449 US 411, 418, 101 S Ct 690, 66 L Ed 2d 621; *In re Tony C.* (1978) 21 C3d 888, 893, 148 CR 366. See, *e.g., People v Brown* (1985) 169 CA3d 159, 163–165, 215 CR 101 (in officer's experience, no one had ever reacted to seeing him in the manner that the defendant did); *People v Perez* (1985) 175 CA3d Supp 8, 11, 221 CR 776 (training and experience justified officer in stopping driver who weaved within traffic lane).

Consideration of these matters does not undermine the objective nature of the standard; it is for the courts to determine what inferences and conclusions the officer could reasonably draw from the articulated facts in light of his experience. *Terry v Ohio* (1968) 392 US 1, 27, 88 S Ct 1868, 20 L Ed 2d 889.

### 3. Sources of Information

#### a. [§3.38] Informants

Information that would not justify an arrest often suffices for an investigative stop. *Alabama v White* (1990) 496 US 325, 330, 110 S Ct 2412, 110 L Ed 2d 301; *Adams v Williams* (1972) 407 US 143, 147, 92 S Ct 1921, 32 L Ed 2d 612; *People v Johnson* (1991) 231 CA3d 1, 11, 282 CR 114; *People v Lissauer* (1985) 169 CA3d 413, 422, 215 CR

335. The reliability of the information, however, remains a relevant issue. A tip from an anonymous informer is usually inherently unreliable and normally requires some corroboration. *Alabama v White, supra*; *People v Johnson, supra.* But an unverified tip from a known informant may carry enough "indicia of reliability" to justify an investigative stop. *Adams v Williams, supra*; *People v Avalos* (1996) 47 CA4th 1569, 1577, 55 CR2d 450. The appropriate inquiry is whether, based on the information, a reasonable police officer would suspect "that a particular person is engaged or has engaged in criminal conduct. . . ." *People v Superior Court* (McBride) (1981) 122 CA3d 156, 164, 175 CR 723.

An accurate description of the subject's appearance and location does not make an anonymous tip reliable; the reasonable suspicion necessary for a detention "requires that a tip be reliable in its assertion of illegality, not just in its tendency to identify a determinate person." *Florida v J.L.* (2000) 529 US 266, 272, 120 S Ct 1375, 146 L Ed 2d 254. There is no exception to this requirement for tips alleging unlawful possession of firearms. *Florida v J.L., supra.*

*Florida v J.L., supra*, and *People v Coulombe* (2000) 86 CA4th 52, 102 CR 798, both involve tips that a suspect matching defendant's description and at a specified location had a gun. In *Florida v J.L.*, the tip came in the form of an anonymous telephone call and the court held it was not sufficiently reliable to support a detention. 529 US at 268–269. In *Coulombe*, the tips came from two persons who independently approached the police officers and provided the information face-to-face. 86 CA4th at 54–55. The court held that the tips were sufficiently reliable to support the defendant's detention. 86 CA4th at 59.

### b. [§3.39] Police Reports; Information and Requests From Other Officers

Police reports often serve as a basis for a temporary detention. But failure to recall them reasonably accurately at the time of making the stop and at the suppression hearing may leave insufficient facts "to support an objectively reasonable suspicion," especially when the inaccurate recollection goes to description of suspects. *Williams v Superior Court* (1985) 168 CA3d 349, 360, 213 CR 919; but see *People v Fields* (1984) 159 CA3d 555, 563, 205 CR 888 (detaining officer got clothing description via police radio; officer who took initial report could not recall what clothing description victim gave, nor could victim, but failure to recall cured by testimony of communications officer who took and remembered initial report, including the clothing description).

When a detention rests on information from or a request by another officer, the prosecution must corroborate the information. *In re Eskiel S.* (1993) 15 CA4th 1638, 1644, 19 CR2d 455 (radio message); *People v Johnson* (1987) 189 CA3d 1315, 1319, 235 CR 62. The originating officer should be produced unless other evidence negates the risk of "do-it-yourself" cause to detain. *People v Lazanis* (1989) 209 CA3d 49, 59, 257 CR 180 (officer's broadcast adequately corroborated by police department record of burglary report by citizen moments before broadcast); *People v Johnson, supra.*

☛ **Judicial Tip**: Judges should not assume that corroboration will always validate a stop. For example, a detention based on an inadequate description is invalid and "no amount of corroboration" makes it otherwise. *In re Eskiel S., supra,* 15 CA4th at 1644. For discussion of description, see §§3.42–3.47.

### 4. Detentions Within the Home

#### a. [§3.40] General Principles

The police can seek interviews with persons at their homes, but a demand to open the door turns the interview into a detention. *People v Poole* (1986) 182 CA3d 1004, 1012, 227 CR 594. Detentions within the home are unlawful in the absence of exigent circumstances. *People v Poole, supra*; *People v Williams* (1979) 93 CA3d 40, 57, 155 CR 414; *People v Mendoza* (1979) 87 CA3d 1008, 1012, 151 CR 489. This is an application of the *Ramey* rule, which prohibits warrantless arrests in the home barring emergencies. *People v Ramey* (1976) 16 C3d 263, 275, 127 CR 629.

A detention on a private driveway is permitted. *In re Gregory S.* (1980) 112 CA3d 764, 774, 169 CR 540. In *People v Gee* (1982) 130 CA3d 174, 181 CR 524, officers knocked on a suspect's door and he came out to talk to them; the detention was upheld. Conversely, a person subject to detention who runs into his house can be ordered to come out. *People v Superior Court* (Bowden) (1976) 65 CA3d 511, 520, 135 CR 306.

#### b. [§3.41] Detentions Related to Search Warrants

A temporary detention within the home while the police seek a search warrant is lawful only when the entry is justified by exigent circumstances and probable cause to search. See *People v Gentry* (1992) 7 CA4th 1255, 1261, 9 CR2d 742. A detention for such a purpose that is not limited in scope and duration amounts to an arrest. 7 CA4th at 1266 (three-and-one-half hour detention of handcuffed occupants is a de facto arrest).

During the execution of a search warrant, persons on the premises may be detained because the warrant makes the occupants "sufficiently suspect" to justify the detention. *Florida v Royer* (1983) 460 US 491, 499, 103 S Ct 1319, 75 L Ed 2d 229; *Michigan v Summers* (1981) 452 US 692, 703, 101 S Ct 2587, 69 L Ed 2d 340. For further discussion, see §2.110.

### 5. Descriptions of Suspects and Vehicles

#### a. Guidelines

##### (1) [§3.42] Description Not Always Necessary

A person who is the only one in view at the scene of a crime that has just been reported may be detained without a description of the suspect. *People v Castaneda* (1995) 35 CA4th 1222, 1229, 42 CR2d 18 (prowler call; defendant sitting in parked car close to source of call; defendant and his passenger were the only visible persons in the area); *People v Conway* (1994) 25 CA4th 385, 389–390, 30 CR2d 533 (burglary-in-progress report; car leaving burglary location two minutes after report at 3 a.m.; officer saw no one else in area). Under circumstances that fall short of a detention, no description is needed to question a person. *People v Juarez* (1973) 35 CA3d 631, 635, 110 CR 865. See also *People v Blackmon* (1969) 276 CA2d 346, 348, 80 CR 862.

##### (2) [§3.43] Descriptions Sufficient for Selective Investigation

Detentions may be made on more general descriptions than arrests. *People v Harris* (1975) 15 C3d 384, 389, 124 CR 536; *People v Mickelson* (1963) 59 C2d 448, 454, 30 CR 18. When courts ask whether a description is "sufficiently unique" or whether the match between description and actuality is close enough, "the description cannot be considered in a vacuum. The ultimate question is whether the description affords a sufficient basis for 'selective investigation procedures,' vis-a-vis a universe made up of all persons within fleeing distance of the crime in question." *People v Fields* (1984) 159 CA3d 555, 565, 205 CR 888. The phrase "selective investigation procedures" in *Fields* comes from *People v Flores* (1974) 12 C3d 85, 92, 115 CR 225, which contrasted such procedures with a "dragnet approach."

##### (3) [§3.44] Time and Place of Detention in Relation to Crime

When the detention occurs close to the crime in time and place, courts are inclined to uphold broad descriptions and imperfect matches. Stops within a few minutes of a crime report have been sustained on descriptions of "two armed Black men wearing dark clothing with hoods" (*People v Overten* (1994) 28 CA4th 1497, 1504, 34 CR2d 232 (no vehicle description; car stopped five to seven minutes from robbery location; passengers' heads popping up and ducking out of sight while car in motion)) and a "light brown" vehicle, "possibly a Chevrolet." (*People v Rico* (1979) 97 CA3d 124, 128, 158 CR 573 (car stopped by the police was a black-on-gold Cadillac; vehicle stopped moments after report of shooting)). For further illustrations, see chart in §3.46.

Some descriptions are too general even for a detention in the immediate aftermath of the reported incident and near its location. *In re Eskiel S.* (1993) 15 CA4th 1638, 1641, 1644, 19 CR2d 455 (10 to 12 Black persons fighting, then reported leaving, specified park). See chart in §3.47.

Courts are more concerned with the adequacy of descriptions and matches when the time lapse is longer. In *Williams v Superior Court* (1985) 168 CA3d 349, 360, 213 CR 919, the officer had heard a robbery report the previous night. It described the suspects as two Black males, mid-twenties, medium-to-above-average in height and weight, one man fully bearded, driving a yellow, newer, larger sedan. The car the officer stopped was white, neither occupant had a beard, and one looked more like 45 years old. The court held that the detention was unreasonable as a matter of law. See also *People v Collins* (1970) 1 C3d 658, 660, 83 CR 179, in which a grand theft auto had occurred several days earlier. The suspect was described as a male Negro, 6 feet tall, weighing 160 pounds. The court expressed "grave doubts" as to the lawfulness of a detention based on this general description, but decided the case on other grounds. Contrast *People v Atmore* (1970) 13 CA3d 244, 246, 91 CR 311, distinguishing *Collins* and upholding a detention upon a broad description primarily on the ground that the offense giving rise to the stop had just been committed.

A description of a highly unusual car justifies a stop several days after the offense, even though the description is not entirely accurate. *People v Flores* (1974) 12 C3d 85, 92, 115 CR 225 (stop four days after offense permitted on description of vintage car used by suspect).

### (4) [§3.45] Broad Descriptions Adequate in Context

A general description, such as race, gender, and approximate age, suffices when it refers to a suspect who is detained in the company of other, more adequately described persons. *In re Lynette G.* (1976) 54 CA3d 1087, 1092, 126 CR 898; *People v Craig* (1978) 86 CA3d 905, 912 n1, 150 CR 676. Similarly, a very broad description is adequate in conjunction with a detailed vehicle description. See *People v Ramirez* (1996) 41 CA4th 1608, 1611, 1619, 49 CR2d 311 (three Hispanic males in two-color Buick with specified California license plate number); *In re Dung T.* (1984) 160 CA3d 697, 713, 206 CR 772 (home invasion robbery; witness had previously identified vehicle in which suspects were detained; only description of persons was young Vietnamese males; detention proper but not arrest). See also *People v Gonzales* (1998) 64 CA4th 432, 438–439, 75 CR2d 272 (accurate description of car used in robbery; persons described as Black male and Hispanic male; detention nine days after crime valid, but may not continue detention of passenger after officer identified another occupant as registered owner of vehicle).

### b. [§3.46] Chart: Illustrative Cases Finding Descriptions Adequate

| ***Case*** | ***Crime Reported*** | ***Description*** | ***Time and Place of Stop in Relation to Crime*** | ***Match*** | ***Other Factors Mentioned by Court*** |
|---|---|---|---|---|---|
| *People v Ramirez* (1996) 41 CA4th 1608, 49 CR2d 311 | "Narcotics activity" | 3 Hispanic males in 2-door blue Buick, license 1MBK445, at specified location | 5 minutes after dispatch; at reported location | Exact | Narcotics-dealing area |
| *People v Overten* (1994) 28 CA4th 1497, 34 CR2d 232 | 211 | 2 Black men wearing dark clothing with hoods; no vehicle description | 5–7 minutes from crime scene | Racial match; front passenger wore dark jacket, with a possible hood | Passengers' heads popped up and ducked out of sight |
| *People v Fields* (1984) 159 CA3d 555, 205 CR 888 | 261 | Slender thin young Black male possibly wearing jogging clothes | 6 hours, one-to-one-and-a-half blocks | Black male wearing jogging pants and light blue jacket | Seriousness of crime, time of stop (7:00 a.m.). Suspect could have been hiding until daylight and then tried to look normal in his running clothes; minimal intrusion |

| ***Case*** | ***Crime Reported*** | ***Description*** | ***Time and Place of Stop in Relation to Crime*** | ***Match*** | ***Other Factors Mentioned by Court*** |
|---|---|---|---|---|---|
| *People v McCluskey* (1981) 125 CA3d 220, 178 CR 7 | 211 | Chicano, 19–21, 5'10", brown hair with center part, mustache, blue jacket | 5 minutes, 2–3 blocks | Male Mexican, 20, dark hair, dark jacket (passenger in moving vehicle at night) | Vehicle traveling in direction consistent with involvement in the robbery |
| *People v Craig* (1978) 86 CA3d 905, 150 CR 676 | 211 | 3 suspects: (1) Black male, small Afro, 5'9", medium build, blue jeans; (2) Black male, medium, Afro, yellow beanie-type hat with "Cheerios" on the back, torn shirt; (3) Black male, small Afro | Not stated; victims had followed robbers into apartment complex; detention at exit from complex | 3 Black male suspects, 1 with pink curlers in his hair. No "Cheerios" beanie, no torn shirt | |
| *People v Huff* (1978) 83 CA3d 549, 147 CR 316 | 211 | 2 Black males in their early 20s driving an older model blue pickup | 3 minutes, 13 blocks | Older model blue pickup with 2 Black male occupants | |

| *Case* | *Crime Reported* | *Description* | *Time and Place of Stop in Relation to Crime* | *Match* | *Other Factors Mentioned by Court* |
|---|---|---|---|---|---|
| *People v Natale* (1978) 77 CA3d 568, 143 CR 629 | Residential 459 | White male adult, 6'3", 180 lbs., black, shoulder-length hair, black mustache (seen walking "in the direction of " victim's house and seen driving one-half mile away) | "A couple of hours later . . . in a nearby community" | Good | Victim named defendant; officer knew him; defendant was only person seen in area at time of burglary; officer knew that defendant was a parolee |
| *People v Harris* (1975) 15 C3d 384, 124 CR 536 | Residential 459 | Male Caucasian, dark hair, mustache, about 5'8" and 150 lbs., light cardigan, dark trousers | 30 minutes, 3 blocks | Physical appearance and clothing "approximated the description" | Presence in residential area at 11:00 p.m. |
| *People v Flores* (1974) 12 C3d 85, 115 CR 225 | Residential 459 | 2 Mexican-Americans, dark clothing, wide-brimmed hats, 5'8" to 5'9", 160–165 lbs., driving a GMC 1940s sedan | 4 days, 2 miles | 4 Hispanic males in 1947 Pontiac; defendant driver "wore a wide-brimmed hat and fit the general description of the suspects" | "Uniqueness" of the described vehicle; officer concentrated on looking for it |

| ***Case*** | ***Crime Reported*** | ***Description*** | ***Time and Place of Stop in Relation to Crime*** | ***Match*** | ***Other Factors Mentioned by Court*** |
|---|---|---|---|---|---|
| *People v Watson* (1970) 12 CA3d 130, 90 CR 483 | 211 | Black male and female, riding in a yellow 1958 or 1959 Cadillac, bearing partial license number "OCX"; female: 5'3," black dress | 24 hours, distance not stated (same city) | Parked yellow 1959 Cadillac, license number XQC335; 3 Black males in vehicle, one talking to a Black woman on curb | |

### c. [§3.47] Chart: Illustrative Cases Finding Descriptions Inadequate

| *Case* | *Crime Reported* | *Description* | *Time and Place of Stope in Relation to Crime* | *Match* | *Other Factors Mentioned by Court* |
|---|---|---|---|---|---|
| *In re Eskiel S.* (1993) 15 CA4th 1638, 19 CR2d 455 | Gang fight | 10–12 Black persons on foot in specified park | Apparently soon after broadcast; area of park | Not discussed | Description by race and general area insufficient |
| *Williams v Superior Court* (1985) 168 CA3d 349, 213 CR 919 | 211 | 2 Black males, mid-20s, medium to above average height, one fully bearded, driving yellow, newer, larger sedan | 1 day; same general area | White car; neither occupant bearded; one looked 45 | Court stressed lack of match |
| *People v Collins* (1970) 1 C3d 658, 83 CR 179 (dictum) | Auto theft | Male Negro, 6', 160 lbs. | Several days; within one block of theft; defendant on foot | Generally matched | Description failed to distinguish defendant from substantial portion of people in area. (*Comment*: The description would not have mattered if defendant had been stopped in or near the stolen car. See §3.44.) |

## 6. "Fit" and Group Characteristics

### a. [§3.48] Ethnicity; Gang Membership

A detention is improper when its sole basis is that the detainee does not ethnically "fit" into the area or for other reasons primarily related to ethnicity or identification with a suspect group. *U.S. v Brignoni-Ponce* (1975) 422 US 873, 885, 95 S Ct 2574, 45 L Ed 2d 607 (vehicle may not be stopped to enforce immigration laws near Mexican border for sole reasons that occupants look Hispanic; court noted that many Hispanics live near border and that most are law abiding); *People v Bower* (1979) 24 C3d 638, 644, 156 CR 856 (Caucasian in predominantly African-American neighborhood may not be detained on that ground even at night); *People v Rodriguez* (1993) 21 CA4th 232, 238–240, 26 CR2d 660 (suspected gang members who are talking to each other may not be detained merely because the police want to identify and photograph them).

Ethnicity or other group characteristics, such as gang membership or youthful appearance, can be considered in conjunction with other pertinent information. See discussion in *People v McCluskey* (1981) 125 CA3d 220, 227, 178 CR 7 (recent crime; race properly part of suspect's description); *In re Hector R.* (1984) 152 CA3d 1146, 1153, 200 CR 110 (officer knew that person stopped was juvenile gang member; this, together with facts such as suspected curfew violation, provided grounds for detention); *In re James D.* (1987) 43 C3d 903, 916, 239 CR 663 (youthful appearance of pedestrian during school hours justifies stop to investigate possible truancy). But see *U.S. v Montero-Camargo* (9th Cir 2000) 208 F3d 1122, 1131–1135 (unless Hispanic appearance is part of a description given to police, it is generally of so little probative value that it may not be considered as a relevant factor where particularized or individualized suspicion is required).

### b. [§3.49] Drug Courier Profile

Drug enforcement agents at airports may properly detain persons whose behavior is consistent with a DEA drug courier profile. *U.S. v Sokolow* (1989) 490 US 1, 10, 109 S Ct 1581, 104 L Ed 2d 1. *Sokolow* holds that, as with any temporary detention, the agents must articulate the factors giving rise to reasonable suspicion; the fact that these factors are contained in a profile does not diminish their significance as seen by a trained agent. 490 US at 7–10.

☛ **Judicial Tip**: Stops that reflect targeting of particular groups or vehicles may need careful scrutiny to prevent police abuses. See, *e.g.*, *U.S. v Hill* (6th Cir 1999) 195 F3d 258, 267 (officer made practice of stopping U-Hauls; court noted that they tend to be used by young and poor people and targeting such vehicles is especially distasteful; court upheld particular stop after extensive scrutiny); *U.S. v Montero-Camargo* (9th Cir 2000) 208 F3d 1122, 1135 (classifications based on race carry danger of stigmatic harm; anomalous to consider race as factor when it harms people, but not when it helps them; court upheld stop by finding it based on adequate grounds other than defendants' Hispanic appearance).

### 7. [§3.50] Effect of Mistakes

A mistake as to what offense was committed is not fatal as long as the true situation permits a *Terry* stop. *People v Smith* (1984) 151 CA3d 89, 98, 198 CR 623; *Ojeda v Superior Court* (1970) 12 CA3d 909, 919, 91 CR 145. Thus, an officer's factual mistake does not necessarily destroy the lawfulness of the detention; the question remains what a reasonable police officer would have done under the same circumstances. See, *e.g., People v Superior Court* (McBride) (1981) 122 CA3d 156, 162, 175 CR 723 (officer erroneously thought person stopped was murder suspect; detention upheld in light of information officer had). The mistake is more likely to be considered unreasonable when it stems from the officer's misrecollection of information. *Williams v Superior Court* (1985) 168 CA3d 349, 360, 213 CR 919. For further discussion, see §1.41.

### 8. [§3.51] Burden of Proof

As with all warrantless searches and seizures, the prosecution has the burden of proving the validity of a temporary detention; proof is by a preponderance of the evidence. Evid C §115; *People v Bower* (1979) 24 C3d 638, 644, 156 CR 856; *People v Wilkins* (1986) 186 CA3d 804, 809, 231 CR 1.

### 9. [§3.52] Reasonable Suspicion as a Question of Law

Reasonableness issues under the Fourth Amendment are generally questions of law. This is also true as to questions whether particular circumstances give rise to a reasonable suspicion of defendant's involvement in criminal activity; reviewing courts must therefore independently determine such questions. *People v Leyba* (1981) 29 C3d 591, 597, 174 CR 867; *People v Jackson* (1990) 218 CA3d 1493, 1501, 267 CR 841; *People v Shandloff* (1985) 170 CA3d 372, 380, 215 CR 916. See *Ornelas v U.S.* (1996) 517 US 690, 699, 116 S Ct 1657, 134 L Ed 2d 911 (federal courts' review of determinations of reasonable suspicion and probable cause is *de novo*; findings of fact are reviewed only for clear error).

## C. Illustrative Situations

### 1. [§3.53] Reasonable Suspicion and Past Conduct

Initially the U.S. Supreme Court permitted stops of persons reasonably suspected of planning to commit a crime. *Terry v Ohio* (1968) 392 US 1, 22, 88 S Ct 1868, 20 L Ed 2d 889. *U.S. v Hensley* (1985) 469 US 221, 234, 105 S Ct 675, 83 L Ed 2d 604, extended *Terry* to the temporary detention of persons reasonably suspected of having committed a crime.

*Hensley* applied a balancing test widely used to measure reasonableness under the Fourth Amendment, weighing "the nature and quality of the intrusion on personal security against the importance of the governmental interests alleged to justify the intrusion." 469 US at 228. The court noted that when past rather than ongoing conduct is involved, the crime prevention factor stressed in *Terry* is weaker, immediate police intervention may not be as necessary, public safety may be less threatened, and the officer may have other alternatives. Nevertheless, the court held that the high public interest in promptly solving serious crimes outweighs the individual's interest in not being stopped. 469 US at 228–229.

The court in *Hensley* limited its decision to felonies and crimes involving public safety, leaving the question open as to less serious offenses. California courts have upheld stops based on suspicion that the detainee committed a minor offense. *People v Williams* (1995) 33 CA4th 467, 477, 39 CR2d 358 (failure to appear on expired registration charge); *People v DeCosse* (1986) 183 CA3d 404, 409–411, 228 CR 114 (littering).

### 2. [§3.54] Persons Carrying Objects

The detention of persons carrying objects is usually lawful when an officer's observations are closely coupled with information about a recent crime. Thus, in *People v Dolliver* (1986) 181 CA3d 49, 54–56, 225 CR 920, the officer knew that a silent alarm at a jewelry store had gone off. He telephoned the store and was told that the owner was in the bathroom. In the officer's experience, if a silent alarm is false, the owner tells the police, and difficulty in establishing contact with the owner is indicative of a robbery in progress. The officer went to the location and saw defendants 10 or 15 feet from the store, hurriedly walking away from it. One defendant carried a large bag over his shoulder. In the officer's experience, jewelry store robbers often use a bag to carry the stolen goods. There was no other foot traffic. The court upheld the defendants' detention.

The information may be about suspicious conduct rather than a crime. In *People v Vasquez* (1983) 138 CA3d 995, 998–1000, 188 CR 417, a citizen phoned the police to report that he saw two men, one standing on the sidewalk, the other on the walkway of the building next door, inside a padlocked gate. When they realized they were being watched they left. Neither was carrying anything at the time. Twenty minutes later, and before the men had been detained, the citizen pointed them out to the police a block away. They were now carrying pillowcases apparently containing bulky items. They told the officer they had found them.

*Vasquez* upheld the detention. The court also ruled that the warrantless search of the pillowcases was proper because defendants manifested no expectation of privacy. Further, the contents (a fan, cassette recorder, clock radio, and binoculars) provided probable cause to arrest even though the officers were unaware of a specific burglary from which these items might have come. 138 CA3d at 1000.

Mere observation of a person carrying an object without a prior report can justify a detention. In *People v Garcia* (1981) 121 CA3d 239, 245, 175 CR 296, disapproved on other grounds in 21 C4th 846, 866 n21, the officers saw two persons loading a TV set into a car trunk, at 7:00 p.m., in a commercial area that had no TV rental or repair shops but many burglaries. The men looked shocked when they saw the officers, walked away, and ignored requests to stop. The court held that the initial observation, given the time and area, justified the detention, and that the suspects' hurried departure was an additional relevant factor.

Observing a person "carrying a television set down the street at 8:30 p.m. in a high burglary neighborhood" suffices for a detention. *People v Myles* (1975) 50 CA3d 423, 430, 123 CR 348. In accord is *People v West* (1956) 144 CA2d 214, 217, 300 P2d 729 (detention proper when officer at 9:20 p.m. in high burglary area saw defendant carrying large bundle of clothes carelessly wadded together).

The context of the observation, however, is important. Thus, an officer may not detain a man who is walking down the street on a summer day without shirt or shoes, carrying a 35mm camera, a duffel bag, and a grocery bag, and looking nervously over his shoulder. *People v Raybourn* (1990) 218 CA3d 308, 310–312, 266 CR 884.

A pedestrian's mere presence at a location, even late at night, usually does not justify a detention. See, *e.g., People v Roth* (1990) 219 CA3d 211, 215, 268 CR 66 (person who walks across parking lot of shopping center at 1:20 a.m. when center's stores were closed may not be detained). But a person standing, at 3 a.m., astride a bicycle to which a large axe is attached may be detained. *People v Foranyic* (1998) 64 CA4th 186, 189, 74 CR2d 804.

### 3. [§3.55] Observation of Exchanges

A pedestrian who merely receives money from another person in an area known for drug activity may not be detained. *People v Jones* (1991) 228 CA3d 519, 524, 279 CR 56. The result is different, however, when, before or after the exchange, the defendant walked to an apparent hiding place and reached into it. *People v Limon* (1993) 17 CA4th 524, 533, 21 CR2d 397.

An exchange of unidentified objects by pedestrians in a high narcotics area at night warrants detention. *Santos v Superior Court* (1984) 154 CA3d 1178, 1184, 202 CR 6. *Santos* said that a contrary dictum in *Cunha v Superior Court* (1970) 2 C3d 352, 356, 85 CR 160, is not binding. Similarly, the police may detain a person who leans into a car and exchanges objects with the occupants in an area where pedestrians often sell drugs to buyers in vehicles. *People v McGriff* (1990) 217 CA3d 1140, 1144, 266 CR 429.

Two men dividing coins on a park bench in broad daylight do not arouse a reasonable suspicion that their activity is related to crime. *People v Henze* (1967) 253 CA2d 986, 989–990, 61 CR 545. The court noted that little more would be needed to justify the detention, such as a recent burglary report or the known use of the park for narcotics transactions. 253 CA2d at 990.

### 4. [§3.56] Presence in High Crime Area

An individual's presence in a high crime area or one of expected criminal activity, standing alone, is not enough to justify a detention. *Illinois v Wardlow* (2000) 528 US 119, 124, 120 S Ct 673, 145 L Ed 2d 570; *Brown v Texas* (1979) 443 US 47, 52, 99 S Ct 2637, 61 L Ed 2d 357; *People v Verin* (1990) 220 CA3d 551, 558, 269 CR 573.

Such presence, however, combined with other observations, may give rise to a reasonable suspicion of criminal activity. *Illinois v Wardlow, supra*; *People v Souza* (1994) 9 C4th 224, 240, 36 CR2d 569. See cases discussed in §§3.54, 3.57.

### 5. [§3.57] Unprovoked Flight

Unprovoked flight at the approach of the police justifies a detention when it occurs in a high crime area (*Illinois v Wardlow* (2000) 528 US 119, 124, 120 S Ct 673, 145 L Ed 2d 570 (neighborhood known for heavy narcotics trafficking)) or under other circumstances giving rise to a reasonable suspicion of criminal activity (*People v Souza* (1994) 9 C4th 224, 235, 36 CR2d 569, superseding *People v Aldridge* (1984) 35 C3d

473, 198 CR 538, and *People v Bower* (1979) 24 C3d 638, 156 CR 856).

For example, in *Souza* adequate circumstances were that the defendant, a pedestrian, was talking to occupants of a parked car at 3:00 a.m. in a high crime area, the people in car ducked when the police car approached, and the defendant took off. 9 C4th at 242.

In *People v Brown* (1990) 216 CA3d 1442, 1450, 265 CR 552, defendant, holding a brown paper bag, was part of a group standing in front of a dance hall. As the police approached, someone yelled "roller" and the group, including defendant, scattered. When the officers returned a few minutes later, defendant was again in front of the dance hall and again quickly left on seeing them. The court held that defendant's behavior not only raised, but almost compelled, a reasonable suspicion that conduct consistent with criminal activity was taking place.

The flight of others may cast suspicion on a person who stays put. In *People v Holloway* (1985) 176 CA3d 150, 155, 221 CR 394, defendant was huddled with four others at 3:00 a.m. outside an apartment complex. The officers knew he did not live in the area. At their approach, his companions fled, but he stayed, apparently unaware of the officers. The court held that "the unprovoked flight" of defendant's "sleepless companions" at that time and place justified defendant's detention.

☛ **Judicial Tip**: *Holloway* should not be turned into a damned-if-you-do and damned-if-you-don't approach to detentions. See also §§3.58–3.61.

*Wardlow* and *Souza* declined to adopt a bright line rule that flight justifies detention. Rather, "flight from police is a proper consideration—and indeed may be a key factor—in determining whether in a particular case the police have sufficient cause to detain." *People v Souza, supra,* 9 C4th at 235.

*Wardlow* emphasized that its ruling did not affect the right of an individual approached by the police without reasonable suspicion or probable cause to ignore the police and go about his or her business, nor the principle that refusal to cooperate, without more, does not furnish grounds to detain. For a decision that scrupulously honors the right to walk away, see *U.S. v Davis* (10th Cir 1996) 94 F3d 1465, 1468–1470 (no basis for detention where defendant, whom the officers recognized as an ex-con, made eye contact with them in a high crime area, walked away, and kept walking with his hands in his pockets after being told to stop).

In short, flight is a suspicious factor, walking away is not. Of course, once the basis for a detention exists and the defendant attempts to leave the presence of the police, the consequences are very different. Such an effort justifies *arrest. People v Abes* (1985) 174 CA3d 796, 805, 220 CR 277.

For discussion of attempts to evade the police, see §3.58.

### 6. Other Reactions to Police Presence

#### a. [§3.58] Evasive Conduct

An attempt to evade police, such as taking an erratic path through an airport or driving in an evasive manner, is a pertinent factor in determining reasonable suspicion. *Florida v Rodriguez* (1984) 469 US 1, 6, 105 S Ct 308, 83 L Ed 2d 165; see *U.S. v Brignoni-Ponce* (1975) 422 US 873, 885, 95 S Ct 2574, 45 L Ed 2d 607. Although such behavior may be highly probative, it does not have "ironclad significance." *U.S. v Sokolow* (1989) 490 US 1, 8, 109 S Ct 1581, 104 L Ed 2d 1.

☛ **Judicial Tip**: As in the case of flight, evasive conduct plus other circumstances may create the requisite level of suspicion. Evasive conduct might have little significance when the officers are not in uniform or driving an unmarked police vehicle.

#### b. [§3.59] Furtive Gestures

A furtive gesture, such as a vehicle passenger's turning around and apparently placing something in the back seat, "can be deemed suspicious only when there are additional facts known to the officer that reasonably give it a guilty connotation," such as prior reliable information or the officer's observation of contraband. *People v McGaughran* (1979) 25 C3d 577, 590, 159 CR 191; *Williams v Superior Court* (1985) 168 CA3d 349, 361, 213 CR 919.

#### c. [§3.60] Nervousness

Generally, "[n]ervousness in the presence of a police officer does not furnish a reasonable basis for a detention." *People v Loewen* (1983) 35 C3d 117, 125, 196 CR 846; *People v Raybourn* (1990) 218 CA3d 308, 312, 266 CR 884.

Some reactions to seeing police, however, are so unusual that they justify a detention for questioning. Thus, in *People v Brown* (1985) 169 CA3d 159, 164, 215 CR 101, the officer saw the defendant come out of a corridor leading to a bank, running as fast as he could. When the defendant saw the officer, he immediately slowed down, kept his eyes on the officer, turned pale, and his hands started to shake. The officer testified that in his six years' experience he had never seen anyone react in such an extreme manner to his presence. No crime had been reported; the officer stopped the defendant because he thought he might have just robbed the bank. The court upheld the detention, saying that the officer's suspicion that the defendant was connected with criminal activity was objectively reasonable.

#### d. [§3.61] Eye Contact

Whether a person looks at an officer or fails to look at an officer should be accorded little or no weight alone or in combination with other factors. *U.S. v Montero-Camargo* (9th Cir 2000) 208 F3d 1122, 1135–1136; *U.S. v Moreno-Chaparro* (5th Cir 1998) 180 F3d 629, 632; *U.S. v Davis* (10th Cir 1996) 94 F3d 1465, 1468. In some cases, the prosecution argues that it is suspicious for a person to look at an officer and on other occasions that it is suspicious not to look. In *Moreno-Chaparro, supra,* the court said that to condone such arguments "would put the officers in a classic 'heads I win, tails you lose' position. The driver, of course, can only lose." 180 F3d at 632.

### 7. [§3.62] Driving Under the Influence

Courts analyze DUI detentions like other *Terry* stops. See, *e.g., People v Perez* (1985) 175 CA3d Supp 8, 10–11, 221 CR 776 (pronounced weaving within lane is ground for stopping car on suspicion of DUI); *Marvin v DMV* (1984) 161 CA3d 717, 719, 207 CR 793 (reasonable to stop car driving in circles at 2:40 a.m.; odor of alcohol justifies further investigation, including field sobriety tests); *People v Bennett* (1983) 139 CA3d 767, 769, 189 CR 77 (weaving, odor of alcohol, bloodshot eyes, slurred speech are abundant grounds to administer field sobriety tests).

### 8. Other Traffic Stops

#### a. [§3.63] Stop for Traffic, Equipment, and Registration Violations

A vehicle stop based on the officer's observation of a traffic violation, such as speeding or running a light, is technically not a *Terry* detention. The officer has probable cause to issue a citation, not mere suspicion that the driver has committed an offense. A stop for a traffic violation, however, "is analogous to a so-called *Terry* stop" because of its brevity and atmosphere. *Berkemer v McCarty* (1984) 468 US 420, 439, 104 S Ct 3138, 82 L Ed 2d 317. It is treated like a *Terry* stop for the purpose of determining its permissible length and scope and the officer's right to search.

The underlying principle governing traffic stops is that an officer who observes a Vehicle Code violation may stop a motorist to conduct a brief investigation and to give the driver a ticket. *People v Franklin* (1985) 171 CA3d 627, 633, 217 CR 529. As to the meaning of "brief" in this context, see §3.72. The principle applies to moving violations (*see, e.g., New York v Class* (1986) 475 US 106, 116, 106 S Ct 960, 89 L Ed 2d 81; *Colorado v Bannister* (1980) 449 US 1, 3, 101 S Ct 42, 66 L Ed 2d 1), as well as to equipment and registration violations, such as a cracked or illegally tinted windshield (*New York v Class, supra*; *People v Hanes* (1997) 60 CA4th Supp 6, 72 CR2d 212; but see *People v Butler* (1988) 202 CA3d 602, 606, 248 CR 887), no working headlights or taillights (*People v Superior Court* (Simon) (1972) 7 C3d 186, 191, 101 CR 837), or expired registration tags (*People v Carter* (1985) 163 CA3d 1183, 1185, 210 CR 103), and an apparent seat belt violation. *Kodani v Snyder* (1999) 75 CA4th 471, 474, 89 CR2d 362.

#### b. [§3.64] Speed Traps

A traffic stop based on a speed trap is illegal, and evidence derived from it is inadmissible. Veh C §§40803–40808. Vehicle Code §40808 expressly renders Proposition 8 inapplicable. *People v Munoz* (1992) 11 CA4th 1190, 1191–1192, 15 CR2d 21. Before the enactment of Veh C §40808, *People v Sullivan* (1991) 234 CA3d 56, 57–58, 285 CR 553, had held that Proposition 8 eliminated the exclusion of speed trap evidence. Vehicle Code §40808 supersedes *Sullivan*. See *People v Munoz, supra*. For discussion of the speed trap law, see 4 Witkin & Epstein, California Criminal Law, *Pretrial Proceedings* §46 (3d ed 2000).

#### c. [§3.65] License Check

The police may not pull a car over solely to check on license or registration. *Delaware v Prouse* (1979) 440 US 648, 657–663, 99 S Ct 1391, 59 L Ed 2d 660. For discussion of inspection checkpoints, see §3.88.

#### d. [§3.66] Pretext Stop

An officer who observes a traffic violation may stop the vehicle even when the stop is a pretext for a narcotics investigation. *Whren v U.S.* (1996) 517 US 806, 809–813, 116 S Ct 1769, 135 L Ed 2d 89. See §§1.43 and 3.34.

### 9. [§3.67] No Suspicious Conduct by Driver; Suspicion Relates Only to Passenger

An officer may stop a car when he or she reasonably believes there is an arrest warrant for the passenger but has no basis for detaining the driver. *In re William J.* (1985) 171 CA3d 72, 77, 217 CR 163 ("criminals throughout the land could hire drivers . . . to chauffeur them around . . ."). The court applied the same balancing test as in *U.S. v Hensley* (1985) 469 US 221, 228, 105 S Ct 675, 83 L Ed 2d 604, but did not mention what offense the passenger was wanted for. Similarly, a vehicle stop is proper when the passenger matches the description of the perpetrator of a recent robbery. *People v McClusky* (1981) 125 CA3d 220, 226, 178 CR 7.

The converse does not follow. Grounds to detain the driver do not automatically create a right to detain the passenger. *People v Spicer* (1984) 157 CA3d 213, 220–221, 203 CR 599.

#### 10. [§3.68] Weapons Violations

An officer may detain a person on reasonable suspicion that the person is carrying an illegal firearm or other deadly weapon. Pen C § 833.5. The purpose of the statute is unclear because such detentions are proper under *Terry.* See, *e.g., People v May* (1973) 33 CA3d 888, 890, 109 CR 396 (detention and frisk of pedestrian proper when officer saw four- to five-inch bulge in detainee's rear pocket and observed that the top of the object was silver). *May* long preceded enactment of Pen C §833.5.

For discussion of weapons searches incident to a temporary detention, see §§3.95–3.104.

#### 11. [§3.69] Detention To Interview Detainee About Crimes of Others

There is very little law on whether a person may be detained because the police want to question him or her as a witness. *U.S. v Ward* (9th Cir 1973) 488 F2d 162, 169, held that such a detention is improper, at least in the absence of exigent circumstances. Of course, the police can always seek a consensual interview. See, *e.g., People v Rosales* (1989) 211 CA3d 325, 330, 259 CR 503. See also *People v Lloyd* (1992) 4 CA4th 724, 733, 6 CR2d 105 (detention of defendant as possible witness upheld because of factual basis for suspecting defendant of burglary).

*LaFave* favors a narrow right to detain likely witnesses briefly in order to seek information from them. 4 LaFave, Search and Seizure, p 24 (3d ed 1996) (hereafter cited as LaFave).

### D. Duration and Scope of Detention

#### 1. [§3.70] In General

*Terry* and its progeny permit *brief* investigatory detentions. The essence of a temporary detention is that it is temporary and that it is a detention rather than arrest or akin to one. Sections 3.71–3.73 discuss time limits. Sections 3.74–3.84 focus on police activities that are within or beyond the ambit of a temporary detention. Searches incident to a detention are the topic of §§3.95–3.107.

Preliminarily, two points bear noting:

(1) When a detention exceeds appropriate limits, it does not automatically follow that the evidence must be excluded. It would be admissible if the officer had probable cause to arrest (see §3.30) or if the detention had become a consensual encounter (see §§3.75–3.76).

(2) Questioning during a detention that exceeds its proper scope can raise both Fourth and Fifth Amendment problems. Questioning during a lawful temporary detention is exempt from *Miranda*. *Berkemer v McCarty* (1984) 468 US 420, 435, 104 S Ct 3138, 82 L Ed 2d 317; *In re Victor B.* (1994) 24 CA4th 521, 525, 29 CR2d 362 (*Miranda* only becomes applicable when point of arrest or accusation has been reached or when questioning ceases to be brief or casual and becomes sustained and coercive); *People v Vasquez* (1993) 14 CA4th 1158, 1161, 18 CR2d 277 (pedestrian stopped on suspicion of making "curb service" drug sales may be questioned without *Miranda* admonition).

Statements made during a detention that has become unlawful are inadmissible, regardless of *Miranda* compliance, like any other evidence resulting from an illegal detention. But the existence of probable cause for arrest may provide an independent basis for admission of the statements. In such situations, *Miranda* admonitions must be given whenever the suspect is questioned under circumstances that have the earmarks of a custodial interrogation. *Berkemer v McCarty, supra*; *People v Taylor* (1986) 178 CA3d 217, 229, 223 CR 638. A suspect's responses during a lawful detention often provide grounds for prolonging it or to search or arrest. *People v Russell* (2000) 81 CA4th 96, 102, 96 CR2d 568.

☛ **Judicial Tip**: In resolving problems relating to the length or scope of a detention, it often helps to separate the issues clearly: Did the stop exceed its appropriate time or scope? If so, did the officers have probable cause to arrest? If they did, at what stage did they acquire it? Probable cause helps only if it existed at the time the officers went beyond the bounds of a valid detention.

### 2. Time Limits

#### a. [§3.71] Investigative Stops

The duration of an investigative stop is important because "the brevity of the invasion of the individual's Fourth Amendment interests is an important factor in determining whether the seizure is so minimally intrusive as to be justifiable on reasonable suspicion." *U.S. v Place* (1983) 462 US 696, 709, 103 S Ct 2637, 77 L Ed 2d 110. Although "some instances create difficult line-drawing problems" (*U.S. v Sharpe* (1985) 470 US 675, 685, 105 S Ct 1568, 84 L Ed 2d 605), the following principles have emerged:

(1) An investigative detention can last no longer than necessary to effectuate the purpose of the stop. *Florida v Royer* (1983) 460 US 491, 500, 103 S Ct 1319, 75 L Ed 2d 229. If it "continues indefinitely, at some point it can no longer be justified as an investigative stop." *U.S. v Sharpe, supra,* 470 US at 685. It "becomes illegal when it extends beyond the time reasonably necessary under the circumstances for the police to wind up their investigation." *People v Paz* (1981) 118 CA3d 332, 334, 173 CR 272. Courts should "consider the law enforcement purposes to be served by the stop as well as the time reasonably needed to effectuate those purposes." *U.S. v Sharpe, supra,* 470 US at 685.

(2) To decide whether a detention was unduly prolonged, it is necessary to assess "whether the police diligently pursued a means of investigation that was likely to confirm or dispel their suspicions quickly." *U.S. v Sharpe, supra,* 470 US at 686. *Sharpe* also said that in making this assessment, courts "should take care to consider whether the police are acting in a swiftly developing situation, and in such cases, the court should not indulge in unrealistic second-guessing." 470 US at 686. Hindsight might indicate the availability of a swifter alternative, but this is not fatal. This last point made by *Sharpe* supersedes contrary comments in *Florida v Royer, supra. Royer* invalidated a drug suspect's 15-minute airport detention partly on the ground that the use of drug-sniffing dogs would have been quicker. 460 US at 506.

(3) Delays caused by the suspect's evasive conduct do not "count" against the police. *U.S. v Sharpe, supra,* 470 US at 688. A detention can reasonably be extended when the detainee provides false information that needs to be checked out. *People v Huerta* (1990) 218 CA3d 744, 750, 267 CR 243.

(4) Questioning must "be strictly limited to the purpose of the stop." *In re James D.* (1987) 43 C3d 903, 915, 239 CR 663; *Pendergraft v Superior Court* (1971) 15 CA3d 237, 93 CR 155 (officers stopped defendant because they thought he might be under age; after getting satisfactory identification they asked him if he had any weapons; court held detention unlawfully prolonged). Of course, "[t]he dynamics of the detention-for-

questioning situation may justify further detention, further investigation, search, or arrest." 15 CA3d at 242; *People v Remiro* (1979) 89 CA3d 809, 828, 153 CR 89.

Detentions lasting 5 minutes (*People v Paz, supra*), 10 minutes (*People v Trudell* (1985) 173 CA3d 1221, 1226, 219 CR 679), and 20 minutes (*U.S. v Sharpe, supra*) have been upheld on their particular facts. Even longer ones have been sustained when the police acted diligently. See, *e.g., People v Soun* (1995) 34 CA4th 1499, 1520, 40 CR2d 822 (over one-half hour detention of homicide suspects); *In re Carlos M.* (1990) 220 CA3d 372, 382 n4, 269 CR 447 (30 minutes); *People v Avalos* (1996) 47 CA4th 1569, 1577, 55 CR2d 450 (25 minutes; much of that time was spent waiting for an officer who spoke defendant's language); *U.S. v Simmons* (11th Cir 1999) 172 F3d 775, 780 (50 minutes to determine whether driver was subject of outstanding warrant).

In *U.S. v Place* (1983) 462 US 696, 709–710, 103 S Ct 2637, 77 L Ed 2d 110, law enforcement agents detained the defendant and his luggage for 90 minutes while they waited for a drug-sniffing dog. The court held that the detention was unreasonable. *Sharpe* explains *Place* by saying that the agents knew of the defendant's arrival several hours in advance and could have arranged for a trained dog with less delay. 470 US at 685.

☛ **Judicial Tip**: It is useful to bear in mind that the number of minutes of a detention is not necessarily determinative of its lawfulness. Even a detention of a few minutes is unlawful when it lasts beyond the point at which the officer had effectuated the purpose of the stop. A substantially longer detention may be justified when the officers diligently check out their suspicions.

Successive stops of the same person are permitted, at least when the second detention is for a reason unrelated to the first. *People v DeCosse* (1986) 183 CA3d 404, 409–411, 228 CR 114.

#### b. Traffic Stops

#### (1) [§3.72] Basic Principles

When a driver has produced a valid license, proof of insurance, and proof of entitlement to operate the vehicle, the officer may issue a warning or a citation, but then must usually allow the driver to proceed without further delay or questioning. *People v McGaughran* (1979) 25 C3d 577, 585–586, 159 CR 191; see *U.S. v Hill* (6th Cir 1999) 195 F3d 258, 264; *U.S. v Patten* (10th Cir 1999) 183 F3d 1190, 1193. As to proof of insurance, see Veh C §16028. The officer may check the validity of the driver's license and the registration papers by computer. See, *e.g.*, *U.S. v Anderson* (10th Cir 1997) 114 F3d 1059, 1064; *U.S. v Hill, supra* (initiating driver's license check late in the stop reasonable under the particular circumstances).

The stop may not lawfully be prolonged by running a check for outstanding warrants (*People v McGaughran, supra*) or by imposing a crime investigation on the car's occupants without reasonable suspicion (*Williams v Superior Court* (1985) 168 CA3d 349, 358, 213 CR 919). For further discussion of warrant checks, see §3.74, of questioning during the stop, §3.75, and of requesting consent to search, §3.76.

### (2) [§3.73] Extension of Traffic Stop

Events during the initial stop often furnish grounds for expanding its scope and duration. Examples of such events include:

- The failure of a driver to produce a license or satisfactory proof of identity. *People v Valencia* (1993) 20 CA4th 906, 918, 24 CR2d 883.

- Observations that give rise to a reasonable suspicion that the driver is under the influence of alcohol. See §3.62.

- Behavior by vehicle occupants, including answers to proper questions, that create a reasonable suspicion of criminal activity, such as the transportation of drugs. *People v Russell* (2000) 81 CA4th 96, 102, 96 CR2d 568; *People v Bell* (1996) 43 CA4th 754, 768, 51 CR2d 115; see also §3.75.

- Observations of weapons in the vehicle. *New York v Class* (1986) 475 US 106, 114, 106 S Ct 960, 89 L Ed 2d 81; *Michigan v Long* (1983) 463 US 1032, 1048, 103 S Ct 3469, 77 L Ed 2d 1201.

- Seeing items in the car that closely resemble ones described in a recent robbery report. *People v Franklin* (1985) 171 CA3d 627, 634, 217 CR 529.

- Valid consent to a search. See §3.76.

Extending a stop on the basis of suspected criminal activity must, of course, rest on a reasonable factual basis. See, *e.g., Williams v Superior Court* (1985) 168 CA3d 349, 360, 213 CR 919 (prolonging traffic stop to investigate vehicle occupants' possible involvement in robbery unreasonable because descriptions did not match vehicle or occupants).

### 3. Scope of Detention: Officer's Actions

#### a. [§3.74] Warrant Checks

The principle that a traffic stop can last no longer than necessary to effectuate the purpose of the stop invalidates few warrant checks because of the following:

- Events during the initial detention often furnish grounds for extending it; a warrant check completed during a lawful extension of the stop is itself lawful. See, *e.g., People v Castaneda* (1995) 35 CA4th 1222, 1228, 42 CR2d 18. For discussion of grounds to prolong a traffic stop, see §3.73.
- Time limitations on warrant checks do not apply to traffic violations for which the officer is authorized to take the driver into custody; the right to custody includes the right to detain for a warrant check. *People v McGaughran* (1979) 25 C3d 577, 583, 159 CR 191.
- Warrant checks are permissible as long as they do not prolong the stop beyond the time it would otherwise take. 25 C3d at 584; *People v Brown* (1998) 62 CA4th 493, 498, 72 CR2d 793. Experienced officers often initiate the check soon after they spot the traffic violation.
- The prohibition against any extension of a stop to complete a check may be easing. See *People v Brown, supra* (warrant check permissible as long as it "does not unreasonably prolong the detention"); *U.S. v Simmons* (11th Cir 1999) 172 F3d 775, 778 (stop may be extended to await results of warrant check properly initiated and pursued diligently).

An arrest on a warrant that turned up as a result of an improperly prolonged stop does not bar prosecution of the underlying offense. *People v McGaughran, supra,* 25 C3d at 583.

#### b. [§3.75] Questioning During Traffic Stop

Despite the principle that questioning during a *Terry* stop must be limited to the purpose of the stop (*In re James D.* (1987) 43 C3d 903, 915, 239 CR 663; see §3.71), some courts have permitted questioning in traffic stops that has little or no relation to the purpose of the stop, as long as the question-and-answer process does not prolong it. See, *e.g., People v Brown* (1998) 62 CA4th 493, 499, 72 CR2d 793 (questions about probation status); *People v Bell* (1996) 43 CA4th 754, 765–768, 51 CR2d 115 (asking passenger about origin and destination of trip); *U.S. v Hill*

(6th Cir 1999) 195 F3d 258, 268 (questioning driver of U-Haul about his moving plans).

When the officer has completed the work related to the stop—typically, checking license, registration, and proof of insurance, and issuing a ticket or warning—further questioning is generally unlawful because it runs afoul of the basic principle that the length of a detention must be reasonably related to the circumstances that justified it in the first place. See *People v Brown, supra,* and cases there discussed. Circumstances during the stop, however, may give rise to a reasonable suspicion of criminal activity; in such situations the duration of the stop may be extended. See §3.73. Delayed questioning is also permitted even in the absence of reasonable suspicion during a time, if any, when the encounter between the officer and the driver ceases to be a detention and becomes consensual. *U.S. v Patten* (10th Cir 1999) 183 F3d 1190, 1193–1194; *U.S. v Anderson* (10th Cir 1997) 114 F3d 1059, 1064.

### c. [§3.76] Consent Searches

Officers often seek a consent to search during a traffic stop. Courts that uphold unrelated questioning also tend to uphold uncoerced consent given during the period justified by the stop. *People v Brown* (1998) 62 CA4th 493, 499–500, 72 CR2d 793; see *People v Bell* (1996) 43 CA4th 754, 765–768, 51 CR2d 115. For further discussion of voluntary and coerced consent, see §§5.112–5.127.

The validity of a consent requested *after* completion of the traffic investigation depends not just on its voluntariness but on the lawfulness of the extended police-civilian contact. The extension may be lawful because of reasonable suspicion of criminal activity (see §3.73). It also may be lawful if the detention has been transformed into a consensual encounter. *Ohio v Robinette* (1996) 519 US 33, 39, 117 S Ct 417, 136 L Ed 2d 347 (no bright line rule that limits such transformation to situations in which officer advised driver of right to leave).

An important factor in determining whether the encounter has become consensual is the return of papers to the driver before the officer asks to search; until that is done, a driver would neither feel nor be free to leave. For decisions upholding consents following return of documents, see, *e.g., U.S. v Patten* (10th Cir 1999) 183 F3d 1190, 1193–1194; *U.S. v Zapata* (11th Cir 1999) 180 F3d 1237, 1239–1242; *U.S. v Chan* (7th Cir 1998) 136 F3d 1158, 1159.

Handing back documents does not automatically produce a consensual encounter or a voluntary consent. Under many circumstances, a reasonable driver would not feel free to leave or decline consent. See *U.S. v Elliott*

(10th Cir 1997) 107 F3d 810, 814 (coercive show of authority); *U.S. v Mesa* (6th Cir 1995) 62 F3d 159, 163 (consent while locked in squad car invalid); see discussion of *Mesa* in *U.S. v Guimond* (6th Cir 1997) 116 F3d 166, 171.

☛ **Judicial Tip**: Some judges suggest alertness to the widespread practice of questioning and searching in the aftermath of routine traffic stops because this practice underlies many of the complaints from drivers about being pulled over for driving because they are Black, Hispanic, young, or poor.

### d. [§3.77] Ordering out of Car

During a traffic stop, officers can order the driver and passenger(s) to get out of the car and move to the curb. *Maryland v Wilson* (1997) 519 US 408, 410, 117 S Ct 882, 137 L Ed 2d 41 (passenger); *Pennsylvania v Mimms* (1977) 434 US 106, 110, 98 S Ct 330, 54 L Ed 2d 331 (driver); *People v Padilla* (1982) 132 CA3d 555, 557, 183 CR 97; *People v Superior Court* (Galbreath) (1980) 104 CA3d 988, 990, 164 CR 116. An officer who is alone can order the vehicle occupants to stand by the patrol car and keep their hands in view. *People v Rico* (1979) 97 CA3d 124, 131, 158 CR 573.

### e. [§3.78] Preventing Reentry

Police can prevent a suspect from reentering a car when reentry might pose a danger. *Michigan v Long* (1983) 463 US 1032, 1045–1049, 103 S Ct 3469, 77 L Ed 2d 1201 (officers had seen a large knife in car). *People v Gonzalez* (1992) 7 CA4th 381, 386, 8 CR2d 640, dealt with the converse: ordering a passenger back into the car. The court held that such an order, when obeyed, creates a detention that is only lawful when it is based on a reasonable suspicion of criminal activity by the passenger. But see *People v Castellon* (1999) 76 CA4th 1369, 1373, 91 CR2d 204 (may order passenger to remain in car when order is based on reasonable concern for officer safety). *Castellon* aside, some judges think that *Maryland v Wilson* (1997) 519 US 408, 412, 117 S Ct 882, 137 L Ed 2d 41, supersedes *Gonzalez,* at least when the order to reenter is reasonable in light of safety concerns.

### f. [§3.79] Placing Detainee Into Patrol Car

Detainees can be held briefly in a police vehicle on the scene pending identification by the victim. *People v Craig* (1978) 86 CA3d 905, 912, 150 CR 676; *People v Natale* (1978) 77 CA3d 568, 572, 143 CR 629.

In traffic stops, it is not uncommon to ask the driver to sit in the patrol car until the matter is completed. See, *e.g., U.S. v Hill* (6th Cir 1999) 195 F3d 258, 263. On the other hand, keeping defendants in the patrol car for more than three hours while officers obtain a search warrant is an arrest. *People v Freund* (1975) 48 CA3d 49, 53–56, 119 CR 762. Earlier cases had indicated that any placement of a suspect into a police car is an arrest. See, *e.g., People v Hatcher* (1969) 2 CA3d 71, 75, 82 CR 323; *People v Gibson* (1963) 220 CA2d 15, 21, 33 CR 775.

#### g. [§3.80] Handcuffing

Usually a person who has been handcuffed has been subjected to the equivalent of an arrest rather than detained. See *People v Campbell* (1981) 118 CA3d 588, 596, 173 CR 442. But handcuffing has been permitted when circumstances make it reasonable, especially when the detention is brief. *People v Glaser* (1995) 11 C4th 354, 369, 45 CR2d 425 (unidentified, unresponsive person approaching house being searched through backyard; detention of two minutes or less); *People v Johnson* (1991) 231 CA3d 1, 12, 282 CR 114 (detainee tried to put something in his mouth and attempted to flee); *People v Brown* (1985) 169 CA3d 159, 167, 215 CR 101 (defendant resisted pat search).

*People v Bowen* (1987) 195 CA3d 269, 274, 240 CR 466, upheld a detention of a handcuffed purse snatch suspect while awaiting the victim. Handcuffing combined with a prolonged detention amounts to an arrest. *People v Gentry* (1992) 7 CA4th 1255, 1264–1266, 9 CR2d 742 (three-and-one-half-hour detention while police obtain search warrant).

#### h. [§3.81] Use of Force

Officers "may use reasonable force to make an investigatory stop," and they may draw a weapon "if the circumstances call for it." *People v Brown* (1985) 169 CA3d 159, 167, 215 CR 101; *U.S. v Hensley* (1985) 469 US 221, 229, 105 S Ct 675, 83 L Ed 2d 604 (wanted flyer stated that suspect was armed and dangerous); *People v Glaser* (1995) 11 C4th 354, 369, 45 CR2d 425 (suspect who approaches residence being searched through backyard and does not respond to officers may be detained briefly at gunpoint). Detention at gunpoint, however, increases the intrusiveness of the detention and may be deemed an arrest when not necessary for the officer's safety. 11 C4th at 366.

The police may physically stop a suspect from leaving. A person who is lawfully "detained is not free to leave at will and may be kept in the officer's presence by physical restraint, threat of force or assertion of authority." *In re Gregory S.* (1980) 112 CA3d 764, 778, 169 CR 540.

In accord is *People v Johnson* (1991) 231 CA3d 1, 12, 282 CR 114. *People v Rivera* (1992) 8 CA4th 1000, 1007, 10 CR2d 785, held that using a police dog who found the suspect and, without warning, bit him in the scalp, was consistent with a temporary detention.

#### i. [§3.82] Transporting Suspect From Scene

As noted in §3.30, taking a person from the scene of the stop to the police station for fingerprinting or questioning exceeds the bounds of a temporary detention. This is generally also the case when the suspect is transported to be viewed by the victim. *People v Harris* (1975) 15 C3d 384, 389, 124 CR 536. Courts make exceptions when it is not feasible to bring the victim to the suspect's location. *In re Carlos M.* (1990) 220 CA3d 372, 383, 269 CR 447 (rape victim being examined in hospital); *In re Lynette G.* (1976) 54 CA3d 1087, 1094, 126 CR 898 (victim injured); *People v Gatch* (1976) 56 CA3d 505, 508–509, 128 CR 481 (no officers available to pick up victim). Only rarely, such as when a hostile crowd gathers, can the detainee be taken to the station house for further investigation. *People v Courtney* (1970) 11 CA3d 1185, 1191, 90 CR 370.

The transportation to another location need not be in a police vehicle or the location need not be very far to transform the detention into an arrest. *People v Parker* (1978) 85 CA3d 439, 445, 148 CR 513 (officers took defendant who had been stopped on school grounds to school's security office); *People v Gonsoulin* (1971) 19 CA3d 270, 274–275, 96 CR 548 (police asked motorist to drive his car to gas station under police escort).

#### j. [§3.83] Production of Identification

Officers can ask a moderate number of questions to determine the identity of the detained person. *Berkemer v McCarty* (1984) 468 US 420, 439, 104 S Ct 3138, 82 L Ed 2d 317; *In re Gregory S.* (1980) 112 CA3d 764, 779–780, 169 CR 540. They can probably also demand written identification. *People v Loudermilk* (1987) 195 CA3d 996, 1001, 241 CR 208; *People v Long* (1987) 189 CA3d 77, 85–89, 234 CR 271. For discussion of searches for identification, see §§3.106–3.107.

#### k. [§3.84] Combination of Coercive Circumstances

Even when several of the factors discussed in §§3.79–3.83 are present, a detention does not necessarily become an arrest. See, *e.g.*, *People v Glaser* (1995) 11 C4th 354, 369, 45 CR2d 425 (defendant detained at gunpoint, ordered to the ground, and handcuffed); *People v Soun* (1995) 34 CA4th 1499, 1517, 40 CR2d 822 (homicide suspect removed from car at gunpoint by many officers, forced to lie on ground, handcuffed, placed in patrol car, transported three blocks to parking lot, and held there for half an hour without being told reason for stop).

☛ **Judicial Tip**: Caution is advisable in applying *Soun.* Homicide situations are not necessarily compelling precedent for cases that involve less serious offenses.

## V. DETENTIONS NOT BASED ON SUSPICION OF CRIMINAL ACTIVITY

### A. Vehicle Roadblocks and Checkpoints

#### 1. [§3.85] Basic Principles

Courts use the words "roadblock" and "checkpoint" interchangeably to refer to law enforcement action that consists of systematically stopping cars and detaining their occupants. See *City of Indianapolis v Edmond* (2000) 531 US 32, 121 S Ct 447, 148 L Ed 2d 333, 339; *Ingersoll v Palmer* (1987) 43 C3d 1321, 1333, 241 CR 42. Drawing lines in this area has proved difficult. The following principles emerge from the cases, particularly from the comprehensive analyses in *Edmond* and *Ingersoll.*

A detention at a roadblock or checkpoint that does not meet the standard of individualized suspicion must meet three conditions in order to be lawful:

(1) It must generally be for a purpose other than capturing criminals or uncovering evidence of crime. Conversely, if that is the purpose, the rules governing *Terry* stops apply. *City of Indianapolis v Edmond, supra,* 148 L Ed 2d at 343–345; *Ingersoll v Palmer, supra,* 43 C3d at 1327. See §§3.86–3.89. *Edmond* indicates that there is an exception for serious emergencies. 148 L Ed 2d at 345. See §3.87.

(2) It must satisfy a test that "balances the public interest served by the seizure, the degree to which the seizure advances the public interest and the severity of the interference with individual liberty." *Ingersoll v Palmer, supra,* 43 C3d at 1329; see §3.90.

(3) The stop must be "carried out pursuant to a plan embodying explicit, neutral limitations on the conduct of individual officers." *Ingersoll v Palmer, supra*; *Brown v Texas* (1979) 443 US 47, 51, 99 S Ct 2637, 61 L Ed 2d 357; *Delaware v Prouse* (1979) 440 US 648, 663, 99 S Ct 1391, 59 L Ed 2d 660. This condition substitutes for suspicion of individual wrongdoing. *Ingersoll v Palmer, supra*; see §3.91.

#### 2. Purpose of Detention

##### a. [§3.86] Dragnets

Dragnet searches, undertaken for the purpose of uncovering evidence of crime without reason to believe that a crime has occurred, are unlawful. *People v Gale* (1956) 46 C2d 253, 256, 294 P2d 13; see *Ingersoll v Palmer* (1987) 43 C3d 1321, 1335, 241 CR 42. In *Gale*, sheriff's deputies set up a roadblock to "curb the juvenile problem and also check for, well, anything that we might find, anything that looked suspicious." The court held that the mere possibility that some automobiles may have been involved in criminal activity did not justify the stopping and searching of all passing vehicles. 46 C2d at 256.

#### b. [§3.87] Dangerous Crime

The Fourth Amendment "almost certainly" does not require individualized suspicion for "an appropriately tailored roadblock set up to thwart an imminent terrorist attack or to catch a dangerous criminal who is likely to flee by way of a particular route. [Citation.] The exigencies created by these scenarios are far removed from the circumstances under which authorities might simply stop cars as a matter of course to see if there just happens to be a felon leaving the jurisdiction." *City of Indianapolis v Edmond* (2000) 531 US 32, 121 S Ct 447, 148 L Ed 2d 333, 345.

#### c. [§3.88] Inspections

Standards for *Terry* stops do not apply to checkpoints for vehicle, license, and registration inspections. Their aim is not crime detection but ensuring that qualified persons drive cars fit for safe operation. *Delaware v Prouse* (1979) 440 US 648, 663, 99 S Ct 1391, 59 L Ed 2d 660. *Prouse* strongly suggests that checkpoints for such purposes are valid. California has long upheld them in decisions approved by *Ingersoll v Palmer* (1987) 43 C3d 1321, 1327, 241 CR 42. *People v De La Torre* (1967) 257 CA2d 162, 165, 64 CR 804; *People v Washburn* (1968) 265 CA2d 665, 670, 71 CR 577. See also *People v Perez* (1996) 51 CA4th 1168, 1178, 59 CR2d 596, upholding checkpoints during hunting season in hunting areas for inspection by game wardens of licenses, tags, and any wildlife taken, and *People v Dickinson* (1980) 104 CA3d 505, 512, 163 CR 575, upholding agricultural inspection checkpoints.

#### d. [§3.89] Sobriety and Drug Checkpoints

The primary purpose of a lawful sobriety checkpoint is to deter people who have been drinking from driving out of fear of encountering a roadblock, rather than to arrest drunk drivers. *Ingersoll v Palmer* (1987) 43 C3d 1321, 1327, 241 CR 42; see *City of Indianapolis v Edmond* (2000) 531 US 32, 121 S Ct 447, 148 L Ed 2d 333, 346.

In contrast, a checkpoint whose primary purpose is the discovery and interdiction of drugs is not lawful. *City of Indianapolis v Edmond, supra.* Even if such a roadblock has, in addition, purposes similar to those of a sobriety checkpoint, it remains in essence one designed to detect evidence of criminal wrongdoing; if it were upheld, "there would be little check on the ability of the authorities to construct roadblocks for almost any conceivable law enforcement purpose." *City of Indianapolis v Edmond, supra,* 148 L Ed 2d at 343–344.

### 3. [§3.90] Balancing Test: Minimizing Intrusiveness

*Ingersoll v Palmer* (1987) 43 C3d 1321, 1327, 241 CR 42, viewed sobriety checkpoints as analogous to administrative or regulatory searches, such as airport screening searches of departing passengers (upheld in *People v Hyde* (1974) 12 C3d 158, 165, 115 CR 358) and housing inspections (*Camara v Municipal Court* (1967) 387 US 523, 536–537, 87 S Ct 1727, 18 L Ed 2d 930). For that reason *Ingersoll* applied the balancing test used in those cases and first developed in *Camara v Municipal Court, supra.* As to administrative and regulatory searches, see 4 LaFave, chap 10.

The test has three factors: (1) the strength of the public interest in combating the problem at hand, (2) the extent to which the program advances that interest compared to approaches based on particularized suspicion or probable cause, and (3) the severity of the interference with individual liberty. *Michigan State Police v Sitz* (1990) 496 US 444, 454, 110 S Ct 2481, 110 L Ed 2d 412; *Ingersoll v Palmer, supra,* 43 C3d at 1329; *Camara v Municipal Court, supra.*

In *Ingersoll,* the court noted that "[d]eterring drunk driving and identifying and removing drunk drivers from the roadways undeniably serves a highly important governmental interest." 43 C3d at 1338. The court also said that traditional methods catch a small percentage of DUI offenders and that the available data, although limited, indicate that sobriety checkpoints are effective. The court then focused extensively on the third factor, setting out "functional guidelines for minimizing the intrusiveness of the sobriety checkpoint stop" (43 C3d at 1341):

(a) Supervisors, rather than officers in the field, select the site and establish procedures.

(b) The procedure includes a neutral formula to determine what drivers are stopped (*e.g.,* every fifth driver).

(c) The checkpoint maintains safe conditions.

(d) Subject to safety factors, the checkpoint is located "on roads having a high incidence of alcohol related accidents and/or arrests." 43 C3d at 1343. Temporary roadblocks are permitted.

(e) Law enforcement officials "exercise good judgment in setting times and durations." 43 C3d at 1345. Nighttime stops are permitted (the checkpoint held in *Ingersoll* operated from 9:30 p.m. to 2:30 a.m.).

(f) High visibility is important.

(g) "Minimizing the average time each motorist is detained is critical. . . ." 43 C3d at 1346. The *Ingersoll* roadblock detained the average motorist 28 seconds; the average time for those given field sobriety tests was a little over six minutes. 43 C3d at 1327.

(h) Advance publicity decreases intrusiveness and increases the effectiveness of the program. It is not, however, a prerequisite to a valid checkpoint. *People v Banks* (1993) 6 C4th 926, 934–935, 25 CR2d 524.

An important limit on intrusiveness is that persons may not be questioned on matters unrelated to the purpose of the checkpoint in the absence of objective individual suspicion. *People v Valenzuela* (1994) 28 CA4th 817, 826, 33 CR2d 802 (border patrol agents may not detain and question driver at agricultural inspection station unless they reasonably suspect that driver is an illegal alien). See also §3.92.

### 4. [§3.91] Explicit, Neutral Limitations on Officer Discretion

A plan embodying limits on officer discretion is important for two reasons. First, action pursuant to such a plan is a requirement in addition to the balancing test (*Ingersoll v Palmer* (1987) 43 C3d 1321, 1329, 241 CR 42):

> The federal test for determining whether a detention or seizure is justified balances the public interest served. . . . In addition, federal constitutional principles require a showing of *either* the officer's reasonable suspicion that a crime has occurred or is occurring *or,* as an alternative, that the seizure is "carried out pursuant to a plan embodying explicit, neutral limitations on the conduct of individual officers." [Emphasis in original.]

Second, in analyzing whether sobriety checkpoints unreasonably invade drivers' privacy, *Ingersoll* gives considerable weight to severe restraints on the discretion of field officers as to whom to stop and in what manner.

☛ **Judicial Tip**: Some judges believe that the need for "a plan embodying explicit, neutral limitations" is a major part of the balancing test rather than a separate requirement. The point may be academic. In either event it is crucial to inquire whether a roadblock or checkpoint was conducted in accord with such a plan. The *Ingersoll* court's separate treatment of this issue serves to underscore its importance.

The carefully operated drunk driving roadblock in *Ingersoll* should be contrasted with an officer acting alone. Such action was condemned in *Delaware v Prouse* (1979) 440 US 648, 663, 99 S Ct 1391, 59 L Ed 2d 660.

## B. Border Detentions

### 1. [§3.92] Near the Border

The principles discussed in §§3.90–3.91 apply equally to detentions near the border that are not grounded on suspicion that the vehicle occupants are illegal aliens or engaged in an unlawful activity. *U.S. v Martinez-Fuerte* (1976) 428 US 543, 561, 96 S Ct 3074, 49 L Ed 2d 1116, upheld a fixed checkpoint, using the balancing test discussed in §3.90. The court stressed that the location was chosen by supervising officials rather than field officers, and that the latter had little or no discretion, thus minimizing the risk of abusive or harassing stops.

In the absence of a valid checkpoint, vehicle stops require particular suspicion of illegal immigration or other unlawful conduct. For example, without such suspicion,

- Patrolling officers may not legally pull over cars near the border merely because the occupants look Hispanic. *U.S. v Brignoni-Ponce* (1975) 422 US 873, 885–886, 95 S Ct 2574, 45 L Ed 2d 607; see *U.S. v Montero-Camargo* (9th Cir 2000) 208 F3d 1122, 1131.

- Officers may not stop all cars that activate a vehicle intrusion sensor on a public road near the border. *People v Hokit* (1998) 66 CA4th 1013, 1018, 78 CR2d 412.

- A border patrol agent parked at a closed checkpoint may not pull over a car merely because its driver had glanced at him in passing. *U.S. v Moreno-Chaparro* (5th Cir 1998) 180 F3d 629, 632; see *U.S. v Montero-Camargo, supra,* 208 F3d at 1136.

- A border patrol agent may not detain a driver at an agricultural inspection station on the basis of an increase in apprehending drug smugglers at the particular inspection station, the driver's nervousness, his inability to speak English well, and the fact that his car had a large trunk capable of concealing aliens. *People v Valenzuela* (1994) 28 CA4th 817, 826, 33 CR2d 802 (facts, singly or in combination, do not constitute reasonable suspicion).

An occasional threshold issue is whether the contact between civilian and law enforcement officer is a detention or a consensual encounter. See *People v Sanchez* (1987) 195 CA3d 42, 47, 240 CR 413 (brief questioning of pedestrian one-half mile from border by border patrol agent in civilian clothes held to be consensual encounter; narcotics task force agent could properly participate). In contrast, a motorist at an agricultural inspection station who pulls over and parks at the direction of a border patrol agent has been detained. *People v Valenzuela, supra,* 28 CA4th at 824.

### 2. [§3.93] At the Border

At the border itself travelers may, of course, not only be detained, but their possessions may be searched. *U.S. v Ramsey* (1977) 431 US 606, 97 S Ct 1972, 1978, 52 L Ed 2d 617; *U.S. v Vance* (9th Cir 1995) 62 F3d 1152, 1156 (as search becomes more intrusive and extends beyond luggage, purse, and contents of pockets, more suspicion is required).

For persons arriving by plane or ship, the first stop in the United States is the functional equivalent of the border. *U.S. v Moore* (9th Cir 1980) 638 F2d 1171, 1173 (aircraft); *U.S. v Prince* (5th Cir 1974) 491 F2d 655, 657 (vessel). The prosecution need not prove that the journey originated abroad as long as the plane crossed the U.S. border (*U.S. v Haley* (11th Cir 1984) 743 F2d 862, 864) or the vessel came from international waters (*U.S. v Solmes* (9th Cir 1975) 527 F2d 1370, 1372).

A border detention beyond the time needed for routine customs inspection must be justified by reasonable factual grounds, but once these exist, even a long and uncomfortable detention is permitted under appropriate circumstances. *U.S. v Montoya de Hernandez* (1985) 473 US 531, 542, 105 S Ct 3304, 87 L Ed 2d 381 (upholding detention of suspected alimentary canal smuggler for over 16 hours).

In light of *U.S. v Ramsey, supra,* a random search of incoming international mail does not contravene the Fourth Amendment even if it violates federal regulations. *People v Blardony* (1998) 66 CA4th 791, 794, 78 CR2d 29.

## C. [§3.94] Juveniles

School officials, including campus security guards, may detain students *on school grounds* without reasonable suspicion of criminal activity or violation of a school rule. *In re Randy G.* (2001) 26 C4th 556, 110 CR2d 516. The only limitation is that the officials do not act in "an arbitrary, capricious, or harassing manner." 26 C4th at 559.

Street detention of juveniles on suspicion of conduct that would be criminal if committed by an adult is governed by the principles applicable to *Terry* stops. See, *e.g., Florida v J.L.* (2000) 529 US 266, 271, 120

S Ct 1375, 146 L Ed 2d 254; *In re Eskiel S.* (1993) 15 CA4th 1638, 1641, 19 CR2d 455.

When the officer reasonably suspects truancy rather than involvement in crime, the detention is also proper. *In re James D.* (1987) 43 C3d 903, 239 CR 663. The court applied the same balancing test as in the administrative search and sobriety roadblock cases and developed a standard analogous to the one used to evaluate *Terry* stops (43 C3d at 916): "A detention to investigate whether a person is a truant is justified when there are specific and articulable facts causing an officer to suspect, reasonably, that a truancy violation is occurring, and that the person he intends to detain is a truant."

Youthful appearance "is a highly relevant . . . factor in determining the propriety of a truancy detention." 43 C3d at 917.

As with any temporary detention, "[q]uestioning must, of course, be strictly limited to the purpose of the stop"; the detention may not be used as a pretext for investigating criminal matters. 43 C3d at 915; *In re Miguel G.* (1980) 111 CA3d 345, 349, 168 CR 688. Thus, while truants can be "arrested" for the purpose of being returned to school as quickly as possible, they cannot be taken to the police station and questioned about unsolved crimes. *In re Jorge S.* (1977) 74 CA3d 852, 856, 141 CR 722; but see *In re Humberto O.* (2000) 80 CA4th 237, 242, 95 CR2d 248 (truancy arrest justifies search). Similarly, once a suspected juvenile has provided identification showing that he is not under age, he cannot be asked whether he has weapons, absent a factual basis for suspecting that he may be armed. *Pendergraft v Superior Court* (1971) 15 CA3d 237, 240, 93 CR 155.

Detentions on suspicion of curfew violation are treated as *Terry* stops. *People v Teresinski* (1982) 30 C3d 822, 829, 180 CR 617; *In re Hector R.* (1984) 152 CA3d 1146, 1152–1153, 200 CR 110. For discussion of *arrests* for truancy and curfew violations, see §4.17. For discussion of searches of students by school authorities, see §§5.157–5.160.

## VI. SEARCHES INCIDENT TO TEMPORARY DETENTIONS

### A. [§3.95] In General

During a temporary detention, police officers may, under certain conditions, conduct a limited search for weapons. A search of the person for this purpose is variously called a pat-down, pat search, *Terry* frisk, or weapons frisk. It is not automatically permitted whenever the police detain a person. Sections 3.96–3.97 discuss the conditions for initiating a pat-down. Sections 3.98–3.103 address questions of what officers may properly do when conducting such a search: (1) what the initial scope of the search is; (2) when an officer can reach into the suspect's clothing, and (3) to what extent the officers can examine objects removed from the subject, such as containers. Under limited circumstances, a weapons search can properly extend beyond the detainee's person to his or her effects of vehicle. See §§3.104–3.105. Sections 3.106–3.107 discuss identification searches of the person and of vehicles.

Events during a detention often give rise to probable cause to arrest the subject. The officers may then conduct a fuller search incident to the arrest. See §§3.102, 4.103–4.136.

## B. Searches for Weapons

### 1. Pat Search

#### a. [§3.96] Purpose and Grounds

The purpose of a pat "search is not to discover evidence of crime, but to allow the officer to pursue his investigation without fear of violence . . ." *Adams v Williams* (1972) 407 US 143, 146, 92 S Ct 1921, 32 L Ed 2d 612; see *Minnesota v Dickerson* (1993) 508 US 366, 373, 113 S Ct 2130, 124 L Ed 2d 334. Pat searches, when authorized, are an exception to the principle that warrantless searches are unreasonable per se. 508 US at 372.

Not every *Terry* stop justifies a pat search, no matter how limited it may be. *Sibron v New York* (1968) 392 US 40, 62, 88 S Ct 1889, 20 L Ed 2d 917; *People v Hill* (1974) 12 C3d 731, 744, 117 CR 393, overruled on other grounds in 18 C3d 889, 896; *People v Superior Court* (Kiefer) (1970) 3 C3d 807, 829, 91 CR 729. Two conditions must be met before a pat search is permitted:

(1) The underlying detention must be valid. *Terry v Ohio* (1968) 392 US 1, 21, 88 S Ct 1868, 20 L Ed 2d 889. See, *e.g., Florida v J.L.* (2000) 529 US 266, 271, 120 S Ct 1375, 146 L Ed 2d 254 (anonymous tip that person is carrying gun does not justify stop and frisk); *In re Eskiel S.* (1993) 15 CA4th 1638, 1644, 19 CR2d 455 (drugs found in pat search inadmissible because officer lacked basis for detaining suspect).

(2) The officer must have "reason to believe that he is dealing with an armed and dangerous individual. . . . [T]he issue is whether a reasonably prudent man in the circumstances would be warranted in the belief that his safety or that of others was in danger." *Terry v Ohio, supra,* 392 US at 27; *People v Avila* (1997) 58 CA4th 1069, 1074, 68 CR2d 432. For applications of this condition, see §3.97.

The officer must have specific facts indicating that the person stopped is armed (*People v Superior Court* (Simon) (1972) 7 C3d 186, 208, 101

CR 837; *People v Barnes* (1983) 141 CA3d 854, 856, 190 CR 591), but need not be certain that this is so (*Terry v Ohio, supra*; *People v Avila, supra*). The critical question is whether this is "the kind of confrontation in which the officer can reasonably believe in the possibility that a weapon may be used against him" or her. *People v Superior Court* (Simon), *supra,* 7 C3d at 204 (routine traffic stop does not, without more, justify weapons frisk).

The officer need not question the suspect or otherwise investigate as long as the circumstances justify the detention and frisk. *Adams v Williams, supra*; *People v Rosales* (1989) 211 CA3d 325, 330, 259 CR 503; *People v May* (1973) 33 CA3d 888, 891, 109 CR 396 (officer properly detained and immediately frisked pedestrian whose rear pocket bulged four to five inches with an object that was visibly silver on top).

☛ **Judicial Tip**: As *Florida v J.L.* and *People v May* illustrate, occasionally the facts on which the police rely to justify the frisk are identical to the facts that were the basis for the stop. Most of the time, however, a dual, if sometimes overlapping, set of facts needs to be analyzed, one to determine the validity of the initial stop and another to adjudicate the weapons frisk.

### b. [§3.97] Reason To Believe That Detainee Is Armed

The following decisions illustrate how courts have dealt with the "reason to believe" requirement. A routine daytime traffic stop does not, without more, warrant a pat-down, even if the driver or passenger makes a furtive gesture such as reaching under the seat. *Kaplan v Superior Court* (1971) 6 C3d 150, 154, 98 CR 649; *People v Superior Court* (Kiefer) (1970) 3 C3d 807, 829, 91 CR 729. The result changes when the stop is at night, the officer is outnumbered, and the responses to the officer's questions are vague or unusual. *People v Satchell* (1978) 81 CA3d 347, 354, 146 CR 307 (vague answers); *People v Barnes* (1983) 141 CA3d 854, 856, 190 CR 591 (driver said his license was in his sock). A daytime stop to investigate a suspected drug deal warrants a pat search when the officers are outnumbered, know that drug dealers often carry weapons, and weapons are prevalent in the area. *People v Limon* (1993) 17 CA4th 524, 534, 21 CR2d 397.

☛ **Judicial Tip**: Most judges consider group characteristics, such as the habit of drug users or dealers to carry guns, insufficient standing by themselves to justify a weapons frisk.

A weapons frisk is justified when the officer sees bulges in clothing that make it reasonable to suspect the presence of a weapon (*Pennsylvania v Mimms* (1977) 434 US 106, 111, 98 S Ct 330, 54 L Ed 2d 331; *People v Snyder* (1992) 11 CA4th 389, 393, 13 CR2d 837), when the officer observes a weapon in the suspect's vehicle (*Michigan v Long* (1983) 463 US 1032, 1049, 103 S Ct 3469, 77 L Ed 2d 1201; *People v Superior Court* (Torres) (1977) 67 CA3d 620, 624–625, 136 CR 779), when the suspect reaches inside his jacket at the sight of police officers (*People v Lee* (1987) 194 CA3d 975, 983, 240 CR 32), when the officer has reason to suspect that the detainee was involved in a violent crime (*People v Franklin* (1985) 171 CA3d 627, 635, 217 CR 529 (armed robbery); *People v Orozco* (1981) 114 CA3d 435, 445, 170 CR 604 ("shots fired" report)), or after a dangerous high-speed chase (*People v Hill* (1974) 12 C3d 731, 745, 117 CR 393, overruled on other grounds in 18 C3d 889, 896).

Even minor offenses can give rise to the right to frisk. *In re Reginald C.* (1985) 171 CA3d 1072, 1075, 217 CR 768, upheld the pat search of a shoplift suspect who wore a zipped-up jacket on a hot day. In *People v Superior Court* (Brown) (1980) 111 CA3d 948, 956, 168 CR 915, the court approved the weapons pat-down of a jaywalker at 3:30 a.m.; he initially failed to comply with the officer's order to stop and when he finally stopped, he held his hands clasped together in front of a bulge in his waistband.

A weapons frisk of juvenile gang members is justified when members of the gang are known to have carried weapons in the past. *In re Stephen L.* (1984) 162 CA3d 257, 260–261, 208 CR 453.

Vehicle *passengers* can also be frisked upon reasonable suspicion that they may be armed. *People v Suennen* (1980) 114 CA3d 192, 199, 170 CR 677 (officer sees knife in car and makes other observations indicating that occupants might be burglars); *People v Satchell, supra*; *People v Superior Court* (Torres), *supra.*

Officers who search an apartment for drugs pursuant to a search warrant may pat search the occupants (*People v Thurman* (1989) 209 CA3d 817, 823, 257 CR 517), as well as persons who enter during the search (*People v Huerta* (1990) 218 CA3d 744, 750, 267 CR 243). In contrast, a search of business premises open to the public does not, without more, give rise to a right to frisk persons found there. *Ybarra v Illinois* (1979) 444 US 85, 93–96, 100 S Ct 338, 62 L Ed 2d 238.

Most cases, responsive to police officers' concerns for their safety, uphold weapons pat searches. There are limits, however. For example, an inability to produce written identification does not justify a weapons pat-down, even when combined with refusal to consent to a vehicle search, nervousness, and the discovery of baking soda in a film canister. *People v Dickey* (1994) 21 CA4th 952, 956, 27 CR2d 44. In *Santos v Superior Court* (1984) 154 CA3d 1178, 1184–1186, 202 CR 6, the defendant was detained at 10:00 p.m. after the officer saw him exchanging unidentified objects with another person. The defendant had no identification. The court held that there was no basis for assuming that he was dangerous, especially since the police officer did not express a belief that he was armed. The court concluded that the officer pat searched defendant to determine what he had been exchanging with the other person. See also *People v Hana* (1970) 7 CA3d 664, 669, 86 CR 721 (officer had no reason to believe that occupants of car stopped for faulty brake light were armed or dangerous); *People v Adam* (1969) 1 CA3d 486, 492, 81 CR 738 ("daylight encounter, between a young man, possibly under the influence of something, alone and apparently cooperative, with two police officers who were presumably armed" does not justify weapons frisk).

### c. [§3.98] Scope of Pat-down

The limited search permitted incident to a temporary detention is one for weapons, not for contraband or other objects. *Minnesota v Dickerson* (1993) 508 US 366, 373, 113 S Ct 2130, 124 L Ed 2d 334; *Terry v Ohio* (1968) 392 US 1, 17, 88 S Ct 1868, 20 L Ed 2d 889; *Kaplan v Superior Court* (1971) 6 C3d 150, 154, 98 CR 649. That purpose delineates the scope of the allowable search. As *Terry* put it, the frisk must "be confined in scope to an intrusion reasonably designed to discover guns, knives, clubs, or other hidden instruments for the assault of the police officer." 392 US at 29. In accord is *People v Hill* (1974) 12 C3d 731, 746, 117 CR 393, overruled on other grounds in 18 C3d 889, 896; see *People v Avila* (1997) 58 CA4th 1069, 1075, 68 CR2d 432.

The initial pat search is limited to a careful exploration of the outer clothing. *People v Collins* (1970) 1 C3d 658, 662, 83 CR 179. The officer may not, in lieu of a pat-down, reach forward and flip open the suspect's coat (*People v Aviles* (1971) 21 CA3d 230, 233–234, 98 CR 316), but during the frisk he may lift the back of a jacket that extends below the waist (*People v Todd* (1969) 2 CA3d 389, 391, 394, 82 CR 574). A weapons frisk is not limited to the upper body. See, *e.g., People v Avila, supra* (legs); *U.S. v Walker* (6th Cir 1999) 181 F3d 774, 779 (groin area). Occasionally, the pat-down can be of clothing not worn by the suspect. *People v Wright* (1988) 206 CA3d 1107, 1111, 254 CR 369 (naked suspect with known history of carrying concealed weapons is detained in motel room and asks for his pants; officer can pat search pants before handing them to suspect).

Once an officer concludes that the object felt is not a weapon, the pat-down may not be continued in an effort to determine whether the object is contraband. *Minnesota v Dickerson, supra*; *People v Dickey* (1994) 21 CA4th 952, 957, 27 CR2d 44 (squeezing object from outside to determine whether it is incriminating not permitted). As to seizure of contraband detected by touch during a properly limited weapons frisk, see §3.79.

The officer may normally not reach into the suspect's pockets without first pat searching him. *Sibron v New York* (1968) 392 US 40, 65, 88 S Ct 1889, 20 L Ed 2d 917; *People v Collins, supra*; *People v West* (1973) 31 CA3d 175, 177, 107 CR 127. Courts make exceptions when it would be dangerous for the officer not to take more direct action or when the detainee frustrates a frisk. *Adams v Williams* (1972) 407 US 143, 147–148, 92 S Ct 1921, 32 L Ed 2d 612 (officer had information that suspect in vehicle had gun at his waist; suspect refused to get out of car; officer properly reached through window and removed revolver from waistband); *In re John C.* (1978) 80 CA3d 814, 819, 145 CR 228 (defendant reached to waistband, removed object that he secreted in his hand, and refused to drop it; officer properly forced suspect's hand open); *People v Wigginton* (1973) 35 CA3d 732, 737, 111 CR 26 (defendant failed to comply with repeated orders to raise his hands); *People v Superior Court* (Holmes) (1971) 15 CA3d 806, 813, 94 CR 728 (detainee reached into rear pants pocket; officer properly grabbed his arm, reached into pocket, and removed automatic pistol); *People v Woods* (1970) 6 CA3d 832, 837, 86 CR 264 (defendant kept his hand concealed in his jacket pocket and would not answer questions as to what he had in pocket). But see *People v McKelvy* (1972) 23 CA3d 1027, 1039, 100 CR 661 (officer saw defendant place a small object into his pocket and ordered him to hand it over; held improper because no pat-down was first conducted).

A sudden move by a person, such as thrusting a hand into a bulging pocket as officers approach, can concurrently create the basis for detention and the emergency that justifies bypassing the pat search. *People v Rosales* (1989) 211 CA3d 325, 330, 259 CR 503.

☛ **Judicial Tip**: The judge should be wary of arguments that the legitimate concern that the suspect may be armed justifies bypassing a pat search. Such concern is precisely what gives rise to a right to frisk the defendant, as discussed in §3.97. Bypassing the weapons frisk is allowable only under the exceptional circumstances illustrated above.

#### d. [§3.99] Effect of Exceeding Proper Scope of Pat-down

When a "protective search goes beyond what is necessary to determine if the suspect is armed, it is no longer valid under *Terry* and its fruits will be suppressed." *Minnesota v Dickerson* (1993) 508 US 366, 373, 113 S Ct 2130, 124 L Ed 2d 334; *Sibron v New York* (1968) 392 US 40, 65–66, 88 S Ct 1889, 20 L Ed 2d 917; *People v Avila* (1997) 58 CA4th 1069, 1075, 68 CR2d 432. For discussion of when it is proper to search beyond the scope of the initial frisk, see §§3.100–3.107.

## 2. Search Beyond Pat-down

### a. Reaching Into Suspect's Clothing

#### (1) [§3.100] Basic Principles

During a weapons frisk the officer may generally reach into a suspect's pockets or clothing only to remove what reasonably feels like a weapon. *Sibron v New York* (1968) 392 US 40, 64–66, 88 S Ct 1889, 20 L Ed 2d 917; *People v Mosher* (1969) 1 C3d 379, 394, 82 CR 379 ("an object which a prudent man could believe was . . . usable as an instrument of assault"). The officer must be able to point to specific articulable facts supporting the suspicion that the item the officer touches is a weapon. *People v Leib* (1976) 16 C3d 869, 876, 129 CR 433; *People v Collins* (1970) 1 C3d 658, 662, 83 CR 179. The fact that an object feels hard is usually sufficient. See §3.101.

The officer may reach into clothing to recover items that do not feel like weapons, such as soft objects, under two circumstances:

(1) The officer may do so when the incriminating character of the object is "immediately apparent." *Minnesota v Dickerson* (1993) 508 US 366, 375, 113 S Ct 2130, 124 L Ed 2d 334; *People v Dickey* (1994) 21 CA4th 952, 957, 27 CR2d 44.

(2) When the officer has probable cause to arrest the defendant, the pat-down may be expanded to the full search that is permitted incident to arrest. *People v Dibb* (1995) 37 CA4th 832, 836–837, 43 CR2d 823; *People v Lee* (1987) 194 CA3d 975, 983–984, 240 CR 32. For further discussion, see §3.102.

#### (2) [§3.101] Objects That Feel Like Weapons

*Hard objects.* Courts generally sustain the officer's judgment when he or she feels a hard object that might be a weapon. Here the courts' operating philosophy is "better safe than sorry." *U.S. v Brown* (7th Cir 1999) 188 F3d 860, 866. The officer may reach into clothing to remove any hard object that feels like a weapon. *People v Allen* (1975) 50 CA3d 896, 902, 123 CR 80. For example, the officer may reach for items that feel like:

- A knife (*People v Orozco* (1981) 114 CA3d 435, 445, 170 CR 604; *In re Donald L.* (1978) 81 CA3d 770, 774, 146 CR 720);
- Sharp, like a knife blade (*People v Mosher* (1969) 1 C3d 379, 393, 82 CR 379);
- A hypodermic needle (*People v Autry* (1991) 232 CA3d 365, 368, 283 CR 417);
- A large bottle (*People v Snyder* (1992) 11 CA4th 389, 393, 13 CR2d 837);
- Flashlights and screwdrivers (*People v Suennen* (1980) 114 CA3d 192, 200, 170 CR 677; *People v Myles* (1975) 50 CA3d 423, 430, 123 CR 348);
- An ammunition clip (*People v Smith* (1971) 17 CA3d 604, 606, 95 CR 229);
- A shotgun shell (*People v Atmore* (1970) 13 CA3d 244, 247–248, 91 CR 311).

The officer may also remove other objects hard to the touch that the officer cannot identify but that he believes may be weapons. *People v Hill* (1974) 12 C3d 731, 741, 117 CR 393, overruled on other grounds in 18 C3d 889, 896 ("hard, square object" that turned out to be a three-inch matchbox; but see below as to matchboxes generally); *People v Huerta* (1990) 218 CA3d 744, 747, 267 CR 243 (large bulge in breast pocket that felt like small caliber weapon wrapped in handkerchief, but turned out to be money, as detainee had asserted); *People v Watson* (1970) 12 CA3d 130, 135, 90 CR 483 (hard object that proved to be a pipe); *Amacher v Superior Court* (1969) 1 CA3d 150, 152, 81 CR 558 ("hard object").

Officers are allowed greater leeway when the items are felt through boots or heavy clothing. *In re Willy L.* (1976) 56 CA3d 256, 262, 128 CR 592 (bulky objects in defendant's zip-up boots); *People v Allen, supra* (hard object felt through heavy jeans); *People v Watson, supra* (hard object felt through leather-type jacket).

It is not fatal if the officer is mistaken and the item turns out upon examination not to be a weapon. *People v Hill, supra*; *People v Mosher, supra*; *People v Huerta, supra*; *People v Allen, supra* (hard object proved to be car keys taped together).

*Soft objects.* In contrast to hard objects, courts are considerably more skeptical when an officer in the course of a *Terry* frisk feels soft items or objects that could feel like a weapon only "in some fanciful or extraordinary circumstances." *People v Leib* (1976) 16 C3d 869, 876, 129 CR

433 (small plastic pill bottle does not reasonably feel like a weapon). In *People v Mosher, supra,* 1 C3d at 394, the court said that "[a] box of matches, a plastic pouch, a pack of cigarettes, a wrapped sandwich, a container of pills, a wallet, coins, folded papers, and many other small items usually carried in an individual's pockets do not ordinarily feel like weapons."

Courts are concerned that allowing officers to reach into clothing for such objects by speculating that they may be or may contain weapons (a handkerchief could conceal a razor blade) "invites a plenary search" and "would render meaningless *Terry*'s requirement that pat-downs be limited in scope absent articulable grounds for an additional intrusion." *People v Collins* (1970) 1 C3d 658, 663, 83 CR 179. A suspicion that the suspect is armed with "an atypical weapon" must be supported by "specific and articulable facts." *People v Collins, supra.*

Accordingly, officers cannot usually reach into clothing for items that feel like a lump (*Kaplan v Superior Court* (1971) 6 C3d 150, 154, 98 CR 649; *People v Collins, supra*) or a plastic container (*People v Leib, supra*). However, *Mosher*'s statement as to what ordinarily feels like a weapon applies only when the officer's touch tells him what the object is likely to be. Thus, as noted above, an officer who feels merely a hard object can reach into clothing for what may turn out to be a large matchbox (*People v Hill, supra*) or a flip-top cigarette package (*Amacher v Superior Court* (1969) 1 CA3d 150, 154, 81 CR 558).

### (3) [§3.102] Objects That Feel Like Contraband Rather Than Weapons

As noted in §3.100, *Minnesota v Dickerson* (1993) 508 US 366, 113 S Ct 2130, 124 L Ed 2d 334, created an exception to the principle that an officer during a weapons frisk may only remove objects from the detainee that feel like possible weapons. The court permitted officers to remove contraband detected by touch, establishing a "plain touch" rule analogous to the so-called "plain view" doctrine. Under the latter, "if police are lawfully in a position from which they view an object, if its incriminating character is immediately apparent, and if the officers have a lawful right of access to the object, they may seize it without a warrant." 508 US at 375; for further discussion of plain view, see §§5.9–5.24.

The key limitation is that the contraband nature of the object felt must be "immediately apparent." (508 US at 375). When an officer has concluded that an item in defendant's pocket is not a weapon, the officer may not continue to explore it with his or her fingers in order to determine what it is; such exploration is not "plain touch" (508 US at 378–379;

officer manipulated small lump in defendant's pocket). Similarly, squeezing an object from the outside to determine whether it is incriminating is not permitted. *People v Dickey* (1994) 21 CA4th 952, 957, 27 CR2d 44; see *Bond v U.S.* (2000) 529 US 334, 338–339, 120 S Ct 1462, 146 L Ed 2d 365.

The "immediately apparent" requirement has two components. The police must have probable cause to believe by sight or touch that the object is contraband, and probable cause must arise immediately on seeing or touching the object "without conducting some further search of it." *Minnesota v Dickerson, supra*, 508 US at 375–376. Feeling a small lump is probably not sufficient. 508 US at 378–379. Nor is feeling a bulge that "led me to believe that it might be a controlled substance." *People v Dickey, supra,* 21 CA4th at 955. In contrast, the sensation of plastic sliding against a granular substance, without manipulating the object, makes the probable contraband nature immediately apparent. *U.S. v Mattarolo* (9th Cir 2000) 209 F3d 1153, 1158. Additional facts known to the officer may also provide sufficient immediate probable cause. *People v Dibb* (1995) 37 CA4th 832, 836–837, 43 CR2d 823 (before pat search detected lumpy object beneath defendant's pants, officer had found scale smelling of methamphetamine, two beepers, and a plastic bag).

California courts anticipated *Minnesota v Dickerson* in decisions holding that the sense of touch, like the sense of smell, may provide probable cause to arrest. *People v Lee* (1987) 194 CA3d 975, 983–984, 240 CR 32 (officer felt what he believed to be heroin-filled balloons); *People v Thurman* (1989) 209 CA3d 817, 825, 257 CR 517 (experienced officer felt what he believed to be rock cocaine). On occasion, touch plus other lawful observations provide probable cause. *People v Dibb, supra* (methamphetamine odor). Many common containers, such as pill bottles, cigarette packs, film canisters, and aluminum foil-wrapped packages, may not be seized merely because they might be used to store narcotics. *People v Holt* (1989) 212 CA3d 1200, 1205, 261 CR 89; *People v Valdez* (1987) 196 CA3d 799, 807, 242 CR 142; see *People v Nonnette* (1990) 221 CA3d 659, 666, 271 CR 329.

### b. [§3.103] Removing Objects From Suspect and Examining Them

When a frisk reveals a hard object that might be a weapon, the officer is justified in removing it into view. *People v Limon* (1993) 17 CA4th 524, 535, 21 CR2d 397; see §3.101. The officer can properly remove other items in the same pocket as a suspected weapon only under the following three limited circumstances:

(1) Accidentally, *i.e.,* when the officer's "hand emerged with more than he intended to remove from the pocket." *People v Atmore* (1970) 13 CA3d 244, 248, 91 CR 311 (officer reached into suspect's pocket for hard cylindrical object and at same time pulled out marijuana cigarette).

☛ **Judicial Tip**: Experienced judges suggest viewing with caution a contention that an item was removed "accidentally."

(2) When objects fall within the "plain touch" rule. See §3.102.

(3) On probable cause to arrest the detainee. See §3.102.

Although a police officer does not have to ignore items that properly come into plain view, such as the marijuana cigarette in *People v Atmore, supra,* he or she cannot open containers or packages not likely to contain weapons in the absence of probable cause. *People v Limon, supra* (discovery of hide-a-key box in context of suspected street drug sale provides probable cause to arrest); *People v Valdez* (1987) 196 CA3d 799, 806, 242 CR 142 (film canister); *In re John C.* (1978) 80 CA3d 814, 819, 145 CR 228 (package of cigarette papers); *Amacher v Superior Court* (1969) 1 CA3d 150, 154, 81 CR 558 (cigarette package). But see *People v Farlow* (1975) 52 CA3d 414, 416–417, 125 CR 118 (permissible for officer to look inside cigarette package that feels from outside as if it contained items other than cigarettes that might be weapons).

*Inquiry before removal.* When the officer does not know whether a bulky and somewhat hard object is a weapon, he or she may ask about the nature of the object. *People v Avila* (1997) 58 CA4th 1069, 1076, 68 CR2d 432. Inquiry is improper, however, when the officer has no reason to believe that the felt object is a weapon. *People v Valdez, supra.*

### 3. [§3.104] Search of Belongings

It is not entirely clear under what conditions and to what extent an officer who has the right to pat search a person can also search the suspect's accessories, such as purses, briefcases, and knapsacks for weapons. Few appellate courts have considered these questions in contrast to problems related to searches incident to custodial arrest.

Preliminarily, an officer who has *no* right to pat search a defendant cannot conduct a search of the suspect's belongings. *People v Lawler* (1973) 9 C3d 156, 161, 107 CR 13. In *People v Brisendine* (1975) 13 C3d 528, 119 CR 315, the court recognized a very limited right to search a knapsack for weapons under the unusual circumstances of the case. Two sheriff's deputies came across four campers in a national forest who had an illegal campfire at night. The deputies planned to take the campers out of the forest to the patrol car and cite them. Before doing so, they searched the persons and effects of the campers. The outer layer of defendant's knapsack was too solid to ascertain whether it contained weapons, and the deputy searched inside. He removed a frosted plastic bottle that contained marijuana and envelopes in which drugs were found.

The court held that a pat-down of the campers and their effects was justified because the officers had to escort them and their belongings a considerable distance over difficult terrain at night and could not be sure that the campers would not obtain access to their gear during the trek. The court also held that, because feeling the knapsack's exterior proved insufficient to allay the officers' fears, they could look in the interior. As in other weapons search situations, however, they could not lawfully examine the contents of the opaque bottle and of the envelopes because the officers had no reason to believe that they contained weapons and no probable cause to suspect that they contained contraband. 13 C3d at 535.

Although in *Brisendine* the campers were technically under arrest, the court used a pat search analysis, and the decision is therefore germane to *Terry* stops. The strong implication of *Brisendine* is that effects can be searched only if the officers cannot keep them away from the suspect during the detention.

*People v Ritter* (1997) 54 CA4th 274, 280, 62 CR2d 686, upheld a weapons search of a fanny pack that defendant had set on the ground. The officer had observed what he suspected was the outline of a handgun in the outer compartment of the fanny pack. *Ritter* indicates that the belongings of a detainee may be searched for weapons under circumstances analogous to those that permit a vehicle search for weapons. As to the latter, see §3.105.

### 4. [§3.105] Search of Vehicles for Weapons

An officer may search a car's passenger compartment incident to a *Terry* stop "if the police officer possesses a reasonable belief based on 'specific and articulable facts which, taken together with the rational inferences from those facts, reasonably warrant' the officers in believing that the suspect is dangerous and the suspect may gain immediate control of weapons." *Michigan v Long* (1983) 463 US 1032, 1049, 103 S Ct 3469, 77 L Ed 2d 1201.

The specific and articulable facts that made the vehicle search lawful in *Michigan v Long* were that defendant drove at excessive speed, swerved into a ditch, and appeared to be intoxicated. As the defendant walked back to the car and was about to reenter it, the officer saw a large hunting knife on the floor board. 463 US at 1035–1036.

Other situations in which a vehicle weapons search has been upheld include:

- Stop for lack of registration sticker on rear license plate. Search based on 6-year-old report of weapons violation; dispatcher did not inform the officer on scene of the age of the report. *People v Bush* (2001) 88 CA4th 1048, 1052–1053, 106 CR2d 439.
- Detention of two people in a parked car to investigate reported drug use; the officer recognized that the passenger had recently been arrested for possession of drugs and of a dangerous weapon. *People v Brueckner* (1990) 223 CA3d 1500, 1506, 273 CR 292.
- Stop for expired registration tags; the officer saw the driver reach under the driver's seat and heard the sound of metal on metal. *People v King* (1989) 216 CA3d 1237, 1240, 265 CR 370.
- Stop for inoperable headlight; officer sees legal four-inch knife in a sheath. *People v Lafitte* (1989) 211 CA3d 1429, 1431, 259 CR 915.
- Traffic stop that lawfully escalated into an investigation of an armed robbery in which a sawed-off shotgun had been used; a frisk of the defendant had turned up a shotgun shell. *People v Franklin* (1985) 171 CA3d 627, 634, 217 CR 529.

The search must be limited to those areas of the vehicle's passenger compartment where a weapon may be placed or hidden. *Michigan v Long, supra.* The police may seize contraband discovered in the course of a proper weapons search. *People v Brueckner, supra* (open paper bag containing drugs).

In *Michigan v Long,* the court stressed that its decision did "not mean that the police may conduct automobile searches *whenever* they conduct an investigative stop." 463 US at 1049 n14 (emphasis in original). In accord is *Knowles v Iowa* (1998) 525 US 113, 114, 119 S Ct 484, 142 L Ed 2d 492 (stop for traffic violation does not, without more, permit vehicle search).

For discussion of vehicle searches for identification, see §3.107.

## C. Search for Identification

### 1. [§3.106] Persons

*Terry* only addressed searches for weapons during an investigative stop. The U.S. Supreme Court has not decided whether police officers can require a detainee to produce identification and, upon his refusal, search him for identification papers. Two California decisions, however, recognize a limited right to do so.

In *People v Long* (1987) 189 CA3d 77, 234 CR 271, the defendant denied having any identification on him. The officer noticed a wallet-sized bulge in his rear pants pocket and directed defendant to look through his wallet. While defendant did that, the officer observed several bindles in the wallet that he recognized as common methamphetamine packaging. The defendant said that nothing in the wallet would identify him. The officer asked the defendant to hand over the wallet and found the bindles, which formed the basis for the defendant's prosecution. He also found identifying papers.

The court upheld the search, saying that requiring the production of identification is a minimal intrusion, that the defendant's oral statement of his name was suspect when he insisted he had no identification while appearing to carry a wallet, and that the officer was entitled to watch the defendant go through the wallet to prevent destruction of evidence or injury from a concealed weapon. 189 CA3d at 88.

*People v Loudermilk* (1987) 195 CA3d 996, 241 CR 208, went a step further. As in *Long,* the defendant denied having any identification when asked to produce it. During a *Terry* frisk, the officer felt a wallet, removed it, and went through it for identification. Defendant blurted out a confession and later argued that the confession was the fruit of the allegedly unlawful search and seizure of his wallet.

In rejecting this contention, the court said that as part of an investigative stop, the police can require proof of identification and the seizure and examination of the wallet is proper when defendant lies about having identification. 195 CA3d at 1002. This holding is weakened by the court's alternative ruling that the officer had probable cause to arrest defendant and that the seizure of the wallet was justified as incident to the arrest. 195 CA3d at 1004.

*Long* and *Loudermilk* are clear that during a lawful detention, officers have the right to request written identification. The officers' right to proceed further and either demand production of a wallet or seize it hinges, according to the two decisions, on defendant's untruthful denial of having written identification. *Loudermilk* states (195 CA3d at 1004):

> We must emphasize that we do *not* hold that a suspect may be detained and searched merely because he either refused to identify himself or refused to produce proof of identification. Nor do we hold that each time an officer conducts a *Terry* stop he may immediately conduct a search for identification. The rule we announce does not provide officers with unfettered discretion and does not open citizens

> to harassment. Our decision, allowing the officer to seize the wallet, is limited to the unique facts of this case, where defendant lied to the officer and himself created the confusion as to his own identity. [Emphasis in original.]

What an officer may do when the suspect does not lie but merely refuses to produce identification is left for future decisions. Many judges doubt that the line will ultimately be drawn at lying. *State v Flynn* (1979) 92 Wis2d 427, 446, 285 NW2d 710, on which *Long* relied, upheld removal and search of a wallet when the defendant admitted having identification in his wallet but refused to produce it. Inability to produce identification does not justify a frisk. See §3.97.

The U.S. Supreme Court has expressly left open two questions: (1) Whether a person lawfully detained has a legitimate expectation of privacy in his identity, and (2) whether compelled identification during a *Terry* stop violates the Fifth Amendment. *Kolender v Lawson* (1983) 461 US 352, 362, 103 S Ct 1855, 75 L Ed 903.

In contrast, when probable cause to arrest exists, the officer clearly has a right to take the defendant's wallet to look for identification. *People v Adams* (1985) 175 CA3d 855, 860, 221 CR 298; *People v Sanchez* (1985) 174 CA3d 343, 346, 220 CR 53. This is even though the officer has not yet placed the defendant under arrest. *People v Adams, supra,* 175 CA3d at 861.

### 2. [§3.107] Vehicles

In the course of a traffic stop the officer has the right to examine the car's vehicle identification number (VIN). *New York v Class* (1986) 475 US 106, 113, 106 S Ct 960, 89 L Ed 2d 81. When papers in the car obscure the number located on top of the dashboard, the officer can reach in and move the papers, at least under the following conditions: (1) The driver has gotten out of the car; (2) the officer cannot find the second VIN, which is normally on the door jamb; and (3) the officer does not rummage around the interior of the car but limits his intrusion to his objective. *New York v Class, supra.* When the VIN has been tampered with, the officer can examine the secret VIN in the engine compartment. *People v Lindsey* (1986) 182 CA3d 772, 777, 227 CR 550.

To avoid a potential threat to safety, an officer can enter the vehicle to retrieve a driver's license or registration papers rather than let the driver who has exited the car go back and get them. *People v Faddler* (1982) 132 CA3d 607, 610, 183 CR 328 (DUI stop at 2:00 a.m. of vehicle with three occupants, one of whom was intoxicated and another boisterous). In *People v Hart* (1999) 74 CA4th 479, 488, 86 CR2d 762, an officer talked to the occupants of a parked van at night. After defendant unsuccessfully looked for identification in the van for several minutes, the officer ordered her out, entered the van, removed her purse from the floor, searched it, and found drugs and an identification card. The court upheld the search on officer safety grounds.

# 4

# Arrest and Searches Incident to Arrest

## I. [§4.1] SCOPE OF CHAPTER

Sections 4.2–4.4 place arrests in the context of the Fourth Amendment and summarize the Amendment's major requirements for a valid arrest. Sections 4.5 and 4.6 discuss the meaning of the term "arrest." Sections 4.7–4.41 cover warrantless arrests, with particular focus on the authority of peace officers and private persons to make arrests and on the underlying requirements of probable cause. Sections 4.42–4.58 deal with arrest warrants and supporting affidavits. Requirements concerning the time, place, and manner of arrests, *i.e.*, nighttime service of warrants, *Payton-Ramey* and knock-notice rules, notice of arrest, and limitations on the use of force, are the topics of §§4.59–4.91.

Sections 4.92–4.102 discuss principles that come into play *after* an arrest, such as a defendant's rights to telephone, to be taken before a magistrate without unnecessary delay, and to a prompt judicial determination of probable cause. Sections 4.103–4.136 cover searches incidental to arrest.

## II. ARREST AND THE FOURTH AMENDMENT

### A. [§4.2] Role of Fourth Amendment

An arrest is a seizure of the person within the meaning of the Fourth Amendment. *Terry v Ohio* (1968) 392 US 1, 16, 88 S Ct 1868, 20 L Ed 2d 889. Fourth Amendment case law does the following:

- Prescribes the standards for a lawful arrest. For a summary, see §4.3.
- Governs the consequences of an unlawful arrest. See §4.4.
- Mandates a prompt postarrest determination of probable cause to arrest under the circumstances discussed in §4.95.
- Delineates the permissible scope of searches incident to arrest. See §§4.103–4.136.

The Fourth Amendment and statutory meanings of the term "arrest" differ. See §§4.5–4.6. Many statutes impose requirements for arrests, particularly Pen C §§834–851.6. Some statutes, such as Pen C §844 (knock-notice), overlap the Fourth Amendment. Others do not. Statutory rules are discussed at appropriate places in this chapter.

### B. [§4.3] Key Requirements for Valid Arrest

Major Fourth Amendment requirements for any lawful arrest include:

- Probable cause to arrest. See §§4.24–4.41.
- The use of only reasonable force in effecting the arrest. See §§4.90–4.91.

In addition, residential arrests must generally be based on an arrest warrant (see §§4.61–4.79) and comply with knock-notice rules. See §§4.81–4.88.

### C. [§4.4] Consequences of Arrest in Violation of Fourth Amendment

An invalid arrest does not bar prosecution of the defendant on the underlying charges. *U.S. v Alvarez-Machain* (1992) 504 US 655, 657, 112 S Ct 2188, 119 L Ed 2d 441; *People v Bradford* (1969) 70 C2d 333, 344, 74

CR 726. But a search incident to an unlawful arrest is also unlawful, and the exclusionary rule generally renders evidence from an arrest in violation of the Fourth Amendment inadmissible. See, *e.g.*, *Payton v New York* (1980) 445 US 573, 584–587, 100 S Ct 1371, 63 L Ed 2d 639; *Brown v Illinois* (1975) 422 US 590, 601, 95 S Ct 2254, 45 L Ed 2d 416; see §§4.79 (consequences of *Payton* violation), 4.90 (application of exclusionary rule uncertain in excessive force cases). For discussion of good faith and the limits of the exclusionary rule, see §§1.28–1.43.

## III. MEANING OF ARREST

### A. [§4.5] Differences Between Fourth Amendment and Statutory Meaning

An arrest for purposes of the Fourth Amendment differs significantly from an arrest as defined by statute. Although the two concepts overlap, there are critical differences between them:

(1) A person can be under arrest for purposes of the Fourth Amendment without being taken into custody and brought to the police station. Fourth Amendment analysis treats as an arrest any restraint on a person's liberty more serious or extensive than that permitted for a temporary detention. See §3.4; for statutory meaning, see §4.6. When police officers exceed the permissible scope of a temporary detention, the Fourth Amendment inquiry becomes whether they had proper grounds to arrest the defendant.

(2) Statutory law may describe a particular police-civilian encounter as an arrest while Fourth Amendment law treats it as a temporary detention for the purpose of determining what kind of search, if any, the police may conduct. The most common example is a traffic stop in order to issue a citation. The Vehicle Code refers to this situation as an arrest (Veh C §§40303, 40500, 40501); however, this type of "arrest" only permits the limited search that *Terry* and its progeny authorize for temporary detentions, unless appropriate grounds for a more extensive search develop during the encounter. See §4.104.

The thrust of the courts is to focus on reality rather than labels. The first principle reflects the fact that some police activities are tantamount to an arrest no matter what they are formally called. The second recognizes the unreasonableness of allowing extensive searches following every routine traffic stop. See *Knowles v Iowa* (1998) 525 US 113, 117–119, 119 S Ct 484, 142 L Ed 2d 492.

### B. [§4.6] Arrest as Custody and Restraint

"The essential elements of an arrest" are

- "[T]aking a person into custody" (Pen C §834), and
- "[A]ctual restraint of the person or his submission to custody" (Pen C §835). *People v Hatcher* (1969) 2 CA3d 71, 75, 82 CR 323; see *Evans v City of Bakersfield* (1994) 22 CA4th 321, 330, 27 CR2d 406.

In *Hatcher,* the court used this "essential elements" analysis to decide that a defendant was under arrest when he was transported to the police station, ordered to empty his pockets, and taken to the squad room for interrogation. The police lacked probable cause for an arrest. The court ruled that therefore the defendant's statement at the station was inadmissible. Using the Fourth Amendment meaning of arrest, rather than the statutory meaning, would also lead to the conclusion that the defendant had been arrested because, as *Hatcher* noted, the restraint went far beyond a temporary detention for the purpose of making reasonable inquiries. 2 CA3d at 75–76.

*People v Parker* (1978) 85 CA3d 439, 443, 148 CR 513, and *People v Freund* (1975) 48 CA3d 49, 53, 119 CR 762, followed *Hatcher* to find an arrest when a trespasser on school grounds was taken to the school security office and there "detained," questioned, and searched (*Parker*), and when defendants were "detained" in a police car for more than three hours while the police obtained a search warrant (*Freund*). In these two cases, however, the court found that the officers had probable cause to arrest and that therefore the searches were lawful.

The use of the Fourth Amendment rather than the "essential elements" analysis to determine whether an arrest had occurred is illustrated by *People v Campbell* (1981) 118 CA3d 588, 595, 173 CR 442. The court held that handcuffing the defendant and taking him to an office was the "functional equivalent of arrest" because "the restraint employed by the police [went] beyond that which is reasonably necessary for a detention." As in *Parker* and *Freund*, the court further found that the officers had probable cause to arrest at the time they engaged in the "functional equivalent" of an arrest. Probable cause was not negated by the officers' erroneous characterization of their conduct as a detention.

*Transfer on unrelated charge.* The transfer of an arrested person to another facility for questioning on a charge unrelated to the initial arrest is not a new arrest and therefore does not require probable cause. *People v Hill* (1992) 3 C4th 959, 978, 13 CR2d 475.

## IV. ARREST WITHOUT WARRANT: AUTHORITY AND GROUNDS

### A. [§4.7] Authority To Arrest

California statutory law delineating authority to arrest is complex. Authority to arrest varies by the status of the person making the arrest, by the type of offense, and by the location of the arrest. Everyone in the state is empowered to arrest under certain conditions depending on whether the arrestor is a peace officer, a public officer or employee, or a private person. Pen C §§836–836.5, 837. Statutory provisions differentiate between several categories of peace officers. See Pen C §§830–832.8; Pub Res C §5008 (delegation of peace officer powers to employees of Department of Parks and Recreation); Pub Util C §21252; 4 Witkin & Epstein, California Criminal Law, *Pretrial Proceedings* §§3–8 (3d ed 2000).

### 1. Authority of Peace Officers To Arrest

#### a. [§4.8] Felony Arrests

Under Pen C §836(a)(3), a peace officer may arrest a person with or without a warrant upon probable cause to believe that the arrestee has committed a felony "whether or not a felony, in fact, has been committed." Residential arrests, however, usually require a warrant. See §§4.61–4.79.

Penal Code §836(a)(2) seems to provide an additional basis for felony arrests: "When a person arrested has committed a felony. . . ." This provision, however, does not create an alternative to probable cause. *People v Dupee* (1957) 151 CA2d 364, 366, 311 P2d 568 (reasonable grounds, *i.e.*, probable cause, required under Pen C §836(a)(2)); *People v Vice* (1956) 147 CA2d 269, 271–272, 305 P2d 270 (same). See *Michigan v Summers* (1981) 452 US 692, 699, 101 S Ct 2587, 69 L Ed 2d 340 (under Fourth Amendment arrest must be supported by probable cause).

#### b. Misdemeanors and Infractions

##### (1) [§4.9] Statutory Requirements; Effects of Violation

Penal Code §836(a)(1) authorizes warrantless arrests for misdemeanors and infractions upon probable cause to believe that the suspect committed the offense "*in the officer's presence.*" (Emphasis added.) The italicized limitation is not grounded in the Fourth Amendment, thus failure to comply with it does not bring the exclusionary rule into play (*People v Donaldson* (1995) 36 CA4th 532, 536, 42 CR2d 314; *People v Trapane* (1991) 1 CA4th Supp 10, 13, 3 CR2d 423), although the common law at the time the Fourth Amendment was adopted required an arrest warrant unless the misdemeanor was committed in the officer's presence. 3 LaFave, Search and Seizure, p 13 (3d ed 1996) (hereafter cited as LaFave).

The legislature has created a growing number of exceptions to the in-the-presence mandate, including many DUI offenses (Veh C §§40300.5, 40300.6), domestic violence (Pen C §836(c), (d)), certain other assaults and batteries (Pen C §§243.5(a)(2), 836.1), and certain firearm offenses (Pen C §§836(e), 12031(a)). In addition, the in-the-presence requirement does not apply to the arrest of a minor. See §4.16.

The in-the-presence requirement, however, continues to apply in such situations as state law false arrest suits and administrative proceedings to suspend or revoke a person's driving privilege under Veh C §13353. The latter must be predicated on a lawful arrest under Pen C §836(a)(1) or Veh C §40300.5. *Mercer v DMV* (1991) 53 C3d 753, 280 CR 745; *Johanson v DMV* (1995) 36 CA4th 1209, 1216, 43 CR2d 42; see *People v Donaldson, supra,* 36 CA4th at 538.

*Special limitation for infractions.* Custodial arrests are generally not permitted for infractions. Pen C §853.5 (mandating release on promise to appear). See also §4.13.

### (2) [§4.10] Components of In-the-Presence Rule

The in-the-presence requirement of Pen C §836(a)(1) has two components:

(1) The person making the arrest must be able to "testify, based on his or her senses, to acts which constitute every material element" of the offense. *Music v DMV* (1990) 221 CA3d 841, 848, 270 CR 692; *People v Welsch* (1984) 151 CA3d 1038, 1042, 199 CR 87; *In re Alonzo C.* (1978) 87 CA3d 707, 713, 151 CR 192. For further discussion, see §4.11.

(2) The arrest "must be made at the time of the offense or within a reasonable time thereafter." *People v Hampton* (1985) 164 CA3d 27, 30, 209 CR 905; *People v Williams* (1971) 17 CA3d 554, 562, 95 CR 234, disapproved on other grounds in 16 C3d 263, 276 n7; *Jackson v Superior Court* (1950) 98 CA2d 183, 185, 219 P2d 879. Unless the arrest is "reasonably contemporaneous" with the commission of the offense, the statutory basis for the arrest (*i.e.,* "reasonable cause to believe that the person to be arrested has committed a public offense in his presence" (Pen C §836(a)(1)) "has evaporated." *People v Williams, supra.* For further discussion, see §4.12.

### (3) [§4.11] Ability To Testify to Elements of Offense

The offense need not occur in the immediate proximity of the person making the arrest; the test, rather, "is whether the misdemeanor is apparent to the officer's senses." *In re Alonzo C.* (1978) 87 CA3d 707, 712, 151

CR 192 (interior quotation marks omitted); *People v Brown* (1955) 45 C2d 640, 642, 290 P2d 528; *Mann v Mack* (1984) 155 CA3d 666, 674, 202 CR 296. The officer may rely on any of his or her senses, such as smell, sight, or hearing. See cases cited in *In re Alonzo C., supra.*

The following situations are illustrative:

(a) *DUI.* To justify a drunk driving arrest the officer must observe some movement of the car, however slight. *Mercer v DMV* (1991) 53 C3d 753, 762, 280 CR 745. But there are many exceptions. See Veh C §40300.5 (traffic accident, obstruction of road, danger that driver won't be apprehended unless arrested immediately, or that driver might injure himself or herself or damage property or conceal evidence). Movement is not required to justify an arrest for attempted drunk driving or public intoxication. See *Mercer v DMV, supra.*

(b) *Hit-and-run.* A warrantless hit-and-run arrest is not justified when the officer sees defendant running, hears others say that there had been a hit-and-run accident, chases defendant, and arrests him. *People v Welsch* (1984) 151 CA3d 1038, 1042, 199 CR 87. In this situation, unlike drunk-driving arrests, there is no statutory permission to arrest on probable cause alone when an accident has occurred. See Veh C §40300.5.

(c) *Noise complaint.* An officer, investigating a noise complaint, who hears loud music coming from a garage can properly arrest an occupant for violation of a local noise ordinance. *Mann v Mack, supra*; see *People v Goldberg* (1969) 2 CA3d 30, 33, 82 CR 314 (officer who hears loud music late at night has basis for Pen C §415 arrest).

(d) *Obscene film showing.* An officer, acting on a report that obscene films would be shown in a motel room, climbs onto a trellis, peeks into the window of the room and, though the curtains are drawn, sees an obscene film through a small aperture. Here the major problem is not the adequacy of the sense data, but the fact that the officer had no right to be where he was; the peeking is an unreasonable infringement of privacy. *Pate v Municipal Court* (1970) 11 CA3d 721, 724, 89 CR 893; *Bielicki v Superior Court* (1962) 57 C2d 602, 605, 21 CR 552 (arrest invalid when based on spying into public toilet booth to observe homosexual activity).

(e) *Glue sniffing.* An officer smells paint on defendant's breath and sees traces of paint in his nostrils and on his hands. At the time Pen C §381 prohibited willfully sniffing the fumes of glue and paint. The observations are insufficient for an arrest. They show only that defendant had been sniffing, but not that he was doing so at the time the officer arrived. *In re Alonzo C.* (1978) 87 CA3d 707, 715, 151 CR 192. The officer observed only the aftermath of the offense, not its commission.

(f) *Drunk in public.* In contrast to glue sniffing, some offenses, such as violations of Pen C §647(f) (drunk in public), are continuing. The offense necessarily takes place in the presence of the officer who encounters the inebriate. *In re Alonzo C., supra.* The occasional issue in drunk arrests is whether the officer observed all of the elements of the offense, particularly facts justifying the conclusion that the defendant was unable to care for himself. See *People v Engleman* (1981) 116 CA3d Supp 14, 16, 172 CR 474.

### (4) [§4.12] Reasonable Contemporaneity

A warrantless misdemeanor arrest must be made within a reasonable time after the offense is committed in the officer's presence. Thus, a warrantless misdemeanor arrest made the day after the offense is too late. *Jackson v Superior Court* (1950) 98 CA2d 183, 188, 219 P2d 879. But an officer who drove an intoxicated woman home and saw her drive away less than 15 minutes later was found to have arrested her within a reasonable time after the offense was committed. This finding was upheld even though he pursued her and then lost sight of her and only arrested her after her return to her apartment. *People v Hampton* (1985) 164 CA3d 27, 31, 209 CR 905.

In the case of citizens' arrests, greater leeway is granted because courts consider it wise to encourage civilians to enlist the aid of the police before making arrests. *Green v DMV* (1977) 68 CA3d 536, 541, 137 CR 368 (35–40 minutes); *Hill v Levy* (1953) 117 CA2d 667, 671, 256 P2d 622 (less than half hour).

The contemporaneity requirement does *not* apply to felony arrests. *People v Williams* (1971) 17 CA3d 554, 562, 95 CR 234, disapproved on other grounds in 16 C3d 263, 276 n7.

### (5) [§4.13] Custodial Arrest for Minor Offenses

*Statutes.* Authority to make custodial arrests for minor traffic and other offenses is circumscribed by statutory cite-and-release procedures. Pen C §§853.5–853.6; Veh C §§40302–40304, 40500, 40504. See *People v Superior Court* (Simon) (1972) 7 C3d 186, 208–211, 101 CR 837; *People v Monroe* (1993) 12 CA4th 1174, 1180–1182, 16 CR2d 267.

*Fourth Amendment.* "If an officer has probable cause to believe that an individual has committed even a very minor criminal offense in his presence, he may, without violating the Fourth Amendment, arrest the offender." *Atwater v City of Lago Vista* (2001) 532 US 318, 121 S Ct 1536, 149 L Ed 2d 549, 577.

### c. [§4.14] Arrest on "Suspicion of" Offense or for Investigation

The "apparently common practice for police officers to arrest and book persons for 'suspicion of' a particular offense . . . is not authorized by law." *McMahon v Municipal Court* (1970) 6 CA3d 194, 197 n1, 85 CR 782. The court added that the practice "is the result of the fact that a peace officer under certain circumstances may arrest a person '[w]henever he has reasonable cause to believe that the person to be arrested has committed' a crime. But the fact remains that the person is arrested, for example, for burglary (which is a crime) and not for 'suspicion of burglary' (which is not a crime)." Similarly, an arrest may not lawfully be made merely for investigation of a crime. *People v Superior Court* (Johnson) (1971) 15 CA3d 146, 152, 92 CR 916. Arresting a person for investigation, like making an arrest on suspicion, "is foreign to our system." *Papachristou v City of Jacksonville* (1972) 405 US 156, 169, 92 S Ct 839, 31 L Ed 2d 110.

☛ **Judicial Tip**: The court should test such arrests for probable cause as if they had been made for the actual offense underlying the suspicion. Such testing should not consider matters the police developed in the course of any postarrest investigation. See §4.27.

### d. [§4.15] Warrantless Arrest of Probationer

A peace officer or probation officer may arrest a probationer upon probable cause to believe that the arrestee is violating a condition of probation. Pen C §1203.2. By its terms this provision covers defendants released on conditional sentence or summary probation, as well as those on formal probation.

☛ **Judicial Tip**: Failure to pay court-ordered restitution is probably a basis for arrest only *after* the court has determined willful failure and ability to pay. See Pen C §1203.2.

As to parolees, see Pen C §§3060 (arrest upon written order of parole authority) and 3067 (parolee subject to search or seizure at any time with or without cause).

### e. Authority To Arrest Minors

#### (1) [§4.16] For Criminal Conduct

Under Welf & I C §625(a), a peace officer may arrest ("take into temporary custody") a minor without a warrant "when such officer has reasonable cause for believing that such minor is a person described in Section 601 or 602." Welfare and Institutions Code §602 brings a minor within the jurisdiction of the juvenile court "when he or she violates any law . . . defining crime other than an ordinance establishing a curfew based solely on age."

The arrest of a minor for conduct that would be a felony when committed by an adult requires the same probable cause as adult arrests under Pen C §836(a)(2). *In re Brian A.* (1985) 173 CA3d 1168, 1173, 219 CR 361. However, authority to arrest juveniles for misdemeanors is broader than for adult arrests. An officer can arrest a minor on probable cause to believe that the juvenile committed the offense; the officer is not limited to probable cause to believe that the minor's violation occurred in the officer's presence. A statute that imposed the in-the-presence requirement on minors' arrests has been repealed. See *In re Thierry S.* (1977) 19 C3d 727, 735, 139 CR 708; *In re Gregory S.* (1980) 112 CA3d 764, 772, 169 CR 540. The broader authority to arrest minors is constitutional. *In re Samuel V.* (1990) 225 CA3d 511, 516, 277 CR 14.

A minor can also be arrested without a warrant on probable cause that he or she has violated a juvenile court order or escaped from a commitment ordered by the court. Welf & I C §625(b).

### (2) [§4.17] For Noncriminal Conduct, Curfew Violations, Truancy, or Sickness

The reference to Welf & I C §601 in Welf & I C §625(a) permits arrest on reasonable cause for believing that the minor comes within §601, *i.e.,* that he or she has habitually refused to obey his parents, is beyond their control, has violated a curfew ordinance based on age, is a habitual truant, or has habitually failed to obey orders of the school authorities. Section 601 should be read carefully for its definitions of prohibited conduct. Runaways come within Welf & I C §601. *People v Rice* (1970) 10 CA3d 730, 736, 89 CR 200. An arrest under Welf & I C §625(a) triggers the requirement of a *Miranda* admonition. Welf & I C §625.

*Curfew violations.* A violation of a local curfew ordinance only permits the officer to transport the minor to his or her residence, parents, or legal guardians. Welf & I C §625.5 (statutory authority is "to temporarily detain," in contrast to Welf & I C §625 which is framed in terms of taking the minor "into temporary custody"). However, by its terms, Welf & I C §625.5 applies only when the local governing body adopts "a resolution to implement this section." Welf & I C §625.5(b).

*Truancy.* As to arrests for truancy, in addition to Welf & I C §601 referred to above, see also Ed C §48264 (peace officers and designated others may arrest, during school hours, "any minor subject to compulsory full-time education or to compulsory continuation education found away from his or her home and who is absent from school without valid excuse . . ."). Education Code §48265 requires the person making the arrest to deliver the minor "forthwith" to his or her parent, guardian, or designated school authorities. A violation of Ed C §48265 renders the arrest illegal. *In re Jorge S.* (1977) 74 CA3d 852, 857, 141 CR 722 (minor's postarrest confession suppressed).

The sole purpose of a truancy arrest is to return the student to school as quickly as possible. This "severely limited type of arrest . . . may not be used as a pretext for investigating criminal matters." *In re James D.* (1987) 43 C3d 903, 915, 239 CR 663, quoting with approval from *In re Miguel G.* (1980) 111 CA3d 345, 349, 168 CR 688.

*Sick or injured minor.* Welfare and Institutions Code §625(c) authorizes custody of a minor "who is found in any street or public place suffering from any sickness or injury which requires care, medical treatment, hospitalization, or other remedial care." This subsection has not been interpreted by the courts.

#### f. [§4.18] Authority To Take Mentally Ill Person Into Custody

Welfare and Institutions Code §5150 authorizes peace officers and certain others to take "into custody" a person who "as a result of mental disorder, is a danger to others or to himself or herself, or gravely disabled."

The statute expressly requires probable cause. *People v Triplett* (1983) 144 CA3d 283, 288, 192 CR 537, held that this means probable cause to believe "that the person detained is mentally disordered and is a danger to himself or herself or is gravely disabled." In accord is *Heater v Southwood Psychiatric Center* (1996) 42 CA4th 1068, 1080, 49 CR2d 880. Although *Triplett* speaks of a "5150 *detention,*" the decision explicitly adapts "the test for probable cause for a warrantless arrest." *People v Triplett, supra,* 144 CA3d at 287.

Many judges believe that the compelling conclusion from *Triplett* is that the exclusionary rule comes into play when a person is taken into custody under Welf & I C §5150 without probable cause and subsequently charged with a crime. In contrast, the exclusionary rule does not apply to conservatorship proceedings. *Conservatorship of Susan T.* (1994) 8 C4th 1005, 1012–1013, 36 CR2d 40.

#### g. Territorial Limitations

#### (1) [§4.19] Penal Code §830.1

Certain peace officers have statewide authority to make any arrest permitted by Pen C §836, among them, state narcotics agents and CHP officers. Pen C §§830.1(b), 830.2(a). The arrest powers of city police officers and deputy sheriffs also extend throughout the state but not as broadly. Penal Code §830.1(a) governs arrests by police officers outside the city that employs them and by sheriffs outside their county. It does not restrict arrests by sheriffs in incorporated areas within their county because the jurisdiction of the sheriff is countywide. *People v Pina* (1977) 72 CA3d Supp 35, 39–40, 140 CR 270; *People v Scott* (1968) 259 CA2d 268, 280, 66 CR 257.

Penal Code §830.1(a) limits power to arrest only for offenses committed *outside* the political subdivision that employs the arresting officer. When the crime occurs inside the political subdivision, the officer has the same authority to make an arrest beyond the officer's political subdivision as within it. Penal Code §830.1(a)(1) specifies that the officer's authority "extends to any place in the state . . . [a]s to any public offense committed or which there is probable cause to believe has been committed within the political subdivision which employs the peace officer."

When the offense takes place outside the officer's political subdivision, an arrest generally requires either the prior consent of the appropriate law enforcement agency or the officer's presence at the offense plus exigent circumstances. Penal Code §830.1(a)(2) authorizes an officer to make an arrest in any place in the state

> [w]here the peace officer has the prior consent of the chief of police . . . , or person authorized by him or her to give consent, if the place is within a city or of the sheriff, or person authorized by him or her to give consent, if the place is within a county.

Consent can be informal. *People v Woods* (1970) 7 CA3d 382, 387–388, 86 CR 508 (oral consent by deputy sheriff to conduct investigation). Blanket advance consents are permitted. *People v Superior Court* (Freeberg) (1981) 117 CA3d 650, 653, 172 CR 903. One appellate department decision empowers sheriffs to give consent in incorporated as well as unincorporated areas. *People v Pina, supra.* Agreements conferring consent

- Also permit a temporary detention of a vehicle and its occupants outside the officer's territorial jurisdiction. See *People v Overton* (1994) 28 CA4th 1497, 1504, 34 CR2d 232.

- Do not apply to off-duty police officers working as private security guards. *Cervantez v J. C. Penney Co.* (1979) 24 C3d 579, 587, 156 CR 198.

Penal Code §830.1(a)(3) confers statewide authority to arrest

> [a]s to any public offense committed or which there is probable cause to believe has been committed in the peace officer's presence, and with

respect to which there is immediate danger to person or property, or of the escape of the perpetrator of the offense.

An infraction is a public offense within the meaning of this provision. *People v Hamilton* (1986) 191 CA3d Supp 13, 17–18, 236 CR 894; *People v Tennessee* (1970) 4 CA3d 788, 791, 84 CR 697. But see *People v Battle* (1975) 50 CA3d Supp 1, 6–7, 123 CR 636, and discussion in §§4.9, 4.13.

Only one of the specified three exigent circumstances, danger to person or property or of escape, needs to be shown. *People v Hamilton, supra.* One or more are usually present when the officer observes a moving vehicular offense. See *Lofthouse v DMV* (1981) 124 CA3d 730, 735, 177 CR 601 (DUI arrest); *People v Hamilton, supra,* 119 CA3d Supp at 19 (DUI arrest). An offense committed in a parked car does not necessarily create an exigency. *People v Bush* (1974) 37 CA3d 952, 955, 112 CR 770 (marijuana sale in parked vehicle created no danger to safety of others or flight risk). A parole condition search and arrest is not an exigent circumstance under Pen C §830.1(a)(3) and therefore is not authorized outside the officer's political subdivision. *People v Alesi* (1979) 89 CA3d 537, 543–544, 152 CR 623; *People v Pina, supra.*

Penal Code §1551.1 creates an additional exception to the principle against warrantless arrests for offenses committed outside the officer's political subdivision. It permits a warrantless arrest of a person charged with a felony in another state.

For discussion of the consequences of violating territorial limitations, see §4.20.

### (2) [§4.20] Status of Arrest Unauthorized by Pen C §830.1(a)

An arrest that violates territorial limitations is not necessarily invalid. It is treated as if it had been made by a private citizen. *Cervantez v J. C. Penney Co.* (1979) 24 C3d 579, 587, 156 CR 198; *People v Alesi* (1979) 89 CA3d 537, 544, 152 CR 623. A citizen's authority to arrest is narrower than a peace officer's, as discussed in §4.23, and a citizen's right to search incidental to an arrest is much more limited. Essentially, it is restricted to weapons searches. See Pen C §846; for further discussion, see §4.107.

### h. [§4.21] Arrests by Federal Law Enforcement Officers

While state law enforcement officials can arrest for federal law violations to the same extent as they can for state law crimes (*U.S. v Bowdach* (5th Cir 1977) 561 F2d 1160, 1168; *Wartson v U.S.* (9th Cir 1968) 400 F2d 25, 27), the converse depends on state authorization (*Connolly v*

*U.S. Dep't of Justice* (Fed Cir 1985) 766 F2d 507, 512–513). Penal Code §830.8 provides broad authorization. Federal law enforcement officers may make arrests in "[a]ny circumstances specified in Section 836 or Section 5150 of the Welfare and Institutions Code for violations of state or local laws." Pen C §830.8(a)(1).

An arrest by a federal law enforcement officer for a crime under state law is treated as a citizen's arrest when it does not fall within Pen C §830.8. *People v Lacey* (1973) 30 CA3d 170, 175, 105 CR 72.

The authority of federal officers to arrest for federal crimes is governed by United States Code provisions similar to Pen C §836. See, *e.g.,* 18 USC §§3052 (FBI), 3053 (U.S. marshals). In the absence of an applicable federal statute, the law of the state where the arrest takes place determines its validity, subject to the requirements of the Fourth Amendment. *Ker v California* (1963) 374 US 23, 31, 83 S Ct 1623, 10 L Ed 2d 726; *U.S. v Di Re* (1948) 332 US 581, 587, 68 S Ct 222, 92 L Ed 210.

The right of peace officers from other states to make "fresh pursuit" arrests are discussed in Pen C §§852–852.4 (Uniform Act on Fresh Pursuit).

### 2. Authority of Private Persons To Arrest

#### a. [§4.22] In General

Private persons have authority to arrest. Pen C §834. The most general authorization is for the so-called citizen's arrest, discussed in §4.23. In addition, a person who has bailed a defendant may arrest him or her and may authorize others to do so as provided in Pen C §1301. On the oral order of a magistrate a private person may arrest anyone committing or attempting to commit a public offense in the magistrate's presence. Pen C §838.

Private persons designated by Pen C §830.7 have peace officer powers within the scope of their employment if they have satisfactorily completed a peace officer training course. Persons summoned to aid a uniformed officer have the powers of a peace officer that are delegated to them by the summoning officer or that are reasonably necessary to assist the officer. Pen C §830.6(c). As to the right of persons making an arrest to summon aid, see Pen C §§723, 839.

#### b. [§4.23] Citizen's Arrest

The term "citizen's arrest" is widely used, but should not obscure the fact that authority to arrest is not limited to citizens, but extends to private persons generally. Pen C §837. It is, however, narrower than the authority of police officers in two significant respects:

(1) While a peace officer can arrest a person on probable cause to believe that the suspect committed a felony (Pen C §836(a)(3)), a valid citizen's arrest requires, in addition to probable cause, that "a felony has been in fact committed." Pen C §837(3). This latter requirement "can only be met if there is evidence of the corpus delicti and it is an offense known by the arresting party to have been committed." *People v Aldapa* (1971) 17 CA3d 184, 188, 94 CR 579. In addition, the person making the arrest must have evidence of the corpus delicti prior to the arrest. *People v Aldapa, supra* (narcotics found after an arrest for possessing narcotics for sale by arresting officers whose authority to arrest was that of private persons could not be used to prove corpus delicti). But see *People v Wilkins* (1972) 27 CA3d 763, 769, 104 CR 89, suggesting that a felony arrest by a private person on probable cause alone is valid.

(2) A "private person may arrest for a misdemeanor only if one actually is committed or attempted in his presence (Pen. Code §837, subd. 1); a reasonable belief that a misdemeanor has been committed or attempted is insufficient." *People v Lacey* (1973) 30 CA3d 170, 175, 105 CR 72.

The actual arrest is sometimes made by a police officer at the request of the citizen. This is permissible. *People v Johnson* (1981) 123 CA3d 495, 499, 176 CR 684; *People v Sjosten* (1968) 262 CA2d 539, 544, 68 CR 832. The request need not be express; it may be inferred from the conduct of the person making the arrest. *Padilla v Meese* (1986) 184 CA3d 1022, 1030–1032, 229 CR 310; *People v Campbell* (1972) 27 CA3d 849, 854, 104 CR 118. In contrast, *People v Richards* (1977) 72 CA3d 510, 514, 140 CR 158, criticizes the resort to treating an arrest as a citizen's arrest when in reality it is made by a police officer who lacks proper grounds.

Penal Code §837 applies to citizens' arrests of minors. *In re Roland K.* (1978) 82 CA3d 295, 298, 147 CR 96.

For discussion of searches by private citizens incidental to arrest, see §§4.107–4.111.

## B. Probable Cause

### 1. [§4.24] Comparison to Probable Cause To Search

Probable cause to arrest has important similarities to, as well as significant differences from, probable cause to search.

*Similarities*

Both kinds of probable cause

- Require the same level of suspicion (see §4.26);

- Are evaluated by a totality-of-the-circumstances approach (see §4.29); and
- Are measured by an objective standard.

*Differences*

- Probable cause to arrest requires only a proper linkage between a suspect and a crime. In contrast, probable cause to search requires a double linkage that connects the items to be seized to an offense and to the place to be searched. See §2.23.
- Probable cause to arrest does not disappear absent new facts, while information that property is likely to be in a particular place grows stale with time.
- Finally, facts that justify an arrest may not permit a search and vice versa. Thus, a valid arrest for a minor traffic offense does not ordinarily authorize a search of the driver or the vehicle (see §4.5). Information that drugs are located in a particular place often serves as a basis for a search warrant, but would not permit an arrest without additional facts linking the drugs to a person. Probable cause to arrest relates to a suspect's conduct; grounds to search hinge on the existence and location of property that is subject to seizure. See *People v Cook* (1978) 22 C3d 67, 84 n6, 148 CR 605 (superseded on other points by Proposition 8 and *Franks v Delaware* (1978) 438 US 154, 98 S Ct 2674, 57 L Ed 2d 667). However, in many cases, the circumstances justifying the arrest are also those furnishing probable cause for the search. See, *e.g., Chambers v Maroney* (1970) 399 US 42, 47 n6, 90 S Ct 1975, 26 L Ed 2d 419 (same set of facts provided probable cause to arrest robbery suspects and to search their getaway car).

### 2. [§4.25] Objective Standard

Probable cause to arrest exists when the facts and circumstances known to the arresting officer at the time of the arrest justify a prudent person in believing that the suspect committed or was committing an offense. *Hunter v Bryant* (1991) 502 US 224, 228, 112 S Ct 534, 116 L Ed 2d 589; *Gerstein v Pugh* (1975) 420 US 103, 111, 95 S Ct 854, 43 L Ed 2d 54; *People v Souza* (1994) 9 C4th 224, 230, 36 CR2d 569.

A classic, often cited, statement is that of *Brinegar v U.S.* (1949) 338 US 160, 175, 69 S Ct 1302, 93 L Ed 1879:

> In dealing with probable cause, however, as the very name implies, we deal with probabilities. These are not technical; they are the factual

> and practical considerations of everyday life on which reasonable and prudent men, not legal technicians, act. The standard of proof is accordingly correlative to what must be proved. "The substance of all the definitions" of probable cause "is a reasonable ground for belief of guilt." [Citations.] And this "means less than evidence which would justify condemnation" or conviction . . . . Since Marshall's time, at any rate, it has come to mean more than bare suspicion: Probable cause exists where "the facts and circumstances within their [the officers'] knowledge and of which they had reasonably trustworthy information [are] sufficient in themselves to warrant a man of reasonable caution in the belief that" an offense has been or is being committed.

### 3. [§4.26] Degree of Suspicion

Probable cause to arrest requires the same level of suspicion as probable cause for a search warrant, *i.e.,* a "fair probability" that the defendant is committing a crime or has committed one. See *Bailey v Superior Court* (1992) 11 CA4th 1107, 1111, 15 CR2d 17; *U.S. v Buckner* (9th Cir 1999) 179 F3d 834, 838. This is a higher level than that needed for a *Terry* stop; it requires more information, as well as more reliable information.

To differentiate probable cause from the reasonable suspicion necessary for a temporary detention, courts often say that probable cause requires a "strong" or "honest and strong" suspicion that the person arrested is guilty of a crime. *People v Price* (1991) 1 C4th 324, 410, 3 CR2d 106; *People v Harris* (1975) 15 C3d 384, 389, 124 CR 536; *In re Justin B.* (1999) 69 CA4th 879, 887, 81 CR2d 852; *People v Gorrostieta* (1993) 19 CA4th 71, 83–84, 23 CR2d 92. Fair probability equals strong suspicion. See §2.36.

### 4. [§4.27] Knowledge at Time of Arrest

The inquiry used to determine whether an officer had probable cause to arrest is what did the officer know and when did he or she know it? For example, in *People v Price* (1991) 1 C4th 324, 409, 3 CR2d 106, the court said:

> Determining whether an officer had cause to arrest requires two analytically distinct steps, . . . First, the court ascertains when the arrest occurred and what the arresting officer then knew; second, the court decides whether the officer's knowledge at the time of arrest constituted adequate cause.

*People v Richards* (1977) 72 CA3d 510, 513–514, 140 CR 158, illustrates how facts that the arresting officer did not know are excluded in determining probable cause. Defendant and another man entered a check-cashing establishment together. The other presented a check that aroused the cashier's suspicion. The manager called the bank and was told the check was stolen. The manager then called the police who came and arrested both men. The court held that there was no probable cause to arrest defendant merely because he entered at the same time as the other man. The additional fact, which the cashier had not told the arresting officer, was that defendant introduced the other man to the cashier.

Knowledge means the totality of the circumstances presented to the arresting officer. For further discussion, see §4.29.

☛ **Judicial Tip**: The judge should keep distinct (1) what victims and witnesses knew, (2) what officers other than the arresting officer knew, and (3) what the arresting officer knew at the time of the arrest. As to the sharing of information between officers, see §4.31.

The risk of confusion is particularly serious when a suppression motion is heard together with a preliminary examination. The basic standard for a holding order is very similar to that for probable cause to arrest (*Rideout v Superior Court* (1967) 67 C2d 471, 474, 62 CR 581; see *McCutchen v City of Montclair* (1999) 73 CA4th 1138, 1145, 87 CR2d 95), with one major difference. Grounds for a holding order hinge on what the *magistrate* knows from the record of the preliminary hearing; grounds for arrest, as discussed above, depend on what the *arresting officer* knew at the time of arrest.

### 5. [§4.28] Subjective Belief of Officer

An officer's subjective beliefs as to the significance of facts known to him or her at the time of arrest is immaterial in determining probable cause to arrest. *People v Limon* (1993) 17 CA4th 524, 539, 21 CR2d 397; *People v Boissard* (1992) 5 CA4th 972, 980, 8 CR2d 738; *People v Adams* (1985) 175 CA3d 855, 862–863, 221 CR 298. Therefore, objective probable cause permits a search incident to an arrest even when the officer believed that there were only grounds for a detention or when the officer was mistaken about the specific offense for which probable cause to arrest exists. See, *e.g., Peters v New York* (1968) 392 US 40, 66–67, 88 S Ct 1889, 20 L Ed 2d 917; *People v Lively* (1992) 10 CA4th 1364, 1371–1373, 13 CR2d 368 (blood test after invalid DUI arrest admitted because officer could have arrested defendant for public intoxication); *People v Adams, supra* (search of detained robbery suspect proper because officer had probable cause to arrest defendant for robbery). See also *Florida v Royer* (1983) 460 US 491, 507, 103 S Ct 1319, 75 L Ed 2d 229 (fact that officer did not believe he had probable cause to arrest "would not foreclose the State from justifying Royer's custody by proving probable cause. . . .").

Language in cases that appear to require a subjective belief that the defendant committed an offense (see particularly *People v Miller* (1972) 7 C3d 219, 226, 101 CR 860) refers to the knowledge of the officer at the time: In *Miller* and similar cases, the officer knew no facts at the time of the arrest indicating that the defendant had committed the offense for which the prosecution later claimed there was probable cause to arrest. *People v Adams, supra.*

The subjective motivation and intent of the officer are also irrelevant (*People v Boissard, supra*), as is subjective good faith. *Beck v Ohio* (1964) 379 US 89, 97, 85 S Ct 223, 13 L Ed 2d 142. See *Maryland v Macon* (1985) 472 US 463, 470, 105 S Ct 2778, 86 L Ed 2d 370 (whether Fourth Amendment violation occurred turns on objective assessment of officer's actions and not on officer's state of mind at time actions were taken).

### 6. [§4.29] Totality of Circumstances

Courts ascertain probable cause to arrest, like probable cause to search, by deciding each case on its own facts and on the totality of circumstances. *People v Ingle* (1960) 53 C2d 407, 412, 2 CR 14 ("total atmosphere"); *People v Boissard* (1992) 5 CA4th 972, 979, 8 CR2d 738 ("total atmosphere"); *People v Rosales* (1987) 192 CA3d 759, 768, 237 CR 558 ("totality-of-the-circumstances approach applies to analyses for arrest"); *People v Superior Court* (Orozco) (1981) 121 CA3d 395, 402, 175 CR 322 (totality of ambient circumstances presented to officers at the time they needed to act).

Totality of circumstance is a concept that includes not only all the facts known to the arresting officer "at the time he acted, but also his special training, experience and expertise," as well as the seriousness of the offense. *People v Profit* (1986) 183 CA3d 849, 881, 229 CR 148.

☛ **Judicial Tip**: The judge should beware of arguments that Fact A is not sufficient to constitute probable cause, Fact B is not sufficient, Fact C is not sufficient, . . . and that, therefore, there is no probable cause. The question is not whether any isolated observation or piece of information is sufficient, but whether the totality of circumstances gives rise to probable cause. *People v Stanfill* (1985) 170 CA3d 420, 423, 426, 216 CR 472.

### 7. [§4.30] Training, Experience, and Expertise of Officer

As mentioned in §4.29, the training, experience, and expertise of the arresting officer are often important factors in assessing whether the officer had probable cause to arrest. "Circumstances and conduct which would not excite the suspicion of the man on the street might be highly significant to an officer who had had extensive training and experience. . . ." *People v Superior Court* (Kiefer) (1970) 3 C3d 807, 827, 91 CR 729, quoting with approval from *People v Williams* (1961) 196 CA2d 726, 728, 16 CR 836; *People v Medina* (1972) 7 C3d 30, 37, 101 CR 521; *People v Knutson* (1976) 60 CA3d 856, 860, 131 CR 846; see §2.25.

For example, when an officer properly stops a vehicle and observes a hand-rolled cigarette inside, such an observation, standing alone, does not justify the arrest of the driver for possessing marijuana. *Thomas v Superior Court* (1972) 22 CA3d 972, 976, 99 CR 647. But probable cause to arrest exists when the officer testifies to extensive experience viewing hand-rolled cigarettes and inspecting them and contrasts "the appearance of normal hand-rolled cigarettes to the appearance of joints." *People v Poole* (1975) 48 CA3d 881, 885–886, 122 CR 87. See also *People v Lilienthal* (1978) 22 C3d 891, 898, 150 CR 910 (suppression denied where officer testified to distinctive appearance of paper bindle and experience in making many arrests where heroin or cocaine was transported in similar bindles). Testimony concerning such contrasts in appearance is not crucial when other suspicious circumstances are present. *People v Stanfill* (1985) 170 CA3d 420, 425, 216 CR 472.

Similarly, manifestations of being under the influence of drugs, such as dilated pupils and slurred speech, give an experienced officer grounds for arrest. *People v Sawkow* (1984) 150 CA3d 999, 1009, 198 CR 374; *People v Low* (1983) 148 CA3d 89, 91, 196 CR 18; *People v Knutson, supra.*

Lack of sufficient experience is not fatal when other circumstances supply probable cause. For example, in *People v Limon* (1993) 17 CA4th 524, 538, 21 CR2d 397, the defendant had a magnetic key case in his pocket. The arresting officer had seen narcotics in a hide-a-key case once before. The court said the officer's experience alone might not be adequate, but that the nature of the container gained added significance from defendant's prior conduct in removing something from a nearby truck, engaging in a hand exchange (see §4.33), and replacing something on or near the truck. The court also noted that people do not ordinarily carry magnetic key cases in their pockets.

In general, the officer's experience is of little help when the officer observes a common container (*People v Chapman* (1990) 224 CA3d 253,

256–357, 274 CR 47 (cosmetics compact; officer's past experience in finding narcotics in similar containers does not make object sufficiently suspicious); *People v Valdez* (1987) 196 CA3d 799, 806, 242 CR 142 (film canister)) in the absence of other suspicious circumstances.

Occasionally the officer's expertise is not in the appropriate area. For instance, defendant is charged with possession for sale after an arrest for being under the influence of drugs. In that situation, an officer's testimony about his experience as to the packaging of drugs is relevant to the possession-for-sale charge but does not help to justify the initial arrest. *People v Dunkel* (1977) 71 CA3d 928, 932–933, 139 CR 685.

At other times the officer's experience leads to a very reasonable conclusion that nevertheless falls short of probable cause. For instance, observations plus experience may indicate that a person is experiencing withdrawal symptoms from opiate use. But exhibiting such symptoms does not provide probable cause to believe that the person is under the influence of a controlled substance in violation of Health & S C §11550. It is, instead, an indication that the person has discontinued use of the narcotic. *People v Gutierrez* (1977) 72 CA3d 397, 401–403, 140 CR 122. For a discussion of *Gutierrez*, see *People v Jones* (1987) 189 CA3d 398, 404, 234 CR 408. What is true of withdrawal symptoms also applies to needle marks, but the observation of marks supplemented by additional evidence suggesting narcotics use may provide probable cause. *People v Cardenas* (1982) 31 C3d 897, 911, 184 CR 165 (droopy eyelids, lethargic movements, dilated pupils); *People v Ibarra* (1963) 60 C2d 460, 463 n1, 34 CR 863; *People v Meyers* (1970) 6 CA3d 601, 606, 86 CR 252.

For a case the court called close, see *People v Gonzales* (1989) 216 CA3d 1185, 1188–1189, 265 CR 507. Defendant, a known drug user, moved his hand to his front pants pocket. The officer saw one-half inch of a rolled up clear plastic baggie protruding from the pocket, identical in appearance to over 1300 bindles of cocaine or heroin the officer had seen, including several where only the top portion was visible. The court held that the officer had probable cause to arrest.

### 8. [§4.31] Information and Directives Obtained by the Arresting Officer From Others

Police officers routinely and necessarily make arrests based on information they received from other persons, such as victims, witnesses, informants, and fellow law enforcement officers. Issues of the reliability and credibility of information are "basically the same" in determining probable cause to arrest as "in the situation involving a search warrant." *People v Madden* (1970) 2 C3d 1017, 1023, 88 CR 171; *People v Rosales* (1987)

192 CA3d 759, 767, 237 CR 558 (applies the standards of *Illinois v Gates* (1983) 462 US 213, 225–230, 103 S Ct 2317, 76 L Ed 2d 527, developed in the context of search warrants to the question of probable cause to arrest on information from an anonymous informant). See §§2.31–2.35.

The following principles govern arrests made at the direction of or on information received from another officer:

(1) For purposes of the exclusionary rule, an arrest on the basis of a directive or request received through official channels is valid only if the originator of the request had probable cause at the time of issuing it. *Whiteley v Warden* (1971) 401 US 560, 568, 91 S Ct 1031, 28 L Ed 2d 306. Otherwise placement of an arrest request into the police communications network would permit arrests without probable cause. *People v Ford* (1984) 150 CA3d 687, 697, 198 CR 80.

(2) The prosecution has the burden of proving that the originating officer had probable cause. *People v Madden, supra,* 2 C3d at 1021; *People v Lara* (1967) 67 C2d 365, 373, 62 CR 586; *People v Ford, supra.* See *People v Ramirez* (1997) 59 CA4th 1548, 1553–1558, 70 CR2d 341 (initiating officer had probable cause for traffic stop; executing officer directed to stop car for narcotics investigation; stop proper). For discussion of good faith relating to warrant information, see §1.39.

(3) An arrest on "a directive from an officer or agency without probable cause is not validated by information obtained after the issuance of the directive." *People v Ford, supra,* 150 CA3d at 701. While hindsight cannot validate an arrest, information developed by the arresting officer between receipt of the directive and the actual arrest may properly be considered in evaluating probable cause. See 2 LaFave, pp 44–45.

(4) In the absence of a request or directive to arrest, only the information in the possession of the arresting officer is considered for probable cause. "[T]he People must prove not only that the collective knowledge of the investigating authorities justified the arrest, but that such knowledge was funneled to the arresting officer either by imparting it to him or, more simply, by the giving of an order or request to make the arrest by someone who, in turn, was possessed of such collective knowledge." *People v Rice* (1967) 253 CA2d 789, 792, 61 CR 394.

In other words, sufficient information to constitute probable cause must exist in one place. *People v Ford, supra,* 150 CA3d at 698. In an arrest based on a directive or request, that one "place" is the originating officer. *People v Rice, supra.* Occasional language in decisions about imputing to the arresting officer the collective knowledge of law enforcement agencies (*People v Ramirez* (1983) 34 C3d 541, 547, 194 CR

454) should be understood in light of the foregoing. *People v Ford, supra.*

(5) When the arresting officers act on information from other officers, the prosecution must on request show the basis of the latter's information (*Remers v Superior Court* (1970) 2 C3d 659, 667, 87 CR 202; *People v Madden, supra*) or present other evidence corroborating the information. *People v Johnson* (1987) 189 CA3d 1315, 1320, 235 CR 62; *People v Orozco* (1981) 114 CA3d 435, 444, 170 CR 604. This requirement is designated to prevent the manufacture of arrest grounds, sometimes called "do-it-yourself probable cause." *People v Orozco, supra*; *Remers v Superior Court, supra.*

### 9. [§4.32] Disappearance of Probable Cause After Arrest

When the police make an arrest on probable cause and later develop information that destroys probable cause, any continued custody and search of the defendant is illegal. The arrest is not unlawful at the outset, but once probable cause has disappeared, the defendant is entitled to be released. See 2 LaFave, p 46.

### 10. [§4.33] Observation of Hand-to-Hand Exchanges

Observations of an exchange of unidentified objects at night in a high narcotics area justifies a *Terry* stop. See §3.55. An exchange of what "appears" to be an object, however, does not provide probable cause for an arrest, even when it occurs in a high crime area and the suspects keep looking around to see if anyone is watching. *Cunha v Superior Court* (1970) 2 C3d 352, 356–357, 85 CR 160. See also *Remers v Superior Court* (1970) 2 C3d 659, 665, 87 CR 202 (observations in same area as *Cunha* of person who shows small tinfoil package to companion and nods to him to go into an establishment "provide less justification for arrest" than facts in *Cunha*; officers' knowledge that dangerous drugs are often wrapped in tinfoil does not make the package suspicious because many legitimate items are packaged in that manner).

The fact that the officer sees that the exchange involves money and a small unidentified object does not provide probable cause to arrest. *People v Knisely* (1976) 64 CA3d 110, 114, 134 CR 269. Not much more is necessary, however. In *People v Stanfill* (1985) 170 CA3d 420, 423, 216 CR 472, officers saw defendant sitting in a park area where the police knew sales of marijuana took place. An apparent stranger drove up, got out of his car, walked over to the defendant, "gave him at least $1 in exchange for two small, thin, white filterless cigarettes," and left. The court held that the officers had observed all the elements of a completed sale and therefore had probable cause to arrest. In accord is *People v Garrett* (1972) 29 CA3d 535, 539–540, 104 CR 829.

☛ **Judicial Tip**: *Stanfill* distinguished *Cunha, Remers,* and *Knisely* on the ground that they did not involve observation of an identifiable object. *Cunha* and *Remers* may be at variance with the totality-of-the-circumstances approach to probable cause and may force courts to draw fine-line distinctions inconsistent with the admonition that probable cause deals with probabilities that "are not technical," but are, rather, the "practical considerations of everyday life on which reasonable and prudent men, not legal technicians, act." See *Illinois v Gates* (1983) 462 US 213, 231, 103 S Ct 2317, 76 L Ed 2d 527, quoting approvingly from *Brinegar v U.S.* (1949) 338 US 160, 176, 69 S Ct 1302, 93 L Ed 1879.

Probable cause to arrest was found in the following situations:

- An attempted exchange of a sandwich baggie for currency in an area of frequent drug transactions, followed by flight when a third person shouts "Police!" *People v Mims* (1992) 9 CA4th 1244, 1248–1251, 12 CR2d 335.

- In an area known for a high rate of street drug sales, defendant, arrested a month earlier for selling narcotics, hands a small object to a companion who places it into a cigarette pack that he puts into his shirt pocket. *People v Guajardo* (1994) 23 CA4th 1738, 1742–1743, 29 CR2d 21.

Patient officers sometimes obviate *Cunha* difficulties by additional observations. In *People v Low* (1983) 148 CA3d 89, 91–92, 196 CR 18, the officers saw a car stop by a phone booth. A person leaned into the car; the driver's arm moved toward the person, but nothing was seen to be exchanged by them. The officers, their suspicion aroused, followed the car, which speeded and weaved. They stopped the vehicle and noticed that the driver displayed clear symptoms of being under the influence of drugs. The court summarily concluded that there was probable cause to arrest the driver and to search the car.

### 11. Description of Suspect

#### a. [§4.34] Key Inquiries

When an arrest is based in whole or in part on a suspect's description, the following questions are often pertinent:

- How detailed is the description? Does it fit many persons or only a few? Is there also a vehicle description?
- How reliable is the source of information?
- How closely does the description match the defendant? Are there discrepancies? How significant are they?
- How close to the offense was the arrest in terms of time and place?
- Did the arresting officer know any facts in addition to the description and match that support probable cause? If so, did any negate probable cause?

### b. [§4.35] Illustrations

*Adequate Descriptions and Matches*

In *People v Adams* (1985) 175 CA3d 855, 859, 221 CR 298, a robbery victim described the assailant as a light-skinned Black male, about 40, over six feet, wearing a white straw hat, dark pants and a light shirt, and driving a gray Lincoln Continental with Arizona plates. Two hours later, an officer saw defendant in the vicinity in which the robbery had occurred. He matched the description in every detail, including the white straw hat. A green Continental with Arizona plates was parked 100 feet away.

In finding probable cause to arrest, the court noted the detailed description, the fact that it came from a citizen-victim rather than a police informer, and the nearly perfect match of person and vehicle with the description. However, the court also relied on defendant's conduct when he was stopped—his attempt to flee, nervousness, and vague answers concerning identity. 175 CA3d at 861.

*In re Brian A.* (1985) 173 CA3d 1168, 1171, 219 CR 361, is a closer case. The arrest was made two days after a cab robbery solely on the basis of descriptions. The police broadcast descriptions, which were less detailed than the victim's description, were of two White males, 13 to 15 years of age, both wearing jeans, one wearing a shiny colored, red-hooded sweatshirt, the other wearing a light blue sweatshirt, and one carrying a black sports-type duffel bag. The officer saw two White juveniles, 13 to 15, both wearing jeans. One carried a black sports-type duffel bag. One wore a jacket with a red nylon hood, the other a pale lavender sweatshirt with a hood.

The court noted that the observations matched the descriptions on many points. The court's main concern was whether the descriptions were sufficiently unique so that they "would be inapplicable to a great many others."

In the court's view only the shiny red hood was "fairly unique." The arrests were saved by the fact that the two juveniles were apprehended together. "Where, as here, there were two perpetrators and an officer stops two suspects who match the descriptions he has been given, there is much greater basis to find probable cause for arrest." 173 CA3d at 1174.

The victim's identification of one suspect sometimes supplies probable cause to arrest a second suspect whose description and match is quite general. In *People v Bowen* (1987) 195 CA3d 269, 271–275, 240 CR 466, two purse snatch suspects had been detained together. In a street show-up, the victim identified one. The description of defendant, the second suspect, was of a White female with red hair who was wearing a three-quarters length coat. Defendant was a female impersonator wearing a long red wig. The victim merely stated at the show-up that defendant was wearing a jacket similar to the jacket her assailant wore. In holding that there was clearly probable cause to arrest defendant, the court relied on the facts that (1) defendant generally matched the description, (2) he was in the company of the suspect identified by the victim, and (3) he had been stopped shortly after the crime near the place where it had been committed.

Other circumstances often substitute for a description. For example, in *People v Ableman* (1970) 7 CA3d 548, 549–550, 86 CR 700, Officer Wells was on his way to answer a hotel burglary call when he heard a radio report that another officer had stopped a car in front of the hotel for a hit-and-run. The car was occupied by members of a motorcycle group. At the hotel Wells found that a member of a rival group had been shot. The victim and his friends told Wells that the shooting had been done by the "Misfits" who had fled in a car. Wells saw that the occupants of the hit-and-run vehicle all wore insignia identifying them as "Misfits." The court held that despite the lack of information identifying any one man as the assailant, all were properly arrested for the shooting.

For other cases illustrating how a broad description can be supplemented by additional information so as to provide probable cause, see, *e.g., People v Loudermilk* (1987) 195 CA3d 996, 1005, 241 CR 208 (defendant hitchhiking at a late hour; during a lawful pat search officer found wallet in defendant's rear pocket after he denied having any identification on his person); *People v Bowen, supra.*

*Inadequate Descriptions*

In *In re Dung T.* (1984) 160 CA3d 697, 206 CR 772, robbers were described as six Vietnamese males in their twenties, driving a Dodge and a yellow Capri. Two nights after the robbery, the officers stopped a Dodge occupied by eight young Vietnamese males, including appellant, then 15 years old. The court held that the descriptions limited to age and nationality permitted only an investigative stop and not an arrest. The fact that eight people were in the car but only six had been reported as robbers further supported the court's holding as to the inadequacy of the descriptions. 160 CA3d at 713.

*In re Jorge S.* (1977) 74 CA3d 852, 855, 141 CR 722, held that a general description ("male Latin, dark hair, five foot eight, maybe 150 pounds, and in his early twenties") does not provide probable cause to arrest anyone 11 days after the offense, even when there is a close match, especially in a neighborhood with a large Hispanic population. 74 CA3d at 857. Such a description is probably too general to permit an arrest even a day after the offense. Police officers often resolve the problem by making an investigative stop for the purpose of a field identification by the victim. General descriptions too broad to constitute probable cause may be adequate to permit a temporary detention. See *People v Curtis* (1969) 70 C2d 347, 350, 358, 74 CR 713 (description of reported prowler as Black man, 6', white shirt, tan trousers is sufficient to warrant detention but not arrest of person matching the description in the neighborhood of the report).

### 12. Probable Cause To Arrest Companion of Principal Suspect

#### a. [§4.36] Persons on Foot

In *People v Profit* (1986) 183 CA3d 849, 856–860, 229 CR 148, a federal narcotics agent was talking with three airline passengers who had entered the ticket counter area with little luggage and had separated there while one of them bought three tickets. All of them had been nervously looking around. During the conversation Profit referred to the tickets as "our tickets." Profit let the agent look in his briefcase, where the agent saw a yellow tablet with certain notations that made the agent suspect, on the basis of extensive experience, that the tablet was a narcotics sales ledger sheet. A second agent joined the conversation. Profit suddenly struck him, ran, took a bottle from his waistband, opened it, and threw it at the second agent. The content smelled strongly of ether, and the first agent immediately formed the belief that the bottle contained liquid PCP.

The agents arrested all three persons for conspiracy to transport PCP. The court held that there was probable cause to arrest the persons who were with Profit. Using a "total atmosphere of the case" approach, the court found that the facts viewed in light of the agent's expertise gave rise to a strong suspicion that the three men were engaged in a joint criminal venture. 183 CA3d at 881–883.

Such a suspicion does not follow from mere togetherness. For example, in *People v Simon* (1955) 45 C2d 645, 649, 290 P2d 531, defendant "was walking on a street with a 20-year-old friend who had a bottle" of alcohol. The court held that this did not constitute reasonable cause to believe that defendant was "either aiding or abetting his friend in committing a crime or contributing to the delinquency of a minor."

Similarly, in *People v Richards* (1977) 72 CA3d 510, 514, 140 CR 158, the mere fact that defendant entered a check-cashing establishment with a man who attempted to cash a forged check was not probable cause to arrest defendant. The court indicated that the result would be different if additional evidence linked the two men, such as defendant's introducing the other man to the cashier.

### b. [§4.37] Vehicle Occupants

A passenger who is merely present in a vehicle with an offender is not, without more, subject to arrest for an offense other than a possessory one. *U.S. v Di Re* (1948) 332 US 581, 584–587, 68 S Ct 222, 92 L Ed 210 (informant in back seat had counterfeit ration coupons bought from driver; no probable cause to arrest front seat passenger); *In re Justin B.* (1999) 69 CA4th 879, 887, 81 CR2d 852 (probable cause to arrest driver for auto burglary does not justify arrest of passenger of whom officer made no inquiry and who did not say or do anything suspicious); *People v Williams* (1970) 9 CA3d 565, 568, 88 CR 349 (auto theft; no evidence that officer knew anything about relation of driver and passenger).

In many circumstances a vehicle occupant's presence or conduct is highly suspicious. For example, probable cause to arrest one or more occupants for a robbery or other offense an hour after it was reported is also probable cause to arrest all others in the vehicle. *Chambers v Maroney* (1970) 399 US 42, 46, 90 S Ct 1975, 26 L Ed 2d 419 (gas station robbery; car matching description stopped one hour later; arrest of all four persons in car proper); *People v Chandler* (1968) 262 CA2d 350, 354, 68 CR 645. Probable cause to arrest all the occupants was supported by common knowledge that one or more persons often remain in the getaway car. *People v Chandler, supra.*

Additional observations may provide probable cause. For instance, in *People v Williams* (1971) 17 CA3d 275, 279, 94 CR 735, the defendant was not merely a passenger in a stolen car, as had been the case in the unrelated *Williams* case cited earlier in this section, but the officer had observed him and two others loitering near a school for an hour before all three were stopped in the car. The court said the police could reasonably conclude that defendant was not merely a passenger but had participated in the theft. Similarly, in *People v Esparza* (1969) 2 CA3d 245, 248, 82 CR 467, the defendant was not only seated on the passenger side of a parked car, he opened the passenger side door through which the person in the driver's seat threw a narcotics kit. The court held that the officer could reasonably infer that defendant opened the door to facilitate disposition of the kit and that this conduct indicated joint possession. For discussion of probable cause to arrest a passenger when the police observe drugs in a vehicle, see §4.38.

#### c. [§4.38] Passenger in Vehicle With Contraband

The observation of contraband in a vehicle is probable cause to arrest any occupant who has access to it. *In re James M.* (1977) 72 CA3d 133, 137, 139 CR 902 (beer can on dashboard and nunchaku sticks on driver's side floor are probable cause to arrest passenger for both violations); *People v Vermouth* (1971) 20 CA3d 746, 756, 98 CR 65. See also *People v Hill* (1974) 12 C3d 731, 749, 117 CR 393, overruled on other grounds in 18 C3d 889, 896 n5 (marijuana cigarettes found on floorboard of car stopped after high-speed chase in aftermath of minor traffic violation are probable cause to arrest both driver and passenger for unlawful possession of marijuana); *Rideout v Superior Court* (1967) 67 C2d 471, 475, 62 CR 581; *People v Lovejoy* (1970) 12 CA3d 883, 887, 91 CR 94 (odor of burning marijuana emanating from vehicle permits arrest of all occupants).

#### d. [§4.39] Contraband in Residence

The observation of contraband in a residence is probable cause to arrest any occupant who has access to it. *People v Gabriel* (1986) 188 CA3d 1261, 1266, 233 CR 769 (methamphetamine in bedroom of apartment in which five people are present permits arrest of defendant who is in bedroom when officer enters; court relies on *In re James M.* (1977) 72 CA3d 133, 137, 139 CR 902 (see §4.34)). See also *Frazzini v Superior Court* (1970) 7 CA3d 1005, 1016, 87 CR 32 (drugs in shirt hanging in closet in which defendant's suitcase is found give rise to inference that shirt belongs to defendant).

In *Ker v California* (1963) 374 US 23, 36, 83 S Ct 1623, 10 L Ed 2d 726, the police had probable cause to arrest the male defendant for selling marijuana. As they entered his apartment, the female defendant came from the kitchen where a brick of marijuana was in plain view. The court held that there was probable cause to arrest the woman. In contrast, information that a particular person has narcotics in an apartment is not, without more, probable cause to arrest another person who answers the door. *People v Shelton* (1964) 60 C2d 740, 745, 36 CR 433. Visitors at a place where a search warrant is being executed and narcotics found are not automatically subject to arrest. See *Ybarra v Illinois* (1979) 444 US 85, 93–96, 100 S Ct 338, 62 L Ed 2d 238; 2 LaFave, p 316.

### C. [§4.40] Flight Plus Grounds To Detain

When the police have a proper basis for detaining a suspect temporarily and the suspect flees, probable cause to arrest arises. *People v Abes* (1985) 174 CA3d 796, 805, 220 CR 277; *People v Bigham* (1975) 49 CA3d 73, 122 CR 252. See also *People v Mims* (1992) 9 CA4th 1244, 1248–1251, 12 CR2d 335 (attempted hand-to-hand exchange; lookout shouts "police"; flight of one participant justifies arrest of the other one).

### D. [§4.41] Effect of Mistakes

Reasonable mistakes of *fact,* such as reasonable reliance on erroneous information or arrest of the wrong person generally do not invalidate an arrest. For discussion, see §1.41.

When considering mistakes of *law,* it is important to differentiate between several kinds of mistake, including the following:

- An arrest based on an officer's erroneous interpretation of California law or of a local ordinance is generally unreasonable and therefore invalid. See §1.42.
- An arrest for violating a statute or ordinance that is subsequently declared unconstitutional is valid. See §1.37.
- The arrest is also valid when the arresting officer is mistaken as to *what* offense the defendant committed as long as the officer knew facts that constitute probable cause to arrest for an offense. See §4.28.
- Finally, an officer's mistaken belief that he or she is only detaining the suspect or only had grounds to detain is not fatal, provided probable cause to arrest existed at the time of the arrest. See §4.28.

## V. ARREST WARRANTS

### A. [§4.42] Need for Arrest Warrant

The Fourth Amendment does not require an arrest warrant for an arrest in a public place, even when there is ample opportunity to obtain one. *U.S. v Watson* (1976) 423 US 411, 413, 423, 96 S Ct 820, 46 L Ed 2d 598.

The police need an arrest warrant in the following three instances:

(1) To make a residential arrest absent exigent circumstances (see §§4.61–4.79);

(2) To arrest for most misdemeanors that occurred outside the officer's presence (see §4.9); and

(3) To arrest for most offenses not committed within the political subdivision that employs the arresting officer. Pen C §§816, 830.1(a), 836; *People v Ramirez* (1988) 202 CA3d 425, 427, 248 CR 396 (bench warrant may be served in any county in same manner as arrest warrant); see §§4.19–4.20.

### B. Types of Arrest Warrants

#### 1. [§4.43] Felony and Misdemeanor Warrants

Courts encounter several distinct kinds of arrest warrants:

(1) *Felony complaint warrants*

Arrest warrants issued by a magistrate when the prosecutor files a felony complaint. Pen C §813(a).

(2) *Postindictment warrants*

Arrest warrants for persons who have been indicted and are not in custody. The Penal Code specifies that these are bench warrants. Pen C §§945, 979. The form is prescribed in Pen C §981.

(3) *Misdemeanor complaint warrants*

Arrest warrants issued by a judge to whom a misdemeanor or infraction complaint is presented. Pen C §1427(a). A warrant form is set out, but not mandated, in Pen C §1427(b).

(4) *Ramey warrants*

Arrest warrants that precede a formal complaint and authorize a residential arrest based on an affidavit of probable cause. Pen C §817. Such warrants developed in response to *People v Ramey* (1976) 16 C3d 263, 270–276, 127 CR 629, and *Payton v New York* (1980) 445 US 573, 576, 100 S Ct 1371, 63 L Ed 2d 639, which held that a warrantless *residential* arrest violates the Fourth Amendment absent exigent circumstances. See *People v Bittaker* (1989) 48 C3d 1046, 1070, 259 CR 630. For further discussion, see §§4.61–4.79.

#### 2. [§4.44] Failure-To-Appear Warrants

(1) *Traffic cases*

In traffic cases warrants for failure to appear, sometimes called FTA warrants, are authorized by Pen C §853.8 (warrant to be issued within 20 days of FTA); see also Pen C §853.7 (FTA is a misdemeanor regardless of disposition of charge upon which defendant originally arrested). Such warrants can no longer be used in cases that involve parking violations. See present and former Veh C §40220.

"Failure to appear" warrants are usually ordered by the clerk, are computer generated, and bear a judge's facsimile signature. *People v Weitzer* (1969) 269 CA2d 274, 282–286, 75 CR 318; *People v Superior Court* (Copeland) (1968) 262 CA2d 283, 284–285, 68 CR 629.

(2) *Non-traffic cases*

In non-traffic cases the court can order a bench warrant when a defendant fails to appear as required by law. Pen C §§813(c), 978.5 (bench warrant upon failure to appear after proper service of summons). See also Pen C §977 (misdemeanant may appear by counsel; felony defendant can waive personal presence except as to specified mandatory appearances). Bench warrants may be signed by the magistrate or clerk. Warrants may also be issued for nonappearing witnesses. CCP §§1993–1994. A bench warrant to compel attendance of a witness is invalid after the underlying proceeding has terminated, but the arrest can be saved if the officer who served the warrant relied on it in good faith. *People v Palmer* (1989) 207 CA3d 663, 672, 255 CR 55.

☛ **Judicial Tip**: Before ordering a bench warrant for a nonappearing defendant, the judge should make sure that the circumstances permit a warrant under Pen C §§977 and 978.5. A defendant who signed a promise to appear in a misdemeanor case can nevertheless appear by counsel. *Simmons v Superior Court* (1988) 203 CA3d 71, 76–77, 249 CR 721. An order to appear in person must be based on the specific facts and circumstances of the case. *Olney v Municipal Court* (1982) 133 CA3d 455, 459–463, 184 CR 78 (invalidating court policy to require misdemeanor defendants to appear in person at readiness and sentencing hearings).

### 3. [§4.45] Other Arrest Warrants

(1) *Probation violation warrants*

The court may issue a warrant for the arrest of a person released on probation upon probable cause to believe that the probationer is violating any term or condition of probation. This authority extends to formal probation, conditional sentences, and "summary probation not under the care of a probation officer." Pen C §1203.2(a).

(2) *Order to return parolee to custody*

The parole authority may issue a written order to return a parolee to custody. Pen C §3060; see also Pen C §§3062 (Governor's similar authority); 3081 (county parole board's equivalent authority). Such orders function as warrants. Pen C §§3060–3061. As to probable cause for such orders, see §4.50.

"Parole holds" placed by parole officers on defendants who are in custody on unrelated charges have the same effect as arrest warrants. See *In re Law* (1973) 10 C3d 21, 24 n2, 109 CR 573. The most common reason for a hold is that defendant was arrested on new charges.

(3) *Extradition warrants*

California authorizes two kinds of extradition warrants, one signed by magistrates, the other by the Governor or his agent. Pen C §§1548.2, 1549.2, 1551–1552.

(4) *Arrest warrants from other states*

An arrest warrant from another state may be served in California if it meets California requirements for a valid warrant. *People v McGraw* (1990) 226 CA3d 346, 348–350, 276 CR 208 (arrest on Washington State warrant with notation not to extradite from other than an adjoining state valid).

(5) *Telegraphic, telephonic, and electronic warrants*

These phrases do not refer to a distinct type of warrant, but either to

- A copy or abstract of an arrest warrant transmitted electronically; see Pen C §850 permitting service of such a copy; see also *People v McGraw, supra* (existence of warrant confirmed by telephone and teletype); or

- A warrant issued upon a sworn oral statement over the telephone and using fax or e-mail transmission. Pen C §817(c); for discussion, see §4.53.

(6) *John Doe warrants*

A John Doe warrant designates the defendant by a fictitious name because defendant's real name is unknown. Pen C §815. For discussion, see §4.55.

## C. Arrest Warrant Differentiated From Other Process

### 1. Summons

#### a. [§4.46] Corporations

Corporations, as distinguished from their officers, directors, and employees, cannot be arrested in the common meaning of that term. Instead of an arrest warrant, the judge issues a summons when a corporation is charged with an offense. Pen C §§1390, 1427(b). The summons must be substantially in the form prescribed by Pen C §1391 and "signed by the judge with his name of office, requiring the corporation to appear before him, at a specified time and place, to answer the charge, the time to be not less than 10 days after the issuing of the summons." Pen C §1390.

The summons must be served at least 5 days before the appearance date. Pen C §1392. Service is made by showing the original summons and "delivering a copy" to one of the persons designated in Pen C §1392, except that the clerk may serve a summons involving a traffic violation by mail. Pen C §1427(b). As to how a corporation appears in response to a summons, see Pen C §1427(b).

### b. [§4.47] Individuals

The prosecutor has discretion to request a summons instead of an arrest warrant when a felony complaint is filed; upon such a request, a summons "shall be issued" by the magistrate. Pen C §813(a). The contents of the summons are prescribed in Pen C §813(b). Penal Code §813(e) lists the following cases for which the prosecution may not request a summons:

- For offenses involving violence, use of a firearm, or resisting arrest;
- When one or more arrest warrants are outstanding against the defendant;
- When it would jeopardize the prosecution of the underlying offense(s) or of any other offenses;
- When there is a reasonable likelihood that the offenses would continue or resume;
- When the safety of persons or property would be imminently endangered; or
- When there is reason to believe that the defendant will not appear.

There are no time constraints for service of summons on individuals. Summons is served by delivery of a copy to the defendant; a duplicate copy is filed with the magistrate. Pen C §816(a).

☛ **Judicial Tips**:

- At defendant's first appearance, the judge should ascertain whether the defendant has been booked. If he or she has not been booked, the judge should order him or her to complete the booking process. Pen C §813(d). Courts often supplement such an order with a handout sheet containing instructions.
- If the defendant fails to appear in response to a summons, the

judge should first ascertain whether the summons was served. If it was, the judge should order a bench warrant. Pen C §813(c).

#### 2. [§4.48] Citation

The citation procedure, unlike use of a summons, is not an alternative to an arrest warrant. Rather, it is a widely used *post*arrest or detention procedure for traffic and misdemeanor violations. See Pen C §§853.5–853.9; Veh C §§40303, 40303.5, 40500. For discussion, see 4 Witkin, California Criminal Law, *Pretrial Proceedings* §§45–58 (3d ed 2000).

### D. Probable Cause

#### 1. [§4.49] Basic Principles

Arrest warrants, like search warrants, must comply with the mandate of the Fourth Amendment that warrants issue only on probable cause. *Giordenello v U.S.* (1958) 357 US 480, 485, 78 S Ct 1245, 2 L Ed 2d 1503; *People v Campa* (1984) 36 C3d 870, 879, 206 CR 114; Pen C §§813(a), 817(a)(1), 1427(a). The standard for probable cause is generally the same as for making a warrantless arrest, *i.e.,* facts that would lead a person of ordinary prudence to entertain a strong suspicion of defendant's guilt. *People v Campa, supra*; *People v Sesslin* (1968) 68 C2d 418, 424–426, 67 CR 409; see *Gerstein v Pugh* (1975) 420 US 103, 111, 95 S Ct 854, 43 L Ed 2d 54.

As to probable cause for extradition warrants, see Pen C §§1548.2, 1551; for warrants based on probation or parole revocation, see §4.50; for the requirement of an affidavit to show probable cause, see §4.51.

*Good faith.* Good faith principles apply to arrests based on recalled or invalid warrants. For discussion, see §§1.28–1.29.

#### 2. [§4.50] Probation or Parole Violation

Probable cause for a warrant based on probation violation means probable cause to believe that the probationer is violating any term or condition of probation. Pen C §1203.2(a). Probable cause for an order to return a parolee to custody means "such a state of facts as would lead a person of ordinary caution or prudence to believe and conscientiously entertain a strong suspicion that the parolee has conducted himself in such a way that his condition of release should be terminated." *People v Anderson* (1975) 49 CA3d 869, 874, 123 CR 209.

#### 3. Showing of Probable Cause

##### a. [§4.51] General Need for Affidavit

A magistrate must be presented with competent facts that establish probable cause to arrest. *In re Walters* (1975) 15 C3d 738, 748, 126 CR 239. A complaint on information and belief couched in statutory language fails to apprise the magistrate of the underlying facts. *Whiteley v Warden* (1971) 401 US 560, 564–565, 91 S Ct 1031, 28 L Ed 2d 306; *Giordenello v U.S.* (1958) 357 US 480, 485–486, 78 S Ct 1245, 2 L Ed 2d 1503; *People v Sesslin* (1968) 68 C2d 418, 424–425, 67 CR 409.

*Sesslin* led to the current practice of attaching to the complaint an affidavit, generally accompanied by copies of police reports, so that the magistrate can ascertain the factual basis for the charges. *People v Case* (1980) 105 CA3d 826, 832, 164 CR 662. A complaint alone suffices as long as it recites competent facts showing probable cause (*In re Walters, supra*; *People v Cressey* (1970) 2 C3d 836, 842–845, 87 CR 699), but accompanying affidavits have become the norm.

☛ **Judicial Tips**:

- The judge should be wary of complaints that do not have an affidavit with them.
- Despite heavy workloads, issuing arrest warrants deserves at least as serious attention as search warrants; arrest is usually a far graver intrusion on a person's freedom and privacy than search.
- Such admonition is much easier to give than to follow, but the task can be made relatively manageable. Some judges allot specific times for it. The job can be rotated or divided among judges. Large stacks of complaints, warrants, and reports can be handled a few at a time during the day.
- *Ramey* warrant affidavits should be given particularly close attention because they may not have been reviewed by a prosecutor before being presented to the magistrate.
- The judge should be on the lookout for missing elements, such as a Veh C §23152(b) complaint (driving with a blood alcohol of .08 or more) without accompanying information about the chemical test result, and for mischarged offenses, but should avoid second guessing the prosecutor who prepared the charges.
- The charging deputy, not the judge, should correct serious typographical errors in a complaint before the warrant issues.
- When rejecting a warrant, the judge should briefly inform the prosecutor of the reason.

- The judge should initial at least the first page of the affidavit and preferably each of the following pages while reading them. This is widely done with search warrant affidavits.
- The judge should make it a practice to dispose of all requests for arrest warrants not later than the next court day.

#### b. [§4.52] Types of Warrant for Which Affidavit Is Not Required

The requirement that the magistrate determine probable cause before signing an arrest warrant does not apply to grand jury indictments. *Ex parte U.S.* (1932) 287 US 241, 250, 53 S Ct 129, 77 L Ed 283. The requirement is met in the case of failure-to-appear warrants because the offense occurred before the magistrate and is reflected in the court's docket. *People v Superior Court* (Copeland) (1968) 262 CA2d 283, 285, 68 CR 629; *People v Weitzer* (1969) 269 CA2d 274, 282–284, 75 CR 318. These decisions also approve the practice of issuing FTA warrants without the magistrate's participation or signature. See *Shadwick v City of Tampa* (1972) 407 US 345, 351–354, 92 S Ct 2119, 32 L Ed 2d 783 (upholding statute authorizing court clerk to issue arrest warrants for municipal ordinance violations).

Warrants based on contempt consisting of a witness's or attorney's failure to appear in court do not need an affidavit. *People v Palmer* (1989) 207 CA3d 663, 673, 255 CR 55. But an affidavit is essential when a warrant is based on indirect contempt. CCP §1211; see *People v Palmer, supra.*

#### c. [§4.53] Sworn Oral Statement; Transmission of Affidavit by Fax or E-mail

For *Ramey* warrants, the following are permissible alternatives to written affidavits:

- Sworn and transcribed oral statements;
- Sworn oral statements made over the telephone; and
- Telephonic oath plus electronic transmission of affidavit. Pen C §817(c).

The procedure for issuing telephonically or electronically authorized *Ramey* warrants is the same as for telephonic or electronic search warrants. For detailed discussion, see §§2.130–2.131.

#### d. [§4.54] Lost Affidavit

Loss or destruction of the original affidavit is not fatal if the arrest would have been valid without a warrant or if the contents of the affidavit are established by secondary evidence. *People v Wright* (1990) 52 C3d 367, 391, 276 CR 731.

#### e. [§4.55] Inadequate or No Showing of Probable Cause

An arrest under an arrest warrant issued without the requisite showing of probable cause is not necessarily invalid. The prosecutor may prove that the arresting officer at the time of the arrest knew the facts that constituted probable cause; the arrest is lawful if it would have been valid without a warrant. *People v Chimel* (1968) 68 C2d 436, 440–442, 67 CR 421, rev'd on other grounds (1969) 395 US 752, 89 S Ct 2034, 23 L Ed 2d 685; see *Giordenello v U.S.* (1958) 357 US 480, 488, 78 S Ct 1245, 2 L Ed 2d 1503 (government may seek to justify arrest without relying on warrant).

An insufficient affidavit, however, cannot be rehabilitated by evidence of information that the affiant had when he or she sought the warrant but did not disclose to the magistrate. *Whiteley v Warden* (1971) 401 US 560, 565 n8, 91 S Ct 1031, 28 L Ed 2d 306.

Alternatively, good faith principles may apply. Thus, the lack of an affidavit is not fatal when the arresting officer could reasonably conclude that no affidavit was required for issuance of the warrant. *People v Palmer* (1989) 207 CA3d 663, 670, 255 CR 55 (applying the *Leon* good-faith exception). See also §§1.28–1.29.

### 4. [§4.56] John Doe Warrants; Description of Person To Be Arrested

Penal Code §815 permits an arrest warrant to designate a defendant who is unknown "by any name." A warrant using a fictitious name, however, complies with the Fourth Amendment requirements only if it describes the person to be arrested with reasonable particularity. *People v Montoya* (1967) 255 CA2d 137, 143, 63 CR 73. *Montoya* invalidated a John Doe warrant that described defendant as a White male adult, 30–35 years, 5'10", 175 lbs, dark hair, medium build. The court held that the description fit too many people. See *People v Patterson* (1979) 94 CA3d 456, 462, 156 CR 518.

Particularity can be supplied by stating defendant's "occupation, his personal appearance, peculiarities, place of residence or other means of identification." *People v Montoya, supra,* 255 CA2d at 142. The police can also supplement the description in a warrant by sending a teletype that contains additional facts pertaining to identification. 255 CA2d at 144.

## E. [§4.57] Attack on Arrest Warrant Affidavit for Misstatements or Omissions

An affidavit in support of an arrest warrant, like a search warrant affidavit, may be challenged for misstatements and omissions. *People v Anderson* (1983) 149 CA3d 1161, 1164, 197 CR 413; *In re Larry C.* (1982) 134 CA3d 62, 67–68, 184 CR 505. The substantive bases for such attacks as well as the procedural hurdles in the path of the defendant are the same for both kinds of affidavit. *People v Anderson, supra* (arrests after June 8, 1982, *i.e.*, post-Proposition 8, governed by *Franks v Delaware* (1978) 438 US 154, 98 S Ct 2674, 57 L Ed 2d 667). For further discussion, see §2.44; for the effect of misstatements on the applicability of the *Leon* good-faith exception, see §1.35.

## F. [§4.58] Checklist: Statutory Requirements for Arrest Warrant Contents

(1) The warrant must be directed to any peace officer in the state or to a person authorized to enforce the charged violation. Pen C §816.

(2) The warrant must specify defendant's name or, if it is unknown and defendant is named fictitiously, the warrant must include an adequate description. Pen C §815; see §4.56.

(3) The warrant must "state the time of issuing it," as well as "the city or county where it is issued." Pen C §815. For required contents of an abstract of a warrant, see Pen C §850(b).

(4) The magistrate must fix bail at the time of issuing the warrant. Pen C §815a. Warrants usually contain a blank for that purpose. Penal Code §815a requires that bail be set "in accordance with the provisions of section 1275." The latter lists the factors that the magistrate is to consider and provides that "public safety shall be the primary consideration."

☛ **Judicial Tip**: The judge should not leave the bail portion of the warrant blank. If the offense is not bailable, the judge should write "None" in that space.

(5) When the warrant is for a misdemeanor or infraction, the magistrate should decide whether to endorse it for night service. Pen C §840(4); see §§4.59–4.60. Warrant forms commonly have a space for the magistrate's initials. Felony warrants do not require night service authorization. Pen C §840.

(6) The warrant "shall be signed by the magistrate, . . . with the title of his office and the name of the court. . . ." Pen C §815. For exceptions, see §4.52.

## VI. TIME, PLACE, AND MANNER OF ARREST

### A. Nighttime Arrest

#### 1. [§4.59] When Permitted

Under Pen C §840, a *felony* arrest can be made at any time. A *misdemeanor* or *infraction* arrest cannot be made between 10 p.m. and 6 a.m., except in the following instances:

- A warrantless arrest (Pen C §840(1));
- An arrest in a public place (Pen C §840(2));
- An arrest "made when the person is in custody pursuant to another lawful arrest" (Pen C §840(3)); or
- An arrest pursuant to a warrant that "for good cause shown, directs that it may be served at any time of the day or night." Pen C §840(4); see §4.60.

In effect Pen C §840 only limits night service of misdemeanor or infraction warrants and then only if the arrest is not made in a public place.

#### 2. [§4.60] Judicial Authorization

Penal Code §840(4) requires an exercise of discretion by the magistrate whether good cause for night service is present. Rubber-stamped night service endorsements placed on failure-to-appear warrants by the court clerk are invalid. *People v Dinneen* (1974) 45 CA3d Supp 5, 8–11, 119 CR 186; *Paddleford v Biscay* (1971) 22 CA3d 139, 142–143, 99 CR 220.

Factors that support night service of arrest warrants are generally the same as in the case of search warrants. *People v Ramirez* (1988) 202 CA3d 425, 429, 248 CR 396; see §§2.84–2.88. An additional factor is a history of failure to appear. *People v Ramirez, supra* (11 outstanding bench warrants provided sufficient ground for night service authorization).

☛ **Judicial Tips**: The magistrate should avoid routine authorization of night service of misdemeanor warrants. Warrant forms with printed night service endorsements should have adjoining space for the magistrate's initials. On a form with preprinted endorsement but no such space, the magistrate's initials can be placed next to the endorsement if it is decided to authorize night service; the printed wording can be struck if it is decided not to permit night service. The magistrate should make certain that failure-to-appear warrants issued by the clerk do not allow night service. Felony warrants do not require night service authorization, and most misdemeanor warrants do not need it.

*Effect of unauthorized night service.* Before Proposition 8, courts suppressed evidence resulting from arrests that substantially violated the statute. *People v Dinneen, supra*; see *People v Koelzer* (1963) 222 CA2d 20, 23, 34 CR 718. In *People v Whitted* (1976) 60 CA3d 569, 572, 131 CR 639, the court said that the limitation of night service "is of statutory, rather than constitutional origin." The court also said that Pen C §840 recognized "the constitutional concern about the 'midnight knock on the door.' " To date, appellate courts have not addressed the effect of Proposition 8 in this area. One court has held that a violation of Pen C §1533, the statute governing night service of *search* warrants, does not compel suppression. *Rodriguez v Superior Court* (1988) 199 CA3d 1453, 1468–1470, 245 CR 617; for discussion, see §2.89.

## B. Residential Arrests: *Payton-Ramey-Steagald* Requirements

### 1. Arrests in Suspect's Residence

#### a. [§4.61] Need for Arrest Warrant

The Fourth Amendment prohibits a warrantless entry into a suspect's home to make an arrest absent consent or exigent circumstances. *Payton v New York* (1980) 445 US 573, 576, 100 S Ct 1371, 63 L Ed 2d 639; *People v Ramey* (1976) 16 C3d 263, 276, 127 CR 629; see *People v Bennett* (1998) 17 C4th 373, 384, 70 CR2d 850. The Amendment gives privacy within the home the highest degree of constitutional protection; accordingly, courts have "drawn a firm line at the entrance to the house" against warrantless arrests and searches. *Payton v New York, supra,* 445 US at 590. *Payton* does not apply to the arrest of a parolee. *People v Lewis* (1999) 74 CA4th 662, 671, 88 CR2d 231. For discussion of consent, see §§5.102–5.140; for discussion of exigent circumstances, see §§4.73–4.78.

#### b. Reason To Believe Suspect Is at Home

#### (1) [§4.62] Basic Principles

Possession of an arrest warrant is a necessary but not a sufficient condition for entering a residence. Officers armed with a warrant may "enter a dwelling in which the suspect lives where there is reason to believe that the suspect is within." *Payton v New York* (1980) 445 US 573, 603, 100 S Ct 1371, 63 L Ed 2d 639.

The U.S. Supreme Court has not decided whether "reason to believe" is the same as probable cause. In the view of most federal circuits, "reason to believe" as used in *Payton* means something less: the arresting officers only need a reasonable basis for believing that the suspect lives in the residence and that he or she is at home when the officers arrive to execute the warrant. See, *e.g., U.S. v Boyd* (8th Cir 1999) 180 F3d 967, 977; *Valdez v McPheters* (10th Cir 1999) 172 F3d 1220, 1225; *U.S. v Lauter* (2d Cir 1995) 57 F3d 212, 214–215. But see *U.S. v Harper* (9th Cir 1991) 928 F2d 894, 896 (officers need probable cause).

At a minimum, California requires a reasonable basis for believing that the suspect is at home. *People v White* (1986) 183 CA3d 1199, 1206, 228 CR 672 (court notes that whether officers need probable cause is an open question). Dictum in *People v Hoxter* (1999) 75 CA4th 406, 414 n7, 89 CR2d 259, speaks of a "reasonable basis for believing" without discussing what that means or contrasting it to probable cause. In *People v Jacobs* (1987) 43 C3d 472, 478–479, 233 CR 323, the court interpreted Pen C §844 (to make an arrest officers "may break open the door or window of the house in which the person to be arrested is, *or in which they have reasonable grounds for believing him to be*" after knock-notice) and held that the emphasized words impose a probable cause requirement.

The officers' belief may be reasonable without specific information that the suspect is at home. For instance, it is reasonable to look for a person at home at 10 p.m. See *Dorman v U.S.* (DC Cir 1970) 435 F2d 385, 393.

#### (2) [§4.63] Objective Standard; Mistakes

Whether or not the *Payton* standard mandates probable cause, "it is at least an objective standard requiring the officer to have enough to reasonably infer the suspect is at home." *People v White* (1986) 183 CA3d 1199, 1206, 228 CR 672. In *White,* a victim had told the police she had been raped at defendant's home an hour or so earlier. The court said that from this information the police might reasonably have believed that the defendant was still at home. But the victim had also stated that the defendant had left home in a particular car and the police saw no car fitting the description anywhere in the vicinity. The court said that this information made any belief that defendant could be found in his home at the time the police went there unreasonable. 183 CA3d at 1209.

The standard does not require that the officers' belief be correct, as long as it is reasonable. *People v Dyke* (1990) 224 CA3d 648, 658, 274 CR 66 (occupant resembled defendant); *Valdez v McPheters* (10th Cir 1999) 172 F3d 1220, 1225; *U.S. v Lovelock* (2d Cir 1999) 170 F3d 339, 343.

## 2. Arrests in Residence of Third Party

### a. [§4.64] Need for Search and Arrest Warrants

To look for a suspect in another person's home requires a search warrant in addition to an arrest warrant in the absence of consent or exigent circumstances. *Steagald v U.S.* (1981) 451 US 204, 211–213, 101 S Ct 1642, 68 L Ed 2d 38; *People v Codinha* (1982) 138 CA3d 167, 171–173, 187 CR 682. The reason is that an arrest warrant protects only the person named in it against unreasonable seizure; it does not protect the privacy of the person whose residence the police enter. *Steagald v U.S., supra,* 451 US at 213. As to problems relating to the arrestee's standing in this situation, see §§6.28–6.33.

*Differentiating suspect's residence from that of third parties.* In the real world, people often live with others and move frequently. "*Payton* and *Steagald* cannot be understood to divide the world into residences belonging solely to the suspect on the one hand, and third parties on the other." *Valdez v McPheters* (10th Cir 1999) 172 F3d 1220, 1225. If the suspect is merely a guest of the third party, the police need a search warrant. *U.S. v Risse* (8th Cir 1996) 83 F3d 212, 216; *U.S. v Litteral* (9th Cir 1990) 910 F2d 547, 553. But if the suspect is a co-resident of the third party, *Steagald* does not apply. *U.S. v Risse, supra* (suspect's statement that she was "staying with" Risse can reasonably be interpreted as meaning that she is a co-resident); *Washington v Simpson* (8th Cir 1986) 806 F2d 192, 196 (suspect who kept clothing and other belongings at third party's place and stayed there two to four nights a week can properly be found to reside there). *Payton,* rather than *Steagald,* applies "so long as the suspect possesses common authority over, or some other significant relationship to, the residence entered by the police." *Valdez v McPheters, supra,* 172 F3d at 1225 (interior quotation marks omitted); *U.S. v Risse, supra,* 83 F3d at 217.

The officers' assessment need not be correct; it need only be reasonable. *U.S. v Risse, supra*; see §4.62.

### b. [§4.65] Probable Cause To Believe Suspect Is Present

Entry into a third party's residence requires probable cause to believe that the suspect is present. *Steagald v U.S.* (1981) 451 US 204, 213, 101 S Ct 1642, 68 L Ed 2d 38 (probable cause that "object of search," *i.e.,* the suspect, is located in a particular place). Probable cause is an indispensable element even in the presence of exigent circumstances. *Fisher v Volz* (3d Cir 1974) 496 F2d 333, 339.

### 3. [§4.66] Arrests in Motel Rooms, Motor Homes, and Other Places

*Payton-Ramey-Steagald* requirements do not apply to public places. *U.S. v Watson* (1976) 423 US 411, 423, 96 S Ct 820, 46 L Ed 2d 598 (upholding warrantless arrest in public restaurant). The following locations are *not* considered public places and *Payton-Ramey-Steagald* standards apply:

- Hotel and motel guest rooms. *People v Kilpatrick* (1980) 105 CA3d 401, 410, 164 CR 349; *People v Lopez* (1979) 99 CA3d 754, 765, 160 CR 774; see *Stoner v California* (1964) 376 US 483, 490, 84 S Ct 889, 11 L Ed 2d 856; *People v Bennett* (1998) 17 C4th 373, 384, 70 CR2d 850.

- Rented rooms in a boarding house. See *McDonald v U.S.* (1948) 335 US 451, 454–456, 69 S Ct 191, 93 L Ed 153.

- Business premises not open or visible to the public. *People v Lee* (1986) 186 CA3d 743, 746–751, 231 CR 45 (locked inner office of law office); *U.S. v Driver* (9th Cir 1985) 776 F2d 807, 810–811 (closed private office in warehouse).

The warrant requirements do not apply to vehicles. *Carroll v U.S.* (1925) 267 US 132, 149, 45 S Ct 280, 69 L Ed 543; for discussion, see §§5.66–5.67. Accordingly, *Payton* does not cover motor homes or houseboats that are readily movable and in a setting that indicates use for transportation. *California v Carney* (1985) 471 US 386, 393, 105 S Ct 2066, 85 L Ed 2d 406; *U.S. v Albers* (9th Cir 1998) 136 F3d 670, 673 (houseboat in open water on large lake; court suggests result might be different if boat were permanently moored or if it were otherwise reasonably apparent that the houseboat was being used as a home and not as a vehicle).

Similarly, *Payton* is inapplicable to a sleeping compartment in a train. *U.S. v Whitehead* (4th Cir 1988) 849 F2d 849, 853.

### 4. [§4.67] Permitted and Prohibited Police Activities

Sections 4.68–4.72 discuss the legality of residential warrantless nonemergency arrests in the following situations:

- Defendant answers the door and is arrested at or near the threshold. See §4.68.

- Defendant answers the door, sees the officers, and runs into the house. The officers follow and arrest defendant. See §4.69.

- The officers ask defendant to step outside in order to talk and then make the arrest outside. See §4.70.
- The officers *order* defendant to come out and then make the arrest outside. See §4.70.
- Officers gain entry by a ruse and arrest defendant inside the residence. See §4.71.
- Officers enter to buy narcotics and arrest defendant in the residence immediately after the buy. See §4.72.

### a. [§4.68] Arrest at or Near Threshold

The police knock, defendant opens the door and is arrested standing directly in the doorway; one more step would have taken defendant outside. The warrantless arrest is lawful: courts treat the threshold of a dwelling as a public place. *U.S. v Santana* (1976) 427 US 38, 42, 96 S Ct 2406, 49 L Ed 2d 300; see *People v Hampton* (1985) 164 CA3d 27, 35, 209 CR 905. This principle is inapplicable when defendant comes to the door in response to a demand by the police. See, *e.g., U.S. v Conner* (8th Cir 1997) 127 F3d 663, 665 (officer shouted "open up"; observations after defendant opened door inadmissible); 3 LaFave, p 260.

As to arrests *near* the threshold, *Payton* states the controlling principle: "the Fourth Amendment has drawn a firm line at the entrance to the house. Absent exigent circumstances, that threshold may not be crossed without a warrant." *Payton v New York, supra,* 445 US at 590. Police officers on occasion successfully finesse the problem by asking the suspect to step outside (see §4.70), but when this tactic is unsuccessful, an officer cannot reach into the residence, pull defendant out, and make the arrest. *James v Superior Court* (1978) 87 CA3d 985, 989, 151 CR 270.

When the police are able to make a lawful arrest at the threshold, they must probably do so without entering the residence. *U.S. v Albrektsen* (9th Cir 1998) 151 F3d 951, 955.

### b. [§4.69] Arrest of Person Who Retreats Into House

The police knock, defendant opens the door, sees the officers, and runs back into the house. The right of the officers to follow defendant and arrest him or her depends on whether the police could have made a lawful arrest at the door before defendant retreated. If defendant stood in the doorway before turning back into the house, the officers can properly follow and make the arrest. *U.S. v Santana* (1976) 427 US 38, 42–43, 96 S Ct 2406, 49 L Ed 2d 300. This result is an application of the "hot pursuit" exception discussed further in §§4.74–4.75.

Similarly, when the police encounter the suspect in the yard of the house and he or she flees into the house before the arrest can be made, the officers can properly enter the house to arrest the suspect. *People v Spain* (1984) 154 CA3d 845, 849, 201 CR 555; *Mann v Mack* (1984) 155 CA3d 666, 674–675, 202 CR 296. The same is true when the police encounter the suspect on the stairwell of an apartment building and the suspect flees into an apartment. *People v Abes* (1985) 174 CA3d 796, 806, 220 CR 277.

*Spain* said that a person cannot thwart an "*otherwise lawful arrest* by retreating into the house." 154 CA3d at 849 (emphasis added). In many situations the arrest would *not* have been "otherwise lawful." When defendant never stood on the threshold before retreating into the interior, the police, absent exigent circumstances, could not have lawfully arrested defendant without a warrant when he opened the door, and the situation is not changed by his retreat. *People v Ramey* (1976) 16 C3d 263, 268, 275, 127 CR 629. To hold otherwise would allow the police to create their own emergencies.

When someone other than the suspect opens the door and the officers see the suspect inside, they cannot enter to make the arrest in the absence of preexisting exigent circumstances or valid consent or a warrant. *Payton v New York* (1980) 445 US 573, 576–578, 100 S Ct 1371, 63 L Ed 2d 639.

### c. [§4.70] Arrest After Defendant Is Asked or Ordered To Step Outside

*Request to come out.* The police knock and ask defendant to step outside so they can talk. Defendant complies and is arrested. The arrest is lawful. The privacy interests protected by *Payton* and *Ramey* are satisfied when defendant "voluntarily" steps outside. *People v Tillery* (1979) 99 CA3d 975, 979, 160 CR 650; *People v Green* (1983) 146 CA3d 369, 377, 194 CR 128. In accord is *People v Jackson* (1986) 187 CA3d 499, 505, 231 CR 889.

The police are permitted to trick defendant not only into leaving a residence but also into providing probable cause to arrest at the same time. *People v Martino* (1985) 166 CA3d 777, 789, 212 CR 45 (officer made anonymous call to suspected narcotics dealer that police were coming and that he had better get the drugs out of the house; observation of defendant rushing out with a plastic bag containing white crystalline substance gave officers grounds to arrest him); *People v Porras* (1979) 99 CA3d 874, 877–879, 160 CR 627 (similar ruse).

*Order to come out.* In *People v Trudell* (1985) 173 CA3d 1221, 1225,

219 CR 679, the officer ordered the defendant to come out and to keep his hands in plain view. Five other officers were at the scene, some with weapons drawn. When defendant stepped out he was arrested. One of the alternative holdings of the court was that this procedure and the ensuing arrest were lawful. The court ruled this was akin to tricking the defendant into leaving his residence and said it could not "agree that had appellant refused to exit the residence the officers axiomatically would have forcibly entered the residence." 173 CA3d at 1230. The dissent noted that if the majority opinion is a correct statement of the law, little remains of *Payton* and *Ramey.* 173 CA3d at 1232. The prevailing view is that a warrantless arrest is illegal if the police coerce the defendant to leave his or her residence or cause defendant to do so by a false claim of authority, such as a threat that otherwise the officers would come into the house. *Sharrar v Felsing* (3d Cir 1997) 128 F3d 810, 819–820; 3 LaFave, p 262.

#### d. [§4.71] Entry Into Residence by Ruse

When, instead of asking defendant to step out for the purpose of talking, the officers ask defendant or whoever answers the door for permission to enter in order to speak with the defendant, and they are allowed in and arrest defendant, the arrest is illegal. The officers' "right to enter is limited to the scope of the consent. A consent to enter for the purpose of *talking* with a suspect is *not* a consent to enter for the purpose of making an arrest of the suspect." *In re Johnny V.* (1978) 85 CA3d 120, 130, 149 CR 180 (emphasis in original); *People v Superior Court* (Kenner) (1977) 73 CA3d 65, 69, 139 CR 343.

The distinction between two kinds of subterfuge, one to gain entry, the other to have the suspect exit, is stated in *People v Trudell* (1985) 173 CA3d 1221, 1229, 219 CR 679: "Clearly, police use of subterfuge or ruse is prohibited to gain an otherwise impermissible entry of a residence. . . . By contrast, post-*Ramey* decisions have upheld the use of subterfuge to trick a defendant into *leaving* a residence." (Emphasis in original.) In accord is *In re Danny E.* (1981) 121 CA3d 44, 51, 174 CR 123.

An officer's statement that he wants to talk to the defendant is not automatically a ruse. The police frequently interview persons during an ongoing investigation. The officer may have no plans to arrest the defendant at the time; the arrest might be made only in light of developments after a consent entry. In that event there is no *Payton* problem. See *In re Danny E., supra*; §4.72.

Failure to disclose the reason for seeking entry is treated differently from giving a false reason. Entry and arrest after the following dialogue is lawful, assuming that the person answering the door has authority to consent (*People v Newton* (1980) 107 CA3d 568, 578, 166 CR 60):

Officer, seeking to make a warrantless residential arrest of a rape suspect, to woman who answers the door: "Is John Newton home? Does he live here?"

Woman: "I haven't seen him for four months."

Officer: "Can we come in and look around?"

Woman: "Yes, come on in, but you are not going to find anything. I am here by myself."

### e. [§4.72] Entry for Purposes Other Than Arrest

*Payton-Ramey-Steagald* limit entries for the purpose of making an arrest. When the police are admitted to a person's residence for another purpose and then develop grounds to arrest, they are free to make an arrest. Undercover narcotics purchases provide a rich variety of examples.

The simplest case is one in which the officers who make the buy immediately arrest the seller. The arrest is clearly lawful; courts have rejected the argument that consent to police entry was obtained by subterfuge. See *Toubus v Superior Court* (1981) 114 CA3d 378, 383, 170 CR 697.

When one of the "buyers" steps out and gives a prearranged signal to an officer outside who enters and makes the arrest, the arrest is also lawful. *Toubus v Superior Court, supra.*

In *People v Cespedes* (1987) 191 CA3d 768, 770–771, 236 CR 649, an undercover officer purchased cocaine from defendant, walked to the door, signaled over his radio transmitter that the transaction was complete, and left the building. Either the undercover officer or other officers reentered the building and arrested defendant. The court upheld the arrest on the ground that it was almost simultaneous with the sale. But see *People v Garcia* (1982) 139 CA3d Supp 1, 6–8, 188 CR 868.

In *People v Evans* (1980) 108 CA3d 193, 195–196, 166 CR 315, probable cause to arrest defendant existed before the entry. The buy was not completed; after two minutes of conversation uniformed officers who listened by radio entered. The undercover officers who had initially been admitted to defendant's motel room arrested him, saying: "Well, if you're not going to sell it to us, you're under arrest anyway." The court upheld the arrest; the officers who initially entered did so with the intent to continue their investigation by making a drug purchase, even though they had probable cause to arrest at the time.

☛ **Judicial Tip**: *Evans* should be used with caution. Language in the decision seems to suggest that entry by ruse is proper, contrary to other California cases. See §4.71. The court in *Evans* also stressed the nature of "the open to the public, commercial motel premises . . . used as much for a place of business as for a place of residence." 108 CA3d at 196. Motel rooms are covered by *Payton-Ramey-Steagald.* See §4.66.

Another incomplete sale case is *People v Robinson* (1986) 185 CA3d 528, 531, 229 CR 851, although it does not involve an entry for a purpose other than arrest. An officer went to defendant's apartment to buy marijuana. Defendant did not let him in, but through the partially open door the officer saw a large plastic bag containing brown vegetable matter. The officer put his foot in the door, demanded entry, entered, and arrested defendant. The court held the arrest lawful for two reasons. First, defendant committed an offense in the officer's presence; Pen C §836 permits a warrantless arrest under such circumstances. The court said Pen C §836 acts as an exception to *Payton.* The court did not explain how a statute can undercut a constitutional rule. Other California decisions recognize no such exception. *People v Ortiz* (1995) 32 CA4th 286, 291, 38 CR2d 59; *People v Hampton* (1985) 164 CA3d 27, 31, 209 CR 905; *Mann v Mack* (1984) 155 CA3d 666, 675, 202 CR 296. The *Robinson* court's alternative reason was that exigent circumstances, namely, forestalling the destruction of evidence, justified the arrest. 185 CA3d at 531. See §§4.76–4.77.

### 5. Exigent Circumstances

#### a. [§4.73] Basic Principles

When the prosecution claims that exigent circumstances justify a warrantless residential arrest, the underlying issue is whether there was "an emergency situation requiring swift action to prevent imminent danger to life or serious damage to property, or to forestall the imminent escape of a suspect or destruction of evidence. There is no ready litmus test for determining whether such circumstances exist, and in each case the claim of an extraordinary situation must be measured by the facts known to the officers" and inferences that may reasonably be drawn from them. *People v Ramey* (1976) 16 C3d 263, 276, 127 CR 629; see *People v Frye* (1998) 18 C4th 894, 989, 77 CR2d 25; *People v Ortiz* (1995) 32 CA4th 286, 291–292, 38 CR2d 59.

In determining whether there was a sufficient exigency, courts consider all the factual circumstances. *People v Ortiz, supra,* 32 CA4th at 293. However, two primary considerations in making this determination are the gravity of the offenses and the extent to which delay in obtaining "a warrant would pose a threat to police or public safety." *Conway v Pasadena Humane Soc'y* (1996) 45 CA4th 163, 172, 52 CR2d 777. For discussion of other factors, see §§4.75–4.78. Courts undertake an objective assessment of the officers' actions in light of the facts and circumstances known to them; their subjective motivation is irrelevant. *People v Hull* (1995) 34 CA4th 1448, 1456, 41 CR2d 99; *People v Ortiz, supra,* 32 CA4th at 292. The emergency cannot be one created by the police. *People v Bellizzi* (1995) 34 CA4th 1849, 1852, 41 CR2d 163.

☛ **Judicial Tip**: Appropriate exigent circumstances only excuse the absence of a warrant, not lack of probable cause or of reasonable grounds to believe that the suspect is in the dwelling.

### b. Hot Pursuit

#### (1) [§4.74] General Rule; Chase Not Required

One kind of emergency that justifies a warrantless residential arrest is hot pursuit of a fleeing felon. *U.S. v Santana* (1976) 427 US 38, 42–43, 96 S Ct 2406, 49 L Ed 2d 300; *Warden v Hayden* (1967) 387 US 294, 298, 87 S Ct 1642, 18 L Ed 2d 782; *People v Johnson* (1981) 30 C3d 444, 452, 179 CR 209 ("fresh pursuit of a fleeing felon").

The phrase "hot pursuit" conjures up an image of police officers chasing a suspect in close pursuit, but the exception is considerably broader. For example, there was no chase in *Warden v Hayden, supra* (police informed of armed robbery and that suspect had entered a particular house less than five minutes before they reached it) or in *People v Johnson, supra* (road rage shooting; police found defendant's car at his father's house, and father directed them to house in which defendant arrested 75 minutes after shooting; for further discussion, see §4.75).

#### (2) [§4.75] Conditions

The essential conditions for application of the hot pursuit exceptions are:

(1) The pursuit must "be substantially continuous and afford the law enforcement authorities no reasonable opportunity to obtain a warrant," but "it is not necessary that the suspect be kept physically in view at all times." *People v Escudero* (1979) 23 C3d 800, 808–810, 153 CR 825 (on-view residential burglary reported immediately, police identified suspect through description and vehicle, and defendant arrested at his home about 45 minutes later with no preceding chase; arrest upheld); *People v Johnson* (1981) 30 C3d 444, 452, 179 CR 209 (shooting suspect arrested without chase at girlfriend's house 75 minutes after incident;

during that time police got description of suspect and his car, located car at house of suspect's father, made a consent search of that house for the suspect, and were directed by the father to the girlfriend's house; arrest upheld). See also *Steagald v U.S.* (1981) 451 US 204, 211, 101 S Ct 1642, 68 L Ed 2d 38 (no exigent circumstances when officers entered two days after obtaining information of suspect's location; there was ample time to obtain warrant); *Minnesota v Olson* (1990) 495 US 91, 100–101, 110 S Ct 1684, 109 L Ed 2d 85 (no exigent circumstances when police learned of suspect's location in morning, surrounded house so there was no risk of escape, but did not enter to arrest suspect until 3:00 p.m.).

(2) The offense must be grave and the suspect must pose an imminent danger if allowed to remain temporarily at large. *People v Keltie* (1983) 148 CA3d 773, 779, 196 CR 243 (hot pursuit justification cannot be used in vehicular manslaughter by drunk driver because he no longer poses a danger once he is separated from his vehicle). Some judges believe that *Keltie* overstates the requirements; gravity of the offense and danger are not absolutes but factors to be considered. See *People v Ramey* (1976) 16 C3d 263, 276, 127 CR 629; *People v Hampton* (1985) 164 CA3d 27, 32–35, 209 CR 905; §4.61.

Occasionally, courts use "hot pursuit" language in arrests for minor offenses. See, *e.g., In re Lavoyne M.* (1990) 221 CA3d 154, 158–160, 270 CR 394; *People v Lloyd* (1989) 216 CA3d 1425, 1429–1430, 265 CR 422. In both cases traffic offenders ran into a residence when the officer attempted to stop them. These decisions, however, are applications of the principle that when the police encounter the suspect near her or his residence, the defendant cannot frustrate the arrest by running inside. See §4.69. *Minnesota v Olson, supra,* confirms that the fresh pursuit exception is limited to fleeing felons.

(3) The pursuing officers must have at least a reasonable belief that the suspect is present in the residence at the time they enter. *People v White* (1986) 183 CA3d 1199, 1204–1209, 228 CR 672; see §§4.62–4.63.

### c. Danger of Destruction or Disappearance of Evidence

#### (1) [§4.76] Factors

When destruction or disappearance of evidence is the basis for claiming exigent circumstances to justify a warrantless residential arrest, courts consider several factors, such as (*People v Ortiz* (1995) 32 CA4th 286, 292, 38 CR2d 59):

- The degree of urgency and the amount of time needed to obtain a warrant;

- The reasonableness of believing that evidence is about to be destroyed or to disappear;
- The possibility of danger to officers guarding the site while the police seek a warrant;
- Information indicating the suspects are aware that the police are on their trail;
- The ready destructibility of the contraband.

In addition, the gravity of the offense is an important consideration. *Welsh v Wisconsin* (1984) 466 US 740, 753, 104 S Ct 2091, 80 L Ed 2d 732 (exigent circumstances rarely sanctioned in arrest for minor offense and cannot be used to justify warrantless residential arrest for violation of Wisconsin drunk-driving statutes that treated first offense as civil forfeiture matter). But see *People v Hampton* (1985) 164 CA3d 27, 31–35, 209 CR 905 (exigent circumstance exception applies to DUI arrests; *Welsh* distinguished on ground that California statutes treat DUI more seriously than the Wisconsin law involved in *Welsh*). For further discussion, see §4.77.

The presence or absence of a particular factor is not conclusive; "the determination of exigent circumstances turns upon whether, in light of all the facts of the particular case, there was an urgent need justifying a warrantless entry." *People v Ortiz, supra,* 32 CA4th at 292–293.

Worry that a suspect will destroy evidence exists in many cases and does not suffice by itself. *People v Edwards* (1981) 126 CA3d 447, 457, 178 CR 876. As time to get rid of incriminating evidence passes, this exigency tends to disappear. *James v Superior Court* (1978) 87 CA3d 985, 992–993, 151 CR 270. Lack of a showing that defendant knows of police interest in him or her mitigates against the exigency. *James v Superior Court, supra.*

### (2) [§4.77] Illustrations

*Observation of narcotics.* The danger of imminent destruction of evidence is particularly acute when officers see drugs or narcotics through a partially open door and have reason to believe that the occupants may have seen the officers. *People v Ortiz* (1995) 32 CA4th 286, 293, 38 CR2d 59 (officer three to six feet away from woman counting out tinfoil bindles; officer as visible to her as she to him; entry to make arrest lawful); *People v Robinson* (1986) 185 CA3d 528, 531, 229 CR 851 (officer trying to make marijuana buy sees contraband through partially open door; warrantless arrest lawful). Similar exigencies may arise with respect to the observation of other contraband. *People v Hull* (1995) 34 CA4th 1448, 1456, 41 CR2d 99 (officer tracked stolen car stereo speakers by alarm signal and saw them through residence window; entry to arrest proper).

The emergency cannot be one created by the police. For example, when officers spot heroin while they unlawfully burst into a person's room, their observation does not give rise to a proper exigency. *People v Bellizzi* (1995) 34 CA4th 1849, 1852, 41 CR2d 163. Officers who do not have a warrant may not rely on observations they make without entering the premises but after the occupant opened the door in response to a demand under color of authority; here the Fourth Amendment violation precedes any exigency. See *U.S. v Conner* (8th Cir 1997) 127 F3d 663, 666, and cases there discussed. The observations are lawful, however, when the occupant opened the door voluntarily. *U.S. v Conner, supra.*

*DUI suspects.* The danger that the evidence will dissipate is acute in DUI cases. The fact that they are misdemeanors does not prevent a residential warrantless arrest. See §4.76. This exigency is available when (1) there is probable cause to believe that the suspect engaged in a DUI offense and (2) a reasonable basis for believing that he or she is at home, and (3) the time interval between the offense and the entry into the dwelling is "brief enough so that evidence of drinking would still remain in the blood." *People v Keltie* (1983) 148 CA3d 773, 780, 196 CR 243; *People v Hampton* (1985) 164 CA3d 27, 31–35, 209 CR 905. *Keltie* also holds that hot pursuit cannot justify noncompliance with *Ramey* in an alcohol-related offense.

*Minor offenses.* No exigency justifies a warrantless entry to seize a dog that had violated a local leash law (*Conway v Pasadena Humane Soc'y* (1996) 45 CA4th 163, 170–177, 52 CR2d 777) or bitten a person. *In re Quakenbush* (1996) 41 CA4th 1301, 1306, 49 CR2d 147. In *Welsh v Wisconsin* (1984) 466 US 740, 753, 104 S Ct 2091, 80 L Ed 2d 732, the court noted "that it is difficult to conceive of a warrantless home arrest that would not be unreasonable under the Fourth Amendment when the underlying offense is extremely minor."

### d. [§4.78] Other Exigencies

Courts have excused compliance with *Payton-Ramey-Steagald* in several other circumstances, including the following:

- Warrantless residential arrests soon after violent offenses involving firearms. *People v Bacigalupo* (1991) 1 C4th 103, 120–123, 2 CR2d 335, judgment vacated on other grounds (1992) 506 US 802, 113

S Ct 32, 121 L Ed 2d 5; *People v Williams* (1989) 48 C3d 1112, 1138, 259 CR 473; *People v Johnson* (1981) 30 C3d 444, 452, 179 CR 209. *Bacigalupo* and *Williams* applied factors enunciated in *Dorman v U.S.* (DC Cir 1970) 435 F2d 385, 392–393: gravity of the offense, reasonable belief that the suspect is armed, strength of probable cause to arrest, likelihood that the suspect is on the premises, and risk of imminent escape.

- Warrantless residential arrests after officers respond to a domestic violence call, when there is a significant risk that the victim would suffer additional harm unless the assailant were arrested on the scene. *People v Frye* (1998) 18 C4th 894, 989, 77 CR2d 25; *People v Wilkins* (1993) 14 CA4th 761, 771, 17 CR2d 743; see *People v Higgins* (1994) 26 CA4th 247, 251, 31 CR2d 516.
- Warrantless residential arrests based on specific and articulable facts known to the officers that indicate a risk of imminent escape if the arrest is delayed while the officers obtain a warrant. *People v Kilpatrick* (1980) 105 CA3d 401, 410, 164 CR 349; *People v Lopez* (1979) 99 CA3d 754, 766, 160 CR 774. In *Kilpatrick,* a kidnap-rape victim had escaped her assailant, notified the police, and told them the suspect was asleep in a specified motel room. Defendant's temporary residence made it particularly likely that he would get away unless apprehended immediately. In *Lopez,* a homicide suspect had left the state, returned, and was arrested 24 days after the crime. The officers had been informed that he knew the police were looking for him, was planning to leave again, and was raising money for that purpose. In both cases the courts upheld the warrantless residential arrest.

*Kilpatrick* and *Lopez* should be contrasted with the more common situation in which the officers have no specific facts relating to the danger of escape. The seriousness of the crime alone is not enough. For instance, in *People v Edwards* (1981) 126 CA3d 447, 457, 178 CR 876, a rape suspect was arrested at home three-and-one-half hours after the victim reported the crime. The arresting officer testified that he feared the suspect might flee or destroy evidence by discarding clothing or taking a shower. The court said: "Those generalized misgivings present in every case do not, however, constitute exigent circumstances. Here, as in *Ramey,* the suspect was known and nearly four hours had elapsed since the attack. If the defendant intended to flee or to destroy evidence he had ample opportunity to do so before the police arrived at his residence."

Similarly, in *James v Superior Court* (1978) 87 CA3d 985, 992, 151

CR 270, a robbery case, the court rejected the contention that defendant might flee if the officers sought a warrant. Defendant had already had sufficient time to escape and there was no indication that he was about to do so. The facts that he came home and went to bed suggest that he thought he had successfully evaded capture.

### 6. [§4.79] Effect of *Payton-Ramey-Steagald* Violation

The mandates of *Payton-Ramey-Steagald* are not "technicalities." The U.S. Supreme Court has said repeatedly that "[i]t is axiomatic that the 'physical entry of the home is the chief evil against which the wording of the Fourth Amendment is directed.' " *Welsh v Wisconsin* (1984) 466 US 740, 748, 104 S Ct 2091, 80 L Ed 2d 732, quoting *U.S. v U.S. District Court* (1972) 407 US 297, 313, 92 S Ct 2125, 32 L Ed 2d 752. Accordingly, when the police unlawfully enter residential premises to make a warrantless arrest, even evidence in plain view is inadmissible. *Payton v New York* (1980) 445 US 573, 586–601, 100 S Ct 1371, 63 L Ed 2d 639.

The limits of the fruit-of-the-poisonous-tree rule discussed in §§1.44–1.62, however, mean that not all evidence obtained in the aftermath of an unlawful arrest must be suppressed. Thus, for example, in *People v Ramos* (1982) 30 C3d 553, 571, 180 CR 266, rev'd on other grounds (1983) 463 US 992, 103 S Ct 3446, 77 L Ed 2d 1171, the police obtained a search warrant after an arrest that arguably contravened *Payton-Ramey.* The court found that the police had all the necessary information for the search warrant before the arrest. Hence the arrest, even if illegal, did not affect or taint the warrant. Similarly, an arrest in violation of *Payton* does not make the arrestee's subsequent statement inadmissible if the arrest was based on probable cause. *New York v Harris* (1990) 495 US 14, 17, 110 S Ct 1640, 109 L Ed 2d 13; *People v Marquez* (1992) 1 C4th 553, 568, 3 CR2d 710; *People v Watkins* (1994) 26 CA4th 19, 28, 31 CR2d 452.

## C. Knock-Notice

### 1. [§4.80] Elements

The Penal Code and the Fourth Amendment require knock-notice for residential arrests (Pen C §844) as well as for the service of search warrants (Pen C §1531; as to the Fourth Amendment basis of knock-notice, see §2.90). The existence of an arrest warrant does not obviate the need to comply with Pen C §844. *People v Hoxter* (1999) 75 CA4th 406, 410, 89 CR2d 259. Arrest knock-notice has four components:

(1) *Reasonable grounds for believing that the person to be arrested is present.* See §4.85.

(2) *Demand for admittance.* Pen C §844.

(3) *Notice of authority.* The officers must identify themselves as law enforcement officers. Penal Code §844, unlike Pen C §1531, does not expressly require such notice, but case law does. *Duke v Superior Court* (1969) 1 C3d 314, 319, 82 CR 348; *People v Franco* (1986) 183 CA3d 1089, 1094, 228 CR 527. This requirement derives from the Fourth Amendment. *People v Constancio* (1974) 42 CA3d 533, 542, 116 CR 910.

(4) *Explanation of purpose.* Pen C §844.

### 2. [§4.81] Chart: Relation of Pen C §§844 and 1531

**KNOCK-NOTICE REQUIREMENTS FOR ARRESTS AND FOR EXECUTION OF SEARCH WARRANTS**

| Requirements to be met before "breaking" into "house"[1] | Arrest (Pen C §844) | Search Warrant (Pen C §1531) |
|---|---|---|
| Arrestee present or reasonable grounds for believing him to be | Yes. See §4.85. | No[2] |
| Demand for admittance | Yes | No |
| Notice of authority (identify selves as police officers) | Yes[3] | Yes |
| Explanation of purpose | Yes | Yes |
| Refusal of admittance after notice | No. See §4.86. | Yes |

1. For meaning of "breaking" and "house," see §§2.93, 2.97.
2. However, probable cause to search a particular location arises only upon facts making it probable that property subject to seizure is presently situated at the particular location. See §2.22.
3. Required by case law. See §4.80.

### 3. [§4.82] Right To Challenge Knock-Notice Violation ("Standing")

A defendant may challenge a violation of Pen C §844 only if he or she had an expectation of privacy in the area the police entered. *People v Ooley* (1985) 169 CA3d 197, 201–203, 215 CR 112 (unexpected presence of defendant in hotel room occupied by another does not establish reasonable privacy expectation); *People v Hamilton* (1985) 168 CA3d 1058, 1064–1065, 214 CR 596 (guest or visitor in private home lying on bed in a bedroom has reasonable privacy expectation in that room). For further discussion, see §§6.28–6.33.

Defendant has the burden of establishing that he or she had a legitimate expectation of privacy. *Rakas v Illinois* (1978) 439 US 128, 131 n1, 99 S Ct 421, 58 L Ed 2d 387; *People v Ooley, supra.* But the prosecution must raise the issue at the suppression hearing. The failure to do so is a waiver. *Steagald v U.S.* (1981) 451 US 204, 209, 101 S Ct 1642, 68 L Ed 2d 38; *People v Lindsey* (1986) 182 CA3d 772, 776, 227 CR 550. For further discussion, see §6.120.

### 4. [§4.83] Parolees and Probationers

Penal Code §844 applies to the arrest of parolees (*People v Ford* (1975) 54 CA3d 149, 155, 126 CR 396) and probationers (*People v Negrete* (1978) 82 CA3d 328, 336, 147 CR 101).

### 5. [§4.84] Investigative Entries

Penal Code §844 is not limited to entries for the purpose of making an arrest. It also applies to entries "sought merely to investigate possible criminal activity." *People v Bruce* (1975) 49 CA3d 580, 584 n3, 122 CR 648; see *People v Galan* (1985) 163 CA3d 786, 794, 209 CR 837.

### 6. [§4.85] Reasonable Grounds To Believe Arrestee Is Present

Penal Code §844 contains one requirement not found in Pen C §1531, *i.e.,* to make an arrest officers can "break" into a house only if the person to be arrested is present or they have reasonable grounds for believing him to be. This part of Pen C §844 imposes a special probable cause standard, requiring facts that would lead a prudent person to believe and to conscientiously entertain a strong suspicion that the person to be arrested was in the house at the time of the officers' entry. *People v Jacobs* (1987) 43 C3d 472, 479, 233 CR 323; *People v Cagle* (1971) 21 CA3d 57, 64, 98 CR 348.

In *Jacobs,* officers sought to serve an arrest warrant in the afternoon. They knew defendant's address and that he was not employed at a daytime job. The court held these facts insufficient to "support a finding that the officers had reasonable grounds to believe defendant was in fact home." 43 C3d at 479. Information about defendant's address, standing alone, provides even less justification for a forcible entry. *People v Bennetto* (1974) 10 C3d 695, 700, 111 CR 699.

In contrast, the police can rely on information from a landlady that the car of the person to be arrested was parked outside the person's residence and that the person was inside. *People v Hill* (1974) 12 C3d 721, 758, 117 CR 393, overruled on other grounds in 18 C3d 889, 896 n5.

An officer who sees the defendant in a residence during the night has grounds to believe the defendant is there at 6:15 a.m. See *People v Wader* (1993) 5 C4th 610, 633, 20 CR2d 788. But knowledge of defendant's presence cannot lawfully be acquired by means that violate the suspect's reasonable expectations of privacy. *People v Cagle, supra,* 21 CA3d at 65 (peering through bathroom window).

### 7. [§4.86] Refusal of Admittance

Unlike Pen C §1531, Pen C §844 does not require that the officers be refused admittance before they can enter by breaking. This difference between the two statutes is intentional. *People v Schmel* (1975) 54 CA3d 46, 50, 126 CR 317 (court speculates that 1872 legislature concluded that arrest may call for quicker action than search).

### 8. [§4.87] Exceptions

The following exceptions apply to the knock-notice requirement:

(1) *Substantial compliance.* The officer need not announce his purpose if the circumstances make it clear to the persons inside or if further announcement would be futile. See §2.104.

(2) *Conduct complying with statutory objectives of minimizing infringement of privacy and risk of violent confrontations.* See §2.105.

(3) *Exigent circumstances.* Compliance with Pen C §844 is excused when "specific facts known to the officer before his entry are sufficient to support his good faith belief that compliance will increase his peril, frustrate the arrest, or permit destruction of evidence." *People v Dumas* (1973) 9 C3d 871, 877, 109 CR 304; see §2.106. Exigent circumstances that justify a warrantless entry under the *Payton-Ramey* rule (see §§4.73–4.78) also justify noncompliance with Pen C §844. *People v Abes* (1985) 174 CA3d 796, 807 n3, 220 CR 277; *People v Galan* (1985) 163 CA3d 786, 795, 209 CR 837.

One decision declined to apply the exigent circumstances exception to misdemeanor arrests. *People v Hughes* (1966) 240 CA2d 615, 49 CR 767. Some judges believe that a proper reading of *Hughes* only requires closer scrutiny of emergency conditions asserted in a misdemeanor case to excuse compliance with the statute. See also *People v Hampton*

(1985) 164 CA3d 27, 31–35, 209 CR 905 (applies *Payton-Ramey* exigent circumstances exception to misdemeanor DUI arrest); *Welsh v Wisconsin* (1984) 466 US 740, 753, 104 S Ct 2091, 80 L Ed 2d 732 (gravity of underlying offense is important factor in determining exigency under *Payton*; exigent circumstances should rarely be sanctioned for minor offenses).

(4) *Consent.* Ruses to obtain consent to enter are permissible. See §2.96.

### D. [§4.88] Notice of Arrest; Showing Warrant

Penal Code §841 requires the person making the arrest to inform the arrestee "of the intention to arrest him, of the cause of the arrest, and the authority to make it. . . ." For discussion of exceptions to these requirements, see *Johanson v DMV* (1995) 36 CA4th 1209, 1218, 43 CR2d 42; *People v Braun* (1973) 29 CA3d 949, 968, 106 CR 56. Upon request the officer must also inform the arrestee "of the offense for which he is being arrested." Pen C §841.

A violation of Pen C §841 "is not a ground for excluding evidence obtained after an otherwise lawful arrest." *People v Hall* (1964) 62 C2d 104, 108 n5, 41 CR 284.

Officers who serve an arrest warrant need not have the warrant in their possession at the time, "but if the person arrested so requests it, the warrant shall be shown to him as soon as practicable." Pen C §842.

### E. Limitations on the Use of Force

#### 1. [§4.89] Basic Principles

The Fourth Amendment prohibits the use of deadly force to prevent a suspect's escape unless "the officer has probable cause to believe that the suspect poses a significant threat of death or physical injury to the officer or others." *Tennessee v Garner* (1985) 471 US 1, 11, 105 S Ct 1694, 85 L Ed 2d 1 (officer may not shoot unarmed nighttime burglar who attempts to flee by climbing fence).

California courts had earlier imposed a similar limitation on the basis of statutory construction. *Kortum v Alkire* (1977) 69 CA3d 325, 333, 138 CR 26; *People v Piorkowski* (1974) 41 CA3d 324, 328, 115 CR 830; see Pen C §§196(3), 197(4), 835, 835a. The limitation applies to citizen arrests to the same extent as to arrests by police officers. *Kortum v Alkire, supra*; see Pen C §490.5(f)(2) (merchant detaining shoplifter "may use a reasonable amount of nondeadly force necessary to protect himself or herself and to prevent escape of the person detained or the loss of . . . property").

For illustrations of situations in which firearms were used in connection with an arrest, contrast *In re Walker* (1974) 10 C3d 764, 774–777, 112 CR 177 (physical struggle with defendant who is armed with submachine gun and is murder suspect; defendant not subdued until shot in shoulder; court upheld reasonable use of force), with *Tennessee v Garner, supra,* and *People v Piorkowski, supra* (citizen chases youths involved in store burglary and shoots one who refuses to halt; court held use of deadly force not justified).

Nondeadly excessive force also violates the Fourth Amendment. *Graham v Connor* (1989) 490 US 386, 395, 109 S Ct 1865, 104 L Ed 2d 443; see *Weaver v State of California* (1998) 63 CA4th 188, 203–207, 73 CR2d 571. Courts determine whether the police used reasonable or excessive force by balancing the nature and quality of the intrusion on Fourth Amendment interests against the governmental interests at stake. *Graham v Connor, supra,* 490 US at 396. Key factors are the severity of the crime, the existence of a threat to the safety of officers or others, resistance to arrest, and attempted flight. *Graham v Connor, supra*; *Seekamp v Michaud* (1st Cir 1997) 109 F3d 802, 806. The police are not required to use the least intrusive degree of force possible. *Seekamp v Michaud, supra,* 109 F3d at 807; *Forrester v City of San Diego* (9th Cir 1994) 25 F3d 804, 807–808. The determination of reasonableness is made in light of all the facts and circumstances facing the officers and without regard to their underlying intent and motivation. *Graham v Connor, supra*; *Seekamp v Michaud, supra,* quoted with approval in *Weaver v State of California, supra,* 63 CA4th at 205.

*Resistance to excessive force.* There is no right to resist any arrest, lawful or unlawful, except that one "may use reasonable force to defend life and limb against excessive force. . . ." *People v Curtis* (1969) 70 C2d 347, 357, 74 CR 713; *People v Henderson* (1976) 58 CA3d 349, 356–357, 129 CR 844; see also Pen C §§243, 834a.

### 2. [§4.90] Effect of Using Excessive Force on Admissibility of Evidence

Excessive force issues are usually raised in the context of civil litigation. See, *e.g.,* the decisions discussed in §4.89. There is virtually no case law on whether the use of excessive force in making an arrest results in the exclusion of evidence. The reasonableness of the force affects the voluntariness of a subsequent confession. See *In re Walker* (1974) 10 C3d 764, 777, 112 CR 177. LaFave suggests that the Fourth Amendment exclusionary rule should apply by analogy to *Schmerber v California* (1966) 384 US 757, 771–772, 86 S Ct 1826, 16 L Ed 2d 908, which held that evidence seized from the body by procedures involving unreasonable pain or risk of injury is subject to suppression. 3 LaFave, p 34.

### F. [§4.91] Detention of Occupants During Service of Arrest Warrant

When the police serve an arrest warrant, they may briefly detain persons on the premises to ascertain who they are and whether they have information concerning the subject of the warrant, as well as for officer safety. *People v Hannah* (1996) 51 CA4th 1335, 1343–1347, 59 CR2d 805; see *People v Castellon* (1999) 76 CA4th 1369, 1376 n3, 91 CR2d 204. The right to detain and pat search persons under these circumstances is essentially the same as during the service of a search warrant. See *People v Hannah, supra*; §§2.110–2.111.

## VII. POSTARREST REQUIREMENTS

### A. [§4.92] Right To Make Telephone Calls

Penal Code §851.5 gives a person who has been arrested and booked the right to make three free completed telephone calls within the local dialing area. Such "calls should be allowed immediately upon request, or as soon thereafter as practical." *People v Locke* (1984) 152 CA3d 1130, 1133, 200 CR 20. See also Pen C §851.5(a) ("Immediately upon being booked, and, except where physically impossible, no later than three hours after arrest . . .").

An arrestee who elects to remain silent until he or she has obtained counsel must be advised of the right to phone an attorney. *People v Locke, supra.*

Violation of Pen C §851.5 is a violation of procedural due process under the 14th Amendment. *Carlo v City of Chino* (9th Cir 1997) 105 F3d 493, 496–500 (civil action for breach of constitutional rights). But violation of the statute results in reversal of a conviction only on a showing that it deprived defendant of a fair trial or prevented defendant from obtaining or presenting evidence of innocence. *In re Newbern* (1961) 55 C2d 508, 513, 11 CR 551; *People v Moreland* (1971) 15 CA3d 269, 275, 92 CR 563. A violation of this statute is also a factor in assessing the validity of a consent to search (*People v Leib* (1976) 16 C3d 869, 877, 129 CR 433) and in determining whether a postarrest statement by the defendant should be excluded on the ground that defendant was denied counsel. See *People v Stout* (1967) 66 C2d 184, 197–198, 57 CR 152.

For discussion of police monitoring of calls made by persons in custody, see §5.34.

## B. Duty To Take Arrestee Promptly Before Magistrate

### 1. [§4.93] 48-Hour Rule

A person who has been arrested must be taken before a magistrate within 48 hours after the arrest. Pen C §825(a)(1); see Cal Const art I, §14; Pen C §§821, 822, 849(a) (duty to bring arrestee promptly before magistrate).

A two-day wait is not automatically lawful; unreasonable delay even within that time frame is improper. *People v Turner* (1994) 8 C4th 137, 175, 32 CR2d 762; *People v Thompson* (1980) 27 C3d 303, 329, 165 CR 289; *Youngblood v Gates* (1988) 200 CA3d 1302, 1319, 246 CR 775.

*Computation of time.* The 48-hour period of Pen C §825(a)(1) is computed as follows (Pen C §825(a)(1), (2)):

- Sundays and holidays are excluded.
- If the period expires at a time when the court in which the magistrate sits is not in session, time is "extended to include the duration of the next regular court session on the judicial day immediately following."
- If the period expires at a time when court is in session, arraignment may take place at any time during the session.
- A defendant arrested after close of court on Wednesday must normally be arraigned not later than the following Friday.

For discussion of the requirement of a probable cause determination within 48 hours after arrest, see §§4.95–4.102.

### 2. [§4.94] Consequences of Unreasonable Delay

Unreasonable delay does not invalidate the initial arrest; even evidence obtained during such delay is not automatically excluded. Confessions are inadmissible only if they are the product of the unlawful incarceration or there is an "essential connection" between the illegality and the confession. *People v Turner* (1994) 8 C4th 137, 176, 32 CR2d 762 (statements admissible); *People v Thompson* (1980) 27 C3d 303, 329–330, 165 CR 289 (confession admissible). Lineup evidence obtained during improper custodial prearraignment delay has been excluded when the defendant was denied the right to have counsel present during the lineup. *People v Williams* (1977) 68 CA3d 36, 45, 137 CR 70; *People v Reese* (1981) 121 CA3d 606, 613, 175 CR 214.

The admissibility of physical evidence obtained during a period of improperly prolonged detention hinges on whether the evidence "has been come at by exploitation of that illegality or instead by means sufficiently distinguishable to be purged of the primary taint." *People v Gordon* (1978) 84 CA3d 913, 925, 149 CR 91, quoting *Wong Sun v U.S.* (1963) 371 US 471, 488, 83 S Ct 407, 9 L Ed 2d 441. In *Gordon,* the unlawful delay was caused by a parole hold that was not followed by a prompt parole revocation hearing. The hold blocks a claim of a Pen C §825 violation (*O'Neal v Superior Court* (1986) 185 CA3d 1086, 1090, 230 CR 257; *People v Gordon, supra*), but failure to conduct a prompt parole revocation hearing makes defendant's continued incarceration unlawful. *People v Gordon, supra.*

Extreme delays impact speedy trial rights and can necessitate dismissal. *People v Hughes* (1974) 38 CA3d 670, 674, 113 CR 508 (case dismissed because of 132-day delay between arrest and arraignment).

When the delay is less than two days, defendant "bears the burden of producing evidence suggesting that the arraignment delay" was unreasonable. Once defendant makes such a showing, the prosecution must demonstrate justification. *People v Cook* (1982) 135 CA3d 785, 792, 185 CR 576. When the delay is longer, defendant "arguably" has no such burden. *People v Cook, supra*; *People v Williams, supra,* 68 CA3d at 43. Defendant has the burden of showing that a confession was the product of the illegal detention. *People v Thompson, supra*; *People v Cook, supra.* As to physical evidence, "[t]he burden is on the prosecution, once the initial illegality has been established, to show that the taint has been attenuated." *People v Gordon, supra.*

## C. Postarrest Judicial Determination of Probable Cause

### 1. [§4.95] 48-Hour Rule

In case of a warrantless arrest, the Fourth Amendment requires a judicial determination of probable cause within 48 hours after arrest as a prerequisite to defendant's continued detention. *County of Riverside v McLaughlin* (1991) 500 US 44, 56, 111 S Ct 1661, 114 L Ed 2d 49. *McLaughlin* makes specific the promptness requirement first imposed by *Gerstein v Pugh* (1975) 420 US 103, 114–126, 95 S Ct 854, 43 L Ed 2d 54; see also *In re Walters* (1975) 15 C3d 738, 743–755, 126 CR 239; Pen C §991.

*McLaughlin* also holds that the 48-hour period is *not* extended for weekends, that a delay beyond that time is unreasonable unless the government demonstrates "the existence of a bona fide emergency or other extraordinary circumstances," and that even when the hearing is held within 48 hours, the defendant is entitled to prove unreasonable delay. 500 US at 56–57. Examples of unreasonable delay include "delays for the purpose of gathering additional evidence to justify the arrest, a delay motivated by ill will against the arrested individual, or delay for delay's sake." 500 US at 56. Another example is delay to investigate the arrestee's involvement in other crimes. *U.S. v Davis* (8th Cir 1999) 174 F3d 941, 944; *Willis v City of Chicago* (7th Cir 1993) 999 F2d 284, 288.

☛ **Judicial Tip**: A duty judge should be available during hours that the court is not open. It is helpful to equip the duty judge with a pager. See *U.S. v Fullerton* (6th Cir 1999) 187 F3d 587, 590.

*Juvenile court.* In juvenile court, the outside time period to determine probable cause is 72 hours because minors are entitled to a formal adversarial hearing within 72 hours after a warrantless arrest. *Alfredo A. v Superior Court* (1994) 6 C4th 1212, 1216, 26 CR2d 623; see *In re Angel M.* (1997) 58 CA4th 1498, 1505, 68 CR2d 825.

### 2. [§4.96] Conditions That Necessitate Timely Probable Cause Determination

*Fourth Amendment conditions.* The prompt probable cause determination required by the Fourth Amendment and discussed in §4.95 needs to be made only if both the following conditions exist:

(1) The defendant was arrested without an arrest warrant; and

(2) The defendant is in custody at arraignment or 48 hours after arrested, whichever happens earlier. *County of Riverside v McLaughlin* (1991) 500 US 44, 57, 111 S Ct 1661, 114 L Ed 2d 49; see *Gerstein v Pugh* (1975) 420 US 103, 95 S Ct 854, 43 L Ed 2d 54; see §§4.95, 4.97.

*Statutory conditions.* Penal Code §991 requires a probable cause determination on motion under the following conditions:

(1) Defendant was arrested for a misdemeanor. Penal Code §991 includes arrests with a warrant. Pen C §991(c).

(2) Defendant is in custody at the time of arraignment.

(3) Defendant has pleaded not guilty.

☛ **Judicial Tips**:

- Penal Code §991 should not be used to limit the right to a timely probable cause determination. This determination may have to be made before arraignment; when it coincides with the arraignment, the entry of a plea should not be made a prerequisite.
- In addition to complying with *County of Riverside v McLaughlin, supra,* and *Gerstein v Pugh, supra,* the court should conduct a

probable cause hearing under Pen C §991 upon the motion of a misdemeanor defendant who was arrested on a warrant, is in custody, and has pleaded not guilty.

### 3. Procedural Matters

#### a. [§4.97] Time of Determination

The court may make the probable cause determination discussed in §4.95 at the time of arraignment as long as the arraignment takes place within 48 hours after arrest. *County of Riverside v McLaughlin* (1991) 500 US 44, 58, 111 S Ct 1661, 114 L Ed 2d 49. But a person arrested on a Thursday, Friday, or early Saturday cannot be made to wait until a Monday arraignment. *County of Riverside v McLaughlin, supra.*

Under Pen C §991, the probable cause determination must be made immediately upon motion "unless the court grants a continuance for good cause not to exceed three court days." Pen C §991(b). A request for a continuance by the prosecution requires a showing of a bona fide emergency or other extraordinary circumstances. See §4.95.

#### b. [§4.98] Advisement of Right to Determination

At the time of arraignment the court should advise eligible defendants of their right to a determination of probable cause, unless there was a prearraignment determination. *Sundance v Municipal Court* (1986) 42 C3d 1101, 1117, 232 CR 814 (affirming judgment that required such advice for in custody Pen C §647(f) defendants); *In re Walters* (1975) 15 C3d 738, 750, 126 CR 239 ("it is incumbent upon the defendant to move the court to make or continue the determination. His failure to do so at the time of arraignment, *with notice of his right thereto,* will be deemed to constitute a waiver of that right" (emphasis added)). When defendants are arraigned in a group, they may be informed of this right as a group. *Sundance v Municipal Court, supra.*

☛ **Judicial Tip**: Some judges also inform defendants of the nonadversarial nature of the hearing (see §4.99).

#### c. [§4.99] Nonadversary Determination

The court makes the determination of probable cause in a nonadversary proceeding; defendant has no right to confront and cross-examine witnesses or to challenge any factual statements in supporting documents. *Gerstein v Pugh* (1975) 420 US 103, 121–122, 95 S Ct 854, 43 L Ed 2d 54; *In re Walters* (1975) 15 C3d 738, 752–753, 126 CR 239.

The determination is made in much the same way and upon the same standard of probable cause that a magistrate uses to decide whether an arrest warrant presented to the magistrate for issuance is supported by probable cause. *Gerstein v Pugh, supra*; *In re Walters, supra*. The court may also receive testimonial evidence. *In re Walters, supra*, 15 C3d at 752; Pen C §991(c) (determination by review of documents or reports).

Reading police reports to make the probable cause determination does not disqualify the judge from further participation in the case. See *In re Walters, supra*, 15 C3d at 752 n7; *O'Neal v Superior Court* (1986) 185 CA3d 1086, 1094, 230 CR 257.

#### d. [§4.100] Issues Court May Consider

Decisions by superior court appellate departments hold that in considering a motion under Pen C §991, the trial court may decide the constitutionality of an ordinance under which the defendants were arrested (*People v Scott* (1993) 20 CA4th Supp 5, 9–10, 26 CR2d 179) and the lawfulness of a *Terry* stop (*People v Ward* (1986) 188 CA3d Supp 11, 14, 235 CR 287). As to the validity of an ordinance, facial challenges are treated differently than attacks on the particular application of an ordinance. The latter are permissible only after conviction of a violation of the ordinance. *Tobe v City of Santa Ana* (1995) 9 C4th 1069, 1085, 40 CR2d 402.

#### e. [§4.101] Dismissal; Refiling

A determination that probable cause to arrest is lacking requires the court to dismiss the complaint and to discharge the defendant. Pen C §991(d). The prosecution may refile the complaint within 15 days, but a second dismissal under Pen C §991 bars further prosecution. Pen C §991(e).

### 4. [§4.102] Consequences of *McLaughlin* Violation

The U.S. Supreme Court has specifically declined to address the issue of the appropriate remedy of a violation of *County of Riverside v McLaughlin* (1991) 500 US 44, 111 S Ct 1661, 114 L Ed 2d 49. *Powell v Nevada* (1994) 511 US 79, 85, 114 S Ct 1280, 128 L Ed 2d 1; see *U.S. v Fullerton* (6th Cir 1999) 187 F3d 587, 590.

Evidence lawfully seized in a search incidental to the arrest does not become inadmissible when a *subsequent* improper delay occurs. *U.S. v Fullerton, supra*. Delay may affect the voluntariness of a confession. *U.S. v Van Metre* (4th Cir 1998) 150 F3d 339, 348. A *McLaughlin* violation for the purpose of investigating other crimes that defendant may have committed renders defendant's statements concerning such crimes inadmissible when the statements were made during the period of improper delay. *U.S. v Davis* (8th Cir 1999) 174 F3d 941, 946.

The fact that a motion under Pen C §991 was granted has no bearing on a subsequent suppression motion. See *People v Ward* (1986) 188 CA3d Supp 11, 17, 235 CR 287 ("The purpose of Penal Code section 991 is *not* to suppress evidence, but to provide a prompt means of protecting an accused's Fourth Amendment rights, by allowing a neutral magistrate to look at . . . documents to determine whether probable cause to hold a misdemeanant in custody exists" (emphasis in original)).

## VIII. SEARCHES INCIDENT TO ARREST

### A. Search of the Person

#### 1. At Scene of Arrest

##### a. Basic Principles

##### (1) [§4.103] Custodial Arrest

A lawful arrest in which the defendant is taken into custody gives the police the right to search the defendant for weapons or evidence at the scene. *Gustafson v Florida* (1973) 414 US 260, 263–266, 94 S Ct 488, 38 L Ed 2d 456; *U.S. v Robinson* (1973) 414 US 218, 225–236, 94 S Ct 467, 38 L Ed 2d 427. This is a bright line rule; no further showing is required. *Gustafson v Florida, supra*; *U.S. v Robinson, supra.*

The *Robinson-Gustafson* rule permits "a full search of the person taken into custody, without regard to the nature of the offense for which the arrest was made." *People v Monroe* (1993) 12 CA4th 1174, 1195, 16 CR2d 267. For example, the rule extends to custodial arrests for failure to have a driver's license in possession (*Gustafson v Florida, supra*), public intoxication (*People v Sanchez* (1985) 174 CA3d 343, 347, 220 CR 53), and possessing an open container of alcohol. *People v Monroe, supra.* The right to search defendant also may be exercised in cases in which the police have discretion to issue a citation but lawfully elect to make a custodial arrest. *Gustafson v Florida, supra*; *People v Monroe, supra.*

The police may search a minor arrested for truancy (*In re Humberto O.* (2000) 80 CA4th 237, 242, 95 CR2d 248) or for a curfew violation. *In re Charles C.* (1999) 76 CA4th 420, 424, 90 CR2d 430; *In re Demetrius A.* (1989) 208 CA3d 1245, 1248, 256 CR 717 (search lawful even though officer intended to take minor home). For discussion of searches of such minors at the police station, see §4.116.

The right to search extends to items on the person of the arrestee. In *Robinson* and *Gustafson,* the officer looked into cigarette packages that the defendants had on their persons. In *People v Gutierrez* (1984) 163 CA3d 332, 334, 209 CR 376, the arresting officer opened a small pill box that the defendant had in his pants pocket; the box contained stolen jewelry. The court upheld the search. In *People v Limon* (1993) 17 CA4th 524, 538, 21 CR2d 397, the court held that the officer was entitled to seize and open a hide-a-key box in defendant's pocket incident to defendant's arrest for possession of drugs.

The search is usually conducted at the scene of the arrest, but may also be made at the police station. *U.S. v Edwards* (1974) 415 US 800, 803, 94 S Ct 1234, 39 L Ed 2d 77; *In re Charles C.* (1999) 76 CA4th 420, 424, 90 CR2d 430.

### (2) [§4.104] Noncustodial Arrest

The *Robinson-Gustafson* rule discussed in §4.103 is inapplicable to a noncustodial "arrest," such as the issuing of a traffic ticket. *Knowles v Iowa* (1998) 525 US 113, 116–119, 119 S Ct 484, 142 L Ed 2d 492. The court said that the reasons for allowing a search of a person placed in custody are officer safety and the need to discover or preserve evidence. The court concluded that the safety of an officer issuing a citation is adequately protected by the more circumscribed rights to search during a *Terry* stop and that there usually is no evidence to look for.

*Knowles* applies to routine traffic stops. Other noncustodial arrests, however, may give rise to a need to secure evidence, *e.g.*, a citation for possessing a small amount of marijuana. See *People v Coleman* (1991) 229 CA3d 321, 326, 280 CR 54.

### b. [§4.105] Search Preceding Arrest

When probable cause to arrest exists, defendant may be searched before being arrested, even when the officer had not decided to make the arrest at the time of the search. *People v Fay* (1986) 184 CA3d 882, 892, 229 CR 291; *People v Brown* (1989) 213 CA3d 187, 192, 261 CR 612. "The fact defendant was not formally arrested until after the search does not invalidate the search if probable cause to arrest existed prior to the search and the search was substantially contemporaneous with the arrest." *People v Adams* (1985) 175 CA3d 855, 861, 221 CR 298; *Rawlings v Kentucky* (1980) 448 US 98, 111, 100 S Ct 2556, 65 L Ed 2d 633; *People v Limon* (1993) 17 CA4th 524, 538, 21 CR2d 397. A search that precedes the arrest, however, cannot be justified as one incident to the arrest when the search itself provides the probable cause for the arrest. *Smith v Ohio* (1990) 494 US 541, 543, 110 S Ct 1288, 108 L Ed 2d 464.

Occasionally, despite the existence of probable cause to arrest, the defendant is not arrested until long after the search or not at all. For example, an injured DUI suspect may be taken to the hospital without being arrested and a blood sample obtained from him or her there. Or a murder suspect voluntarily goes to the police station for an interview and the police, without the suspect's consent, take fingernail scrapings from him or her. Such searches are upheld on an exigent circumstance rationale due to the evanescent nature of the evidence. *Cupp v Murphy* (1973) 412 US 291, 295, 93 S Ct 2000, 36 L Ed 2d 900 (fingernail scrapings); *People v Deltoro* (1989) 214 CA3d 1417, 1422–1426, 263 CR 305 (blood test in hospital); *People v Trotman* (1989) 214 CA3d 430, 432, 262 CR 640 (same). *Deltoro* and *Truman* hold that the contrary rule of *People v Superior Court* (Hawkins) (1972) 6 C3d 757, 100 CR 281, was abrogated by Proposition 8. A hospital blood test of an injured, unarrested DUI suspect has also been upheld by treating it as substantially contemporaneous with the arrest. *People v Nieto* (1990) 219 CA3d 1275, 1278, 268 CR 893 (accident at 3:00 a.m.; arrest at 5:00 a.m.; no discussion as to time of taking blood sample).

Another kind of exigent circumstance occasionally justifies the search of a person when there are otherwise no grounds for an arrest. Thus, a person who is found unconscious may be searched for identification and the police need not close their eyes to what they find in the process. *People v Gomez* (1964) 229 CA2d 781, 783, 40 CR 616. This type of search differs from a search incident to arrest in purpose and justification.

#### c. [§4.106] Use of Force; Choke Holds

A search becomes unlawful when performed with excessive force, such as a choke hold to prevent swallowing. *People v Allen* (1978) 86 CA3d 948, 951, 150 CR 568; *People v Sanders* (1969) 268 CA2d 802, 805, 74 CR 350. A choke hold is designed to stop the blood flow to the head and produce unconsciousness. *People v Sanders, supra.* Courts differ on what kind of throat and neck pressure constitutes excessive force. See *People v Fulkman* (1991) 235 CA3d 555, 561, 286 CR 728; *People v Johnson* (1991) 231 CA3d 1, 15, 282 CR 114; *People v Jones* (1989) 209 CA3d 725, 729, 257 CR 500; *People v Cappellia* (1989) 208 CA3d 1331, 1336, 256 CR 695. One decision prohibits even "pressure sufficient to prevent swallowing but not sufficient to cut off air." *People v Trevino* (1977) 72 CA3d 686, 691, 140 CR 243. But see *People v Fulkman, supra*; *Carleton v Superior Court* (1985) 170 CA3d 1182, 1188–1192, 216 CR 890.

Another swallow-blocking technique, forcing defendant's chin against his chest, was approved in *People v Lara* (1980) 108 CA3d 237, 166

CR 475. Unlike the situation in *Trevino,* this tactic avoids the dangers of pressure to the neck. 108 CA3d at 242.

Pointing a gun at defendant's head and telling him: "Spit it out or I'll blow your head off" was found to constitute excessive force in *People v Allen, supra.* As the court observed in *People v Lara, supra,* "Apart from the terror engendered by such an act, its consequences might well prove fatal were the suspect to physically react in startled alarm. . . ."

Factors "to be utilized in fixing the parameters of permissible police conduct" include (*People v Lara, supra,* 108 CA3d at 241):

- "[T]he amount of fear, physical trauma, embarrassment, indignity, etc., to which an innocent person would necessarily be subjected before his innocence could be clarified."
- The need for swift action.
- The seriousness of the offense.

### d. Citizen's Arrest

#### (1) [§4.107] Purely Private Arrest

A private person who makes an arrest "is authorized only" to search the arrestee for weapons, "not to conduct a search for contraband 'incidental' to the arrest, or to seize such contraband upon uncovering it." *People v Sandoval* (1966) 65 C2d 303, 311 n5, 54 CR 123; *People v Zelinski* (1979) 24 C3d 357, 363, 155 CR 575; Pen C §846.

This principle is of little help in a criminal prosecution to a defendant who has been illegally arrested or searched by a private person. As a general proposition, the Fourth Amendment and the exclusionary rule based thereon are applicable only to searches and seizures by the government or its agents, not to the actions of private individuals. *Burdeau v McDowell* (1921) 256 US 465, 475, 41 S Ct 574, 65 L Ed 1048; *People v Taylor* (1990) 222 CA3d 612, 619, 271 CR 785; *People v De Juan* (1985) 171 CA3d 1110, 1120, 217 CR 642; see §1.25. Thus, in *People v Cheatham* (1968) 263 CA2d 458, 461, 69 CR 679, the court held that it was immaterial whether a citizen's arrest was valid because "[t]he cases uniformly hold that evidence, illegally obtained by private citizens, does not come within the exclusionary rule." It is equally immaterial whether a purely private search or seizure was lawful. *People v De Juan, supra.*

#### (2) [§4.108] Joint Action by Police and Citizen

Insulation from the exclusionary rule disappears when private individuals act jointly with the police (*Stapleton v Superior Court* (1968) 70 C2d 97, 101–102, 73 CR 575), at the direction or request of the authorities (*People v Fierro* (1965) 236 CA2d 344, 347, 46 CR 132), or as agents of the police (*People v Tarantino* (1955) 45 C2d 590, 595, 290 P2d 505). Suppression will also be ordered when police officers sit idly by and do nothing when they have knowledge that a private citizen is violating or about to violate the private rights of another, but mere consultation between victim and police does not create a joint operation. *People v North* (1981) 29 C3d 509, 513–516, 174 CR 511.

#### (3) [§4.109] Store Detectives and Other Private Security Personnel

*Right to search.* Merchants, theater owners, librarians, and their agents may

- Examine items in plain view upon probable cause to believe that they were unlawfully taken from the premises (Pen C §490.5(f)(3));
- Request the suspect to surrender any item upon probable cause to believe that the suspect removed or attempted to remove it from the premises (Pen C §490.5(f)(4)); and
- Conduct a reasonable search for such an item if the suspect refuses to surrender it. The search must be limited to packages, bags, and other property in the immediate possession of the suspect and may not extend to clothing worn by him or her. Pen C §490.5(f)(4).

*Application of exclusionary rule. People v Zelinski* (1979) 24 C3d 357, 155 CR 575, held the exclusionary rule applicable to searches of shoplift suspects by security personnel on the grounds that "here the store security forces did not act in a purely private capacity but rather were fulfilling a public function in bringing violators of the law to public justice" and that "illegal conduct of privately employed security personnel poses a threat to privacy rights of Californians that is comparable to that which may be posed by the unlawful conduct of police officers." 24 C3d at 366. The court explicitly based its decision on the California Constitution rather than the Fourth Amendment. Subsequent court of appeal decisions hold that in light of Proposition 8, the exclusionary rule no longer applies to searches by private security guards who exceed the limited search rights of civilians. *In re Christopher H.* (1991) 227 CA3d 1567, 1570, 278 CR 577; *People v Taylor* (1990) 222 CA3d 612, 619, 271 CR 785; *People v Brouillette* (1989) 210 CA3d 842, 846, 258 CR 635. In accord is *Collins v Womancare* (9th Cir 1989) 878 F2d 1145, 1154. For an extensive discussion of private policing, see Sklansky, *The Private Police*, 46 UCLA L Rev 1165 (1999).

Even before the adoption of Proposition 8, *Zelinski* was held not to apply to a company's internal investigations by its security personnel. Such conduct is treated as purely private; arrests and searches in that setting are not subject to the exclusionary rule. *People v Leighton* (1981) 124 CA3d 497, 502, 177 CR 415. This is also true of other private investigators. See, *e.g., People v Mangiefico* (1972) 25 CA3d 1041, 1047, 102 CR 449 (fire insurance investigator). On the other hand, the considerations underlying *Zelinski* apply to the security personnel of public agencies. *Dyas v Superior Court* (1974) 11 C3d 628, 633–636, 114 CR 114 (uniformed patrolman of Los Angeles Housing Authority).

#### (4) [§4.110] Police Officers as Citizens

Off-duty officers who work as store detectives have only the authority of citizens to arrest and search (*Cervantez v J. C. Penney Co.* (1979) 24 C3d 579, 587, 156 CR 198); police officers' conduct while working in this capacity is governed by the Fourth Amendment and the exclusionary rule (*People v Millard* (1971) 15 CA3d 759, 761–762, 93 CR 402, disapproved on other grounds in 24 C3d 579, 589). The same holds true when an arrest by officers is treated as a citizen's arrest because it occurred outside their geographic jurisdiction (see §4.20); the exclusionary rule applies. *People v Martin* (1964) 225 CA2d 91, 96, 36 CR 924.

Actions by off-duty police officers as purely private citizens do not fall within the exclusionary rule. *People v Wachter* (1976) 58 CA3d 911, 920–923, 130 CR 279 (officer on social visit during his day off); *People v Wolder* (1970) 4 CA3d 984, 993, 84 CR 788 (search by off-duty policeman for reasons of parental concern of suspicious boxes stored on his daughter's rented premises).

#### (5) [§4.111] Bail Bondsmen

Arrests and searches by bail bondsmen are acts of private citizens and not subject to the exclusionary rule in the absence of evidence of action in concert with the police. *People v Houle* (1970) 13 CA3d 892, 91 CR 874.

## 2. At Police Station and Other Places of Pretrial Detention

### a. Booking Search

#### (1) [§4.112] Purposes

Booking searches of arrestees and their personal effects have long been permitted. They serve three purposes: maintaining jail security, discovering evidence, and safeguarding prisoners' personal belongings. *People v Maher* (1976) 17 C3d 196, 200, 130 CR 508; *People v Bundesen* (1980) 106 CA3d 508, 515, 165 CR 174.

### (2) [§4.113] Scope

The permissible scope of a booking search is at least coextensive with that of a search at the scene of arrest. *U.S. v Edwards* (1974) 415 US 800, 803, 94 S Ct 1234, 39 L Ed 2d 771 ("searches and seizures that could be made on the spot at the time of arrest may legally be conducted later when the accused arrives at the place of detention"). It extends to any container or article in defendant's possession. *Illinois v Lafayette* (1983) 462 US 640, 642, 645–649, 103 S Ct 2605, 77 L Ed 2d 65 (cigarette package inside shoulder bag carried by person arrested for disturbing the peace); *People v Miranda* (1987) 44 C3d 57, 81, 241 CR 594 ("The permissible scope of a booking search is broad: it may 'involve an item-by-item examination of everything in the arrestee's pockets or otherwise on his person, including looking into his wallet or into containers on the person; it may even extend to a strip search' "). As to strip searches, see §4.123.

*Lafayette* also noted (462 US at 645):

> The governmental interests underlying a station-house search of the arrestee's person and possessions may in some circumstances be even greater than those supporting a search immediately following arrest. Consequently, the scope of a station-house search will often vary from that made at the time of arrest. Police conduct that would be impractical or unreasonable—or embarrassingly intrusive—on the street can more readily—and privately—be performed at the station. For example, the interests supporting a search incident to arrest would hardly justify disrobing an arrestee on the street, but the practical necessities of routine jail administration may even justify taking a prisoner's clothes before confining him, although that step would be rare. This was made clear in *United States v Edwards,* 415 US 800, 804, 39 L Ed 2d 771, 94 S Ct 1234 (1974): "With or without probable cause, the authorities were entitled [at the station house] not only to search [the arrestee's] clothing but also to take it from him and keep it in official custody."

The police can read, as well as inventory, papers in defendant's possession. *People v Clark* (1992) 3 C4th 41, 142, 10 CR2d 554 (telephone numbers in defendant's wallet); *People v Hovey* (1988) 44 C3d 543, 571, 244 CR 121; *People v Miranda, supra.* Clothing and articles taken from the defendant can be tested to determine whether they were used in the commission of a crime. *U.S. v Edwards, supra* (clothing); *People v Remiro* (1979) 89 CA3d 809, 826, 835, 153 CR 89 (keys matched to locks of buildings involved in investigation); *People v Rogers* (1966) 241 CA2d 384, 388, 50 CR 559 (defendant arrested for one burglary; keys in his possession tested later to locks of place where another burglary had been committed).

The proper scope of a booking search does not extend to items that were not in defendant's possession at the time of the arrest and that the police, rather than the defendant, brought to the station. *People v Ingham* (1992) 5 CA4th 326, 330–333, 6 CR2d 756.

#### (3) [§4.114] Time

A booking search usually takes place soon after defendant's arrival at the station house, but it need not do so. See *People v Clark* (1992) 3 C4th 41, 142–143, 10 CR2d 554 (defendant placed in holding cell at 1:30 p.m.; booking search after interrogation completed at 10:45 p.m.). For discussion of further searches after a booking search, see §4.117.

#### (4) [§4.115] Custodial Traffic Arrest: Opportunity To Post Bail

Persons taken into custody on nonfelony traffic offenses and traffic warrants must be given an opportunity to post bail before they can be booked or subjected to a booking search. *People v Superior Court* (Simon) (1972) 7 C3d 186, 209, 101 CR 837; *People v Collin* (1973) 35 CA3d 416, 421–424, 110 CR 869.

It is sufficient for the police to advise defendant of the amount of bail, without advising him or her about the right to telephone a bail bondsman. *People v Archuleta* (1975) 47 CA3d 555, 559–561, 120 CR 919; *People v Collin, supra.* It is not necessary for the police to delay booking and searching in order to wait for the arrival of a bondsman. *People v Archuleta, supra.* These decisions have been modified by Veh C §40304.5, which states that a person arrested for not more than two traffic infraction failure-to-appear warrants must be informed of the right to make three completed telephone calls, given the opportunity to do so, and also be allowed at least three hours to arrange for bail before being booked. See also Pen C §851.5(b) (information about right to call must be conspicuously posted at police station).

Penal Code §4030(e) provides that, notwithstanding Veh C §40304.5, custodial arrests permit "pat-down searches, metal detector searches, and thorough clothing searches in order to discover and retrieve concealed weapons and contraband substances prior to [the arrestee] being placed in a booking cell."

Vehicle Code §40307(b) provides that persons arrested for failure to present a valid driver's license or other identification may be kept at the police station up to two hours in order to verify their identity. A person so kept is subject to the equivalent of a booking search. *People v Benz* (1984) 156 CA3d 483, 488–489, 203 CR 28. But see *People v Salinas* (1980) 111 CA3d Supp 27, 31–32, 169 CR 16.

#### (5) [§4.116] Arrest of Minor for Truancy or Curfew Violation

*Truancy.* A minor arrested for truancy must generally be taken "forthwith" to his or her parent, guardian, or school, or to a school counselor or attendance officer located at the police station. Educ C §48265. Otherwise bringing the minor to the police station is unlawful. *In re Jorge S.* (1977) 74 CA3d 852, 857, 141 CR 722 (minor's statements at station suppressed; pre-Proposition 8 decision). Search of the truant at the scene of the arrest is proper. See §4.103.

*Curfew violation.* Courts disagree whether the police may take a minor arrested for violating curfew to the police station. Yes: *In re Charles C.* (1999) 76 CA4th 420, 425, 90 CR2d 430 (search at station upheld). No: *In re Justin B.* (1999) 69 CA4th 879, 888, 81 CR2d 852 (custodial questioning at station not authorized; statement suppressed). *In re Charles C.* held that the minor's Fourth Amendment rights were not violated; hence, the evidence was admissible in light of Proposition 8. 76 CA4th at 426; for discussion of Proposition 8, see §1.7. *In re Justin B.* did not discuss this point. As with truants, a curfew violator may be searched at the scene of arrest. See §4.103.

### b. [§4.117] Search After Initial Booking

Courts have been liberal in permitting further warrantless searches long after booking, *i.e.,* after defendant has been processed for incarceration. *U.S. v Edwards* (1974) 415 US 800, 804, 94 S Ct 1234, 39 L Ed 2d 771 (clothing taken from defendant for examination the morning after his arrest); *People v Earls* (1980) 109 CA3d 1009, 1011–1012, 167 CR 685 (defendant's jeans taken for examination several days after his arrest on unrelated charges).

The defendant and his or her property may be searched when defendant is transferred to another jail and rebooked. *People v Hovey* (1988) 44 C3d 543, 571, 244 CR 121. See also *People v Panfili* (1983) 145 CA3d 387, 392–394, 194 CR 1. Officers investigating a crime can lawfully examine the clothing and personal effects of a person arrested and booked for a wholly different offense. *People v Superior Court* (Gunn) (1980) 112 CA3d 970, 974–979, 169 CR 559 (defendant arrested for possession of cocaine; 10 hours later homicide investigators examined ring defendant had in his possession and that had been taken from him at booking); *People v Earls, supra.* Officers investigating the crime for which defendant was booked can take a second look after booking at items he had in his possession when arrested. *People v Dominguez* (1988) 201 CA3d 345, 348, 247 CR 81; *People v Bradley* (1981) 115 CA3d 744, 750, 171 CR 487. Contrary to the above cases, *People v Smith* (1980) 103 CA3d 840, 843, 163 CR 322, holds that once an arrestee's personal effects have been examined during a booking search, they do not remain "fair game" for the period of incarceration. Dictum in *People v Laiwa* (1983) 34 C3d 711, 727, 195 CR 503, is to the same effect ("the legitimate purposes of the booking search exception do not justify a belated search after the booking process had ended . . .").

*People v Smith, supra,* sought to distinguish the United States Supreme Court's decision in *Edwards* on the ground that in *Edwards* defendant had been arrested late at night and allowed to keep his clothes overnight, so that the booking process had not been completed. But other decisions permit a second look after, and sometimes long after, booking was clearly completed. *People v Earls, supra*; *People v Superior Court* (Gunn), *supra*; *People v Dominguez, supra*; *People v Bradley, supra. People v Davis* (2000) 84 CA4th 390, 394–396. 100 CR2d 835, limits *Smith* and *Laiwa* to prohibiting "second look" searches for items that the police had not noted during the booking search; postbooking retrieval of items known to the police is not unlawful.

### 3. Bodily Intrusions and Strip Searches

#### a. [§4.118] Basic Principles

The broad right to search the arrestee incident to arrest does not extend to searches and seizures that involve intrusions below the surface of the body. Because of the Fourth Amendment's "particular solicitude for personal dignity and privacy" (*People v Scott* (1978) 21 C3d 284, 292, 145 CR 876), such intrusions must meet considerably more stringent requirements:

(1) A bodily intrusion is permitted only upon probable cause to believe that it will provide probative evidence. *Winston v Lee* (1985) 470 US 753, 759, 105 S Ct 1611, 84 L Ed 2d 662; *Schmerber v California* (1966) 384 US 757, 769–770, 86 S Ct 1826, 16 L Ed 2d 908; *People v Scott, supra.* In contrast, routine searches of and seizure from the person incident to lawful arrest require no grounds for believing that they will be produc-

tive (see §4.113); procedures such as fingerprinting, taking fingernail scrapings, and obtaining saliva and hair samples fall within the routine category because they involve "virtually no risk, trauma or pain" (*People v Thomas* (1986) 180 CA3d 47, 52, 225 CR 277).

(2) Bodily intrusions can normally only be made upon prior court authorization. *Winston v Lee, supra*; *People v Scott, supra.* The court order, which functions like a search warrant, must authorize the specific procedure; a search warrant permitting search of the person does not suffice. *People v Bracamonte* (1975) 15 C3d 394, 400, 124 CR 528; *Jauregui v Superior Court* (1986) 179 CA3d 1160, 1164–1167, 225 CR 308. In this area an overly broad search warrant is *not* saved by the *Leon* good-faith exception. *Jauregui v Superior Court, supra.*

An invasion of the body without court authorization "must be incident to a valid arrest and may occur only under a limited range of exigent circumstances." *People v Scott, supra,* 21 C3d at 291–292 [citations]. The most common exigency is the need to prevent loss or destruction of evidence. For this reason the warrantless removal of a blood sample from persons arrested for alcohol-related offenses is permitted. *Schmerber v California, supra.* Another exigency is a medical emergency, such as stomach pumping after a doctor's determination that the arrestee may have swallowed a lethal dose of barbiturates. *People v Jones* (1971) 20 CA3d 201, 205, 97 CR 492. This should be contrasted to the situation in which the arrestee ingested heroin balloons, which, unlike alcohol in blood, will not dissipate but will pass unchanged through the digestive tract; such ingestion normally does not pose serious health hazards. Hence, there are no exigent circumstances that justify the warrantless, nonconsensual removal of the evidence by stomach pumping or administration of an emetic. *People v Bracamonte, supra*; *Jauregui v Superior Court, supra.*

A visual rectal cavity search does not require a search warrant. *People v Wade* (1989) 208 CA3d 304, 307, 256 CR 189.

(3) Court authorization of a bodily intrusion must be based on more than a finding of probable cause to believe the intrusion will reveal evidence of crime. The magistrate "must apply an additional balancing test to determine whether the character of the requested search is appropriate." *People v Scott, supra,* 21 C3d at 293; *People v Melton* (1988) 44 C3d 713, 738, 244 CR 867. *Scott* listed the significant factors:

> Factors which must be considered include the reliability of the method to be employed, the seriousness of the underlying criminal offense and society's consequent interest in obtaining a conviction [citations], the strength of law enforcement suspicions that evidence of crime will be revealed, the importance of the evidence sought, and the possibility that

> the evidence may be recovered by alternative means less violative of Fourth Amendment freedoms. [Citation.]

These considerations must, in turn, be balanced against the severity of the proposed intrusion. Thus, the more intense, unusual, prolonged, uncomfortable, unsafe or undignified the procedure contemplated, or the more it intrudes upon essential standards of privacy, the greater must be the showing for the procedure's necessity.

The U.S. Supreme Court uses a similar balancing process. *Winston v Lee, supra.* This process renders some bodily invasions impermissible, regardless of probable cause, *e.g.,* surgical removal of a bullet under general anesthesia, when the medical risks are uncertain and the prosecution has other strong evidence tying defendant to the crime (*Winston v Lee, supra*); prolonged rectal massage of the prostate gland to produce involuntary ejaculation, when the test to be performed on the semen sample lacks reliability (*People v Scott, supra*).

### b. Blood Samples

#### (1) [§4.119] General Rule

A compulsory, warrantless seizure of a defendant's blood incident to a lawful arrest is permissible if it meets three conditions:

(1) The blood is taken in a reasonable manner;

(2) The police have probable cause to believe that a blood test will reveal material evidence against the defendant; and

(3) Exigent circumstances require prompt testing and make it impractical to obtain a search warrant. *Schmerber v California* (1966) 384 US 757, 766–772, 86 S Ct 1826, 16 L Ed 2d 908; *Mercer v DMV* (1991) 53 C3d 753, 757, 280 CR 745. For discussion of these conditions, see §§4.120–4.122.

When these conditions are present, defendant's consent is not required. *People v Ford* (1992) 4 CA4th 32, 35–36, 5 CR2d 189; see *Mercer v DMV, supra.* Compulsory blood testing does not violate the privilege against self-incrimination. *Schmerber v California, supra,* 384 US at 760–765; *Quintana v Municipal Court* (1987) 192 CA3d 361, 365–366, 237 CR 397.

*Schmerber* does not apply to *postconviction* blood testing that requires neither probable cause nor exigent circumstances. *People v McVickers* (1992) 4 C4th 81, 88, 13 CR2d 850 (upholding mandatory AIDS blood testing of convicted sex offenders); *Roe v Marcotte* (2d Cir 1999) 193 F3d 72, 78 (mandatory blood testing of convicted sex offenders for inclusion in DNA database proper).

### (2) [§4.120] Reasonable Manner of Taking Sample

A reasonable manner of taking blood means use of medically trained personnel. *People v Superior Court* (Hawkins) (1972) 6 C3d 757, 761, 100 CR 281; see *Mercer v DMV* (1991) 53 C3d 753, 757, 280 CR 745. The procedure need not be performed in a hospital or by a doctor. *Carleton v Superior Court* (1985) 170 CA3d 1182, 1189–1192, 216 CR 890 (sample taken in jail by registered nurse).

Taking a sample without defendant's consent does not violate accepted medical practice. *People v Ford* (1992) 4 CA4th 32, 36, 5 CR2d 189. Reasonable force may be used to restrain defendants who resist having a blood sample taken. *Carleton v Superior Court, supra*; *People v Ryan* (1981) 116 CA3d 168, 182, 171 CR 854.

### (3) [§4.121] Probable Cause

The requirement that a warrantless seizure of blood rest on probable cause that a test will produce material evidence rests on privacy considerations enunciated in *Schmerber v California* (1966) 384 US 757, 769–770, 86 S Ct 1826, 16 L Ed 2d 908: "The interests in human dignity and privacy which the Fourth Amendment protects forbid any such intrusion on the mere chance that desired evidence might be obtained."

This requirement overlaps probable cause to arrest. The same observations that justify an arrest for driving under the influence of alcohol or drugs are usually grounds for believing that chemical test will reveal material evidence. See, *e.g., People v Ritchie* (1982) 130 CA3d 455, 457, 181 CR 773 (drugs). The main difference between the two kinds of probable cause is that the latter disappears with time.

A blood test may be material to issues other than intoxication or being under the influence. See, *e.g., People v Clark* (1993) 5 C4th 950, 993, 22 CR2d 689 (probable cause to take blood of murder suspect who admitted ingesting drugs on night of murder; defendant arrested same day); *U.S. v Edmo* (9th Cir 1998) 140 F3d 1289, 1291–1292 (circumstances indicated use of controlled substance by defendant arrested for firearms violation; federal statute prohibited possession of firearm while using controlled substance).

Probable cause under *Schmerber,* like probable cause to arrest, is determined by considering the totality of circumstances known to the officer at the time of ordering the taking of the sample. See, *e.g., U.S. v Edmo, supra.*

### (4) [§4.122] Exigent Circumstances

The exigent circumstance for warrantless blood-alcohol or blood-drug tests after arrest is the evanescent nature of the evidence sought; alcohol and drugs in blood disappear over time. *Schmerber v California* (1966) 384 US 757, 770, 86 S Ct 1826, 16 L Ed 2d 908.

*Failure to honor DUI arrestee's test choice.* When a person arrested for DUI requests but is denied the choice of a breath or urine test, the exigency used to justify a blood test continues only because of the failure to perform the alternative test; honoring the arrestee's request would end the exigency, and failure to do so when the alternative tests are available violates the Fourth Amendment. *Nelson v City of Irvine* (9th Cir 1998) 143 F3d 1196, 1204–1205.

*Nelson* does *not* hold that the police must generally use the least intrusive alternative. See 143 F3d at 1204 (decision does not turn on relative intrusiveness of tests); see also *Schmerber v California, supra,* 384 US at 771. Nor does *Nelson* require the police to advice DUI arrestees of their choice of tests; the court held that failure to do so does not violate the Fourth Amendment. 143 F3d at 1203. In accord is *People v Bloom* (1983) 142 CA3d 310, 317, 190 CR 857.

When a DUI arrestee has provided proper urine samples, the officer cannot insist on obtaining a blood sample. *People v Fiscalini* (1991) 228 CA3d 1639, 1642, 279 CR 682.

*Blood sample for purposes unrelated to alcohol or drug testing.* In the view of most judges, when the defendant's blood is needed for typing or for another reason not related to the presence of a disappearing substance in the blood, no exigency exists. See *Schmerber v California*, *supra*, 384 US at 770–771; 3 LaFave, pp 138–139, and other cases there noted.

### c. [§4.123] Strip and Body Cavity Searches

The U.S. Supreme Court has not addressed "the circumstances in which a strip search of an arrestee may or may not be appropriate." *Illinois v Lafayette* (1983) 462 US 640, 646 n2, 103 S Ct 2605, 77 L Ed 2d 65. Intermediate federal courts have concluded that to be reasonable under the Fourth Amendment, "strip and visual body cavity searches must be justified by at least a reasonable suspicion that the arrestee is concealing contraband or weapons." *Swain v Spinney* (1st Cir 1997) 117 F3d 1, 7 (damage action), and cases there cited. For example, it is unreasonable to strip search every person arrested for driving under the influence of alcohol or drugs. *Foote v Spiegel* (10th Cir 1997) 118 F3d 1416, 1425 (damage action).

Penal Code §4030 restricts strip and body cavity searches of persons arrested for misdemeanors or infractions. Major limitations include a requirement of a search warrant specifically authorizing a physical body cavity search (Pen C §4030(h)), prohibition against touching specified bodily parts during a strip or visual body cavity search (Pen C §4030(j)), and a requirement that physical body cavity searches be conducted by specified medical personnel (Pen C §4030(k)). Except for such personnel, only persons of the same sex as the arrestee may be present during a strip search or a visual or physical body cavity search and the search must be held in an area that precludes observation by nonparticipants. Pen C §4030(*l*), (m). See also Educ C §§49050–49051, prohibiting body cavity and other degrading searches by school employees.

Violation of Pen C §4030 does not compel suppression of the evidence. *People v Wade* (1989) 208 CA3d 304, 307, 256 CR 189.

## B. Search Beyond Person of Arrestee

### 1. Areas Within Arrestee's Immediate Control

#### a. [§4.124] *Chimel* Rule

At or near the time of arrest, the police can search not only the person whom they arrested but also the area within the lunging distance of the arrestee, *i.e.,* "the area from within which he might gain possession of a weapon or destructible evidence." *Chimel v California* (1969) 395 US 752, 763, 89 S Ct 2034, 23 L Ed 2d 685.

A *Chimel* search does not require a search warrant or probable cause to believe that it will turn up a weapon or evidence. The rationale for this exception to the warrant requirement of the Fourth Amendment is "the threat posed by the arrestee"; the rationale defines and narrowly limits the scope of the permissible search. *Guidi v Superior Court* (1973) 10 C3d 1, 7, 109 CR 684; *Chimel v California, supra.* An arrest does not justify the routine search of rooms other than the one in which the arrest took place. *Chimel v California, supra*; *People v Mendoza* (1986) 176 CA3d 1127, 1132, 224 CR 145 (arrest of person in bathroom does not permit search of shoulder bag located near front door; court upheld search on ground that defendant had denied ownership of bag at time of arrest and hence given up any reasonable expectation of privacy). But an officer may accompany an arrestee who is looking for personal items and seize contraband in plain sight. *People v Breault* (1990) 223 CA3d 125, 132, 273 CR 110 (officer has same right as to juvenile being taken into protective custody).

An arrest that occurs outside a house does not provide a basis for a search of the house. *Dillon v Superior Court* (1972) 7 C3d 305, 311, 102 CR 161.

#### b. [§4.125] Illustrative Cases

(1) *Illegal drugs in the store.* Police investigating a store burglary see

barbiturates in plain view, arrest the store owner, search the entire store, and discover many more unlawful drugs. The search after the arrest cannot be justified under *Chimel. People v Rios* (1976) 16 C3d 351, 356–357, 128 CR 5.

(2) *Bag at defendant's feet.* Upon being arrested, defendant lunged toward a shoulder bag at this feet. Search of the bag is proper and would be even without lunging. *People v Flores* (1979) 100 CA3d 221, 230–233, 160 CR 839. See also *People v Mendoza* (1986) 176 CA3d 1127, 1132, 224 CR 145 (shoulder bag in different room cannot be searched under *Chimel* rationale).

(3) *Odor of hashish.* Defendants are arrested in the living room and immediately handcuffed. The officer goes to the kitchen, smells hashish, and finds it in a bag behind the kitchen counter. None of the arrestees are ever closer than eight feet from the counter. *Chimel* does not permit such a search because any evidence or weapons in the kitchen "were clearly beyond the reach of the arrestees." *Guidi v Superior Court* (1973) 10 C3d 1, 7, 109 CR 684. The court agreed with the prosecution that evidence in "plain smell" may be seized like evidence in plain sight, but noted that the real issue is whether the officer had a right to be where he was when he saw or smelled the object. As to when the officers may go beyond the area within the arrestee's immediate control to look for other suspects, see §4.127.

(4) *Pretext for search.* Officers cannot move a person from room to room "as a pretext for seizing items open to their view." *Sanderson v Superior Court* (1980) 105 CA3d 264, 273, 164 CR 290.

(5) *Delayed search.* In *People v Ingham* (1992) 5 CA4th 326, 331, 6 CR2d 756, the police could have searched defendant's purse when they arrested her. Instead they took the purse to the station house and searched it there. The search is illegal; there was no longer any danger that defendant could gain access to the purse. In *People v Summers* (1999) 73 CA4th 288, 86 CR2d 388, the police saw a sawed-off shotgun within a few feet of the arrestee who was being removed from a trailer, but they did not seize it until they secured the area about 10 minutes after the arrest. The court upheld the search, saying that the discovery of the illegal weapon was within *Chimel* and that the delay in seizing it was justified by the need to take "reasonable precautions for the safety of everyone involved." 73 CA4th at 291.

### 2. Vehicles

#### a. [§4.126] *Belton* Rule

When the occupant of a car is arrested and placed into custody, a contemporaneous search of the passenger compartment of the vehicle and any containers found in it is proper. *New York v Belton* (1981) 453 US 454, 460, 101 S Ct 2860, 69 L Ed 2d 768. There is no need to show that the arrestee, who has usually been removed from the car by the time the search takes place, still had access to the vehicle or to a particular object in it. The court formulated this extension of *Chimel* to develop a bright line rule. For further discussion, see §4.127.

### b. [§4.127] Conditions for Applicability of Rule

A search is justified under *Belton* if it meets the following conditions:

(1) *Lawful custodial arrest of a vehicle occupant.* "Occupant" includes a person who, as in *Belton,* was ordered out of the car and then arrested, as well as a vehicle owner seen near but not inside the car. *People v Stoffle* (1991) 1 CA4th 1671, 1680, 3 CR2d 257; see *People v Boissard* (1992) 5 CA4th 972, 982, 8 CR2d 738. A noncustodial arrest for a traffic violation does not, without more, permit a vehicle search. *Knowles v Iowa* (1998) 525 US 113, 114, 119 S Ct 484, 142 L Ed 2d 492.

(2) *Search limited to passenger compartment and objects found in it. Belton* does not provide a rationale for searching the trunk of a vehicle or other areas beyond the passenger compartment. The court stressed that "articles inside the relatively narrow compass of the passenger compartment of an automobile are in fact generally, even if not inevitably, within 'the area into which an arrestee might reach in order to grab a weapon or evidentiary item.' " *New York v Belton* (1981) 453 US 454, 460, 101 S Ct 2860, 69 L Ed 2d 768.

As to articles within the passenger compartment, the right to search extends to a passenger's purse, even when the passenger is not arrested or suspected of a crime. *People v Mitchell* (1995) 36 CA4th 672, 674, 42 CR2d 537; see *People v Prance* (1991) 226 CA3d 1525, 1531–1534, 277 CR 567.

(3) *Search contemporaneous with arrest. Belton* used the phrase "a contemporaneous incident" of the arrest. *New York v Belton, supra,* 453 US at 460. This condition stems from underlying concern for what the arrestee might do. A car cannot be searched incident to arrest long after the arrest has been completed. *People v Hill* (1974) 12 C3d 731, 750, 117 CR 393, overruled on other grounds in 18 C3d 889, 896 n5.

The contemporaneity requirement does not apply to vehicle searches that rest on a basis other than arrest. *U.S. v Johns* (1985) 469 US 478, 105 S Ct 881, 885, 83 L Ed 2d 890; *People v Salih* (1985) 173 CA3d

1009, 1020, 219 CR 603. For discussion of such bases, see §§5.48–5.53, 5.55–5.59.

### 3. Protective Sweep

#### a. [§4.128] Definition and Purpose

A protective sweep "is a quick and limited search of premises, incident to an arrest and conducted to protect the safety of police officers or others." *Maryland v Buie* (1990) 494 US 325, 327, 110 S Ct 1093, 108 L Ed 2d 276. It differs from a *Chimel* search discussed in §§4.124–4.127 in that (1) it may extend to portions of the premises that are beyond the arrestee's immediate control and (2) it requires a factual basis in addition to a valid arrest. See §4.129. A protective sweep is not a search for additional suspects, although some cases speak in those terms. See *People v Mack* (1980) 27 C3d 145, 151, 165 CR 113; *Guidi v Superior Court* (1973) 10 C3d 1, 8, 109 CR 684; *People v Block* (1971) 6 C3d 239, 245, 103 CR 281 (search for "more defendants"). Rather, it is a search for persons who might endanger those on the scene (*Maryland v Buie, supra,* 494 US at 327) or who might destroy evidence. *People v Seaton* (2001) 26 C4th 598, 632, 110 CR2d 441. Such persons are not inevitably suspects, although they often are.

#### b. [§4.129] Conditions for Valid Sweep

A protective sweep must meet three conditions in order to be valid:

(1) *Arrest.* The sweep must be incident to a lawful arrest. *Maryland v Buie* (1990) 494 US 325, 327, 110 S Ct 1093, 108 L Ed 2d 276; *U.S. v Hawkins* (8th Cir 1995) 59 F3d 723, 727. Officers who seek to interview a suspect may not conduct a protective sweep, at least in the absence of probable cause to arrest. *U.S. v Wilson* (5th Cir 1994) 36 F3d 1298, 1306–1307.

(2) *Factual basis.* The searching officers must have "a reasonable belief based on specific and articulable facts that the area to be swept harbors an individual posing a danger to those on the arrest scene" (*Maryland v Buie, supra,* 494 US at 337) or to evidence that is probably on the premises. *People v Seaton* (2001) 26 C4th 598, 632, 110 CR2d 441. This standard is lower than probable cause, but does not legitimate a protective sweep incident to every residential arrest. *Maryland v Buie, supra.* For further discussion of what constitutes an adequate factual basis for a sweep, see §§4.130–4.135.

(3) *Limited scope.* The sweep "may extend only to cursory inspection of those spaces where a person may be found" and last "no longer than

is necessary to dispel the reasonable suspicion of danger." *Maryland v Buie, supra,* 494 US at 335–336; see §4.136.

### c. Factual Basis for Sweep

#### (1) [§4.130] Slight Showing Often Sufficient

The arresting officers' reasons to be concerned for their safety need not be strong (*U.S. v Brown* (7th Cir 1995) 64 F3d 1083, 1086) as long as they are reasonable under the particular circumstances. Examples of protective sweeps found lawful include:

*Pot party.* In *People v Block* (1971) 6 C3d 239, 245, 103 CR 281, the officers interrupted a pot party on the main floor of a house. They noticed marijuana smoke, a roach, and several people who had been using marijuana. The stairs going to the upper floor were lit, as well as the second floor hallway. The court said it was reasonable to suspect that others might be upstairs. But a protective sweep of the story above the location of the arrest is unreasonable when the officers fail to point to any basis for believing that dangerous persons might be upstairs. *U.S. v Akrawi* (6th Cir 1990) 920 F2d 418, 420.

*Others present at drug sales.* In *U.S. v Hromada* (11th Cir 1995) 49 F3d 685, 689–690, officers had negotiated a marijuana sale by phone and heard defendant talk to another man. They also knew that the defendant's girlfriend lived on the premises.

*Chase into building.* In *U.S. v Jones* (8th Cir 1999) 193 F3d 948, 950, defendant brandished a shotgun at police who were arresting others. Officers chased him into an apartment building and observed a rifle during the chase. The court said the presence of "the rifle could certainly have signaled to a reasonable mind the presence of another assailant."

Stronger indicia of possible danger include:

- Information that the defendant and confederates are making methamphetamine on the premises. *U.S. v Smith* (10th Cir 1997) 131 F3d 1392, 1396.
- Sounds coming from other rooms and the presence of a large amount of contraband giving rise to the possibility that any occupants would violently defend it. *Guidi v Superior Court* (1973) 10 C3d 1, 8, 109 CR 684.
- Occupants heard moving about while refusing officers entry; officers observe movement in an upstairs window. *U.S. v Burrows* (7th Cir 1995) 48 F3d 1011, 1017 (defendants arrested downstairs; sweep of second floor upheld).

### (2) [§4.131] Protective Sweep After Defendant Removed From Premises or Arrested Outside

Police officers have the right to ensure their safety not only during the arrest itself but also during the remainder of the time that they are lawfully on the premises or its environs. *U.S. v Burrows* (7th Cir 1995) 48 F3d 1011, 1017. A protective sweep may be justified after the arrestee is no longer on the premises, as long as the officers have fact-based reasons to fear they are exposed to danger from persons on the premises. *People v Maier* (1991) 226 CA3d 1670, 1675, 277 CR 667 (defendant ordered out of building and arrested; sweep proper because possible presence of accomplices); see *Maryland v Buie* (1990) 494 US 325, 328, 110 S Ct 1093, 108 L Ed 2d 276 (defendant handcuffed and removed from premises; remanded to determine whether sweep justified). Fact-based reasons to fear that persons on the premises might destroy evidence also justifies a brief sweep. *People v Seaton* (2001) 26 C4th 598, 632, 110 CR2d 441.

There is no bright line rule that prohibits a sweep when the arrest took place outside but in close vicinity to the arrestee's residence. *U.S. v Colbert* (6th Cir 1996) 76 F3d 773, 776–777; *U.S. v Biggs* (6th Cir 1995) 70 F3d 913, 915–916; see *People v Maier, supra. Biggs* and *Colbert* are particularly instructive. In both cases officers had defendant's place of residence under surveillance, a motel room in *Biggs* and the apartment of defendant's woman companion in *Colbert.* Before the police had made their presence known, each defendant walked out of the building and to his vehicle parked nearby. The police arrested each defendant next to his vehicle and then made a sweep of the premises from which the defendants had emerged. The court upheld the sweep in *Biggs,* but not in *Colbert.*

In *Biggs,* the court held that the following circumstances made the sweep reasonable: the police had information that another person would be meeting defendant at his room; anyone present in the room would have a clear view of the officers; and defendant had been arrested on two previous occasions in the presence of persons who possessed firearms. In *Colbert,* the court held that the police had no reasonable basis for a sweep: the sole fact that arguably supported it—defendant's girlfriend running out of the house in a frantic and upset manner—did not suggest a threat from anyone who might be inside. In addition, the officers had no reason to think that any person was in the apartment.

### (3) [§4.132] Arrest of Confederates

When the police arrest and secure all the defendant's associates, a protective sweep is not proper, at least in the absence of information about possible danger from others. *Sharrar v Felsing* (3d Cir 1997) 128 F3d 810, 825. A different situation is presented when the police articulate reasons for believing that, despite the arrest of some confederates, others may well be still at large. See *People v Mack* (1980) 27 C3d 145, 149, 165 CR 113; *People v Coffee* (1980) 107 CA3d 28, 34, 165 CR 676.

#### (4) [§4.133] Delay in Conducting Sweep

A substantial time lapse between the arrest and the protective sweep negates the basis for a sweep. *U.S. v Chaves* (11th Cir 1999) 169 F3d 687, 692 (45-minute delay too long); see *U.S. v Hogan* (10th Cir 1994) 38 F3d 1148, 1150 (sweep occurred at some point during officers' two-hour postarrest presence on premises; court said extended stay and uncertainty at what point during stay the protective sweep took place threw doubt on its validity; court decided case on other grounds).

#### (5) [§4.134] Dangerousness of Arrestee

The dangerousness of the arrestee has no bearing on the possible presence of others in the absence of information about confederates. *U.S. v Colbert* (6th Cir 1996) 76 F3d 773, 777; *U.S. v Ford* (DC Cir 1995) 56 F3d 265, 269; *U.S. v Henry* (DC Cir 1995) 48 F3d 1282, 1284.

Particular categories of crime do not justify a protective sweep any more than they create an exception to knock-notice requirements. *U.S. v Hatcher* (6th Cir 1982) 680 F2d 438, 444 (allowing sweep on ground that drug-related arrestees are dangerous would permit wholesale abrogation of Fourth Amendment); see *U.S. v Calhoun* (6th Cir 1995) 49 F3d 231, 234 n3 (arrest following controlled delivery of cocaine does not warrant protective sweep); for discussion of knock-notice, see §§2.90–2.109 and §§4.80–4.87.

#### (6) [§4.135] Lack of Information

Lack of information whether anyone is inside the premises cannot be used to justify a protective sweep. *U.S. v Chaves* (11th Cir 1999) 169 F3d 687, 692; *U.S. v Colbert* (6th Cir 1996) 76 F3d 773, 778 (absence of information not an articulable factual basis); *U.S. v Calhoun* (6th Cir 1995) 49 F3d 231, 234. But see *U.S. v Boyd* (8th Cir 1999) 180 F3d 967, 975 (sweep upheld although police had previously removed only person other than defendant of whom they knew).

### d. [§4.136] Scope of Protective Sweep

The police may seize weapons, contraband, or evidence in plain view, "plain smell," or "plain touch" during a lawful protective sweep. See, *e.g., People v Mack* (1980) 27 C3d 145, 149, 165 CR 113 (stolen property in plain sight in garage); *Guidi v Superior Court* (1973) 10 C3d 1, 5, 109 CR 684 (odor of hashish coming from shopping bag). Other examples include:

- A gun in an open suitcase. *U.S. v Biggs* (6th Cir 1995) 70 F3d 913, 915.
- Clear plastic bags containing white powder residue that the officers had probable cause to believe was cocaine. *U.S. v Buchanan* (5th Cir 1995) 70 F3d 818, 826.
- The stock of a shotgun protruding from underneath a bed. *U.S. v Lauter* (2d Cir 1995) 57 F3d 212, 216–217.
- A handgun in a bag when the nature of the weapon is apparent by touch. *People v Maier* (1991) 226 CA3d 1670, 1674, 277 CR 667.

On the other hand, a checkbook seized from a waste basket is not within the scope of the cursory visual inspection that is permitted during a protective sweep. *U.S. v Wilson* (5th Cir 1994) 36 F3d 1298, 1306–1307.

The discovery of seizable objects does not justify a further warrantless search. *U.S. v Ford* (DC Cir 1995) 56 F3d 265, 272 (search under mattress after discovery of gun clip improper because that is not a place from which attack on officers could be launched).

*Reentry to seize.* Reentry to seize an item observed earlier cannot be justified as part of a protective sweep. *People v Keener* (1983) 148 CA3d 73, 78, 195 CR 733 (officers observed gun, left building; second entry unlawful in absence of search warrant or exigent circumstances; no exigent circumstances present); see *People v Duncan* (1986) 42 C3d 91, 100–101, 227 CR 654.

# 5

# Warrantless Searches

## III. WARRANTLESS SEARCHES OF MOTOR VEHICLES

## I. [§5.1] INTRODUCTION AND SCOPE OF CHAPTER

The Fourth Amendment generally requires the police to secure a warrant before conducting a search. *Maryland v Dyson* (1999) 527 US 465, 466, 119 S Ct 2013, 144 L Ed 2d 442; *California v Carney* (1985) 471 US 386, 390–391, 105 S Ct 2066, 85 L Ed 2d 406. Decisions often state that the requirement is subject only to a few "narrow and well-delineated" exceptions. See, *e.g., Flippo v West Virginia* (1999) 528 US 11, 13, 120 S Ct 7, 145 L Ed 2d 16; *Minnesota v Dickerson* (1993) 508 US 366, 372, 113 S Ct 2130, 124 L Ed 2d 334; *People v Woods* (1999) 21 C4th 668, 674, 88 CR2d 88; *In re Tyrell J.* (1994) 8 C4th 68, 76, 32 CR2d 33.

In reality there are many exceptions to the warrant requirement, some of them quite broad. This chapter discusses several of the major ones: warrantless vehicle searches (§§5.48–5.83); entries to preserve life or property (§§5.84–5.101); consent searches (§§5.102–5.140); searches of probationers and parolees (§§5.141–5.156); and searches by school authorities (§§5.157–5.160). Warrantless searches incident to temporary detention and arrest are discussed, respectively, in §§3.95–3.107 and 4.103–4.136.

In addition, there is a wide range of police conduct that does not come within the scope of the Fourth Amendment because it does not interfere with reasonable expectations of privacy. This matter is discussed in §§5.2–5.47.

## II. PLAIN VIEW AND MISCELLANEOUS INVESTIGATIVE TECHNIQUES

### A. Reasonable Expectation of Privacy

#### 1. [§5.2] Basic Principles

A court determines the lawfulness of any investigative technique, whether an observation of objects in plain view, an aerial sighting of marijuana cultivation, the installation of beepers to track an item or a vehicle, or the examination of the contents of a trash container, by whether it interferes with the defendant's reasonable expectation of privacy.

Fourth Amendment analysis of warrantless law enforcement activities considers two underlying questions: Did the activity interfere with the defendant's reasonable expectation of privacy? If so, should it be allowed as an exception to the warrant requirement? The material in §§5.2–5.47 addresses the first question; the second is discussed in the balance of the chapter, as well as in §§3.95–3.107 (searches incident to temporary detention) and §§4.103–4.136 (searches incident to arrest).

Under this analysis there is no Fourth Amendment violation in the absence of police conduct that infringes on a defendant's reasonable expectation of privacy. See, *e.g., California v Ciraolo* (1986) 476 US 207, 213, 106 S Ct 1809, 90 L Ed 2d 210 (overflight of backyard for observational purposes is not an infringement); *Katz v U.S.* (1967) 389 US 347, 356–359, 88 S Ct 507, 19 L Ed 2d 576 (electronic eavesdropping is an infringement and, in the absence of a warrant authorizing it, an unreasonable one); *People v Camacho* (2000) 23 C4th 824, 831–832, 98 CR2d 232 (entering side yard of residence is infringement). Thus, observations and other information-gathering techniques are searches within the meaning of the Fourth Amendment only when a defendant's reasonable expectations of privacy are violated. See, *e.g., Maryland v Macon* (1985) 472 US 463, 469, 105 S Ct 2778, 86 L Ed 2d 370 (nonuniformed officer who browsed through adult bookstore open to public and bought porno magazine not engaged in search); *Arizona v Hicks* (1987) 480 US 321, 324–325, 107 S Ct 1149, 94 L Ed 2d 347 (officer who looked at stereo equipment while lawfully present in apartment on other business not engaged in search, but turning equipment over is a search and lawful only if officer had probable cause to consider it stolen). See also *People v Mayberry* (1982) 31 C3d 335, 341, 182 CR 617 ("It is commonly accepted that a 'search' is a governmental intrusion upon, or invasion of, a citizen's personal security in an area in which he has a reasonable expectation of privacy").

☛ **Judicial Tip**: It is important to focus on the relation of the police activity to reasonable privacy expectations, rather than on the definition of "search." Some police conduct that is clearly a search in the ordinary meaning of the word, such as walking onto defendant's land to look for growing marijuana, does not interfere with such expectations (see §5.23); calling the activity not a search is the shorthand conclusion of Fourth Amendment analysis and not the beginning. Conversely, the observation of an object in plain view may not appear to be a search in the common meaning of the word, but it is a search for Fourth Amendment purposes (and not necessarily a lawful one) unless the officer's vantage point did not infringe reasonable privacy expectations. See §§5.10, 5.14–5.24.

### 2. [§5.3] Threshold Questions for Determining Presence of Reasonable Privacy Expectations

The two threshold questions that a court must answer to determine whether there is a reasonable expectation of privacy are:

(1) Did the defendant exhibit an actual, subjective expectation of privacy? *People v Camacho* (2000) 23 C4th 824, 830–831, 98 CR2d 232;

see *Bond v U.S.* (2000) 529 US 334, 338, 120 S Ct 1462, 146 L Ed 2d 365; *California v Ciraolo* (1986) 476 US 207, 211, 106 S Ct 1809, 90 L Ed 2d 210. For further discussion, see §5.4.

(2) Is the defendant's expectation of privacy "objectively reasonable, that is, is the expectation one society is willing to recognize as reasonable?" *People v Camacho, supra*; *Bond v U.S., supra*; *Oliver v U.S.* (1984) 466 US 170, 177, 104 S Ct 1735, 80 L Ed 2d 214. For discussion, see §§5.5–5.8.

In cases involving other parties, an additional inquiry may be necessary, that is, "whether the defendant, rather than someone else, had a reasonable expectation of privacy in the place searched or the items seized." *People v Ayala* (2000) 23 C4th 225, 254 n3, 96 CR2d 682; see *Rakas v Illinois* (1978) 439 US 128, 148–150, 99 S Ct 421, 58 L Ed 2d 387. Courts have referred to this inquiry as one of "standing," but in *Ayala* the court said that the term "standing" should not be used. For further discussion, see §§6.28–6.41.

### 3. [§5.4] Subjective Expectation of Privacy

The requirement of an actual, subjective expectation of privacy expresses the idea that one has no privacy interest in what one exposes to the view of others. *Katz v U.S.* (1967) 389 US 347, 361, 88 S Ct 507, 19 L Ed 2d 576 (concurring opinion of Harlan, J); *People v Deutsch* (1996) 44 CA4th 1224, 1229, 52 CR2d 366. Law enforcement officers do not have to shield their eyes when passing by a house on a public thoroughfare. *U.S. v Dunn* (1987) 480 US 294, 304, 107 S Ct 1134, 94 L Ed 2d 326; *California v Ciraolo* (1986) 476 US 207, 213, 106 S Ct 1809, 90 L Ed 2d 210.

Courts place less emphasis on this requirement than the one of objective reasonableness. *Hudson v Palmer* (1984) 468 US 517, 525 n7, 104 S Ct 3194, 82 L Ed 2d 393 ("constitutional rights are generally not defined by the subjective intent of those asserting the right"; court has always emphasized the requirement that the privacy expectation be objectively reasonable); *Sacramento County Deputy Sheriffs' Ass'n v County of Sacramento* (1996) 51 CA4th 1468, 1478 n8, 59 CR2d 834. Courts at times assume that there was a subjective privacy expectation and proceed quickly to the question of reasonableness. See, *e.g.*, *Sacramento County Deputy Sheriffs' Ass'n v County of Sacramento, supra* (deputies have no objectively reasonable expectation of privacy in release office of county jail, "even assuming" that they have subjective expectation).

Subjective expectations are not always an adequate index of Fourth Amendment protection. For example, a refugee from a police state might expect his phone to be tapped. Such "subjective expectations obviously could play no meaningful role in ascertaining what the scope of Fourth Amendment protection was." *Smith v Maryland* (1979) 442 US 735, 740 n5, 99 S Ct 2577, 61 L Ed 2d 220.

The process of determining a defendant's subjective expectation of privacy is similar to ascertaining subjective intent: courts draw inferences from the defendant's actions. For example, in *Bond v U.S.* (2000) 529 US 334, 338, 120 S Ct 1462, 146 L Ed 2d 365, the court held that a law enforcement agent's squeezing of a bus passenger's bag violated the Fourth Amendment. The court found that the defendant's use of an opaque bag and placement of the bag directly above his seat demonstrated a subjective expectation of privacy in the bag's contents. But in *Rawlings v Kentucky* (1980) 448 US 98, 104–105, 100 S Ct 2556, 65 L Ed 2d 633, the court held that a person who dumped drugs into the purse of a short-term acquaintance just before arrival of the police had no subjective expectation of privacy.

### 4. Reasonableness of Expectation

#### a. [§5.5] Basic Principles

The reasonableness of an expectation of privacy depends on "whether the government's intrusion infringes upon the personal and societal values protected by the Fourth Amendment." *Oliver v U.S.* (1984) 466 US 170, 182–183, 104 S Ct 1735, 80 L Ed 2d 214. No single factor is determinative; the U.S. Supreme Court "has given weight to such factors as the intention of the Framers of the Fourth Amendment [citation], the uses to which an individual has put a location [citation], and our societal understanding that certain areas deserve the most scrupulous protection from government invasion [citation]." 466 US at 177–178; *O'Connor v Ortega* (1987) 480 US 709, 715, 107 S Ct 1492, 94 L Ed 2d 714; *Sacramento County Deputy Sheriffs' Ass'n v County of Sacramento* (1996) 51 CA4th 1468, 1477, 59 CR2d 834.

The home is the place given the highest degree of protection and in which a resident's expectation of privacy will almost always be reasonable. See, *e.g., U.S. v Karo* (1984) 468 US 705, 713–715, 104 S Ct 3296, 82 L Ed 2d 530; *Steagald v U.S.* (1981) 451 US 204, 211–212, 101 S Ct 1642, 68 L Ed 2d 38.

#### b. [§5.6] Common Habits in Use of Property

Common habits in the use of property are a key factor in determining whether there is a reasonable expectation of privacy in a given situation. *People v Edelbacher* (1989) 47 C3d 983, 1015, 254 CR 586; *In re Deborah C.* (1981) 30 C3d 125, 137–138, 177 CR 852 (reasonableness of privacy expectation "is measured by common habits in the use of domestic and business properties"; store "employees' normal-view observations through fitting room doors whose design and location almost invite inspection" does not run counter to common habits).

#### c. [§5.7] Efforts To Conceal

Efforts to conceal are not determinative but are a factor in determining reasonableness of a privacy expectation. *U.S. v Dunn* (1987) 480 US 294, 301, 107 S Ct 1134, 94 L Ed 2d 326 (effort to protect area from observation relevant in determining extent of curtilage). Lack of effort to keep one's activities or conversations private may bear on whether the defendant has a subjective expectation of privacy. See, *e.g., California v Ciraolo* (1986) 476 US 207, 211, 106 S Ct 1809, 90 L Ed 2d 210.

#### d. [§5.8] Matters Observable by Public

An expectation of privacy is generally not objectively reasonable if members of the public could use their senses to detect what the officers observed. See *California v Ciraolo* (1986) 476 US 207, 213–214, 106 S Ct 1809, 90 L Ed 2d 210. But this is not always the case. In *Bond v U.S.* (2000) 529 US 334, 338–339, 120 S Ct 1462, 146 L Ed 2d 365, an officer squeezed a bus passenger's luggage to ascertain whether it might contain drugs. The court held that while a traveler expects members of the public to actually touch and handle luggage, he or she would not expect that anyone would feel the bag in an exploratory manner. The court concluded that the defendant's expectation of privacy was objectively reasonable and that therefore, the officer's physical manipulation of the bag violated the Fourth Amendment.

## B. Plain View

### 1. [§5.9] Basic Principles

The warrantless seizure of an object in plain view does not violate a reasonable expectation of privacy when the following three conditions are met:

(1) The officers made their observations from a place where they had a right to be. *People v Camacho* (2000) 23 C4th 824, 832, 98 CR2d 232 (observations unlawful because officers were not in area where they had right to be); *Lorenzana v Superior Court* (1973) 9 C3d 626, 634, 108 CR 585. See §§5.10, 5.14–5.24.

(2) The incriminating character of the objects was "immediately appar-

ent." *Horton v California* (1990) 496 US 128, 136, 110 S Ct 2301, 110 L Ed 2d 112. See §5.11.

(3) The officers had "a lawful right of access to the object itself." *Horton v California, supra.* See §5.12.

The plain view doctrine extends to the use of senses other than sight. See §5.13.

### a. [§5.10] Place Where Officers Had Right To Be

It is "an essential predicate to any valid warrantless seizure that the officer did not violate the Fourth Amendment in arriving at the place from which the evidence could be plainly viewed." *Horton v California* (1990) 496 US 128, 136, 110 S Ct 2301, 110 L Ed 2d 112. Officers have a right to be in a particular place if their location either does not infringe on the defendant's reasonable expectations of privacy or is justified by one of the established exceptions to the warrant requirement. *People v Camacho* (2000) 23 C4th 824, 832, 98 CR2d 232; *Lorenzana v Superior Court* (1973) 9 C3d 626, 634, 108 CR 585.

As a general rule, a police officer's presence in a place open to the public or to the occupants and visitors of a building does not violate reasonable privacy expectations. *In re Deborah C.* (1981) 30 C3d 125, 135, 177 CR 852; *Lorenzana v Superior Court, supra.* See *People v Camacho, supra,* 24 C4th at 833. This rule applies even if "the individual has taken measures to restrict some view of his activities" as long as the officer's lawful vantage point "renders the activities clearly visible." *California v Ciraolo* (1986) 476 US 207, 213, 106 S Ct 1809, 90 L Ed 2d 210.

For discussions of particular locations, see §§5.14–5.24.

### b. [§5.11] Incriminating Character Immediately Apparent

The plain view doctrine's requirement that the incriminating character of the observed objects be immediately apparent means that the police must have probable cause that the objects are contraband or evidence of crime. *Soldal v Cook County* (1992) 506 US 56, 66, 113 S Ct 538, 121 L Ed 2d 450. Officers may not move objects to obtain probable cause; it must exist *before* they move an item to verify whether the item is contraband or evidence. *Arizona v Hicks* (1987) 480 US 321, 324–325, 107 S Ct 1149, 94 L Ed 2d 347 (officer lawfully present in apartment on other business may look at stereo equipment but may not turn it over to examine its serial numbers in the absence of probable cause to believe it was stolen); see *People v Rios* (1988) 205 CA3d 833, 838, 252 CR 653 (officer lawfully present in residence may seize TV set in plain sight closely matching description of stolen set; match of description provides probable cause and distinguishes case from *Arizona v Hicks*).

The "immediately apparent" requirement does not mean that the discovery must be inadvertent (*Horton v California* (1990) 496 US 128, 136, 110 S Ct 2301, 110 L Ed 2d 112) or that the police may not use, within limits, artificial aids to expand their sensory capacities. See §§5.26–5.32.

### c. [§5.12] Right of Access

Police can only seize an object in plain view if they have a lawful right of access to it. *Horton v California* (1990) 496 US 128, 136, 110 S Ct 2301, 110 L Ed 2d 112. An illustration of the lawful access requirement is the case of the officer who sees narcotics through the window of a residence from a place where he had a right to be: the officer may not enter and seize the contraband without consent or exigent circumstances. *People v Ortiz* (1995) 32 CA4th 286, 291, 38 CR2d 59; see *Soldal v Cook County* (1992) 506 US 56, 66, 113 S Ct 538, 121 L Ed 2d 450; *People v Robles* (2000) 23 C4th 789, 801, 97 CR2d 914.

A right to seize does not always create a right to search further without a warrant. Thus, an officer who is lawfully on the premises and sees a cocaine pipe in plain sight may seize it, but may not search for other evidence in the absence of exigent circumstances or consent. *People v LeBlanc* (1997) 60 CA4th 157, 167, 70 CR2d 195.

### d. [§5.13] Senses Other Than Sight

Plain view principles apply by analogy to senses other than sight, such as:

- "Plain smell." *U.S. v Place* (1983) 462 US 696, 707, 103 S Ct 2637, 77 L Ed 2d 110; *People v Gale* (1973) 9 C3d 788, 794, 108 CR 852 (strong odor of marijuana in vehicle). See also §§5.35–5.36.

- "Plain touch." *Minnesota v Dickerson* (1993) 508 US 366, 375, 113 S Ct 2130, 124 L Ed 2d 334; *People v Snyder* (1992) 11 CA4th 389, 393, 13 CR2d 837; *People v Lee* (1987) 194 CA3d 975, 984, 240 CR 32. For limitations, see, *e.g., Bond v U.S.* (2000) 529 US 334, 338, 120 S Ct 1462, 146 L Ed 2d 365 (law enforcement agent squeezing bus passenger's bag violates reasonable privacy expectation). See §5.36.

- "Plain hearing." *People v Kaaienapua* (1977) 70 CA3d 283, 286, 138 CR 651 (officer lawfully present in room adjacent to defendant's may place ear to wall to overhear conversation in defendant's room); *People v Guerra* (1971) 21 CA3d 534, 537–538, 98 CR 627. For discussion of the use of technology, see §§5.33–5.34.

## 2. Particular Locations

### a. No Violation of Reasonable Privacy Expectations

#### (1) [§5.14] Public Street or Sidewalk; Temporary Shelter

Public streets and sidewalks are the clearest examples of places open to the public in which an officer's presence does not infringe reasonable privacy expectations. *People v Warren* (1984) 152 CA3d 991, 996, 199 CR 864; *People v Superior Court* (Reilly) (1975) 53 CA3d 40, 45, 125 CR 504. But see *People v Lovelace* (1981) 116 CA3d 541, 551–554, 172 CR 65, discussed in §5.24.

Similarly, an officer who peers into a makeshift shelter illegally erected on a sidewalk does not violate reasonable privacy expectations. *People v Thomas* (1995) 38 CA4th 1331, 45 CR2d 610. The shelter occupant would, however, have a reasonable expectation of privacy in closed containers. 38 CA4th at 1335. The *Thomas* situation should also be differentiated from legal temporary shelters, such as tents in public campgrounds, that are entitled to Fourth Amendment protection. 38 CA4th at 1334.

#### (2) [§5.15] Residential Locations Open to Public or Tenants

Officers generally have a right to be in places implicitly open to the public or to tenants, such as the following:

- Private driveways and paths leading to the front door of a house. *People v Superior Court* (Bowden) (1976) 65 CA3d 511, 520, 135 CR 306; *People v Moore* (1975) 51 CA3d 610, 617, 124 CR 290; *People v Superior Court* (Irwin) (1973) 33 CA3d 475, 481, 109 CR 106.

- Common areas of apartment houses. *People v Berutko* (1969) 71 C2d 84, 91, 77 CR 217 (observation from common area through small aperture between drapes and bottom of apartment window); *Cowing v City of Torrance* (1976) 60 CA3d 757, 760–761, 131 CR 830 (inspector went to recreation room of apartment complex, gaining entry to building by following mailman who entered locked lobby with key); see *People v Camacho* (2000) 23 C4th 824, 833, 98 CR2d 232.

- Open carports of an apartment complex or motel. *People v Arango* (1993) 12 CA4th 450, 454–455, 15 CR2d 629 (police may enter carport by climbing over fence); *People v Kilpatrick* (1980) 105 CA3d 401, 409, 164 CR 349.
- Apartment house garages used by residents. *People v Szabo* (1980) 107 CA3d 419, 429, 165 CR 719. As to private residential garages, see §5.21.
- Motel hallways. *People v Zabelle* (1996) 50 CA4th 1282, 1287, 58 CR2d 105 (view from hallway through open door of motel room). But climbing from a hallway onto a trellis or sun screen of motel room window violates reasonable expectations of privacy. *Pate v Municipal Court* (1970) 11 CA3d 721, 724–725, 89 CR 893.

#### (3) [§5.16] Adjacent Room; Neighboring Property

Listening to conversations audible from adjacent rooms does not infringe reasonable privacy expectations. For example, in *People v Kaaienapua* (1977) 70 CA3d 283, 286–287, 138 CR 651, the manager of a boardinghouse suspected defendant of illegal activities and invited the police into a vacant room next to defendant's room. The officers overheard incriminating conversation by placing their ears to the wall dividing the two rooms. The court held that the officers had a right to be where they were and that speech loud enough to be overheard is not protected.

Similarly, observations from a neighbor's property generally do not infringe on reasonable privacy expectations. *Dillon v Superior Court* (1972) 7 C3d 305, 311, 102 CR 161 ("The view of the backyard was vulnerable to observation by any of petitioner's neighbors, in essence open to public view"; observation from neighbor's second-story window at her invitation); *People v Superior Court* (Stroud) (1974) 37 CA3d 836, 839, 112 CR 764, disapproved on other grounds in 41 C3d 373, 385. In *Stroud*, officers, apparently without seeking consent, walked over a neighbor's front lawn to look over a five-foot fence into defendant's backyard. But see *People v Fly* (1973) 34 CA3d 665, 667, 110 CR 158, discussed in §5.24.

#### (4) [§5.17] Commercial Premises Open to Public

Officers may observe activities from areas in a store that are open to the public without infringing privacy expectations. *In re Deborah C.* (1981) 30 C3d 125, 135, 177 CR 852 (observation of fitting room from public corridor); *People v Freeman* (1977) 66 CA3d 424, 428, 136 CR 76, disapproved on other grounds in 25 C3d 238, 257 n13 (observation of booths in movie arcade of adult bookstore). In *People v Doty* (1985) 165 CA3d 1060, 1066, 212 CR 81, the court said "what is observable by the general public at a commercial establishment is also observable by police officers without a warrant. Moreover, such a search is not unreasonable even if the officers enter the premises purely for an investigative purpose."

The police also have a right to be present in the hallway of a public storage facility. *People v Campobasso* (1989) 211 CA3d 1480, 1483, 260 CR 202.

Some observations of commercial premises, however, may violate reasonable expectations of privacy. See, *e.g., Jacobs v Superior Court* (1973) 36 CA3d 489, 494–496, 111 CR 449 (officer stepped onto planter area of closed business establishment to peer through slight gap in curtained-off window).

#### (5) [§5.18] Public Airspace

Observations from public airspace in a physically nonintrusive manner do not interfere with privacy expectations, even if the flight is at a much lower altitude than commercial flights and has the specific purpose of viewing defendant's property. *Florida v Riley* (1989) 488 US 445, 448–450, 109 S Ct 693, 102 L Ed 2d 835 (helicopter at 400 feet); *California v Ciraolo* (1986) 476 US 207, 213, 106 S Ct 1809, 90 L Ed 2d 210 (plane at 1000 feet); *People v Romo* (1988) 198 CA3d 581, 587–588, 243 CR 801 (helicopter flight over backyard at not less than 500 feet).

In *Ciraolo,* the court stressed that "[a]ny member of the public flying in this airspace who glanced down could have seen everything that these officers observed." 476 US at 213–214. See also discussion of *Ciraolo* in *California v Greenwood* (1988) 486 US 35, 41, 108 S Ct 1625, 100 L Ed 2d 30.

In *Florida v Riley, supra,* the court stressed the lawful altitude of the flight, the fact flights at such altitude are not rare, and the absence of undue noise, wind, dust, threat of injury, or interference with normal activities. *People v Romo, supra*, relied on three factors (198 CA3d at 587):

(1) Lawful altitude;

(2) Absence of visual or optical aids; and

(3) "Most importantly," the nonintrusive manner of the flight (no hovering).

### b. Violation of Reasonable Privacy Expectations

#### (1) [§5.19] Yard of Residence

An uninvited entry into the backyard or side yard of a single-family residence infringes on reasonable privacy expectations; such areas are not implicitly open to the public. *People v Camacho* (2000) 23 C4th 824, 832–838, 98 CR2d 232 (side yard); *Lorenzana v Superior Court* (1973) 9 C3d 626, 634–636, 108 CR 585; *People v Winters* (1983) 149 CA3d 705, 707, 196 CR 918 (backyard).

The result is not altered by the absence of any gate, fence, or shrubbery suggesting that entrance is forbidden. *People v Camacho, supra.*

☛ **Judicial Tip**: Entry into yards of private residences should be differentiated from apartment building yards open to tenants (see §5.15) and from observation of a yard from the street, air, or adjacent property. See §§5.16, 5.18.

#### (2) [§5.20] Planter Areas; Trellises

Planter areas of a building and trellises are not usually places open to the public; observations from such locations infringe on reasonable privacy expectations. See *Jacobs v Superior Court* (1973) 36 CA3d 489, 494–496, 111 CR 449 (planter area outside business establishment); *Pate v Municipal Court* (1970) 11 CA3d 721, 724–725, 89 CR 893 (officer proceeded along trellis or sunscreen to motel room window).

#### (3) [§5.21] Private Residential Garage

The police may not enter the garage of a single-family dwelling without consent, exigent circumstances, or a warrant. *People v Baker* (1986) 187 CA3d 562, 567, 231 CR 877; *People v Morgan* (1987) 196 CA3d 816, 820, 242 CR 140. However, looking through the cracks in a garage door from the driveway is permissible. *People v Superior Court* (Irwin) (1973) 33 CA3d 475, 481, 109 CR 106.

### c. [§5.22] Borderline Situations

The existence of a reasonable expectation of privacy in the following locations depends on the specific facts:

- *Workplace. O'Connor v Ortega* (1987) 480 US 709, 715–719, 107 S Ct 1492, 94 L Ed 2d 714 (question of reasonable privacy expectation in work environment must be addressed on case-by-case basis; doctor employed by public hospital has such expectation as to desk and file cabinet not shared with other employees); *Sacramento County Deputy Sheriffs' Ass'n v County of Sacramento* (1996) 51 CA4th 1468, 1476, 59 CR2d 834 (videotaping in release office of county jail did not violate reasonable privacy expectations of deputies, although videotaping in certain other portions of jail may); *People v Thompson* (1988) 205 CA3d 1503, 1508, 253 CR 266 (employees have reasonable privacy expectation in their desks, notebooks, and other personal work areas; store employee has no such expectation in area under store's front counter).

- *Hospital room. People v Brown* (1979) 88 CA3d 283, 290–291, 151 CR 749 (for some purposes room is under full control of medical staff, for others it is patient's room; no privacy violation when nurse consents to officer's presence, patient does not object, and presence is for purpose unrelated to search); *U.S. v George* (9th Cir 1993) 987 F2d 1428, 1432 (person taken to hospital by police after arrest lacks reasonable privacy expectation as to police observations in hospital room).
- *Outside fire escape of apartment house. Cohen v Superior Court* (1970) 5 CA3d 429, 435, 85 CR 354 (reasonableness of privacy expectations depends "on the customary use or nonuse of the fire escape platforms for purposes other than emergency escape . . ."; remanded to trial court for determination).
- *Premises damaged by fire.* See §5.46.

### d. [§5.23] "Open Fields" and "Curtilage"

There is no reasonable expectation of privacy in "open fields," regardless of the owner's efforts, such as constructing fences and posting "No Trespassing" signs, to keep the public out. *Oliver v U.S.* (1984) 466 US 170, 179, 104 S Ct 1735, 80 L Ed 2d 214 (upholding warrantless entry on defendant's farmlands to look for marijuana). Society has no interest "in protecting the privacy of those activities, such as the cultivation of crops, that occur in open fields." 466 US at 179. As to the ineffectiveness of fences, see *U.S. v Dunn* (1987) 480 US 294, 297–298, 107 S Ct 1134, 94 L Ed 2d 326 (officers climbed over perimeter and interior fences to look into defendant's barn).

"Open fields" need neither be "open" nor "fields"; the expression is a term of art applying to land beyond the "curtilage." *U.S. v Dunn, supra,* 480 US at 300. Traditionally, "curtilage" refers to the area immediately surrounding a dwelling that is treated like the home itself in terms of societal recognition of privacy expectations. *U.S. v Dunn, supra*; *Oliver v U.S., supra. Oliver* speaks of the curtilage "as the area around the home to which the activity of home life extends." 466 US at 182 n12. *Dunn* says that the task of defining the extent of a home's curtilage "should be resolved with particular reference to four factors: the proximity of the area claimed to be curtilage to the home, whether the area is included within an enclosure surrounding the home, the nature of the uses to which the area is put, and the steps taken by the residents to protect the area from observation by people passing by." 480 US at 301. In *Dunn*, the court held that a barn located 50 yards from the fence surrounding the residence and 60 yards from the residence itself was not within the curtilage.

The police may lawfully observe objects within the curtilage from an open field. *People v Channing* (2000) 81 CA4th 985, 990–994, 97 CR2d 405; *People v Freeman* (1990) 219 CA3d 894, 902, 268 CR 603. It may also be observed from public air space. *California v Ciraolo* (1986) 476 US 207, 213, 106 S Ct 1809, 90 L Ed 2d 210. See §5.18.

### e. [§5.24] Unusual Vantage Points

Even in places that are not private property, a particular vantage point can be so unusual that it infringes on reasonable privacy expectations. For example, "a clandestine, unexpected vantage point to spy" on all who enter a public restroom infringes on reasonable expectations of privacy. *In re Deborah C.* (1981) 30 C3d 125, 137, 177 CR 852; *People v Triggs* (1973) 8 C3d 884, 891–892, 106 CR 408, disapproved on other grounds in 22 C3d 891, 896 n4.

A more difficult case is *People v Lovelace* (1981) 116 CA3d 541, 172 CR 65, in which an officer peered into defendant's solidly fenced yard from a public alley by putting his face within an inch or two of small knotholes and gaps in the fence. The court concluded that although the officer was on public property, he viewed the yard "from a vantage point not expected to be used by the public at large" and that this violated the privacy expectations that defendant had gone to considerable trouble to safeguard. 116 CA3d at 554.

*Lovelace* bears comparison with *People v Superior Court* (Irwin) (1973) 33 CA3d 475, 481, 109 CR 106 (peering through cracks in garage door from driveway lawful), *People v Guerra* (1971) 21 CA3d 534, 537–538, 98 CR 627 (officer in hallway can place ear to door in order to listen to conversation), and *People v Berutko* (1969) 71 C2d 84, 90–91, 77 CR 217 (officer in common area of apartment building can look though small aperture in draped window). On the other hand, *People v Fly* (1973) 34 CA3d 665, 667, 110 CR 158, is consistent with *Lovelace*. In *Fly*, an officer observed defendant's yard from a narrow area between a neighbor's garage and defendant's fence, stooping down to look through a small opening in heavy foliage. The court held that this was a vantage point from which the defendant had a reasonable expectation of privacy.

## C. Investigative Techniques

### 1. Aiding the Senses

#### a. [§5.25] Basic Principles

Observations made with mechanical or electronic aids to the senses are subject to the same prohibition against violating reasonable privacy expectation as are unaided observations. *Dow Chem. Co. v U.S.* (1986) 476 US 227, 238, 106 S Ct 1819, 90 L Ed 2d 226; *People v Arno* (1979) 90 CA3d 505, 509, 153 CR 624. Thus, unprotected areas, such as open fields, may be viewed through binoculars (*People v Joubert* (1981) 118 CA3d 637, 647, 173 CR 428). Technologically assisted observations of the interior of a residence or business, however, may violate reasonable privacy expectations even if made from a place where the officers had a right to be if the equipment does more than "somewhat" enhance human vision or hearing or if it reveals intimate details. *Dow Chem. Co. v U.S., supra*, 476 US at 238. More recently, the U.S. Supreme Court has said that in the home "*all* details are intimate details." *Kyllo v U.S.* (2001) 533 US 27, 121 S Ct 2038, 150 L Ed 2d 94, 104 (prohibiting warrantless use of thermal imaging device to gather heat use information from residence; emphasis in original).

In general, without a search warrant the police may not use sense-enhancing technology to gather information regarding the interior of a home that could not otherwise have been obtained without physical intrusion, at least where the technology in question is not in general public use. 150 L Ed 2d at 106.

#### b. Optical Aides

#### (1) [§5.26] Flashlights

Under the plain-view doctrine (see §5.9), the police may use flashlights to improve vision. Courts have permitted their use in a variety of situations, including the following:

- To look into a vehicle that has been lawfully stopped. *Texas v Brown* (1983) 460 US 730, 739, 103 S Ct 1535, 75 L Ed 2d 502 (court also held officer could bend down to improve his view); *People v Rogers* (1978) 21 C3d 542, 549, 146 CR 732.
- To view the contents of an open garage from a lawful vantage point outside the garage. *People v Wheeler* (1972) 28 CA3d 1065, 1069, 105 CR 56; *U.S. v Dunn* (1987) 480 US 294, 303–305, 107 S Ct 1134, 94 L Ed 2d 326 (barn).
- To see the face of a person validly detained at night. *People v Bene-*

*dict* (1969) 2 CA3d 400, 403–404, 82 CR 759. See also *People v Snider* (1978) 76 CA3d 560, 565, 142 CR 900, implying that if the purpose is to determine whether the person is under the influence of drugs, as distinguished from the purpose of identification, a factually based suspicion is a prerequisite. The court likened this situation to field sobriety tests.

- To illuminate the interior of a pedestrian's jacket pocket during a proper *Terry* stop without spreading the pocket or pulling it open. *People v Woods* (1970) 6 CA3d 832, 838, 86 CR 264.
- To shine into the handbag of a woman who is retrieving her driver's license during a consensual encounter. *People v Capps* (1989) 215 CA3d 1112, 1123, 263 CR 791.

☛ **Judicial Tip**: If the officer in *Woods* had pulled the pocket open in order to shine his flashlight into it, that would be the equivalent of reaching into the pocket, an act permissible only under the limited circumstances discussed in §§3.100–3.102.

Flashlights, unlike cameras or binoculars, may be used to make visible what could not be seen with the naked eye. See *People v Szabo* (1980) 107 CA3d 419, 429, 165 CR 719.

### (2) [§5.27] Binoculars

The police may use binoculars to see more clearly what is visible to the unaided eye, but not to view activities or objects that are otherwise invisible. *Cooper v Superior Court* (1981) 118 CA3d 499, 509, 173 CR 520; *People v Arno* (1979) 90 CA3d 505, 153 CR 624. "[T]he reasonable expectation of privacy extends to that which cannot be seen by the naked eye or heard by the unaided ear." *People v Arno, supra,* 90 CA3d at 511–512.

For example, *Cooper v Superior Court, supra,* upheld the use of binoculars to look into an apartment in which the officer could clearly see the suspects weighing objects and used the binoculars only to determine the nature of items weighed. 118 CA3d at 510. By contrast, in *People v Arno, supra,* an officer, suspecting that defendants were operating a wholesale porno film business, looked into their suite from a hilltop 200 to 300 yards away. With the unaided eye, he could see people in the suite but could identify only the color of their clothing. Using binoculars, the officers saw the defendants handle a distinctively marked box displaying a label with a picture of a nude woman; the box contained film. The court held that the activity seen "was not observable to anyone not using an optical aid" and that its observation was, therefore, unlawful. 90 CA3d at 509, 512.

Plants visible to the naked eye from a lawful vantage point may be viewed through binoculars. *People v St. Amour* (1980) 104 CA3d 886, 893, 163 CR 187; *People v Vermouth* (1974) 42 CA3d 353, 361, 116 CR 675. The use of binoculars to observe open fields does not violate reasonable privacy expectations. *People v Joubert* (1981) 118 CA3d 637, 647, 173 CR 428.

### (3) [§5.28] Cameras: Aerial Photography

Aerial photography of an industrial complex by the EPA with a precision mapping camera does not violate reasonable privacy expectations. *Dow Chem. Co. v U.S.* (1986) 476 US 227, 106 S Ct 1819, 90 L Ed 2d 226. The court said that anyone "with an airplane and an aerial camera could readily duplicate" the photographs, that they advance human vision only somewhat, and that they are limited to an outline of buildings and equipment without revealing intimate details. 476 US at 231, 238.

The court also noted that Dow Chemical Co. had a reasonable expectation of privacy in the interior of its covered buildings, but a reduced one in its extensive outdoor facilities. 476 US at 236–238. The court also said that it "may well be, as the Government concedes, that surveillance of private property by using highly sophisticated surveillance equipment not generally available to the public, such as satellite technology, might be constitutionally proscribed absent a warrant." 476 US at 238.

Aerial photography of marijuana plants in a backyard with a standard 35 mm camera does not violate reasonable privacy expectations, as long as the photographs were taken from a plane flying in public airspace, the officers could see and identify the plants from the plane, and any "member of the public flying in this airspace who glanced down could have seen everything that these officers observed." *California v Ciraolo* (1986) 476 US 207, 209–214, 106 S Ct 1809, 90 L Ed 2d 210; see *People v Mayoff* (1986) 42 C3d 1302, 1316, 233 CR 2.

### (4) [§5.29] Magnetometers and X Rays

Aids such as magnetometers (metal detectors) and X rays enable law enforcement agents to observe what would otherwise be invisible; their use is a violation of a privacy expectation. Thus, their employment is always a search within the meaning of the Fourth Amendment and the proper inquiry is whether the search was lawful. See, *e.g., People v Hyde* (1974) 12 C3d 158, 164–167, 115 CR 358 (upholding use of magnetometers at airports as a reasonable administrative search); *People v Ayala* (2000) 23 C4th 225, 250–253, 96 CR2d 682 (overruling Fourth Amendment and other constitutional objections to magnetometer use at public entrance of courtroom in which defendant is on trial).

#### (5) [§5.30] Thermal Imaging Devices

The use of a thermal imaging device to detect whether a residence emits an unusual amount of heat impinges on reasonable privacy expectations and is therefore unlawful without a search warrant. *Kyllo v U.S.* (2001) 533 US 27, 121 S Ct 2038, 150 L Ed 2d 94, 106; *People v Deutsch* (1996) 44 CA4th 1224, 1228–1232, 52 CR2d 366. A warrantless thermal scan of an outbuilding 200 to 300 yards from a home is lawful when the structure scanned is in an open field. *U.S. v Ishmael* (5th Cir 1995) 48 F3d 850, 857.

#### (6) [§5.31] Surveillance Meters

Use of a surveillance meter, installed on a utility pole within the curtilage to measure electricity consumption in a residence, does not violate reasonable expectations of privacy. *People v Stanley* (1999) 72 CA4th 1547, 86 CR2d 89. The court based its decision on the conclusion that the "surveillance meter neither measures nor reveals anything about the intimate details of activities within the house." 72 CA4th at 1553. In contrast, in *People v Deutsch* (1996) 44 CA4th 1224, 1231, 52 CR2d 366, discussed in §5.30, the court was concerned with the fact that the heat detector used there disclosed information that the police could not have observed or learned without obtaining a search warrant.

#### (7) [§5.32] Electronic Tracking Devices ("Beepers")

Beepers aid or substitute for visual observation of the movement and location of objects. Monitoring such a device without a warrant or consent is lawful while the object is in a moving vehicle or other place where the officers could follow it visually, but not while it is inside a residence. *U.S. v Karo* (1984) 468 US 705, 713–718, 104 S Ct 3296, 82 L Ed 2d 530; *U.S. v Knotts* (1983) 460 US 276, 282–285, 103 S Ct 1081, 75 L Ed 2d 55; *People v Erwin* (1997) 55 CA4th 15, 18, 63 CR2d 617. In short, monitoring beepers is lawful unless it "reveals information that could not have been obtained through visual surveillance." *People v Salih* (1985) 173 CA3d 1009, 1015, 219 CR 603; see *U.S. v Karo, supra.*

### c. Aural Aids: Wiretaps and Other Listening Devices

#### (1) [§5.33] Basic Principles

The use of electronic or mechanical equipment to hear what the unaided ear cannot hear generally violates reasonable expectations of privacy and is unlawful without prior judicial authorization. *Katz v U.S.* (1967) 389 US 347, 354–357, 88 S Ct 507, 19 L Ed 2d 576. Wiretapping and other forms of electronic surveillance are comprehensively regulated and broadly proscribed by Title III of the Omnibus Crime Control and Safe Streets Act of 1968, 18 USC §§2510–2522. *Gelbard v U.S.* (1972) 408 US 41, 46, 92 S Ct 2357, 33 L Ed 2d 179 (Title III provides "comprehensive scheme" for regulation); *People v Otto* (1992) 2 C4th 1088, 1097, 9 CR2d 596. See also Pen C §§629.50–637.7. For discussion of exceptions, see §5.34.

An interception of a communication within Title III is "the aural or other acquisition of the contents of any wire, electronic, or oral communication through the use of any electronic, mechanical, or other device." 18 USC §2510(4).

The contents of an illegally intercepted communication and any "evidence derived therefrom" are inadmissible. 18 USC §2515; *People v Otto, supra,* 2 C4th at 1098.

#### (2) [§5.34] Exceptions

The prohibition of electronic and mechanical eavesdropping does not apply to the following situations:

(1) *Nonconfidential communications. Katz v U.S.* (1967) 389 US 347, 511, 88 S Ct 507, 19 L Ed 2d 576; 18 USC §§2510(2), 2511(2)(g).

(2) *Informant wired for sound. U.S. v White* (1971) 401 US 745, 750–751, 91 S Ct 1122, 28 L Ed 2d 453; *People v Murphy* (1972) 8 C3d 349, 361, 105 CR 138. "A defendant has no constitutionally protected expectation that his confidant will not reveal a conversation to the police, and the recording merely corroborates and assures the accuracy of the confidant's later testimony." *People v Phillips* (1985) 41 C3d 29, 52, 222 CR 17.

(3) *Consensual monitoring.* Interception and recording of a conversation with the consent of a party to it is lawful. *People v Phillips, supra*; *People v Murphy, supra*; 18 USC §2511(2)(d). See *People v Velasquez* (1976) 54 CA3d 695, 698–699, 126 CR 656 (consent while in custody raises factual issue of voluntariness).

Sixth Amendment problems that may ensue from monitoring conversations are beyond the scope of this book. See *Maine v Moulton* (1985) 474 US 159, 106 S Ct 477, 88 L Ed 2d 481; *U.S. v Henry* (1980) 447 US 264, 100 S Ct 2183, 65 L Ed 2d 115; *Massiah v U.S.* (1964) 377 US 201, 84 S Ct 1199, 12 L Ed 2d 246; *People v Lowery* (1988) 200 CA3d 1207, 246 CR 443.

(4) *Recording by party to communication.* 18 USC §2511(2)(d); see *People v Otto* (1992) 2 C4th 1088, 1097, 9 CR2d 596. But nonconsensual recording of a conversation by a person who is not a party to it is unlawful and inadmissible. *People v Otto, supra,* 2 C4th at 1099 (no exception for interspousal wiretapping).

(5) *Jail conversations and telephone calls from jail. People v Riel* (2000) 22 C4th 1153, 1184, 96 CR2d 1 (jail conversation between defendant and his mother recorded by jail officials); *People v Plyler* (1993) 18 CA4th 535, 542, 22 CR2d 772 (telephone call from jail recorded by recipient at direction of police). Wiretapping a jail telephone does not violate an inmate's Fourth Amendment rights, but violates the Fifth Amendment in the absence of advance judicial approval. *People v Zepeda* (2001) 87 CA4th 1183, 1192–1207, 105 CR2d 187. The application for approval must contain facts showing that "normal investigative procedures have been tried and have failed or reasonably appear to be unlikely to succeed if tried or to be too dangerous." 87 CA4th at 1196; 18 USC §2518(3)(c).

When the police tell a jail inmate that he may talk privately with another person, a reasonable expectation of privacy arises; evidence of the conversation based on police eavesdropping is inadmissible. *People v Hammons* (1991) 235 CA3d 1710, 1715, 5 CR2d 317.

(6) *Pen registers that record the numbers dialed from a particular telephone. Smith v Maryland* (1979) 442 US 735, 741–746, 99 S Ct 2577, 61 L Ed 2d 220 (no Fourth Amendment violation); *U.S. v N.Y. Telephone Co.* (1977) 434 US 159, 166–167, 98 S Ct 364, 54 L Ed 2d 376 (no statutory violation); *People v Larkin* (1987) 194 CA3d 650, 653–657, 239 CR 760; 18 USC §2511(2)(h).

(7) *Random monitoring by operators of switchboards or providers of communication services.* 18 USC §2511(2)(a)(i) (limited to normal cause of business while engaged in activity necessarily incident to rendition of service or to protection of the service provider).

(8) *Foreign intelligence surveillance permitted by specified statutes.* 18 USC §2511(2)(e).

### d. Aiding the Sense of Smell

#### (1) [§5.35] Canine Sniffs

The use of specially trained dogs to sniff luggage for narcotics does not violate reasonable expectations of privacy. *U.S. v Place* (1983) 462 US 696, 706–707, 103 S Ct 2637, 77 L Ed 2d 110; *People v Mayberry* (1982) 31 C3d 335, 337, 182 CR 617; *People v Bell* (1996) 43 CA4th 754, 768–769, 51 CR2d 115. In these cases, unlike those involving visual and aural aids, courts are not concerned with the fact that dogs detect odors where humans smell nothing. *Place* said that a canine sniff "is much less intrusive than a typical search" and reveals only the presence of contraband. 462 US at 707.

The validity of a sniff, like that of other police observations, depends on whether it occurs in a place where the officers have a right to be. See §5.10. For instance, sniffs during a temporary detention are lawful only if the detention itself is valid, *i.e.*, if it meets the requirement of a *Terry* stop as to grounds, scope, and duration. *U.S. v Place, supra*, 462 US at 709 (detention of luggage for 90 minutes excessive); *People v Bell, supra.* Consent can provide an adequate basis for a sniff; factual issues concerning the scope of the consent may arise if the defendant has no reason to know that the officers would use a dog. See *People v Bell, supra,* 43 CA3d at 771. For discussion of the scope of consent to search, see §5.110.

A positive reaction by the dog authorizes a warrantless search only with consent or under exigent circumstances. *People v Mayberry, supra*, 31 C3d at 342. Evidence of a sniff is admissible only on a showing of the dog's training. *People v Mayberry, supra.*

Courts are divided whether canine sniffs of *persons*, as distinguished from luggage, violate reasonable privacy expectations. *Yes*: *B.C. v Plumas Unified Sch. Dist.* (9th Cir 1999) 192 F3d 1260, 1265; *Horton v Goose Creek Indep. Sch. Dist.* (5th Cir 1982) 690 F2d 470, 479. *No*: *Doe v Renfrow* (7th Cir 1980) 631 F2d 91, 92.

#### (2) [§5.36] Manipulating Baggage To Aid Officer's Sense of Smell

Squeezing luggage to smell the air that is expelled was held lawful in *People v Santana* (1998) 63 CA4th 543, 545–549, 73 CR2d 886. *Bond v U.S.* (2000) 529 US 334, 338, 120 S Ct 1462, 146 L Ed 2d 365, held, however, that a law enforcement agent's squeezing of a bus passenger's bag in order to feel the contents violated the passenger's reasonable expectations of privacy.

### 2. [§5.37] Videotaping

Videotaping inside a residence violates reasonable privacy expectations absent a search warrant or consent. *People v Henderson* (1990) 220 CA3d 1632, 1649, 270 CR 248. But videotaping activities in the release room of a county jail does not. *Sacramento County Deputy Sheriffs' Ass'n v County of Sacramento* (1996) 51 CA4th 1468, 1476, 59 CR2d 834 (deputies have reasonable privacy expectations in some portions of jail, but not in release room to which inmate trustees have access).

### 3. [§5.38] Controlled Deliveries

In a controlled delivery "the authorities . . . permit a package of known contraband to be delivered to its intended recipient for the purpose of discovering narcotics importers." *People v Hampton* (1981) 115 CA3d 515, 521, 171 CR 312. As long as the initial discovery of the contraband was lawful, for instance during an agricultural, customs, or airport inspection, a search warrant is generally not required to seize and search the package following delivery. *Illinois v Andreas* (1983) 463 US 765, 771, 103 S Ct 3319, 77 L Ed 2d 1003; *People v Salih* (1985) 173 CA3d 1009, 1020, 219 CR 603; *People v Hampton, supra*; *People v Matthews* (1980) 112 CA3d 11, 169 CR 263.

*Illinois v Andreas, supra,* explained this rule by saying that no protected privacy interest remains once government officers have lawfully opened the package and identified the contents as contraband.

Between the initial discovery and the delivery, additional warrantless inspections may be made. *People v Hampton, supra.*

Brief gaps in surveillance are fatal only if there was a substantial likelihood that the contents of the package were changed during the interruption. *Illinois v Andreas, supra.*

☛ **Judicial Tip**: Loss of privacy protection in the *container* does not equate to loss of reasonable expectation of privacy in the place where the container is located. A nonconsensual entry into defendant's home to seize the package normally requires a search warrant. See *Illinois v Andreas, supra.* It is often simpler to analyze the seizure as one incident to defendant's arrest.

### 4. [§5.39] Inspection of Bank and Other Third Party Records

A person has no protected privacy interest under the Fourth Amendment in banking records in the possession of the bank (*U.S. v Miller* (1976) 425 US 435, 440, 96 S Ct 1619, 48 L Ed 2d 71), or in information the person gave the telephone company (*People v Bencomo* (1985) 171 CA3d 1005, 1014, 217 CR 826 (name and address of unlisted subscriber)), or the postal service (*People v Pearson* (1985) 169 CA3d 319, 323, 215 CR 147 (release of box renter's name and address upheld despite regulations that limit giving out such information and absence of search warrant)).

The rationale underlying these decisions is that information voluntarily revealed to a third party does not fall within the zone of protected privacy expectations. See, *e.g., People v Slaton* (1990) 222 CA3d 1041, 1046, 271 CR 617 (applying *Miller* to loan applications and other documents submitted to institutional lenders); *People v Pearson, supra,* 169 CA3d at 322.

*U.S. v Miller, supra,* permitted the subpoena of bank records without a search warrant. In response, Congress enacted the Right to Financial Privacy Act of 1978 (12 USC §§3401–3422), which gives bank customers the right to contest such subpoenas unless a "protective order" is obtained. California also has a Right to Financial Privacy Act (Govt C §§7460–7493), which contains an exclusionary rule. Govt C §7489. Proposition 8 made Govt C §7489 inoperative. *People v Meyer* (1986) 183 CA3d 1150, 1162, 228 CR 635.

### 5. Search of Abandoned, Discarded, or Disclaimed Property

#### a. [§5.40] Basic Principle

The police may search abandoned property without a warrant. See, *e.g., California v Hodari D.* (1991) 499 US 621, 624, 111 S Ct 1547, 113 L Ed 2d 690 (rock-like object tossed away by defendant during foot chase by police); *Abel v U.S.* (1960) 362 US 217, 241, 80 S Ct 683, 4 L Ed 2d 668 (items left in wastebasket of vacated hotel room); *Hester v U.S.* (1924) 265 US 57, 58, 44 S Ct 445, 68 L Ed 898 (jug and bottle dropped in field by participants in illegal liquor sale during pursuit by law enforcement agents). For searches of discarded items, see §5.43; for discussion of the effect of disclaimers, see §5.47.

#### b. Meaning of Abandonment

##### (1) [§5.41] Relinquishment of Privacy Expectation

Fourth Amendment law and property law differ as to the meaning of abandonment. Abandonment in the property law sense is a voluntary, intentional, and unconditional relinquishment of interest in property, so that a finder could assert a superior claim to it; in Fourth Amendment law it is the relinquishment of one's reasonable expectation of privacy with respect to an object in a particular location. *In re Baraka H.* (1992) 6 CA4th 1039, 1048, 8 CR2d 221 (abandonment for Fourth Amendment purposes not meant in strict property-rights sense; if defendant treated object so "as to relinquish a reasonable expectation of privacy, it does not matter whether formal property rights have also been relinquished"); *U.S. v Jackson* (9th Cir 1976) 544 F2d 407, 409.

To demonstrate abandonment the prosecution must establish by a preponderance of the evidence that the defendant's voluntary words or conduct would lead a reasonable person to believe that the defendant relinquished his or her reasonable expectation of privacy in the item searched or seized. *U.S. v Basinski* (7th Cir 2000) 226 F3d 829, 836.

#### (2) [§5.42] Illustrative Cases

The following cases illustrate the Fourth Amendment meaning of abandonment:

- A street drug dealer keeps his stash in a paper bag on a street corner among some leaves. This effort to establish "deniability" is not a common law abandonment, but a surrender of reasonable privacy expectations. *In re Baraka H.* (1992) 6 CA4th 1039, 1045–1046, 8 CR2d 221 (defendant's subjective expectation of privacy not reasonable because paper bags are often casually discarded).
- A burglar sees a police officer and hides a box in the bushes of a stranger's yard. The defendant might expect or at least hope that the box will not be found. His expectation of privacy, however, is not one that society accepts as reasonable. *People v Ketchum* (1975) 45 CA3d 328, 330, 119 CR 368. See *People v Roybal* (1998) 19 C4th 481, 506–507, 79 CR2d 487 (hiding plastic bag and contents in backyard wall of mother's home is tantamount to abandonment). In contrast, a person who, at the approach of the police, hides an object on his or her own property retains a reasonable expectation of privacy. *People v Haines* (1981) 123 CA3d 861, 867, 177 CR 41 (storage bin in defendant's carport).

### c. Discarding

#### (1) [§5.43] Discarding as Abandonment

Fourth Amendment law often treats discarding an object as relinquishing any reasonable expectation of privacy concerning the object and, hence, as abandoning it. See, *e.g., California v Hodari D.* (1991) 499 US 621, 624, 111 S Ct 1547, 113 L Ed 2d 690 (object thrown during police pursuit); *People v Patrick* (1982) 135 CA3d 290, 292–293, 185 CR 325; *People v Stafford* (1972) 28 CA3d 405, 410, 104 CR 754. For discussion of limitations, see §5.44.

#### (2) [§5.44] Limitations

There are two important limitations to the treatment of discarded objects as abandoned:

(1) Discarding only operates as a relinquishment if it is "not caused

by improper police conduct," such as an unlawful detention. *In re Baraka H.* (1992) 6 CA4th 1039, 1047, 8 CR2d 221; see *Michigan v Chesternut* (1988) 486 US 567, 574, 108 S Ct 1975, 100 L Ed 2d 565; *People v Brown* (1990) 216 CA3d 1442, 1451, 265 CR 552; *U.S. v Stephens* (9th Cir 2000) 206 F3d 914, 917 (disclaimer of bag ownership by bus passenger not abandonment when officers gave passenger Hobson's choice of staying on bus and consenting to luggage search or getting off bus).

(2) The particular circumstances may show that the defendant retained a reasonable expectation of privacy. For example, a person who throws a paper bag on his or her parked car in response to an officer's inquiry and tries to protect the bag from inspection "clearly has not abandoned that property." *Smith v Ohio* (1990) 494 US 541, 544, 110 S Ct 1288, 108 L Ed 2d 464. Similarly, a taxi passenger who lets a package drop to the floor of the cab "can hardly be said to have 'abandoned' it. An occupied taxicab is not to be compared to an open field or a hotel room." *Rios v U.S.* (1960) 364 US 253, 262 n6, 80 S Ct 1431, 4 L Ed 2d 1688 [citations].

In addition to the location of an object, its nature may be significant. A person on the street who places a paper bag some distance away is viewed as having abandoned it, but the result might be different if the object were a suitcase rather than a paper bag. See *In re Baraka H., supra,* 6 CA4th at 1046. But there are no "worthy" and "unworthy" containers; under appropriate circumstances, a paper bag is entitled to Fourth Amendment protection against claims of abandonment. 6 CA4th at 1045–1048; *People v Haines* (1981) 123 CA3d 861, 867, 177 CR 41; see *Smith v Ohio, supra.* For discussion of disposal of garbage, see §5.45.

### d. [§5.45] Garbage

There is no reasonable expectation of privacy in the contents of garbage bags set out at curbside for pickup by the trash collector. *California v Greenwood* (1988) 486 US 35, 40, 108 S Ct 1625, 100 L Ed 2d 30; see *People v Stanley* (1999) 72 CA4th 1547, 1552, 86 CR2d 89. Even if people expect that their garbage bags would not become known to the police, "garbage bags left on or at the side of the public street are readily accessible to animals, children, scavengers, snoops, and other members of the public" and are placed "at the curb for the express purpose of conveying [them] to a third party"; such exposure defeats a claim to Fourth Amendment protection. *California v Greenwood, supra,* 486 US at 40.

Similarly, items placed in a neighbor's garbage can or into a trash can used by apartment house tenants in common are not subject to a reasonable expectation of privacy. *People v Superior Court* (Barrett) (1972) 23 CA3d 1004, 1009–1011, 100 CR 604; see *People v Gray* (1976) 63 CA3d 282, 290, 133 CR 698; *People v Stewart* (1973) 34 CA3d 695, 700, 110 CR 227. Nor is there such an expectation as to the garbage collector. *People v Gray, supra* (trash collector acted as police informant on his own initiative).

#### e. [§5.46] Fire Damage

Property damaged by fire is not automatically treated as abandoned; reasonable privacy expectations may remain. *Michigan v Clifford* (1984) 464 US 287, 292, 104 S Ct 641, 78 L Ed 2d 477; *Michigan v Tyler* (1978) 436 US 499, 505, 98 S Ct 1942, 56 L Ed 2d 486. The recognition of such expectations is important in determining the lawfulness of warrantless searches for the purpose of investigating the causes of fires.

Privacy expectations "vary with the type of property, the amount of fire damage, the prior and continued use of the premises, and in some cases the owner's efforts to secure it against intruders. Some fires may be so devastating that no reasonable privacy interests remain in the ash and ruins, regardless of the owner's subjective expectations." *Michigan v Clifford, supra,* 464 US at 292. For discussion of postfire entries by arson investigators, see §5.98.

In *Clifford,* the court held that homeowners retained reasonable privacy expectations in their residence, which fire had rendered uninhabitable, because the upstairs rooms were largely undamaged, personal belongings remained in the house, and the owners had arranged to have the house secured against intrusion in their absence. 464 US at 295.

#### f. [§5.47] Disclaimers

Disclaiming an interest in an item has occasionally been viewed as evidence of abandonment. *People v Ketchum* (1975) 45 CA3d 328, 330, 119 CR 368. When property does not appear to be abandoned, such as a shoulder bag on the floor of an occupied residence, a disclaimer does not create an abandonment, but nevertheless functions as a surrender of any reasonable expectation of privacy. *People v Mendoza* (1986) 176 CA3d 1127, 1133, 224 CR 145 (even though police do not credit disclaimer but believe or know that bag belongs to defendant). See also *People v Dasilva* (1989) 207 CA3d 43, 48, 254 CR 563 (driver has no reasonable expectation of privacy in items in trunk that he says he knows nothing about); *People v Vasquez* (1983) 138 CA3d 995, 1001, 188 CR 417 (no reasonable privacy expectations as to pillowcases and contents carried by defendants who state they found them in bushes).

## III. WARRANTLESS SEARCHES OF MOTOR VEHICLES

### A. [§5.48] Bases for Searches

There is a wide array of justifications for warrantless nonconsensual vehicle searches. Although some are discussed in other chapters, they are summarized in §§5.49–5.59 in order to provide an overview in a single place. Courts apply the warrant requirement of the Fourth Amendment far less rigorously to automobiles than to homes and offices for three reasons. The mobility of cars makes rigorous application impossible. Pervasive and continuing regulation of automobiles reduces one's expectation of privacy with respect to them. The expectation is further diminished by the public nature of automobile travel. *South Dakota v Opperman* (1976) 428 US 364, 367–368, 96 S Ct 3092, 49 L Ed 2d 1000.

#### 1. [§5.49] Examination of Vehicle From Outside

Examining the exterior of a car, or viewing its contents from the outside is such a minimal infringement of privacy that courts do not regard it as a search. *New York v Class* (1986) 475 US 106, 119, 106 S Ct 960, 89 L Ed 2d 81; *Cardwell v Lewis* (1974) 417 US 583, 591, 94 S Ct 2464, 41 L Ed 2d 325; *People v Gale* (1973) 9 C3d 788, 794, 108 CR 852.

But this does not place all such examinations beyond the reach of the Fourth Amendment. An observation after an unlawful vehicle stop is itself unlawful and subject to exclusion because it is the product of an illegal seizure. See §3.3. Examination from the exterior of a vehicle parked in a public place is permissible. See, *e.g., People v Lindsey* (1986) 182 CA3d 772, 779, 227 CR 550; *People v Sandoval* (1985) 164 CA3d 958, 965, 211 CR 1. The use of a flashlight to aid vision is also permissible. *People v Sandoval, supra*; see §5.26. Scraping a paint sample from a car's exterior, however, is unlawful in the absence of probable cause. *People v Robinson* (1989) 209 CA3d 1047, 1055, 257 CR 772.

As to the objects in a car, the line of demarcation between searches and nonsearches is physical intrusion into the vehicle's interior. *New York v Class, supra* (reading VIN from outside is not a search; reaching into car to move papers obscuring the VIN is a search, but a permissible one under the particular circumstances).

#### 2. [§5.50] Abandoned Vehicle

Searching an abandoned vehicle is lawful on the ground that defendant gave up any legitimate expectation of privacy. *People v Smith* (1966) 63 C2d 779, 801, 48 CR 382. See §5.40.

### 3. [§5.51] Examination of Vehicle Identification Number

The police may examine a car's vehicle identification number (VIN) in the course of a traffic stop. *New York v Class* (1986) 475 US 106, 119, 106 S Ct 960, 89 L Ed 2d 81; see §3.107.

Observation of a suspicious VIN plate from the exterior provides probable cause to enter the car in order to look for secondary plates; a search of this kind must be limited to places in which such plates are likely to be found. *People v Lindsey* (1986) 182 CA3d 772, 779, 227 CR 550. This is not a *New York v Class* search but one based on probable cause. See also *People v Burnett* (1980) 107 CA3d 795, 799, 165 CR 781 (officer can touch VIN plate to see if it is securely attached to car).

### 4. [§5.52] Entries Into Vehicles To Look for Registration or License

Entries into vehicles to look for licenses or registration information have been permitted under limited circumstances discussed in §§5.78–5.81.

### 5. [§5.53] Search Incident to Temporary Detention

A traffic stop or other temporary detention of a vehicle's occupant does not automatically justify a search of the vehicle. The conditions for a valid car search for weapons are stated in *Michigan v Long* (1983) 463 US 1032, 1049, 103 S Ct 3469, 77 L Ed 2d 1201:

> [T]he search of a passenger compartment of an automobile, limited to those areas in which a weapon may be placed or hidden, is permissible if the police officer possesses a reasonable belief based on "specific and articulable facts which, taken together with the rational inferences from those facts, reasonably warrant" the officer in believing that the suspect is dangerous and the suspect may gain immediate control of weapons.

The sole justification for this type of search is the protection of police officers and others nearby. *Michigan v Long, supra.* For further discussion, see §3.105.

### 6. [§5.54] Search Incident to Arrest

When the police arrest a vehicle occupant, they can properly make a contemporaneous search of the car's passenger compartment for weapons or destructible evidence. *New York v Belton* (1981) 453 US 454, 457–458, 101 S Ct 2860, 69 L Ed 2d 768. No factual basis for the search other than the lawful arrest of an occupant needs to be shown. The right to search extends to containers found in the passenger compartment. 453 US at 460. For discussion, see §§4.127–4.128. "Arrest" in this context means custodial arrest. *Knowles v Iowa* (1998) 525 US 113, 114, 119 S Ct 484, 142 L Ed 2d 492 (stop for traffic violation does not authorize car search incident to arrest even if state law characterizes stop as arrest).

### 7. [§5.55] Inventory Search of Impounded Vehicle

Once the police lawfully impound a vehicle, they can search it and every item in it, including closed containers, as long as they follow standard police department procedures and do not conduct the search as part of a criminal investigation. *Colorado v Bertine* (1987) 479 US 367, 375, 107 S Ct 738, 93 L Ed 2d 739; see §§5.60–5.65.

### 8. [§5.56] Search Under "Automobile Exception"

Independently of the detention or arrest of a vehicle's occupant, officers have the right to search a car when they have probable cause to believe that it contains contraband or evidence of a crime. *U.S. v Johns* (1985) 469 US 478, 482–483, 105 S Ct 881, 83 L Ed 2d 890; *U.S. v Ross* (1982) 456 US 798, 823, 102 S Ct 2157, 72 L Ed 2d 572. The permissible scope of such a search depends on the nature of the particular probable cause. For further discussion, see §§5.66–5.76.

### 9. [§5.57] Search Under "Instrumentality Exception"

The police have the right to search a vehicle when they reasonably believe that the car itself is evidence of a crime for which an arrest was made. *People v Griffin* (1988) 46 C3d 1011, 1024, 251 CR 643. See §5.77.

### 10. [§5.58] Safety Inspections

Officers may inspect vehicles on reasonable grounds to believe that they lack required equipment or are so unsafe as to endanger any person. Veh C §§2804, 2806. For further discussion, see §5.82. The CHP can also set up checkpoints at which cars are pulled over and inspected. See §3.88.

### 11. [§5.59] Border Searches

Vehicles may be searched at the border. See §3.93. As to detentions and searches near the border, see §3.92.

## B. Inventory Searches of Impounded Vehicles

### 1. [§5.60] Basic Principles

Warrantless inventory searches are lawful under the following three conditions:

(1) The vehicle was lawfully impounded for reasons other than a criminal investigation (see §§5.61–5.63);

(2) The inventory search is *not* for contraband or evidence of crime (see §5.64); and

(3) The inventory is conducted under standardized procedures (see §5.65). *Colorado v Bertine* (1987) 479 US 367, 372–375, 107 S Ct 738, 93 L Ed 2d 739.

### 2. Requirements for Lawful Impoundment Not Based on Probable Cause

#### a. [§5.61] Limited Purpose of Impoundment

In the absence of probable cause, warrantless seizures of vehicles for impounding are permitted when they serve a public safety or community caretaking function, such as removing damaged vehicles, cars that block traffic, or cars that cannot be safely locked and left by the side of the road. *South Dakota v Opperman* (1976) 428 US 364, 368–369, 96 S Ct 3092, 49 L Ed 2d 1000. Such seizures are exceptions to the warrant and probable cause requirements of the Fourth Amendment because they are not conducted to further a criminal investigation. *South Dakota v Opperman, supra.* In short, an impoundment without probable cause is lawful only if it is conducted "on the basis of something other than suspicion of evidence of criminal activity." *Colorado v Bertine* (1987) 479 US 367, 375, 107 S Ct 738, 93 L Ed 2d 739; *People v Aguilar* (1991) 228 CA3d 1049, 1053, 279 CR 246.

#### b. [§5.62] Right To Impound

The statutory authority for the right to impound is Veh C §§22651–22711. In addition, officers may impound a car that cannot be secured at the scene, such as one without a windshield. *People v Scigliano* (1987) 196 CA3d 26, 29, 241 CR 546 (officer performed community caretaking function that includes duty to protect vehicle). See also *People v Trejo* (1994) 26 CA4th 460, 462, 31 CR2d 302 (tow from private property and impound upheld despite apparent lack of statutory authority).

☛ **Judicial Tips**: Judges should determine the validity of the impound before ruling on the inventory search. When the driver was arrested, the issues often are whether there was any need for police custodial care of the vehicle and whether the police made the decision to impound under standard criteria. See §5.63.

#### c. [§5.63] Standard Criteria

Statutes and ordinances usually give an officer discretion whether to impound a vehicle or park and lock it. See, *e.g.,* Veh C §22651. In order for an impound to be lawful that discretion must be "exercised according to standard criteria." *Colorado v Bertine* (1987) 479 US 367, 375–376, 107 S Ct 738, 93 L Ed 2d 739 (local police department procedures provided adequate criteria because they set out conditions to be met before officers could pursue park-and-lock alternative).

"Standard criteria" has been interpreted broadly. *People v Benites* (1992) 9 CA4th 309, 318, 11 CR2d 512 (verbal directive to use discretion and follow guidelines established in Vehicle Code); *People v Steeley* (1989) 210 CA3d 887, 891–892, 258 CR 699 (written policies or procedures not essential as long as officer has reasonable factual basis for impoundment and did not impound for investigative purposes). An established routine may substitute for written procedures. See *U.S. v Duguay* (7th Cir 1996) 93 F3d 346, 351. But a police policy, even if written, is not necessarily reasonable. *People v Aguilar* (1991) 228 CA3d 1049, 1053, 279 CR 246; *People v Steeley, supra,* 210 CA3d at 891.

### 3. Additional Requirements for Inventory Search

#### a. [§5.64] Not To Further Criminal Investigation

Inventory searches of impounded vehicles are exempt from the warrant and probable cause requirements of the Fourth Amendment as long as they are not made to further a criminal investigation, but rather "to protect an owner's property while it is in the custody of the police, to insure against claims of lost, stolen, or vandalized property, and to guard the police from danger." *Colorado v Bertine* (1987) 479 US 367, 372, 107 S Ct 738, 93 L Ed 2d 739. Inventory "searches are unreasonable and therefore violative of the Fourth Amendment when used as a ruse to conduct an investigatory search." *People v Steeley* (1989) 210 CA3d 887, 891–892, 258 CR 699; see *People v Williams* (1999) 20 C4th 119, 138, 83 CR2d 275. "However, the fact that an officer suspects that contraband may be found does not defeat an otherwise proper inventory search." *U.S. v Lumpkin* (6th Cir 1998) 159 F3d 983, 987; *U.S. v Lewis* (8th Cir 1993) 3 F3d 252, 254.

#### b. [§5.65] Standardized Procedures

The inventory must be conducted under standardized police department procedures that leave little or no discretion regarding the scope of the search. *Colorado v Bertine* (1987) 479 US 367, 372–374, 107 S Ct 738, 93 L Ed 2d 739. Officers, however, are not required to pursue or offer the driver less intrusive alternatives, such as letting the driver arrange for the safekeeping of personal property, regardless of the feasibility of such an alternative. *Colorado v Bertine, supra.*

Some discretion is permissible, as long as it is exercised according to standard procedures. *Florida v Wells* (1990) 495 US 1, 3–4, 110 S Ct 1632, 109 L Ed 2d 1; *Colorado v Bertine, supra.* Thus, closed containers may not be opened during an inventory search unless the police agency has a policy concerning this matter, but the policy can allow or forbid the opening of all containers, or permit officers to open those whose contents cannot be ascertained by external examination. *Florida v Wells, supra*; see *People v Williams* (1999) 20 C4th 119, 126–127, 83 CR2d 275 (policy requiring inventory before tow inadequate because absence of policy on opening closed containers); *People v Needham* (2000) 79 CA4th 260, 266, 93 CR2d 899.

A written policy is not required. *Florida v Wells, supra*; *People v Williams, supra.* An established routine followed by the police may substitute for standardized criteria. *Florida v Wells, supra*; *People v Williams, supra*; see *People v Needham, supra.*

The policy should be designed to produce an inventory. The need for standardized criteria rests on the principle that taking an inventory must not be a ruse for rummaging through a car to discover incriminating evidence. *Florida v Wells, supra*; see §5.64.

### C. Automobile Exception

#### 1. [§5.66] Basic Principles

The automobile exception to the warrant requirement of the Fourth Amendment makes it lawful to search a readily mobile vehicle, without a warrant or consent, upon probable cause to believe that the vehicle contains contraband or evidence of crime. *Pennsylvania v Labron* (1996) 518 US 938, 940, 116 S Ct 2485, 135 L Ed 2d 1031; *U.S. v Ross* (1982) 456 US 798, 799–800, 102 S Ct 2157, 72 L Ed 2d 572; *Carroll v U.S.* (1925) 267 US 132, 155–157, 45 S Ct 280, 69 L Ed 543.

Probable cause for purposes of the automobile exception means objective facts known to the officer that would justify the issuance of a search warrant. *U.S. v Ross, supra,* 456 US at 808. For a detailed discussion of probable cause to support a search warrant, see §§2.22–2.43.

When a search is lawful under the automobile exception, the court should uphold it, even if the officer who conducted the search relied on another, inadequate, ground. See *People v Dey* (2000) 84 CA4th 1318, 1321–1322, 101 CR2d 581; *People v Decker* (1986) 176 CA3d 1247, 1250, 222 CR 689.

#### 2. [§5.67] Justifications

Courts initially based the automobile exception on the ready mobility of cars that make it impractical to secure a search warrant. *Carroll v U.S.* (1925) 267 US 132, 153, 45 S Ct 280, 69 L Ed 543; see *California v Carney* (1985) 471 US 386, 390, 105 S Ct 2066, 85 L Ed 2d 406. Ready mobility remains a part of the automobile exception (§5.68), but the practicability of securing a search warrant in a given situation is immaterial. See §5.72.

More recent cases stress a second justification, namely, the diminution of privacy expectations in cars due to their pervasive regulation. *Pennsylvania v Labron* (1996) 518 US 938, 940, 116 S Ct 2485, 135 L Ed 2d 1031; *California v Carney, supra,* 471 US at 393. Courts have used this rationale to apply the automobile exception to motor homes, houseboats, and even to bicycles. See §§5.69–5.71.

A third justification likens warrantless car searches to warrantless searches of vessels that were lawful when the Fourth Amendment was adopted. *Florida v White* (1999) 526 US 559, 563–565, 119 S Ct 1555, 143 L Ed 2d 748; *Wyoming v Houghton* (1999) 526 US 295, 300, 119 S Ct 1297, 143 L Ed 2d 408; *Carroll v U.S., supra,* 267 US at 149–151. The court used this rationale in *Florida v White, supra,* to extend the automobile exception to the seizure of a car on the basis of probable cause to believe that car is subject to forfeiture.

### 3. Applications to Particular Vehicles

#### a. [§5.68] Parked Cars

The automobile exception applies to parked vehicles and is not limited to those pulled over by the police. *U.S. v Johns* (1985) 469 US 478, 482, 105 S Ct 881, 83 L Ed 2d 890; *People v Carrillo* (1995) 37 CA4th 1662, 1665–1668, 45 CR2d 16. For example, in *People v Superior Court* (Overland) (1988) 203 CA3d 1114, 1119, 250 CR 458, the defendant was taken into custody while he was in an office. His parked truck was 150 to 200 yards away. The court upheld the search under the automobile exception.

The vehicle must, however, be "readily mobile" in order for the automobile exception to apply. See *Pennsylvania v Labron* (1996) 518 US 938, 940, 116 S Ct 2485, 135 L Ed 2d 1031; *California v Carney* (1985) 471 US 386, 394, 105 S Ct 2066, 85 L Ed 2d 406 (automobile exception turns on ready mobility of vehicle).

#### b. [§5.69] Motor Homes

The automobile exception applies to motor homes being operated on the highway or readily capable of such use and "found stationary in a place not regularly used for residential purposes." *California v Carney*

(1985) 471 US 386, 392, 105 S Ct 2066, 85 L Ed 2d 406 (motor home parked in downtown lot); *People v Black* (1985) 173 CA3d 506, 509, 219 CR 355 (mobile home being driven on public street).

In *California v Carney, supra,* the court said that the vehicle "exception has historically turned on the ready mobility of the vehicle and on the presence of the vehicle in a setting that objectively indicates that the vehicle is being used for transportation." 471 US at 394. The court left open the question of the application of the automobile exception to a motor home "situated in a way or place that objectively indicates that it is being used as a residence" and suggested that the factors "that might be relevant in determining whether a warrant would be required in such a circumstance" include "its location, whether the vehicle is readily mobile or instead, for instance, elevated on blocks, whether the vehicle is licensed, whether it is connected to utilities, and whether it has convenient access to a public road." 471 US at 394 n3.

#### c. [§5.70] Houseboats

The automobile exception applies to a houseboat when it is objectively apparent that the houseboat is being used as a vehicle and not as a home. *U.S. v Albers* (9th Cir 1998) 136 F3d 670, 673, subseq. op. after remand and trial, 226 F3d 989 (houseboat floating on lake subject to automobile exception); *U.S. v Hill* (10th Cir 1988) 855 F2d 664, 668 (boat in motion on large lake at night subject to automobile exception).

#### d. [§5.71] Bicycles

The automobile exception applies to bicycles being ridden on a public street. *People v Allen* (2000) 78 CA4th 445, 449, 92 CR 869. The court stressed the mobility of bicycles and the extensive regulations pertaining to their use.

### 4. [§5.72] Opportunity To Obtain Search Warrant

A vehicle search based on probable cause is lawful even if the police could have obtained a search warrant without jeopardizing the search. *Cardwell v Lewis* (1974) 417 US 583, 592–593, 94 S Ct 2464, 41 L Ed 2d 325; *People v Superior Court* (Overland) (1988) 203 CA3d 1114, 1119–1120, 250 CR 458. Probable cause suffices; there is no requirement of an exigency that would preclude the police from getting a search warrant. *Maryland v Dyson* (1999) 527 US 465, 466, 119 S Ct 2013, 144 L Ed 2d 442; *Pennsylvania v Labron* (1996) 518 US 938, 940, 116 S Ct 2485, 135 L Ed 2d 1031.

## 5. Scope of Search

### a. [§5.73] Basic Principles

Two key principles governing the scope of a search under the automobile exception are (*U.S. v Ross* (1982) 456 US 798, 102 S Ct 2157, 72 L Ed 2d 572):

(1) The search can be "as thorough as a magistrate could authorize in a warrant 'particularly describing the place to be searched.'" 456 US at 800.

(2) The scope of the search "is defined by the object of the search and the places in which there is probable cause to believe that it may be found. . . . [P]robable cause to believe that undocumented aliens are being transported in a van will not justify a warrantless search of a suitcase. Probable cause to believe that a container placed in the trunk of a taxi contains contraband or evidence does not justify the search of the entire cab." 456 US at 824. Similarly, probable cause to look for a stolen TV set "would not justify the search of the glove compartment; probable cause to search for identification would extend to the glove compartment, but would not permit cutting open the car's seat cushions." *People v Chavers* (1983) 33 C3d 462, 470, 189 CR 169. The proper scope of a search for open containers of alcohol is the passenger compartment and any containers in it. See *People v Molina* (1994) 25 CA4th 1038, 1042–1043, 30 CR2d 805. Observing marijuana seeds on the floor of a car and detecting a slight odor of marijuana provides probable cause to search the passenger compartment, but not to believe that additional contraband is located in the trunk. *Wimberly v Superior Court* (1976) 16 C3d 557, 566–573, 128 CR 641. But see *People v Dey* (2000) 84 CA4th 1318, 1321, 101 CR2d 581 (*Wimberly* is no longer controlling).

### b. [§5.74] Containers

The lawful scope of the search extends to closed containers, packages, suitcases, and others, when there is probable cause to believe that they contain the object of the search. *California v Acevedo* (1991) 500 US 565, 574, 111 S Ct 1982, 114 L Ed 2d 619 (upholding search of lunch bag in trunk of car on probable cause that it contained marijuana; court overruled previous limitations on certain container searches); *U.S. v Johns* (1985) 469 US 478, 481–482, 105 S Ct 881, 83 L Ed 2d 890 (packages wrapped in dark green plastic and sealed with tape can be seized and opened on probable cause to believe they contain marijuana); see *Wyoming v Houghton* (1999) 526 US 295, 300, 119 S Ct 1297, 143 L Ed 2d 408, discussed in §5.75.

The permissible scope of the search is not defined by the type of container or the degree of expectation of privacy as to its contents, but by the reasons for the search. *U.S. v Ross* (1982) 456 US 798, 824, 102 S Ct 2157, 72 L Ed 2d 752 (reliable information that defendant sold narcotics kept in trunk of his car authorizes warrantless search of closed paper bag and leather pouch found in trunk of vehicle); *People v Sandoval* (1985) 164 CA3d 958, 964–966, 211 CR 1 (observation of vehicle occupant with Frisbee on which there is white powder on a razor blade justifies search of canvas bag on front seat).

#### c. [§5.75] Belongings of Passengers; Search of Persons

Police officers with probable cause to search a car may search a passenger's belongings found in the car that are capable of concealing the object of the search. *Wyoming v Houghton* (1999) 526 US 295, 307, 119 S Ct 1297, 143 L Ed 2d 408. But the automobile exception does not extend to a search of persons in the vehicle or of clothing worn by them. 526 US at 303; *People v Temple* (1995) 36 CA4th 1219, 1224–1227, 42 CR2d 888 (smelling marijuana in car does not justify search of passenger).

### 6. [§5.76] Time and Place of Search

The vehicle or the contents for which probable cause exists can be removed and searched later. *U.S. v Johns* (1985) 469 US 478, 487, 105 S Ct 881, 83 L Ed 2d 890; *U.S. v Ross* (1982) 456 US 798, 800, 102 S Ct 2157, 72 L Ed 2d 572; *People v Nicholson* (1989) 207 CA3d 707, 711–712, 255 CR 27; *People v Decker* (1986) 176 CA3d 1247, 1251, 222 CR 689. In *U.S. v Johns, supra,* the court noted that the officers cannot retain the vehicle and its contents indefinitely before they complete the search, but the limits have not been defined. *Johns* upheld a search of packages that took place three days after they were seized from a truck.

It is an open question whether delay between the time the police developed probable cause to search or seize the vehicle and the time the search or seizure actually occurred might render probable cause stale. *Florida v White* (1999) 526 US 559, 565 n4, 119 S Ct 1555, 143 L Ed 2d 748.

## D. [§5.77] Instrumentality Exception

A vehicle that is the instrumentality of a crime may be searched and seized without a warrant. *People v Griffin* (1988) 46 C3d 1011, 1024, 251 CR 643. The prerequisites are a lawful arrest and probable cause to believe that the vehicle "*is itself evidence of the commission of the crime for which the arrest is made. . . .*" *People v Rogers* (1978) 21

C3d 542, 549, 146 CR 732 (emphasis in original). The search is limited "to a scientific examination of the object itself, for example for fingerprints, bloodstains, or the taking of tire impressions or paint scrapings." *People v Minjares* (1979) 24 C3d 410, 422, 153 CR 224. See also *People v Griffin, supra* (bloody footprint). The search need not be contemporaneous with its seizure. *People v Teale* (1969) 70 C2d 497, 507, 75 CR 172 (search 10 days later upheld).

The instrumentality exception does not apply when the vehicle is "merely a container of evidence." *People v Griffin, supra,* 46 C3d at 1025. A car does not become an instrumentality simply because it was used during a crime. *People v Minjares, supra* (robbery getaway car not an instrumentality); *People v Gee* (1982) 130 CA3d 174, 182, 181 CR 524 (vehicle used by residential robber not instrumentality). Illustrations of motor vehicles as instrumentalities include situations in which vehicles ran over or struck the victim (*People v Wolf* (1978) 78 CA3d 735, 741–742, 144 CR 344; *People v Robinson* (1974) 41 CA3d 658, 674, 116 CR 455), the car transported a kidnapping victim (*North v Superior Court* (1972) 8 C3d 301, 306, 104 CR 833), and a rape or homicide took place in the vehicle (*People v Bittaker* (1989) 48 C3d 1046, 1075, 259 CR 630; *People v Teale, supra*).

The instrumentality exception has been used relatively little. After Proposition 8 there is even less need for it because alternative grounds for a vehicle search are usually available. See *People v Griffin, supra,* 46 C3d at 1023 n3.

## E. Entries Into Vehicles for Other Purposes

### 1. To Look for Registration or License

#### a. [§5.78] Basic Principles

Courts have upheld warrantless police entries into vehicles to look for registration in a variety of situations. Although the underlying principles have not been clearly enunciated, the following conditions emerge from the cases:

- The vehicle was lawfully stopped (*e.g., People v Webster* (1991) 54 C3d 411, 428–431, 285 CR 31) or abandoned (*e.g., People v Turner* (1994) 8 C4th 137, 181–183, 32 CR2d 762) or parked under circumstances making further investigation reasonably necessary. See, *e.g., People v Hart* (1999) 74 CA4th 479, 489, 86 CR2d 762 (occupied, illegally parked van; entry to retrieve driver's license); *People v Gale* (1973) 9 C3d 788, 795, 108 CR 852 (circumstances indicated vehicle tampering or auto burglary).

- The officer had good reason to determine ownership. See, *e.g., People v Webster, supra* (need to ascertain owner in order to decide whether to release or impound car); *People v Gale, supra.* Drivers are required to produce their license and registration for examination upon a peace officer's demand. *People v Webster, supra*; Veh C §§4462, 12951.

- The driver was given an opportunity to produce registration and could not do so (*e.g., People v Vermouth* (1971) 20 CA3d 746, 752, 98 CR 65) or could not be allowed back into the vehicle for articulable safety concerns. See, *e.g., People v Faddler* (1982) 132 CA3d 607, 610, 183 CR 328 (intoxicated driver). A driver's contradictory answers about ownership of the car substituted for an opportunity to produce registration in *People v Webster, supra.* The police need not accept a driver's denial that registration papers are in the vehicle, at least when the driver's conduct casts doubt on the veracity of the statement. 3 LaFave, Search and Seizure, p 566 (3d ed 1996).

- The search is confined to places where registration papers can be reasonably expected to be found. See, *e.g., People v Turner, supra,* 8 C4th at 182. When the vehicle is occupied, the officer should first ask about the location of the registration slip (*Jackson v Superior Court* (1977) 74 CA3d 361, 367, 142 CR 299), at least unless it is clear under the circumstances that the occupant does not know where it is. See *People v Turner, supra.*

### b. [§5.79] Use of Less Intrusive Means

When a vehicle is unoccupied or has been abandoned, the police need not check its registration by radio or computer before entering the car to look for it, assuming the entry is otherwise proper. *People v Turner* (1994) 8 C4th 137, 183, 32 CR2d 762.

The law is not settled whether the police must first use less intrusive alternatives when they deal with a vehicle that is not unoccupied or abandoned; greater privacy concerns are involved in such a situation. See *People v Turner, supra*; *People v Gale* (1973) 9 C3d 788, 795, 108 CR 852; *Jackson v Superior Court* (1977) 74 CA3d 361, 368, 142 CR 299.

### c. Illustrative Cases

#### (1) [§5.80] Lawful Entries

The following cases illustrate lawful entries by the police into vehicles to look for licenses or registration information:

- The driver had fled after a chase in the middle of the night, and the person observed to have been a passenger, identified as a parolee, disclaimed any knowledge of the vehicle. *People v Turner* (1994) 8 C4th 137, 182, 32 CR2d 762 (death penalty case).

- The driver of a car stopped for speeding was wanted on a warrant and denied ownership, stating that the car belonged to one of the passengers, but also said that the passengers were hitchhikers. The passengers denied ownership. *People v Webster* (1991) 54 C3d 411, 430–431, 285 CR 31 (death penalty case).
- The vehicle was unoccupied, the defendant who had been standing by it denied ownership, and the car appeared to have been tampered with or burglarized. *People v Gale* (1973) 9 C3d 788, 795, 108 CR 852.
- The vehicle was apparently abandoned and parked in a manner creating a traffic hazard. *People v Grubb* (1963) 63 C2d 614, 618, 47 CR 772.
- A van was parked illegally at night, occupied by the defendant and another person. Defendant unsuccessfully searched the van floor for several minutes for her license. *People v Hart* (1999) 74 CA4th 479, 488–490, 86 CR2d 762 (officer safety concern).
- Boisterous and intoxicated occupants of a car had exited and could not safely be allowed to reenter. *People v Faddler* (1982) 132 CA3d 607, 610, 183 CR 328.
- The driver of a car with California plates presented an out-of-state license, could not produce registration, and said the car belonged to a friend. *People v Vermouth* (1971) 20 CA3d 746, 752, 98 CR 65.

#### (2) [§5.81] Unlawful Entries

The following cases illustrate unlawful entries:

- The driver of a car stopped for weaving produced a license and was not asked for registration. After the driver's DUI arrest the officer looked for registration in the car, apparently assuming that the search was simple standard procedure and without first making a radio check. *Jackson v Superior Court* (1977) 74 CA3d 361, 367, 142 CR 299. But see *New York v Belton* (1981) 453 US 454, 460, 101 S Ct 2860, 69 L Ed 2d 768 (custodial arrest of driver justifies contemporaneous search of passenger compartment).

- The officers observed an apparent auto burglary of a parked car. *People v Superior Court* (Fishback) (1969) 2 CA3d 304, 309–310, 82 CR 766 (no necessity to enter locked car because police could readily have obtained registration information by other means).

### 2. [§5.82] Safety Inspections

Under Veh C §2806, an officer "having reasonable cause to believe that any vehicle . . . is not equipped as required by this code or is in such unsafe condition as to endanger any person, may require the driver to stop and submit the vehicle . . . to an inspection and such tests as may be appropriate to determine the safety to persons and compliance with the code." Vehicle Code §2804 gives the same authority to CHP officers.

*People v May* (1977) 76 CA3d 543, 546, 143 CR 45, held that reasonable cause under the statute is broader than probable cause in criminal law and that "once an officer has observed the unsafe condition of a vehicle, he has authority to make whatever inspection is necessary to protect the public safety by inspecting the affected mechanical devices." *May* held further that when the affected device, in *May* the hydraulic system, is usually located in the trunk, the officer may open the trunk in order to carry out the inspection. See also *U.S. v Portillo* (9th Cir 1980) 633 F2d 1313, 1317, applying Veh C §2806 to permit inspection of the trunk upon observing a malfunctioning taillight.

## F. [§5.83] Chart: Comparison of Permitted Warrantless Vehicle Searches

| | | ***Car Search*** | | | |
|---|---|---|---|---|---|
| ***Asserted Justification*** | ***Major Conditions for Valid Search*** | ***Passenger Compartment*** | ***Trunk*** | ***Containers*** | ***Time Limits*** |
| Examination of or from exterior | Car parked in public place or lawfully stopped. No physical intrusion into interior | No[1] | No[1] | No[1] | Within period of lawful detention |
| Abandonment | Vehicle in fact abandoned | Yes | Yes | Yes | |

1. But probable cause to search may result from observations.

| *Asserted Justification* | *Major Conditions for Valid Search* | *Car Search* | | | *Time Limits* |
|---|---|---|---|---|---|
| | | *Passenger Compartment* | *Trunk* | *Containers* | |
| Examination of VIN | Valid stop; VIN not on door jamb or visible from outside | Only to move objects obscuring VIN | No[1] | No[1] | Within period of lawful detention |
| To look for registration papers | Valid stop or unoccupied vehicle; exigent circumstances or probable cause that car has been stolen, burglarized, or tampered with | Limited to areas where such papers are usually kept | No[1] | No[1] | |
| Incident to temporary detention | Valid stop; factual basis for belief that suspect is dangerous and may gain immediate control of weapons | Yes, for weapons | No[1] | As in *Terry* frisk of person[2] | Within period of lawful detention |
| Incident to arrest | Lawful custodial arrest | Yes | No[1] | Yes, containers in passenger compartment | Contemporaneous with arrest |
| Inventory of impounded vehicle | Lawful impound; inventory of contents under standard procedures and not as part of a criminal investigation | Yes | Yes | Yes | |

1. But probable cause to search may result from observations.

| | | Car Search | | | |
|---|---|---|---|---|---|
| ***Asserted Justification*** | ***Major Conditions for Valid Search*** | ***Passenger Compartment*** | ***Trunk*** | ***Containers*** | ***Time Limits*** |
| Probable cause | Lawfully obtained probable cause to believe that vehicle contains contraband or evidence of crime | Scope of search depends on nature of probable cause and is as broad as magistrate could authorize | | | Excessive delay may render probable cause stale |
| Instrumentality of crime | Lawful arrest and reasonable belief that the vehicle is evidence of the crime for which defendant was arrested | Yes | Yes | No | Seizure probably contemporaneous with arrest; search can be deferred |
| Safety inspection | Reasonable grounds to believe that vehicle lacks required equipment or is dangerously unsafe | Areas in which mechanical devices suspected of being unsafe are likely to be found[1] | | | |
| To look for illegal aliens | Fixed checkpoint near border or reasonable suspicion | Yes | No[1] | No[1] | Within period of lawful detention |
| Customs | Vehicle entering or leaving U.S. | Yes | Yes | Yes | |

1. But probable cause to search may result from observations.
2. See §§3.100–3.103.

## IV. ENTRIES TO PRESERVE LIFE OR PROPERTY

### A. [§5.84] Imminent Danger

Imminent danger to life or property is an exigent circumstance—an emergency—that justifies police entry of premises. *Mincey v Arizona* (1978) 437 US 385, 392, 98 S Ct 2408, 57 L Ed 2d 290; *People v Duncan* (1986) 42 C3d 91, 104, 227 CR 654; see *People v Ray* (1999)

21 C4th 464, 468–472, 88 CR2d 1. Exigent circumstances and consent are the two major exceptions to the warrant requirement of the Fourth Amendment relating to entries of premises. *People v Frye* (1998) 18 C4th 894, 989, 77 CR2d 25. For discussion of consent searches, see §§5.102–5.140. For discussion of other exigent circumstances such as fresh pursuit, risk of imminent escape, and danger of imminent destruction of evidence, see §§4.73–4.78.

In addition to exigent circumstances and consent, a community caretaking exception to the warrant requirement may be emerging, and entries to preserve life or property may come within that exception. *People v Ray, supra* (lead opinion by three justices; concurring opinion by three justices relies on exigent circumstances). See Note, *People v Ray: The Fourth Amendment and the Community Caretaking Exception*, 35 U San Francisco L Rev 135 (2000). Community caretaking entries do not always require the existence of an emergency. See §5.85.

### B. Factual Basis for Entry

#### 1. [§5.85] Basic Principles

The police may enter a residence without a warrant or consent for the purpose of preserving life or property if they have knowledge of "specific, articulable facts indicating the need for swift action to prevent imminent danger to life or serious damage to property." *People v Ray* (1999) 21 C4th 464, 472, 88 CR2d 1 (interior quotation marks omitted); *People v Duncan* (1986) 42 C3d 91, 97, 227 CR 654. The rule is the same whether such "imminent danger" is treated as one of the exigent circumstances that are exceptions to the warrant requirement or as part of the police's community caretaking function that the lead opinion in *Ray* also regards as an exception. *People v Ray, supra*; *People v Duncan, supra*.

The difference between exigent circumstances and community caretaking is not entirely academic, however, for the latter also permits police entries under other circumstances short of a perceived emergency. *People v Ray, supra*, 21 C4th at 473. The standard for community caretaking entries other than to render emergency aid is whether, given the known facts, a prudent and reasonable officer would have perceived a need to act in the proper discharge of the particular caretaking function. 21 C4th at 476–477.

#### 2. [§5.86] Victim's Denial of Problem

A victim's statement that he or she is all right is a factor the police must consider, but it does not destroy the justification of an entry for purposes of rendering emergency aid when the victim's appearance or other circumstances reasonably indicate the need for such aid. *People v Higgins* (1994) 26 CA4th 247, 251, 31 CR2d 516 (discussed in §5.91); *People v Poulson* (1998) 69 CA4th Supp 1, 5–6, 82 CR2d 605 (discussed in §5.93).

### 3. [§5.87] Failure To Take Steps Short of Entry

The officers' failure to take reasonable steps short of entry to determine the necessity for entering "must be viewed in the totality of the circumstances to determine the ultimate reasonableness of the intrusion." *People v Ray* (1999) 21 C4th 464, 478–479, 88 CR2d 1 (failure not fatal under the particular circumstances); see *People v Coddington* (2000) 23 C4th 529, 580, 97 CR2d 528 (fact that FBI had time and probable cause to obtain telephonic warrant before breaking into home not fatal because defendant precipitated emergency after probable cause arose, and officers did not deliberately wait for exigent circumstances to develop; death penalty case).

## C. [§5.88] Belief and Motive of Officer

Entries to protect life or property are lawful only if they are actually made for that purpose, rather than as pretexts to look for evidence of criminal conduct. *People v Ray* (1999) 21 C4th 464, 477, 88 CR2d 1; *People v Duncan* (1986) 42 C3d 91, 104, 227 CR 654.

Mixed motives are treated differently under the exigent circumstances and the community caretaking rationales. Under the former, as long as the officer reasonably believes that there is an emergency necessitating quick action and acts reasonable in accord with that belief (see §5.89), the officer's concurrent concern with collecting evidence and capturing criminals is proper. *People v Duncan, supra*; *People v Osuna* (1986) 187 CA3d 845, 856, 232 CR 220. But "[a]ny intention of engaging in crime-solving activities will defeat the community caretaking exception even in cases of mixed motives." *People v Ray, supra,* 21 C4th at 477 (lead opinion by three justices).

## D. [§5.89] Conduct Consistent With Asserted Justification

An officer's conduct must be consistent with the justification and with the objectives on which the officer relies. *People v Ray* (1999) 21 C4th 464, 477, 88 CR2d 1; *People v Duncan* (1986) 42 C3d 91, 104, 224 CR 654.

Conduct before the entry may negate the officer's asserted belief that there was an emergency. See, *e.g.*, *People v Baird* (1985) 168 CA3d

237, 244–245, 214 CR 88 (officer waited five hours after smelling ether before entering premises without any attempt to warn or remove persons known to be inside). This does not mean that the officer must rush in immediately. The nature of the emergency may make it advisable to await the arrival of backup officers or other assistance. *People v Stegman* (1985) 164 CA3d 936, 945, 210 CR 855.

After entry, the officer's conduct must be carefully limited: the officer may only ascertain whether someone is in need of assistance or property is at risk, and to provide that assistance or protect the property. *People v Ray, supra,* 21 C4th at 477. A search for a person in distress merely permits a cursory look through the premises. *People v Roberts* (1956) 47 C2d 374, 378–380, 303 P2d 721. Once the emergency or other justification for the entry ends, so does the right to enter, search, or seize. *People v Duncan, supra*; *People v Keener* (1983) 148 CA3d 73, 77–78, 195 CR 733; *People v Blackwell* (1983) 147 CA3d 646, 651, 195 CR 298. Entries subsequent to the initial entry often involve this issue. See §§5.98–5.101.

## E. Homicides and Other Violent Offenses

### 1. [§5.90] Basic Principles

There is no homicide or crime scene exception to the warrant requirement of the Fourth Amendment: the police may not conduct a warrantless nonconsensual search of premises on which a murder or other violent crime occurred. *Flippo v West Virginia* (1999) 528 US 11, 14, 120 S Ct 7, 145 L Ed 2d 16; *Mincey v Arizona* (1978) 437 US 385, 389–391, 98 S Ct 2408, 57 L Ed 2d 290.

But the "police may make warrantless entries if they reasonably believe a person is in need of immediate aid and may make prompt warrantless searches for possible other victims" or perpetrators. *Flippo v West Virginia, supra*, 528 US at 14; *Mincey v Arizona, supra,* 437 US at 392.

### 2. Illustrations

#### a. [§5.91] Police Conduct Lawful

The following cases illustrate lawful police conduct:

- A radio call informs an officer of a residential robbery and that a victim is believed to be injured or bleeding. The officer goes to the apartment in question, gets no response to his knock, kicks in the door, and is met by a bleeding man in a bathrobe. Unsure whether the man is a suspect or victim, the officer walks through the apartment to determine whether there are other injured persons. In the process he sees cocaine residue and the narcotics paraphernalia in plain sight. The observations are lawful. *Tamborino v Superior Court* (1986) 41 C3d 919, 226 CR 868. A reasonable concern for human life justifies the brief walk-through without making any inquiry of the injured man. 41 C3d at 923–924.

- Officers respond to a domestic violence report. They see a man in the residence, hear a shout, knock on the door, and are met by a frightened, nervous woman with a small red mark under one eye, who says she is all right, that she had fallen down the stairs, and that her boyfriend had been there but had left. The officers enter, observe marijuana, and arrest the boyfriend and the victim. The entry and observations are lawful. *People v Higgins* (1994) 26 CA4th 247, 250–251, 31 CR2d 516; see *People v Frye* (1998) 18 C4th 894, 989, 77 CR2d 25. The officer's belief that the woman had been injured and was under threat of continued violence is reasonable; spousal abuse is a serious offense that justifies immediate police intervention; the police need not delay until an arrest warrant can be obtained. *People v Higgins, supra,* 26 CA4th at 251–255. In accord is *People v Wilkins* (1993) 14 CA4th 761, 773, 17 CR2d 743; see *People v Neighbours* (1990) 223 CA3d 1115, 1121, 273 CR 32 (entry to prevent danger of injury to child).

#### b. [§5.92] Police Conduct Unlawful

The following cases illustrate unlawful police conduct:

- Responding to a 911 call, the police find a body in a cabin and a wounded man outside. After securing the area and taking the injured man to the hospital, they search the cabin. In the absence of consent the warrantless search is unlawful. *Flippo v West Virginia* (1999) 528 US 11, 12, 120 S Ct 7, 145 L Ed 2d 16.

- A drug raid goes awry; an undercover officer is shot and killed. The police enter, quickly look for other victims, and subsequently search the apartment without a warrant or consent. The search is unlawful, except for the cursory search for possible victims. *Mincey v Arizona* (1978) 437 US 385, 390, 98 S Ct 2408, 57 L Ed 2d 290.

### F. [§5.93] Others Who May Need Aid

Persons other than victims of crime may need emergency aid justifying a warrantless entry. See, *e.g., People v Poulson* (1998) 69 CA4th Supp

1, 5, 82 CR2d 605 (blood at scene of severe car crash and on walkway leading to residence; in response to shout of "police," officer sees woman with blood on her face; emergency entry proper even though woman said she was all right and that she did not want officer to come in); *People v Snead* (1991) 1 CA4th 380, 385, 1 CR2d 892 (motel guest cut himself, wife called front desk employee, who called 911; motel employees, firemen, a police officer, and paramedics responded, in that order; officer's brief entry justified for limited purpose of ensuring safety of those present).

A report of an open door and shambles inside the residence, even when confirmed by the officer's observation, would not lead a reasonable person to believe that entry was immediately necessary to aid life or limb. *People v Ray* (1999) 21 C4th 464, 473, 88 CR2d 1 (but entry upheld under protection of property rationale).

Injured and unconscious persons may be searched for identification. *People v Gomez* (1964) 229 CA2d 781, 783, 40 CR 616; *People v Gonzales* (1960) 182 CA2d 276, 279, 5 CR 920.

### G. [§5.94] Missing Persons; Unattended Children

Courts have often upheld entries related to missing or unattended children. *People v Lucero* (1988) 44 C3d 1006, 1017, 245 CR 185 (fire of unknown origin and discovery of blood stains inside justifies search for two girls missing from park across street from house); *People v Miller* (1999) 69 CA4th 190, 199, 81 CR2d 410 (two-year-old walking on street calling for his mother; neighbors point out house; no response to repeated knock and announcement); *People v Sutton* (1976) 65 CA3d 341, 347–348, 134 CR 921; *In re Dawn O.* (1976) 58 CA3d 160, 163, 128 CR 852.

A report of a missing adult may also justify an entry. For example, in *People v Ammons* (1980) 103 CA3d 20, 30–31, 162 CR 772, the officers had information that one of the occupants of a house had not shown up for work or called, although he was always punctual, that he had a heart condition, and that he had not been seen by neighbors for two days. The court held that the officer properly made an emergency entry after he received no response to knocking and announcing and could see nothing from the outside. In *People v Wharton* (1991) 53 C3d 522, 577, 280 CR 631, an entry was held proper when neighbors had not seen the victim for two weeks, her aunt had telephoned police voicing concern for her welfare, and the police had been called to the residence earlier in the month to quell a domestic disturbance.

There are limits, however. In *People v Smith* (1972) 7 C3d 282, 286–287, 101 CR 893, a downstairs neighbor had taken in a six-year-old girl who had been sitting outside the girl's upstairs flat crying. After a while the neighbor called the police. An officer knocked on the door of the upstairs flat and entered after receiving no response. The court held that there was no emergency, and no substantial threat to life, health, or property.

### H. [§5.95] Burglary in Progress

A warrantless entry is justified when officers reasonably believe that a burglary is in progress or has recently occurred. *People v Ray* (1999) 21 C4th 464, 473 (community caretaking), 481 (conc. op.; exigent circumstance), 88 CR2d 1; *People v Duncan* (1986) 42 C3d 91, 97, 227 CR 654.

In *People v Ray, supra,* police promptly responded to a report that the door of a residence had been open all day and that it was a shambles inside. The officers' observations from the outside confirmed the report. The court held that the entry into the residence and observations made inside were lawful. In *People v Duncan, supra,* the officer responded to a radio call that a residential burglary was in progress or had just occurred. The officer checked outside of the house in question. He found an open window with a TV set and other articles beneath it. The court held these facts to be sufficient to justify entry in order to protect property; the officer's surmise that one or more burglars might still be inside was reasonable under the circumstances, though it turned out to be incorrect. In *People v Ray, supra,* there was no such surmise, but the court upheld the entry on the ground that it was reasonable for the police to investigate whether a burglary had occurred (lead opinion) or because the officer reasonably believed that there had been a burglary and that there may be injured persons inside (concurring opinion).

### I. [§5.96] Chemical Odors

A strong odor of a volatile or toxic chemical such as ether has often been held to justify an emergency entry. *People v Duncan* (1986) 42 C3d 91, 97, 227 CR 654; *People v Osuna* (1986) 187 CA3d 845, 852, 232 CR 220; *People v Messina* (1985) 165 CA3d 937, 942, 212 CR 75; *People v Stegman* (1985) 164 CA3d 936, 942–944, 210 CR 855. While "each situation must be evaluated on its own facts" (*People v Duncan, supra,* 42 C3d at 103), courts recognize that "[t]he extremely volatile nature of chemicals, including ether, involved in the production of drugs such as PCP and methamphetamine creates a dangerous environment. . . ." *People v Duncan, supra,* 42 C3d at 105.

A long delay between smelling the chemical and entry may indicate a lack of belief that an emergency existed. *People v Baird* (1985) 168 CA3d 237, 244–245, 214 CR 88. See also *People v Blackwell* (1983) 147 CA3d 646, 653, 195 CR 298.

### J. [§5.97] Fires

"A burning building of course creates an exigency that justifies a warrantless entry by fire officials to fight the blaze." *Michigan v Clifford* (1984) 464 US 287, 293, 104 S Ct 641, 78 L Ed 2d 477; *People v Avalos* (1988) 203 CA3d 1517, 1521, 251 CR 36. As to subsequent entries, see §5.98.

Smoke is not always indicative of a fire. In *People v Brown* (1989) 210 CA3d 849, 856, 260 CR 293, officers went to an apartment in response to the manager's report of suspicion that the occupants were selling narcotics. The only observations of the officers were of two persons coming from a back bedroom, one of them under the influence of a stimulant, and of smoke coming from the same room. The smoke was not identified as coming from marijuana, a chemical, or fire. The court held that there were no exigent circumstances.

### K. Subsequent Entries

#### 1. [§5.98] After a Fire

Nonconsensual entries and searches to investigate the cause of a fire require a warrant unless no reasonable expectations of privacy remain in the damaged building or there are exigent circumstances. *Michigan v Clifford* (1984) 464 US 287, 293, 104 S Ct 641, 78 L Ed 2d 477. In addition, firefighters may remain for "a reasonable time to investigate the cause of the blaze," including entries and reentries. *Michigan v Tyler* (1978) 436 US 499, 510, 98 S Ct 1942, 56 L Ed 2d 486; *Michigan v Clifford, supra*, 464 US at 296–298 (delay of six hours between time last fireman leaves and arson investigator arrives is not within *Tyler*); *People v Lucero* (1988) 44 C3d 1006, 1017, 245 CR 185. Exigent circumstances include an immediate threat that the blaze might rekindle and the need to preserve evidence from intentional or accidental destruction. *Michigan v Clifford, supra*; *Michigan v Tyler, supra*; *Cleaver v Superior Court* (1979) 24 C3d 297, 305, 155 CR 559 (subsequent entries justified by need to preserve evidence threatened with destruction by fire or water in the basement).

A police officer who is a trained arson investigator may enter the damaged premises shortly after the fire has been put out in order to investigate its cause. *People v Glance* (1989) 209 CA3d 836, 846, 257 CR 522.

The police "cannot search any areas the firefighters were not justified in searching. They may only venture into areas affected by the flames and places where evidence of arson might reasonably be found." 209 CA3d at 845–846 (dictum).

### 2. After Other Emergencies

#### a. [§5.99] Reentry Generally Unlawful

As in case of a fire, once the emergency that justified the entry has passed, a second warrantless entry is generally unlawful. *Conway v Pasadena Humane Soc'y* (1996) 45 CA4th 163, 173, 52 CR2d 777; *People v Boragno* (1991) 232 CA3d 378, 386, 283 CR 452; *People v Bradley* (1982) 132 CA3d 737, 744, 183 CR 434 (unlawful to reenter to seize evidence observed during lawful entry in response to burglary-in-progress report). See *People v Duncan* (1986) 42 C3d 91, 99, 227 CR 654. For discussion of circumstances under which reentry is lawful, see §§5.100–5.101.

#### b. [§5.100] Continuing Emergency

A subsequent entry to deal with a continuing or newly arisen emergency is permitted. *People v Duncan* (1986) 42 C3d 91, 98, 227 CR 654 (subsequent entry lawful to cope with chemical danger); *People v Ngaue* (1992) 8 CA4th 896, 904, 10 CR2d 521 (police arrest attempted-murder suspect in residence; see gun on floor but leave it there; suspect escapes from patrol car; reentry justified by officer's safety). But see *People v Blackwell* (1983) 147 CA3d 646, 653, 195 CR 298 (proper initial entry led to discovery of PCP lab; firemen ventilated premises and took action to prevent explosion; reentry and seizure of evidence by officers three hours later unlawful because claim of ongoing emergency not supported by evidence).

#### c. [§5.101] Uninterrupted Police Presence

A subsequent entry to seize evidence is valid if it is part of an uninterrupted police presence. *People v McDowell* (1988) 46 C3d 551, 564, 250 CR 530; *People v Duncan* (1986) 42 C3d 91, 100, 227 CR 654; *People v Amaya* (1979) 93 CA3d 424, 431, 155 CR 783.

The police presence does not have to be literally uninterrupted; repeated entries and exits may be reasonable under the particular circumstances. *Michigan v Tyler* (1978) 436 US 499, 510, 98 S Ct 1942, 56 L Ed 2d 486 (fire investigation); *People v McDowell, supra.* The crux of *McDowell* "is the lack of intent by the officer to abandon the items in plain view and his inability to seize them immediately." *People v Ngaue* (1992) 8 CA4th 896, 905, 10 CR2d 521.

The length of delay between observation of the evidence and its retrieval is an important consideration. *People v Ngaue, supra,* 8 CA4th at 904 (20 minutes not too long); *People v Boragno* (1991) 232 CA3d 378, 392, 283 CR 452 (4 to 5 hours too long).

The continuity of police presence is broken once officers leave the premises and permit a resident to enter it. *People v Duncan, supra.* See also *People v Justin* (1983) 140 CA3d 729, 736, 189 CR 662.

## V. CONSENT SEARCHES

### A. [§5.102] Overview

Consent is a major exception to the warrant requirement of the Fourth Amendment. Assertions that the defendant or another person consented to a search may raise any of the following issues (see Caskey, Benchguide to California Search and Seizure Cases §V(F) (Specialized Legal Publications 2d ed 1995)):

(1) Was there consent? How was it manifested? Was it withdrawn? See §§5.103–5.107.

(2) What was the scope of the consent? Was it limited? Were the limits exceeded? See §§5.108–5.111.

(3) Was the consent valid? This is a frequently litigated issue in the consent area. See §§5.112–5.127.

(4) Did the person who gave consent have actual or apparent authority to do so? This question often arises when consent was given by a person other than the defendant. See §§5.128–5.140.

The principles applicable to consent to search also govern consent to enter (*e.g., People v Machupa* (1994) 7 C4th 614, 632, 29 CR2d 775; *People v Poole* (1986) 182 CA3d 1004, 1012, 227 CR 594), surrender of an object by defendant to the police (*People v Epperson* (1986) 187 CA3d 115, 120, 232 CR 16 (issue of voluntariness)), and consent by a person who has been temporarily detained to be transported to the police station (*People v Farley* (1979) 90 CA3d 851, 865, 153 CR 695).

Consent discussed here, in essence, voluntary consent given in the context of a specific search, should be differentiated from mandatory or "implied" consent. Among the latter are consents required of probationers, consent under implied consent statutes such as Veh C §13353, consent imputed to persons who engage in particular activities (*e.g., Almeida-Sanchez v U.S.* (1973) 413 US 266, 270, 93 S Ct 2535, 37 L Ed 2d 596 (implied consent to inspection by person in pervasively regulated business)), and court-ordered "consent" (*Doe v U.S.* (1988) 487 US 201, 215,

108 S Ct 2341, 101 L Ed 2d 184 (target of grand jury investigation ordered to sign consent authorizing foreign banks to disclose records of his accounts)).

## B. Manifestation and Withdrawal of Consent

### 1. Manifestation

#### a. [§5.103] Basic Principles

A threshold issue is whether there was consent to a police entry or search. The courts resolve this issue by determining whether the officers' belief that they had consent is objectively reasonable under the circumstances. *People v Machupa* (1994) 7 C4th 614, 632, 29 CR2d 775. A "yeah" by defendant suffices, provided it comes in response to a clear and simple request (*People v James* (1977) 19 C3d 99, 113, 137 CR 447); so do "I don't care" and "Do what you want" (*People v James, supra,* and cases there cited). But, "I guess" said by a defendant in response to an officer's statement that the officer would have to accompany defendant into the house is not a consent to enter; a police officer's belief that it is would not be objectively reasonable. *People v Machupa, supra.*

#### b. [§5.104] Nonverbal Consent

Consent can be manifested by actions as well as by words. *People v Harrington* (1970) 2 C3d 991, 995, 88 CR 161; *People v Hamilton* (1985) 168 CA3d 1058, 1067, 214 CR 596. Thus, consent to enter can be given by opening the door and stepping aside in response to a request to enter. *People v Harrington, supra*; *People v Hamilton, supra*; *People v Martino* (1985) 166 CA3d 777, 791, 212 CR 45. A nonverbal manifestation raises the same issues of voluntariness as a verbal one. See, *e.g., People v Poole* (1986) 182 CA3d 1004, 1012, 227 CR 594 (opening door in response to police command); *People v Brown* (1975) 53 CA3d Supp 1, 4, 125 CR 739 (opening door of private club after officer's assertion of right to enter). In addition, the absence of unambiguous consent is itself a negative factor in assessing voluntariness. *People v Superior Court* (Peck) (1974) 10 C3d 645, 649, 111 CR 565.

When one person is asked for consent, the silence of another who is present is not a consent by the latter. *People v Stage* (1970) 7 CA3d 681, 684, 86 CR 701.

### 2. Withdrawal

#### a. [§5.105] Right To Withdraw

Consent may be withdrawn any time before the search is completed.

*People v Hamilton* (1985) 168 CA3d 1058, 1067, 214 CR 596; *People v Gurtenstein* (1977) 69 CA3d 441, 451, 138 CR 161. The revocation can be expressed by actions inconsistent with consent if they are positive in nature. *People v Botos* (1972) 27 CA3d 774, 779, 104 CR 193.

#### b. [§5.106] Effective Withdrawals

The following cases illustrate effective withdrawal of consent:

- Officers have a warrant for the defendant. They go to the apartment of defendant's female friend (a lessee), advise her of the warrant, and she reluctantly admits them. An officer goes toward the bedroom. She runs ahead of him and starts to close the bedroom door. The officer pushes the door open and finds the defendant. The friend's "active attempt to exclude the officers from the bedroom . . . constituted a withdrawal of consent to enter the bedroom." *People v Hamilton* (1985) 168 CA3d 1058, 1068, 214 CR 596.
- Defendant consents to a search of the trunk of his car and then throws the key into the bushes. He has revoked his consent. *People v Escollias* (1968) 264 CA2d 16, 18, 70 CR 65.
- Defendant consents to a search of his person and portfolio. The officer finds a plastic card and defendant immediately struggles to retrieve the portfolio in which it had previously been. This is an effective revocation of consent; the search may lawfully continue only if the officer has probable cause to arrest defendant at the time consent is withdrawn. *U.S. v Ho* (5th Cir 1996) 94 F3d 932, 934–936.

#### c. [§5.107] Ineffective Withdrawals

Efforts to revoke consent were found ineffective in the following cases:

- Defendant verbally consents to a residential search. Halfway through the search he is asked to sign a written consent and refuses. The mere refusal to sign, unaccompanied by any statement that he is withdrawing his consent, is not a revocation. *People v Gurtenstein* (1977) 69 CA3d 441, 451, 138 CR 161.
- An air passenger consents to a luggage search, becomes increasingly nervous, denies he has the key, but produces it when the officer questions him about a large bulge in his pocket. Denial by itself is not a withdrawal of consent, particularly in light of the subsequent production of the key. *People v Botos* (1972) 27 CA3d 774, 779, 104 CR 193. See also *People v Johnson* (1980) 108 CA3d 175,

180, 166 CR 419 (defendant's silence when asked for key is not a withdrawal of consent).

Aside from the question of withdrawal, defendant's noncooperation after purportedly consenting occasionally sheds light on whether the consent was voluntary. See §5.123.

### C. Scope of Consent

#### 1. [§5.108] Consent To Enter

The scope of a consent to *enter* the premises is limited to the stated purpose of the entry. Thus, an invitation to enter after an emergency call for help is not a consent to search. *People v Timms* (1986) 179 CA3d 86, 91–92, 224 CR 434; see *People v Boragno* (1991) 232 CA3d 378, 387, 283 CR 452. When officers say they want to talk to the defendant, consent to enter does not encompass arresting defendant. *In re Johnny V.* (1978) 85 CA3d 120, 130, 149 CR 180; *People v Superior Court* (Kenner) (1977) 73 CA3d 65, 69, 139 CR 343. See also *People v Villa* (1981) 125 CA3d 872, 878, 178 CR 398 (arrest valid where grounds do not arise until after entry). However, the officers who enter "do not have to blind themselves as to what is in plain sight simply because it is disconnected with the purpose for which they entered the premises." *People v Szabo* (1980) 107 CA3d 419, 431, 165 CR 719.

#### 2. Consent To Search

##### a. [§5.109] Objective Reasonableness

The scope of a suspect's consent to search is measured by a standard of objective reasonableness; the inquiry is what a reasonable person would have understood by the exchange between the officer and the person giving consent. *Florida v Jimeno* (1991) 500 US 248, 251–252, 111 S Ct 1801, 114 L Ed 2d 297 (permission to search car for narcotics includes consent to search paper bag found on floorboard but probably not locked briefcase in trunk); *People v Jenkins* (2000) 22 C4th 900, 974–976, 95 CR2d 377 (consent extended to brother's briefcase when person giving it was told that police were looking for evidence that her brother murdered a police officer, she consented to search of residence, disclosed location of briefcase, and handed it to officer).

##### b. [§5.110] Broad Scope

Consent to search, particularly for narcotics, is broad in scope unless limited by the person giving it or by officers' statements. *People v Miller*

(1999) 69 CA4th 190, 203, 81 CR2d 410 (consent to search for narcotics extends to writings and a videotape in places where narcotics or narcotic-related evidence could have been secreted); *People v $48, 715 U.S. Currency* (1997) 58 CA4th 1507, 1515, 68 CR2d 829 (scope of consent to search pickup for narcotics includes moving it to off-highway location and using drug-sniffing dog); *People v Crenshaw* (1992) 9 CA4th 1403, 1408–1415, 12 CR2d 172 (scope of consent to search car for drugs extends to removal of screw from plastic door vent and disengaging of vent).

A consent to look "in the back of [a] pickup truck where the boxes [are]" authorizes a search of all containers in the back of the truck. *People v Carvajal* (1988) 202 CA3d 487, 494, 497, 249 CR 368. Consent to search suitcases extends to envelopes found in them. *People v Shandloff* (1985) 170 CA3d 372, 384, 215 CR 916 (court stressed that defendant who had consented was present during the search and at no time attempted to limit or revoke it).

#### c. [§5.111] Searches Not Within Scope

Examples of searches that exceed their legitimate scope include:

- Interception of phone calls while officers search an apartment pursuant to a consent to search for cocaine and money. *People v Harwood* (1977) 74 CA3d 460, 467, 141 CR 519.

- A thorough search of a residence and its closets pursuant to consent to enter in order to look for a person. *People v Superior Court* (Arketa) (1970) 10 CA3d 122, 127, 89 CR 316.

☛ **Judicial Tip**: It is sometimes easy to confuse an issue concerning the *scope* of consent with one concerning the *authority* to consent. These issues should be analyzed separately. See *People v Jenkins* (2000) 22 C4th 900, 974–977, 95 CR2d 377. For example, when an officer searches articles in a car knowing that they belong to persons other than the one who gave consent, the question is one of authority to consent, not of scope. See *People v Stage* (1970) 7 CA3d 681, 683, 86 CR 701. For discussion of authority to consent, see §§5.128–5.140.

## D. Validity of Consent

### 1. [§5.112] Basic Principles

Valid consent has two components:

(1) It must be free and voluntary rather than a mere submission to a claim of lawful authority or the result of coercion or duress. *Florida v Royer* (1983) 460 US 491, 497, 103 S Ct 1319, 75 L Ed 2d 229;

*Schneckloth v Bustamonte* (1973) 412 US 218, 233–234, 93 S Ct 2041, 36 L Ed 2d 854; *People v James* (1977) 19 C3d 99, 106, 137 CR 447.

(2) The consent cannot be the result of unlawful police activity such as an illegal detention, entry, or arrest. *Florida v Royer, supra*; *Wilson v Superior Court* (1983) 34 C3d 777, 791, 195 CR 671; *Burrows v Superior Court* (1974) 13 C3d 238, 251, 118 CR 166. Courts speak of such consents as involuntary (*e.g., People v James, supra*; *Burrows v Superior Court, supra*; *People v Bailey* (1985) 176 CA3d 402, 405, 222 CR 235); the underlying reason for their invalidity is that consents obtained in this way exploit unlawful police conduct. For further discussion, see §5.125.

The determination of voluntariness in the first sense requires careful examination of all the circumstances surrounding the consent. *Schneckloth v Bustamonte, supra*; *People v James, supra.* For the most part, no single factor determines the outcome. Trial court resolutions are given great deference and are rarely reversed. See, *e.g., People v Ratliff* (1986) 41 C3d 675, 686, 224 CR 705. In contrast, when consent follows unlawful police conduct, a *per se* rule of invalidity applies unless the prosecution shows attenuation. See §5.125. Determinations regarding voluntariness in the second sense involve conclusions of law that are not binding on appellate courts. See, *e.g., People v Loewen* (1983) 35 C3d 117, 123, 196 CR 846.

☛ **Judicial Tip**: When a case presents issues concerning both kinds of voluntariness, some judges recommend deciding the second one first, *e.g.,* whether defendant was unlawfully arrested. If the answer is no, the judge should determine whether the total atmosphere in which consent was given was coercive. Some judges also suggest briefly stating key factual determinations and legal conclusions; this helps to give reviewing courts a clearer picture.

### 2. Factors Affecting Voluntariness

#### a. [§5.113] Giving Directions or Orders

Compliance with an assertion of police authority does not constitute voluntary consent. Giving directions or orders usually vitiates consent, such as:

- Asking a vehicle passenger to open the trunk, rather than requesting permission to search. *People v Fields* (1979) 95 CA3d 972, 976, 157 CR 578; but see *In re D.M.G.* (1981) 120 CA3d 218, 224–227, 174 CR 557 (officer asked passenger to unlock vehicle; passenger was not a suspect and search did not occur shortly after vehicle stop; consent voluntary).

- Shouting to persons inside a building to open the door. *People v Poole* (1986) 182 CA3d 1004, 1008–1012, 227 CR 594.
- Directing a person to yield the key to a residence. *People v Engel* (1980) 105 CA3d 489, 499, 164 CR 454.

In contrast, the following actions do not render consent involuntary:

- Asking a person whether he or she objects to a search. *People v Ratliff* (1986) 41 C3d 675, 686, 224 CR 705. It is coercive, however, to ask reluctant persons why they object to a search and to tell them they should have no objections if nothing is wrong. *Crofoot v Superior Court* (1981) 121 CA3d 717, 725, 175 CR 530.
- Displaying the officer's badge at the door of a residence and stating the officer's business. *People v Martino* (1985) 166 CA3d 777, 783, 212 CR 45.
- Asking, "Do you mind if we look around," in a manner that leaves the hearer free to deny permission. *People v Parker* (1975) 45 CA3d 24, 30, 119 CR 49.

#### b. [§5.114] Statements Concerning Search Warrants

A statement by the police that they have a search warrant renders consent involuntary whether the statement is true or false. *Bumper v North Carolina* (1968) 391 US 543, 548, 88 S Ct 1788, 20 L Ed 2d 797 (consent under such circumstances is no more than acquiescence to a claim of lawful authority; assertion was apparently true, but the prosecution chose not to rely on the search warrant); *People v Baker* (1986) 187 CA3d 562, 570, 231 CR 877 (same result when officers say that search warrant is on the way). But see *People v Terrill* (1979) 98 CA3d 291, 302, 159 CR 360 (officers who had search warrant limited to daytime execution told resident they had a warrant and obtained consent for search before time permitted by warrant; consent upheld).

In contrast, statements that the officers would apply for or seek a search warrant if defendant did not consent do not render consent involuntary; courts treat such expressions as mere declarations of the officer's legal remedies should defendant refuse to cooperate. *People v Goldberg* (1984) 161 CA3d 170, 188, 207 CR 431; *People v Ward* (1972) 27 CA3d 218, 224, 103 CR 671. Similarly, courts have upheld consents given after statements that the officer had never failed to get a search warrant in similar situations (*People v Mayberry* (1982) 31 C3d 335, 338, 182 CR 617), that the officers would impound the vehicle if consent were refused (*People v Gee* (1982) 130 CA3d 174, 182, 181 CR 524 (but circumstances must show that the police had the right to impound)), and that failure to permit an inspection would subject defendant to arrest, provided the statement is true (*People v Woolsey* (1979) 90 CA3d 994, 1003, 153 CR 746).

The problem is more difficult when an officer says he will *get* or *obtain* a search warrant, rather than *apply* for one. The principal case upholding a consent based on such a statement stressed that "in the same breath the officer expressly informed defendant that he need not consent to the search, that the search was expected to reveal incriminating evidence, and that such evidence would be admissible against him." *People v Ruster* (1976) 16 C3d 690, 701, 129 CR 153. Other decisions, however, simply permit such statements on the ground that they "threatened nothing more than what the officers had a legal right to do." *People v McClure* (1974) 39 CA3d 64, 69, 113 CR 815; see *People v Ratliff* (1986) 41 C3d 675, 687, 224 CR 705.

A district attorney's publication comments that this is "wrong" because officers do not have a legal right to "get" or "obtain" a search warrant, but only to apply for one. "A statement that officers can simply 'obtain' or 'get' a search warrant falsely implies that a warrant will be automatically granted"; such a statement is "misleading and arguably more coercive than a statement that a search warrant will be sought." 16 *Point of View* 78 (Alameda County District Attorney's Office, Fall 1988).

☛ **Judicial Tip**: While "we will get a search warrant if you refuse to consent" is not impermissibly coercive under all circumstances, such a statement makes careful scrutiny of the entire atmosphere surrounding the purported consent particularly important.

### c. [§5.115] Display of Weapons

When officers point their guns at the defendant, his or her consent at such a moment is highly suspect and very likely to be involuntary. *People v Challoner* (1982) 136 CA3d 779, 782, 186 CR 458. See also 16 *Point of View* 77 (Alameda County District Attorney's Office, Fall 1988) ("It may safely be assumed that consent given at gunpoint is never voluntary").

This does not mean that every situation in which an officer drew a weapon at some stage results in a coerced consent. For instance, in *People v Martino* (1985) 166 CA3d 777, 791, 212 CR 45, an officer who sought consent to enter had his gun drawn but concealed behind his leg. The court affirmed the trial court's finding of voluntary consent, distinguishing "those cases where consent was vitiated by the officer's display of weapons. . . ." In *People v Ratliff* (1986) 41 C3d 675, 686, 224 CR 705, the court held that the initial drawing of guns by the officers when they confronted defendant did not vitiate consent where "the evidence did not indicate that any of them kept their guns drawn when . . . the actual request for consent to search was made." A consent limited in scope indicates that it was not coerced, despite a display of weapons. *People v Aguilar* (1996) 48 CA4th 632, 640, 55 CR2d 716.

#### d. [§5.116] Advice That Consent Can Be Refused

Advice that consent can be refused is not required (*U.S. v Watson* (1976) 423 US 411, 424–425, 96 S Ct 820, 46 L Ed 2d 598; *People v James* (1977) 19 C3d 99, 115, 137 CR 447; *People v Ramirez* (1997) 59 CA4th 1548, 1558, 70 CR2d 341), but it is germane, and when such advice is given, that fact weighs heavily in favor of voluntariness (*People v James, supra,* 19 C3d at 118; see also *People v Profit* (1986) 183 CA3d 849, 877, 229 CR 148 (police-civilian encounter more likely to be found consensual rather than detention when civilian so advised)).

Similarly, a motorist need not be advised that he or she is free to leave in order for consent to search to be voluntary. *Ohio v Robinette* (1996) 519 US 33, 35, 117 S Ct 417, 136 L Ed 2d 347. The absence of such advice is simply one facet of the fact-specific nature of the inquiry. 519 US at 39. In contrast, an officer who holds defendant's identification papers while requesting consent is placing the defendant in a much more coercive situation, especially when the defendant is a foreigner. *People v Valenzuela* (1994) 28 CA4th 817, 832, 33 CR2d 802 (holding defendant's green card while seeking consent inherently coercive under circumstances).

#### e. [§5.117] *Miranda* Admonition

Officers need not give a *Miranda* admonition to a person in custody before obtaining his or her consent to search. *People v James* (1977) 19 C3d 99, 114–115, 137 CR 447; *People v Ramirez* (1997) 59 CA4th 1548, 1558–1559, 70 CR2d 341; see *People v Ratliff* (1986) 41 C3d 675, 686, 224 CR 705. But giving the admonition tends to show voluntariness. See *U.S. v Carbajal* (9th Cir 1992) 956 F2d 924, 930.

Consent after interrogation in violation of *Miranda,* however, is invalid in the absence of attenuation. *People v Superior Court* (Keithley) (1975) 13 C3d 406, 409, 118 CR 617; for discussion of attenuation, see §§1.45–1.57. On the other hand, invocation of *Miranda* rights by a defendant does not block police from seeking his or her consent. *People v Ruster* (1976) 16 C3d 690, 699, 129 CR 153, disapproved on other grounds in 28 C3d 494, 503 n9.

### f. [§5.118] Custody; Handcuffs

The fact that defendant was handcuffed or in custody when his or her consent was obtained is to be weighed with all other circumstances bearing on voluntariness, but is not determinative. *People v Siripongs* (1988) 45 C3d 548, 566, 247 CR 729; *People v Ratliff* (1986) 41 C3d 675, 686, 224 CR 705; *People v Llamas* (1991) 235 CA3d 441, 447, 286 CR 467; see *People v James* (1977) 19 C3d 99, 109, 137 CR 447 (defendant's custody at time of giving consent is circumstance of particular significance); *People v Valenzuela* (1994) 28 CA4th 817, 832, 33 CR2d 802.

"[I]t is axiomatic that consent to search produced by an illegal arrest or detention is not voluntary." *People v Valenzuela, supra,* 28 C4th at 833; see §§5.112, 5.125.

### g. [§5.119] Number of Officers; Time

Relevant, but not decisive, circumstances bearing on the voluntariness of consent include the number of officers present and whether it was day or night. *People v James* (1977) 19 C3d 99, 110, 137 CR 447; *People v Gurtenstein* (1977) 69 CA3d 441, 451, 138 CR 161 (presence of seven or eight officers did not render consent involuntary where it did not contribute to defendant's giving consent).

### h. [§5.120] Condition of Person Consenting

The maturity and emotional condition of the person whose consent is in issue is relevant. *Schneckloth v Bustamonte* (1973) 412 US 218, 226, 93 S Ct 2041, 36 L Ed 2d 854 (definition of voluntariness takes into account the possibly vulnerable subjective state of the person who consents, as well as evidence of minimal schooling and low intelligence). Officers can, however, rely on "ostensibly rational statements," even by a defendant who is hysterical and who had recently ingested substantial amounts of heroin and alcohol. *People v Gurley* (1972) 23 CA3d 536, 553, 100 CR 407. Defense testimony that defendant was nervous, upset, and confused at the time he gave consent does not preclude a finding of voluntariness. *People v Williams* (1980) 114 CA3d 67, 71, 170 CR 433.

### i. [§5.121] Ambiguous Manifestation of Consent

An ambiguous manifestation of consent (*e.g.*, opening the door and stepping back) supports a finding that the defendant acted through fear or submission to authority; it also supports a finding of tacit consent. *People v Superior Court* (Peck) (1974) 10 C3d 645, 648, 111 CR 565.

☛ **Judicial Tip**: Ambiguous conduct may also raise questions of whether there was actual consent and whether it was withdrawn.

#### j. Efforts To Mislead

##### (1) [§5.122] By Police

Use of a ruse by the police is a factor to be considered, but is not inherently incompatible with voluntariness. *People v Avalos* (1996) 47 CA4th 1569, 1577, 55 CR2d 450 (deceptive statements regarding purpose of search; consent valid in light of totality of circumstances). But a ruse that an honest person would be likely to fall for makes the defendant's cooperation, including his or her consent, involuntary. *People v Reyes* (2000) 83 CA4th 7, 10, 98 CR2d 898 (luring defendant outside by officer's false statement that officer had hit defendant's parked truck renders consent involuntary).

##### (2) [§5.123] By Person Consenting

Postconsent efforts to mislead the police or refusal to cooperate with the officers can show that apparent consent was not voluntarily given. *People v James* (1977) 19 C3d 99, 108, 137 CR 447, and cases cited there. See also *People v Ibarra* (1980) 114 CA3d 60, 65, 170 CR 440 (upholding voluntariness despite effort to mislead police).

### 3. [§5.124] Factors Entitled to Little or No Weight

Circumstances given little or no weight in the determination of voluntariness include:

- A mistake of fact by the consenting party. *People v Patterson* (1979) 94 CA3d 456, 461, 156 CR 518 (defendant was expecting friends when police knocked; called out, "Come in"; lack of knowledge did not vitiate consent to enter).
- Consent obtained after the search. *People v Parrison* (1982) 137 CA3d 529, 536, 187 CR 123.
- The argument that defendant had no logical reason to consent. *People v James* (1977) 19 C3d 99, 113, 137 CR 447.

### 4. [§5.125] Unlawful Police Conduct

Consent produced by unlawful police conduct is involuntary. See, *e.g., Florida v Royer* (1983) 460 US 491, 497, 103 S Ct 1319, 75 L Ed 2d

229; *People v Valenzuela* (1994) 28 CA4th 817, 833, 33 CR2d 802. For example:

- Consent to search obtained soon after an illegal entry. *People v Brown* (1989) 210 CA3d 849, 856, 260 CR 293; *People v Poole* (1986) 182 CA3d 1004, 1012, 227 CR 594. But see *In re Reginald B.* (1977) 71 CA3d 398, 403, 139 CR 465 (consent to enter after minor, nonintrusive entry by police is valid).
- Consent to search obtained during an unlawful detention. *Florida v Royer, supra*; *People v Gallant* (1990) 225 CA3d 200, 211, 275 CR 50.
- Consent to search given after several hours of unlawful arrest and incarceration. *People v Leib* (1976) 16 C3d 869, 877, 129 CR 433.
- Consent to search a vehicle following illegal search of office. *Burrows v Superior Court* (1974) 13 C3d 238, 251, 118 CR 166.
- Consent after interrogation in violation of *Miranda. People v Superior Court* (Keithley) (1975) 13 C3d 406, 409, 118 CR 617; see *People v Rich* (1988) 45 C3d 1036, 1079, 248 CR 510; *People v Carvajal* (1988) 202 CA3d 487, 497, 249 CR 368.

The prosecution is entitled to prove attenuation, *i.e.*, to show that there is no causal connection between the unlawful police conduct and the consent. For discussion, see §1.55.

### 5. [§5.126] Consent by Represented Defendant

Consent obtained from the defendant in the absence of defense counsel is invalid when it is given after the defendant was arraigned and counsel retained or appointed. *People v Williams* (1980) 114 CA3d 67, 75, 170 CR 433; *Tidwell v Superior Court* (1971) 17 CA3d 780, 789, 95 CR 213. This limitation on the validity of consent stems from the Sixth Amendment right to the aid of counsel. *People v Williams, supra,* 114 CA3d at 76.

### 6. [§5.127] Race Discrimination

Consent searches initiated solely on racial considerations may violate the Equal Protection Clause. *U.S. v Travis* (6th Cir 1995) 62 F3d 170, 173; see *U.S. v Woods* (8th Cir 2000) 213 F3d 1021, 1022; *U.S. v Avery* (6th Cir 1997) 137 F3d 343, 352.

## E. Third Party Consent

### 1. Actual and Apparent Authority

#### a. [§5.128] Basic Principles

A warrantless entry and search is lawful if the officers have obtained the voluntary consent of a third party

- "[W]ho possesses common authority over the premises," or
- "[W]hom the police, at the time of the entry, reasonably believe to possess common authority over the premises, but who in fact does not do so." *Illinois v Rodriguez* (1990) 497 US 177, 179, 110 S Ct 2793, 111 L Ed 2d 148; *U.S. v Matlock* (1974) 415 US 164, 170, 94 S Ct 988, 39 L Ed 2d 242; *People v Jenkins* (2000) 22 C4th 900, 976–980, 95 CR2d 377; *People v Jacobs* (1987) 43 C3d 472, 481, 233 CR 323.

#### b. [§5.129] Common Authority

The authority of a third party to consent does not rest on the law of property but "on mutual use of the property by persons generally having joint access or control for most purposes, so that it is reasonable to recognize that . . . [they have] the right to permit the inspection . . . and that the others have assumed the risk that one of their number might permit the common area to be searched." *U.S. v Matlock* (1974) 415 US 164, 171 n7, 94 S Ct 988, 39 L Ed 2d 242; see *People v Jenkins* (2000) 22 C4th 900, 979, 95 CR2d 377 (joint access and control may establish apparent authority to consent to search of personal property, regardless of mutual use; death penalty case).

#### c. [§5.130] Objective Standard

Apparent authority is determined by an objective standard: whether the facts available to the officer would warrant a reasonable cautious person in believing that the person who gave consent had authority over the property. *Illinois v Rodriguez* (1990) 497 US 177, 188, 110 S Ct 2793, 111 L Ed 2d 148; *People v Jenkins* (2000) 22 C4th 900, 977, 95 CR2d 377.

#### d. [§5.131] Knock-Notice

A consent to enter or search premises given by a third party who is absent from them at the time does not excuse compliance with knock-notice requirements. *People v Haskett* (1982) 30 C3d 841, 857, 180 CR 640 ("an absent cotenant cannot authorize the police to burst into occupied premises unannounced if there is no emergency . . ."); *Duke v Superior Court* (1969) 1 C3d 314, 322, 82 CR 348.

## 2. Applications

### a. Landlords and Innkeepers

#### (1) [§5.132] No Authority To Consent

A landlord has no actual or apparent authority to allow the police to enter premises lawfully occupied by tenants, whether or not the tenants are present at the time. *Chapman v U.S.* (1961) 365 US 610, 612, 81 S Ct 776, 5 L Ed 2d 828; *People v Escudero* (1979) 23 C3d 800, 808, 153 CR 825 (ranch owner who provides housing for farm workers lacks authority to permit police entry); *People v Roman* (1991) 227 CA3d 674, 680, 278 CR 44 (tenant who paid part of one month's rent lawfully occupies premises during that month; landlord's consent invalid). For exceptions, see §5.133.

Similarly, hotel employees cannot validly consent to a police entry of occupied guest rooms. *Stoner v California* (1964) 376 US 483, 487, 84 S Ct 889, 11 L Ed 2d 856. An officer's reliance on such consent is unreasonable. *Krauss v Superior Court* (1971) 5 C3d 418, 422, 96 CR 455, overruled on other grounds in 22 C3d 67, 99.

The same principles apply to owners of personal property who rent it to others. For example, in *People v Smith* (1977) 67 CA3d 638, 647, 136 CR 764, the owner of an airplane who had rented it to defendant allowed police to enter the plane and install a transponder designed to track its flight. The court held that (1) the owner lacked actual authority because the plane was in the possession and under the control of defendant at time the owner gave consent, and (2) there was no apparent authority, and the police were aware of the rental arrangement and therefore could not claim they made a good faith mistake. See also *People v Baker* (1970) 12 CA3d 826, 836, 96 CR 760 (police cannot rely on consent of bowling alley manager to search locker and its contents).

#### (2) [§5.133] Exceptions

Consent by landlords has been upheld in two kinds of situations:

(1) An apartment house manager has authority to give a police officer a key to the locked outside door for the purpose of entering the common areas of the building. *People v Howard* (1976) 63 CA3d 249, 254, 133 CR 689. Entries into such areas do not violate protected privacy expectations. See §5.15.

(2) Police officers can rely on a property owner's consent as to premises

that have apparently been vacated if facts known to the officers reasonably support this conclusion. See, *e.g.*, *People v Carr* (1972) 8 C3d 287, 298, 104 CR 705 (duplex); *People v Ingram* (1981) 122 CA3d 673, 679, 176 CR 199 (hotel room); *People v Superior Court* (York) (1970) 3 CA3d 648, 658, 83 CR 732 (landlord had physically evicted tenant; officer did not know that property owner had failed to comply with legal requirements; court found apparent authority; officer is not obligated to ascertain legality of eviction).

### b. Joint Owners, Occupants, and Spouses

#### (1) [§5.134] Actual Authority

A person with common authority over premises may validly consent to their search. *U.S. v Matlock* (1974) 415 US 164, 170, 94 S Ct 988, 39 L Ed 2d 242 (consent to search rented room by woman who told police that she and defendant occupied it together); *People v Wilkins* (1993) 14 CA4th 761, 775, 17 CR2d 743 (consent by cotenant); *People v Hamilton* (1985) 168 CA3d 1058, 1067, 214 CR 596 (consent by tenant of apartment to search it for a guest); *People v Haskett* (1982) 30 C3d 841, 855, 180 CR 640 (consent by wife whose husband had been arrested to search their residence).

Similarly, joint users of personal property may validly consent to its search. *Frazier v Cupp* (1969) 394 US 731, 740, 89 S Ct 1420, 22 L Ed 2d 684 (joint user of duffel bag); *People v Nelson* (1985) 166 CA3d 1209, 1214, 212 CR 799 (nonowner permissive driver of car and absent owner both have authority to consent to vehicle search).

A spouse's consent is effective even when the defendant-spouse refuses to consent. *People v Haskett, supra.* The consent of one co-resident on the premises suffices, whether or not defendant's consent was sought or refused. See *People v Haskett, supra*; *People v Redmond* (1981) 29 C3d 904, 908, 176 CR 780.

Consent by an *absent* cotenant is valid, at least when there is no express objection by a cotenant who is present at the premises. *People v Veiga* (1989) 214 CA3d 817, 827, 262 CR 919; see *People v Haskett, supra*; *Tompkins v Superior Court* (1963) 59 C2d 65, 69, 27 CR 889. *Tompkins* invalidated the consent when there was such an objection, no prior warning by the police, and no emergency. *Veiga* leaves the effect of an objection undecided, but suggests that it has no relevance to the validity of the consent. 214 CA3d at 829. When both occupants are present, consent may be valid even if one of them objects, at least as long as the person giving the consent does not know of the objection. See *People v Oldham* (2000) 81 CA4th 1, 7, 96 CR2d 343.

### (2) [§5.135] Apparent Authority

Illustrations of apparent authority include:

- Consent of a wife to search the family residence that she had left three weeks earlier. She had moved into a battered women's shelter, taking most of her belongings with her. The police knew these facts. *People v Bishop* (1996) 44 CA4th 220, 236–239, 51 CR2d 629 (murder prosecution); see *Illinois v Rodriguez* (1990) 497 US 177, 182, 110 S Ct 2793, 111 L Ed 2d 148 (former cotenant who had moved out lacks actual authority but may have apparent authority).

- Consent by defendant's sister to search his briefcase. The police had come to her residence and asked her whether it contained any property belonging to her brother. She said there was a briefcase belonging to him, handed it to an officer, and consented to a search of the residence. *People v Jenkins* (2000) 22 C4th 900, 969–980, 95 CR2d 377 (apparent authority to consent to search of personal property located on premises of person consenting may be found on the basis of access and control rather than mutual use; death penalty case). But see *U.S. v Basinski* (7th Cir 2000) 226 F3d 829, 834–836; *U.S. v Welch* (9th Cir 1993) 4 F3d 761, 764–765; *U.S. v Salinas-Cano* (10th Cir 1992) 959 F2d 861, 865.

- Consent by the tenant of an apartment to search a closet in which the defendant, the tenant's nephew, kept his belongings. The tenant had invited defendant to stay at his place temporarily. *People v McClelland* (1982) 136 CA3d 503, 506, 186 CR 365.

- Consent by the occupant of a hotel room (not the defendant) to search the room under the following circumstances. The police had gone to the hotel to talk to defendant. The desk clerk told the officers that defendant was a registered guest and had been living in several different rooms. The clerk gave them the room numbers. The officers went to one of those rooms and obtained consent from the only person in it, a man who was lying on the bed. *People v Parker* (1975) 45 CA3d 24, 30, 119 CR 49.

### (3) [§5.136] No Authority

There is no actual or apparent authority to consent to the search of personal property as to which there is no joint possession or control, and common authority over personal property may not be implied from a proprietary interest in the premises. *In re Scott K.* (1979) 24 C3d 395, 404–405, 155 CR 671.

A driver who tells the police that suitcases in the trunk belong to a passenger lacks actual or apparent authority to consent to a search of the luggage. *U.S. v Jaras* (5th Cir 1996) 86 F3d 383, 384. Such a statement by the driver denies joint access and control over the property. *People v Jenkins* (2000) 22 C4th 900, 980, 95 CR2d 377.

The fact that the person giving consent answered the door and appeared to be alone in the apartment is insufficient to show actual or apparent authority to consent, especially when the officers did not even ask the person whether he lived there. *U.S. v Reid* (9th Cir 2000) 226 F3d 1020, 1025–1026.

#### c. Parents and Children

##### (1) [§5.137] Consent by Parent

Parents generally have authority to permit a search of a room in their house occupied by their child, even an adult child, unless the child has exclusive control over the room. *People v Oldham* (2000) 81 CA4th 1, 10, 96 CR2d 343; *People v Daniels* (1971) 16 CA3d 36, 44, 93 CR 628. In *Oldham,* the son, apparently an adult who stayed in his parents' residence from time to time, objected to the search prior to his father's consent but not at the time the father consented. 81 CA4th at 7. The court held that the father had apparent authority to consent. 81 CA4th at 10.

Authority to consent is not unlimited. A parent has no actual or apparent authority to permit a search of their son's locked toolbox (*In re Scott K.* (1979) 24 C3d 395, 404, 155 CR 671 (no joint possession or control)) or suitcase (*People v Daniels, supra*); see *People v Oldham, supra,* 81 CA4th at 16.

##### (2) [§5.138] Consent by Child

Children generally lack actual or apparent authority to allow the police into the family residence. *People v Jacobs* (1987) 43 C3d 472, 481, 233 CR 323 (11-year-old). Parents' privacy is not subject to the discretion of their children. 43 C3d at 482.

The *Jacobs* rule has exceptions. Two are suggested in *Jacobs*: consent by teenagers and consent in emergency situations. A 16-year-old has apparent authority to consent. *People v Hoxter* (1999) 75 CA4th 406, 411–413, 89 CR2d 259. Other exceptions are:

- A child's initiation of the events that lead to the investigation and to the child's consent. *People v Santiago* (1997) 55 CA4th 1540,

1543, 64 CR2d 794 (12-year-old complained to neighbor of child abuse).

- Consent related to the minor's own conduct. *In re Robert H.* (1978) 78 CA3d 894, 899, 144 CR 565 (police acted on information that minor had stolen motorcycles; his consent was upheld).

#### d. [§5.139] Real Estate Agents

A real estate agent holding an open house may consent to the entry of persons the agent believes to be possible buyers, but has no actual or apparent authority to permit others, such as the police, to enter. *People v Jaquez* (1985) 163 CA3d 918, 927, 209 CR 852.

#### e. [§5.140] Bailees

A bailee's authority to consent "depends upon whether the nature of the bailment is such that the bailor has assumed the risk [that the bailee would let the police examine the property] [citation]. Crucial factors are the extent to which the bailor has surrendered control and the length of the bailment." *In re Javier A.* (1984) 159 CA3d 913, 924, 206 CR 386 (apartment resident has at least apparent authority to show officers photo album belonging to another person who had temporarily stayed there).

In *People v Pranke* (1970) 12 CA3d 935, 942, 91 CR 129, defendant left some property at the apartment of a former neighbor while defendant was moving. The court found that defendant had made no efforts to restrict the ex-neighbor's "rights as a citizen to cooperate with the authorities" and upheld the neighbor's consent to search the property.

## VI. PROBATION AND PAROLE SEARCHES

### A. [§5.141] Validity in Absence of Individualized Suspicion

A warrantless search under a search condition imposed on a probationer or parolee does not require reasonable grounds to suspect that the person searched has violated the law or possesses evidence of a crime. *People v Reyes* (1998) 19 C4th 743, 751, 80 CR2d 734 (parolee), overruling *People v Burgener* (1986) 41 C3d 505, 224 CR 112; *In re Tyrell J.* (1994) 8 C4th 68, 83, 32 CR2d 33 (juvenile probationer); *People v Bravo* (1987) 43 C3d 600, 609, 238 CR 282 (adult probationer). See *Griffin v Wisconsin* (1987) 483 US 868, 871, 107 S Ct 3164, 97 L Ed 2d 709 (search of probationer's home must be reasonable; court did reach question whether reasonableness in this context requires particularized suspicion).

## B. Nature and Validity of Search Conditions

### 1. [§5.142] Nature

Search clauses in probation and parole release orders typically specify that the defendant, any property under the defendant's control, and defendant's residence may be searched without a warrant at any time by any law enforcement officer. See, *e.g., People v Reyes* (1998) 19 C4th 743, 746, 80 CR2d 734; *People v Lewis* (1999) 74 CA4th 662, 666 n1, 88 CR2d 231. Judges may limit the breadth of a probationer's search condition. See §5.150.

### 2. Validity

#### a. [§5.143] Parolees

Search conditions are valid for parolees. *People v Burgener* (1986) 41 C3d 505, 532, 224 CR 112, overruled on other grounds in 19 C4th 743, 756. This principle covers parolees from state prison (*People v Burgener, supra*), the California Rehabilitation Center (*People v Guerrero* (1978) 85 CA3d 572, 581, 149 CR 555; *People v Howard* (1978) 79 CA3d 46, 49, 143 CR 342), and the California Youth Authority (*People v Anglin* (1971) 18 CA3d 92, 95, 95 CR 588).

#### b. [§5.144] Probationers

Courts disagree whether a search condition is valid only if it is reasonably related to the probationer's offense. Yes: *People v Burton* (1981) 117 CA3d 382, 390–391, 172 CR 632 (invalid as to defendant convicted of assault with a deadly weapon who had not concealed weapon before committing offense and had no history of using concealed weapons); *People v Mayers* (1980) 110 CA3d 809, 816, 168 CR 252 (not reasonable as to defendant convicted of running three-card monte game); *People v Keller* (1978) 76 CA3d 827, 833, 143 CR 184 (invalid as to defendant convicted of petty theft). No: *People v Balestra* (1999) 76 CA4th 57, 67, 90 CR2d 77 (elder abuse; court said that probation search conditions are always intended to ensure that probationer obeys laws and are, therefore, rehabilitative). See also Pen C §1203.1(j) (court may impose reasonable conditions "generally and specifically for the reformation and rehabilitation of the probationer").

#### c. [§5.145] O.R. Release Orders

Search conditions in O.R. release orders are valid if the court makes an "individualized determination" of their reasonableness based on the specific facts and circumstances of a defendant's case. *In re York* (1995) 9 C4th 1133, 1139, 40 CR2d 308.

#### d. [§5.146] Deferred Entry of Judgment/Diversion

The statutes permitting courts to defer entry of judgment following a guilty plea by certain first time drug offender (Pen C §§1000–1000.8) do not authorize imposition of a search condition. *Terry v Superior Court* (1999) 73 CA4th 661, 666, 86 CR2d 653; see *People v Fleming* (1994) 22 CA4th 1566, 1569, 28 CR2d 78 (reaching same conclusion under predecessor drug diversion statute "with considerable misgivings"). The court may, however, impose a drug testing condition. *Terry v Superior Court, supra.*

The corresponding deferred entry of judgment statutes for certain child abuse and neglect cases (Pen C §§1000.12–1000.17) *mandate* the imposition of a search condition. Pen C §1000.12(c)(4)(D).

The misdemeanor pretrial diversion statutes (Pen C §§1001–1001.9) do not include a provision that authorizes search conditions.

#### e. [§5.147] Reliance on Invalid Search Condition

A search based on an invalid search condition is lawful if the police in good faith relied on a facially valid condition. *People v Fleming* (1994) 22 CA4th 1566, 1573, 28 CR2d 78; see §1.38.

## C. Scope of Search

### 1. [§5.148] Limited by Scope of Search Condition

A search under a search condition may not exceed the scope of the condition. *People v Woods* (1999) 21 C4th 668, 682, 88 CR2d 88; *People v Bravo* (1987) 43 C3d 600, 605, 238 CR 282. For example, a search clause for narcotics and drugs does not authorize a search for stolen property. *People v Howard* (1984) 162 CA3d 8, 19, 208 CR 353.

### 2. [§5.149] Construction of Search Conditions

Most search clauses are broad. See §5.142. They are interpreted on the basis of what a reasonable person would understand from the language of the search condition itself, not narrowly on the basis of defendant's subjective understanding. *People v Bravo* (1987) 43 C3d 600, 606, 238 CR 282. Examples include:

- A clause that authorizes search of a probationer's residence extends to a residence occupied by the probationer and others and all areas within it under the full or joint control of the probationer. *People v Woods* (1999) 21 C4th 668, 682, 88 CR2d 88.

- A clause that authorizes search of a probationer's person and property also authorizes a search of his or her residence. *Russi v Superior Court* (1973) 33 CA3d 160, 166, 108 CR 716.
- A provision in a juvenile probationer's home supervision agreement giving the probation officer "access to the minor" permits the probation officer to enter the minor's home, but not to search it. *In re Curtis T.* (1989) 214 CA3d 1391, 1394, 263 CR 296.
- A clause that authorizes a search for narcotics and dangerous drugs does not authorize a search for stolen property. *People v Howard* (1984) 162 CA3d 8, 19, 208 CR 353.

A search condition imposed by a court in another state is interpreted under California law when the challenged search took place in California. *People v Reed* (1994) 23 CA4th 135, 143, 28 CR2d 509.

### 3. [§5.150] Authority To Limit Search Conditions

Judges have authority to limit the conditions under which a probationer may be searched, for example, by requiring reasonable cause for a search (see *People v Bravo* (1987) 43 C3d 600, 608, 238 CR 282) or notice (*People v Mason* (1971) 5 C3d 759, 763, 97 CR 302, disapproved on other grounds in 15 C3d 481, 486 n1) or by restricting the operation of the clause to a particular category of objects. *People v Howard* (1984) 162 CA3d 8, 19, 208 CR 353 (narcotics and dangerous drugs).

In the absence of expressly mandating notice, a search under a search condition does not require notice. *People v Lilienthal* (1978) 22 C3d 891, 900, 150 CR 910. But a search clause does not excuse compliance with knock-notice requirements. *People v Constancio* (1974) 42 CA3d 533, 544, 116 CR 910.

## D. [§5.151] Change of Probationary Status

Reversal of the underlying conviction after a probation search does not render the search invalid. *People v Fields* (1981) 119 CA3d 386, 388, 174 CR 49.

Summary revocation does not itself terminate probation or its conditions. *People v Barkins* (1978) 81 CA3d 30, 33, 145 CR 926; *People v Pipitone* (1984) 152 CA3d 1112, 1117, 201 CR 18. A probation search following a restoration of probation is valid if probation was restored with no change in the terms of the original probation and those terms included a search condition. *People v Pipitone, supra.* However, when probation is restored on new terms that do not include a search clause, a subsequent probation search is invalid. *Freytes v Superior Court* (1976) 60 CA3d 958, 962–963, 132 CR 26.

### E. [§5.152] Use of Search Condition as Pretext

A search clause that authorizes the search of a probationer's residence may lawfully be used as a pretext to search for incriminating evidence against a co-resident. *People v Woods* (1999) 21 C4th 668, 676–681, 88 CR2d 88. For limitations, see §5.153.

### F. [§5.153] Arbitrary or Harassing Searches

A search under a search condition may not be "arbitrary, capricious or harassing." *People v Reyes* (1998) 19 C4th 743, 752, 80 CR2d 734; see *People v Woods* (1999) 21 C4th 668, 682, 88 CR2d 88; *In re Tyrell J.* (1994) 8 C4th 68, 87, 32 CR2d 33. Evidence of numerous fruitless warrantless searches of the defendant in the months preceding the search in question is relevant to the issue of harassment. *People v Clower* (1993) 16 CA4th 1737, 1741, 21 CR2d 38.

Use of a search condition as a pretext to look for evidence against a joint occupant does not make the search arbitrary or unreasonable (*People v Woods, supra*), unless the police did not know of the search condition at the time (see §5.154), or the search is so intrusive that the cotenant cannot reasonably be said to have contemplated its occurrence. See *People v Haskett* (1982) 30 C3d 841, 857, 180 CR 640, cited with approval by *Woods* at 682.

Absence of suspicion does not make a search under a search condition arbitrary or capricious. *In re Tyrell J., supra.*

### G. Police Information Concerning Search Condition

#### 1. [§5.154] Lack of Information

Evidence from an otherwise unlawful search of a probationer or parolee is admissible against that person if he or she was subject to a search condition at the time of which the police were unaware. *In re Tyrell J.* (1994) 8 C4th 68, 83–90, 32 CR2d 33 (juvenile probationer); *People v Viers* (1991) 1 CA4th 990, 993, 2 CR2d 667 (adult probationer). But an unknown search clause does not make evidence from an otherwise unlawful residential search admissible against a co-resident of a probationer or parolee. *People v Robles* (2000) 23 C4th 789, 799, 97 CR2d 914 ("cohabitants need not anticipate that officers with no knowledge of the probationer's existence or search condition may freely invade their residence in the absence of a warrant or exigent circumstances").

### 2. [§5.155] Erroneous Information

Searches based on erroneous information that defendant is subject to a search condition are lawful if the mistake originated with a probation officer, but not if it originated with the police. See §1.40.

A police officer is entitled to rely on defendant's erroneous statement that he or she is subject to search. *In re Jeremy G.* (1998) 65 CA4th 553, 555, 76 CR2d 585.

### H. [§5.156] Detention of Others During Search

The police may briefly detain other persons during a residential probation search. *People v Matelski* (2000) 82 CA4th 837, 846–853, 98 CR2d 543 (holding lawful 15-minute detention of persons to ascertain whether probationer was violating probation by associating with convicted felons).

## VII. SEARCHES BY SCHOOL AUTHORITIES

### A. [§5.157] Basic Principles

The Fourth Amendment applies to searches by school authorities, but the warrant requirement does not. Moreover, such searches can be conducted on less than probable cause. *New Jersey v T.L.O.* (1985) 469 US 325, 341, 105 S Ct 733, 83 L Ed 2d 720; *In re William G.* (1985) 40 C3d 550, 558–566, 221 CR 118.

*New Jersey v T.L.O.* specified two conditions for a valid search by teachers or school officials. The first concerns the grounds for the search, the second its scope:

(1) At the inception of the search, the school authorities must have "reasonable grounds for suspecting that the student has violated or is violating either the law or the rules of the school." For exceptions, see §5.160.

(2) The search is "permissible in its scope when the measures adopted are reasonably related to the objectives of the search and not excessively intrusive in light of the age and sex of the student and the nature of the infraction." 469 US at 342.

A third condition is that the underlying detention of the pupil must be valid. *In re Frederick B.* (1987) 192 CA3d 79, 84, 237 CR 338, disapproved on other grounds in 26 C4th 556, 567 n2. For discussion of *detentions* by school authorities, see §3.94.

School officials need not give a *Miranda* warning before questioning or searching a student. *In re Corey L.* (1988) 203 CA3d 1020, 1023, 250 CR 359.

### B. [§5.158] Illustrative Applications

(1) *The smoking student.* A teacher discovers a student smoking in a lavatory in violation of school rules. The teacher takes her to the vice principal, but the student denies having smoked. The vice principal takes her purse, opens it, finds a package of cigarettes, sees cigarette rolling papers, examines the purse more thoroughly, and finds a small amount of marijuana as well as evidence that the pupil had been selling marijuana. Subsequently, the student confesses to selling. The items from her purse and her confession are admissible in delinquency proceedings in juvenile court; the search is valid. *New Jersey v T.L.O.* (1985) 469 US 325, 343–347, 105 S Ct 733, 83 L Ed 2d 720.

(2) *The student with the calculator case.* A vice principal of a high school sees two students walking across campus at 1:10 p.m. One is carrying a vinyl calculator case that the vice principal thinks has an unusual bulge and at which the students are looking. The vice principal stops them, inquires why they are late for class, and sees that the student with the case puts it in a palmlike gesture to his side and then behind his back. The vice principal searches the case and discovers marijuana in it. The student is not late for class; he has no classes after 12:00 p.m. The search is invalid because the vice principal had no prior information the student was engaging in illegal activities, and furtive gestures alone do not provide sufficient cause to search. *In re William G.* (1985) 40 C3d 550, 566, 221 CR 118.

*William G.,* a pre-Proposition 8 case, developed a standard for school authority searches that is essentially the same as that formulated by *New Jersey v T.L.O., supra.* Some judges believe that the application of the standard might produce a different result today in a situation similar to *William G.*. In any event, the outcome is very different when a school official has information that a student possesses contraband or a weapon. See *In re Joseph G.* (1995) 32 CA4th 1735, 1740–1742, 38 CR2d 902, discussed below; *In re Alexander B.* (1990) 220 CA3d 1572, 1577, 270 CR 342, disapproved on other grounds in 26 C4th 556, 567 n2.

(3) *The armed student.* A parent calls the vice principal and reports that her son had seen a fellow student with a pistol five days earlier. On the day after the call, the vice principal searches the student's locker, but no weapon is found. A few hours later, he sees the student putting a backpack in the locker and searches again and finds a loaded handgun. Both searches are valid. They rested on information from a citizen infor-

mant, the information was not stale as a matter of law, and there was adequate cause for the second search. *In re Joseph G., supra.*

## C. Additional Issues

### 1. [§5.159] Application of Exclusionary Rule

*New Jersey v T.L.O.* (1985) 469 US 325, 327–328, 105 S Ct 733, 83 L Ed 2d 720, expressly left open the question whether the exclusionary rule applies to the fruits of unlawful searches by school authorities. The court said it did not have to decide that question because it found the particular search to be lawful. *In re William G.* (1985) 40 C3d 550, 567 n17, 221 CR 118, held that the exclusionary rule is the only appropriate remedy when the evidence is sought to be admitted in a juvenile or criminal prosecution.

The exclusionary rule is inapplicable to school disciplinary proceedings. *Gordon J. v Santa Ana Unified Sch. Dist.* (1984) 162 CA3d 530, 531, 208 CR 657.

### 2. [§5.160] Individual Suspicion

*New Jersey v T.L.O.* (1985) 469 US 325, 342 n8, 105 S Ct 733, 83 L Ed 2d 720, also explicitly left open the question "whether individualized suspicion is an essential element of the reasonableness standard we adopt for searches by school authorities." But the court observed (469 US at 342 n8):

> Exceptions to the requirement of individualized suspicion are generally appropriate only where the privacy interests implicated by a search are minimal and where "other safeguards" are available "to assure that the individual's reasonable expectation of privacy is not 'subject to the discretion of the official in the field.' " [Citations.]

Absence of suspicion focused on a particular student was held not to invalidate a search for weapons when one minor pointed to a group of five or six others and told the dean of students: "Don't pick on us; one of those guys has a gun." *In re Alexander B.* (1990) 220 CA3d 1572, 1576, 1577, 270 CR 342, disapproved on other grounds in 26 C4th 556, 567 n2. School officials and police assisting them need not articulate individual suspicion to detain an outsider to determine whether the detainee has a right to be present in the school. *In re Joseph F.* (2000) 85 CA4th 975, 986, 102 CR2d 641.

Despite the absence of individualized suspicion, random drug testing of student athletes is lawful. *Vernonia Sch. Dist. 47J v Acton* (1995) 515 US 646, 664, 115 S Ct 2386, 132 L Ed 2d 564. Similarly, random metal detector weapon searches of high school students are constitutional. *In re Latasha W.* (1998) 60 CA4th 1524, 1527, 70 CR2d 886.

On testing of school *employees,* see, *e.g., United Teachers of New Orleans v Orleans Parish Sch. Bd.* (5th Cir 1998) 142 F3d 853, 856 (school board cannot require injured employees to provide urine samples); *Aubrey v School Bd. of Lafayette Parish* (5th Cir 1996) 92 F3d 316, 319 (random urinalysis requirement can be applied only to employees in safety-sensitive positions).

# 6

# Handling Penal Code §1538.5 Motions

## I. [§6.1] SCOPE OF CHAPTER

Sections 6.2–6.4 discuss the purposes and main features of Pen C §1538.5, followed in §§6.5–6.27 by a discussion of what motions come within the statute and must be made under Pen C §1538.5 or not at all. The topic of "standing"—the condition that the challenged search or seizure violated the defendant's own reasonable expectations of privacy and not those of another person—is considered in §§6.28–6.41.

The time and manner of making motions, especially the requirements of notice, are discussed in §§6.42–6.53, particular motions in §§6.54–6.99, and issues related to the hearing in §§6.100–6.131. Appellate review is covered in §§6.132–6.142, and proceedings related to Pen C §1538.5 proceedings, such as suppression motions in juvenile court, suppression issues litigated by nonparties under Pen C §1524(c), and motions for the return of property, in §§6.143–6.159.

## II. PURPOSES AND PRINCIPAL FEATURES OF STATUTE

### A. [§6.2] Purposes

The enactment of Pen C §1538.5 was chiefly

> aimed at redressing defects identified in the previously existing procedures: (i) the unnecessary expenditure of time and effort in allowing repeated challenges to the legality of a search or seizure during the course of a criminal proceeding; (ii) the waste of jury time in permitting search and seizure questions to be raised during trial, since the determination of these issues takes place outside the presence of the jury; and (iii) the lack of adequate opportunity for the prosecution to obtain appellate review of an adverse decision on a search and seizure question before trial commences and jeopardy attaches. [Citations.]

*People v Brooks* (1980) 26 C3d 471, 475–476, 162 CR 177; *People v Sherwin* (2000) 82 CA4th 1404, 1409, 98 CR2d 888. The principal objective is to require a defendant to raise search and seizure issues early. See *People v Cagle* (1971) 21 CA3d 57, 60, 98 CR 348.

### B. [§6.3] Principal Features

Penal Code §1538.5 "provides a comprehensive and exclusive procedure for the final determination of search and seizure issues prior to trial." *People v Brooks* (1980) 26 C3d 471, 475, 162 CR 177. The main features of the procedure in felony cases are as follows:

- The defendant may make a motion to suppress under Pen C §1538.5 at the preliminary hearing by giving written notice. Pen C §1538.5(f). The motion is restricted to evidence that the prosecution offered at the preliminary hearing. Pen C §1538.5(f)(1). For discussion, see §§6.54–6.59.
- The defendant may make a suppression motion after the filing of the information. Pen C §1538.5(i). The defendant is entitled to a full evidentiary hearing, unless a motion was also made at the preliminary hearing, in which event the evidence is limited to the preliminary hearing transcript, evidence that could not have been produced at the preliminary hearing, and witnesses recalled by the prosecution. Pen C §1538.5(i); for discussion, see §§6.60–6.76.
- "The defendant is not entitled to renew his pretrial motion to suppress at trial and, subject to a narrowly circumscribed exception (subd. (h)), he is not permitted to raise search and seizure issues for the first time at trial." *People v Brooks, supra*, 26 C3d at 476. For discussion, see §§6.77–6.84.
- Penal Code §1538.5 does not affect the substantive law, including the law of standing to raise a Fourth Amendment issue. Pen C §1538.5(n).

### C. [§6.4] Exclusive Remedy

Penal Code §1538.5, when applicable, provides "the sole and exclusive remedy" for a defendant to seek suppression of evidence on Fourth Amendment grounds. Pen C §1538.5(m); *People v Brooks* (1980) 26 C3d 471, 475, 162 CR 177. Under Pen C §1538.5(m), the court must deny untimely and nonstatutory suppression motions. *People v Takencareof* (1981) 119 CA3d 492, 496, 174 CR 112; *People v Harris* (1974) 39 CA3d 965, 970, 114 CR 892.

Penal Code §1538.5 does not apply to claims that the Fourth Amendment was violated unless the claim is made in a criminal case as the basis for suppressing evidence or returning property. Pen C §1538.5(a). Examples of matters not covered by Pen C §1538.5 include motions to set aside an indictment or information under Pen C §995 (see Pen C

§1538.5(m)), postarrest determinations of probable cause (see §§4.95–4.102), Fourth Amendment issues litigated by a nonparty under Pen C §1524(c) (see §§6.144–6.147), civil litigation, juvenile court proceedings (see §6.7), and administrative proceedings (see §6.9).

## III. WHAT MOTIONS COME WITHIN PENAL CODE §1538.5

### A. [§6.5] Overview

A suppression motion under Pen C §1538.5 can be made only

(1) by a defendant in a criminal case,

(2) who seeks to exclude evidence

(3) that the prosecution offers at the defendant's preliminary hearing or may offer at trial,

(4) on the ground that the evidence was obtained in violation of the Fourth Amendment. Pen C §1538.5(a), (f)–(i); for discussion, see §§6.6–6.27.

### B. Statute May Be Invoked Only by Criminal Defendant

#### 1. [§6.6] Uncharged Persons

Penal Code §1538.5 may be invoked only by a defendant in a criminal case. *Goldin v PUC* (1979) 23 C3d 638, 668, 153 CR 802; Pen C §1538.5(a). Persons whose property has been seized but who have not been charged may seek its return under other statutory provisions. For discussion, see §§6.144–6.147, 6.152–6.155.

#### 2. [§6.7] Juvenile Offenders

Juvenile courts have their own statutory suppression procedure; Pen C §1538.5 is inapplicable. Welf & I C §700.1; *In re Michael V.* (1986) 178 CA3d 159, 169, 223 CR 503; *In re David G.* (1979) 93 CA3d 247, 252, 155 CR 500. For further discussion, see §6.143. The exclusionary rule does not apply to dependency (as distinguished from delinquency) proceedings. *In re Robert P.* (1976) 61 CA3d 310, 320, 132 CR 5.

#### 3. [§6.8] Party to Civil Proceeding

Neither Pen C §1538.5 nor the exclusionary rule apply to actions that are purely civil, such as a conservatorship proceeding. The exclusionary rule, however, but not Pen C §1538.5, applies to quasi-criminal proceedings, such as narcotics commitment proceedings. *People v Bourdon* (1970) 10 CA3d 878, 882, 89 CR 415. See §1.23.

If the exclusionary rule is invoked, the court should determine, outside the presence of the jury, whether the challenged evidence is admissible. 10 CA3d at 882.

#### 4. [§6.9] Party to Administrative Proceeding

Penal Code §1538.5 does not apply in administrative hearings even when the exclusionary rule does. *Goldin v P.U.C.* (1979) 23 C3d 638, 668, 153 CR 802.

### C. Motion Must Seek To Exclude Evidence

#### 1. [§6.10] Motion To Disclose Informant

Penal Code §1538.5 covers only motions to return property or to exclude evidence. A motion to disclose an informant's identity does not come within the statute, even when the informant provided information that led to the search in issue. See *Honore v Superior Court* (1969) 70 C2d 162, 167 n5, 74 CR 233; *People v Martin* (1969) 2 CA3d 121, 125, 82 CR 414; Evid C §§1041–1042. For discussion of motions to disclose an informant, see California Criminal Law Procedure and Practice, chap 21 (5th ed 2000).

#### 2. [§6.11] Meaning of Evidence

Penal Code §1538.5 applies to all evidence, tangible and intangible, that the police assertedly obtained in violation of the Fourth Amendment. Pen C §1538.5(a). Intangible evidence includes the following:

- Observations by police officers. See, *e.g., People v Camacho* (2000) 23 C4th 824, 831, 98 CR2d 232; *Kirby v Superior Court* (1970) 8 CA3d 591, 595, 87 CR 577.
- Conversations overheard or recorded. *Lorenzana v Superior Court* (1973) 9 C3d 626, 637–640, 108 CR 585 (eavesdropping); *North v Superior Court* (1972) 8 C3d 301, 104 CR 833 (secret monitoring and tape recording of jail visit conversation).
- Witness testimony. *People v Superior Court* (Sosa) (1982) 31 C3d 883, 887, 185 CR 113.

In short, evidence is anything that a party offers at trial to prove or disprove a fact. See Evid C §140 and Law Revision Commission comment on the section.

### D. [§6.12] Posttrial Proceedings

Suppression issues cannot be relitigated or raised for the first time in posttrial hearings such as a motion for a new trial. Pen C §1538.5(m).

By its express terms, Pen C §1538.5 is a *pretrial* motion. Pen C §1538.5(f)–(g). Under limited circumstances it can be made at trial. Pen C §1538.5(m). For discussion of the use of evidence suppressed before trial under Pen C §1538.5 in posttrial sentencing and probation or parole revocation proceedings, see §§1.20–1.21.

## E. Grounds for Motion

### 1. Need To Make Fourth Amendment Claim

#### a. [§6.13] Basic Principle

Penal Code §1538.5 applies to motions for the return of property or, more commonly, for the suppression of evidence assertedly obtained in violation of the Fourth Amendment. Pen C §1538.5(a). The section is "restricted to Fourth Amendment issues" (*People v Avalos* (1996) 47 CA4th 1569, 1576, 55 CR2d 450; *People v Campa* (1984) 36 C3d 870, 885, 206 CR 114); it "does not provide for pretrial determination of rulings on evidentiary questions generally." *People v Rawlings* (1974) 42 CA3d 952, 956, 117 CR 651; *People v Pham* (1987) 189 CA3d 1531, 1534, 235 CR 99.

Penal Code §1538.5 applies to motions to quash a search warrant, for example, to claims that the warrant is insufficient on its face, lacks probable cause, or resulted in the seizure of evidence not described in the warrant, as well as to motions to traverse a search warrant, that is, to claims that the supporting affidavit contained fatal mistakes or omissions. Pen C §1538.5(a)(1); Caskey, Benchguide to California Search and Seizure Cases §I(A) (Specialized Legal Publications 2d ed 1995).

#### b. [§6.14] Procedure When Pen C §1538.5 Unavailable

The procedure for raising suppression issues not based on the Fourth Amendment is a common law motion to exclude or suppress evidence. *People v Superior Court* (Zolnay) (1975) 15 C3d 729, 734, 125 CR 798; *People v Temple* (1995) 36 CA4th 1219, 1223, 42 CR2d 888; see Evid C §402(b) (challenge to admission of confession heard outside presence of jury).

When a defendant mistakenly makes a Pen C §1538.5 motion instead of a common law motion, the trial court may treat it as a nonstatutory motion under Evid C §402. *People v Stansbury* (1993) 4 C4th 1017, 1049, 17 CR2d 174, rev'd on other grounds (1994) 511 US 318, 114 S Ct 1526, 128 L Ed 2d 293.

☛ **Judicial Tip**: Judges should not, however, treat the determination whether a defendant must utilize Pen C §1538.5 or a nonstatutory motion as a minor technicality. Important consequences flow from the determination. See §6.15.

### c. [§6.15] Consequences of Procedure Used

Different consequences follow from the procedure the defendant must use to challenge the admissibility of particular evidence. For example:

(1) When Pen C §1538.5 is available it is the exclusive remedy; failure to use it at the time and in the manner required by the section results in the admission of the evidence. See §6.4.

(2) Denial of a Pen C §1538.5 motion made after an information has been filed can be reviewed on appeal following a guilty plea. *People v Pettingill* (1978) 21 C3d 231, 235, 145 CR 861; Pen C §1538.5(m). See §6.135. But in the absence of a proper Pen C §1538.5 motion, a guilty plea forecloses appellate review of suppression issues. *People v DeVaughn* (1977) 18 C3d 889, 895, 135 CR 786; see *In re Ricardo C.* (1995) 37 CA4th 431, 435, 43 CR2d 585.

(3) The defendant cannot relitigate Pen C §1538.5 issues in a second trial, but can relitigate determinations made under Evid C §402(b). *People v Mattson* (1990) 50 C3d 826, 850–852, 268 CR 802.

## 2. Confessions and Admissions

### a. [§6.16] Products of Unlawful Detention or Arrest

Whether a challenge to the admissibility of a confession or admission comes within Pen C §1538.5 depends on the ground of the challenge. If the defendant claims that the confession or admission is the product of an unlawful detention or arrest, Pen C §1538.5 provides the only appropriate procedure because the defendant raises a Fourth Amendment issue. *People v Campa* (1984) 36 C3d 870, 885, 206 CR 114; *People v DeVaughn* (1977) 18 C3d 889, 896–897, 135 CR 786. But substantively, an unlawful arrest does not automatically invalidate ensuing statements. See *New York v Harris* (1990) 495 US 14, 18, 110 S Ct 1640, 109 L Ed 2d 13 (warrantless arrest in defendant's home unlawful, but subsequent statement at police station admissible if arrest based on probable cause; see §4.79).

### b. Other Statements

#### (1) [§6.17] Penal Code §1538.5 Unavailable

Penal Code §1538.5 may generally not be used to suppress admissions or confessions on grounds that they are the product of Fifth or Sixth Amendment violations. *People v Mattson* (1990) 50 C3d 826, 851, 268

CR 802; *People v Superior Court* (Zolnay) (1975) 15 C3d 729, 734, 125 CR 798 (Pen C §1538.5 "can be properly employed only to shield a defendant from Fourth Amendment violations; it has no part in protecting against Fifth Amendment infringements such as the one at hand"); *In re Ricardo C.* (1995) 37 CA4th 431, 435, 43 CR2d 585. For an exception, see §6.18.

Penal Code §1538.5 is not the proper vehicle for a *Miranda* challenge to questioning in the course of executing a valid search warrant (*People v Simpson* (1998) 65 CA4th 854, 856, 76 CR2d 851) or to litigate the contention that defendant's statement was obtained in violation of corpus delicti rules. *People v Saunders* (1994) 26 CA4th Supp 21, 24, 32 CR2d 195.

#### (2) [§6.18] Exception: Statement That Led to Other Evidence

Courts have long held that Pen C §1538.5 is the proper procedure to litigate dual contentions that defendant's statements were the product of unlawful interrogation and that the evidence defendant seeks to suppress is the product of these statements. *People v Superior Court* (Zolnay) (1975) 15 C3d 729, 735, 128 CR 798 ("Since admissibility of the evidence depended upon whether or not a *Miranda* violation had occurred, a ruling on the *Miranda* issue necessarily became part of the section 1538.5 hearing"); *People v Carter* (1980) 180 CA3d 127, 130, 166 CR 304 (*Miranda* determination "inextricably bound up" in resolution of search and seizure issues); see *People v Pettingill* (1978) 21 C3d 231, 237, 145 CR 861.

*People v Brewer* (2000) 81 CA4th 442, 453, 96 CR2d 786, states that this exception no longer exists as to noncoercive *Miranda* violations because as a matter of substantive law such violations do not result in the exclusion of evidence that flow from them.

## 3. Chemical Tests

### a. [§6.19] Penal Code §1538.5 Applicable

The heavy volume of drunk driving cases underscores the importance of understanding when Pen C §1538.5 must be invoked to challenge the admission of a chemical test. The basic principles concerning the applicability of Pen C §1538.5 in drunk driving cases are the same as govern motions to exclude confessions and are as follows:

- Penal Code §1538.5 applies when the defendant contends that the police lacked probable cause for arrest (*People v Deltoro* (1989) 214 CA3d 1417, 1419, 263 CR 305; *People v Trotman* (1989) 214 CA3d 430, 432, 262 CR 640) or that the chemical test violated the Fourth Amendment for other reasons. *People v Ford* (1992) 4 CA4th 32, 35, 5 CR2d 189; *People v Fiscalini* (1991) 228 CA3d 1639, 1642, 279 CR 682.

- When the chemical test followed an arrest based on an asserted *Miranda* violation, the Pen C §1538.5 motion is the proper procedure. *People v Carter* (1980) 108 CA3d 127, 130, 166 CR 304. Challenges to tests on due process grounds, *i.e.*, tests administered under brutal circumstances, probably come within Pen C §1538.5, at least when the challenge overlaps, as it often does, a Fourth Amendment claim. See *Carleton v Superior Court* (1985) 170 CA3d 1182, 1188, 216 CR 890.

#### b. Penal Code §1538.5 Inapplicable

##### (1) [§6.20] Denial of Choice of Tests

A denial of a choice of a blood, breath, or urine test in violation of Veh C §13353 violates due process rather than the Fourth Amendment, and Pen C §1538.5 is therefore inapplicable. *People v Superior Court* (Scott) (1980) 112 CA3d 602, 605, 169 CR 412; see *People v Fiscalini* (1991) 228 CA3d 1639, 1645 n7, 279 CR 682. Contra: *Nelson v City of Irvine* (9th Cir 1998) 143 F3d 1196, 1203.

A different result follows when the defendant supplied a proper sample and the police nevertheless insist on a different test: the second sample is the product of an unreasonable search in violation of the Fourth Amendment. *People v Fiscalini, supra.*

☛ **Judicial Tip**: When a Pen C §1538.5 motion combines Fourth Amendment and due process claims, the judge should dispose of them in a single hearing, but with a clear statement of the basis for the ruling.

##### (2) [§6.21] Other Claims

Penal Code §1538.5 is not available

- To challenge the administration of a breath test by an allegedly inadequately trained officer. *People v Rawlings* (1974) 42 CA3d 952, 956, 117 CR 651 (no search and seizure issue involved; question was not whether police could constitutionally administer test but only mechanical circumstances of its administration).

- To litigate a defendant's contention that a statement that violated corpus delicti principles led to the defendant's arrest and to the chemical test. The corpus delicti rule applies only to the admissibility of the statement at trial; it does not affect probable cause to arrest. *People v Saunders* (1994) 26 CA4th Supp 21, 24, 32 CR2d 195.

### 4. [§6.22] Racial Profiling

It is not clear whether Pen C §1538.5 is appropriate for challenging a search or seizure on the ground that the defendant was singled out because of his or her race. Such a contention rests on the Equal Protection Clause (*U.S. v Travis* (6th Cir 1995) 62 F3d 170, 173), but it could be argued that the discriminatory conduct violates defendant's reasonable expectation of privacy or invalidates any consent to search, thus implicating the Fourth Amendment.

☛ **Judicial Tip**: Pending appellate clarification, it may be wise to hear the motion on the merits regardless of defendant's choice of procedure.

### 5. [§6.23] Identification Evidence

Objections to identification evidence generally cannot be raised by a Pen C §1538.5 motion. *People v Stearns* (1973) 35 CA3d 304, 306, 110 CR 711 (claim of unfair lineup); *People v Vanbuskirk* (1976) 61 CA3d 395, 401, 132 CR 30 (claim that in-court identification was tainted by suggestive photo identification). Impermissibly suggestive lineups violate due process and are properly challenged by an *in limine* motion. See *People v Brandon* (1995) 32 CA4th 1033, 1050–1051, 38 CR2d 751.

But a contention that the identification is the consequence of an unlawful arrest raises Fourth Amendment issues and Pen C §1538.5 is the proper procedure. *People v Teresinski* (1982) 30 C3d 822, 833, 180 CR 617.

### 6. [§6.24] Searches by Private Citizens

The Fourth Amendment and its exclusionary rule generally do not apply to the actions of private individuals, subject to limited exceptions. See §§1.25–1.27. A criminal defendant who asserts an exception must raise the issue by a Pen C §1538.5 motion. See, *e.g., People v North* (1981) 29 C3d 509, 513, 174 CR 511; *People v Zelinski* (1979) 24 C3d 357, 360–362, 155 CR 575.

### 7. [§6.25] Lost or Destroyed Evidence

Exclusion of lost or destroyed evidence, such as suppression of a blood test result when the police destroyed the blood sample, does not rest on the Fourth Amendment but on due process grounds. *People v Hitch* (1974) 12 C3d 641, 645, 117 CR 9. Thus, a *Hitch* motion does not raise a question of unreasonable search and cannot be made in a Pen C §1538.5 proceeding (*People v Wakefield* (1987) 194 CA3d 67, 71, 239 CR 277; *People v Galan* (1985) 163 CA3d 786, 796, 209 CR 837), except when the lost evidence is essential to the decision of the suppression motion (*People v Swearingen* (1978) 84 CA3d 570, 572–574, 148 CR 755 (suppression issue turned on whether vial observed by officer and later lost was transparent or opaque)).

Substantively, loss or destruction of potentially exculpatory evidence by the police violates due process only if the police acted in bad faith. *Arizona v Youngblood* (1988) 488 US 51, 57, 109 S Ct 333, 102 L Ed 2d 281; *People v Huston* (1989) 210 CA3d 192, 213, 258 CR 393 (*Youngblood* probably retroactive).

#### 8. [§6.26] Possession of Contraband

A claim that the defendant did not possess the contraband in issue is not a ground for a Pen C §1538.5 motion. *People v Gale* (1973) 9 C3d 788, 793, 108 CR 852. This matter should be litigated by a motion under Pen C §995 or at trial. *People v Gale, supra.*

At a Pen C §1538.5 hearing, the only connection that need be shown between the evidence and the moving party is one sufficient to give the latter standing to make the motion. *People v Gale, supra.*

#### 9. [§6.27] Out-of-State Searches

Penal Code §1538.5 procedure applies to a criminal defendant's challenge to the lawfulness of a search that took place in another state. See *People v Blair* (1979) 25 C3d 640, 650, 159 CR 818. The search is lawful if it complied with the law of that state and with federal law. *People v Phillips* (1985) 41 C3d 29, 79, 222 CR 127; *People v Blair, supra*, 25 C3d at 654–657. But the outcome is uncertain if the search complied with California and federal law but not with the law of the other state. As to searches abroad, see *U.S. v Verdugo-Urquidez* (1990) 494 US 259, 274, 110 S Ct 1056, 108 L Ed 2d 222 (Fourth Amendment inapplicable to search and seizure by U.S. agents of property located abroad and owned by nonresident; result would be different if owner were U.S. citizen or resident).

## IV. "STANDING": DEFENDANT MAY ONLY CONTEST VIOLATION OF OWN RIGHTS

### A. [§6.28] Nature of Inquiry

Fourth Amendment rights are personal. *Minnesota v Carter* (1998) 525 US 83, 88, 119 S Ct 469, 142 L Ed 2d 373. A defendant may not successfully assert that the contested evidence stemmed solely from a violation of another person's rights. The "nature of the inquiry" is "whether the defendant, rather than someone else, had a reasonable expectation of privacy in the place searched or the items seized." *People v Ayala* (2000) 23 C4th 225, 254 n3, 96 CR2d 682; *Minnesota v Carter, supra,* 525 US at 88. Formerly, California had a broader rule that allowed defendants to contest evidence obtained in violation of another's Fourth Amendment rights. *People v Martin* (1955) 45 C2d 755, 761, 290 P2d 855. The *Martin* rule was abrogated by the adoption of Cal Const art I, §28(d) (Proposition 8). *In re Lance W.* (1985) 37 C3d 873, 885–891, 210 CR 631.

The inquiry as to whether a defendant has a reasonable expectation of privacy is one of substantive Fourth Amendment law rather than being a procedural matter. *Rawlings v Kentucky* (1980) 448 US 98, 104, 100 S Ct 2556, 65 L Ed 2d 633; *Rakas v Illinois* (1978) 439 US 128, 139–140, 99 S Ct 421, 58 L Ed 2d 387; *People v Ayala, supra,* 23 C4th at 255. Although courts have often referred to the inquiry as one of standing, such usage is disfavored. *People v Ayala, supra,* 23 C4th at 254 n3. For discussion of the burden of proof, see §§6.118–6.120.

### B. [§6.29] Factors

There is no set formula for determining whether the defendant rather than another person had a reasonable expectation of privacy in the place or object searched. *People v Koury* (1989) 214 CA3d 676, 686, 262 CR 870. Factors that the courts consider include whether the defendant

- Has a property or possessory interest in the place searched or the items seized;
- Has a right to exclude others from the place;
- Has exhibited a subjective expectation of privacy;
- Has taken normal precautions to maintain privacy; and
- Was legitimately on the premises. *People v Roybal* (1998) 19 C4th 481, 507, 79 CR2d 487; *People v Thompson* (1996) 43 CA3d 1265, 1269–1270, 51 CR2d 334; *People v Koury, supra.*

### C. Residential Premises

#### 1. [§6.30] Range of Privacy Expectations

A person may have a reasonable expectation of privacy in the residence of another. *Minnesota v Carter* (1998) 525 US 83, 89, 119 S Ct 469, 142 L Ed 2d 373; *Minnesota v Olson* (1990) 495 US 91, 95–100, 110

S Ct 1684, 109 L Ed 2d 85. The reasonableness of such privacy expectations varies. At one end of the range are overnight guests and baby-sitters whom the courts view as having a reasonable expectation of privacy in the premises. *Minnesota v Olson, supra* (overnight guest); *People v Hamilton* (1985) 168 CA3d 1058, 1064, 214 CR 596 (overnight guest); *People v Moreno* (1992) 2 CA4th 577, 584, 3 CR2d 66 (baby-sitter has even greater privacy expectation than overnight guest).

At the other end of the continuum are casual visitors without control over the premises, persons who are merely present legitimately and others whose presence is unlawful. *Minnesota v Carter, supra,* 525 US at 90–91; *People v Cowan* (1994) 31 CA4th 795, 798, 37 CR2d 469; *People v Koury* (1989) 214 CA3d 676, 690, 262 CR 870. An illustration of unlawful presence is a motel guest who uses a stolen credit card to register or who does not pay the room rent when it is due. *People v Satz* (1998) 61 CA4th 322, 325, 71 CR2d 433. Tenants, however, retain a reasonable expectation of privacy as to their personal possessions in their rooms or apartments until they are lawfully evicted. *People v Thompson* (1996) 43 CA4th 1265, 1270–1271, 51 CR2d 334 (restraining order requiring boarding house tenant who had his own room and key under rental agreement to stay away from premise does not destroy reasonable expectation of privacy).

The reasonableness of other persons' privacy expectations is between that of overnight guests and casual visitors and is determined by examining the particular circumstances. For example, in *Minnesota v Carter, supra,* defendants were packaging cocaine in an apartment with the permission of the tenant. In concluding that the visitors lacked a reasonable expectation of privacy in the premises, the court stressed that they came from out-of-state, had been in the apartment only 2 1/2 hours, and had never been there previously. The court did not base its conclusion on the defendant's illicit activity, but on the short-term commercial nature of their presence.

A repeat visitor to an apartment who neither stays overnight nor has permission to come and go on his own has no reasonable expectation of privacy. *People v Cowan, supra*; see also *People v Dimitrov* (1995) 33 CA4th 18, 27, 39 CR2d 257 (defendant could not contest apartment search when he testified he did not live there, had no key, and had no clothes or other possessions in the apartment).

### 2. [§6.31] Co-occupants

A co-occupant's reasonable expectation of privacy extends only to those portions of the residence to which he or she has legitimate access. *People v McPeters* (1992) 2 C4th 1148, 1172, 9 CR2d 834 (defendant who stayed in cousin's house failed to show legitimate access to cousin's bedroom); *People v Hernandez* (1988) 199 CA3d 1182, 1189, 245 CR 513 (temporary resident has no reasonable privacy expectation in bedroom he did not occupy and had no permission to enter).

A defendant may challenge the voluntariness of a co-occupant's consent to search the premises, but may not raise the issue of whether the consent was invalidated by the co-occupant's unlawful detention. *People v Llamas* (1991) 235 CA3d 441, 446–448, 286 CR 467. See *People v Jenkins* (2000) 22 C4th 900, 972–973, 95 CR2d 377 (court considered apparent authority of defendant's sister to consent; defendant was not a co-occupant). A joint occupant who was temporarily absent at the time of the search may challenge a knock-notice violation. *People v Hoag* (2000) 83 CA4th 1198, 1203–1206, 100 CR2d 556.

### 3. [§6.32] Reasonable Privacy Expectation in Objects Rather Than Premises

A defendant who lacks a reasonable expectation of privacy in the premises may have such an expectation in the item searched, so that he or she may object to the search. *People v Jenkins* (2000) 22 C4th 900, 972–973, 95 CR2d 377 (court assumes defendant has reasonable privacy expectation in his briefcase moved by sister to her house without his request; sister has apparent authority to consent to search of briefcase); *People v Ybarra* (1991) 233 CA3d 1353, 1361, 285 CR 200 (person who leaves padlocked toolbox in friend's motel room may challenge search of box); *People v Koury* (1989) 214 CA3d 676, 689, 262 CR 870 (casual visitor without reasonable privacy expectation in premises can nevertheless challenge search of his locked suitcase that he had brought to the premises).

An important factor in *People v Jenkins, supra,* was that the defendant had not asked his sister to take possession of the suitcase (she had taken it from his jeep after his arrest). Had defendant voluntarily relinquished control over the briefcase to his sister without instructions concerning safeguarding, he would usually no longer have a reasonable expectation of privacy in its contents. 22 C4th at 973 n10; *People v McPeters* (1992) 2 C4th 1148, 1172, 9 CR2d 834 (defendant who asks resident relative to hold his gun for him loses privacy expectation).

### 4. [§6.33] Privacy Expectation in Premises But Not in Items Searched or Seized

Courts state the requisite reasonable expectation of privacy in the alternative: the defendant must have a reasonable expectation of privacy in the place searched or the items seized. *People v Ayala* (2000) 23 C4th

between conspirators or being in charge of transportation has no bearing on Fourth Amendment rights); see *People v Workman* (1989) 209 CA3d 687, 696, 257 CR 753 (persons delivering documents to coconspirators have reasonable privacy expectation in them only on proof that they "retained an ownership or possessory interest in the documents after they were delivered" or had joint control over the premises from which the papers were seized).

## V. TIME AND MANNER OF MAKING MOTIONS

### A. Written Motion

#### 1. [§6.42] Basic Principles

A motion by the defendant under Pen C §1538.5 must be in writing and accompanied by a memorandum of points and authorities. Pen C §1538.5(a)(2). See Cal Rules of Ct 4.111 (written criminal pretrial motions). Before enactment of Pen C §1538.5(a)(2) and court consolidation, Pen C §1538.5 motions in lower courts were often oral, without written notice. See *Cox v Superior Court* (1993) 19 CA4th 1046, 1050, 23 CR2d 751 (local court rule requiring written suppression motion at preliminary hearing invalid); former Cal Rules of Ct 227.5 (predecessor of Rule 4.111 was expressly limited to superior courts); *People v Hansel* (1992) 1 C4th 1211, 1222, 4 CR2d 888. The statute does not specify whether a *prosecution* motion under Pen C §1538.5(j) must be in writing, but Cal Rules of Ct 4.111 imposes such a requirement.

#### 2. Specificity

##### a. [§6.43] Statutory Requirements

The memorandum of points and authorities accompanying a Pen C §1538.5 motion must set out (Pen C §1538.5(a)(2)):

- The specific items of property or evidence that the defendant seeks to suppress, and
- "[T]he factual basis, and
- The legal authorities that demonstrate why the motion should be granted."

Penal Code §1538.5(a)(2) begs the question of how specific the parties must be in specifying the precise grounds for the motion or the justification for the search or seizure. *People v Williams* (1999) 20 C4th 119, 135, 83 CR2d 275. For further discussion of specificity, see §§6.44–6.46.

### b. Case Law

#### (1) [§6.44] Burden of Raising Issue

In motions under Pen C §1538.5, the defendant has the burden of raising the issue he or she wants the court to decide, notwithstanding the fact that the prosecution may have the burden of proof on the particular issue, such as the burden to prove the lawfulness of a warrantless search. *People v Williams* (1999) 20 C4th 119, 128, 83 CR2d 275.

The burden of raising an issue means a party's obligation to bring it to the attention of the trial court and the opposing party, with the consequence that a party that fails to do so waives the right to raise the issue on appeal. The specificity requirement reflects the burden of raising an issue and "does not depend on the allocation of the burden of proof." *People v Williams, supra.*

#### (2) [§6.45] Warrantless Searches

In the event of a warrantless search or seizure, the defendant initially meets the burden of raising the issue by simply asserting the absence of a search or arrest warrant. *People v Williams* (1999) 20 C4th 119, 130, 83 CR2d 275 (defendant need not guess in advance what justification prosecution may offer for warrantless search). But when the defendant has an argument that is independent of the lack of a warrant, such as a knock-notice violation, the defendant must specify that contention in the moving papers. 20 C4th at 130.

In its reply papers the prosecution must offer its justification for the warrantless search or seizure, and defendant must then "present any arguments as to why that justification is inadequate." *People v Williams, supra,* 20 C4th at 130, 134; *Wilder v Superior Court* (1979) 92 CA3d 90, 96–97, 154 CR 494. For example, if the prosecution claims consent to search and the defendant asserts lack of authority to consent, the defendant may not contend for the first time on appeal that the search also exceeded the scope of consent. *People v Oldham* (2000) 81 CA4th 1, 13–15, 96 CR2d 343.

Although *Williams* requires the defendant to specify "the inadequacy of the prosecution's response" (20 C4th at 130), the court often does not learn of this specification before the hearing because Pen C §1538.5 does not require a reply memorandum by the defendant. See Pen C §1538.5(f), (i).

☛ **Judicial Tips**:

- The prosecution usually should not be permitted to assert a new justification in response to defendant's specification of inadequacy.

- Posthearing briefs are occasionally helpful in complex cases, but the judge needs to be on guard against attempts by any party to expand the issues.
- The court should clearly state what issues, if any, are not properly before the court. The absence of such a statement is likely to complicate subsequent proceedings, especially on appeal.

#### (3) [§6.46] Search Warrants

Penal Code §1538.5(a)(1)(B) lists the grounds for challenging search warrants and searches based on them; the defendant needs to specify and amplify the particular ground or grounds.

## B. Time for Filing Motion and Response

### 1. Felonies

#### a. [§6.47] Motion at Preliminary Hearing

Defendant must file and serve the motion at least five *court* days before the preliminary hearing; the motion must be "personally served on the people." Pen C §1538.5(f)(2).

Alternatively, the court may grant defendant a continuance of the preliminary hearing for the purpose of filing the motion upon a showing that the defendant was unaware of the evidence or the grounds for the motion before the hearing. In that event the motion is to be filed and served at least five court days before the resumed hearing. Pen C §1538.5(f)(2).

The prosecution's written response, if any, is to be filed and served personally on the defendant or his attorney at least two *court* days before the hearing. Pen C §1538.5(f)(3).

#### b. Motion After Filing of Information or Indictment

#### (1) [§6.48] 10-Day Notice

Defendant must file and serve the motion at least 10 *court* days before the hearing "unless the people are willing to waive a portion of this time." Pen C §1538.5(i). As to untimely notice, see §6.75(h).

Any prosecution response is to be filed and served personally on the defendant or his attorney at least two *court* days before the hearing, unless the defendant waives a portion of this time. Pen C §1538.5(i).

☛ **Judicial Tip**: The court should set a hearing date for any Pen C §1538.5 motion at defendant's arraignment on the information or indictment. See Cal Rules of Ct 4.100. The court should use the time frames of Pen C §1538.5(i), rather than the 10-5-2 calendar days scheme set forth in Rule 4.111; the rule by its terms applies "unless otherwise . . . specifically provided by law." Some judges find it useful to seek a stipulation that the parties will adhere to the time frames of Rule 4.111. One benefit is the increased likelihood of a reply memo by the defendant that may aid the court in pinpointing the issues early in the hearing.

#### (2) [§6.49] 60-Day Rule

The Pen C §1538.5(i) motion must be made not later than 60 days following defendant's arraignment on the information or indictment to preserve the right to pretrial appellate review, unless the defendant was unaware of the issue or had no opportunity to raise it. Pen C §1510. For further discussion, see §6.134.

☛ **Judicial Tip**: The judge should avoid setting the hearing close to the trial date to prevent last minute writs and delays, and also to encourage early disposition. See *People v Rodriguez* (1988) 199 CA3d 1453, 1459, 245 CR 617 (suppression motion denied on day of trial; writ proceedings still pending a year later).

#### c. [§6.50] Prosecution Motion

A prosecution motion ("request") to relitigate a ruling for the defendant on a Pen C §1538.5(f) motion must be made "upon the filing of an information . . . [and] within 15 days after the preliminary hearing." Pen C §1538.5(j). The 15-day requirement is jurisdictional: The court may not entertain a late request even if the defense does not object. *People v Lankford* (1976) 55 CA3d 203, 209, 127 CR 408.

The statute does not specify times for serving the motion and responses; Pen C §1538.5(a)(2) appears to deal only with defense motions.

☛ **Judicial Tip**: The court should set a hearing date for any Pen C §1538.5(j) motion at arraignment on the information. See Cal Rules of Ct 4.100. The court should order compliance with Cal Rules of Ct 4.111 (10-5-2 calendar days for service).

#### d. [§6.51] Motion During Trial

Penal Code §1538.5 and the Rules of Court do not require advance notice for a Pen C §1538.5 motion made during trial. See Pen C §1538.5(h), (j).

### 2. [§6.52] Misdemeanors

Penal Code §1538.5(g) provides that a suppression motion in a misdemeanor case must be made and heard before trial. The defendant must make the motion within 45 days after arraignment to preserve his or her right of pretrial appellate review. Pen C §1510.

Penal Code §1538.5 does not specify the notice periods for misdemeanor motions. Cal Rules of Ct 4.111 probably applies to require that the motion, accompanied by points and authorities, be served at least 10 *calendar* days, opposing papers at least 5 *calendar* days, and reply papers at least 2 *calendar* days before the hearing date. For discussions of motions during trial, see §6.51.

When a misdemeanor is charged with a felony, the felony procedure applies. Pen C §1538.5(g).

☛ **Judicial Tip**: Courts should not permit defendants to notice the motion for hearing just before the trial. Such a motion is a trial motion (see *People v Young* (1976) 62 CA3d 49, 51, 133 CR 22) and is permissible only under the limited circumstances provided in Pen C §1538.5(h).

### 3. [§6.53] Chart: Summary of Notice Requirements

| *Charge* | *Motion Under* | *Time* |
|---|---|---|
| Felony (and misdemeanor charged with felony) | Pen C §1538.5(f) | Motion—5 *court* days<br>Response—2 *court* days |
| | Pen C §1538.5(i) | Motion—10 *court* days<br>Response—2 *court* days |
| | Pen C §1538.5(j) | Probably:<br>Motion—10 *calendar* days<br>Opposition—5 *calendar* days<br>Reply—2 *calendar* days |
| | Pen C §1538.5(h) | Advance notice not required |
| Misdemeanor (other than misdemeanor charged with felony) | Pen C §1538.5(g) | Probably:<br>Motion—10 *calendar* days<br>Opposition—5 *calendar* days<br>Reply—2 *calendar* days |
| | Pen C §1538.5(h) | Advance notice not required |

# VI. MOTIONS IN FELONY CASES

## A. By Defendant

### 1. At Preliminary Hearing

#### a. [§6.54] Basic Principles

A defendant whose prosecution was initiated by complaint, rather than by indictment, may make a Pen C §1538.5 motion "at the preliminary hearing." Pen C §1538.5(f)(1). "At the preliminary hearing" means during the hearing. *People v Ciraco* (1986) 181 CA3d 1142, 1145, 226 CR 541. For discussion of notice, see §6.47.

Penal Code §1538.5(f) is permissive; the defendant may choose to make a suppression motion first after the filing of an information. See *People v Ramsey* (1988) 203 CA3d 671, 678, 250 CR 309; Pen C §1538.5(i).

A suppression motion at the preliminary hearing is "*restricted to evidence sought to be introduced by the people at the preliminary hearing.*" Pen C §1538.5(f)(1) (emphasis added).

#### b. [§6.55] Issues at Hearing

The procedural setting of a motion under Pen C §1538.5(f) may necessitate the resolution of several issues before reaching the merits, such as:

- What issues does the motion raise?
- Does the defendant have "standing" to raise them?
- What evidence does the motion challenge?
- Is the prosecution offering the evidence that the defendant seeks to suppress?
- What evidence at the preliminary hearing is relevant to whether the magistrate should hold defendant to answer? What evidence is relevant to the motion? To both? To neither?

☛ **Judicial Tips**:

(1) Read the motion papers before starting the hearing.

(2) Ascertain at the outset whether the parties agree what the issues are.

(3) Take thorough notes; suppression issues are often very fact-specific.

(4) Do not permit the prosecution to prevent a Pen C §1538.5 hearing by not offering physical evidence. Any evidence linking defendant to the charge(s) is subject to a suppression motion. See §6.11.

(5) Endeavor to resolve any disparities between the evidence identified

in the moving papers and the evidence at the hearing. Occasionally a workable resolution is to permit an amendment to conform.

(6) Take the motion under submission in case of any doubt.

#### c. [§6.56] Continuances

Penal Code §1538.5(f)(2) authorizes the court to grant the defendant a continuance to file a suppression motion. The statute requires a showing that the defendant was unaware of the evidence or the grounds for suppressing it. Delayed or skimpy discovery is the main ground for a continuance.

A continuance may also be necessary when the prosecution has not filed a reply memorandum (Pen C §1538.5(f) does not explicitly require such a memo) or when there is inadequate notice of defendant's motion.

☛ **Judicial Tip**: When the court grants a continuance, it should put over both the motion and the preliminary hearing to the same time and place. Otherwise the principle that the motion be heard at the preliminary hearing would be violated.

#### d. [§6.57] Findings

A magistrate's findings in ruling on a motion under Pen C §1538.5(f) will be upheld on appeal if supported by substantial evidence and are binding in a subsequent suppression hearing under Pen C §1538.5(i), subject to limitations. *People v Fulkman* (1991) 235 CA3d 555, 560, 286 CR 728; *People v Ramsey* (1988) 203 CA3d 671, 679, 250 CR 309; Pen C §1538.5(i). Express findings are not required; the findings to which the appellate courts and Pen C §1538.5(i) refer may be implicit. See *People v Bishop* (1993) 14 CA4th 203, 211, 17 CR2d 657; *People v Fulkman, supra*; Evid C §402(c) ("A ruling on the admissibility of evidence implies whatever finding of fact is prerequisite thereto; a separate or formal finding is unnecessary unless required by statute"). For limitations on implied findings, see §6.71.

☛ **Judicial Tip**: While trial judges differ on the general desirability of making express findings in Pen C §1538.5 hearings, explicit findings are particularly useful in some situations. One such situation arises when the court resolves a factual issue in favor of the defendant or leaves it undecided, but rules for the prosecution as a matter of law. For example, there may be conflicting testimony about how long the police waited after knocking before breaking down the door. The magistrate accepts the defense version, but concludes that the police waited long enough. Or the magistrate says (or thinks): "Even if the time interval was as short as the defense testimony indicates, it was long enough under the circumstances." In either case, in the absence of an express finding, the reviewing court will erroneously assume that the magistrate accepted the prosecution's version of how long the police waited. Failure to make an express finding in this kind of situation may be easy and safe, but it is hard to justify leading reviewing courts astray.

#### e. Relitigation in Trial Court

##### (1) [§6.58] By the Defendant

In the trial court, the defendant may relitigate the issues raised in a Pen C §1538.5(f) motion as follows:

- By motion to set aside the information under Pen C §995. See, *e.g., People v Messina* (1985) 165 CA3d 937, 940, 212 CR 75. See Pen C §1538.5(n) (Pen C §1538.5 does not affect a Pen C §995 motion). The court that hears the Pen C §995 motion functions like a reviewing court; it is bound by the magistrate's finding of fact. *People v Laiwa* (1983) 34 C3d 711, 718, 195 CR 503.
- By a suppression motion under Pen C §1538.5(i). For discussion, see §§6.60–6.76.
- By a suppression motion under Pen C §1538.5(g) as to any charge that the court reduced to a misdemeanor at the conclusion of the preliminary hearing. *Chivers v Municipal Court* (1976) 59 CA3d 929, 932, 131 CR 221. For discussion, see §6.94.
- By a suppression motion at trial under the "narrow grounds" provided in Pen C §1538.5(h). *People v Nelson* (1981) 126 CA3d 978, 981, 179 CR 195. For discussion, see §§6.90–6.91.

##### (2) [§6.59] By the Prosecution

When the court grants the defendant's Pen C §1538.5(f) motion, the prosecution has several options: to refile, to seek an indictment, to move to reinstate the complaint, or, if the evidence was suppressed but the defendant was held to answer, to relitigate the suppression issues after the prosecution has filed an information. Pen C §1538.5(j). These options lead to a de novo relitigation of the Fourth Amendment issues. Pen C §1538.5(j).

### 2. After Filing of Information or Indictment

#### a. [§6.60] Basic Principles

A defendant who was held to answer at the preliminary hearing may "renew or make the motion in the superior court at a special hearing. . . ." Pen C §1538.5(i). So may a defendant who has been indicted. Pen C §1538.5(i).

When the defendant made a suppression motion at the preliminary hearing, the evidence at the Pen C §1538.5(i) hearing is limited to the preliminary hearing transcript, evidence that the defendant could not reasonably have presented at the preliminary hearing, and witnesses recalled by the prosecution. The court is bound by the magistrate's findings "as to evidence or property not affected by evidence presented at the special hearing." Pen C §1538.5(i). For discussion of findings, see §§6.57, 6.70–6.73. In the absence of a suppression motion at the preliminary hearing, the parties are entitled to a full evidentiary hearing on the Pen C §1538.5(i) motion.

Giving the prosecution the right to recall witnesses who testified at the preliminary hearing without affording defendant a similar opportunity does not render the statute unconstitutional. *People v Hansel* (1992) 1 C4th 1211, 1216–1222, 4 CR2d 888 (overruling restrictions on such witness recall imposed by *People v Anderson* (1989) 210 CA3d 24, 258 CR 125).

### b. [§6.61] New Legal Theories

When the defendant made a suppression motion at the preliminary hearing, he or she may not advance theories at the Pen C §1538.5(i) hearing "that were not raised or litigated during" the earlier hearing. *People v Bennett* (1998) 68 CA4th 396, 407, 80 CR2d 323 (at preliminary hearing defendant argued only one of three grounds that his moving papers had raised; court held other two grounds are waived and defendant may not introduce evidence at the Pen C §1538.5(i) hearing to support them, despite sketchy preliminary hearing record). A criminal defendant is generally "afforded only one evidentiary hearing in which to contest the legality of searches and seizures." 68 CA4th at 398–399.

☛ **Judicial Tip**: A different result is necessary when the defendant could not have litigated the new theory at the preliminary hearing because it did not relate to the evidence the prosecution presented at that hearing.

### c. Admissibility of Additional Evidence

#### (1) [§6.62] Basic Principle

When the defendant initially made a suppression motion at the preliminary hearing, the right to introduce additional evidence at the Pen C §1538.5(i) hearing is limited. The prosecution may recall witnesses; the defendant may only introduce "evidence that could not reasonably have been presented at the preliminary hearing." Pen C §1538.5(i). For further discussion, see §§6.63–6.69.

#### (2) [§6.63] Evidence Inadmissible at Preliminary Hearing

The clearest example of evidence that could not reasonably have been presented at the preliminary hearing is evidence that was not offered by the prosecution at that hearing. Pen C §1538.5(f)(1) (motion at preliminary hearing "restricted to evidence sought to be introduced by the people . . .").

An illustration is the case in which there were several searches of defendant's property, the prosecution offered only the products of one of them at the preliminary hearing, and the defendant moved to suppress them under Pen C §1538.5(f). The defendant then moves under Pen C §1538.5(i) to suppress the remaining items. The defendant is permitted to offer evidence relevant to the Pen C §1538.5(i) motion, even if the issues are the same as at the preliminary hearing. The same result applies to the case of a single search when the prosecution offers only some of the items at the preliminary hearing and the defendant seeks to suppress all of them at the Pen C §1538.5(i) hearing. See Pen C §1538.5(i).

#### (3) [§6.64] Unavailable Witnesses

It also seems clear that the parties can call witnesses who were unavailable at the time of the preliminary hearing. As to the criteria for determining unavailability, see Evid C §240. The testimony of a witness who was not available at the preliminary hearing may be excluded if it is cumulative or if it does not focus on the issues. *People v Drews* (1989) 208 CA3d 1317, 1327–1328, 256 CR 846.

A witness who was asked to appear voluntarily at the preliminary hearing but who was not subpoenaed was not unavailable. 208 CA3d at 1326.

#### (4) [§6.65] Controverting New Evidence

When one party presents new evidence at the Pen C §1538.5(i) hearing, the other party is entitled to rebut it because such rebuttal evidence could not reasonably have been presented at the preliminary hearing. *People v Hansel* (1992) 1 C4th 1211, 1222, 4 CR2d 888.

### d. Procedure To Determine Whether Evidence Could "Reasonably Have Been Presented at the Preliminary Hearing"

#### (1) [§6.66] Preliminary Fact

The question whether the evidence could reasonably have been presented at the preliminary hearing is a "preliminary fact," that is, a fact on which the admissibility of evidence depends. Evid C §400. The procedure for deciding the question is set out in Evid C §405(a):

> When the existence of a preliminary fact is disputed, the court shall indicate which party has the burden of producing evidence and the burden of proof on the issue as implied by the rule of law under which the question arises. The court shall determine the existence or nonexistence of the preliminary fact and shall admit or exclude the proffered evidence as required by the rule of law under which the question arises.

### (2) [§6.67] Burden and Degree of Proof

"The Evidence Code does not allocate the burden of proof between parties on preliminary fact issues." 1 Jefferson, California Evidence Benchbook §25.5 (3d ed 1997). Nevertheless, it seems clear that the burden of proof, as well as of producing evidence, should be on the party claiming that it has evidence that could not reasonably have been presented at the preliminary hearing. See comment to Evid C §405.

The degree of proof is probably preponderance of the evidence. See *People v Farley* (1979) 90 CA3d 851, 869, 153 CR 695; *People v James* (1977) 19 C3d 99, 106 n4, 137 CR 447.

### (3) [§6.68] Evidentiary Problems

In the hearing about whether the evidence could have been presented at the preliminary hearing, testimony from counsel may or may not help. Often the attorneys who appear at the Pen C §1538.5(i) hearing are not those who appeared at the preliminary hearing, and much of their testimony would therefore be hearsay or opinion. When attorneys have to be called specially to testify, other cases are likely to be disrupted and the court may be confronted with time-consuming continuances. The judge may be able to ameliorate these difficulties somewhat by encouraging the use of declarations.

### (4) [§6.69] In Camera Hearing

"If the people object to the presentation of evidence at the special hearing on the grounds that the evidence could reasonably have been presented at the preliminary hearing, the defendant shall be entitled to an in camera hearing to determine that issue." Pen C §1538.5(i).

"In camera" means outside the presence of the prosecutor. Under Pen C §1538.5(i), in trying to show that the evidence could not reasonably have been presented at the preliminary hearing, the defendant must also disclose what the evidence is. The in camera hearing is designed to protect the attorney-client privilege and to preclude prosecutorial discovery. *People v Drews* (1989) 208 CA3d 1317, 1324, 256 CR 846.

Penal Code §1538.5(i), unlike Evid C §1042(d) (in camera hearing on motion to disclose informant), does not specify how or whether the in camera hearing is to be reported. Pending clarification, probably the soundest course is to follow the Evid C §1042(d) procedure: The judge should have a reporter present and make an order (1) that any transcription of the in camera proceedings and any physical evidence received during them shall be sealed, and (2) that only the court shall have access to the sealed matters. See also *People v Hertz* (1980) 103 CA3d 770, 777, 163 CR 233 (in camera hearing under Evid C §915(b) must be in presence of court reporter although the statute does not expressly provide for one; otherwise, record would be unreviewable).

☛ **Judicial Tip**: The judge may want to give the prosecution a chance to rebut the in camera showing, as long as this can be done without disclosing the evidence in issue. For example, if the matter turns on when the defense discovered certain information, the court may give the prosecution the opportunity to establish when and what it gave the defense pursuant to discovery.

### e. Extent to Which Findings Are Binding

#### (1) [§6.70] Basic Principles

The findings, express or implied, at the Pen C §1538.5(f) hearing are binding at the Pen C §1538.5(i) hearing to the extent that

- They are express or may properly be implied (see §6.71); and
- They are factual (see §6.72); and
- They are supported by substantial evidence (*People v Trujillo* (1990) 217 CA3d 1219, 1223, 266 CR 473; *People v Ramsey* (1988) 203 CA3d 671, 678–679, 250 CR 309); and
- They are "not affected by evidence presented at the" Pen C §1538.5(i) hearing. Pen C §1538.5(i); for discussion, see §6.73.

When the magistrate's findings are "binding," the court at the Pen C §1538.5(i) hearing acts as a reviewing court, drawing all presumptions in favor of the magistrate's factual determinations. *People v Bishop* (1993) 14 CA4th 203, 214, 17 CR2d 657; *People v Ramsey, supra.*

#### (2) [§6.71] Finding Implied Only on Grounds Ruled On

A court may imply findings only on grounds or theories that underlie the motion and that the magistrate ruled on. Thus, when a search is challenged or defended on alternative grounds and the magistrate at the preliminary hearing based the decision on one of them, there are no findings on the other ground and none may be implied. See *People v Manning* (1973) 33 CA3d 586, 603–605, 109 CR 531. Absent findings, the court at the Pen C §1538.5(i) hearing may base its decision on the ground not ruled on by the magistrate only if

- That ground is established as a matter of law, or
- Evidence concerning that ground is presented at the Pen C §1538.5(i) hearing. See *People v Rios* (1976) 16 C3d 351, 356, 128 CR 5.

In contrast, when only a single ground was asserted at the Pen C §1538.5(f) hearing, the decision at that hearing "necessarily" ruled on that ground, and findings are implied. *People v Bittaker* (1989) 48 C3d 1046, 1074, 259 CR 630.

☛ **Judicial Tip**: In the case of a summary ruling by the magistrate, the court should assume that the magistrate considered all theories that the parties had raised.

#### (3) [§6.72] Factual and Legal Matters

A finding is a factual determination either made expressly or implied from the ruling. See *People v Manning* (1973) 33 CA3d 586, 599, 601, 109 CR 531; see §6.57. "Reasonableness" in search and seizure law is not a fact but a legal standard that is to be applied to the facts. *Terry v Ohio* (1968) 392 US 1, 27, 88 S Ct 1868, 20 L Ed 2d 889; *People v Matelski* (2000) 82 CA4th 837, 846, 98 CR2d 543. Hence, a court's conclusions about the reasonableness of a search are not findings. *People v Manning, supra,* 33 CA3d at 599. Similarly, a determination at the Pen C §1538.5(f) hearing that a detention was reasonable is not a finding, and the court that hears the Pen C §1538.5(i) motion exercises its independent judgment on that issue. See *People v Holguin* (1989) 213 CA3d 1308, 1315, 262 CR 331.

Factual determinations often underlie legal ones. For example, the *validity* of consent is a legal matter; the *existence* of consent is a factual one. *People v Memro* (1995) 11 C4th 786, 847, 47 CR2d 219.

#### (4) [§6.73] "Not Affected by Evidence Presented" at Pen C §1538.5(i) Hearing

The introduction of evidence at the Pen C §1538.5(i) hearing on issues on which there was evidence at the Pen C §1538.5(f) hearing raises the question of the effect of the new evidence on the findings. Penal Code §1538.5(i) makes only "findings . . . not affected by evidence presented at the" Pen C §1538.5(i) hearing binding. Findings are not "affected" by the new evidence merely because the evidence is relevant to them. *People v Bishop* (1993) 14 CA4th 203, 210, 17 CR2d 657. The test is whether the magistrate would probably have made different findings in light of "the total evidence, new and old." 14 CA4th at 212.

The test is objective; the proper inquiry is analogous to determining the effect of newly discovered evidence in deciding whether to grant a motion for a new trial: would it render a different outcome probable? *People v Bishop, supra,* 14 CA4th at 212–213 (cumulative evidence on officer's credibility would probably not cause magistrate to change finding under particular facts of case).

### f. Renewal or Reconsideration of Motion

#### (1) [§6.74] No Reconsideration After Decision on Merits

Once the court has decided a Pen C §1538.5(i) motion *on its merits,* it has no discretion to reconsider it or to entertain a second motion. *Madril v Superior Court* (1975) 15 C3d 73, 77, 123 CR 465 ("We hold that the determination of a §1538.5 motion at a special hearing in the superior court—whether in the defendant's or in the People's favor—deprives that court of jurisdiction to reconsider the matter . . ."); *People v Superior Court* (Edmonds) (1971) 4 C3d 605, 611, 94 CR 250; *People v Sotelo* (1996) 47 CA4th 264, 269, 54 CR2d 643. Penal Code §1538.5(i) provides that the only pretrial review is by writ. Applications of the rule against reconsideration are discussed in §6.75, exceptions in §6.76; for discussion of writ review, see §§6.134, 6.136.

#### (2) [§6.75] Applications of Rule

(a) *Newly discovered evidence.* After the judge has decided the motion, the defendant, before trial, renews it or wants the judge to reconsider because of newly discovered evidence. The court has no jurisdiction. *People v Dubose* (1971) 17 CA3d 43, 47, 94 CR 376.

(b) *In light of new case law.* Counsel may attempt to renew the motion in light of a new decision that would require a different ruling. Whether or not counsel is correct, the court cannot reconsider. This is essentially the same situation as *Dubose.* Defendant's remedy is to seek a writ or to make a suppression motion at trial. See §§6.78, 6.81, 6.134.

(c) *When there is a change of counsel during trial.* This is not a valid argument for renewing the motion. See *People v Superior Court* (Green) (1970) 10 CA3d 477, 479–481, 89 CR 223.

(d) *When counsel offers new grounds.* The judge cannot accept such a contention. See *People v Brooks* (1980) 26 C3d 471, 483, 162 CR 177 ("during the pretrial hearing all parties [are] obligated to present all testimony and legal theories relevant to the admissibility of the evidence," summarizing the holding of *Lorenzana v Superior Court* (1973) 9 C3d 626, 640, 108 CR 585); *People v Nelson* (1981) 126 CA3d 978, 981, 179 CR 195.

(e) *When alternative grounds are raised.* Contrast the above situation with one in which the motion initially states alternative grounds and the defense presents evidence on both. If the motion is granted on one ground, without reaching the other one, and the ruling is reversed later on appeal, the court has jurisdiction to rule on the defendant's second basis and should do so. *People v Brooks, supra.* The defendant is entitled to have all the grounds that were properly raised in the original motion ruled on. A more common problem with a motion on alternative grounds occurs when the judge decides ground A and puts ground B over. According to *People v Lopez* (1981) 116 CA3d 600, 604, 172 CR 236, the judge can reconsider the ruling on A before deciding B. In this instance, the ruling on A is tentative and the hearing has not been completed. *Lopez* should be viewed with caution, however. Its reference to the court's inherent powers is unique in cases within this area.

(f) *Reconsideration in the court's own motion.* If the court has ruled on the motion but then concludes that its ruling was wrong, it cannot reconsider the ruling on its own motion. *Madril v Superior Court* (1975) 15 C3d 73, 77, 123 CR 465, overruling *People v Leighter* (1971) 15 CA3d 389, 93 CR 136. This underscores the uncertain status of *People v Lopez, supra,* because *Madril* rejected an inherent power argument very similar to that used by the *Lopez* court.

(g) *When a timely motion is continued too long.* If the defendant makes a proper motion under Pen C §1538.5(i), asks that it be continued, and requests a ruling after jury selection starts, the judge probably cannot decide the motion. *People v Pangelina* (1981) 117 CA3d 414, 417, 172 CR 661, suggests this answer without explaining it.

This may seem inconsistent with the principle that the parties are entitled to a ruling on the merits. However, that refers to a *pretrial* ruling. Taking up the motion during jury selection would frustrate one of the key purposes of Pen C §1538.5. See *People v Brooks, supra.*

☛ **Judicial Tip**: To avoid this situation, when counsel requests a continuance, the judge should put the motion over to a date certain and hear it on that date.

(h) *Insufficient notice.* When a motion is denied on the ground that the required 10 days' notice was not given, the defendant has the right to file a new motion, give proper notice, and have the motion decided on the merits. *Moreno v Superior Court* (1978) 80 CA3d 932, 935, 146 CR 35 ("Since the petitioner never received a hearing on the merits of his first motion, the court had jurisdiction to entertain the second motion").

(i) *Untimely service of points and authorities.* This situation can be contrasted with that in which the defendant has given insufficient notice. The new factor in this situation is Cal Rules of Ct 4.111(b): "The court may consider the failure without good cause of the moving party to serve and file points and authorities within the time permitted as an admission that the motion is without merit."

Here the judge must first decide whether there was good cause for the failure. If the judge finds that good cause was lacking, he or she must next determine, and state on the record, whether the violation is considered an admission that the motion is without merit. If it is regarded as an admission, the motion is denied on its merits and cannot be reconsidered. However, it is usually better for the judge to give the moving party a chance to cure the defect.

(j) *Error in denying the motion as a ground for a new trial.* The court cannot grant a new trial on the basis that an earlier ruling on the Pen C §1538.5 motion was erroneous. *People v Cardenas* (1981) 114 CA3d 643, 648–649, 170 CR 763. Nor can the motion be renewed after a mistrial. *People v Williams* (1979) 93 CA3d 40, 59, 155 CR 414.

(k) *Defendant's absence.* When the court denies a motion because of defendant's unexcused absence, the court has jurisdiction to decide a subsequent motion on its merits. *People v Schunk* (1991) 235 CA3d 1334, 1337, 1 CR2d 438. The situation is analogous to that in *Moreno v Superior Court, supra.*

(*l*) *Conflict of interest.* The court may not entertain a renewed motion on the ground that prior counsel had a conflict of interest (*People v Superior Court* (Green) 10 CA3d 477, 481, 89 CR 223), except after a reversal of defendant's conviction on a finding that the conflict resulted in ineffective representation of counsel that affected the entire original proceedings. *People v Superior Court* (Corona) (1981) 30 C3d 193, 200, 178 CR 334. See *People v Ramos* (1997) 15 C4th 1133, 1163, 64 CR2d 892; §6.76.

#### (3) [§6.76] Exceptions

The court may reconsider a Pen C §1538.5(i) motion decided on the merits under the following circumstances:

(a) *Immediate reconsideration to correct clear legal error. People v Ramirez* (1992) 6 CA4th 1583, 1590, 8 CR2d 529 (trial court mistakenly imposed clear-and-convincing-evidence standard on prosecution and reconsidered next day at prosecution's request; held: reconsideration proper because "court applied clearly erroneous legal standard in its original ruling").

(b) *Prosecution wins but seeks reconsideration of adverse factual finding. People v Jackson* (1996) 13 C4th 1164, 1200–1205, 56 CR2d 49 (death penalty case; contrary ruling might have necessitated reversal).

(c) *After conviction reversed for ineffectiveness of counsel. People v Superior Court* (Corona) (1981) 30 C3d 193, 200, 178 CR 334 (ineffectiveness of counsel infected first suppression hearing and deprived defendant of opportunity for full determination of issues). In the absence of a reversal, it is not clear whether the defendant may seek reconsideration on the ground of ineffective representation. See *People v Sotelo* (1996) 47 CA4th 264, 272, 54 CR 2d 643; *People v Camilleri* (1990) 220 CA3d 1199, 1203, 269 CR 862; *People v Superior Court* (Green) (1970) 10 CA3d 477, 479, 89 CR 223.

*Corona* does not mean that a reversal of a conviction on grounds other than inadequate representation entitles the defendant to renew the suppression motion. *People v Ramos* (1997) 15 C4th 1133, 1163, 64 CR2d 892.

A defendant has no right to insist that defense counsel make a suppression motion. *People v Turner* (1992) 7 CA4th 1214, 1219–1220, 10 CR2d 358.

### 3. At Trial

#### a. [§6.77] Motion Disfavored

A major objective of Pen C §1538.5 is to prevent suppression motions at trial. *People v Pham* (1987) 189 CA3d 1531, 1534, 235 CR 99; see §6.2. Hearing untimely motions at trial, even with the prosecutor's acquiescence, is disapproved; such practice "thwarts one of the statute's purposes [citation] and misuses judicial resources." *People v Jackson* (1992) 7 CA4th 1367, 1370 n3, 10 CR2d 5.

#### b. [§6.78] Basic Principles

Under Pen C §1538.5(h), a defendant may make a suppression motion "during the course of the trial" if "prior to the trial . . . opportunity for this motion did not exist or the defendant was not aware of the grounds for the motion. . . ." Penal Code §1538.5(h) has been interpreted as permitting the defendant to make a suppression motion at trial in only two situations:

(1) A change in the applicable law. *People v Superior Court* (Edmonds) (1971) 4 C3d 605, 611, 94 CR 250; see §6.81.

(2) The discovery of new evidence that could not have been obtained

earlier by using due diligence. *People v Martinez* (1975) 14 C3d 533, 537, 121 CR 611; *People v Robbins* (1980) 103 CA3d 34, 42, 162 CR 780, rev'd on other grounds (1981) 453 US 420, 101 S Ct 2841, 69 L Ed 2d 744.

Penal Code §1538.5(h) does not permit the defendant to relitigate a prior suppression motion. *People v Superior Court* (Edmonds), *supra*, 4 C3d at 609; *People v O'Brien* (1969) 71 C2d 394, 403, 79 CR 313. For a contrary suggestion, see *Green v Superior Court* (1985) 40 C3d 126, 139 n11, 219 CR 186.

The motion does not have to be made literally "during the course of trial." It may be made before the trial judge just before the start of the trial. *People v Young* (1976) 62 CA3d 49, 51, 133 CR 22.

### c. Illustrative Cases

#### (1) [§6.79] Officer Testifies for First Time at Trial

In a grand theft auto case, at issue is the admissibility of the pink slip to the victim's car. At the preliminary hearing, officer A testified that officer B told him that he had observed the pink slip on the defendant's person. During trial, officer B testifies that he found the pink slip by searching the defendant's pockets. Defense counsel moves to suppress the pink slip, arguing that officer A's testimony during the preliminary hearing did not clearly indicate whether the pink slip was the product of a search and that he had no basis for a suppression motion until officer B testified at trial.

The judge should not hear the motion. Counsel could have learned that there had been a search by interviewing the defendant. In addition, officer A's testimony during the preliminary hearing put counsel on notice that it was advisable to look further into the pink slip matter before trial. *People v Martinez* (1975) 14 C3d 533, 537, 121 CR 611.

☛ **Judicial Tip**: Many variations arise on the theme of testimony given for the first time during trial. *Martinez* does not stand for the proposition that no such new testimony can give rise to a Pen C §1538.5(h) motion. Rather, the inquiry should always be whether counsel could reasonably have discovered the evidence earlier. For an illustration of a proper Pen C §1538.5(h) motion, see *People v Minjares* (1979) 24 C3d 410, 415 n1, 153 CR 224 (police testimony at trial contradicted testimony at initial suppression hearing).

#### (2) [§6.80] Violation of Discovery Order

At trial, the prosecution offers in evidence a driver's license taken from the defendant's wallet. Before trial, the defendant had obtained a discovery order requiring discovery of "each document, . . . object and photograph . . . which was obtained by search and seizure." The response to the discovery order did not disclose the license. The defendant now moves to suppress the license on the ground of illegal search.

The judge should hear the motion. In *People v Guzman* (1975) 47 CA3d 380, 391, 121 CR 69, the court ruled that defendant did not have a fair opportunity for a pretrial motion. "Although he may have known a wallet was taken on his arrest, he had a definite indication that the People did not consider it material to the case."

#### (3) [§6.81] "New" Case Decision

At trial, the defendant cites a recent decision as the basis for a Pen C §1538.5(h) motion. The judge reads it and while the case is unquestionably new, it merely adopts the reasoning of an old case. In this instance the judge should not hear the motion. *People v Ramos* (1997) 15 C4th 1133, 1163, 64 CR2d 892.

#### (4) [§6.82] Ineffective Representation

Defendant's trial counsel argues that unless the court hears the motion, the defendant would be denied effective representation. It is unclear whether the court may hear a Pen C §1538.5(h) motion on this ground. See §6.76.

#### (5) [§6.83] Confession

Assume the defendant made a pretrial motion to suppress his confession on the ground that it was involuntary, and another judge denied it. At trial, the defendant renews his motion. The trial judge should hear the motion, although it has nothing to do with Pen C §1538.5(h). *People v Memro* (1985) 38 C3d 658, 666 n3, 214 CR 832, stated:

> The admissibility of a confession, standing alone, is outside the scope of a section 1538.5 motion. [Citation.] While such evidence may be the subject of a pretrial common law motion to suppress, a ruling on that type of motion is not binding on the trial judge.

For discussion of the relation of confession issues to Pen C §1538.5, see §§6.16–6.18.

In another instance, the defendant moves for the first time at trial to suppress a confession on the ground that the police lacked probable cause to arrest him. This challenge does come within Pen C §1538.5, and unless the defendant shows good cause under Pen C §1538.5(h), the motion cannot be heard on its merits, even if the prosecution does not object. *People v Takencareof* (1981) 119 CA3d 492, 496, 174 CR 112.

#### (6) [§6.84] Reversal of Conviction

Reversal of defendant's conviction is not a ground for renewing a suppression motion, unless the reversal was based on ineffective representation that affected all the original proceedings, not just the prior trial. *People v Ramos* (1997) 15 C4th 1133, 1163, 64 CR2d 892; *People v Superior Court* (Corona) (1981) 30 C3d 193, 200, 178 CR 334.

## B. By Prosecution

### 1. At Special Hearing Under Pen C §1538.5(j)

#### a. [§6.85] Basic Principles

When the magistrate grants a suppression motion at the preliminary hearing but holds the defendant to answer, the prosecution may relitigate the motion at a special hearing. Pen C §1538.5(j). The statute is phrased in terms of a "request" for such a hearing, but entitles the prosecution to one. See, *e.g., People v Superior Court* (Williamson) (1979) 91 CA3d 789, 791–792, 154 CR 387. The hearing occurs after the prosecution files the information; for discussion of notice, see §6.50.

#### b. Features of Statute

#### (1) [§6.86] De Novo Hearing

At the Pen C §1538.5(j) hearing, "the validity of the search or seizure shall be relitigated de novo" on the basis of evidence presented at that hearing. Pen C §1538.5(j). The fact that the statute gives the prosecution, but not the defendant, a right to a de novo hearing does not render Pen C §1538.5(j) unconstitutional. *People v Weaver* (1996) 44 CA4th 154, 158–160, 51 CR2d 602.

*Weaver* justifies the different treatment on the ground that it offsets the advantage that the defendant enjoys at the preliminary hearing by being able to surprise the prosecution with an unnoticed motion. 44 CA4th at 160. Unnoticed motions are no longer permitted. Pen C §1538.5(f)(2); for discussion, see §6.47.

#### (2) [§6.87] Continuance

The defendant is "entitled, as a matter of right, to a continuance of the special hearing for a period of time up to 30 days." Pen C §1538.5(j).

☛ **Judicial Tip**: When the defendant asks for the full 30 days, the court should probably grant the request in order to offset the "heads-I-win, tails-you-lose" position of the prosecution under Pen C §1538.5(i) and (j).

### (3) [§6.88] Binding Effect of Prior Ruling

The ruling at the preliminary hearing is binding on the prosecution unless it makes a Pen C §1538.5(j) request. Pen C §1538.5(j). The following cases illustrate the application of this principle.

*Defendant held to answer on all counts.* Assume the defendant is charged with several counts of drug possession. At the preliminary hearing, the court grants the defendant's Pen C §1538.5 motion as to some drugs, denies it as to others, and holds the defendant to answer on all counts. Defendant makes a motion under Pen C §1538.5(i), but the prosecution does not seek a hearing under Pen C §1538.5(j). At the Pen C §1538.5(i) hearing, the court may not reconsider the prior ruling that suppressed some of the drugs. *Eiseman v Superior Court* (1971) 21 CA3d 342, 347, 98 CR 342.

☛ **Judicial Tip**: The court should be wary of prosecution argument that the Pen C §1538.5(i) motion "opened up" all the suppression issues decided at the preliminary hearing: defendant's Pen C §1538.5(i) motion goes only to evidence that was not suppressed at the earlier hearing.

*Defendant held to answer only on some counts.* Suppose the preliminary hearing involved two counts of possession and the magistrate denied the defendant's Pen C §1538.5 motion with respect to count 1, but granted it as to count 2 and did not hold the defendant to answer that count. Normally, the prosecution could not use Pen C §1538.5(j) to challenge the suppression ruling because there was no holding order to count 2. But the prosecution may want to use the suppressed evidence in what remains of the case, such as to negate a defense it expects the defendant to raise. In such a situation, Pen C §1538.5(j) applies. *People v Superior Court* (Williamson) (1979) 91 CA3d 789, 791–792, 154 CR 387. The prosecution not only can, but must, make a Pen C §1538.5(j) request if it wants to use the evidence at trial.

### (4) [§6.89] Renewal of Reconsideration

The same rule applies to Pen C §1538.5(j) hearings as to Pen C §1538.5(i) motions. A decision on the merits cannot be reheard or reconsidered. *Madril v Superior Court* (1975) 15 C3d 73, 77, 123 CR 465; *People v Superior Court* (Sosa) (1982) 31 C3d 883, 895–896, 185 CR 113; see §6.74. The court has no jurisdiction to do so. This applies to the defense as well as the prosecution. When the prosecution prevails on the Pen C §1538.5(j) hearing, the defendant cannot seek reconsideration or make a suppression motion challenging the same evidence. *People v Thomas* (1983) 141 CA3d 496, 501, 190 CR 408. Again, the rule is jurisdictional in the sense that the court lacks "subject matter jurisdiction." Thus, the opposing party need not object to the improper relitigation. *People v Thomas, supra.*

The following situations illustrate the *Thomas* rule:

- The prosecutor makes a Pen C §1538.5(j) request, which is granted. The defendant then files a Pen C §1538.5(i) motion going to the same evidence. The judge should not hear it; this is precisely the kind of practice barred by *Thomas.*

- At the preliminary hearing, some evidence was admitted, some excluded, and the defendant was held to answer. The defendant files a Pen C §1538.5(i) motion, and the prosecution files a Pen C §1538.5(j) request, which the court grants. Before the defense motion is heard, the defendant files an amended motion including a motion to suppress the evidence that has just been ruled on. This is merely an attempt to avoid *Thomas,* which the court should not allow.

- The defendant's statement was suppressed at the preliminary hearing as the product of an unlawful arrest, but the superior court ruled otherwise at the Pen C §1538.5(j) hearing. The defendant then moves to exclude the statement on the basis of *Miranda* violations. The defendant's claim should be decided on the merits (though not necessarily by a pretrial motion); it does not involve Pen C §1538.5 and is therefore unaffected by *Thomas.* See discussion of defendant's motion to suppress a confession in §§6.16–6.18.

## 2. At Trial

### a. [§6.90] Conditions for Relitigation

The prosecution may relitigate a Pen C §1538.5(i) motion at trial when it meets all of the following four conditions (Pen C §1538.5(j)):

(1) The defendant made a successful Pen C §1538.5(i) motion;

(2) The prosecution did not seek appellate review of the Pen C §1538.5(i) ruling;

(3) The prosecution has additional evidence that it did not present at the Pen C §1538.5(i) hearing; and

(4) The prosecution had "good cause" for not presenting the evidence at the earlier hearing.

The prosecution's right to relitigate a Pen C §1538.5(i) motion, albeit limited, is one that the defendant does not have. See *Madril v Superior Court* (1975) 15 C3d 73, 76–78, 123 CR 465; §6.78.

Good cause means grounds "comparable to the justification required of the defendant who seeks to present new evidence on the suppression motion at the special hearing in superior court after a denial at the preliminary hearing." *People v Lopez* (1993) 12 CA4th 1732, 1737, 16 CR2d 177 (remanded to determine whether prosecution can show good cause why its witness repeatedly did not appear at hearing).

It is *not* a condition that the defendant made a suppression motion at the preliminary hearing, as long as there was a Pen C §1538.5(i) motion. *People v Lopez, supra.*

### b. [§6.91] Issues

The prosecution's limited right to relitigate Pen C §1538.5 issues at trial involves a three-part inquiry:

(1) Did the prosecution meet the statutory conditions precedent to endeavoring a showing of good cause, *i.e.,* conditions (1)–(3) discussed in §6.90? The following circumstances fail to meet at least one of the conditions:

- Defendant's Pen C §1538.5 motion was granted at the preliminary hearing. There was no subsequent Pen C §1538.5(i) hearing; thus, the first condition was not met and the prosecution is not entitled to show good cause.

- Defendant prevailed at the preliminary hearing and the prosecution was unsuccessful in its Pen C §1538.5(j) motion. The problem is the same as in the previous illustration: defendant did not make a Pen C §1538.5(i) motion; the first condition was therefore not met.

- Defendant's Pen C §1538.5 motion was granted; the prosecution sought review by writ and lost. In this situation, the second condition was not met.

- The prosecution claims that the Pen C §1538.5(i) ruling was wrong and requests reconsideration on the existing record. Here the third condition is not met; Pen C §1538.5(j) does not provide for such reconsideration.

(2) Assuming the prosecution meets the conditions discussed above, has it shown good cause for not presenting the evidence at the Pen C §1538.5(i) hearing?

(3) Assuming good cause, should the ruling on the suppression be changed in light of all the evidence, including the new evidence?

## VII. MOTIONS IN MISDEMEANOR CASES

### A. Pretrial Motion

#### 1. [§6.92] Basic Principles

A defendant who is charged with one or more misdemeanors may make a pretrial suppression motion. Pen C §1538.5(g). For discussion of notice, see §6.52.

Once the motion is decided on its merits, the court has no authority to rehear it or to consider a renewed or second pretrial motion. *McQuillan v Appellate Dep't* (1977) 71 CA3d 543, 545, 139 CR 514.

#### 2. [§6.93] Continuance

A defendant is entitled to continuance of the trial of up to 30 days when needed to file a Pen C §1538.5(g) motion. Pen C §1538.5(*l*).

☛ **Judicial Tip**: A continuance is preferable to a motion heard on the morning of the trial.

#### 3. [§6.94] Reduced Wobblers Under Pen C §17(b)(5)

When a wobbler is reduced to a misdemeanor after the preliminary hearing under Pen C §17(b)(5), the defendant is entitled to a new suppression hearing. *Chivers v Municipal Court* (1976) 59 CA3d 929, 933, 131 CR 221. *Chivers* does not state whether this is to be a de novo hearing, but the inference from the opinion is that it is. "It is clear that when the felony offenses were reduced to misdemeanors, pursuant to section 17, subdivision (b)(5), they became misdemeanors for *all purposes* [text omitted] The rights and remedies afforded by [the provisions of §1538.5] would be denied [defendants] by reason of the [trial] court's refusal to hear and determine their motion to suppress made pursuant to section 1538.5, subdivision (g)." 59 CA3d at 933–934; emphasis in original.

The unanswered question is whether, once the wobbler has been reduced, the defendant *must* make a motion under Pen C §1538.5(g) if he or she wishes to exclude the evidence. The question is not academic; the answer has practical consequences. For example, assume the defendant's Pen C §1538.5 motion is granted at the preliminary hearing. The court concludes there is other evidence sufficient to support the charge, but reduces it to a misdemeanor. The defendant, satisfied with the result, does not make a Pen C §1538.5(g) motion. The prosecutor offers the suppressed evidence at trial. How the judge should rule depends on whether the ruling at the preliminary hearing applies or whether the defendant must make a new suppression motion after the court reduced the charge.

One line of reasoning is to treat the case analogously to a felony.

If the court had not reduced the charge, the defendant could have relied on the suppression ruling at the preliminary hearing to exclude the evidence at trial. A weakness of this argument is that it rests on statutory language that covers only defendants who are held to answer. Pen C §1538.5(j). A second and perhaps stronger argument against requiring a Pen C §1538.5(g) motion is that it would be inconsistent with the structure and purposes of Pen C §1538.5 to construe the statute as requiring motions that it does not expressly prescribe.

However, *Chivers* made the Pen C §1538.5(g) motion available because the court concluded that the case, once it had been reduced under Pen C §17(b)(5), became a misdemeanor for all purposes. In that regard, Pen C §17(b)(5) provides that on reduction, "the case shall proceed as if the defendant had been arraigned on a misdemeanor complaint." But for defendants arraigned on misdemeanor complaints, a Pen C §1538.5(g) motion is the exclusive remedy for obtaining a suppression order. Pen C §1538.5(m). "Exclusive remedy" means that the evidence cannot be excluded unless a motion under Pen C §1538.5(g) is made and granted. See, *e.g., People v Harris* (1974) 39 CA3d 965, 970, 114 CR 892 (defendant failed to make Pen C §1538.5(i) motion; evidence properly admitted at trial).

A similar problem can arise when the preliminary hearing judge grants the suppression motion in part and denies it in part. After the charge has been reduced, the defendant makes a motion under *Chivers* to exclude the part of the evidence that had been ruled admissible at the preliminary hearing. Whether the prosecutor can offer the evidence excluded at the preliminary hearing at trial again depends on whether the defendant is required to raise the issue as part of the Pen C §1538.5(g) motion.

### 4. Misdemeanor Charged With Felony

#### a. [§6.95] Felony Procedures Apply

When a misdemeanor is charged in the same complaint as a felony, the Pen C §1538.5 procedures governing suppression motions in felony cases apply. Pen C §1538.5(g). Occasionally felony charges are dismissed, giving rise to a question of how suppression motions related to the remaining misdemeanor are handled. This question is discussed in §§6.96–6.98.

#### b. [§6.96] Felony Dismissed Before Preliminary Hearing

When the prosecution dismisses the felony charges before the preliminary hearing, the defendant has not yet had an opportunity to litigate suppression issues relating to the remaining misdemeanor(s). Pen C §1538.5(g) provides that opportunity.

#### c. [§6.97] Felony Dismissed at End of Preliminary Hearing

When the felony charge disappears at the conclusion of the preliminary hearing, a Pen C §1538.5(g) motion lies on the basis of *Chivers v Municipal Court* (1976) 59 CA3d 929, 933, 131 CR 221; see §6.94. This is the case whether or not defendant made a suppression motion at the preliminary hearing. *Chivers v Municipal Court, supra.*

#### d. [§6.98] Felony Dismissed After Pen C §1538.5(i) Hearing

When the felony charge is dismissed at some point after a Pen C §1538.5(i) hearing, it is unclear whether a motion under Pen C §1538.5(g) may be made. One reason *Chivers v Municipal Court* (1976) 59 CA3d 929, 131 CR 221, gave for allowing such a motion after the felony had been reduced to a misdemeanor at the preliminary hearing is that a preliminary hearing "is not the equivalent of a *special hearing* under section 1538.5, subdivision (g)." 59 CA3d at 933; emphasis in original. But a hearing under Pen C §1538.5(i) is a "special hearing" according to the express wording of the subdivision. On this reasoning no Pen C §1538.5(g) motion could be made. There is no case law, however.

### B. [§6.99] Motion at Trial

The defendant may make a suppression motion at a misdemeanor trial under the same limited circumstances as at a felony trial. Pen C §1538.5(h); for discussion, see §§6.77–6.84.

In misdemeanors, unlike felonies, there is no statutory provision that gives the prosecutor an opportunity to relitigate the suppression issue at trial. As to felonies, see Pen C §1538.5(j) and discussion in §§6.90–6.91.

## VIII. HEARING

### A. [§6.100] Hearing by Magistrate Who Issued Search Warrant

In cases involving a search warrant, a Pen C §1538.5 motion "should first be heard by the magistrate who issued the search warrant." Pen C §1538.5(b). This subsection is "a recommendation, not . . . a mandate." *Cuevas v Superior Court* (1976) 58 CA3d 406, 409, 130 CR 238; see *People v Fleming* (1981) 29 C3d 698, 704 n6, 175 CR 604 (language of Pen C §1538.5(b) "is permissive, not mandatory . . .").

☛ **Judicial Tips**:

- The court should not split a Pen C §1538.5(f) motion from the preliminary hearing, having the former heard by the issuing magistrate and the latter by the judge regularly assigned to the preliminary hearing. The motion would then no longer be heard "at the preliminary hearing" as required by Pen C §1538.5(f).

- Nor should the court permit two Pen C §1538.5(f) hearings, one at the preliminary hearing and another before the issuing magistrate. Such procedure is contrary to the statute. *People v Sanchez* (1972) 24 CA3d 664, 689, 101 CR 193. When the court grants a Pen C §1538.5(b) request in connection with a suppression motion at the preliminary hearing, the issuing magistrate should preside at the preliminary hearing, as well as hear the motion.
- A policy requiring early notification of Pen C §1538.5(b) requests will often give the court sufficient time to arrange for the issuing magistrate to hear the motion.
- When the request is first made on or before the hearing date and the requested judge is busy, the court should not lightly grant a continuance, especially when one of the parties has not waived time. Such requests are sometimes made for purposes of delay or judge-shopping.
- When a Pen C §1538.5(b) request cannot be accommodated, the judge should briefly state the reasons on the record so that the party making the request cannot later claim an arbitrary denial.

### B. [§6.101] Challenging Judge Under CCP §170.6

The parties can use CCP §170.6(2) to peremptorily challenge the judge assigned to hear the suppression motion. See, *e.g., People v Rodgers* (1975) 47 CA3d 992, 993, 121 CR 346. This includes the judge who issued the search warrant. Pen C §1538.5(b) ("Subject to the provisions of Section 170 through 170.6 . . .").

Code of Civil Procedure §170.6(2) is available even when the motion hearing is not de novo, as under Pen C §1538.5(i). *Solberg v Superior Court* (1977) 19 C3d 182, 189, 137 CR 460.

When CCP §170.6(2) is not used to challenge a judge at the time of the suppression motion, but the same judge is assigned to try the case, CCP §170.6(2) may be employed at that stage depending on whether a Pen C §1538.5 hearing involved "a determination of contested fact issues relating to the merits." CCP §170.6(2). *In re Abdul Y.* (1982) 130 CA3d 847, 859, 182 CR 146 (overruling *Parnell v Superior Court* (1976) 61 CA3d 430, 132 CR 535), held that "a contested pretrial factual hearing to determine the admissibility of incriminating evidence" is such a determination. Hence, the defendant's attempt to disqualify the trial judge was ruled untimely. The Supreme Court left the question open in *People v Wilks* (1978) 21 C3d 460, 466 n3, 146 CR 364.

*Abdul Y.* does not apply when the defendant has two cases pending and simultaneously files challenges in both against the judge who heard a suppression motion in one of the cases. To avoid an appearance of impropriety, the challenge should be allowed in the case involving the suppression motion if it is granted in the other case. *Woods v Superior Court* (1987) 190 CA3d 885, 886, 235 CR 687.

A suppression hearing does not always resolve disputed facts, *e.g.*, when there is a challenge to the facial sufficiency of a search warrant affidavit. Under those circumstances, CCP §170.6(2) should permit disqualification of the trial judge even though he or she heard the Pen C §1538.5 motion.

As to successive disqualification motions by codefendants, see CCP §170.6(3); *People v Eaker* (1980) 100 CA3d 1007, 1016, 161 CR 417 (one motion per side; codefendant can make additional motion only if he shows he has "substantially adverse interests" to those of the other defendant).

### C. [§6.102] Magistrate as Witness

Defense counsel occasionally attempt to call the magistrate who signed a search warrant as a witness in the suppression hearing. This tactic has been used especially when the warrant is supported by a long affidavit or one with extensive attachments. Counsel questions the magistrate whether he read every word. The practice rests on *Kaylor v Superior Court* (1980) 108 CA3d 451, 457, 166 CR 598, in which the supporting affidavit had 155 pages of attachments and some were illegible. In addition, the issuing magistrate testified that he did not read all the attachments. The appellate court ordered the Pen C §1538.5 motion granted.

However, *Kaylor* has been eroded to the point of being disapproved. First, in *People v Kashani* (1983) 143 CA3d 77, 79–80, 191 CR 562, the court held that in the absence of facial irregularity (such as the illegibility in *Kaylor*), the magistrate is presumed to have considered all the material and that he or she cannot routinely be subpoenaed as a witness. The subpoena must be quashed when the only showing is "sweeping pro forma assertion that the magistrate did not read all material offered in support of the search warrant application." 143 CA3d at 80.

Next, *Kaylor* was distinguished in *People v Aston* (1985) 39 C3d 481, 498, 216 CR 771 (magistrate not required to read redundant material). Finally, *People v Wilson* (1986) 182 CA3d 742, 753, 227 CR 528, stated that "[w]hatever vitality *Kaylor* retained after *Kashani,* it has none after the enactment of Proposition 8. . . ."

*Wilson* stated that before a magistrate can be called as a witness, there must be a prima facie showing that the magistrate has shed the mantle of neutrality and assumed the role of an "adjunct law enforcement officer." *Wilson* also stated that the magistrate should not have to testify when the contention was that he did not read all the attachments to an affidavit and that, in any event, his testimony that he scanned them was sufficient under the circumstances since the attachments added nothing material to the affidavit. 182 CA3d at 753.

☛ **Judicial Tips**: Magistrates can reduce the risk of such challenges by initialing each page of the affidavit and its attachments as they are read and by taking the time to read affidavits carefully. It is sometimes possible to keep affidavits overnight. If called to testify, the magistrate should seek legal help, unless the prosecutor competently moves to quash the subpoena. Motions to disqualify a judge on the ground of intention to call him or her as a witness in the suppression hearing should be denied unless the judge has knowledge of other disputed facts. See CCP §170.1(a)(1).

### D. [§6.103] Open and Closed Suppression Hearings

When the Pen C §1538.5 motion is heard at the preliminary hearing, the proceedings must be open to the public and the press, in the absence of specific findings demonstrating the following:

(1) A substantial probability that an open hearing would prejudice the defendant's right to a fair trial, and

(2) The unavailability of reasonable alternatives to closure that would adequately protect the defendant's rights. *Press-Enter. Co. v Superior Court* (1986) 478 US 1, 17, 106 S Ct 2735, 92 L Ed 2d 1; *KFMB-TV Channel 8 v Municipal Court* (1990) 221 CA3d 1362, 1365, 271 CR 109 (court may not qualify open hearing order by prohibiting witnesses' statements from being broadcast without further court authorization). See *NBC Subsidiary (KNBC-TV), Inc. v Superior Court* (1999) 20 C4th 1178, 1207, 86 CR2d 778; Pen C §§868, 868.7.

Similar principles apply to a Pen C §1538.5 hearing that is not part of a preliminary hearing. *Waller v Georgia* (1984) 467 US 39, 48, 104 S Ct 2210, 81 L Ed 2d 31 (party seeking to close hearing must advance overriding interest likely to be prejudiced, closure must be no broader than necessary to protect that interest, and trial court must consider reasonable alternatives to closing proceedings and must make findings adequate to support closure). In *Waller,* the court said that suppression hearings are often as important as the trial. 467 US at 46–47; see *People v Hobbs* (1994) 7 C4th 948, 981, 30 CR2d 651.

## E. [§6.104] Chart: Statutory Right to Continuance

The chart below summarizes the circumstances that entitle the defendant to a continuance. For further discussion, see §§6.56, 6.87, 6.93.

| ***Motion Under*** | ***Length*** | ***Showing*** | ***What Is Continued*** |
|---|---|---|---|
| Pen C §1538.5(f) | At least 5 court days | Defense unaware of evidence or grounds for motion | Preliminary hearing and motion |
| Pen C §1538.5(g) | Up to 30 days[1] | Defense intends to file motion and needs time to prepare for hearing | Trial |
| Pen C §1538.5(j) | Up to 30 days | None | Hearing of prosecution motion |

1. Right to continuance is contained in Pen C §1538.5(*l*).

## F. Burden and Standard of Proof

### 1. Warrantless Searches

#### a. [§6.105] Initial Showing

The defendant must show initially that the search was without a warrant. *Coolidge v New Hampshire* (1971) 403 US 443, 454–455, 91 S Ct 2022, 29 L Ed 2d 564; *Badillo v Superior Court* (1956) 46 C2d 269, 272, 294 P2d 23; *People v Constancio* (1974) 42 CA3d 533, 538, 116 CR 910. An allegation in the moving papers that a search was warrantless does not satisfy this burden; allegations are not evidence. *People v Garcia* (1981) 115 CA3d 85, 104, 171 CR 169.

This defense burden is often met by a stipulation that there was no search warrant. In the absence of a stipulation, defendant has a duty to support his or her motion. *People v Carson* (1970) 4 CA3d 782, 784–785, 84 CR 699.

☛ **Judicial Tip**: When there is no stipulation or other evidence and both sides insist that the other proceed first, the court should deny the suppression motion.

The defendant must also prove standing. See §§6.118–6.120.

### b. Prosecution Burden

#### (1) [§6.106] Basic Principles

Once a defendant shows that a search was without a warrant, the prosecution has the burden of proving that the search comes within an exception to the warrant requirement of the Fourth Amendment. *Coolidge v New Hampshire* (1971) 403 US 443, 454–455, 91 S Ct 2022, 29 L Ed 2d 564; *People v James* (1977) 19 C3d 99, 106, 137 CR 447; see *People v Williams* (1999) 20 C4th 119, 127, 83 CR2d 275.

The reason for the shift in the burden of proof is that a warrantless search is presumed to be illegal. *People v James, supra*; *People v Bishop* (1996) 44 CA4th 220, 236, 51 CR2d 629. The presumption of illegality does not extend to searches by private persons. See *People v Villalva* (1973) 33 CA3d 362, 368, 109 CR 16 (court will not assume airline employee acted at request of police).

#### (2) [§6.107] Consent

When the prosecution claims that a search was consensual, it has the burden of proving that the search comes within the consent exception to the warrant requirement. A vital aspect of this burden is "proving that the defendant's manifestation of consent was the product of his free will and not a mere submission to an express or implied assertion of authority." *People v James* (1977) 19 C3d 99, 106, 137 CR 447 (leading case); *Bumper v North Carolina* (1968) 391 US 543, 548–549, 88 S Ct 1788, 20 L Ed 2d 797; *Anderson v Superior Court* (1988) 206 CA3d 533, 545, 253 CR 651. The prosecution must also prove that the "search was *within* the scope of the consent given." *People v Harwood* (1977) 74 CA3d 460, 466, 141 CR 519 (emphasis in original); *People v Cooney* (1991) 235 CA3d Supp 1, 6–7, 286 CR 765. The prosecution has the burden of proving the validity of a third party consent. *U.S. v Matlock* (1974) 415 US 164, 177, 94 S Ct 988, 39 L Ed 2d 242; *People v Escudero* (1979) 23 C3d 800, 806, 153 CR 825. See also §6.110.

### c. Meeting the Prosecution's Burden: Illustrative Cases

#### (1) [§6.108] Identification

In a shoplifting case, the store clerk testifies that he identified the defendant at a street corner showup two blocks from the store 20 minutes after the defendant ran out of the store. The motion to suppress the identification should be granted. On this record, the prosecution has not proved either the legality of the showup identification or that the in-court identification was not tainted. *People v Washington* (1984) 161 CA3d Supp 21, 27, 207 CR 795. One case suggests that the judge ask appropriate questions when the prosecution inadvertently omits them. *People v Ferguson* (1981) 126 CA3d Supp 22, 30 n4, 179 CR 437.

☛ **Judicial Tip**: This suggestion should be used with restraint to avoid the appearance of bias.

#### (2) [§6.109] Information From Other Officers; *Harvey-Madden*

In a drug possession case, the police officer testifies that he stopped and searched the defendant's car on information from another officer that the defendant was transporting drugs. Here the prosecution must call the officer who provided the information to prove that it rests on a reasonable basis (*People v Madden* (1970) 2 C3d 1017, 1021, 88 CR 171; *People v Harvey* (1958) 156 CA2d 516, 522, 319 P2d 689; *People v Wooten* (1985) 168 CA3d 168, 172, 214 CR 36 (post-Proposition 8 decision)) or present other evidence "circumstantially proving that the police did not make up the information" (*People v Johnson* (1987) 189 CA3d 1315, 1320, 235 CR 62).

Contrast the following situation: An officer goes to the defendant's apartment to interview him as a result of information from another officer that the defendant is selling drugs. The defendant, who appears to be under the influence of drugs, is arrested and searched. Here the officer's information is germane only to explain why he sought out the defendant. It is not relevant to probable cause to arrest, and hence there is no *Harvey-Madden* burden on the prosecution. See *People v Mendoza* (1982) 129 CA3d Supp 10, 13, 181 CR 387.

#### (3) [§6.110] Landlord's Consent

The prosecution shows that defendant's landlord consented to the search of defendant's apartment. This does not meet the prosecution's burden of showing valid consent. Nor is it sufficient to prove that the landlord was convinced he had authority to consent and that the officer believed him. Generally a landlord has no such authority and the officer's belief is unreasonable unless an exception such as joint control of the premises is shown. *People v Escudero* (1979) 23 C3d 800, 806, 153 CR 825.

## 2. Search and Arrest Warrants

### a. [§6.111] Basic Principles

A search warrant is presumed to have been lawfully issued and executed. Evid C §664. Hence, the burden of establishing its invalidity or improper execution is on the defendant. *People v Wilson* (1967) 256 CA2d 411, 417, 64 CR 172; *Theodor v Superior Court* (1972) 8 C3d 77, 101, 104 CR 226. Similarly, an arrest under an arrest warrant is presumed to be lawful, and the defendant has the burden of overcoming the presumption. Evid C §664; *People v Pipkin* (1971) 17 CA3d 190, 194, 94 CR 595.

In cases involving search warrants courts make additional burden of proof allocations when the prosecution seeks to validate a search despite a facially invalid search warrant and, conversely, when the defense challenges a facially valid warrant because of claimed misstatements or omissions in the supporting affidavit. For discussion, see §§6.113–6.116.

### b. [§6.112] Good Faith; Independent Source

The prosecution may seek to uphold a search made under an invalid warrant on one of two grounds: the "good-faith exception" and the existence of adequate independent grounds.

Under the first, once the defendant shows the invalidity of the warrant, the prosecution has the task of proving that the searching officers relied on the warrant in "objective good faith." *U.S. v Leon* (1984) 468 US 897, 920, 104 S Ct 3405, 82 L Ed 2d 677 (search warrant affidavit failed to establish probable cause); *Massachusetts v Sheppard* (1984) 468 US 981, 989, 104 S Ct 3424, 82 L Ed 2d 737 (search warrant form used in murder case erroneously authorized search for controlled substances rather than for evidence of the murder).

The good-faith exception does not turn on what the officer conducting the search actually believed. Rather, the "good-faith inquiry is confined to *the objectively ascertainable question whether a reasonably well trained officer would have known that the search was illegal despite the magistrate's authorization.* In making this determination, all of the circumstances—including whether the warrant application had previously been rejected by a different magistrate—may be considered." *U.S. v Leon, supra,* 468 US at 922 n23 (emphasis added). See §1.29.

One effect of the good-faith exception is that "the defendant shall be entitled to discover any previous application for a search warrant in the case which was refused by a magistrate for lack of probable cause." Pen C §1539(c).

The prosecution may also prove that the police had a lawful basis for the search independent of the defective search warrant. See §§1.58–1.59.

### c. Attack on Warrant for Misstatements or Omissions

#### (1) [§6.113] Dual Burdens

A defendant who challenges a search warrant based on misstatements or omissions in the supporting affidavit faces two burdens. First, the defendant must make a specific, factual offer of proof that the misstatements or omissions were deliberate or reckless on the affiant's part, and second, that they are material to the finding of probable cause to search. *Franks v Delaware* (1978) 438 US 154, 156, 98 S Ct 2674, 57 L Ed 2d 667; see §§2.44–2.48. Defendant is entitled to an evidentiary hearing only upon making such a threshold showing. *Franks v Delaware, supra.*

At the threshold hearing, the defendant has the burden of proving "the allegation of perjury or reckless disregard . . . by a preponderance of the evidence." *Franks v Delaware, supra.*

#### (2) [§6.114] High Threshold Burden

The standard for the threshold showing is a high one (*Franks v Delaware* (1978) 438 US 154, 171–172, 98 S Ct 2674, 57 L Ed 2d 667):

> There is, of course, a presumption of validity with respect to the affidavit supporting the search warrant. To mandate an evidentiary hearing, the challenger's attack must be more than conclusory and must be supported by more than a mere desire to cross-examine. There must be allegations of deliberate falsehood or of reckless disregard for the truth, and those allegations must be accompanied by an offer of proof. They should point out specifically the portion of the warrant affidavit that is claimed to be false; and they should be accompanied by a statement of supporting reasons. Affidavits or sworn or otherwise reliable statements of witnesses should be furnished, or their absence satisfactorily explained. Allegations of negligence or innocent mistake are insufficient. The deliberate falsity or reckless disregard whose impeachment is permitted today is only that of the affiant, not of any governmental informant. Finally, if these requirements are met, and if, when material that is the subject of the alleged falsity or reckless disregard is set to one side, there remains sufficient content in the warrant affidavit to support a finding of probable cause, no hearing is required.

Even declarations by defendant that directly controvert the affiant's statements may not warrant an evidentiary hearing. *People v Box* (1993) 14 CA4th 177, 182, 17 CR2d 504; *People v Sandlin* (1991) 230 CA3d

1310, 1318, 281 CR 702. The standard is not met by defendant's testimony that an informant's statements recited in the affidavit are false and that no such person as the quoted informant exists. *People v Duval* (1990) 221 CA3d 1105, 1111–1113, 271 CR 240. Affiant's death prior to the hearing does not reduce the requirement of making a substantial preliminary showing. *People v Duval, supra.*

Unless the defendant meets the threshold requirement, he or she is not entitled to examine the affiant in an effort to establish misstatements or omissions. *People v Wilson* (1986) 182 CA3d 742, 747, 227 CR 528; see *People v Duval, supra.* For discussion of discovery, see §6.115.

#### (3) [§6.115] Lesser Showing for Discovery

A defendant is entitled to discovery as to whether omissions or misstatements occurred on a preliminary showing that

(1) Casts reasonable doubt on the veracity of affiant's statements;

(2) Specifies, if possible, the basis for defendant's belief that the information exists, and the purpose for which defendant seeks it; and

(3) Raises a substantial possibility that the allegedly untrue statements were material to the determination of probable cause. *People v Luttenberger* (1990) 50 C3d 1, 20–24, 265 CR 690. For discussion of the materiality of omissions relating to police informants, see §2.45.

The preliminary showing for discovery, unlike the *Franks* threshold showing, need not show that the statements resulted from the affiant's bad faith. 50 C3d at 23.

The preliminary showing specified by *Luttenberger* need not be made if the defendant did not have a reasonable chance to do so because a portion of the search warrant affidavit was sealed. *People v Hobbs* (1994) 7 C4th 948, 965–975, 30 CR2d 651; *People v Seibel* (1990) 219 CA3d 1279, 1292, 269 CR 313.

#### (4) [§6.116] In Camera Hearings

*Franks v Delaware* (1978) 438 US 154, 98 S Ct 2674, 57 L Ed 2d 667, and *People v Luttenberger* (1990) 50 C3d 1, 265 CR 690, give rise to two in camera hearings:

(1) *Discovery hearing.* After defendant has made the showing mandated by *Luttenberger,* the court should conduct an in camera inspection of the documents defendant seeks, determine their materiality, and delete information that might identify the informant. 50 C3d at 20. The court should order production "of only those documents that are relevant to the material inaccuracies asserted by the defendant." 50 C3d at 23.

(2) *Franks hearing.* After defendant has made the requisite preliminary

showing required by *Franks,* the court should conduct a further in camera hearing. *People v Brown* (1989) 207 CA3d 1541, 1547–1548, 256 CR 11. The court first determines whether the informant's identity should be kept confidential. "[D]efendant has no right to discover an informant's identity solely to attack a facially valid search warrant affidavit. That right arises only where defendant shows a reasonable possibility that informant is a witness to guilt or innocence." *People v Luttenberger, supra,* 50 C3d at 13, quoting with approval *People v Kurland* (1980) 28 C3d 376, 387 n5, 168 CR 667.

If the court decides that the informant's identity should not be revealed, then under *People v Brown, supra,* the court further interviews the informant in camera and determines whether the affidavit is materially false.

A reporter should be present at in camera hearings and the transcription ordered sealed. See Evid C §1042(d); *People v Brown, supra.*

### d. [§6.117] Production of Arrest Warrant

The prosecution has the burden of proving the existence of the search warrant. Formerly, the prosecution had to produce the original arrest warrant or a certified copy on request. *People v Romanoski* (1984) 157 CA3d 353, 360, 204 CR 33; *People v Davis* (1986) 187 CA3d 1250, 1253, 232 CR 428. Under present law, these are not the only methods for proving the warrant, at least in the absence of a claim that the warrant had been recalled or did not exist. *People v Armstrong* (1991) 232 CA3d 228, 241–246, 283 CR 429 (production of computer printout received by arresting agency sufficient). In accord is *People v Alcorn* (1993) 15 CA4th 652, 656–660, 19 CR2d 47. Under *Armstrong,* probative evidence may be used to show that the officer who provided the warrant information had in fact received it. The need to make such a showing on request is not obviated by *Leon.*

The prosecution is still required to introduce independent evidence that the warrant exists. *People v Collins* (1997) 59 CA4th 988, 992, 69 CR2d 544.

☛ **Judicial Tip**: It is useful to keep in mind that behind the request to produce an arrest warrant may lie at least four issues: (1) Was a warrant in existence at the time of the arrest? (2) Was defendant in fact arrested on that warrant? (3) Did the warrant authorize the particular arrest (*e.g.,* night service problems)? (4) Was the warrant supported by probable cause? The latter can be ascertained only if the supporting affidavit or other records showing probable cause are before the court.

## 3. Reasonable Expectation of Privacy (Standing)

### a. [§6.118] Basic Principle

The defendant has the burden of proving a reasonable expectation of privacy in the place searched or the items seized. *Minnesota v Carter* (1998) 525 US 83, 88, 119 S Ct 469, 142 L Ed 2d 373; *Rawlings v Kentucky* (1980) 448 US 98, 104, 100 S Ct 2556, 65 L Ed 2d 633; *People v Ayala* (2000) 23 C4th 225, 255, 96 CR2d 682.

This burden exists whether or not there was a search warrant. See, *e.g.*, *Minnesota v Carter, supra* (no warrant at time of challenged observations); *People v Williams* (1992) 3 CA4th 1535, 1537, 5 CR2d 372 (search warrant).

### b. [§6.119] Use of Prosecution Evidence

The defendant's burden of proving a reasonable expectation of privacy can be met by prosecution evidence. *People v Dees* (1990) 221 CA3d 588, 595, 270 CR 554 (officer testified that at scene of car search, defendant said car was his). See *People v Williams* (1992) 3 CA4th 1535, 1539–1543, 5 CR2d 372 (documents found by police during apartment search, linking defendant to apartment, admissible on reasonable privacy expectation issue).

In deciding whether the defendant has met the burden, the court must look at all the circumstances, including the prosecution evidence. *People v Dees, supra.* The fact that the burden is on the defense does not mean that defendant must necessarily proceed first. The court has discretion to regulate the order of proof. For discussion, see §6.123.

### c. [§6.120] Waiver and Estoppel

The prosecution must raise the issue of defendant's reasonable expectation of privacy in the court hearing the Pen C §1538.5 motion, so that the defendant has an opportunity to prove standing. Failure to raise it operates as a waiver. *Steagald v U.S.* (1981) 451 US 204, 209, 101 S Ct 1642, 68 L Ed 2d 38; *People v Henderson* (1990) 220 CA3d 1632, 1641, 270 CR 248; *People v Lindsey* (1986) 182 CA3d 772, 776, 227 CR 550. No waiver occurs when the court raises the standing issue at the time of the suppression hearing because that gives defendant a chance to make a record. *People v Dasilva* (1989) 207 CA3d 43, 48, 254 CR 563.

The prosecution may be estopped from asserting lack of standing when it takes contradictory positions. *People v Dees* (1990) 221 CA3d 588,

597–598, 270 CR 554. As to inconsistent positions by the defendant, see §6.40.

☛ **Judicial Tip**: The judge should usually decide the reasonable expectation of privacy issue on the totality of the credible evidence rather than relying on an estoppel theory.

#### 4. [§6.121] Fruit of Poisonous Tree

The defendant has the burden of establishing a causal link between the illegal police conduct, the "primary illegality," and any evidence derived from it. Once the defendant makes a prima facie showing, the burden shifts to the prosecution to prove either attenuation or the independent origin of the evidence. *Alderman v U.S.* (1969) 394 US 165, 181, 89 S Ct 961, 22 L Ed 2d 176; *People v Williams* (1988) 45 C3d 1268, 1300, 248 CR 834. See §§1.44–1.59.

#### 5. [§6.122] Standard of Proof

In a Pen C §1538.5 hearing, the party having the burden of proof may discharge it by a preponderance of the evidence. *U.S. v Matlock* (1974) 415 US 164, 177, 94 S Ct 988, 39 L Ed 2d 242; *People v James* (1977) 19 C3d 99, 106 n4, 137 CR 447. Cases stating a different standard, such as *People v Reynolds* (1976) 55 CA3d 357, 366, 127 CR 561 ("clear and positive evidence"), should be disregarded.

### G. Evidence and Presentation

#### 1. [§6.123] Order of Proof

Penal Code §1538.5(c) directs the court to "receive evidence on any issue of fact necessary to determine the motion." The parties sometimes disagree whether the prosecution or the defense should make the initial presentation of evidence. The prosecution may want to know the basis of the motion, especially when the moving papers contain few details. See *People v Williams* (1999) 20 C4th 119, 129, 83 CR2d 275, and discussion in §6.44. Or the prosecution may insist that the defendant go first to show standing. See *People v Scott* (1993) 17 CA4th 405, 408–409, 21 CR2d 193; *People v Johnson* (1984) 162 CA3d 1003, 1007, 209 CR 78. Occasionally defense counsel wants to start the hearing by calling witnesses; at other times, the defense insists that the prosecution meet its burden of proof.

Two principles help bring order to the hearing:

(1) The burden of producing evidence is initially on the party who has the burden of proof. Evid C §550(b).

(2) The court has discretion to regulate the *order* of proof. Evid C §320. For an illustration, see *People v Contreras* (1989) 210 CA3d 450, 453, 259 CR 290 (court may require prosecution to show validity of search before defendant establishes standing); see *People v Scott, supra*; *People v Williams* (1992) 3 CA4th 1535, 1539 n2, 5 CR2d 372.

☛ **Judicial Tips**:

- It is useful to read the moving and opposing papers before the hearing and to hold a brief prehearing conference if the papers do not focus the issues. Knowledge of the issues is essential to making a sensible allocation of the order of proof.
- It is occasionally helpful to defer the issue of standing to avoid hearing it in a vacuum in which the judge knows virtually nothing about the case. See *People v Scott, supra.* Also, the evidence on reasonable expectation of privacy often overlaps evidence on the lawfulness of the search. In warrantless search cases, it often works best to have the prosecution start, unless the reasonable expectation of privacy issue is factually clearly distinct from other matters. At other times, the court can expedite the hearing by allowing the defense to call and question the officer on the suppression issues.
- In addition to determining the order of proof, the judge should make sure that the record clearly shows from the outset exactly *what* evidence the defense seeks to suppress. See §6.131. The prehearing conference can help to answer that question.

### 2. [§6.124] Practical Problems in Hearing Pen C §1538.5 Motions and Preliminary Hearings Concurrently

When the Pen C §1538.5 motion is heard at the preliminary hearing, there is a risk of confusion. The magistrate hears some testimony germane only to the motion, some germane only to the holding order, and some relevant to both. The record is often unclear as to what evidence is admitted on what issue, making it more difficult when the case is reviewed on the transcript. Finally, it is not always easy for the court to keep evidence addressed only to the motion from affecting its thinking on the preliminary hearing questions. The difficulties are compounded in multiple-defendant, multiple-count cases.

☛ **Judicial Tips**: (1) Take careful notes that separate evidence on the Pen C §1538.5 motion from evidence that bears only on the preliminary hearing. (2) Request counsel to indicate when they are asking questions limited to the motion. (3) When this does not happen, inquire of counsel at appropriate points. (4) Be alert for statements like "these questions are for probable cause." "Probable cause" is ambiguous; counsel may mean probable cause to detain, arrest, or search, or probable cause to believe that the defendant committed the offense.

At the preliminary hearing, defendant cannot offer evidence relevant solely to a suppression motion unless the motion is, in fact, made. Thus, defendant cannot cross-examine the officer on probable cause to detain, arrest, or search in the absence of a motion; defendant has no right to conduct such an examination for the purpose of deciding whether to make a Pen C §1538.5 motion. *People v Barnes* (1990) 219 CA3d 1468, 1473, 269 CR 44; *People v Williams* (1989) 213 CA3d 1186, 1190, 262 CR 303.

### 3. Hearsay

#### a. [§6.125] Applicability of Hearsay Rule

The Evidence Code, including the hearsay rule, applies to Pen C §1538.5 motions. Evid C §§130, 300; *Hewitt v Superior Court* (1970) 5 CA3d 923, 927, 85 CR 493. The admission of hearsay permitted by Cal Const art I, §30(b) is expressly limited to preliminary hearings. Yet apparent hearsay is routinely admitted in Pen C §1538.5 hearings. For discussion of the governing principles, see §§6.126–6.127.

#### b. [§6.126] Statements Providing Grounds To Detain, Arrest, or Search

Testimony about an out-of-court statement is hearsay only when it is offered for the truth of the statement. Evid C §1200(a); 1 Witkin, California Evidence, *Hearsay* §4 (4th ed 2000). Statements and other information on which police officers rely to detain, arrest, or search are not hearsay because they are not offered to prove their truth, but only to provide a basis for the officer's actions. *People v Marsh* (1962) 58 C2d 732, 738, 26 CR 300; *People v Zolin* (1994) 23 CA4th 128, 132–133, 28 CR2d 238.

For example, the following testimony does not constitute hearsay:

- One officer's statement to another that a particular driver was weaving in a snake-like manner. *People v Zolin, supra.*
- An officer's testimony of radio transmissions he heard about a recent crime (*People v Satchell* (1978) 81 CA3d 347, 350, 146 CR 307)

or about the existence of an arrest warrant. See *People v Landa* (1973) 30 CA3d 487, 489, 106 CR 329.

- An officer's testimony about information he received from an informant. See, *e.g., People v Williams* (1988) 45 C3d 1268, 1289, 248 CR 834.
- Testimony that a given area of the city has a high burglary rate. See *People v Baldwin* (1976) 62 CA3d 727, 733, 133 CR 427.

Some decisions misstate the rule as "hearsay evidence may be used to establish probable cause. . . ." See, *e.g., People v Mack* (1979) 89 CA3d 974, 979, 152 CR 882.

### c. [§6.127] Document Relevant Regardless of Truth

A document or statement may justify an inference about a fact in issue regardless of whether the statement is true. In that case it is admissible. *People v Williams* (1992) 3 CA4th 1535, 1542, 5 CR2d 372. *Williams* applied this principle to a suppression hearing in which the defendant sought to prove he had a reasonable expectation of privacy in an apartment that the police had searched. A police officer testified that he found a fishing license and two checks bearing defendant's name in a bedroom in the apartment. The court held the documents were not hearsay because "regardless of the truth of any express or implied statement contained in those documents, they are circumstantial evidence that a person with the same name as the defendant resided in the apartment from which they were seized. Therefore, when introduced for the purpose of showing that residency, they are admissible nonhearsay evidence." 3 CA4th at 1542–1543.

### 4. [§6.128] Physical Production of Evidence; View of Premises

"[T]he physical production of evidence at the suppression hearing is not a prerequisite to a ruling on its admissibility." *People v O'Brien* (1969) 71 C2d 394, 402, 79 CR 313.

Exceptions to this rule are:

(a) When the absence of an item prevents resolution of a factual issue. See *People v Ritchie* (1971) 17 CA3d 1098, 1106, 95 CR 462. *Ritchie* suggests that the hearing should be continued so that the item can be produced. An alternative is to resolve the particular issue against the party who has the burden of proving it. The judge should *not* dismiss, as the judge hearing the motion in *Ritchie* had done.

(b) When the suppression motion is heard at the preliminary examination. Pen C §1538.5(f) (motion "restricted to evidence sought to be introduced by the people at the hearing").

*Viewing by magistrate.* The magistrate may view any relevant place, but only with the entire court, as part of a court session, not ex parte. See *People v Jackson* (1990) 218 CA3d 1493, 1505, 267 CR 841.

### 5. [§6.129] Later Use of Defendant's Testimony

The defendant's testimony at a Pen C §1538.5 hearing is inadmissible at trial as evidence of guilt. *Simmons v U.S.* (1968) 390 US 377, 389–394, 88 S Ct 967, 19 L Ed 2d 1247; *People v Drews* (1989) 208 CA3d 1317, 1325, 256 CR 846; see *People v Clark* (1993) 5 C4th 950, 1006, 22 CR2d 689. The testimony may, however, be used to impeach the defendant at trial. *People v Douglas* (1977) 66 CA3d 998, 1003, 136 CR 358; see *People v Humiston* (1993) 20 CA4th 460, 474, 24 CR2d 515; *People v Drews, supra.*

## H. Orders

### 1. [§6.130] Stating Grounds

Although the judge is not statutorily required to state the grounds for granting or denying the motion, under some circumstances it is especially useful to do so. For example:

(a) When the factual issues are decided in favor of one side, but the motion in favor of the other. See §6.57.

(b) When the decision does not reach the merits of the suppression issue, for instance, when the judge rules that the motion is not cognizable under Pen C §1538.5 or that it was not properly noticed or that it cannot be made at trial.

(c) When the judge decides a standing issue.

When the motion is made or opposed on multiple grounds, announcing that the ruling is based on only some of them may necessitate later proceedings on the undecided grounds (see *People v Brooks* (1980) 26 C3d 471, 475, 162 CR 177), and the order will not have the support of implied factual findings on those grounds (see *People v Manning* (1973) 33 CA3d 586, 603, 109 CR 531).

### 2. [§6.131] Identification of Evidence

The judge "should expressly state for the record the precise evidence" that he or she is suppressing. *People v Superior Court* (Arketa) (1970) 10 CA3d 122, 126, 89 CR 316. Imprecise orders are likely to cause considerable difficulties for reviewing courts. "Motion granted" is usually not an adequate order, especially when the motion is stated broadly ("all evidence resulting from the search of . . . , including but not limited to . . .").

☛ **Judicial Tips**:

- When the physical evidence is extensive, stipulated use of the search inventory can be helpful, so that the judge can frame the order by reference to it.
- If the order refers to exhibit numbers, the judge should either make sure that the exhibits are adequately described in the record or describe them in the order, so that subsequent courts are clearly and fully informed.
- Precision is particularly important when dealing with intangible evidence. The judge may have to pinpoint, for example, exactly what officer observations or identification evidence are being suppressed. In summary, the judge making the order should put himself or herself in the shoes of a judge who gets the case later. Time spent to provide a careful formulation can avoid confusion later on.

## IX. APPELLATE REVIEW

### A. Felonies

#### 1. Motion at Preliminary Hearing

##### a. [§6.132] Review Sought by Defendant

The only appellate court review from a ruling on a suppression motion made at the preliminary hearing (Pen C §1538.5(f)) is on defendant's postconviction appeal. Pen C §1538.5(f), (m). A guilty plea does not preclude review of Fourth Amendment issues. Pen C §1538.5(m); for further discussion, see §6.135.

To preserve the right to raise the issue on appeal, the defendant must make a subsequent suppression motion under Pen C §1538.5(i) (*People v Lilienthal* (1978) 22 C3d 891, 896, 150 CR 910; *People v Hoffman* (2001) 88 CA4th 1, 105 CR2d 372; *People v Hart* (1999) 74 CA4th 479, 485, 86 CR2d 762), unless the defendant pleads guilty before the magistrate. *People v Callahan* (1997) 54 CA4th 1419, 1424, 63 CR2d 684.

##### b. [§6.133] Review Sought by Prosecution

The prosecution may not seek appellate review of an order granting a suppression motion at the preliminary hearing or from a dismissal by the magistrate. *People v Randall* (1973) 35 CA3d 972, 977, 111 CR 590; see *People v Mimms* (1988) 204 CA3d 471, 476–478, 251 CR 672. But the prosecution may obtain appellate review indirectly by moving in the trial court to reinstate the complaint and appealing the denial of the motion to reinstate. Pen C §§871.5, 1538.5(j); see *People v Mimms, supra.* For discussion of other prosecution options after an adverse ruling under Pen C §1538.5(f), see §6.59.

### 2. Penal Code §1538.5(i) Motion

#### a. Review Sought by Defendant

##### (1) [§6.134] Pretrial

A defendant who loses a Pen C §1538.5(i) motion may seek pretrial appellate review by petitioning for a writ of mandamus or prohibition within 30 days after the court denied the motion. Pen C §1538.5(i). The time limit is jurisdictional. *Clifton v Superior Court* (1970) 7 CA3d 245, 252, 86 CR 612; *Gomes v Superior Court* (1969) 272 CA2d 702, 704, 77 CR 539. It begins to run on the day the motion is orally denied and is not extended by service-by-mail statutes. 272 CA2d at 705.

The right to petition for pretrial review is available only if the defendant made the Pen C §1538.5(i) motion within 60 days after arraignment on the information or indictment, unless the defendant was unaware of the issue or had no opportunity to raise it. Pen C §1510. For exceptions, see *Rodriguez v Superior Court* (1988) 199 CA3d 1453, 1459, 245 CR 617 (motion refiled past 60-day period after having been ordered off calendar because of absence of counsel); *Ghent v Superior Court* (1979) 90 CA3d 944, 951, 153 CR 720 (delay in providing preliminary hearing transcript). The motion need only be made within 60 days; it need not be decided within that time. *Rodriguez v Superior Court, supra.* The motion is probably made at the time it is filed. See Pen C §1538.5(a)(2).

Grant of review by the court of appeal is discretionary; a denial of a writ petition without opinion does not preclude later consideration of the suppression issue on appeal of the defendant's conviction. *People v Medina* (1972) 6 C3d 484, 493–494, 99 CR 630.

##### (2) [§6.135] Postconviction

The trial court's ruling on a Pen C §1538.5(i) motion is reviewable on an appeal from a conviction, including a conviction after a plea of guilty or no contest. *People v Lilienthal* (1978) 22 C3d 891, 897, 150 CR 910 (guilty plea); *People v West* (1970) 3 C3d 595, 601, 91 CR 385 (no contest plea); Pen C §1538.5(m). The defendant need not obtain a certificate of probable cause. *People v Jones* (1995) 10 C4th 1102, 1106, 43 CR2d 464; *People v Kaanehe* (1977) 19 C3d 1, 8, 136 CR 409.

Subject to an important exception, an erroneous trial court ruling on the suppression motion will not result in a reversal if the ruling was harmless beyond a reasonable doubt. *People v Tewksbury* (1976) 15 C3d 953, 972, 127 CR 135 (applying harmless error test of *Chapman v California* (1967) 386 US 18, 24, 87 S Ct 824, 17 L Ed 2d 705). But when the conviction is based on a plea, there is no way to determine whether the error was harmless, and reversal is automatic. *People v Hill* (1974) 12 C3d 731, 768, 117 CR 393, overruled on other grounds in 18 C3d 889, 896 n5; see *People v Miller* (1983) 33 C3d 545, 551–556; 189 CR 519; but see *People v Salazar* (1979) 93 CA3d 912, 915, 156 CR 125 (*Hill* rule inapplicable when nearly identical evidence legally seized). The *Hill* exception is inapplicable to a "slow plea," *i.e.,* submitting the matter to the trial judge on the preliminary hearing transcript for a decision on guilt. *People v Ingram* (1981) 122 CA3d 673, 681–682, 176 CR 199.

#### b. [§6.136] Review Sought by Prosecution

When the prosecution loses the suppression motion, its appellate remedies depend on whether the court dismissed the action under Pen C §1385:

- In the event of such a dismissal, the prosecution has a right of appeal to review the suppression order. Pen C §1238(a)(7), (c). In this situation, writ review is unavailable. *People v Superior Court* (Abrahms) (1976) 55 CA3d 759, 769, 127 CR 672; Pen C §1538.5(i). The court's power to dismiss under Pen C §1385 is limited to the time of ruling on the suppression motion. 55 CA3d at 768.

- When there is no dismissal, the prosecution may petition the court of appeal for a writ of mandamus or prohibition. Pen C §1538.5(o). The petition must be filed within 30 days after the court granted the suppression motion. Pen C §1538.5(o). For further discussion, see §6.137.

☛ **Judicial Tip**: After granting the suppression motion, the judge should ask the prosecution whether it can proceed without the suppressed evidence. When the prosecution says that it cannot, the judge should dismiss under Pen C §1385.

### 3. [§6.137] Penal Code §1538.5(j) Motion

The defendant and the prosecution may seek review by way of extraordinary writ of an order under Pen C §1538.5(j) (prosecution motion to relitigate suppression issues) within 30 days after the date of the order. *Nerell v Superior Court* (1971) 20 CA3d 593, 596, 97 CR 702.

The defendant may also obtain review of the trial court's order by appealing the conviction. Pen C §1538.5(m). The right to review is not negated by a guilty plea. Pen C §1538.5(m); for further discussion, see §6.135.

#### 4. [§6.138] Motion at Trial

Suppression motions at trial are not reviewable by writ except when the trial court exceeded its jurisdiction by entertaining the motion. *People v Superior Court* (Edmonds) (1971) 4 C3d 605, 608, 94 CR 250. The defendant may obtain review on appeal from the conviction, notwithstanding a guilty plea. Pen C §1538.5(m); for further discussion, see §6.135.

## B. Misdemeanors

### 1. Appeal by Defendant

#### a. [§6.139] Pretrial Appeal

A misdemeanor defendant may appeal the denial of a suppression motion to the appellate division of the superior court. Pen C §1538.5(j); CCP §77. This right of pretrial review, however, is available only if the defendant made the suppression motion within 45 days after arraignment, "unless within these time limits the defendant was unaware of the issue or had no opportunity to raise the issue." Pen C §1510.

The defendant must file a notice of appeal within 30 days after the court denied the motion. Cal Rules of Ct 182 (appeal may not proceed unless time limit complied with). After the decision of the appellate division, the parties may seek further review only by applying to the court of appeal for certification. Cal Rules of Ct 63.

Appeal as provided in Pen C §1538.5(j) is the exclusive remedy; the parties may not use writ proceedings as an alternative. *Macias v Municipal Court* (1975) 49 CA3d 259, 261, 122 CR 590; Pen C §1538.5(m).

#### b. [§6.140] Postconviction Appeal

The defendant may obtain further review of the ruling on the suppression motion on an appeal from a conviction. Pen C §1538.5(m). This right to review is not affected by a guilty plea (Pen C §1538.5(m)) or by a pretrial appeal. *People v Hallman* (1989) 215 CA3d 1330, 1335, 264 CR 215. For further discussion, see §6.135.

### 2. [§6.141] Appeal by Prosecution

The prosecution has the same right as the defendant to appeal the ruling on a suppression motion in a misdemeanor case to the appellate division of the superior court. Pen C §1538.5(j). The appellate division may affirm or reverse the ruling, but may not order reopening or reconsideration. *McQuillan v Appellate Dep't* (1977) 71 CA3d 543, 545, 139 CR 514.

The prosecution, like the defendant, must file a notice of appeal within 30 days of the order (Cal Rules of Ct 182) and may not proceed by writ application. Pen C §1538.5(m).

The prosecution may also appeal a dismissal order made after the granting of a suppression motion and in that manner obtain review of the suppression order. *People v Rawlings* (1974) 42 CA3d 952, 958, 117 CR 651; Pen C §1238(a)(7), (c).

### [§6.142] Chart: Appellate Review of Pen C §1538.5 Motions

| ***Type of Motion*** | ***Review Sought By*** | | |
|---|---|---|---|
| | ***Defendant*** | | ***Prosecution*** |
| *Felony* | *Pretrial* | *Postconviction* | |
| At preliminary hearing | None | Appeal from conviction[1] if D also made Pen C §1538.5(i) motion[2] | None, but may appeal denial of motion to reinstate complaint |
| Pretrial | Writ; for conditions, see §6.134 | Appeal from conviction[1] | Appeal if trial court dismissed under Pen C §1385; otherwise writ |
| At trial | None | Appeal from conviction[1] | None, except writ when court exceeded jurisdiction |

| ***Type of Motion*** | ***Review Sought By*** | | |
|---|---|---|---|
| | ***Defendant*** | | ***Prosecution*** |
| *Misdemeanor* | *Pretrial* | *Postconviction* | |
| | Appeal to appellate division within 30 days after denial | Appeal from conviction[1] | Appeal to appellate division within 30 days or appeal from dismissal |

1. Including conviction following a plea of guilty or no contest.
2. For exception to requirement of making a Pen C §1538.5(i) motion, see §6.132.

## X. RELATED PROCEEDINGS

### A. [§6.143] Suppression Motions in Juvenile Court

In juvenile court, suppression motions are governed by Welf & I C §700.1, which provides:

- The motion "shall be heard prior to the attachment of jeopardy," unless the minor was unaware of the grounds for the motion.

☛ **Judicial Tip**: The hearing on the motion should not be combined with the adjudication hearing, even by stipulation. See *In re Mitchell G.* (1990) 226 CA3d 66, 69, 276 CR 245.

  - The prosecution is entitled to at least five court days' notice. See Cal Rules of Ct 1419 (suppression motion to be filed at least five court days before jurisdiction hearing; motion "shall be specific, noting the grounds, and supported by points and authorities").

  - If the court grants the motion, it must dismiss all counts except those on which the prosecution elects to proceed without the suppressed evidence.

### B. Suppression Issues Raised by Nonparty Under Pen C §1524(c)

#### 1. [§6.144] Right to Hearing

Penal Code §1538.5 gives only defendants the right to make a suppression motion. Pen C §1538.5. Penal Code §1524(c) extends the right to a hearing to raise Fourth Amendment issues to certain nonparties—doctors, lawyers, psychotherapists, and members of the clergy who are not targets of a criminal investigation—whose records are searched. Pen C §1524(c)(2); see *Gordon v Superior Court* (1997) 55 CA4th 1546, 1549, 65 CR2d 53. For discussion of appointing special masters and issuing search warrants under Pen C §1524(c), see §2.7.

### 2. [§6.145] Notice and Sealing

When the person served with a search warrant issued under Pen C §1524(c) tells the special master "that an item or items should not be disclosed" (Pen C §1524(c)(2)), the special master does the following:

- Gives notice to the person serving the warrant and to the person served of the date, time, and place of the hearing required by Pen C §1524(c) (*Gordon v Superior Court* (1997) 55 CA4th 1546, 1549, 1553–1560, 65 CR2d 53);
- Seals the documents in dispute (Pen C §1524(c)(2)); and
- Takes them to court for a hearing. Pen C §1524(c)(2).

The documents must remain sealed until a hearing is held. *Gordon v Superior Court, supra.*

### 3. [§6.146] Date, Time, and Place of Hearing

The hearing is in court within three days of the service of the warrant, unless impractical. "The court shall provide sufficient time for the parties to obtain counsel and make any motions or present any evidence." Pen C §1524(c)(2).

☛ **Judicial Tip**: At the time of appointing the special master, the judge and the master should agree on the date, time, and place of any hearing that might become necessary. This is essential if the court is going to respect the urgency expressed by the statute.

### 4. [§6.147] Issues at Hearing; In Camera Inspection

At the hearing, the person whose records were searched under the special master procedure "shall be entitled to raise any issues that may be raised pursuant to Section 1538.5 as well as a claim that the item or items are privileged." Pen C §1524(c)(2).

The court determines a privilege claim by inspecting the documents in camera. *Geilim v Superior Court* (1991) 234 CA3d 166, 173, 285 CR 602. See also *People v Superior Court* (Memorial Med. Ctr.) (1991) 234 CA3d 363, 388, 286 CR 478 (in camera inspection proper in Pen C §1524 proceedings; hospital peer review committee records not protected against criminal discovery).

### C. [§6.148] Objection to Motion for Order Authorizing Bodily Intrusion

When the prosecution moves for a court order authorizing a bodily intrusion, the defendant may object to it on Fourth Amendment grounds, among others. See, *e.g., People v Scott* (1978) 21 C3d 284, 289–290, 145 CR 876. The defendant need not renew his or her objection after the test by a Pen C §1538.5 motion, as long as the trial court fully considered the Fourth Amendment issues when it ruled on the prosecution's motion. *People v Scott, supra,* 21 C3d at 290–291.

### D. Return of Property

#### 1. After Grant of Suppression Motion

##### a. [§6.149] Basic Principles

Penal Code §1538.5(e) states that if a suppression motion is granted, "the property shall be returned upon order of the court," subject to two limitations:

(1) The court may order return only after the prosecution's time to seek review or to recharge defendant has expired or such subsequent proceedings have been concluded.

(2) The court may not order return of property that is "otherwise subject to lawful detention." This clause refers to all property that is unlawful to possess, including dangerous or deadly weapons, explosives, narcotics or drugs, and stolen property. *People v Superior Court* (McGraw) (1979) 100 CA3d 154, 157, 160 CR 663; see *Ensoniq Corp. v Superior Court* (1998) 65 CA4th 1537, 1547, 77 CR2d 507; Pen C §1417.6.

☛ **Judicial Tip**: The judge should not sign ex parte orders to return property unless they accurately reflect a prior stipulation or oral court order or unless they include the prosecutor's approval.

##### b. [§6.150] Chart: Time for Return

The time for return of property varies with the stage at which the Pen C §1538.5 hearing was granted, as shown in the following chart:

| *Stage* | *Time* | *See Pen C §1538.5(e)* |
|---|---|---|
| | **Felony** | |
| Preliminary hearing | On court order after 10 days "unless . . . within that time, further proceedings . . . are utilized; if they are utilized," then only after they are concluded | 3rd sentence |
| Superior court under Pen C §1538.5(i) | After expiration of time to initiate review or on its completion, whichever happens last | 2nd sentence |
| At trial | On order of the court | 1st sentence |
| | **Misdemeanor** | |
| Before trial under Pen C §1538.5(g) | After expiration of time to initiate review or on its completion, whichever happens last | 2nd sentence |
| At trial | On order of the court | 1st sentence |

### c. [§6.151] Evidentiary Hearing

The court should resolve disputes about whether property is contraband or otherwise subject to lawful detention by holding an evidentiary hearing. *People v Superior Court* (McGraw) (1979) 100 CA3d 154, 159, 160 CR 663. The prosecution has the burden of proof by a preponderance of the evidence. 100 CA3d at 159.

In cases involving allegedly stolen property, the defendant is entitled to a rebuttable presumption that he or she is the owner. 100 CA3d at 159; Evid C §637.

## 2. [§6.152] Motions Under Pen C §§1536, 1539(a), and 1540

Penal Code §1538.5 is not always available as a procedure to seek return of money or other property seized by the police. No charges might be pending (see, *e.g., People v Superior Court* (Aquino) (1988) 201 CA3d 1346, 1349, 248 CR 50), the case may have been terminated (see, *e.g., People v Superior Court* (Loar) (1972) 28 CA3d 600, 607, 104 CR 876), or the person seeking the return may not be a defendant (Pen C §1538.5 is expressly limited to defendant; see §6.6).

In these situations courts have permitted motions to return property based on Pen C §§1536 (officer to retain property taken on search warrant subject to order of court), 1539(a) (grounds on which search warrant issued are controverted and motion to return "made (i) by a defendant on grounds not covered by Section 1538.5; (ii) by a defendant whose property has not been offered or will not be offered as evidence against him; or (iii) by a person who is not a defendant . . ."), and 1540 (magistrate must cause property to be restored to owner if the property "is not the same as that described in the warrant, or . . . there is no probable cause for believing the existence of the ground on which the warrant was issued . . ."). See, *e.g., People v Superior Court* (Aquino), *supra*; *People v Superior Court* (Chico etc. Health Ctr.) (1986) 187 CA3d 648, 652, 232 CR 165; *People v Icenogle* (1985) 164 CA3d 620, 623, 210 CR 575. See *City of West Covina v Perkins* (1999) 525 US 234, 240, 119 S Ct 678, 142 L Ed 2d 636 (nondefendants may move for return under Pen C §1536 or §1540); *Ensoniq Corp. v Superior Court* (1998) 65 CA4th 1537, 1544, 77 CR2d 507 (motion by uncharged defendant under Pen C §§1536, 1539, and 1540; third party claimant not permitted to intervene).

Such motions should not be permitted when relief under Pen C §1538.5 is available. *People v Superior Court* (Chico etc. Health Center), *supra,* 187 CA3d at 652; *People v Superior Court* (Morton) (1984) 151 CA3d 899, 903, 199 CR 153 (defendant must use Pen C §1538.5 rather than Pen C §1540 to litigate whether description in search warrant was too vague; a Pen C §1540 motion asks only whether the description fits the items seized).

The motion should be addressed to the magistrate who issued the search warrant. *People v Superior Court* (Chico etc. Health Center), *supra.* The district attorney is entitled to contest the motion as a party. *People v Superior Court* (Aquino), *supra.* However, the prosecution may not block the return of money on the ground that it wants to introduce the actual bills into evidence. Testimony about the circumstances of the seizure and the amount seized normally suffices. *Buker v Superior Court* (1972) 25 CA3d 1085, 1089, 102 CR 494.

A court cannot order money returned when the police no longer have it. *City of San Jose v Superior Court* (1987) 195 CA3d 743, 746–750, 240 CR 882 (police turned money over to DEA; court indicated city may be liable in civil action, as well as to sanctions in a properly noticed contempt proceeding for willful violation of Pen C §1536); *Mason v Superior Court* (1981) 121 CA3d 876, 881, 175 CR 462 (funds turned over to Franchise Tax Board under jeopardy assessment); *People v Icenogle, supra.*

The police executing a search warrant need not give property owners information about procedures for reclaiming the property. *City of West Covina v Perkins, supra.*

☛ **Judicial Tip**: Motions to return should be heard only on reasonable notice in order to avoid confusion and unfairness. See *People v Superior Court* (Aquino), *supra.*

### 3. [§6.153] Hearing To Determine Whether Seized Documents Are Privileged

Under Pen C §1536 and the courts' inherent power, courts have "an obligation to consider and determine claims that materials seized pursuant to a search warrant, from attorneys suspected of criminal activity and before charges have been filed, are protected by the attorney-client privilege or work-product doctrine and thus should not be inspected by or disclosed to law enforcement authorities." *People v Superior Court* (Laff) (2001) 25 C4th 703, 713, 720, 107 CR2d 323; see *People v Superior Court* (Bauman & Rose) (1995) 37 CA4th 1757, 44 CR2d 734. A hearing on such claims is called a *Bauman & Rose* hearing. *People v Superior Court* (Laff), *supra,* 25 C4th at 722–723, 725–727.

The court should seal the documents pending determination of the privilege claim in order not to defeat the purpose of the hearing. *People v Superior Court* (Laff), *supra,* 25 C4th at 720 n8.

### 4. [§6.154] Nonstatutory Motions

Penal Code §§1536, 1539(a), and 1540 by their terms apply only to property taken under a search warrant. See *Sims v Superior Court* (1985) 172 CA3d 1065, 1067, 218 CR 723. In situations not covered by these statutes, trial courts have inherent power to entertain a motion for the return of seized items. See *Ensoniq Corp. v Superior Court* (1998) 65 CA4th 1537, 1547, 77 CR2d 507.

A nonstatutory motion is necessary when there was no search warrant and the claimant cannot use Pen C §1538.5 because he or she is not a defendant or for other reasons. Due process entitles a claimant to an early judicial determination. See *Williams v Justice Court* (1964) 230 CA2d 87, 98, 40 CR 724. Another use of a nonstatutory motion to return is by a person who does not contest the legality of the search and seizure, but contends that the property should be returned for other reasons. *People v Superior Court* (Shayan) (1993) 21 CA4th 621, 624, 26 CR2d 173 (claim that seized car stereo components were not contraband and that retention would substantially harm claimant's business).

### 5. [§6.155] Motions Under Forfeiture Statutes

Under the forfeiture statutes of Health & S C §§11469–11495, a criminal defendant may move for the return of the property on the ground that there is no probable cause to believe that it is forfeitable. The motion may be made before, during, or after the preliminary hearing. Health & S C §11488.4(h).

The motion does not adjudicate *admissibility* of the property; lack of probable cause to forfeit is not the equivalent of an illegal search or seizure. *People v Ford* (1985) 163 CA3d 736, 741–742, 210 CR 22.

Persons other than the defendant may contest a forfeiture by filing a claim in accordance with Health & S C §11488.5. For further discussion of forfeitures, see 3 Witkin & Epstein, California Criminal Law, *Punishment* §§201–223 (3d ed 2000); California Criminal Law Procedure and Practice, chap 56 (5th ed 2000).

### 6. [§6.156] Applications for Return of Exhibits

The disposition of exhibits is governed by Pen C §§1417–1417.9. Penal Code §1417.2 permits a motion prior to the final determination of the action under limited circumstances (no prejudice; complete photographic record).

After final determination, claimants must "make application to the court for release of the exhibits within 15 days of receipt of" notification from the court clerk. Pen C §1417.5(a). Persons not notified have 60 days to apply for the return of exhibits. Pen C §1417.5. The persons entitled to apply are those from whom the exhibit was taken and those claiming title to, or a right of possession of, the exhibit. See Pen C §1417.5(b).

Penal Code §1417.6(a) specifies that certain property is not returnable: "[D]angerous or deadly weapons, narcotic or poisonous drugs, explosives, or any property of any kind or character whatsoever the possession of which is prohibited by law and that was used by a defendant in the commission of the crime of which the defendant was convicted, or with which the defendant was armed or that the defendant had upon his or her person at the time of the defendant's arrest." See also Pen C §§1427.8, 1427.9.

## E. [§6.157] Release of Defendant

Penal Code §1538.5(k) states that the defendant must be released on his or her own recognizance under two circumstances:

(1) When the suppression motion is granted and the case dismissed under Pen C §1385.5; and

(2) When the prosecution appeals after losing a misdemeanor Pen C §1538.5 motion.

When the prosecution seeks review by writ, the defendant must be released on his or her own recognizance in all but homicide cases. In noncapital homicides, the defendant is entitled to bail. Pen C §1538.5(k).

The provisions of Pen C §1538.5(k) are mandatory. *People v Superior Court* (Mahle) (1970) 3 CA3d 476, 486, 83 CR 771, disapproved on other grounds in 37 C3d 302, 318.

A misdemeanor defendant who loses a Pen C §1538.5 motion and appeals is entitled to bail as a matter of right and to an O.R. release in the discretion of the court. Pen C §1538.5(l).

### F. [§6.158] Stay of Proceedings

*After grant of* Pen C §1538.5 *motion.* When the court grants a Pen C §1538.5 motion, the court must stay the trial, pending initiation and completion of review proceedings. Pen C §1538.5(*l*).

The defendant must be brought to trial within 30 days after completion of review proceedings. Pen C §1538.5(l). Misdemeanor proceedings are automatically stayed for 30 days; no request for such a stay is required. *Marcotte v Municipal Court* (1976) 64 CA3d 235, 242, 134 CR 314.

*After denial of* Pen C §1538.5 *motion.* In misdemeanor cases, the court has discretion to grant or deny a stay, pending appeal. *Ellis v Municipal Court* (1995) 33 CA4th 653, 656, 39 CR2d 461; Pen C §1538.5(*l*).

### G. [§6.159] Discretionary Dismissal

After granting a Pen C §1538.5 motion at a special hearing (*i.e.,* a hearing under subsections (g), (i), or (j)), the court may dismiss the case on its own motion. Pen C §1538.5(*l*). For dismissal after preliminary examination, see Pen C §§871, 871.5, 1385.

When the superior court hears concurrent Pen C §§995 and 1538.5 motions and grants the latter, dismissal "is the preferred remedy, as it gives the defendant immediate relief and the People immediate review." *People v Laiwa* (1983) 34 C3d 711, 722, 195 CR 503. After granting a Pen C §1538.5 motion, the court may set aside an indictment under Pen C §995 when the court finds that without the suppressed evidence there is insufficient evidence to support the indictment. *People v Sherwin* (2000) 82 CA4th 1404, 1410–1411, 98 CR2d 888.

# Table of Statutes

**PENAL CODE**

**PUBLIC RESOURCES CODE**



**PUBLIC UTILITIES CODE**



**VEHICLE CODE**

**WELFARE AND INSTITUTIONS CODE**



**ACTS BY POPULAR NAMES**



**SESSION LAWS**



**CALIFORNIA RULES OF COURT**



## UNITED STATES

### Constitution



### Statutes

**UNITED STATES CODE**

**Title 12**



**Title 18**



**Title 42**

# Table of Cases

**D**

**E**

**F**

**H**

## I

## J

## K

## L

## N

## O

**Q**

**R**

## S

### W

# Index